SEA POWER
A Naval History

SEA

Editor
E. B. Potter

Assistant Editors
Roger Fredland
Henry H. Adams

Authors
Henry H. Adams
James A. Arnold
William M. Belote
James C. Bradford
Ellery H. Clark, Jr.
Roger Fredland
Edwin M. Hall
Neville T. Kirk
Winston B. Lewis
Philip K. Lundeberg
E. B. Potter
William H. Russell
Craig Symonds
Herman O. Werner

SECOND EDITION

POWER
A Naval History

NAVAL INSTITUTE PRESS
Annapolis, Maryland

Printed in the United States of America
on acid-free paper ♾

Library of Congress Catalog No. 81-81668
ISBN: 978-0-87021-607-7
ISBN: 978-1-61251-767-4 (eBook)

The authors wish to acknowledge sources for the maps,
diagrams, and pictures appearing in the following pages:
page 76, adapted from William Oliver Stevens and Allan
Westcott, *A History of Sea Power* (Garden City, New York:
Doubleday & Company, Inc., 1942); page 210, adapted
from Langhorne Gibson and Vice-Admiral J.E.T. Harper,
RN, *The Riddle of Jutland* (New York: Coward-McCann,
Inc., 1934); and page 215 adapted from Alan Moorehead,
Gallipoli (New York: Harper and Brothers, Publishers, 1956).

22 21 20 19 18 17 16   27 26 25 24 23 22 21

Contents

Preface

This edition of *Sea Power: A Naval History* covers the same ground as the 1960 edition and then extends the narrative through the following two decades and beyond, yet it is only half as long as the 1960 version. The shortening was achieved through tightening the style, omitting minor operations, and deleting tactical details. Such deletion, it was found, makes the decisive maneuvers stand out more clearly.

Though the title page lists 14 authors, this book is not a symposium but a continuous narrative, uniform in style and treatment. All the authors have been closely associated, as instructors of naval history at the U. S. Naval Academy. Most of them began participating in the *Sea Power* project by writing chapters for *The United States and World Sea Power*, a preliminary study published by Prentice-Hall in 1955. Some of the authors withdrew from the project and some were added, but the core group cooperated in refining the subject matter of the 1955 book to produce the 1960 edition of *Sea Power* (also published by Prentice-Hall) and eventually in writing the present, shortened edition. In pursuit of accuracy and uniformity, the authors and editors have so thoroughly revised and rewritten the text that it has become impossible to state with accuracy who wrote what.

Sea Power is offered for general reading, as a reference work, and as a textbook. To assist students, it provides summaries—following consecutive chapters covering a major war and at the ends of all other chapters. *Sea Power* is tailored to meet the teaching requirements of the Naval Academy, but it is not an official publication. The authors wrote it in their own time. The opinions expressed are the authors' own, and they take full responsibility for errors of fact and interpretation.

A major influence on the *Sea Power* project has been the writings of Alfred Thayer Mahan. The authors have in general adopted Mahan's analysis of naval history from the beginnings of the age of sail to the early twentieth century, and where applicable they have also applied his concepts to more recent events. Another important influence has been the advice and guidance of the late Fleet Admiral Chester W. Nimitz, USN, who acted as associate editor and advisor for the 1960 edition, steering the civilian writers away from the pitfalls of amateur military analysis. Guided by his experience and professional insight, they have boldly developed certain concepts that they might otherwise have been hesitant to put forward.

The names of other people, including many now deceased, who have personally influenced or assisted in this work are listed alphabetically below. Unless otherwise indicated, names that are preceded by rank are officers in the U. S. Navy. Nearly a score of the listed officers took the time to read and correct portions of the book describing operations in which they participated. To all who have lent a hand in this enterprise, the authors take this opportunity to express their thanks.

Rear Adm. Walter C. Ansel; Vice Adm. Bernard L. Austin; Comdr. F. Barley, RN; Patrick Beesly; Commo. Howard H. J. Benson; Louis H. Bolander; Vice Adm. Eliot H. Bryant; Adm. Arleigh A. Burke; Adm. Robert B. Carney; Robert W. Daly; Grossadmiral Karl Dönitz, German navy; Philip A. Crowl; Rear Adm. Ernest M. Eller; Charles Fox, Jr.; William M. Franklin; Erick Gröner; Wilhelm Hadler; Fleet Adm. William F. Halsey; Rear Adm. Brooks J. Harral; Adm. H. Kent Hewitt; Gen. Thomas Holcomb, USMC; Adm. James L. Holloway, III; John Jeffries; Lt. Comdr. P. K. Kemp, RN; Maj. Gen. R. W. Keyser, USMC; Adm. Thomas C. Kinkaid; Harvé Kras; Rear Adm. Edwin T. Layton; Vice Adm. Charles A. Lockwood; Henry H. Lumpkin; Gen. of the Army Douglas MacArthur, USA; Vice Adm. A. Stanton Merrill; Grace B. Potter; Grossadmiral Erich Raeder, German navy; Arthur A. Richmond; Capt. Joseph J. Rochefort; Jürgen Rohwer; Vizeadmiral Friedrich Ruge, German navy; Capt. Laurance F. Safford; Comdr. M. G. Saunders, RN; Lt. Gen. Julian C. Smith, USMC; Adm. Raymond A. Spruance; Vernon D. Tate; James P. Thomas; G. A. Titterton; Frank Uhlig, Jr.; David Vanderburgh; Lt. Comdr. D. W. Waters, RN; Richard S. West; Vice Adm. Ralph Weymouth; Micajah Wyatt.

SEA POWER
A Naval History

Chapter 1
The Age of Galley Warfare

When man ceased to look upon streams, rivers, and seas as barriers and learned to use them as highways, he made a giant stride toward civilization. The waterways of the world provided a new mobility—to man himself, later to the products of his toil and skill, and at all times to his ideas.

The mobility provided by rivers and seas both enriched and enlightened their users. River-faring and seafaring peoples could barter their products with other peoples far and near, trading those goods that they were best equipped to produce in exchange for the agricultural and industrial specialties of other lands. In the process they also brought home in their heads an invisible cargo of ideas and information, a form of wealth oftentimes more precious than the trade goods they carried in their ships' holds.

Western man first began to use the broad seas in and around the Mediterranean basin. This use of the great waterways brought into contact the vigorous civilizations of Asia, Europe, and Africa. From the resulting exchange of products and ferment of ideas emerged most of the basic institutions of our Western culture.

Early Navies

The appearance of trade goods on the seas gave rise to piracy and to clashes between rival traders. Because merchant ships manned by their regular crews are ill prepared to defend their cargoes, trading communities early designated certain vessels to carry soldiers for protecting the commercial ships at sea. Such specialization of function early led to specialization of form. Thus the first books of history produced in the Mediterranean world mention two types of vessels: the *round ship*, broad of beam for carrying cargo and propelled mainly by sail; and the *long ship*, or galley, a vessel built specifically for fighting and propelled in combat by oar. Thus navies came into being to protect maritime commerce, and the history of sea power is largely a record of rivalries resulting from conflicting commercial interests.

Whatever the cause of conflict, a principal function of warships has always been to protect one's own sea *communications*, that is, one's freighters and transports and the men and goods they carry, and to block or disrupt the enemy's communications.[1] Achieving this twofold objective confers command (or control) of the sea, and attaining command of the sea is usually a necessary preliminary to a navy's carrying out its other wartime functions: defending the state against seaborne attack, isolating the enemy, and carrying the attack across the sea to the enemy.

Crete (c. 2,500–1,200 B.C.) was one of the earliest and most powerful of the Mediterranean sea powers. With a dense and growing population, the Cretans must early have been forced by the mountainous, inhospitable geography of their island to seek their living on the sea. Here geography was more in their favor, for Crete sits athwart the major sea routes of the eastern Mediterranean. Here she was strategically placed not only for carrying commerce but also for attacking and limiting the operations of her commercial rivals.

The Phoenicians (c. 2,000–300 B.C) were the next major wielders of Mediterranean sea power. They established a flourishing maritime trade that carried their ships into all the inland seas in their part of the world and even beyond the Straits of Gibraltar to seek the tin of Britain, the amber of the Baltic, and the slaves and ivory of western Africa to exchange for the spices, gold, and precious stones of India. In this East–West trade, they made use of the ports of Sidon and Tyre at the termini of caravan routes from the Orient.

The Phoenicians' search for new customers and new sources of raw materials made them the first great colonizers of ancient times. Their trading stations on the shores and islands of the Mediterranean became new centers of civilization. Carthage

---

[1]Not to be confused with another word of the same spelling that refers to the dissemination and exchange of information by whatever means—messenger, post, telegraph, radio, flag hoist, and the rest.

is a notable example. This Phoenician colony came to dominate the western Mediterranean and founded an empire embracing northwest Africa, Sardinia, Corsica, half of Sicily, and much of Spain.

It is of early Greek sea power that we are able to attain the clearest and most accurate picture, thanks to Herodotus and Thucydides, who wrote contemporary histories of the Greco–Persian and Peloponnesian wars. But Greece's naval traditions were already old by then, and her sea trade was well developed. Indeed, there is reason to believe that Homer's *Iliad* is really a poetic description of prehistoric Greek sea power at work—that the siege of Troy was a commercial war to secure control of the Hellespont (modern Dardanelles) and thus of the Black Sea trade. At any rate, the Greeks had by the fifth century B.C. excluded the Phoenicians and the Carthaginians from the Black and Aegean seas and held a virtual monopoly on shipping in the eastern Mediterranean. From their own mountainous, unfertile peninsula they could export few agricultural products but olive oil and wine; these products, however, were of the best quality and much in demand. Moreover, the work of their artisans (pottery, rugs, swords, tiles, and metal work) and their artists (jewelry, painted vases, and statues) gave them a highly favorable balance of trade.

As Greek trading stations developed into colonies, the coasts of Asia Minor to the east, Thrace to the north, and Sicily and southern Italy to the west became virtual extensions of Greece. Other Greek settlements existed as far away as the northern shores of the Black Sea and the Mediterranean coasts of Spain and Gaul (France). All that prevented the ancient Greeks from founding one of the mightiest maritime empires of history was the fatal defect of disunity. Within the Hellenic peninsula the Greek peoples were split up into separate little city-states—Athens, Sparta, Corinth, Thebes, and the rest—more often than not at odds with each other. The overseas Greek settlements were for the most part not true colonies but independent communities, attached to the mother cities of Greece by sentiment, tradition, and commercial ties. This dispersion of power, as much as anything else, was at length to cost the Greeks their freedom.

The Greco–Persian War

The dawn of recorded naval history coincides with one of the great crises in the annals of mankind. As viewed from later times, it can be seen as nothing less than an attack by Asia on Europe. Had the

hordes out of the Middle East succeeded in subduing peninsular Greece, the cradle and first home of Western civilization, we may be sure that subsequent world history would have been very different.

The attacker was Persia, one of a series of empires that through the centuries dominated southwestern Asia. Expanding out of the Iranian highlands, Persian control had by the sixth century B.C. reached the Mediterranean and Aegean seas. The Phoenicians, having no solidarity as a nation or prospect of assistance, submitted easily—as they had earlier submitted to Egyptians, Assyrians, and Babylonians—and provided fleets for the overseas conquests of their new masters. But the Greek cities of Asia Minor resisted and, even when conquered, rose against their conqueror with naval aid from Athens and Eretria across the Aegean. The Persians recaptured the rebellious cities, but suppressing the revolt cost them several years and gave the city-states of the Hellenic peninsula time to prepare for the inevitable attack.

The expanding Empire had already spread across the Hellespont and through Thrace and Macedonia. The first Persian expedition against Greece, in 492 B.C., succeeded in subduing revolt in these areas, but the fleet of galleys that accompanied the Persian army as it marched around the northern shores of the Aegean Sea was heavily damaged in a storm. With the fighting fleet out of action, cargo vessels could not be protected while supplying the troops; hence further advance was out of the question. The army was too large either to live off the land or to subsist upon supplies hauled overland by wagon. Loss of overseas communications thus stopped the first expedition in its tracks.

The second Persian expedition, two years later, came to an even more inglorious end. This was an amphibious operation, an attack from across the Aegean. When the first Persian echelon, numbering about 10,000 troops, landed on the plain of Marathon, some 8,000 Athenians, without waiting for tardy reinforcements from their Spartan allies, marched the 23 miles to the beachhead and hurled the invaders into the sea.

The Persians did not attack Greece again for ten years, partly because the new Persian ruler, King Xerxes, undertook elaborate precautions to ensure that the third expedition would be a success. Choosing the overland approach as probably less vulnerable, Xerxes in 480 B.C. assembled 180,000 troops at Sardis in Asia Minor and marched them to the Hellespont, which they crossed by means of boat bridges. The new expedition followed the example of the first by proceeding along the Aegean coast, while hundreds of cargo vessels kept it supplied from Asian bases. About 1,300 fighting ships, manned by some 175,000 seamen, rowers, and marines, covered the flank of the advancing army and protected the cargo vessels.

Aware of the Persian preparations, the peninsular Greeks had for once united, setting up a Panhellenic Congress to direct the defense. Luckily, Athens had produced an exceptional leader in Themistocles, who correctly saw that the Persian army was no stronger than the fleet that protected its communications back to base. He persuaded his fellow Athenians to invest in an enlarged fleet, which with galleys of other city-states gave the Greeks a naval force of nearly 500 warships. Themistocles expected this force at least to prevent the Persians from using their navy to outflank and put troops behind the Greek army's defense lines. With luck it might win a naval victory that would expose the Persian communications to attack.

When the Greek army failed to hold the Persian hordes at the coastal pass of Thermopylae, it fell back to the Isthmus of Corinth, while the Greek fleet retired south to the narrow waters between the island of Salamis and the mainland not far from Athens. At the same time Xerxes pressed with his army into Attica, laying waste everywhere and at length plundering the abandoned city of Athens. His fleet of some 1,400 ships entered the Bay of Phalerum a few miles east of the Salamis strait.

The Peloponnesians were for withdrawing the Greek ships to the Corinthian Isthmus, where the Greek army had taken a new stand. Themistocles, however, argued for keeping them where they were instead of exposing them to superior numbers in the open sea. To make sure that the ships would not withdraw, he sent a double agent to Xerxes with the information that the Greek fleet was planning to escape. The Persian king thereupon sent 200 ships around to close the narrows west of Salamis, and he blocked the eastern exit from the strait with his main body. When the Greeks learned, during the night, that they were thus entrapped, they sent a detachment to contain the western Persian squadron and with the rest of their ships prepared to do battle with the enemy main fleet.

At dawn the Greek ships east of Salamis were seen withdrawing, as if in retreat. It was a ruse to draw the Persians into the strait, where they could present no broader fighting front than could the heavily outnumbered Greeks. When the leading line of Persian ships, closely followed by several more lines, approached the narrows, the Greeks reversed course. Under the eyes of Athenian evacuees watching from the heights of Salamis and of King Xerxes enthroned on the opposite shore, the Greek ships bore down on the enemy, oars stroking in unison, archers stationed at the bows firing volleys of arrows.

Among the Greeks were no unwilling conscripts, but freemen fighting desperately for their homes and families. Moreover, they had what in the circumstances proved to be a superior tactical plan and suitable ships and skillful seamanship to carry it out. Their galleys were slim, low-lying triremes. On board each were some 40 marines, but its principal weapon was a bronze-sheathed underwater ram projecting from the bow. Each was propelled in combat by 150 rowers, manning oars in three banks. The rowers, able to attain speeds in excess of seven knots, gave the triremes and their rams a powerful forward thrust.

The Persian galleys, less agile, were designed for boarding tactics. Their marines counted on grappling ships together, friend and foe, into a floating battlefield and fighting hand to hand across decks.

As the fleets drew together, the leading Greek ships sped forward and crashed their bronze beaks into the first line of enemy galleys, sinking them or driving them back into their own oncoming reinforcements. The nimble triremes, avoiding Persian grapnels, now circled the enemy ships, forcing them into an unwieldy bunch, and ramming again and again until the outermost ring had become a shambles of wreckage and floating corpses.

When a west wind arose, all the Persian ships that were able hoisted sail and fled. Though still outnumbering the Greeks, they were too demoralized to renew the attack, then or later. Xerxes recognized that with the Greek fleet unassailable in its fastness, his own seaborne communications were no longer secure, and that his army was stranded with insufficient supplies for an extended campaign. So he dispatched what was left of his fleet to Asia Minor and returned the way he had come, leaving behind some 50,000 troops to winter in Thessaly, where grain enough could be found to feed that many but no more. The following summer, land forces of the Panhellenic League attacked and annihilated Xerxes' 50,000 at Plataea, 40 miles northwest of Athens. That summer also the combined Greek fleet hunted down the Persian fleet drawn up aground on the eastern shore of the Aegean Sea, defeated its guard force, and with fire destroyed what was left of Xerxes' armada.

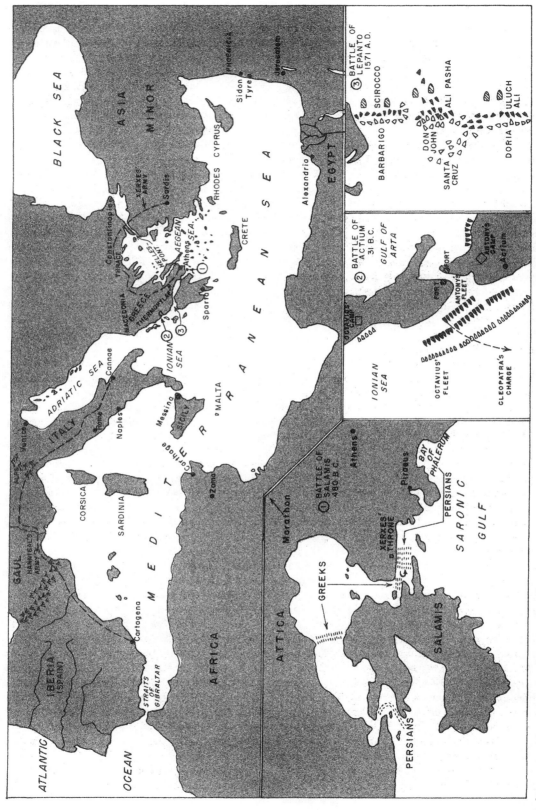

Mediterranean Operations in the Age of Galley Warfare

The Battle of Salamis and its aftermath illustrate as clearly as any operations in history the truth of naval philosopher Alfred Thayer Mahan's famous dictum: "Communications dominate war." An army that cannot live off the land is no stronger than its line of supply, and when its supplies must come across water, a victory at sea can set the stage for a victory on land.

The Greek victory ushered in the Golden Age of Athens, in which the Athenians gained maritime and commercial superiority and achieved an intellectual and artistic preeminence that laid the foundations for Western civilization. Conversely, Salamis marked the beginning of Persia's decline. The Persians never again invaded Greece. In the century following Salamis, Greeks and Macedonians, led by Alexander the Great, overran and conquered the moribund Persian Empire.

The Rise of Rome

For two centuries after Salamis, Carthage and the Greeks of southern Italy and Sicily held each other in check. The Carthaginians controlled the waters west of the Mediterranean narrows as their private lake, but the Greeks consistently blocked their attempts to advance eastward. In 275 B.C., however, the Romans, expanding from the Tiber basin, conquered southern Italy, engulfing the Greek cities.

The Carthaginians at first saw Rome's conquest of the Italian Greeks as their own opportunity and promptly renewed their pressure on the Greeks of Sicily. They were thereby coming to grips with a rival far more formidable than any they had ever encountered. The Romans, sturdy and resolute, originally of farming stock, had developed a genius for administration and the arts of war. When the Carthaginians in 264 B.C. threatened to send troops into Messana (modern Messina), just across the strait from the toe of the Italian boot, the alarmed Romans sent their legions into Sicily and quickly bottled up the Carthaginians in their fortified cities at the western end of the island. They thereby launched the first of three Punic wars (so called from the Latin word for Carthaginian) and took the initial step toward overseas conquests.

Rome's first problem in her century-long conflict with Carthage was how to deal with the Punic navy, which not only guarded Carthage from Roman attack but promptly interdicted Rome's maritime commerce and began to plunder her coasts. The problem was twofold: how to acquire a fleet, and how to handle it. Solving the first proved not

too difficult; Rome's subject and allied Greek cities provided galleys and also shipbuilders to build additional galleys. More perplexing was how to deal with the highly evolved Carthaginian mode of sea fighting, which included ramming, sideswiping, flanking, and breaking the line—distinctly naval tactics, designed to concentrate ships against ships. Rome's only hope was to force a return to the "old tactics" used before Salamis, tactics that concentrated men against men. Rome would then have the advantage of confronting the Punic mercenaries with her own specialty, the well-disciplined legionaries. The crux of the problem was how to get close enough to the agile foe to throw men on board his ships.

The ingenious Roman solution was the corvus, an 18-foot gangway bearing a pointed iron beak under the outboard end. Pivoted from a mast by a topping lift, it could be dropped forward or on either side to grip an unwary enemy vessel that approached close enough to ram or sideswipe. Over the gangway, foot soldiers then surged to convert a naval battle into an infantry battle across decks. The corvus first proved decisive off Mylae in 260, when the Carthaginians, despising their lubberly foe, bore down without bothering to assume a formation. The crashing corvi and the expert legionaries promptly disposed of nearly half the enemy ships and sent the rest scurrying in bewildered flight. In a subsequent battle off Mt. Ecnomus, the Romans not only made deft use of their corvi but, in a dazzling display of teamwork and command control, turned Punic envelopment tactics to their own advantage. But Roman ingenuity and teamwork proved after all no adequate substitute for seamanship. Admonished by a defeat and the loss in storms of several mishandled fleets, the Romans by dogged perseverance at length made themselves such skillful sailors that they brought the First Punic War to a close with a naval battle in which they defeated the enemy through sheer shiphandling.

Such was the ascendancy the Romans had won at sea that in the Second Punic War, the Carthaginian general, Hannibal, chose to attack Rome overland from Spain via the Alps. Though he managed to maintain himself in Italy for 15 years, he did so only by ravaging farm lands to sustain his army, thereby incurring the wrath of the disaffected Roman subject states, on which he had counted for aid. At length when Rome, by virtue of her sea command, carried the war to Africa, Hannibal hastened home to the defense, only to be defeated in the Battle of Zama. The Third Punic War began with a Roman seaborne invasion of Africa and concluded with the razing of Carthage and the utter destruction of the Carthaginian power.

Rome's first war with Carthage gave her Sicily as a province, the second gave her Spain, and the third gave her North Africa. The struggle and the final victory provided the warlike experience that carried Roman armies eastward through the Hellenic Peninsula and the Middle East to the Caspian Sea and the Persian Gulf and northward through Gaul to Britain.

During the period of expansion, the Roman navy, ever the neglected stepchild, cleared the Mediterranean of pirates, covered the overseas transport of the invincible legions, and successfully challenged any hostile fleet that had the temerity to contest Rome's command of the seas. In the process Rome completed her naval education. The legionaries remained her principal weapon on the sea as on land, but these she learned increasingly to support by judicious use of ship tactics and, later, missile tactics—employment of catapults and ballistae to hurl stones, javelins, and combustibles. Out of this combination the methodical Romans developed a fighting team as irresistible at sea as their infantry proved on land.

Rome's far-reaching conquests were at length interrupted by civil war at home. Control of the expanding empire was disputed between Mark Antony, married to Cleopatra, queen of Egypt, and Octavius, grandnephew and adoptive son of the assassinated Julius Caesar. Octavius accused Antony of planning to subdue Rome and make Alexandria the imperial capital. The dispute was decided in 31 B.C. by the Battle of Actium. Fought off the west coast of Greece, it was the last major naval battle of antiquity.

To meet Octavius's fleet of 260 galleys, Antony put to sea with about 200 much larger vessels. The latter were burdened with troops and stores—and carried sails, for flight in event of defeat. Neither Octavius nor his admiral, Agrippa, was overawed by Antony's floating monsters. Aware that their opponent had legionaries every bit as good as theirs, they intended to avoid boarding or being boarded. Correctly estimating that the big ships would prove sluggish, they planned to maneuver and use naval tactics against Antony's infantry and missiles.

Initially the opposing fleets were drawn up facing each other in three squadrons abreast, each squadron composed of galleys in single line abreast. Each galley thus protected its neighbors' vulnerable sides, where the banks of oars were exposed, and at the same time exposed to the enemy its fighting part, the bow, with its ram, its grappling devices, and its missile-hurling apparatus. Behind Antony's line was a reserve of 60 vessels under Cleopatra.

Through the morning the opposing fleets remained inactive. At noon a breeze set Antony's left flank in motion, and soon the fleets were engaged all down the line. Octavius's ships avoided compact formations of the enemy, but attacked vessels that had become isolated, darting in to sweep away oars and then, without pausing to permit boarding, backing off and striking swiftly again. At a crucial moment, Agrippa discharged a terrifying fire of blazing arrows and pots of flaming charcoal that had considerably greater range than his opponent's catapulted stones.

Seeing the battle turning against Antony, Cleopatra came charging through the center of both lines with the wind at her back and her reserve squadron under sail. Octavius's agile ships seem merely to have drawn aside and let her pass, leaving her separated from the main body of Antony's fleet. Since the wind did not permit her to reverse course and repeat her maneuver, she headed south and sailed away to Egypt. Antony boarded one of his smaller craft and managed to join her, but the rest of the fleet, under attack by Agrippa's fiery missiles, could not disengage and follow according to plan. Instead, they fought on until the flaming arrows and fire pots decided the battle in Octavius's favor. After dark that evening what was left of Antony's fleet managed to slip away. A week later all of his surviving ships and his military forces in the area surrendered to Octavius. This victory gave Octavius command of the whole Mediterranean, an indispensable preliminary to his subsequent conquest of Egypt and his assumption of imperial power as Caesar Augustus.

For five centuries after Actium, commercial vessels moved from the Black Sea to the Atlantic protected only by small fleets of police vessels to keep down piracy. The entire Mediterranean and its tributary waters had become a closed sea, with all coasts and naval bases controlled by Rome. On land and sea the *Pax Romana* was established, the longest period of comparative peace in history.

The Decline of Rome and the Rise of Europe

The heavy influx of slaves, which for centuries had offset Rome's declining birthrate, came to an end as the Roman conquest reached its limits. Into the resulting manpower vacuum at first seeped, then poured, the Germanic peoples of northern and eastern Europe—originally by invitation, as farmers and soldiers; then by permission, to escape the inroads of the nomadic Huns out of Central Asia; and at last as conquerors. Under these stresses, the Empire split into two parts, each having its own emperor: the Western Roman Empire, with its capital at Rome, and the Eastern Roman, or Byzantine, Empire, with its capital at Constantinople.

By the end of the fifth century A.D., the Western Empire had disappeared as a political entity. In the next century, the rise of Islam threatened all Roman and former Roman territories. Nomadic Arabs, filled with religious fervor by the eloquence of Muhammad, poured out of the Arabian desert and attacked the neighboring empires. The Persians and the Byzantines quickly gave way as Muslim forces advanced eastward to the Indus and westward to Egypt and the Bosporus.[2] Based securely on the whole Middle East, the Muslims took to the sea, overrunning Cyprus and Rhodes and raiding southern Italy and Sicily. At the same time they pushed westward across North Africa, conquering by the sword and then converting the defeated peoples to Islam. By A.D. 700 the invasion had reached the Straits of Gibraltar, across which Berber converts to Islam advanced to conquer Spain and invade Gaul. It appeared that Muslim power was about to engulf the whole Christian world. In the east, however, Constantinople held firm. An assault by 80,000 Muslims in 717 failed to breach the city walls, and Byzantine galleys scattered the blockading fleet with a new incendiary weapon, the practically inextinguishable Greek fire. In the West, the Muslim thrust into Gaul was repelled in 732 by a Frankish army.

The Franks under Charlemagne, in cooperation with the Papacy, briefly restored order in western Europe, but the Frankish empire fell apart under fresh attacks by the Muslims in the South, by Slavs and kindred peoples in the East, and by Vikings out of Scandinavia in the North. Thus, while the Islamic and Byzantine empires reached peaks of culture and enlightenment, the West entered a period of disorder and confusion.

Out of the ruins of the Frankish empire at length rose the Holy Roman Empire, embracing Germany and most of Italy. The Vikings ceased their raids and blended with the peoples whose lands

they had penetrated. The Slavs settled down in the areas east of the new empire. Only the Muslims continued to pick at the frontiers of Christendom, while their fleets dominated the Mediterranean.

By the eleventh century Christendom was ready to strike back. Christian forces expelled the Muslims from Sardinia and Sicily and thrust them down into southern Spain. In 1095 Pope Urban II preached the First Crusade. By the end of the century the Christians had captured Jerusalem and very nearly swept the Arabs from the seas.

The Crusades, which fired Western imagination for 250 years, were responsible for a prodigious growth of the Italian commercial cities. These cities took over the bulk of the carrying trade between East and West, their merchant fleets picking up spices and fine goods at the termini of the Oriental caravan routes in the Middle East and transporting them to the coastal cities of southern and western Europe.

Venice was especially fortunate in her central position. Situated at the head of the Adriatic, her merchants had ready access to the passes of the Alps, through which they conducted a lucrative commerce with northern Europe. As a result of the sack of Constantinople by the Fourth Crusade, partly instigated by the Venetians, Venice acquired possession of Crete. Subsequently she increased her control over the sea traffic by annexing Cyprus. The great Arsenal of Venice, a sort of assembly-line shipbuilding yard, provided the fleets of galleys whereby she enforced her monopoly. By the year 1400, when Venice was at the height of her power and grandeur, she had 3,000 ships, and in a population of 200,000, had 38,000 seamen.

But prospering Christendom was already under attack by a new surge of Muslim aggression. Political and religious feuds among the Arabs opened the way for the Turks, coming down out of the hills of central Asia, to take over the Arab world and its religion. By 1400 the Turks had swept across the Dardanelles and advanced to the Danube. In 1453 Constantinople, surrounded, fell before a Turkish siege backed by guns.

The Byzantine Empire, which for a thousand years after the fall of Rome had been a bastion of Europe and a preserver of the ancient culture, had at last been extinguished. Thereafter, the Turks overran eastern Europe as far as Vienna, and from their bases in North Africa and the Middle East, increasingly dominated the Mediterranean. Like the Arabs, they gladly served in the profitable capacity of middleman for the trade between Europe and the Orient, but this did not in the least

---

[2]*Muslim*: believer in the faith taught by Muhammad. *Islam*: the whole body of Muslims; also the religion.

hinder their sea rovers from capturing Christian merchant ships and enslaving their crews or from raiding and pillaging the Mediterranean coasts of western Europe.

The Campaign of Lepanto

Against the menace of the Turkish (Ottoman) Empire there was never any such spontaneous uniting of the forces of Christendom as had carried European armies and navies into the Middle East during the Crusades. A Turkish invasion of Cyprus in 1570, however, at length provided the atmosphere of urgency and alarm that drew the Christian Mediterranean powers together. Pope Pius V sponsored the creation of an anti-Muslim Holy League. Neither Portugal nor the Holy Roman Empire would have any part of the alliance, but Spain and the Italian states answered the papal summons and dispatched their fleets for a concentration at Messina, for it was clear that the Christians would have to defeat the Turks at sea before Christian armies could land on Cyprus.

The Christian fleet comprised some 200 galleys, mostly Venetian and Spanish, with a few from the Pope and from Genoa, Savoy, and Malta. Their total complement was about 44,000 seamen, including rowers, and 28,000 soldiers, of whom two-thirds were supplied by Spain. Commander in chief of the fleet was Don John of Austria. Though the choice was dictated by his half brother, Philip II of Spain, it was not an unpopular one, for at the age of 24 Don John was known as an experienced and successful campaigner on land and sea. The Ottoman fleet, commanded by Ali Pasha, numbered about 250 galleys, manned by 50,000 seamen and 25,000 soldiers.

The galleys on both sides were long, slim, flat-bottomed craft like those of ancient Greece and Rome, but they carried an 18-foot spur above the waterline in place of the classic underwater ram. While the Turks still clung to the bow and arrow, many of the Christian soldiers were armed with the arquebus, precursor of the musket. All the galleys carried guns at the bow. The Venetians brought along six galleasses—heavy, sluggish vessels with guns on bow and in broadside.

In mid-September 1571, the ships of the Holy League set out from Messina, crossed to the Greek coast, and worked their way slowly against head winds to an extension of the Gulf of Lepanto, where the Turkish fleet was known to be mobilized. Early in the morning of 7 October, Christian lookouts sighted Ali Pasha's squadrons approaching from within the gulf.

The Battle of Lepanto is especially significant as the first great galley action since the Battle of Actium, and also as the last great galley action. As at Actium, fought 16 centuries earlier only a few miles north of the scene of Lepanto, the opposing fleets were in three squadrons abreast, the ships of each squadron in line abreast. Both Turks and Christians held an additional squadron in reserve in the rear. Don John made an innovation in the ancient battle plan by placing the four galleasses that arrived on time ahead of his squadrons of galleys. When the Turks advanced to attack, they were obliged to sweep around these floating fortresses, taking heavy losses from their broadside guns.

As the opposing lines came together, each galley fired its bow guns two or three times. The battle then became a general melee, particularly at the center, with ramming, grappling, boarding, and fighting across decks. The hottest fighting soon developed between the opposing flagships and their supporters. Twice the Turks entered Don John's ship, and both times they were driven back as additional Christian soldiers came on board from adjoining vessels. At the crucial moment, Santa Cruz, Spanish commander of the Holy League reserve, arrived with 200 additional men. Then one of the Christian galleys, ranging alongside the Turk, swept her deck with arquebus fire, whereupon Italians and Spaniards, including Don John himself, poured on board the enemy flagship and took possession, killing Ali and all that remained of his crew.

At the northern end of the line of battle, the ships of the Turkish right squadron, under Scirocco, attempted to outflank the Christian left by putting in close to the shore, exploiting their superior knowledge of the shallows. But Barbarigo, the Christian squadron commander, concluding that where there was enough water for Turks there was enough for Christians, also closed the beach and planted his left wing impassably against the coast. At the same time, Barbarigo's right wing, taking advantage of the Turkish shift shoreward, enveloped Scirocco's left flank like a closing door. The Turks, thus surrounded and forced against the coast, were defeated in an hour of fierce fighting.

A Turkish attempt to envelop at the opposite end of the line of battle came nearer success. Here the Turkish squadron commander, Uluch Ali, made a feint at the right flank of his opponent, Doria, who to avoid being enveloped edged south.

He thereby opened a broad gap between his squadron and the Christian center. Uluch Ali, seeing his opportunity, shifted course to the northwest and headed for the opening in order to outflank the right wing of Don John's center squadron. In this he partially succeeded, doing fearful carnage among the Christians in that area. But by now Don John's squadron was so near victory that it could swing bows around toward the point of attack. Before Doria, having realized his blunder, could get back into the battle, Santa Cruz had thrown his reserve squadron into the breach, and Uluch Ali was in flight.

When the battle ended late in the afternoon, the Gulf was red with blood. According to contemporary Christian accounts, possibly exaggerated, 30,000 Turks lost their lives and all but 60 of their ships were captured or destroyed. The Christian losses were 12 ships and 7,700 men.

Like most purely naval victories, the triumph of the Holy League at Lepanto was both decisive and indecisive. The Christians had won the moral ascendancy; their dread of the Turk was never again so great as it had been, and the Turks thereafter operated with a prudence that kept their incursions within bounds. They and their subsidiary states of North Africa never again threatened to dominate the Mediterranean.

On the other hand, because the Holy League soon broke asunder and the Christians did not follow up their success at sea with combined intervention ashore, the Turks retained possession of Cyprus, and armed Muslim vessels continued to create an almost intolerable nuisance. The "Barbary System" of raiding excursions and extortion of tribute and ransom from Christian powers continued for centuries.

Summary

Rowed warships called galleys came into being mainly to control communications on the sea by defending friendly freighters and disrupting the movements of enemy freighters. To the extent that they achieved this dual objective, generally by destroying enemy warships, they are said to have attained command of the sea.

A striking example of galleys controlling communications occurred in a Persian expedition against Greece in 480 B.C. In the Battle of Salamis, the Greeks drew the Persian fleet into a narrow strait where the latter could not profit by their superior numbers. Then, avoiding the across-decks tactics of the Persians, the Greeks attacked and defeated them with the rams of their agile, many-oared triremes. The Persian army, its supply ships now menaced by the victorious Greek warships, was obliged to retreat to avoid starvation. Few campaigns more clearly confirm Mahan's dictum: "Communications dominate war."

In the third century B.C., the Romans, expanding out of the Tiber basin, overran the Greek cities of southern Italy and clashed with the Africa-based Carthaginians. From the latter they wrested control of the western Mediterranean, at first by gripping the Carthaginian galleys with the corvus, a pivoted, beaked gangway across which Roman legionaries surged, and later by means of improved naval tactics.

After adding the Carthaginian domains to her growing empire, Rome sent her conquering legions, ofttimes spearheaded by her navy, into Europe, Asia Minor, and Egypt. Rome's far-reaching conquests were at last interrupted by civil war at home. At sea, the climax of the civil war was reached in the Battle of Actium, in 31 B.C. At Actium, the galleys, in the final evolution of naval warfare under oars, began the battle with each fleet in single line abreast. The galleys of Octavius, by virtue of superior maneuverability, defeated those of Mark Antony. Octavius's victory set the stage for unification of the Roman Empire under himself as Caesar Augustus.

Four centuries later, the Empire split in two. The Western Roman Empire was then overrun by Germanic invaders, and the Eastern Roman, or Byzantine, Empire was invaded by Muslim Arabs. In the eighth century A.D., Constantinople, the eastern capital, was saved by the Byzantine galleys, which repulsed a blockading Arab fleet by use of the almost inextinguishable Greek fire.

The Crusades, originally organized to wrest the Holy Land from the Muslims, stimulated the growth and enrichment of the Italian commercial cities, which took over the bulk of the shipping between East and West. Venice, situated at the head of the Adriatic Sea, was especially fortunate in her central position. She brought goods by sea from the Middle East and the Mediterranean and transported them over the passes of the Alps to the cities of northern Europe. By 1400, to carry her maritime trade, Venice owned 3,000 ships protected by fleets of galleys.

Meanwhile, the Turks had overrun the Arab empire, adopted its Muslim religion, and swept across the Dardanelles and advanced to the

Danube. In 1453 Constantinople, surrounded, fell before a Turkish siege. Thereafter the Turks overran eastern Europe as far as Vienna, and from their bases in North Africa and the Middle East increasingly dominated the Mediterranean.

The Mediterranean showdown between the Christians and the Muslims occurred in the naval Battle of Lepanto, in 1571, with the galley fleets of Spain and Italy arrayed against that of the Turks. As at Actium, fought 16 centuries earlier in nearby waters, the opposing fleets fought in single line abreast. The Christians soundly defeated the Turks and thereby gained moral ascendancy in the Mediterranean, but armed Muslim vessels continued to create an almost intolerable nuisance in those waters. The "Barbary System" of seaborne raids and extortion of tribute and ransom from Christian powers continued for centuries.

Chapter 2
The Rise of English Sea Power

Though the Vikings employed combat craft using oars as well as sails, galley warfare did not develop to any great extent in Atlantic waters. Slim, shallow-draft galleys, adequate for the choppy waters of the Mediterranean, were too easily capsized by the long ocean swells. Besides, the kings of medieval western Europe could not afford ships specially designed for fighting. When they wished to contest the seas with their rivals, they usually called on their merchants for cargo sailing vessels—crank, broad-beamed, single-masted ships—and sent them out loaded with soldiers to do the work. Fighting consisted mostly of grappling and boarding, and the action ended when the soldiers on the captured vessels were tossed over the side to drown.

The first structural refinement in men-of-war under sail was the addition of temporary towers fore and aft, called forecastles and aftercastles. When the enemy succeeded in boarding, the defenders retreated into these towers and rained down stones, arrows, hot pitch, and, later, shot upon the intruders in the waist of the ship. From the towers too, missiles could be fired and stones dropped upon the enemy in the ships alongside. The towers, or castles, proved so useful that the merchant owners had them built permanently into new construction, for one never knew when he might have to deal with pirates or other raiders. This is only one of the many structural changes resulting from the occasional use of cargo carriers as men-of-war. The great advances in ship design in the fifteenth century doubtless owed much to this dual employment.

The ancient, relatively frail cargo carrier with one mast and one sail evolved in the fifteenth century into a full-rigged ship with three or four masts, a bowsprit, and five or more sails—a vessel strong enough to cope with Atlantic gales and swift and seaworthy enough to cross vast stretches of ocean without replenishment or repair. The compass, coming into general use in ships, gave the seafarer his approximate direction in any sort of weather. He had learned to measure his approximate speed by observing the time it took his vessel to pass a

bubble or a bit of flotsam. Using these two factors, he was able to find his way reasonably well by dead reckoning.

Though dead reckoning enabled the mariner to guess intelligently, once out of sight of land he was never really sure of his course or position. Contemporary instruments for finding latitude all required a steady platform and some knowledge of mathematics; the sea-tossed mariner rarely had either. In general he found it wise to sail north or south along the coast to the latitude of his destination and then strike out due east or west, hoping to make a recognizable landfall on the far shore. Finding longitude was utterly beyond his means because he had no way of accurately measuring time. Development of the dependable chronometer and the reflecting quadrant, which would solve his navigation problems, was still centuries away. Nevertheless, ships out of western Europe ventured farther and farther afield.

Meanwhile, rising commercial interests along Europe's Atlantic seaboard were observing with envy the Italian and German monopoly of the rich carrying trade from the Orient. The cottons, silks, spices, dyes, perfumes, and gems of the East found a ready market in the West, even though prices quadrupled in transit—chiefly as a result of costly transport from the Persian Gulf or the Red Sea to the Mediterranean. Toward the end of the medieval period, Europeans dwelling on the Atlantic front began to consider old legends and quasi-historical accounts of unbroken water routes to the Orient. The invention of printing made widely available ancient ideas of a spherical world, so that daring thinkers and explorers dreamed of reaching the Far East either around Africa or across the mysterious Atlantic.

Explorers sponsored by Prince Henry "the Navigator" of Portugal inched their way down the west coast of Africa. In 1487 Bartholomeu Dias, by rounding the Cape of Good Hope, raised to a near certainty the belief in an all-water route to the Orient. In 1492 Christopher Columbus, sponsored by the queen of Spain, crossed the Atlantic in search of a competing route and instead discovered the New World. Six years later Vasco da Gama completed the work of Diaz by sailing from Portugal around Africa all the way to India.

Results flowing from these discoveries ushered in the modern period, sometimes known as the Oceanic Age. Portuguese fleets, following in the wake of da Gama, easily defeated the Arab traders in the Indian Ocean, established a trade empire stretching from East Africa to Japan, and secured a monopoly of the rich spice trade of the East Indies. Spanish conquest of Mexico and Peru made available to Spain wealth accumulated over the centuries by the Indian civilizations, and the working of American gold and silver mines assured an apparently inexhaustible flow of precious metal into the Spanish treasury. These changes were bound to have a shattering effect upon the Old World economy.

Europe was already in ferment. The vague internationalism of the feudal system was giving way to national feudalisms with a dominant monarch. National monarchs were abetted in the increase of their power by a rising merchant class that wanted domestic peace, uniform coinage, and a centralized government favorable to commerce and industry. The Church, for centuries a unifying influence, was itself beginning to break asunder in the Protestant Reformation. The new maritime discoveries hastened the breakup of medieval unity by shifting European interests from the East, so long the focus of trade and the source of recurrent threats of conquest, to the West, where nationalism had made its greatest advances. With loss of trade, the Ottoman Empire gradually weakened, and the commercial cities of Italy and Germany went into a decline. The inland seas of Europe and the Middle East, from the Baltic to the Red Sea and from the Mediterranean to the Persian Gulf, became backwaters. The major states of Europe's Atlantic seaboard—Spain, Portugal, France, the Netherlands, and England—began to rise as rival oceanic powers.

The English Navy

King Henry VIII was the first English monarch prosperous enough to be able to build a few national ships, intended exclusively for fighting. Henry's shipbuilding nearly coincided with the development of the big, muzzle-loading ship guns, which eventually displaced the small railing-pieces that were mounted on bulwarks and in the castles to repel or defeat boarders. Because placing the heavy guns so high above the waterline could cause the vessel to capsize, the king's carpenters cut gunports in the sides and mounted most of them on

the "cargo deck." Thus the first broadsides came into being. An action off Shoreham in 1545, demonstrating that the broadsides could destroy ships as well as kill men, introduced a new sort of warfare under sail. "Off-fighting" had become possible; ships no longer had to be in physical contact to "engage."

With the introduction of guns in broadside and King Henry's decision that he would have a fighting fleet apart from the merchant marine, England began to forge ahead of all other nations in warship design. Progress slackened during the brief reigns of Edward VI and Mary Tudor. Under Elizabeth I it came to a standstill until the threat of a Spanish attack impelled her to resume Henry's naval rearmament.

Philip II of Spain took very seriously his role as leading Roman Catholic monarch and champion of the Church of Rome. We have seen how he responded to Pope Pius V's proclamation of 1570 against the Muslims and the part his galley fleet played in the Battle of Lepanto. In 1570 also, the Pope, despairing of reclaiming Protestant England, excommunicated Queen Elizabeth, branded her a heretic and usurper, and called on Philip to launch a crusade against her as well as the Turks. To the Spanish monarch, northern Europe's heretical Protestantism was every bit as detestable as infidel Islam, but against Elizabeth he was not prepared to move. He had his hands full, being at war with both the Turks and his Netherlands subjects, the latter having revolted against his bloody drive to suppress Dutch Protestantism.

Elizabeth realized that Philip's forbearance was only temporary. Once his hands were freed, he would undoubtedly try to oust her from her throne. She therefore set about strengthening England's defenses and undermining the power of Spain. In 1572 she achieved a masterstroke by allying herself with the King of France. Then she secretly released her gold-hungry seamen against Philip's treasure ships and with equal secrecy encouraged her subjects to aid the Dutch. More to the point, she began rebuilding her neglected navy.

Foremost among the semi-pirates that the queen turned loose against Spanish colonies and shipping were John Hawkins and his cousin and protégé Francis Drake. Hawkins's position as chief sea commander of England made his opinions respected long before he was appointed Treasurer and Controller of the Navy in 1577. A prosperous merchant shipowner of Plymouth, he had interspersed peaceful pursuits with periods of freebooting and slave-running in Spanish–American waters, sometimes with royal connivance and profit.

His experiences at sea, which included some hot fighting, had imbued him with a dislike for boarding tactics and an unshakable respect for guns and maneuver. By his advice and, later, under his stewardship, royal combat vessels became floating gun platforms emphasizing speed and mobility. The lofty fore- and aftercastles were reduced, and length was increased relative to beam.

Though armament was outside Hawkins's responsibility, his influence can be detected in this department also. If the new fashion in the English navy was to eschew hand-to-hand fighting for long-range gunnery, then guns of the longest range were desirable. So we find in English ships fewer and fewer stubby, short-range guns firing heavy shot and an increasing proportion of long-barreled guns called culverins that could throw a light 17-pound ball 1¼ miles.

One priceless advantage Elizabeth possessed was her seamen. They had little opportunity to develop tactical niceties, but their freebooting excursions had endowed them with an incomparable knowledge of ships and the sea.

The Challenge of Spain

Nothing infuriated Philip II more than the raiding of Spanish bases and shipping by English privateers, whom the irate Spaniards considered mere pirates. The most famous of such expeditions was that of Drake's *Golden Hind*, which entered the Pacific through the Straits of Magellan in 1578 and raided Spanish cities and shipping up and down the west coast of South America. Drake returned to England via the Cape of Good Hope, arriving in 1581 with gold, silver, and jewels valued at half a million pounds sterling. Queen Elizabeth openly acquiesced in the enterprise by sequestering the bulk of the treasure and knighting Drake on his own quarterdeck. Though Philip raged, he was not yet prepared to risk open warfare. Instead he began secretly conspiring with the large Roman Catholic faction in England to assassinate Elizabeth. Her death would vacate the throne in favor of her Catholic cousin, Mary Stuart, Queen of Scots, whom Elizabeth had held captive since 1568, when Mary had been driven out of Scotland by the Calvinist hierarchy.

Two events in 1584 at length brought this clandestine warfare into the open. France was plunged into civil war by the death of the Catholic heir and the succession of a Protestant claimant to the throne; and an assassin in Spanish pay struck down William "the Silent," Stadtholder of the newly proclaimed Dutch republic. The war in France de-

stroyed the effectiveness of the Anglo–French alliance that had restrained Philip for 12 years; and the assassination of the Stadtholder paved the way for Spanish subjugation of the Netherlands, which would undoubtedly be followed by an invasion of England. Philip now began seizing English merchantmen peacefully trading in his ports. Elizabeth promptly retaliated. To cut down still further the flow of precious metal to Spain, she sent Drake with a fleet of 19 ships to raid the Spanish Indies. She formed an alliance with Philip's rebellious Dutch subjects and dispatched an army to Holland. If there was to be war, she considered, it was better to fight on foreign soil with an ally than alone in her own realm. The Spanish king now stepped up his campaign for the assassination of Elizabeth. To remove the focus for such plots, Elizabeth early in 1587 reluctantly signed the death warrant of Mary Stuart. Philip thereupon openly claimed the crown of England, alleging his descent from Edward III and his marriage to Mary Tudor, Elizabeth's half sister and predecessor on the English throne.

The Spanish monarch proposed nothing less than a descent upon England out of the ports of Spain with an army carried and supported by a great naval armada. In the end he had to compromise by drawing most of his invasion troops from those engaged in Flanders against the Dutch, but his general concept remained. If Philip had any hope of conquering the English fleet with the weapons he had used in 1571 against the Turks, he was presently disabused, for in April 1587 Drake sailed boldly into the Spanish port of Cadiz with 23 ships, easily thrust aside the defending galleys, and destroyed some 18 cargo vessels. The vaunted galleys were clearly no match for England's sailing fleet with its long-range broadside batteries.

Luckily for Philip, he now had at his disposal the warships and armed merchantmen of Portugal and the services of Portugese marine constructors, men well acquainted with Atlantic naval shipbuilding practices. He adopted the sailing man-of-war and the broadside, somewhat grudgingly we may assume, for he could not forget Lepanto. Once more, as at Lepanto, he would rely on his infantry for victory at sea. To cripple the English vessels so that they could not maneuver out of reach of his boarders, he armed his ships with the biggest naval guns he could find, including some firing 50-pound shot.

The Grand Armada, as finally assembled and dispatched against England in July 1588, consisted of 130 vessels carrying 1,100 guns and 27,000 men, more than half of whom were soldiers. In command was the duke of Medina Sidonia, whose chief qualifications were noble rank and reputation for piety. Begging to be excused from so novel an undertaking, Medina had gloomily accepted the command only at Philip's insistence. His assignment was to proceed via the English Channel to Flanders, add 6,000 troops to the 17,000 already there under the duke of Parma, and then cover Parma's invasion force as it crossed in small craft from the Flemish port of Dunkirk to Margate at the mouth of the Thames. The English fleet was of course expected to give battle, probably before Parma's crossing could be carried out. Though Philip knew that the Englishmen intended to fight with guns alone, he specifically directed his Spaniards to "grapple and board and engage hand to hand."

Meanwhile the queen's navy of 34 men-of-war had been heavily reinforced. Armed merchantmen from the seaport towns and artillerymen from all over England had brought it up to the respectable strength of 197 vessels carrying 16,000 men and 2,000 guns. Mere numbers, however, fail to point up the really important differences between the opposing fleets. Though the English ships were in general lighter than the Spanish, they were incomparably handier and better handled. Moreover, they carried no infantrymen, only sailors and gunners. The Armada, with fewer guns, was superior in total weight of broadside, about 17 pounds per gun as compared to an English average of around 7 pounds. But most of the Spanish guns were heavy, medium-range cannon and light, short-range boarder-repelling pieces, while 95 percent of the English guns were long-range intermediate culverin types. Thus the Spaniards had the advantage in striking power; and the English in maneuverability, relatively clear decks, and range.

Like the Armada, the queen's fleet was officially headed by an aristocrat, Charles Howard of Effingham, Lord Admiral of England. An intelligent administrator, Lord Howard had the good sense to take the advice of his subordinates, old seadogs Drake, Hawkins, and Martin Frobisher. At crucial moments in the campaign, Drake virtually exercised command.

The clash, which took place off the English coast, was epochal in two respects. It was an all-out confrontation between the chief champions of Catholicism and of Protestantism, and it was the first major contest between sailing fleets. In the past there had been many small-scale skirmishes under sail, but none had provided experience on which to base a tactical doctrine. The English, however, were well aware of the advantages conferred by possession of the weather gage, the position upwind of the enemy. The windward fleet

could choose the range and decide when to engage, and it could attack the windward part of the enemy's fleet while the rest of his fleet was held in check by the wind. The Spaniards seem to have been less appreciative of these advantages.

A detached force of the English fleet under Lord Henry Seymour watched Parma from Dover, but the main body, under Howard, took station off Plymouth in order to profit by the prevailing southwesterly wind. This was the wind that blew the Spanish Armada into the English Channel, where it caught Howard's fleet beating out of Plymouth Sound. Had Medina Sidonia attacked then, the result might have been disastrous for England. Instead, he sailed majestically past Plymouth, and Howard fell in behind, seizing the weather gage and blocking the line of retreat back to Spain. For a week the Armada sailed slowly up the Channel while the English, holding off beyond the range of the Spanish guns, fired at its weathermost ships. There were three hot engagements, but they were far from general, for such was the bunched condition of both fleets that most broadsides were masked by friendly hulls.

During the run up the Channel, the Spaniards fired more than 100,000 rounds, and the English fired almost as many, yet neither fleet seriously hurt the other. The reason is clear: the range, selected by the English, was too great. The Spaniards, despite their heavy guns, achieved almost nothing because they simply could not get at Howard's nimble ships, which generally managed to keep to windward. The English did little better because, at the range they chose, their light shot could not penetrate Spanish hulls.

For all Howard's attempts to thwart them, the Spaniards had apparently achieved their first objective when on 7 August the Armada, practically intact, dropped anchor in the neutral port of Calais. Actually they were in a poor situation, for Calais was not the logistic base they sorely needed. Howard had won after all, because he could be resupplied with ammunition from England, whereas Medina Sidonia had fired off most of his heavy shot and could get no more. In the dubious hope that the mere presence of the Armada would hold the English fleet in check, Medina sent a messenger posthaste to the duke of Parma urging him to launch the invasion forthwith. But Parma, tightly blockaded by Seymour and the Dutch fleet, could not move.

While Medina was still wondering what to do next, Howard sent eight fireships into Calais Roads, forcing out the Spanish fleet in the middle of the night. The next day, off Gravelines, the English

Western Europe

attacked. They now abandoned long-range fire and closed with impunity because the Spaniards, lacking shot for their big guns, could reply only with small boarder repellers and muskets.

At this critical moment, the shaky English logistic system broke down completely. No more shiploads of powder and shot arrived for the queen's fleet. After Howard had sunk two ships, driven

three others on the shoals, and littered the Spanish decks with casualties, he too ran out of ammunition.

Fortunately for England, the Spaniards were already on the run. With the wind against them and the English behind them, they were convinced that they had no choice but to retreat into the North Sea. Howard plowed the Spanish wake for a few days, spurring the fugitives with a brave show of wanting to attack. But the Grand Armada was already en route back to Spain—the long way, north and west of the British Isles.

In the Atlantic, hunger and thirst completed Spanish demoralization. Storms and inept navigation scattered the Spanish ships. Some 35 or 40 foundered at sea. At least a score were wrecked upon the rocky shores of Scotland and Ireland. In October Philip received back into ports of Spain no more than half the military power he had sent so confidently against England.

"God breathed and they were scattered," so went the inscription on the Protestant victory medals. Yet it was the English fleet that wore down Spanish morale, mauled the Spanish vessels into unseaworthiness, and forced the Spaniards, in a defeatist frame of mind and with insufficient provisions, to take the long voyage home that proved their undoing. In repulsing the Armada, English seamen also took the first major step in devising a tactical doctrine for sailing fleets. For them at least, decisions at sea were henceforth to be reached not by hand-to-hand combat but with the gun.

Historians of later times recognized that the catastrophic failure of the Armada marked the beginning of Spain's decline. The true situation was not so clear to contemporaries. Philip II at once lost some credit as defender of Catholicism, and England was stimulated into those ventures in commerce, exploration, and colonization that, together with the flourishing of literature, mark the Elizabethan Age.

The Anglo–Spanish conflict became a desultory raiding war, neither side daring to take decisive measures against the other. It ended at last in 1603 with the death of Queen Elizabeth and the accession of James I, king also of Scotland and son of Mary Stuart. James soon sealed an alliance with England's erstwhile enemy. In so doing, he abandoned the struggle for Dutch independence and sowed the seeds of future hostilities between England and Holland.

The Challenge of Holland

After the Armada, Englishmen, Frenchmen, and Dutchmen, at first circumspectly and then more and more boldly, infringed on lands and trade that the king of Spain claimed as his own. Englishmen settled the Atlantic seaboard of North America from Nova Scotia and the valley of the St. Lawrence, which the French staked off for themselves, to Florida, which Spaniards occupied. Until past the middle of the seventeenth century, however,

the Dutch claimed the Hudson Valley and maintained on Manhattan Island their prosperous colony of New Amsterdam. In the West Indies English, French, and Dutch adventurers rushed to seize islands that were not firmly in the hands of the Spaniards. The French and Dutch, moreover, obtained footholds in South America; and the English, in Central America.

In the competition for maritime trade, Holland quickly outstripped her rivals. Her long war with Spain, by which she won de facto independence in 1609, had actually nourished Dutch commerce and provided Holland with a formidable fleet to extend and protect it. But her decisive advantage was a business-minded government that steadily encouraged and supported commercial ventures. While England was torn internally by a struggle between king and Parliament, and France by a struggle between king and nobility, Holland more and more dominated commerce in the Baltic, the Middle East, and the Far East, and at the same time by legal and illegal means took over a large part of the American trade. Concurrently Dutchmen made themselves the chief whalers, fishermen, and carriers of Europe. Wherever the English and French turned to enrich themselves on the seas, they met ruinous competition from the enterprising seamen and traders of Holland. When they sought to participate in the spice trade, they found the Dutch so unshakably established in the East Indies that they were obliged to shift their interests to India. Holland's ruthless monopoly turned her seafaring competitors into enemies. The monopoly would have to be broken, insisted the mercantilists, if other sea powers hoped to prosper.

England was first to issue the challenge. It came late, for want of means to back it up. Elizabeth's navy had wasted away under James's mismanagement. When James's son and successor, Charles I, called for "ship money" to restore the fleet, his domestic enemies made his demand an issue in the civil war that broke out in 1642. Only after Charles had been defeated and beheaded by his own subjects, and Oliver Cromwell and the commercial interests had taken over the reins of government, did England seriously prepare to act. The new Commonwealth greatly enlarged the neglected navy, mostly through the sale of estates seized from the aristocracy. It improved the pay and victuals of the sailors, introduced an incentive system of "prize money" for captures or sinkings of enemy vessels, and reorganized and strengthened the naval establishment in every department. At length, armed with a powerful and disciplined fleet, Parliament threw down the gauntlet to Holland. It passed the famous Navigation Act of 1651, which stipulated that goods could be brought into England or English possessions only by English ships or by ships of the country where the goods originated. This Act, aimed directly at the Dutch carrying trade, brought about the first of three naval wars between Holland and England.

These wars revealed the fatal weaknesses underlying Holland's pretensions. First, she was absolutely dependent upon the sea for a livelihood, yet England dominated the sea approaches to her coast. Second, because Holland had a land as well as a sea frontier to guard, she was obliged to divert much of her wealth and manpower to building fortresses and maintaining a standing army. Third, the Dutch fleet, though formidable in numbers of ships, was composed of small, unhandy, relatively flat-bottomed craft built to enter the shallow Dutch harbors. Finally, the English navy usually managed to keep a tactical step ahead of the Dutch.

This last is surprising, for the Dutch admirals were reputed to be the best in the world. The English navy, on the other hand, was initially headed not by admirals at all but by army officers called generals-at-sea—put in command of the fleet by Cromwell, who suspected his naval officers of monarchism.

In the First Anglo–Dutch War (1652–54), the generals-at-sea must have been appalled at the formlessness of naval warfare as they found it. In March 1653 they issued a new set of Fighting Instructions. Included was the epochal Article 3: "All ships in every squadron shall endeavor to keep in line with the chief. . . ." This article did away with bunching of ships and established the column as the standard formation.

The column, also called *line ahead*, is the logical corollary of the broadside. In column no broadside is masked by a friendly ship; all have a clear line of fire. Ships are mutually supporting and hence difficult to board or to defeat in detail. Enemy vessels cannot readily get across their bows or sterns, where they are out of reach of the broadside guns and whence they can send deadly raking fire the length of the ship.

In the second year of the war, the new English fleet and its maritime generals caught their stride, roundly trounced the Dutch fleet twice in succession, and then blockaded Holland into submission. Cromwell let the Dutch off with payment of an indemnity and an agreement to admit the English on equal terms to the East Indies trade.

Charles II, son of the beheaded Charles I, on his restoration to the English throne in 1660, conferred upon England's naval force the title Royal Navy and appointed as Lord High Admiral his brother James, Duke of York. The duke, far from repudiating the innovations of the Commonwealth Navy, adopted them all in the Fighting Instructions under which the second Anglo–Dutch War (1665–67) was fought. Nevertheless there arose a sharp division of opinion about how the Instructions were to be applied. The crux of the dispute had to do with the fleet line ahead. Nobody disparaged its value, at least for the approach, but there arose two rival schools of thought concerning what to do after contact with the enemy.

These groups have been called the Formal School and the Melee School. The formalists, a strictly naval group headed by the duke of York, insisted upon maintaining the line throughout the battle. The meleeists were ready, at a favorable opportunity, to unleash their squadron and ship commanders from the line and send them in on their own initiative to overpower the enemy in a massed attack. This would bring on a melee in which control would slip from the hands of the admiral, but it would produce a greater preponderance of gunfire at the decisive point than could ever be achieved by a battle line stretched out 12 miles or more, with a good many ships out of range of a disorderly enemy.

After the Dutch had suffered defeat at sea and seen their coast raided by the Royal Navy, they requested terms. King Charles dragged out the negotiations and at the same time laid up most of his ships and discharged the crews. This shortsighted action exposed England to humiliating counterattack. In June 1667, a powerful Dutch fleet entered the Thames estuary unopposed, seized naval stores, bombarded Chatham, burned seven large men-of-war, and captured the *Royal Charles*, flagship of the English navy. The Dutch fleet then clapped so tight a blockade on English shipping that the London government was soon ready to discuss peace. This time both sides gained and lost something. England relinquished all claims to the East Indies and modified the Navigation Act. The Dutch recognized the West Indies as an English sphere of influence and ceded the Hudson Valley and the colony of New Amsterdam, which the English renamed New York.

The Third Anglo–Dutch War (1672–74) was a senseless struggle, contrary both to English interests and to English public sentiment. Louis XIV of France (1643–1715), desiring to annex Holland, bribed King Charles into participating. He then invaded the Netherlands while Charles's navy launched a sudden attack on Dutch sea commerce. In Holland, William of Orange, the Stadtholder, checked the French invasion by opening the dikes and flooding the countryside. At sea, the Dutch fleet more than held its own in two skirmishes and two indecisive battles. The poor showing of England's vaunted fleet and the French navy's reluctance to fight turned English dissatisfaction into disgust. Accepting the inevitable, Charles not only made peace but sealed an alliance with Holland by giving the duke of York's daughter Mary in marriage to William of Orange.

Fear of imperialistic France had drawn Spain and several German states to the Dutch cause. King Louis, finding himself isolated against a growing coalition, in 1678 acknowledged his failure and made peace with the Dutch, from whom he had extracted not a foot of territory. England turned out to be the only beneficiary of the war, for more and more of the lucrative carrying trade had passed from exhausted Holland to English merchants.

Ships and Guns

When fleets abandoned bunching tactics for fighting in line ahead, small, lightly armed warships and armed merchantmen too often found themselves opposite men-of-war many times more powerful than themselves. This sort of thing had to be avoided because the strength of a column of ships lies in its coherence. Like a chain, it is no stronger than its weakest link. So, before the end of the seventeenth century, the smaller types were detached for cruising and patrol duty, became in fact the cruisers of the navy, and merchantmen went back to cargo hauling. The tendency thereafter was toward shorter, more homogeneous lines including only heavily gunned men-of-war considered "fit to lie in the line." Such ships were called *ships of the line*.

Men-of-war were divided into six rates according to the number of guns carried, first, second, and third rates being designated ships of the line, and the rest cruisers. Toward the end of the eighteenth century this terminology was replaced by rated number of guns, a system that prevailed until the end of the age of sail and a little beyond. Thus we read about a 74-gun ship of the line or a 36-gun frigate, though the number of guns carried might be somewhat more or less than the rated number. We also find men-of-war named with rated number of guns following: *Victory*, 100; *Constitution*, 44; *Wasp*, 20. To the initiated these figures indicate that the first was a ship of the line; the second, a frigate; and the third, a sloop-of-war.

Flagships of the line carried from 80 to more than 100 guns. In later periods some huge ships managed to crowd up to 140 on board. Ships of 80 guns and upward (first and second rates) were three-deckers; that is, they carried their guns on three complete decks, with additional guns on the forecastle and quarterdeck. A typical 100-gun ship carried 32-pounders (guns firing shot weighing 32 pounds) on her lower gun deck, 24-pounders on her middle deck, 18-pounders on her main deck, and 12-pounders on her forecastle and quarterdeck. All the guns were smoothbore muzzle loaders hurling solid-iron round shot, which were propelled by a charge ignited through a touchhole in the breech.

Most of the "private," or nonflag, ships in the line were two-deckers (third rates) carrying 74 guns. A good many 64s also were built, and some continued in use in the nineteenth century, but these economy-sized ships generally proved inadequate for service in the line.

An in-between and relatively rare type was the 50 (fourth rate), which served mainly as a flagship in cruiser squadrons. The fifth and sixth rates were the cruisers themselves. The most famous and numerous of these were the frigates, which initially carried 28 to 30 guns but were later standardized at 36 and 44. They were ship-rigged (square-rigged on three masts) single-deckers carrying a main battery of 12- and 18-pounders on the gun deck and with a secondary battery of 6-pounders on the forecastle and quarterdeck. The most versatile of men-of-war, the frigates carried out functions varying from commerce raiding to scouting for the fleet. In fleet action they normally took station on the unengaged side of their line to repeat signals or take disabled ships in tow. Smaller types were sloops-of-war—single-deckers, usually ship rigged with no secondary battery; brigs—square-rigged vessels with two masts; and schooners—fore-and-aft-rigged vessels with two masts.

Eighteenth-century warships carried huge complements of seamen, partly to work the great cloud of sail needed to drive such broad-beamed vessels at an acceptable speed (five to ten knots in average winds) but chiefly to manhandle the awkward guns of the period. A dozen men were required to secure, load, run out, and lay a long 32-pounder. Well-trained gun crews in the Royal Navy could fire a broadside every two or three minutes and get off three or four broadsides before exhaustion slowed them down. A few British captains toward the end of the century trained their crews to fire five broadsides in five minutes. French and Spanish gunners did well to get off one broadside every five minutes.

The Challenge of France

The continuing aggressions of Louis XIV so alarmed his continental neighbors that Austria, Spain, Sweden, and several German states banded defensively together in the anti-French League of Augsburg. Into this league England and Holland were soon drawn as the closest of allies. The duke of York had succeeded his brother Charles on the English throne as James II. An avowed Catholic, James undertook to Catholicize England, thereby so outraging parliamentary leaders that they invited William of Orange and his wife Mary (James's daughter) over from Holland to be joint sovereigns of England. William and Mary came, James fled to France, and England and Holland joined hands under a dual head of state. Attempts by Louis XIV to restore the deposed king brought about the War of the English Succession (1689–97), the first of seven successive wars in which England and France were antagonists.

Luckily for England, the accession of William and Mary brought the Dutch and English fleets into combination, for France had built the world's most powerful navy. The chief architect of French sea power was Jean Colbert, Louis XIV's mercantilist minister of finance. Under his patronage, French ship design became a science, far superior to the rather casual practices of the English. By the time of Colbert's death in 1683, the *Marine Française* was equal to any navy on the high seas. By 1689 it was numerically equal to the combined fleets of England and Holland.

French naval superiority was to a large extent offset by two serious handicaps. Because France was a continental power, the *Marine* had to compete with the army for military funds; in a long war it could not count on adequate replacements of men or material. And because France had two coasts, the Paris government felt obliged to divide its sea forces between the Atlantic and the Mediterranean, basing them on Brest and Toulon. The obvious English strategy was to keep France expensively campaigning in Europe and to prevent the two parts of the French fleet from uniting. During most of the Anglo–French wars, England achieved these objectives by encouraging, and even subsidizing, European allies, and by maintaining a fleet off Toulon or near the Straits of Gibraltar.

As regards tactics, Royal Navy commanders now had to deal with deep-draft ships that could easily keep in column. England's experience in the Armada campaign having demonstrated the futility of long-range fire, they now endeavored to get within 600 yards of the enemy. First, they maneuvered to seize the weather gage. They then came opposite but out of range of the enemy column. Next, on signal, the English ships put helms over and bore down on the enemy in line abreast—or, if the enemy had way on, in line of bearing. For the English this was often the most perilous phase of the battle, for it temporarily exposed their bows to raking fire. The French generally seized the advantage, firing on the upward roll and aiming at masts, yards, and rigging so as to impair the English ability

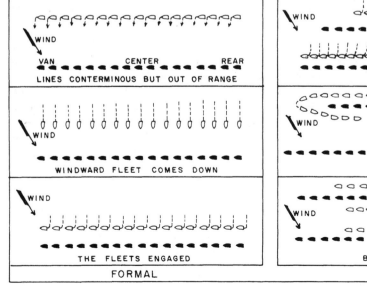

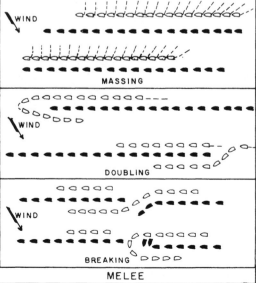

Fleet Tactics under Sail

to pursue. As the Royal Navy ships came within gun range, they turned together once more into line ahead, paralleling the enemy, and opened fire—usually on the downward roll, aiming at hulls.

In a formal battle, the opposing fleets remained in parallel columns, each ship firing at its opposite number until one fleet or the other flinched and withdrew. The meleeists argued that such tactics were likely to produce stalemate, and in fact the Royal Navy in the eighteenth century fought 13 formal battles, with every one a tactical draw—no ship was captured or destroyed on either side.

The meleeists argued that to defeat an enemy column of force equal to one's own, one had to bring more ships against fewer enemy ships at some portion of the enemy's line. This could be achieved by massing, that is, decreasing intervals between one's own ships, or by breaking through the enemy's column or doubling around his van or rear and thus placing a part of his line between two fires. (See diagrams, p. 19.) The formalists argued that such tactics merely invited the enemy to retaliate in like manner against one's own column.

The two naval engagements of the War of the English Succession seemed to support the formalists' objections to melee tactics. In the Battle of Beachy Head (1690), an outnumbered Anglo–Dutch fleet massed on the French rear, whereupon the French van doubled back on the allied van and crushed it. At the Battle of Barfleur (1692), the French attempted to mass on the allied rear, but their line was so stretched out elsewhere with long intervals between ships that the allies were able to break through the French center and achieve a victory.

For the French navy, Barfleur marked the end of offensive operations against fleets. King Louis, recognizing that he could not maintain both a powerful army and a formidable navy, sacrificed his fleet to his continental ambitions. Rotting ships were not replaced, others were laid up, still others joined swarms of French privateers in disputing the allied command of the sea by *guerre de course*—raiding the enemy's sea commerce.[1] Though France's strategy proved a serious nuisance to English shipping, it was far from decisive. England actually prospered. France, on the verge of financial ruin, was obliged to capitulate. By the terms of the peace treaty, Louis was forced to abandon all his continental conquests and to acknowledge William of Orange as king of England.

In the War of the Spanish Succession (1703–13), which broke out six years later, the English began to add to their domains at the expense of France and her allies. England's great strategic acquisition was Gibraltar, taken in 1704 by English and Dutch marines and English seamen, supported by an Anglo–Dutch fleet under Admiral Sir George Rooke. England's possession of Gibraltar apparently guaranteed that the Toulon and Brest fleets should never unite in time of war. Louis, recognizing the extreme gravity of the situation for France, dispatched his Toulon fleet with orders to oust the invaders. Rooke's force barred the way. Having the wind, Rooke bore down on the French and stretched his line alongside theirs. The ensuing engagement, called the Battle of Malaga, was tactically indecisive in that neither line broke and neither could gain any serious advantage over the other. Nevertheless, the English were the strategic victors, for the French flinched under bombardment and slipped back to port under cover of darkness, and Rooke retained his grip on the Rock.

Four years later the Royal Navy buttressed Gibraltar by capturing Minorca and its fine harbor of Port Mahon, an excellent base for blockading Toulon. The long war brought France nothing but financial prostration. England, on the other hand, acquired Nova Scotia, Newfoundland, and the Hudson Bay territory from France; and Gibraltar, Minorca, and a share of the Spanish–American trade from Spain. Moreover, despite the continued efforts of French sea raiders, she had taken a strong lead in maritime commerce and made good her self-conferred title of Mistress of the Seas.

So far as the British Admiralty was concerned, the Battle of Malaga settled the tactical dispute in favor of formalism. The Royal Navy adopted Rooke's Fighting Instructions as Permanent Fighting Instructions, including his rule that the British line must keep conterminous with the enemy's— van opposite van, center opposite center, rear opposite rear. To assure that the fleet commanders should attempt no innovations, they were issued as signals only numbers corresponding to the numbered articles of the Permanent Fighting Instructions.

During the long peace from 1713 to 1740, while top-ranking officers grew old and conservative, formalism acquired the added sanction of tradition. Formal doctrine became dogma; melee tactics were forgotten. If anyone doubted that the conterminous line had become inviolate, he was disabused by official reaction to the first fleet engagement of the War of the Austrian Succession (1740–48). This was the curious Battle of Toulon.

---

[1]Privateer: a privately owned, armed ship commissioned by a government to cruise against enemy commercial ships or warships. Also the commander or one of the ship's company of such a vessel.

Pursuing a Franco–Spanish fleet off Toulon in February 1744, Admiral Thomas Mathews, with a fleet of equal size but with bottoms fouled by long blockade duty, could not overtake the enemy van with his own van. Rather than let the enemy escape, he bore down as he was and engaged while still flying the signal for line ahead. This brought his van against the enemy center and his center against the enemy rear. Mathews had expected Vice Admiral Richard Lestock, commanding the British rear, to do the obvious and commonsense thing: press on all sail and advance into the battle, joining the British center in massing on the enemy rear. But Lestock did nothing of the sort. In literal obedience to Mathews's line signal, he brought his rear squadron down against the open sea and so remained out of the battle. After the engagement, in which ships of the British van and center were severely battered, Mathews placed Lestock under arrest, but in the subsequent courts-martial the tables were turned—Lestock was acquitted, and Mathews was dismissed from the service.

For a good many years after the trials, it was a bold officer indeed who would risk disgrace by failing to maintain a conterminous battle line. Certainly Admiral Sir John Byng, who had sat as a judge on Mathews's court-martial, was no such officer—as we shall presently see.

Abandonment of the line was sanctioned only by Article 25 of the Permanent Instructions, which permitted pursuit when the enemy fleet as a whole was "put on the run." The onus of course was placed on the admiral, for it was up to him to decide (1) whether the enemy was actually in flight, and (2) whether the chances for success warranted the risk of breaking formation. If he signaled "general chase" and won a victory, nobody was going to inquire too closely about the state of the enemy when the signal was given. But if he signaled "chase" and lost, he would have to convince a skeptical court-martial that the enemy had indeed been on the run. Thus the decision for a chase was the touchstone distinguishing those British admirals possessing merely physical courage, which seems to have been the common possession of the breed, from those possessing the rarer quality of moral courage.

Summary

When the rulers of medieval Europe's Atlantic seaboard states wanted to carry out military operations at sea, they commandeered for warships the broad-beamed, single-masted freighters of the times. Combat at sea was conducted by soldiers, who grappled and boarded enemy ships and fought hand to hand across decks.

During the fifteenth century the frail medieval cargo carriers evolved into the sturdy, full-rigged ships that conveyed Columbus from Spain to the New World and da Gama from Portugal around Africa to India. Gold flowing from America to Spain and the bypassing of the lucrative Middle East–Mediterranean trade route broke up the medieval economy and stimulated rivalry among Europe's Atlantic states.

The first major showdown was between Spain and England, the champions respectively of Catholicism and Protestantism. Philip II of Spain proposed to invade England in retaliation for raids by English privateers on Spanish bases and shipping and in order to seize the English throne from Protestant Elizabeth I. The invasion force was to be drawn chiefly from the Spanish army with which the duke of Parma was endeavoring to suppress a Dutch rebellion.

In 1588 Philip sent against England his Grand Armada of 130 ships with reinforcements for Parma. Expecting the English fleet to give battle, he armed his vessels with heavy, short-range guns to disable the English ships so that his embarked soldiers could grapple and board and fight across decks as they had done so victoriously 17 years earlier in the galley Battle of Lepanto. The English, however, since the adoption of the broadside, had learned to fight ship against ship instead of men against men. To deal with the Armada, they armed their warships with long-range, lightly shotted guns.

As the Armada in the summer of 1588 sailed into the English Channel on a southwesterly wind, the English fleet fell in behind it, thereby seizing the weather gage (upwind position), which enabled them to reach the Spaniards with their long-range guns while remaining outside the range of the Spanish guns and grappling hooks. As a result, when the Spaniards dropped anchor in the neutral port of Calais, neither fleet had been seriously hurt. The Spaniards had not been able to reach the English, and the English had not been able, at their chosen range, to penetrate Spanish hulls with their light shot. The Spaniards were at a severe disadvantage, however, because they had fired off their heavy shot and could get no more, whereas the English could be resupplied from nearby England.

The English flushed the Spanish ships from their anchorage with fireships, pounded them severely off Gravelines, and sent them fleeing homeward the long way, north and west of the British

Isles. Storms and inept navigation cost the Spaniards half their vessels, sunk at sea or wrecked upon the rocky coasts of Scotland and Ireland. In the evolution of tactics under sail, the English victory established the gun as the principal weapon, replacing hand-to-hand combat across decks.

In the next half century, the Dutch outstripped all their rivals in the competition for maritime commerce, and attained a near monopoly of the carrying trade. England under the Commonwealth threw down the gauntlet to Holland in the Navigation Act of 1651, whereby imports into England were restricted to English ships or ships of the country of origin. There ensued, between 1652 and 1674, three Anglo–Dutch naval wars, in which the Dutch were at a disadvantage because English bases lay athwart their sea approaches, because they had to guard a land frontier as well as their coasts and seaward approaches, and because their ships, shallow draft to enter their shallow harbors, were too leewardly to be easily controlled in battle. In the end, the bulk of the Dutch carrying trade passed into the hands of the English.

In the Anglo–Dutch Wars, England's Lord Protector, Oliver Cromwell, distrusting naval officers as possibly monarchist, sent his generals to sea to command the fleet. The generals introduced the column, or line ahead, to replace the earlier bunching of ships that masked broadsides. During the wars also there arose in the English fleet two opposing schools of naval tactics, the Formal School, which favored retaining the column throughout the battle, and the Melee School, which preferred dispensing with the column at a favorable opportunity.

The formal–melee division of opinion carried over into the long struggle between England and France. During the War of the English Succession, the English in the Battle of Beachy Head (1690) used melee tactics and lost. In the Battle of Barfleur (1692), the French used melee tactics and lost. Understandably, these defeats cast melee tactics into disrepute. In the ensuing War of the Spanish Succession, England captured Gibraltar and defended her conquest in the formal Battle of Malaga (1704). Malaga was in fact a drawn battle, but Gibraltar remained in English hands.

The above three battles established formal tactics in the Royal Navy. They were prescribed by the Admiralty in the Permanent Fighting Instructions, which required British naval commanders not only to fight in column but in column conterminous with that of the enemy. When Admiral Thomas Mathews in the Battle of Toulon (1744) attacked a Franco–Spanish column with which he was not able to make his line conterminous, he was dismissed from the service for not obeying instructions. Thereafter it was a bold officer indeed who would risk such a fate by failing to conform to the inflexible regulations of the Permanent Fighting Instructions.

Chapter 3
The Seven Years' War

The Seven Years' War (1756–63) was the first true world war. It involved most of the countries of Europe. Military and naval operations were conducted not only on the European continent and in the Mediterranean and Atlantic but also in America, India, Africa, the West Indies, and the Philippines.

The causes of the war were conflicting British and French claims to the lands west of the Appalachians in America, and Austria's commitment to recovering Silesia, a province that she had lost to the upstart Kingdom of Prussia. Hostilities broke out in America in 1754—what the colonists called the French and Indian War was simply the American phase of the Seven Years' War. French forces defeated Colonel George Washington at Fort Necessity in western Pennsylvania. The following year a mixed command of colonial militia and British regulars under Major General Edward Braddock was defeated at nearby Great Meadows.

When Frederick the Great of Prussia learned that Austria had secured alliances with France and Russia specifically to isolate him as a preliminary to recapturing Silesia, he turned to England. Pointing out that Austria's ambitions extended beyond mere recovery of her lost province and doubtless included control of all the German states, including Hanover, he offered to protect Hanover, if the latter would join forces with him. Since George II of England was also Elector of Hanover,[1] the British government agreed, thereby forming what amounted to an Anglo–Prussian defensive alliance.

France lost no time in taking up the challenge, which she saw as an opportunity to revenge herself on her old enemy and perhaps regain some of her territories lost in 1713. Seeing an advantage in speed, she promptly opened hostilities by attacking the British island of Minorca.

In mid-April 1756, one hundred and fifty transports carrying 15,000 troops and twelve ships of the line commanded by the Marquis de la Galissonière

---

[1]On the death of Queen Anne (1714) without issue, the Elector of Hanover, great-grandson of James I, succeeded to the English throne as George I. Hanover remained under the protection of the English crown until the accession of Queen Victoria in 1837.

---

sailed from Toulon and effected a landing. Outnumbering the British garrison by 5 to 1, the French army quickly drove the defenders inside the walls of Fort St. Philip, which covered Port Mahon. The French fleet coasted offshore under light sail, ready for action.

With conflicting intelligence reports, the Admiralty belatedly sent Admiral Sir John Byng to the Mediterranean with a transport squadron carrying a regiment of fusileers and 13 ships of the line. His orders were to use "all possible means in [his] power" to raise the siege of Minorca.

On 19 May, Byng's ships stood off the island. Before Byng could communicate with forces ashore, his lookouts sighted the French fleet. The dying wind prevented the opposing battle lines from coming into range. As the morning mists cleared on the 20th, the French were again sighted, about 12 miles away to the southeast. There was a mild south–southwest wind. Recalling his frigate scouting line, Byng tacked southeast toward the enemy and signaled for line-of-battle. He was in personal command of seven ships; Rear Admiral Temple West commanded six of the rear. The French, carrying all plain sail, held a west–northwest course. Byng spread more canvas and raced to cross the enemy course and thus secure the weather gage.

The Battle for Minorca, 20 May 1756

The adversaries converged on near-collision courses. Shortly after noon, the wind veered to the southwest. Galissonière, realizing that this development favored the British maneuver, shortened sail and fell off to starboard—accepting the lee gage. Byng eased off a little also, and the fleets came abreast on nearly reciprocal courses in not quite parallel columns, the French on the port tack, the British on the starboard.

The orthodoxy of the Permanent Fighting Instructions dictated that Byng should maintain course till his van ship was opposite the enemy rear ship, then wear ships together and attack the enemy ship to ship. The objection to this maneuver was that it compelled each of one's ships to

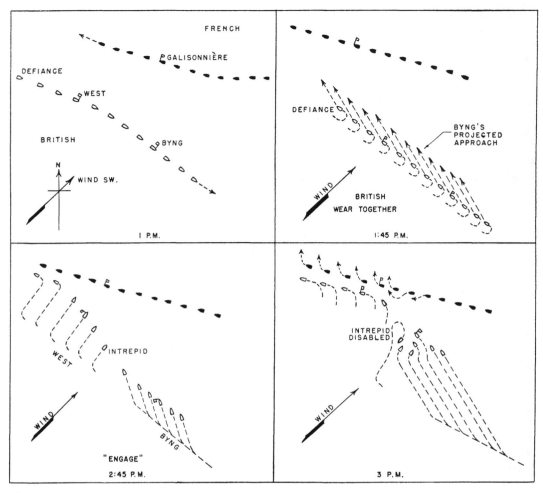

Battle for Minorca, 20 May 1756

approach the enemy's broadsides almost bows-on, exposed to raking fire before one's own guns could bear.

Byng accordingly planned a tactical innovation: he would hold course until his van was well past the enemy rear ship, and only then come about and attack on an angling course that would permit his own guns to be exercised.

At the appropriate moment, Byng backed topsails to kill way. Galissonière did likewise. Byng signaled to wear ship, intending that when his line re-formed on a northwest course, the *Defiance* (which would then be the van ship) should fall off to starboard to engage the lead ship in the French line. This the *Defiance* failed to do, holding to a course parallel to the enemy. Temple West's whole division followed. Hampered by an inadequate sig-

nal system, a frustrated Byng signaled for general action—an order impossible to misunderstand.

So, discarding the tactical advantage Byng had almost gained, West's six ships bore bows-on for the French van, and were three times raked as they approached. They were soon engaged in a murderous gun duel at pistol range. Byng himself in the rear division was too far off for support: it was a full half hour before the British rear could open long-range fire. Meanwhile, all of West's vessels were severely damaged. The *Intrepid*, rearmost ship of the van division, lost her foretopmast overside, and became unmanageable across Byng's line of advance—causing bunching of the rear ships, all way lost.

At this point a bolder commander might well have thrown caution to the winds and brought his ships, melee fashion, to the support of his battered van with as much speed as each individual ship could show. But apart from his training in formalist tactics, Byng, as we have seen, had sat on the court-martial of Admiral Mathews, who earlier off Toulon had been presented with a similar quandary. Mathews had been dismissed from the service for failing to maintain his line. Byng, in turning down his flag-captain's recommendation for the more reckless course, said: "You would not have me, as admiral of the fleet, run down as if I were going to engage a single ship. It was Mr. Mathews' misfortune to be prejudiced by not carrying down his force together, which I shall endeavor to avoid."

Byng delayed long enough to re-form a column, only to find the French breaking off action as he approached. Galissonière must have perceived the wide gap separating the British divisions. He may well have hoped by close-hauling his own line to cut between the British van and rear and then to wear and double on West's division. But if so, Byng maneuvered the rear ships promptly enough to prevent it.

In any event, the French appeared satisfied. They fell off to leeward and re-formed their line out of range. West's ships, badly damaged in spars and rigging, were in no condition to follow. Moreover, the day was far gone. Galissonière, with his ships' fine lines and cleaner bottoms, had the option of further action, or avoiding it. But he regarded covering the beachhead as his primary mission, and he was prepared to fight only for this purpose.

Byng regretted that he could not order "general chase," but the Fighting Instructions enjoined that this was to be initiated only against a markedly inferior force or when "the main body be disabled or run." Neither condition prevailed. Byng set easy sail to cruise the area, while West's crews jury-rigged their wrecked top-hamper.

Byng now found himself in a quandary, with no option particularly inviting. Galissonière would not oblige by another action. The British troop reinforcement, even if Byng could get it ashore, was grossly inadequate against the large French force on the beach. The British fleet was spread all over the world; the loss of many of his battered ships by reckless action might mean endangering Gibraltar. Seeking the advice of a council of war made up of the senior naval and army officers on board, Byng concurred in its defeatist views. He accordingly shifted his fleet to Gibraltar. The stubborn British garrison in Fort St. Philip held out for a month longer, but surrendered before Admiral Sir Edward Hawke superseded Byng as commander in

chief of the Mediterranean. Minorca remained in French hands for the duration.

The news of the loss of Minorca, coming as it did on the heels of Braddock's defeat, threatened the government of the duke of Newcastle. A scapegoat was needed—a role poor Byng seemed born for.

He was ordered home for court-martial. After a lengthy and well-publicized trial, he was found innocent of the charge of cowardice in the face of the enemy, but guilty of failing "to do his utmost" to defeat the enemy—either to destroy the French fleet or to relieve the garrison on Minorca. For this offense a recent revision of the Articles of War made a death penalty mandatory. Refused a royal pardon in spite of petitions from members of the court itself, Byng was shot.

Though Byng was not executed for a purely tactical mistake, the notoriety of this affair refocused service interest on tactics as such, and brought into question the inflexible rules of the Permanent Fighting Instructions. It may not be too much to say that Byng in dying accomplished more for his service than he ever had alive.

Pitt's Plan

The loss of Minorca also combined with other bad news to compel a reshuffling of the British Cabinet. The bumbling duke of Newcastle was obliged to accept his chief parliamentary rival, the elder William Pitt, as secretary of state for war. Despite the hostility of George II, Pitt was able to use his personal popularity and his support in Commons as levers to demand and get practically dictatorial powers over all ship and troop movements.[2] His energy and strategic insights enabled him to gain a string of victories that reshaped the world for centuries to come.

The Prussian alliance, and the fact that the defense of Hanover was a major war aim, prompted the king and his coterie to favor a major commitment of forces to war on the Continent.

Pitt strongly disagreed. To aid Frederick by subsidy, to support Hanover by token forces, to draw off French troops by coastal raids—these were actions consistent with Pitt's Plan. But the great ends of the war as he saw them were the capture and retention of Canada, India, and the Caribbean islands—in short, the creation and consolidation of a world empire. His rationale was

[2]In political infighting against Lord John Carteret (later the Earl of Granville) in Parliament, Pitt had excoriated Lord John's Hanoverian sympathies, and thereby had mortally offended George II's German patriotism.

simple. England throve on trade. The Empire fostered trade. Trade made for wealth. Wealth enhanced military and naval strength. Indeed at this very time Frederick was in effect able to fight England's battles on the Continent by virtue of the chests of specie England was sending him to pay his soldiers.

Whereas Britain's small army could have little effect on the outcome of the war on the Continent, her navy, preponderant in strength, was able to bottle up the French ports by blockade, keeping the enemy fleet divided between France's Mediterranean and Atlantic ports. Any naval margin could be employed in supporting expeditions anywhere in the four corners of the earth. By commanding the seas, the British fleet would of course cut off any support from France to her colonies.[3]

European Coastal Operations

The military successes of Prussia early in the war simply stimulated greater efforts by the French and the Austrians, who together had an overwhelmingly greater force. Not unnaturally, Frederick demanded of his British allies more material assistance than the subsidy and the dubious support of a small English army. A part of England's response was the "conjunct expeditions"—amphibious raids against French ports. These campaigns were aimed incidentally at cleaning out nests of troublesome privateers that preyed on English coastal shipping, but their primary object was to relieve the pressure on Frederick by inducing France to retain troops for shore defense that might otherwise be used against Frederick in central Europe.

The first "conjunct expedition" was directed against Rochefort in the fall of 1757. In spite of the investing and subsequent capture of the island of Aix, lying just offshore, this expedition was correctly accounted a failure. A lack of adequate planning led the commanders to conclude that a landing was impossible. The undertaking did, however, offer a negative object lesson to Lieutenant Colonel James Wolfe, who was serving as chief of staff. Apropos of the ill-starred Rochefort campaign, he remarked in a famous letter:

> I have found out an Admiral should endeavour to run into an enemy's port immediately . . . ; that

previous directions should be given in respect to landing the troops, and a proper disposition made for the boats of all sorts, . . . that pushing on smartly is the road to success . . . ; that nothing is to be reckoned an obstacle to your undertaking which is not found really so upon trial; that in war something must be allowed to chance and fortune, seeing that it is in its nature hazardous, and an option of difficulties; that the greatness of the object should come under consideration, opposed to the impediments that lie in the way; that the honour of one's country is to have some weight; and that, in particular circumstances and times, the loss of a thousand men is rather an advantage to a nation than otherwise, seeing that gallant attempts raise its reputation and make it respectable. . . .[4]

As Wolfe was to demonstrate at Louisburg and Quebec, the lesson was not lost on him.

The British scored a somewhat larger measure of success at St. Malo. Here in June 1758 some 13,000 British troops landed and spent a week ashore, burning more than a hundred privateers. The following August the British took temporary possession of Cherbourg and destroyed fortifications and shipping.

These were relatively small-scale raids, with no design to hold the territory captured. Though they did induce the French to retain for coast defense troops that might have been used against Frederick, their value was mainly psychological, encouraging Frederick to believe in the reality of British military assistance.

Fleet Actions in European Waters

In the summer of 1759, as part of a French plan to invade England, Admiral Sabran de la Clue, commanding the Toulon fleet, received orders to add his ships to France's Brest fleet. This would take some doing, for they were tightly blockaded by a British fleet under Admiral Edward Boscawen. When Boscawen temporarily lifted his blockade to recondition his ships at Gibraltar, de la Clue gambled on being able to escape with his 12 ships of the line into the Atlantic. Under cover of darkness and aided by a strong east wind, he did in fact get his ships safely through the Straits, but he had been spotted by Boscawen's watch frigates, and the British fleet of 15 of the line were promptly in pursuit. They brought the French to bay off Portugal, and Boscawen signaled general chase. In what amounted to a series of bloody single-ship actions, the British overwhelmed the French and drove

[3]Pitt's Plan, which had a lasting influence on British military strategy, may be abstracted thus: (A) Subsidize one or more allies on the Continent. (B) Use own fleet to : (1) raid enemy coasts, thereby holding enemy troops away from allies; (2) blockade enemy and destroy his fleet; (3) convoy and support own troops in seizing enemy's overseas colonies and associated seaborne trade.

[4]Robert Wright, *The Life of Major General James Wolfe* (London, 1864), 396–97.

most of them into Lagos Bay, where de la Clue deliberately grounded his flagship. In the course of the chase, Boscawen captured one of the French ships and then, in violation of Portuguese territorial waters, entered the bay where he captured two more and burned two others that had grounded themselves. No ship of the Toulon fleet reached Brest.

Later that year Admiral Hubert, Comte de Conflans, commanding the Brest fleet, made a similar effort to dodge the persistent blockade of Sir Edward Hawke's fleet. When a northeast gale made the Breton coast a lee shore, the British clawed their way back into their own Channel ports. As soon as the wind moderated, Conflans sallied forth, hoping to sweep up some British frigates off Belle-Île, and then by dodging the Channel fleet to support a possible landing in Scotland. But Hawke, who had quickly returned to station, intercepted the French off Quiberon Bay.

Unmindful of a rising gale and the onset of darkness, Hawke ordered general chase, and the British drove the fleeing French into the dangerous, reef-strewn bay. Lower deck gunports rolled under water; one French vessel foundered when she opened hers. Another French vessel was pounded to pieces by British broadsides. Hawke, losing two vessels himself from grounding, finally anchored when nightfall made further pursuit suicidal. During the night eight of the French ships jettisoned their guns and, thus lightened, escaped over the bar into the shallow Vilaine River, where most of them broke their backs. Eight others slipped their cables under cover of darkness. One, heavily damaged, soon sank, but the rest made good their escape to Rochefort. Conflans, abandoned by his fleet, ran his flagship on the rocks and set her afire to avoid having her captured.

The battles of Lagos and Quiberon Bay, won with general-chase tactics, were decisive British victories. They set at rest any fears of an invasion of England, and they freed the bulk of the British fleet for employment overseas.

The American Campaign

William Pitt, in assuming his wartime ministry, took as his paramount objective the winning of North America. For two years following Braddock's defeat, the French and their Indian allies enjoyed uninterrupted success in that theater. By 1758 they had practically evicted the British colonists from their frontier settlements and confined them to Nova Scotia and the strip between the Appalachians and the Atlantic.

Pitt set out to reverse this course of events. To that end, he obtained almost unlimited funds from Parliament; recruited fresh troops, mainly in the colonies and the Scottish highlands; and searched out capable, aggressive commanding officers, preferably vigorous young men. His ultimate military objective was capture of the city of Quebec, which for a century had been the capital and headquarters of French operations in America.

To block supplies and reinforcements flowing to French America, the Royal Navy swept France's shipping from the Atlantic, and Pitt sent one of his young officers, Sir Jeffrey Amherst, to capture Louisburg. On the shore of Cape Breton Island, Louisburg was well located to serve as a base for blockading the St. Lawrence River, the vital communication route between French America and the ocean.

With 14,000 men, 150 field and siege guns, and the able assistance of Edward Boscawen, who commanded the transports and the supporting fleet of 23 ships, and of James Wolfe, who led the main landing force, Amherst made a successful assault on Cape Breton and took Louisburg under siege. After enduring six weeks of bombardment from land and sea, the garrison surrendered.

The following year, 1759, the British launched a three-prong offensive against Quebec. Amherst with 12,000 men, mostly colonists, struck from the south, using the natural waterway provided by Lake Champlain and the Richelieu River. (See map, p. 34.) This would entail capturing French outposts at Fort Ticonderoga and Crown Point. A smaller British force set out to capture Fort Niagara and converge on Quebec from the west, via the St. Lawrence valley.

Meanwhile a strong amphibious force ascended the St. Lawrence from the sea. Included were 23 ships and 13 frigates, besides auxiliaries and transports, under Admiral Charles Saunders, and 9,200 British regulars, mostly Highlanders, under Major General Wolfe.

By the standards of eighteenth-century colonial warfare, the British had formidable numbers. But the French defenders had important advantages. Quebec is located 400 miles upstream from the sea, where the St. Lawrence begins to broaden into a great tidal estuary. Protected by the St. Charles River to the north and by the cliff-like shoreline of the Plains of Abraham to the west, the rocky bastions of the Upper City were deemed impregnable. The attacking forces approaching from south and west, involved in long marches and a wilderness campaign, were so delayed by harassing French and Indian forces that they failed to reach the combat area in time to aid Wolfe and Saunders. The defense of Quebec was entrusted to General Louis Joseph de Montcalm, an able and experienced officer, who could count on a potential garrison of 14,000 men and 300 artillery pieces.

Admiral Saunders, with the grudging assistance of captured French-Canadian pilots, brought his whole armada of more than a hundred sail up the difficult channel without a loss and anchored just out of cannon shot of Quebec. Wolfe disembarked his troops onto the unfortified Isle of Orleans and then seized the lightly defended heights of Point Levis, where he emplaced heavy siege guns to fire into the Lower City across the river.

Montcalm, leaving the walled city lightly garrisoned, arrayed his major force in earthworks behind the beach all the way from the St. Charles to the turbulent Montmorency River, and blocked the mouth of the St. Charles with sunken hulks. Outposts and a mobile force under Louis Antoine de Bougainville guarded the lofty shores of the St. Lawrence upsteam from the city.

Wolfe, seeing no evident weakness in the French position, unwisely decided to attack the strongly defended French left flank, which was anchored on the Montmorency River. The attack went badly. Shoal water prevented Saunders from getting frigates close enough to the beach to deliver effective covering fire, and it proved impossible to assemble ashore an assault force adequate to storm the high ground. Recognizing his mistake, Wolfe cut his losses and recalled his troops. But he left 500 casualties on the beach.

Soon afterward Wolfe became seriously ill. It appeared that the campaigning season would be

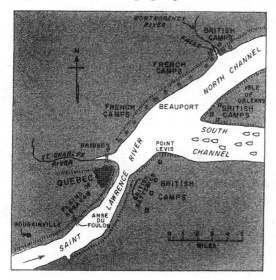

Siege of Quebec, 1759

over before a decisive blow could be struck. Now Wolfe's leadership was put to the test. He had tried a bold stroke and failed. Though perforce the attacker, he was greatly outnumbered. He had not received the reinforcements and relief he had been led to expect from Amherst. He could have sailed for Halifax secure in the reputation of an honorable effort. But the record shows that neither Wolfe nor Saunders nor any of their principal subordinates had any idea of quitting while they had any resources remaining.

Even as Wolfe tossed in delirium, his brigadiers pushed boat expeditions up the river, ever probing for a soft spot. Montcalm, concerned by this possible threat to his right flank, detached 3,000 men to reinforce Bougainville's guard force, whose role was to protect the whole north bank of the river above Quebec by moving troops to any threatened point.

In early September Wolfe was well enough to resume active command, and eager to try a new line of attack. While Saunders feinted a landing at the old beachhead, he would try a surprise attack at the Anse du Foulon, a little boat-landing a bare mile and a half upriver from the city walls. The movement was to begin the evening of 12 September.

Saunders played his role to perfection, bombarding the now-ruined Lower City and the beach below Quebec with every gun that could be brought to bear, ostentatiously loading the ships' boats with marines and seamen as if a new landing were imminent. Meanwhile, a strong infantry force in flat-bottomed boats, supported by frigates and sloops-of-war, worked upriver with the tide as if to effect a lodgment far above the city. It was a fine moonlit night, and Bougainville marched the bulk of his force along the shore to parallel this intentionally visible movement.

But when the tide turned, the British boat force began rowing furiously down river. Aided by the tidal current, it quickly outdistanced Bougainville's exhausted foot soldiers. Shortly before dawn the lead boat scraped ashore at the foot of the narrow, rocky path up the bluff at the Anse du Foulon. The light infantry swarmed up the slope and bayoneted the picket force before they could sound an alarm. Working against time, the officers swiftly disembarked their troops and sent the boats to bring reinforcements across from Point Levis. By clear daylight, Wolfe had spirited 4,500 men up onto the Plains of Abraham and arrayed them in battle order in sight of the walls of Quebec.

The shock of Wolfe's sudden appearance at the city's gates and the chagrin of seeing his nearly perfect defenses so readily breached caused Montcalm for once to abandon his steady good judgment. With a little patience, he might have withdrawn his immediate command behind the solid walls of the Upper City to await the arrival from the west of Bougainville's troops for an assault on the British rear. The odds would scarcely favor the outnumbered British, caught in a powerful pincers.

But Montcalm did not wait. He marched out his garrison pell-mell, forming a battle line as it advanced, its front covered by a swarm of skirmishers and marksmen. The British lines waited stolidly, while the French regulars marched steadily to a drumbeat. A 6-pounder that some sailors had dragged up to the heights began rapid fire and cut swathes in the white-clad French column. But the disciplined troops closed ranks and came on. As they approached small-arms range, they began to fire, individually and by companies. The British accepted the fire without returning it.

When the French were within 30 yards, the swords of the British officers flashed up. Then down. "Fire!" That great double-shotted volley may be said to have won Canada for Britain. It swept windrows of French soldiery to the earth. Exercising superb fire discipline, the British infantry reloaded, and delivered another volley before the French could recover from the shock of the first. After that it was a disorganized melee, rapidly turning into a rout. While the bagpipes of the highland regiments skirled, the demoralized French fled the field before the English bayonets and the Scottish broadswords.

Montcalm was mortally wounded. His second and third in command were killed outright. The British lost their quartermaster-general and one of their brigadiers. Wolfe, leading a charge, was himself fatally wounded, and was dead in the hour of victory.

The advance guard of Bougainville's forces now appeared in the British rear, but Bougainville deemed it prudent to withdraw without a fight. The French garrison inside the city, observing the British putting out siege lines and siting batteries, recognized the hopelessness of its position and surrendered. Quebec taken, Amherst assumed the overall British command and completed the conquest of Canada.

The Campaign in India

The French and British East India companies—virtual sovereignties with their own armies and navies—were at this time able to secure the aid of royal forces in their struggle for India. The British East India Company's troops ashore under Robert Clive were effectively supported by Royal Navy admirals Charles Watson and, after Watson's death, Sir George Pocock.

Following the fall of the French base at Chandernagore in 1757, French admiral the Comte d'Aché was handicapped by having no station for refitting nearer than Mauritius, 2,000 miles to the southwest, across the Indian Ocean. Also, France neglected to send him reinforcements and supplies. Meanwhile, Pocock could refit and wait out the monsoon season in Bombay.

The major naval phase of the Indian campaign occurred between April 1758 and October 1759, when d'Aché sailed his battered fleet from Indian waters for the last time. There were three major engagements between the evenly matched fleets, all conventional line-against-line actions of the formalist variety. In spite of fierce fighting and heavy casualties, all these actions were tactical draws—object lessons in the indecisiveness of formal tactics.

Pocock gained the strategic advantage over his opponent by simple attrition. He could better effect repairs and obtain supplies than could d'Aché. Under the circumstances, it was enough for Pocock to continue *contesting* the seas around the subcontinent to ensure ultimate British victory, Though Pondicherry and some other minor enclaves were restored to the French at the peace, India was to remain substantially a British dependency until after World War II.

Operations in the West Indies

In the eighteenth century the islands of the Caribbean enjoyed an economic importance hard to realize today. West Indian sugar planters made enormous fortunes. Except for the tea and spices of the Far East, the West Indies supplied nearly all the tropical products taken by the European market. As buyers, these islands were also important in the cruel but profitable African slave trade.

Many of the Antilles had changed hands from time to time in earlier wars, but by the time of the Seven Years' War, tradition had sanctified Spain's claim to Cuba; England's, to Jamaica, Antigua, and Barbados; and France's, to Martinique and Guadeloupe. The Netherlands also had some small possessions in the area—Curaçao, Aruba, and the tiny island of St. Eustatius. Santo Domingo was divided between France and Spain. (See map, p. 44.)

Since "filching sugar islands" had become established practice in maritime war, Pitt at the earliest opportunity set about despoiling France of her valuable Caribbean possessions. Apart from his general empire-building objective, Pitt was motivated by the depredations of privateers based on Martinique and Guadeloupe, who from the beginning of the war had raised havoc with British commercial shipping in the area.

The first British joint expedition arrived in the Caribbean in early 1759 and in a three-month campaign succeeded in wresting Guadeloupe from its French defenders. Another such expedition in 1760 took Dominica. In 1762 a powerful joint force captured Martinique, Grenada, St. Lucia, and St. Vincent—a clean sweep of all the French possessions in the Lesser Antilles.

In January 1762 Spain entered the war. Earlier the combination of the Spanish and French fleets could well have presented a mortal danger to England. But by now the French fleet had been broken, and Spain's involvement at this time spelled to England merely opportunity. For Spain's treasure-laden convoys were an open invitation to depredation by the cruisers of the Royal Navy, and Spain had enormously rich dependencies in the West Indies and the Far East.

Since England already had squadrons and soldiers in the West Indies, an operation against Havana was put in train at once. The expedition included 15,000 troops commanded by the earl of Albemarle. Commanding the fleet was Admiral Pocock, who had more than 50 men-of-war. With transports and auxiliaries, the invasion armada amounted to about 200 sail.

To attain surprise Pocock daringly approached Havana from the east, through the little-used, reef-studded Old Bahama Channel north of Cuba. The unexpected appearance of the huge fleet was the first intimation to the governor of Havana that the mother country was at war. His naval commander chose not to sally forth with his 12 of the line to challenge so formidable an armada. Instead, to prevent their capture, he sank 3 of them across the narrow entrance to Havana harbor, thereby locking in the rest, and incidentally freeing Pocock from the responsibility of guarding against a sortie.

In a sandy bay east of the city, Pocock battered down defending blockhouses with ships' gunfire and set the troops ashore. Albemarle then proceeded to use siege tactics against the Morro, one of two forts guarding the harbor and city.

The approach presented formidable problems, because the Morro stood at the end of a rocky peninsula. There was too little earth for entrenchment. The siege lines had to be advanced by means of above-ground works built on the rocky ledges. In an effort to keep down fire from the fort, the attackers laboriously winched fleet guns into position ashore. The process took nearly two months, in which the troops suffered agonies in the tropical summer heat. Many were killed or wounded by enemy fire, but as in all West Indian operations, the most severe toll was from disease, especially yellow fever. Throughout the operation, the fleet played an indispensable role—in both gunfire and logistic support. Like Saunders at Quebec, Pocock at Havana set an example of selfless cooperation for subsequent naval officers.

The British sappers finally completed a tunnel under the shoreward walls of the Morro. Here they exploded a mine, and the redcoats swarmed through the narrow gap it blew out. They then hunted down the defenders in the stone corridors of the fortress. With the Morro in British hands, the city also was obliged to surrender, and possession of Havana conferred control of all Cuba.

Other Operations

Because control of the seas gave the British a virtually free choice of where and when to strike, Britain was able not merely to conduct those major operations that would contribute materially to the outcome of the war. She was able also to invest a fraction of her power in sideshow operations that had only commercial importance or that might slightly improve her bargaining position at the peace table. An example is her seizure in 1758 of the French slave-trading stations of Gorée and Senegal at the western bulge of Africa. And in 1760 Pitt renewed "conjunct operations" against the French coast, sending a considerable force to seize Belle-Île.

The capstone of the British war effort overseas was the Manila expedition of 1762, undertaken by East India Company troops and an eight-ship squadron. Under bombardment and siege, Manila fell in less than two weeks, whereupon the governor surrendered the entire Philippines.

The End of the War

At the outset of 1762 Frederick of Prussia appeared on the brink of defeat, but he was saved by the death of his implacable enemy, the Czarina Elizabeth. Elizabeth was succeeded on the Russian throne by the nearly idiotic Prussophile Peter III, who signed an immediate peace with Frederick. Peter was presently assassinated, but Catherine II, who succeeded him, would not renew the war. Sweden next withdrew from the Grand Coalition.

France and Austria, their allies gone, nearly exhausted, and without further expedient, both sued for peace.

The Peace of Paris (1763) was the high-water mark of Britain's "Old Empire." Everywhere victorious, the British might well have demanded even more than they took. And they took the lion's share. Britain received Canada and a cession of French claims to all the territory east of the Mississippi. She thereby unwittingly defined the boundaries of the then undreamed-of United States of America, to be established 13 years later. From France Britain also received Senegal and had Minorca returned to her. From Spain she received Florida in exchange for Cuba. To France were restored Belle-Île, Guadeloupe, Martinique, St. Lucia, Gorée, the French trading stations in India (which France promised not to fortify), and the little North Atlantic islands of Miquelon and St. Pierre. To Spain were restored Cuba and the Philippines. France helped to make the treaty acceptable to Spain by ceding to her New Orleans and the Louisiana Territory, a primeval empire of unsurveyed dimensions to the west of the Mississippi River.

Summary

The Seven Years' War was the first of the world wars. In it Britain followed the pattern of allying with other continental powers against a major continental power. The distinctive feature, from Britain's point of view, was Pitt's Plan, a strategy toward which Britain had been groping since the Anglo–Dutch wars.

On the worldwide scale, Pitt's strategy, like all strategies that achieve true concentration, had both a *hitting* and a *holding* aspect. The main British offensive, the hitting aspect, was carried out beyond the seas—using England's naval preponderance to support attacks on the colonies of France and Spain. Capture of these colonies expanded the British Empire, promoted trade, and thereby produced wealth. A part of this increased wealth went to subsidize Britain's indispensable allies on the continent of Europe. The holding aspect consisted of (1) the efforts of the Royal Navy in first blockading and then destroying the French fleet and (2) the efforts of Britain's allies, chiefly Frederick the Great of Prussia, in absorbing French wealth and containing French manpower that might otherwise have been used to build up the French navy, break the British blockade, and succor France's overseas possessions.

Within the European theater also, Pitt's Plan had a hitting and holding aspect. Here Frederick's army was the principal hitting element, while British "conjunct expeditions" along the coast of France were intended in part to make the French sufficiently fearful of an invasion to hold back troops that might otherwise have been sent against Frederick.

France's counter-strategy against Britain consisted of (1) raids on British maritime commerce, (2) attempts to defend French colonies, and (3) attempts to invade England. Britain's naval preponderance rendered all such efforts futile. A French invasion plan, requiring the combining of the Toulon and Brest fleets in the English Channel, was nullified when the former was destroyed by Boscawen in the Battle of Lagos Bay (1759) and the latter by Hawke in the Battle of Quiberon Bay (1759).

While France was expending her strength and treasure in the fruitless war in Europe, relatively minor British forces were capturing French possessions all around the world. In 1758 Amherst and Boscawen opened the St. Lawrence River by capturing Louisburg. In 1759 Wolfe and Saunders assured the British conquest of Canada by capturing Quebec. At the same time Clive, with the naval cooperation of Watson and Pocock, was winning control over India, and British army–navy teams were seizing French possessions in the West Indies. When Spain allied herself with France in 1762, she was promptly dispossessed of Havana by Albemarle and Pocock, and of Manila by British East India Company forces.

The naval battles of the Seven Years' War demonstrated that strict adherence to formal tactics, as enjoined by the Permanent Fighting Instructions, precluded decisive victory, since it rendered tactical concentration nearly impossible. The Minorca action and the several engagements of Pocock and d'Aché in Indian waters exemplify this fact. On the other hand, the simple tactics of general chase won smashing victories at Lagos and at Quiberon Bay.

Amphibious war requires careful planning, unstinted interservice cooperation, boldness of leadership, and perseverance. In amphibious assaults prior to World War II, these qualities were often lacking for want of unified command. The usual pattern made the general and the admiral coequal. The cooperative operations of Wolfe and Saunders at Quebec and of Albemarle and Pocock at Havana demonstrated the qualities needed to accomplish this difficult and vulnerable form of warfare.

Pitt is the model of the commander in chief, characterized by unity of purpose, consistency, and decisiveness. In the chess game of war, he saw the board as a whole. He disposed his pieces so that each aided all the others. Because he thought naturally in grand strategic terms, he could not merely ensure victory, but assured that England would attain all her war aims.

Above everything else the great lesson of the Seven Years' War is the pervasive and inexorable power of naval preponderance in a world war. The British navy at once kept the tight little island secure from invasion and made possible winning half the world for empire.

Chapter 4
The War of
the American Revolution, I

Following the Seven Years' War the French set about rebuilding their navy, while the British allowed theirs to decline in strength and efficiency. Although British naval appropriations were far higher than they had been even at the height of the war, inordinate amounts were consumed in the maintenance of vessels that had been hastily built of imported oak, which quickly decayed. More serious, the corruption prevalent in British politics had penetrated the Admiralty. Large sums voted for the repair and refitting of ships disappeared while the vessels rotted in the docks. When war broke out in America, there were not enough ships ready to provide even the modest strength required on the American station.

The Outbreak of the American Revolution

Tightening of the mercantilist system and reassertion of British authority in the colonies after the Seven Years' War led to the defection of the Americans. The Revenue Act of 1764, with its threat of actual collection of a threepence-a-gallon molasses duty, appalled merchants and distillers who had habitually evaded the previous sixpence duty. The Stamp Act of 1765, by asserting Parliament's internal taxing power, united in opposition colonies that had grown accustomed to a large measure of practical independence. Although the Stamp Act was repealed, the Townshend Acts of 1767, providing for import duties on paper, lead, and tea, indirectly brought about the "Boston Massacre" of 1770.

The Boston Tea Party of 1773 began a chain of events that led to war. This act of defiance caused Parliament to pass the Coercive Acts, which among other indignities closed the port of Boston and abolished the long-established liberties of Massachusetts, taking from the people the right of selecting their Council. British attempts to enforce the Coercive Acts led to shooting at Lexington and Concord in April 1775. After that, there was little room for moderation or reconciliation.

For Britain the war presented peculiar difficulties. Moving troops and supplies in quantity across the Atlantic, a passage that might easily take two months, was a stupendous task. Recognizing the

difficulty, Lord Barrington, British Secretary of State for War, suggested a naval blockade to bring the colonists to terms. But Lord George Germain, the Colonial Secretary, who was to direct the war, seems scarcely to have considered such a strategy. The temptation to punish the colonies by conventional occupation was reinforced by a desire to protect the loyalists ("Tories"), who were expected to assist. Britain was thus committed to a course that ultimately proved disastrous.

The American Offensive, 1775

Although the skirmishes at Lexington and Concord had precipitated hostilities, more than a year passed before the colonies declared their independence. While the British were still gathering their forces, the colonials seized the opportunity and initiated a series of military operations that amounted to an American offensive.

Less than a month after Concord, Ethan Allen took Fort Ticonderoga on Lake Champlain, key to communications between the rebellious colonies and Canada. In the autumn of 1775, colonial forces invaded Canada, hoping that the Canadians might join them in resistance to Britain. Brigadier General Richard Montgomery, invading via the Lake Champlain–Richelieu River route exploited by Amherst in the Seven Years' War, took Montreal in November. Then, joined by Benedict Arnold, who had led 600 men across northern Maine, he assaulted Quebec on the last day of the year. With Montgomery killed and Arnold wounded, the attack failed, but Arnold maintained a siege of the city till spring, when melting ice permitted the British to bring in reinforcements via the St. Lawrence River.

In Boston the British found themselves besieged by 16,000 American militia who had swarmed to the city from the surrounding colonies. The defenders were virtually helpless until the arrival in May 1775 of Major General Sir William Howe with 10,000 troops. In July General George Washington assumed command of the American forces and undertook to organize the raw militia into an army, but he had so little gunpowder that

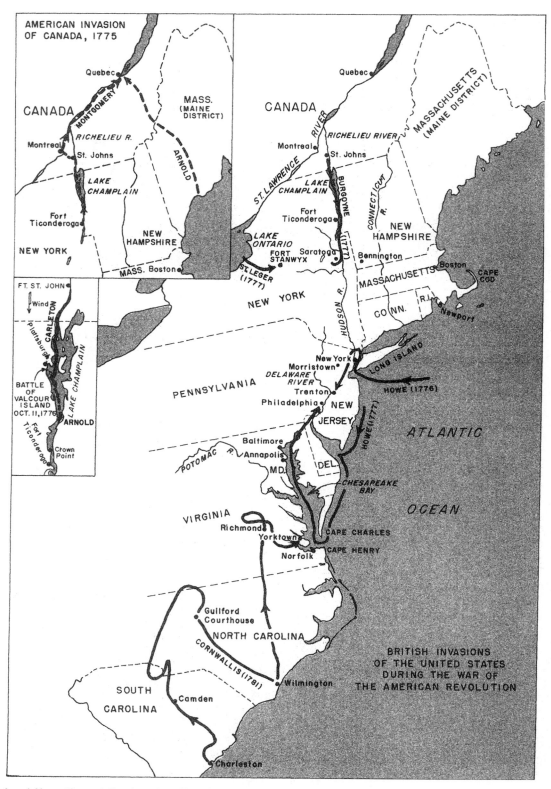

Land Operations of the American Revolution

his troops could scarcely return the British fire. The besieged British, however, lacked for nothing because ships arrived regularly bringing them munitions, provisions, and whatever else they needed.

Washington, on his own initiative and without authorization from Congress, commissioned armed vessels, manning them with troops from New England coastal areas, and sent them to attack this British shipping—with the dual objective of depriving the enemy of supplies and relieving his own army's acute shortage of everything. He thus improvised a makeshift fleet that has been called Washington's Navy. The first of Washington's raiders, the schooner *Hannah*, sailed in September and soon returned with a prize. By October Washington had half a dozen vessels in operation. In its short existence Washington's Navy took 38 prizes.

In early March 1776 General Washington emplaced cannon from Fort Ticonderoga on Dorchester Heights, overlooking Boston from the south. General Howe, having had enough of storming American-held heights at Bunker Hill the year before and finding his position untenable, evacuated Boston by sea and retired to Halifax, Nova Scotia, where he waited till early June for reinforcements from England.

If Washington had needed any lesson on the importance of sea power, the unopposed withdrawal of the British from Boston would have supplied it. So long as the British had free use of the sea, the Americans were helpless to prevent either the evacuation of a beaten army or seaborne forays along their coast.

The British Counteroffensive, 1776

Washington had no doubt that Howe would return from Halifax and estimated that he would attack not Boston but the more centrally located New York, gateway to the strategic Hudson River valley. Accordingly he shifted his own army to New York, where he divided it between Manhattan and Brooklyn Heights, on Long Island. As many weeks passed, Washington was at first puzzled and then alarmed by the failure of the British to appear.

Finally, on 5 July, the day after Congress signed the Declaration of Independence, Howe arrived, escorted by a fleet under the command of his brother, Admiral Richard Lord Howe, and landed his troops on Staten Island. Even then General Howe marked time until the arrival of Hessian mercenaries from Europe and British troops from an abortive diversionary attack on Charleston,

South Carolina gave him 32,000 men to oppose Washington's 17,000.

At last, on 22 August, Howe crossed to Long Island and began a leisurely advance. Washington slowly withdrew, aided by winds that prevented British frigates from supporting Howe's left flank and by a fog that enabled the Americans on the night of the 29th to slip across to Manhattan. Within two months Washington was forced north to White Plains, whence he crossed the Hudson into New Jersey. In another month he was forced across the Delaware into Pennsylvania.

By this time Washington's army had dwindled to a mere 3,000 men, and only the lateness of the season prevented Howe from advancing on and taking Philadelphia, seat of the Continental Congress. It was at this point, when the colonial cause seemed hopeless, that Washington made his dramatic Christmas night crossing of the Delaware to surprise the Hessian garrison and occupy Trenton. After a series of attacks on British outposts and the capture of Princeton, by which he regained control of the greater part of New Jersey, Washington took a position at Morristown in the Jersey highlands, whence he could threaten any British move toward Philadelphia or up the Hudson.

In Canada the war had resumed the preceding May, when melting ice permitted ships to arrive at Quebec with 6,000 reinforcements from England. Arnold and his Americans at once lifted their siege and hastily retreated, pursued by the British under Major General Sir Guy Carleton, governor general of Canada.

On reaching Lake Champlain, Arnold hurriedly began expanding the tiny American fleet already on the lake. This shipbuilding operation forced the British to stop and build a superior fleet, for the lake constituted the only practical line of supply through the area. With materials brought overland and by small boats up the Richelieu River, they constructed a 180-ton ship. In addition they dismantled two schooners on the St. Lawrence and reassembled them on the lake. These vessels gave them a decisive superiority over Arnold's motley collection of smaller craft.

On 11 October, when the British squadron was finally ready to sail, it moved up the lake before a north wind. Arnold, with his force concealed behind Valcour Island, let it pass, thus obliging the enemy to beat back upwind to attack him. Despite this advantage, the Americans suffered so severely in the ensuing Battle of Valcour Island that they were fortunate to succeed that night in slipping past the British squadron toward Crown Point. The

British pursued, and in a running, two-day battle most of the American vessels were either captured or beached and burned, while the survivors took to the woods.

Although the British could congratulate themselves on a tactical victory that rendered Canada secure, their months of shipbuilding had cost them their strategic opportunity, for mid-October was too close to winter for them to resume their advance. "If we had begun our expedition four weeks earlier," lamented one of Carleton's officers, "I am satisfied that everything would have ended this year." In the circumstances, however, there was nothing for the British to do but retire to winter quarters in Canada. American naval power had scored its first and most important success, for it had delayed the invasion when there was little else to do so.

Saratoga, the Turning Point

The British intended to resume their campaigns the following year, but in 1777 they were to find the rebels better prepared to contest their advances. Washington's victory at Trenton had fired American patriotism, and whereas the Americans did not exactly flock to the colors, recruitments picked up. France, ever resentful at having lost her overseas empire to Britain, began providing the rebels with substantial supplies of munitions.

Lieutenant General John Burgoyne, who had succeeded Carleton in command of the British army in Canada, expected to advance southward via Lake Champlain and the Hudson to meet General Howe advancing northward from New York. Between them they would thus cut off New England, the hotbed of the rebellion, from the rest of the American colonies.

But General Howe was worried about Washington's growing army, unassailable at Morristown. He had received no orders to coordinate his movements with those of the northern British force, for it had occurred to no one in London that Burgoyne might run into serious difficulty. Howe concluded that he could best serve the British cause by destroying Washington's army, and that the surest way to draw Washington out of his highland fastness was to seize Philadelphia. To avoid another Trenton, Howe eschewed the overland approach and embarked his troops in transports. To bypass the American defenses on the Delaware River, he moved on Philadelphia by the roundabout route of the Chesapeake Bay.

General Washington was bewildered by the disappearance of Howe and the bulk of his army from New York. For almost two months he was in grave doubt as to the proper disposition of his troops, whether to move to the north or to cover Philadelphia. The dilemma imposed upon him was a striking demonstration of the mobility and initiative conferred by British sea power.

At last Washington received a message that Howe's armada had entered the Chesapeake. He at once transferred his army by forced marches to the Philadelphia area in order to block the British overland advance from the head of the bay. At Brandywine Creek on 11 September Howe defeated Washington (but by no means destroyed his army) and then proceeded to occupy the rebel capital.

Meanwhile, Burgoyne, who had retained control of Lake Champlain, won from Arnold the previous autumn, moved up the lake in June and captured Fort Ticonderoga. By the end of July, he was on the upper Hudson despite obstructions put in his path by the Americans. But in early August British Colonel Barry St. Leger, who was advancing from Lake Ontario via the Mohawk Valley to join Burgoyne, was stopped in a bloody battle with local patriots near Fort Stanwyx. Upon news that General Arnold was approaching with American reinforcements, St. Leger retreated hastily to Canada.

At the same time Burgoyne was finding his long line of communications through the wilderness inadequate to supply his army. So he dispatched some 700 men to cross the Green Mountains near Bennington, seize the stores reported to be in that town, and then raid the Connecticut River Valley for supplies, cattle, and draft animals. This detachment got no farther than Bennington, where in mid-August the Green Mountain Boys destroyed or captured the entire force. After these disasters, Burgoyne pressed on against growing opposition. Finally, surrounded by American militiamen, now stiffened by regulars under Major General Horatio Gates, Burgoyne, at Saratoga on 17 October 1777, surrendered his army of more than 5,000 men.

The American victory at Saratoga was a turning point in the Revolution, for by demonstrating that the colonies had a chance for success it brought France openly into the war—and French assistance was decisive. But that result could not be foreseen in the autumn of 1777. While Howe's army settled down for a comfortable winter in Philadelphia, the despairing remnants of Washington's army endured cold and hunger at Valley Forge.

France Enters the War

After the news of Saratoga, the French, fearful that England might make concessions that would bring peace with the colonies, on 6 February 1778 signed with Benjamin Franklin treaties of commerce and alliance. The entry of France into the war completely altered its character. From a sort of civil war, in which British public opinion had been divided, it was transformed into an international war and at length into a new world war, with fighting in America, at Gibraltar, in the Atlantic, in the Mediterranean, in the West Indies, and in the waters off India.

In Europe Britain found herself at war with a major continental power and with no ally on the Continent, a situation that she had hitherto avoided and which she endeavored ever thereafter to prevent. France, with no land warfare to tax her resources, no threat to her own frontiers to distract her attention, was now free to concentrate on Britain. She intended to exploit this freedom by seizing control of the Channel and invading the British Isles. A successful invasion would even old scores, regain her lost West Indies possessions, and free America at a single stroke. Though her own naval resources appeared sufficient for the task, France set about inducing Spain to join her in the war so as to have a superfluity of power.

General Washington, who had been frustrated when sea power enabled the British to escape him at Boston, at last had the prospect of support from a first-class navy. The history of the Revolution from the American point of view now became the story of Washington's endeavors to secure the cooperation of the French fleet for a decisive action, because he saw clearly that in a combined operation lay the best hope for American victory.

The Early War at Sea

In the spring of 1776 Congress had authorized privateering, and adopted a form of commission to be issued by the colonial governments and by American agents abroad. Massachusetts had already authorized privateers and prize courts, and some of the other colonies followed suit, issuing both their own and the congressional commissions.

Privateers made by far the most effective contribution to the American seagoing effort. After some decline in 1777 as the Royal Navy's frigates took to sea to protect British commerce, American privateering revived in 1778, when France's entry into the war obliged the British to concentrate their

naval forces. Thereafter the number of American vessels engaged in privateering increased, and their effectiveness improved each year until the end of the war, by which time they had captured some 600 British merchant vessels.

Congress had taken the first steps toward creating a Continental Navy by establishing, on 13 October 1775, a "Naval Committee" to acquire and fit out vessels for sea and to draw up regulations. The following month the committee purchased two ships, two brigs, and subsequently two sloops and two schooners, while Congress on 10 November established a Marine Corps by authorizing the raising of two battalions of marines. Esek Hopkins, brother of the Rhode Island member of the Naval Committee, was appointed Commander in Chief of the Fleet, a post corresponding to that of General Washington in the Continental Army. Hopkins seemed a reasonable choice for the command. He had gone to sea at the age of 20 and had become the prosperous commodore of a fleet of 17 merchantmen. In the Seven Years' War he had shown himself a daring privateersman.

Taking advantage of a discretionary clause, Hopkins disregarded his orders to clear the Virginia and Carolina coasts of enemy forces and sailed instead for the Bahamas, where there was reportedly a supply of powder. In early March 1776, he landed a force on New Providence, took two forts guarding Nassau after only token resistance, and then spent two weeks loading the captured munitions.

This was the squadron's only cruise—mainly because Hopkins could not adequately man his vessels, owing to competition from the privateers. The latter, offering greater rewards, lighter discipline, and less danger, attracted seamen away from the Continental Navy. The best Hopkins could do was to send out individual vessels on commerce-raiding cruises. The most successful of the cruiser captains was John Paul Jones, who in the sloop *Providence* captured no fewer than 16 prizes. In a subsequent cruise in the *Alfred*, he took several more, including an armed vessel laden with winter uniforms and other supplies for Carleton's army in Canada.

Commodore Hopkins was making enemies: in Congress, by his inability to obey orders to go to sea and attack the Newfoundland fisheries; among his own officers, who accused him of tyranny; and among New England politicians, who were displeased when he denounced privateering, an enterprise in which many of them were heavy investors. The commodore's critics had the ammunition they needed when, through failure to maintain proper patrols, Hopkins found his squadron blockaded in Providence River, and subsequently, through sheer clumsiness, he botched a chance to capture an investigating British frigate that ran aground in Narragansett Bay. Congress in March 1777 suspended Hopkins from his command and later dismissed him from the service.

Following the raid on New Providence, the Continental Navy participated in only one major operation—the Penobscot Expedition of 1779. This was primarily a Massachusetts enterprise, directed against the British–Tory base at Castine, Maine, but the 16 fighting ships that accompanied the transports were stiffened by three vessels of the Continental Navy, of which the most powerful was the frigate *Warren*, 32, under Captain Dudley Saltonstall, who commanded the expedition. Arriving at Castine in the latter part of July, the ill-managed force made such slow progress that a British relief squadron had time to arrive from New York, whereupon the Americans fled ignominiously up the Penobscot River and beached their vessels.

All the 13 colonies except New Jersey and Delaware created state navies during the war, but these navies consisted principally of small craft and conducted few operations of significance.

The most remarkable accomplishment of the Continental Navy was carrying the war into British waters. The use of French bases for this unneutral purpose presented some inconveniences because the French occasionally had to make concessions to British protests, but the net effect was to embroil France with England.

The first Continental vessel in European waters was the brig *Reprisal*, commanded by Lambert Wickes, who in late 1776 took Benjamin Franklin to France. Sailing from Nantes in January 1777, Wickes took 5 prizes. His bringing them into French ports raised a storm of protest from Britain. The fitting out of the cutter *Dolphin* and the arrival in France of the Continental brig *Lexington* created a little squadron, which Wickes led in a month's cruise around Ireland, netting 18 prizes. On the return voyage to America in the fall, the *Reprisal* foundered in a storm off the Grand Banks, taking her captain with her.

Meanwhile, American agents in France had purchased the lugger *Surprise*, command of which was given to Gustavus Conyngham. Sailing from Dunkirk in May, Conyngham soon returned with two prizes. British protests induced the French government to surrender the captured vessels, seize the *Surprise*, and imprison Conyngham and

his crew. But Franklin procured Conyngham's release in time for him to take command of the cutter *Revenge*. Operating from French and later from Spanish bases, he contributed not a little to increasing tension between the Bourbon powers and England.

If Hopkins's squadron of converted merchantmen was the first Continental Navy, 13 frigates authorized by Congress at the end of 1775 may be considered the second. These were to be not mere conversions but built as real men-of-war from the keel up. But the promise of an effective fleet of genuine combatant vessels was never realized. Six of the frigates for various reasons never got to sea at all, and of the remainder, four had only short careers. The *Hancock*, 32, an exceptionally fine, fast vessel, was taken by a British 44. The *Raleigh* was lost when Captain John Barry was driven ashore in Penobscot Bay by superior forces. The *Warren* was lost in the Penobscot Expedition. Only the *Randolph*, 32, died with glory. Her captain, Nicholas Biddle, had commanded the *Andrew Doria* under Hopkins and had made a successful cruise afterward. He was fortunate in being able to take the *Randolph* out of the Delaware and to sea early in 1777, before the British moved on Philadelphia. In the spring of 1778, Biddle was given a small squadron headed by the *Randolph* to hunt down British cruisers. In March he encountered the 64-gun *Yarmouth* near Barbados. Biddle engaged her and, although unsupported by the rest of his squadron, appeared near victory when the *Randolph*'s magazine exploded, depriving the United States of an outstanding officer.

Thus by 1780 only 3 of the 13 frigates were available. The *Boston* and the *Providence* after a cruise to the south put in at Charleston, shared in the defense of that city, and were lost when it fell to the British. The *Trumbull* alone survived into 1781, mainly because she was unable to get over the Connecticut River bar and to sea before 1780.

Greatest of the officers of the Continental Navy was John Paul Jones. After serving as lieutenant in the *Alfred* under Hopkins and making his successful cruises in command of the *Providence* and the *Alfred*, he was in June 1777 given the new 18-gun *Ranger*. Sailing her to France in the autumn, he was in that country when the Franco–American alliance was signed and had the satisfaction of receiving a salute from a French squadron in Quiberon Bay. In the spring of 1778 he circled Ireland in the *Ranger*, raiding ashore, and captured HMS *Drake*, 20. A year later he was given command of an old, half-rotten East Indiaman, which he named the *Bonhomme Richard*. On board her he sailed in

August 1779 in command of a small squadron consisting of a new American frigate, the *Alliance*, 32—commanded by a half-mad Frenchman, Captain Pierre Landais—and three smaller French vessels. In a clockwise circuit of the British Isles, Jones took several prizes, and in the evening of 4 September off Flamborough Head, on the east coast of England, he fought his most famous battle.

At dusk, while stalking a British convoy, he encountered its two escorts, the new 50-gun frigate *Serapis*, under Captain Richard Pearson, and the *Countess of Scarborough*, 20. While one of the French vessels engaged the *Countess*, Jones in the *Bonhomme Richard* headed for the *Serapis*. At the first exchange of broadsides, two of Jones's heaviest guns burst, knocking out the rest of that battery, and reducing the *Richard*'s weight of broadside to 195 pounds, to combat the *Serapis*'s 300.

Jones, realizing that a gun duel would be fatal to his ship, attempted to board the *Serapis*. The latter nimbly sidestepped and sped ahead to rake the *Richard*. The clumsy old East Indiaman, turning, ran her bow into the *Serapis*'s stern. The British captain, having clearly demonstrated his ship's superiority, peered through the growing darkness and called out disdainfully, "Has your ship struck?"—to which Jones made his famous reply: "I have not yet begun to fight!"

The *Richard* now tried to rake the *Serapis* but fell short, causing the ships to collide. The wind then made them pivot together, bow to stern, stern to bow. Jones, seizing the opportunity, ordered his men to lock the ships together with grappling irons, and he himself seized a broken line from the *Serapis* and made it fast to his mizzenmast. The ships, thus lashed alongside one another, their guns almost muzzle to muzzle, fired into each other for two hours. During this period, the *Alliance* loomed out of the darkness and fired three broadsides into the *Bonhomme Richard*. Captain Landais afterward confided to a friend that he had hoped to sink the *Richard*, capture the *Serapis*, and emerge the victor.

The *Richard* slowly began to sink, all of her battery knocked out but three 9-pounders, one of which Jones himself worked. At this critical point, an American seaman crawled out on a yard of the *Richard* and dropped a grenade through an open hatch onto the gun deck of the *Serapis*, causing loose cartridges to explode and killing many of her gunners. When, shortly afterward, her mainmast began to sway, Captain Pearson's nerve cracked, and he tore down his flag with his own hands. The battered *Richard* went down the next day, and Jones transferred his own flag to the *Serapis*.

Fleet Operations in American Waters, 1778–79

The French, on forming their alliance with the United States, began readying a portion of their Toulon fleet for operations in American waters. In April 1778 twelve ships of the line sailed under the command of Vice Admiral the Comte d'Estaing.

The English recognized the necessity of getting prompt reinforcements to Admiral Lord Howe if the British position in America were to be preserved, but only by taking men and supplies from Admiral Augustus Keppel's Channel fleet was the Admiralty able to provide 13 of the line for Vice Admiral John Byron, who sailed for America in June.

The French alliance made Philadelphia a vulnerable position for the British army because here the troops depended upon seaborne supplies brought via the Delaware River, which a French fleet could readily blockade. General Sir Henry Clinton, who had succeeded to the overall British command in America, was ordered to evacuate the position forthwith and return to New York. Suspecting that a French fleet was on the way, he marched his army overland, leaving his supplies and artillery for Lord Howe to bring by sea. Howe cleared the Delaware with his little fleet on 28 June, reached New York the next day, and immediately stationed frigates to warn of the approach of French naval forces.

D'Estaing, who had proclaimed, "Speed is the foremost of military virtues; to surprise is almost to have conquered," failed to heed his own precept. With a prompt crossing of the Atlantic, he could have caught Howe's fleet still in the Delaware and destroyed it along with Clinton's artillery, but he spent 85 days getting from Toulon to the Capes of the Delaware, where he arrived on 6 July. He was fortunate that "Foul Weather Jack" Byron's British reinforcements, having been scattered by a storm, were even later. Howe was thus left to face a French fleet mounting nearly twice as many guns as his own.

Howe grimly prepared for what promised to be a fight against hopeless odds. He placed his ships in a close line across the main channel into New York harbor, while Clinton mounted a battery at the end of Sandy Hook. On 11 July d'Estaing arrived and anchored about four miles distant. General Washington sent an offer of full cooperation in an attack on New York. It appeared that the stage was set for the kind of combined assault Washington had hoped to achieve since early in the war. This apparent opportunity was foiled by the simple fact that the deep draft of the French ships prevented their crossing the bar, which was under only 22 feet of water. D'Estaing, frustrated, finally sailed away. Washington was deeply disappointed at the failure of what had looked like an unparalleled opportunity to block the British army from contact with the sea, its source of supply and reinforcement, and its potential avenue of escape.

D'Estaing retired to Boston for a leisurely refitting. The scene, as was customary in sailing-ship days, shifted to the West Indies for the good weather of winter months. Early in November d'Estaing sailed for the Caribbean. The British at the same time sent 5,000 troops from New York thither, and early in 1779 the main British fleet followed. The latter was now under Admiral Byron, Lord Howe having surrendered command of his squadron, declaring that he would serve no more "so long as the present Ministers remain in office."

The forces already in the West Indies had been at their old game of "filching sugar islands," and both d'Estaing and Byron were soon involved. The following July the French admiral had occasion to give the English naval commander a lesson in tactics. D'Estaing had just completed the capture of Grenada when he received a report of an approaching fleet. It was Byron, coming to the relief of the island with several transports of troops and 22 ships of the line. The resulting Battle of Grenada demonstrated the danger of falling into the disarray of a general chase upon a competently handled force that intends to stand and fight.

Before dawn on the following day, d'Estaing in a near calm was attempting to get his fleet under way from the harbor, when first light disclosed the British bearing down. Byron, eager to catch the French as they straggled forth, ordered general chase, but the quickening breeze enabled the French to form their line of battle, and the disordered British, dashing in pell-mell, had six ships disabled. The battle then moved westward, but d'Estaing, mindful of his strategic purpose of covering Grenada, wore his fleet, cannonaded the British cripples in passing, and returned to harbor. Next day the battered British withdrew to St. Kitts. Although the French as usual suffered more casualties than the British, they had won not only a strategic victory in preserving their hold on Grenada but a neat tactical victory as well.

D'Estaing now bethought himself of the approaching hurricane season, which in the West Indies lasted from July to October. During that period naval forces in the area cleared for home or for the North American theater. D'Estaing sailed first for Haiti, the last French port of call in the Indies. Letters awaiting him at Cap Français enabled him to plan his next operation. From General Washington he learned that the British had exploited the absence of the French fleet to invade the southern colonies and had held Savannah since the end of 1778. Heeding appeals, D'Estaing prepared to help recapture the port.

On 1 September, the French admiral arrived off Savannah with 20 ships of the line and 3,000 troops in transports. He had generously undertaken the expedition after receiving orders to return to France, and was anxious to get it over with. At his urging, the French and Americans rather prematurely launched their assault on the city on 9 October. The attack failed, the French suffered severely, and D'Estaing himself was wounded. He sailed for France, leaving disappointment and bitterness in his wake.

Relative Advantages of the French and British Fleets

The French navy of 1778 was in many respects the world's finest. With about 45 ships ready to go to sea, France had more ships fit for action than did Britain. These vessels, scientifically designed, had cleaner lines and were faster and heavier, rate for rate, than the British. The French corps of seaman gunners were probably the most accurate marksmen in the world, clearly outshooting the British at long ranges. Finally, the French led the British in the theory and practice of naval tactics. Bigot de Morogue's Tactique Navale, published in 1763, not only expounded various methods of achieving tactical concentration but also spurred development of a practical signal system. Both theory and signals were put into practice in "squadrons of evolution," in which most of the French naval leaders of the war had been trained.

The British, on the other hand, had only the Permanent Fighting Instructions, though as early as the Seven Years' War commanding officers had begun issuing Additional Instructions to provide more flexibility. Lord Howe and Admiral Richard Kempenfelt were interested in producing something still more effective. One of the significant developments of the period was their creation for the Royal Navy of an efficient system of signals and of flexible tactics, which, however, were not adopted generally until several years after the end of the War of the American Revolution. Signals and tactics were inseparable, for so long as an admiral could signal only to execute a given article of the Fighting Instructions, it was obviously impossible to escape the Instructions.

Given the Royal Navy's shortcomings and the *Marine's* advantages in the war, why did the French navy achieve no clear-cut victories? The chief reason seems to have been the inhibiting force of its defensive tradition—developed in earlier wars when French resources were strained by simultaneous warfare on land and sea, and the navy was warned to save its ships. Thus while the British fired at hulls to destroy or capture the enemy's ships and thus gain permanent command of the sea, the French fired at spars and rigging to impair the enemy's ability to pursue and thus gain temporary command. An example is the Battle for Minorca, in which Galissonière, without losing or destroying a ship, removed Byng's fleet from the scene long enough for the French army to complete its conquest of the island.

Fleet Operations in European Waters, 1778–80

The first fleet action of the War of the American Revolution, the Battle of Ushant, followed visual contact, on 23 July 1778, between the Brest and Channel fleets a hundred miles west of Ushant, an island off the tip of Brittany. The French admiral, the Comte d'Orvilliers, with 29 ships, was less interested in combat than in getting his fleet safely back to Brest. For three days he used his windward position to evade action.

At length, on 27 July, Admiral Keppel, commanding the 30 ships of the Channel fleet, lost patience. He signaled general chase, sacrificing an orderly line in an attempt to fall upon the French rear. But d'Orvilliers suddenly wore his fleet together and heavily engaged the disordered British, dismasting several vessels of their van and heavily damaging their rear. This one inconclusive pass effectively ended the battle. Keppel had learned that general chase, indiscriminately employed, was not necessarily the key to victory.

D'Orvilliers, considering he had done well enough, withdrew for Brest as darkness fell. Although the French had suffered the greater number of casualties, they had clearly outmaneuvered the British. Moreover, they enjoyed the unusual experience of bringing home all their ships from an engagement with the Royal Navy. For the underdogs of the Seven Years' War, that was no small victory.

When Keppel, who happened to be a member of Parliament, was court-martialed for his poor showing, the chamber was packed with his partisans. They turned the proceedings into a farce, and he was acquitted with the acclaim of a riotous mob.

To officers of the Royal Navy who forgot, or were unaware of, these circumstances, his acquittal seemed a clear demonstration that the Permanent Fighting Instructions had lost their sacrosanct character. Keppel had been charged simultaneously with the offenses of Mathews in the Battle of Toulon and of Byng in the Battle for Minorca, yet he had been neither dismissed from the service nor shot. The inference seemed clear—an officer might now conduct a battle according to his own best judgment.

France had expected to be joined in the war by Spain, her sister Bourbon power and sister-sufferer in the Seven Years' War. In early June 1779, d'Orvilliers put to sea from Brest with 28 of the line and headed south for a rendezvous with the Spanish fleet, while the Spanish ambassador in London provoked a British declaration of war.

Franco–Spanish plans, already drawn up, had set the summer of 1779 for an invasion of England at the Isle of Wight and Portsmouth. For this operation the French could muster 62 and the Spanish 40 of the line, against a maximum British strength of 80. In this crisis the dearth of leadership in Britain became evident. The Howe brothers and Keppel had resigned in disgust. To take command of the vital Channel fleet the Ministry was reduced to calling out of retirement Sir Charles Hardy, 63 years old and physically unfit.

In something like panic, the English rushed preparations to meet the expected invasion, but speed proved needless. D'Orvilliers had to wait a month for the dilatory Spaniards to join him, and the combined armada of 67 ships was not assembled until late July. By mid-August it lay becalmed off Plymouth. Hardy with his 35 ships had been in and out of port without offering any real challenge, but on board the French and Spanish vessels water and provisions were running short, and sickness was reaching serious proportions. While the French government vacillated and changed plans, d'Orvilliers sighted Hardy and pursued him briefly. Finally, with his supplies exhausted, he returned exasperated to Brest.

While the London government was fully occupied with measures to throw back the invasion, which never came, John Paul Jones was making his raiding circuit of the British Isles with impunity. After defeating the *Serapis,* he made it safely to Holland and at length to France. Here the story of his colorful exploits, in contrast to the miserable performance of the Franco–Spanish fleet, made him the toast of Paris.

At the end of 1779, Admiral George Brydges Rodney sailed from England with 22 sail of the line to relieve Gibraltar, then under blockade by the Spaniards. The British ships, mostly borrowed from the Channel fleet, were newly sheathed with copper, which conferred a speed advantage and inhibited fouling. Rodney had made his reputation in the Seven Years' War, partly for gallantry but more for his partiality for enterprises that promised good prize money. An inveterate gambler, he was in Paris to escape his creditors when the new war broke out. Because he was 60 years old and plagued by poor health, many officers felt that the Admiralty, in selecting him to head the relief expedition, was scraping the bottom of the barrel.

In fact, Rodney carried out his mission with dispatch and considerable flair. Sighting a Spanish fleet of 11 ships near Cape St. Vincent, he crowded on sail before a westerly wind and ordered general chase. The newly coppered British ships slowly overhauled the Spaniards and by evening, as the wind freshened to a half-gale, began action with the rearmost. The fighting continued throughout the night—the famous "Moonlight Battle." One Spanish ship blew up, and Rodney captured 6 others. With the Straits thus cleared, he had no difficulty relieving Gibraltar.

From Gibraltar Rodney sailed in mid-February for the West Indies, detaching on the way those vessels that were to return to the Channel fleet. Although the French and Spaniards occasionally combined to put to sea a fleet outmatching anything the British could muster, naval actions in European waters for the rest of 1780 were confined to *guerre de course*.

Chapter 5
The War of
the American Revolution, II

There was little to relieve the gloom that had descended upon the American leaders in the fall of 1779 after D'Estaing's failure at Savannah and return to France. Washington's army spent the winter of 1779–80 once more at Morristown, where its hardships surpassed those of Valley Forge.

General Clinton, confident that Washington was too weak to threaten New York City, decided at the urging of General Lord Charles Cornwallis to make the southern colonies the area of his principal effort in 1780. At the end of December 1779, as soon as he was certain that d'Estaing was out of the way, he sailed with Cornwallis and 8,000 men for Charleston, which fell early in May 1780. British forces soon had substantial control of South Carolina. In mid-August Cornwallis overwhelmingly defeated the victor of Saratoga, General Gates, near Camden, South Carolina, and followed this success by invading North Carolina. Washington was powerless to interfere with this overrunning of the South.

There was one bright spot in the gloomy picture. Early in 1779 the Marquis de Lafayette had returned to France to advocate the cause of the colonies. In April 1780 he arrived back in America with the welcome news that his government was sending General Rochambeau with French troops.

When transports bringing 5,500 soldiers arrived at Newport in early July, they were escorted by seven ships of the line and three frigates. The departure of this force from Brest had not gone unnoticed by the British Admiralty, which had at once sent a warning to Clinton at Charleston and dispatched Admiral Thomas Graves with six of the line to reinforce the British squadron at the New York station. Clinton left Cornwallis in command in the South and hurried back to New York.

In September Washington met with Rochambeau at Hartford to plan a joint strategy. In response to questions posed by the French, he reiterated the views from which he never deviated:

1st. That there can be no decisive enterprise against the maritime establishments of the English in this country without a constant naval superiority.

2nd. That of all the enterprises which may be undertaken, the most important and decisive is the reduction of New York, which is the center and focus of all the British forces.

Washington returned from the Hartford conference to be confronted with the treason of Benedict Arnold. He found moreover that his little army of 3,500 men near West Point had exhausted its supplies, and he had no money to pay them.

News from the South, however, was improving. General Nathanael Greene, Gates's successor in command of the American Southern forces, was achieving some gains. His Americans had wiped out British detachments in South Carolina at King's Mountain and at Cowpens. At Guilford Courthouse, North Carolina, Cornwallis repulsed Greene's army, but at a cost of a third of his men, killed or wounded. As British generals in difficulty usually did, he retreated to the coast, at Wilmington, and called for the Royal Navy to bring him supplies and take away his wounded. Meanwhile, Greene proceeded to reduce the British outposts in South Carolina and within a few months brought the greater part of the state under American control.

In other areas also Britain's situation was deteriorating. She had united the maritime nations against her. Her seizure of neutral merchant vessels had induced Russia, Denmark, and Sweden to unite in a hostile Armed Neutrality of the North. When the Dutch decided to join the Armed Neutrality, the British government seized upon a mere pretext to declare war on them. The actual basis for the declaration was Britain's resentment of Dutch trade with France and America and the opportunity the rupture offered for Britain to seize weakly held Dutch possessions.

The really decisive factor in the changed situation, however, was the arrival via the West Indies of the effective French naval aid that Washington had so long sought.

The West Indies, 1781

In early January 1781 Rear Admiral Sir Samuel Hood, designated Admiral Rodney's second-in-

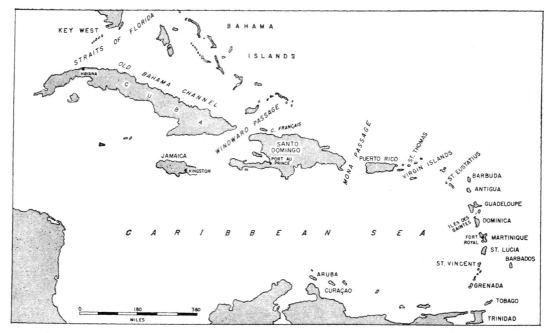

The West Indies

command, arrived in the West Indies with reinforcements that gave Rodney a fleet of 21 ships. Hood was to prove an able and energetic, though somewhat less than loyal, subordinate. Naturally cantankerous, he soon came to detest Rodney, so that relations between the two were far from cordial.

Shortly after Hood's arrival, Rodney received orders from London to attack the Dutch West Indian islands. The most important at that time was St. Eustatius, which served as a main entrepôt for goods, including contraband, from France and neutral countries, and even from disloyal British merchants, for transshipment to the United States and the French West Indies. Because there were always immense quantities of such goods on the island, Rodney, whose greed was notorious, welcomed the opportunity for plunder. Before the authorities at St. Eustatius knew that the mother country was at war, Rodney seized the island with its immense stores and with 120 merchantmen in its harbor.

If the booty, running into millions of pounds, made Rodney wealthy beyond his dreams, it also ended for the time being his usefulness as an officer in the Royal Navy, for he at once became too engrossed in his treasure to pursue the plan for operations against other Dutch possessions. Even word that a strong French fleet was heading for the West

Indies failed to arouse him. He merely ordered Hood to a position from which he could both watch Fort Royal, French Martinique, and also cover the departure for England of a huge treasure convoy from St. Eustatius.

Rear Admiral the Comte de Grasse had sailed from Brest in the latter part of March 1781 with a sizable fleet escorting a large convoy of merchantmen. Aged 58, he was tall, handsome, energetic, and courageous, with a lifetime of experience at sea. Arriving off Martinique after a remarkably rapid passage of 36 days, he beat off Hood's attempt to intercept his convoy, damaging six British ships badly, and pursued the British for two days, turning back only when it became evident that he could not overtake their copper-clad vessels.

Immediately upon reaching Martinique, de Grasse organized expeditions against the British. After an unsuccessful attempt to surprise St. Lucia, he turned to Tobago, which fell on the first of June. He then returned to Fort Royal to repair and replenish his ships. In early July he sailed with his entire fleet of 23 of the line and a convoy of 160 merchant vessels for Cap Français. Here he was joined by four additional ships, and here too he found letters from Rochambeau and from the French minister in Philadelphia requesting his aid in America.

The War in the Colonies, 1781

Cornwallis, contrary to orders from General Clinton at New York, marched his army from Wilmington into Virginia and there added to the remnant of his army a strong British raiding party that had been ravaging the state. With his force thus built up to more than 7,000 men, he did some ravaging of his own and then, on peremptory orders from Clinton, entrenched his army at Yorktown on Chesapeake Bay, where he could have naval support. There he was kept under observation by General Lafayette, commanding 5,000 American troops, mostly ragged, raw militia.

At Newport, Rochambeau had been awaiting the arrival of the rest of his promised force, 5,000 additional men, before committing his services to General Washington. In May 1781, however, a French frigate arrived bringing Admiral de Barras to take command of the Newport squadron and bringing also the unwelcome news that the Royal Navy was watching Brest too closely for France to risk sending any more troops to America from Europe.

Aware now that he would probably have to make do with what he had, Rochambeau and his senior officers met with Washington and his staff at Wethersfield, Connecticut, to plan strategy for a forthcoming joint campaign. With some misgivings, Rochambeau concurred with Washington's proposal that they operate against New York, where Clinton had nearly 13,000 well-supplied, well-equipped troops.

Washington, never doubting that naval superiority was of "essential importance in any offensive operation," wrote to the French minister in Philadelphia, asking him to urge Admiral de Grasse to come north to join the operation against New York. Rochambeau now concluded that the British planned to center operations in the South and was deeply concerned for his countryman Lafayette. He wrote directly to de Grasse:

> There are two points at which an offensive may be made against the enemy: Chesapeake Bay and New York. The southwesterly winds and the state of distress in Virginia will probably make you prefer Chesapeake Bay, and it will be there where we think you may be able to render the greatest service.

In a second letter he strongly urged the Admiral to bring not only his fleet but also French troops from the West Indies.

In early July the main French and American armies met near White Plains to launch their campaign against New York. Rochambeau was not reassured by the sight of his allies. "The army of our neighbors," he reported to France, "has not four thousand men under arms." To assault a city with a force substantially smaller than its garrison was not a promising enterprise. Washington saw no alternatives but to await de Grasse's arrival. If the admiral brought enough troops to make the New York campaign practical, he preferred to put it into effect. If not, they might look to the Chesapeake.

The Forces Converge on Yorktown

Yorktown was one of the most remarkable and decisive campaigns in history. At a time when the British could not effectively coordinate two of their own armies in the colonies—witness Howe and Burgoyne, or Clinton and Cornwallis—it was an example of perfect coordination of the armies of two different nations with a fleet. At a time when communications were slow and unreliable, it demonstrated precise timing on the part of forces 1,500 miles apart. It was the sort of operation of which Washington had dreamed ever since the French entered the war.

The letter on which everything hinged arrived at Washington's headquarters on 14 August. The essence was that de Grasse was sailing from Cap Français on 13 August with more than 3,000 troops embarked in 25 to 29 ships of the line. He would go directly to the Chesapeake, "the place which seems indicated . . . as that most certain to achieve the benefits which you propose." He would be able to remain only till mid-October, for his troops had been promised for other operations.

Washington quickly adjusted his plans to embrace the opportunity. Because some of his American troops would have to remain to protect West Point, he could take only 2,500 men to Virginia, whereas Rochambeau would take about 4,000. Within four days of receiving de Grasse's letter, Washington had his Franco–American army on the march. To prevent the British at New York from attacking his rear or from making any move to extricate Cornwallis, he made an elaborate pretense of preparing for an attack on Staten Island.

Although this stratagem succeeded beyond expectation, the march south was a period of intense anxiety for Washington. Arriving at Philadelphia on the last day of August, he received news that a British fleet—actually Hood's from the West Indies—was off Sandy Hook. There seemed a real danger that it might intercept de Barras, who had just sailed from Newport, or that it might enter the

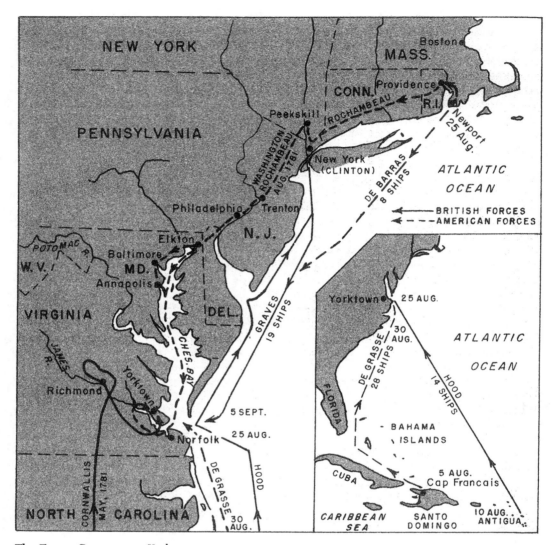

The Forces Converge on Yorktown

Chesapeake before de Grasse, of whom there had been no further word.

By 5 September both the American and the French troops had passed through Philadelphia. General Washington, after concluding his business in the city, followed with his staff at his customary hard pace. On the way he received information that de Grasse was in the Chesapeake, and he at once turned back to Chester to bring the news to Rochambeau, who had been inspecting the Delaware forts by water. As the French general's boat approached shore, he was astonished to see the usually reserved Washington wildly waving his hat in one hand and his handkerchief in the other, and

to be vigorously embraced as soon as he stepped ashore.

On the evening of 14 September, after a furious ride, Washington and Rochambeau arrived at Williamsburg and greeted Lafayette. Early the next morning came news that de Grasse had returned to the Chesapeake after a successful though inconclusive engagement, and that de Barras had arrived safely from Newport with artillery and provisions.

De Grasse, after reading the appeals from North America at Cap Français, had decided to go north with his entire fleet. Sailing on 5 August, he proceeded by the unfrequented Old Bahama Channel, between the north coast of Cuba and the Bahama

Banks, and arrived off the mouth of the Chesapeake on 30 August without any report of his approach having reached the British. After landing the troops he had brought, he transported American soldiers to a position below the James River to cut off Cornwallis's retreat to the Carolinas. He was preparing to send his lighter vessels to the head of the Chesapeake to bring French and American troops down the bay, when at about ten o'clock on the morning of 5 September his frigates posted outside the bay signaled that a fleet had been sighted. There was at first some hope that it might be de Barras's squadron from Rhode Island, but it was soon evident that there were too many sails. The fleet was obviously enemy.

When de Grasse had sailed from Port Royal to Cap Français in early July, his movement had been reported to Rodney, who ordered Hood to prepare to head for New York should the need arise. Then, being in poor health, Rodney sailed on 1 August for England with 4 of the line. The next day Hood proceeded to Antigua, where he found dispatches from Clinton and Graves indicating that de Grasse was expected to come to Rhode Island to join de Barras for an attack on New York. Hood therefore sailed from Antigua on 10 August, five days after de Grasse's departure from Cap Français. Outside the harbor he was joined by 4 of the line, to give him a total of 14 ships.

Hastening north by the direct route, Hood looked into the Chesapeake on the 25th. Finding no trace of the French there, since he was ahead of de Grasse, he looked in at the Delaware and then hurried on to New York. There he found Clinton and Graves, oblivious of the real situation, making leisurely plans for an operation against the French in Rhode Island. Hood's representations, reinforced by news that de Barras had sailed from Newport, brought Graves over the bar with 5 ships. As senior he assumed command of the combined force of 19 of the line and set sail for the Chesapeake, where he arrived on the morning of 5 September. It was a fine, fair day, with a moderate breeze from the north–northeast. At about 9:30 British lookouts sighted the French fleet at anchor just inside Cape Henry, and Graves ordered his ships to form a line of battle.

De Grasse had just detached 4 ships of the line to blockade the York and James rivers, so that only 24 were available for a sortie. His boats with a large part of his crews were absent landing troops, leaving his fleet seriously undermanned. Under these circumstances he might well have taken a defensive position across the mouth of the Chesapeake, but

remaining in the bay would sentence de Barras to almost certain capture on his arrival, with the loss of all the French siege artillery and munitions. Weighing these alternatives, de Grasse decided to leave the bay for battle. But to leave the Chesapeake in the face of a fresh northeasterly wind and against a flood tide was impossible. Therefore de Grasse's order was for ships to get under way about noon when the tide turned.

The Battle of the Virginia Capes, 5 September, 1781

At 12:30 p.m., when the British were 12 or 15 miles northeast of Cape Henry, de Grasse ordered his ships to slip cables and form a line of battle in order of swiftness, without regard to assigned positions. They executed this command with remarkable efficiency, considering their shorthanded condition, but they could hardly avoid straggling out of the bay. The first four vessels emerged in good order, but the next two were a mile to leeward, while the center and rear were almost another two miles to leeward.

The British, by contrast, were coming down from the northeast in a well-formed line at one cable's length. Gradually Graves changed course toward the west until the two fleets were on approximately parallel and opposite courses. At 2 p.m. the French van was three miles south of Graves's flagship *London*, which was at the center of the British line. Soon afterward, as the head of the British line approached the shoals at the entrance to the bay, Graves ordered his fleet to wear together. This maneuver, besides reversing the direction of sailing, reversed the order of the line, putting the former van division in the rear. Fatefully, the new rear division was commanded by Admiral Hood, a somewhat old-fashioned tactician who believed in strict adherence to formal tactics.

By this time the French center and part of the rear division were well clear of Cape Henry. Although the fleets were now on the same tack, the lines were by no means parallel, but formed a seaward-pointing V. As the vans converged, the rearward French vessels tended to lag, and Hood maintained a rigid line ahead behind the flagship. As a result, the battle began with close action at the head of the battle lines, rippling back to the center divisions, and never involving the rear divisions at all.

For the ships engaged, it was a vicious close-range action, devoid of tactical elegance. Nightfall ended the carnage, and the fleets continued east on

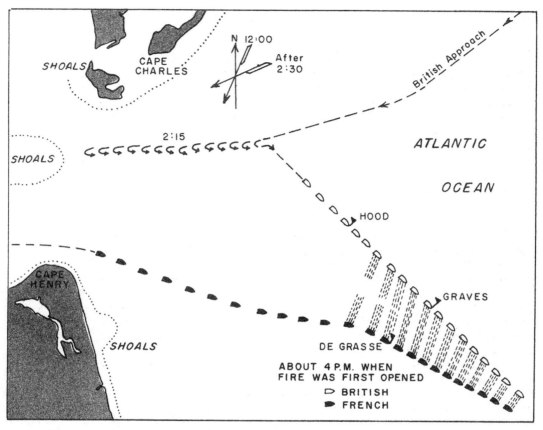

Battle of the Virginia Capes, 5 September 1781

slightly divergent courses. Frigates sent out by Graves to assess the condition of his fleet brought him reports of "such a state of damages that we could only think of preserving the best appearance." One ship was so badly riddled that she had to be sunk, and at least five other ships had sustained serious damage. The French too had suffered severely, but when Graves viewed the French fleet next morning "they had not the appearance of near so much damage as we had sustained." This battle had been no mere French "rigging shoot." The British suffered 336 casualties, the French 230. Rigid adherence to formal tactics had again kept the British rear out of action and denied the Royal Navy a possible victory.[1]

Through the 6th the two fleets remained within sight of each other, repairing their damage, with neither attempting to attack. Indeed, Graves had already decided that his fleet was in no condition to renew the engagement. Consequently, though the fleets continued in visual contact two more days, there was no further action. On the morning of the 9th de Grasse sighted the sails of a squadron on the horizon. It was, as he surmised, de Barras, who anchored safely in the Chesapeake on the 10th. Being now out of sight of the British and conscious of his strategic mission, de Grasse set course for the bay, where he arrived next day. With de Barras's ships, he now had 36 of the line.

When the British on the 13th found the French at anchor inside Chesapeake Bay, Graves had no alternative to returning to New York to repair his fleet as quickly as possible in order to bring back Clinton with 6,000 troops to the aid of Cornwallis. It is a measure of the effectiveness of French fire at Virginia Capes that, despite the extreme urgency, Graves was not ready until 19 October. Sailing with 23 of the line, he arrived off the Chesapeake a week later. But Cornwallis, after losing two of his outer redoubts and failing in an attempt to escape across the York River, had on the 19th surrendered his entire army.

---

[1]Earlier examples were the Battle of Toulon (1744) and the Battle for Minorca (1756). These battles, together with the Battle of the Virginia Capes, when studied in retrospect, went far toward discrediting formalism in naval battles.

For the British the loss of a second army in America was a stunning blow. Lord North announced the resignation of his ministry. George III seriously considered abdicating. The Marquis of Rockingham formed a new government friendly to America and at once sent an emissary to Paris to discuss peace terms with Franklin.

Yorktown practically ended the war in the colonies. General Greene, reinforced after the surrender of Cornwallis, succeeded by the end of 1781 in clearing South Carolina of the enemy, confining the British to Charleston, while Washington lamented the departure of the sea power that might have made the success complete.

The Continental Navy played very little part in the final phase of the war. Indeed, it had very nearly ceased to exist. During 1781 the frigates *Confederacy* and *Trumbull* were captured, and the ship *Saratoga* was lost at sea. By the time of the Battle of Yorktown, the only active Continental vessel was the frigate *Alliance*, veteran of John Paul Jones's battle with the *Serapis* and now commanded by gallant John Barry. In March 1783 in the *Alliance* Barry fought the last naval battle of the war, driving off a superior British force that intercepted him as he was bringing home money and a newly purchased vessel from Havana.

The Battle of the Saints, 12 April 1782

Following the defeat of Cornwallis, de Grasse sailed for the West Indies with his 27 of the line and de Barras's 7, his orders being to join a Spanish fleet from Cuba in an assault on Jamaica, largest and most valuable of the British West Indian possessions. While awaiting supplies for the Jamaican expedition, de Grasse used his time to advantage. Frustrated by the weather in an attempt on Barbados, he turned his attention to St. Kitts. Hood, who had followed de Grasse from North America, appeared on the scene with 22 ships before the island was completely in French hands, but was unable to prevent its capture. Other French expeditions had seized minor islands from the British, who eventually retained only St. Lucia, Antigua, Barbados, and Jamaica. Having lost the war in North America, they appeared well on the way to losing it in the West Indies.

A desperate ministry again called on Rodney to save the situation. "The fate of the empire is in your hands," said Lord Sandwich, First Lord of the Admiralty. Though suffering so severely from gout that his fingers could not hold a pen, the old admiral set out for the West Indies as soon as his ships were ready. Arriving at Barbados in mid-February

1782 with 12 of the line fresh from overhaul, he took command of the fleet, retaining Hood in command of a division. The latter had recently careened his ships, so that all copper bottoms were clean and ready for the utmost speed. The British weather decks, moreover, were now armed with carronades, newly invented short guns of large caliber, which threw a heavy ball with terrific smashing effect at short range. Considerably lighter than long guns, they could be worked by fewer men while adding 25 percent to a ship's weight of metal.

The carronades were well seconded by the British long guns, the effectiveness of which had been vastly increased by the gunnery reforms of Rodney's fleet captain, Sir Charles Douglas. The old rule had been "two or three quick broadsides in passing," but now special tackle enabled British gun crews to train their guns up to four points ahead or astern of the beam. The result was that a British ship could fire two or three broadsides both before and after the guns of a French ship could be brought to bear, and, while they were opposite, the British were able to fire a great deal more rapidly.[2]

The greater rapidity of fire was effected by a series of small improvements initiated by Sir Charles. Inclined planes, called "wedges," and heavy springs and weights in the breeching absorbed the recoil of guns and made their return to battery easier. Flannel-bottomed cartridges and the use of wet wads eliminated the whole process of worming, that is, cleaning out the bore to remove any sparks or burning fragments before recharging the gun with powder. Goose quills, perforated and filled with powder, were quickly inserted in the touchhole, and the gun was then fired with a flintlock similar to that of a musket.

By April both fleets had been strengthened with additional reinforcements. De Grasse was at his base at Fort Royal, Martinique, preparing to escort a convoy of 150 ships with troops and artillery for a rendezvous with the Spaniards at Santo Domingo. Rodney was at nearby St. Lucia determined to break up the French operation.

At daybreak on 8 April de Grasse saw his convoy safely out of port. He then put to sea with his fleet of 33 of the line. By noon Rodney, warned by his frigates, was at sea in pursuit with 36 of the line. That evening the two fleets were in sight of each

---

[2]A "broadside" did not generally involve the simultaneous firing of all the guns on one side of a vessel. That would have severely strained her timbers. Unless the relative positions of the opposing vessels dictated a different order, the forward guns were fired first, followed by the second, and so on down the line.

other. Twice, on the 9th and 10th, de Grasse turned back to rescue laggards. On the first occasion he so severely pounded the British van division, commanded by Hood, that Rodney transferred it to the rear to recuperate. While the convoy headed northwest for Santo Domingo, de Grasse began beating into the easterly trade wind, to draw the British away and into the Saints' Passage between Dominica and Guadeloupe. (See map, p. 44.)

A little after dawn on 12 April, Rodney sent four fast ships in pursuit of the collision-damaged French ship *Zélé*, seen in the distance under tow by a frigate. De Grasse by this time had available only 30 ships to oppose the British 36, but he gallantly turned back to support his threatened vessels. He ordered his fleet to form a line of battle on the port tack and advanced on a south–southwest course to meet the British. Rodney recalled his chasers and ordered a line of battle on the starboard tack, advancing on a northeasterly course. A little before 8 a.m. the head of the French line crossed the British line of advance, thereby winning the windward position.

Ordinarily the passing of two fleets on opposite courses produced no significant results, but during this passage the battle was largely decided because the range was extremely close and the light airs made the passing slow, thus protracting the exposure to enemy fire. The British close-hauled to bring the lines within easy pistol shot, and the French, occupying the windward position, could not fall off to a greater distance, as they ordinarily would have done.

The closeness of the action favored the British. Their heavy-shotted carronades created havoc in the crowded French vessels, which carried 5,500 troops in addition to their regular crews. Worst hit of the French ships was the *Glorieux*, which came reeling down toward Rodney's flagship *Formidable*. Just at this moment, the wind veered four points toward the south, filling the British sails from the stern, but striking the bows of the already close-hauled French. Most of the French vessels swung to starboard in an attempt to keep their sails filled and to preserve steerageway. This movement tended to force them into the British line. Others, taken aback, filled on the starboard tack. Thus the French line, already badly formed, simply disintegrated.

The ship immediately astern of the disabled *Glorieux* fell into the starboard tack, thereby opening a great gap in the French line opposite the *Formidable*. The British flagship, probably to avoid collision with a French ship ahead, swung to starboard through the opening. Despite the absence of a signal, British ships almost simultaneously cut through the French line at other points. *For the first time in a century of naval warfare, a line of battle had been broken.*

"Breaking the line," far from conferring victory on the British, in this instance brought them no advantage. Both fleets were fragmented. Rodney, after passing through the French line, went to windward, out of contact. Before he could tack to rejoin the battle, the breeze, already light, failed completely. Thus at about 10:50 a.m. most of the firing ceased, but smoke hung over the battlefield. Only between a few ships of the British rear and the French van, which were becalmed in contact, did the firing continue for an hour longer.

At about one o'clock that afternoon, a light breeze sprang up, and the battle came back to life. De Grasse, in the *Ville de Paris*, realizing that his fleet was in no condition to renew the action, attempted to make an orderly withdrawal, running generally before the wind. Many of the French ships that were able to do so took to flight, leaving the badly damaged *Ville de Paris* behind.

While Rodney came down in leisurely fashion, a few of his ships raced for the French cripples. They

Battle of the Saints, 12 April 1782

soon surrounded the French flagship, which put up a gallant defense. De Grasse's commanding figure was conspicuous on the quarterdeck, where he almost alone remained unwounded. A little before 6 p.m., when his situation was clearly hopeless, he released the few French vessels still endeavoring to support him. The *Ville de Paris,* stripped of her rigging and without a rudder, was obviously in no condition to continue the fight. When her cartridges were exhausted, her gunners ladled gunpowder into her guns. Soon there was no more shot. At 6:30, as Hood took position to rake, de Grasse struck his colors. Soon afterward Rodney, refusing to order pursuit, signaled his fleet to lie to for the night.

In the battle the British took five ships, three of which had been seriously damaged in the first phase. Five days later Hood, at last released to pursue, overtook and captured two additional French ships in Mona Passage. British casualties totaled slightly over a thousand. There is no reliable tabulation of French casualties, but it is obvious that they amounted to several thousand.

Hood made Rodney's failure to pursue the burden of many critical letters he wrote after the battle, and it appears that his opinion was generally shared in the fleet. But in England, where the details were not known and where news of British victories had been scarce indeed, the capture of five ships was hailed as a triumph. Moreover, in ignorance of the truth, John Clerk of Elden, a layman who had written a book on naval tactics condemning the formal Fighting Instructions and advocating massing, conceived that he had influenced Rodney to break the French line and that the victory was due to that maneuver. In this belief he has since been followed by many naval historians, who have taken the battle as initiating a revolution in the history of tactics.

Yet the truth was that Rodney had not broken the line in any *tactical* sense, and no one in his fleet appears to have considered his maneuver remarkable. Far from regarding their admiral's passing to windward of some of the French ships as the key to success, the men who were there considered it the means by which the opportunity for a smashing victory was thrown away. The windward position was of advantage chiefly in enabling its possessor to force an action. In this instance the French were already irrevocably committed to battle. The leeward position then became desirable from the British point of view because in it the British could hold the French to the action—and bar their way to Santo Domingo. But Rodney threw away the advantage, and as a consequence the greater part of

the French fleet escaped. However, this victory, the only significant success gained over the French in the entire war, went far toward retrieving the British position in the West Indies.

French refugee ships from the Battle of the Saints, added to other French vessels already at Cap Français, made a total of 26. With a dozen Spanish ships, an allied force of 40 of the line was available to escort 8,000 Spanish troops for the attack on Jamaica. Hood, anxiously keeping watch with 25 ships, can hardly be blamed for bitterly lamenting Rodney's failure to make the victory of 12 April complete. But the loss of de Grasse had taken the heart out of the French. The Spaniards were, as ever, indisposed to act, and disease was decimating the troops. The threat to Jamaica had been averted.

Europe, 1782

The change in the British ministry in the spring of 1782 brought Keppel to the Admiralty as First Lord, replacing the wretched Lord Sandwich, and Howe to the Channel fleet. Here Howe was ably seconded by Kempenfelt. This happy combination marked the beginning of another period of British tactical progress, for Howe gave his subordinate a free hand to draw up signals for the fleet. Kempenfelt's first book contained all of Morogue's signals plus a good many innovations, but the significance of the flags, as in the Fighting Instructions, depended upon their location on the ship. It was not till summer, when preparations were being made for the relief of Gibraltar, that he composed a book based on a numerary system whereby signal flags could be hoisted together in one or more lines. Issued for the Channel fleet by Howe, this book marked the end of the Permanent Fighting Instructions far more truly than the "breaking of the line" by Rodney.

In the summer of 1782 France and Spain had again assembled a formidable fleet, but after cruising fruitlessly in the Channel, it returned to Spain to assist in the siege of Gibraltar. Here the Spanish and the French had concentrated a huge force, supported by heavily protected floating batteries, for an autumn assault, but the British fired the batteries with red-hot shot and beat off the attack.

Howe had been ordered to relieve Gibraltar. During his fitting out, Britain suffered an irreparable loss. The *Royal George,* Kempenfelt's flagship, was being slightly careened for repairs to her bottom. Officers, crew, and visitors were on board, and the admiral was at his desk when water rushed into the lower gunports. The ship went down so suddenly that, although she was at dockside, 900 persons were lost, including Kempenfelt.

Howe arrived off Cape St. Vincent in early October with a convoy and 34 of the line. Despite the presence of the Allied fleet of 46, he pressed on to Gibraltar and delivered his supplies without being seriously challenged. When he reentered the Atlantic, the French and Spanish ships made a distant attack, but it was a halfhearted affair. Obviously they had no desire to come to grips.

Suffren in the Far East

Pierre André de Suffren, the only French admiral to emerge from the war with enhanced prestige and lasting fame, won no victories at sea. Sent to India in the spring of 1781, he fought five battles with the British Indian fleet, ably commanded by Sir Edward Hughes. Suffren's plans, which often provided for doubling on the enemy rear, reveal a thorough understanding of concentration, but his captains were unwilling or unable to execute such tactics; the instrument was not equal to his purpose. Consequently, not one of the five battles was tactically decisive; not a single ship of the line was captured by either side. They were, however, among the mostly fiercely fought battles of the war, for Suffren, fully appreciating that sea power was the key to the war in India, aimed at nothing less than the annihilation of the British naval forces.

Although he failed to achieve that aim, Suffren by his sound sense of strategy, his energy, and his timing did in fact reap some of the benefits of command of the sea. After his first battle with Hughes, he established relations with the ruler of Mysore, France's principal ally in India. After his second, he received orders to retire to Mauritius for repairs and refit, but, realizing that the French position in India would collapse if his fleet were withdrawn, he disregarded the orders and continued the campaign. Repairing his ships quickly after a devastating third battle, he captured the Ceylonese port of Trincomalee before the British could react, and subsequently fought a drawn battle to retain it. His fifth battle was also a tactical draw, but it was a French strategic victory, for Suffren was left in a position to raise the siege of Cuddalore. Soon after this action, news of the signing of peace in Europe brought an end to hostilities in India.

The Treaty of Paris

The Treaty of Paris, signed 3 September 1783, closed a war in which Britain had suffered severe defeats. That she suffered no worse than she did at the peace table was due in part to the exhaustion of her opponents, in part to her timely defensive successes at the Saints and at Gibraltar. The terms were surprisingly favorable to the colonies when it is considered that Britain at the time the provisional articles were signed still held New York, Charleston, and Savannah. The treaty recognized the independence of the United States, defined as stretching from the Atlantic to the Mississippi and from the Great Lakes to Florida. Britain retained Gibraltar and her holdings in India. Spain received Florida and Minorca. France restored to Britain most of her West Indian conquests but retained Tobago and received back St. Lucia and her African colony of Senegal.

Summary

Britain's unpreparedness at the outbreak of the American Revolution enabled the Americans in 1775 to invade Canada and attack Quebec and, the following year, to force the British to withdraw from Boston. Later in 1776 the British, having gathered their forces, seized the initiative, which they exercised until the French entered the war. Their command of the sea enabled them to raid or seize almost any American coastal point at will. When they penetrated inland, however, they exposed their communications to American semi-guerrilla tactics and suffered defeats. American independence was achieved mainly by the defeat of British armies at Saratoga (1777) and Yorktown (1781), following British penetrations, respectively, from the north and from the south. A French fleet isolated Cornwallis at Yorktown, making the second, and decisive, American victory possible.

The British penetration from the north was begun in 1776 by Carleton, who drove Arnold from Canada and invaded the colonies via the Hudson—Champlain route. He was unable to use the lake, however, until he had spent the summer building a fleet to overmatch that of Arnold. In October, at last ready, he moved up the lake and defeated Arnold at Valcour Island, but it was now too near winter for him to proceed with the campaign that year. In 1777, when Burgoyne attempted to continue Carleton's strategy, the Americans were better prepared and captured the British army at Saratoga.

Early in the war Washington realized that sea power was the key to the struggle in America, and the strategic aim to which he firmly adhered throughout was to secure a naval superiority that

would make possible a combined sea-and-land operation against one of the British lodgments on the
coast, preferably New York, the center of British
military operations. The arrival of d'Estaing in 1778
offered an opportunity to put this strategy into
effect and did cause the British to abandon Philadelphia. But d'Estaing failed at New York and
again at Savannah, leaving Washington discouraged but with unwavering faith in his own strategy.
His faith was vindicated in 1781 as superior French
and American land and sea forces converged on
Cornwallis's army, entrenched at Yorktown. When
Graves's fleet arrived from New York to support or
evacuate Cornwallis, de Grasse's fleet in the Battle
of the Virginia Capes (5 September) so damaged
the ships of the British van that Graves had to retire
to New York for repairs. Before he could return
with reinforcements, Cornwallis was obliged to
surrender.

The small Continental Navy, after a minor raid
on the Bahamas in 1776, could do no more than
harry British communications, principally by sending out single cruisers. Its only notable influence on
the war was the moral effect of the exploits of a few
individuals: Wickes, Conyngham, Jones. The most
famous American naval action was the Battle off
Flamborough Head (1779), in which Jones in the
old East Indiaman *Bonhomme Richard* captured
the new British frigate *Serapis*.

The French navy had superior ships and a good
signal system but was hampered by a tradition of
caution. Even when joined with the Spanish fleet,
it failed to invade England or prevent the relief of
Gibraltar. At Virginia Capes, de Grasse, with superior force, obliged Graves's fleet to retire but
made no attempt to destroy it. The following year,
in the Battle of the Saints (1782), the British defeated a Franco–Spanish naval expedition against
Jamaica, thereby demonstrating that, thanks to
coppering, gunnery reforms, and the adoption of
the carronade, they had regained naval ascendancy.

Equally important, the War of the American
Revolution saw the Royal Navy cast off the shackles
of the Permanent Fighting Instructions. The battles of Ushant (1778) and Grenada (1779) demonstrated that general chase was not a safe means of
bypassing the Instructions. Keppel's exoneration
following the Battle of Ushant notified officers of
the Royal Navy that henceforth the Instructions
need not be blindly obeyed. The Battle of the
Virginia Capes (1781) demonstrated that blind
obedience to the Instructions could lead to defeat.
The Battle of the Saints (1782) was credited with
demonstrating that breaking the line, which the
Instructions forbade, could lead to victory. The
final release was Kempenfelt's system of tactical
signals, which replaced the Permanent Fighting
Instructions and permitted the admiral to command his fleet as he saw fit.

Chapter 6
The War of the French Revolution

In the period following the American Revolution, the European balance of power inclined steadily in Britain's favor as the French army and navy were undermined, at first by public insolvency and then, after 1789, by revolution and civil war. This disaffection, spreading from Paris, at length touched the fleets at Brest and Toulon. The unrest in the navy soon became mutiny, and for two years French naval power ceased to exist. With aristocratic officers fleeing abroad in large numbers, the government in 1791 averted complete dissolution by a decree of reorganization. The changes, in harmony with the spirit of the times, were carried out along egalitarian lines. Juniors sympathetic to the revolution were promoted, and numerous petty officers and merchant marine officers were given commissions. The corps of seamen gunners, which had come to be regarded as a privileged order of the lower deck, was banned in the name of equality. Finally, in 1793, the navy minister was empowered to promote any individual to any rank. Thereafter political reliability became the principal qualification for command.

This policy, disastrous to the French navy, had little detrimental effect on the army, mainly because the artillery officers, drawn largely from the middle class, supported the revolution from the beginning and hence were not touched by the reorganization. An improvised infantry, caught up by revolutionary fervor and backed by the finest artillery in Europe, was soon to work wonders. But in the navy, enthusiasm proved an inadequate substitute for training. Though French fleets would fight with great courage, and captains would handle individual ships skillfully, the new flag officers lacked the time to master the art of the admiral. They misinterpreted orders, executed maneuvers improperly, failed to achieve mutual support among their fleet divisions, and were plagued by indecision at critical moments.

The Outbreak of War

The rulers of Austria and Prussia, seeing in the political events in France a frightening incitement to revolt at home, proceeded to concert military countermeasures. The British, however, were at first inclined to applaud the revolution, which seemed to be leading France toward a constitutional monarchy like their own. Britain's prime minister, William Pitt the Younger, second son of the great war minister of the Seven Years' War, declared in his budget speech of February 1792 that "unquestionably there never was a time in the history of this country when, from the situation of Europe, we might more reasonably expect 15 years of peace than at the present moment." Less than six weeks later the revolutionary French government declared war on Austria, Prussia, and Sardinia.

In August 1792 an Austro–Prussian army invaded France from the Austrian Netherlands (Belgium), but the deliberateness of its movements gave the revolutionary leaders in Paris time to assemble an army that halted the invaders, forced them into retreat, overran Belgium, and penetrated into Germany. Other French armies were conquering the Rhineland, Nice, and Savoy. The small, professional armies of France's enemies, employing formal tactics and limited moves to attain limited objectives, were clearly outmoded. They were no match for the impetuous offensives of the French republican generals commanding mass armies fired with the new nationalism. Moreover, the Austrians and Prussians had failed to coordinate their military operations—a result of their rulers' unwillingness to subordinate selfish territorial ambitions to the common objective of defeating the French. Last, while suffering defeats in the West, they retained thousands of troops at home in reserve against opportunities in eastern Europe, where the chaotic disunity of Poland and the decadence of the Ottoman Empire invited intervention and annexation.

The setbacks of the Austrians and Prussians in the Low Countries deeply concerned Pitt's cabinet because it had become axiomatic at Westminster that Antwerp must never come into the possession of a dynamic naval power. Public opinion in Britain was further alarmed by decrees of the French National Convention establishing a system of revolutionary propaganda and conquest. The decrees authorized French armies to invade neutral territories and promised assistance to any European revolutionary movements aimed at overthrowing existing governments. Relations between France and England were further embittered when, in violation of treaty commitments England had with Austria, the French opened the Scheldt to navigation. The execution of Louis XVI augmented the crisis. The British government dismissed the French ambassador and shortly afterward, on 1 February 1793, the National Convention declared war on England, thereby launching a struggle that, with a single intermission, continued for 22 years.

As a war leader, the younger Pitt concerned himself primarily with finance, leaving the strategic planning to Henry Dundas, his secretary of state for war. Influenced by Dundas, the British cabinet rejected the continental strategy of landing an army in France to support an allied drive on Paris. It decided instead to revive the peripheral and colonial strategy of the elder Pitt's plan of the Seven Years' War, in order to make optimum use of the mobility and surprise conferred by sea power.

The hard lessons of the War of the American Revolution had driven home the fact that in any war against a continental power, Britain had to have allies on the Continent. The British government therefore promptly concluded treaties of alliance with Austria, Russia, Prussia, Spain, Portugal, Hanover, and the Kingdom of the Two Sicilies (Naples), thereby completing the first of a series of coalitions directed against revolutionary France and the succeeding French Empire. The treaties required Britain to make cash payments in return for specified allied forces to be used in stipulated areas. Since the treaties also provided for British naval support for Austrian and Italian land forces, command of the Mediterranean became a principal British objective.

Britain lost no time in putting into operation her economic weapons. Her cruisers soon hunted the French merchant marine from the high seas. As escorts became available, she herded into convoys her own merchantmen carrying trade to North America, the West Indies, and the Levant. At the same time, she assigned blockade of the French Atlantic and Mediterranean fleets to a pair of able but aging veterans of the war in America. Lord Howe with 26 of the line maintained a distant blockade of Brest. Lord Hood with 16 kept a close watch on Toulon.

French leaders, aware that they were helpless to counter British moves by sea, concentrated their available strength in land operations on continental Europe. Their objective was nothing less than to bring the whole continent into their republican

system. They believed that the British, isolated in their island fortress, would be obliged to yield to the threat of economic ruin. The war between France and Britain thus became, in the contemporary metaphor, a struggle between the Elephant and the Whale, each fruitlessly seeking some means of coming decisively to grips with the other.

Opening Operations

To cooperate with the Austrians in the Netherlands, the duke of York in August 1793 landed at Ostend at the head of 10,000 British soldiers. Adding an equal number of Austrians and Hanoverians, he took the initiative and moved rapidly on the commerce raiders' haven at Dunkirk. Here he found no siege artillery waiting for him off the port, as promised by the Admiralty. Instead, he faced an encirclement of superior enemy reinforcements, for his thrust at the sensitive Channel coast brought quick reaction from War Minister Lazare Carnot at Paris. The duke, thus threatened, withdrew to the Austrian Netherlands, leaving behind all his field artillery and baggage.

This fiasco pointed up not only the defective coordination between the British army and navy but also the nearly fatal lack of cooperation among the allies. It was this lack of cooperation, as much as anything else, that prevented the allies from seizing the opportunities presented by the raging counterrevolution, spreading from western to southern France, that threatened to engulf the republican government.

Britain's greatest opportunity came in August, the month of the Dunkirk expedition, when the royalist naval commander at Toulon simply turned over to Lord Hood the city's arsenal and 31 ships of the line, to be held by the British in custody for the heir of Louis XVI. Hood, assuming the responsibility for the defense, proceeded in a leisurely fashion to prepare the unready ships for sailing. A Spanish fleet numerically equal to Hood's soon arrived, but the commander, Don Juan de Langara, failing to get from Hood recognition of his claim to equal authority, remained sullen and uncooperative in the outer roads.

News of Toulon's surrender to Hood created rage and dismay throughout republican France. The Committee of Public Safety, which had replaced the National Convention as the French executive agency, rushed troops thither. Before Hood had properly organized his defense forces, the Republicans stormed the passes. After a long siege, in which Lieutenant Colonel Napoleon Bonaparte commanded the republican artillery,

Toulon became untenable for the allies. The evacu-ation, beginning in mid-December, was compli-cated by the moral obligation to remove the thousands of royalists from the reach of republican vengeance. Hood, postponing action beyond good judgment, barely managed to bring out four French ships and burn ten more.

Hood's ineptitude in dealing with allied forces influenced the whole course of the war unfavorably for the allies. Had Toulon been held, there would have been no Italian campaign to put Bonaparte in the forefront of French leaders. Had Toulon and its fleet been destroyed, there could have been no French expedition to Egypt. With Toulon lost, Hood soon withdrew from naval history into forced retirement, and Austria braced herself for the in-evitable attack.

British troops that might have held Toulon were dispersed elsewhere. Some were in India, where they captured Chandernagore and Pondicherry. Others were in Flanders with the duke of York. Still others were assigned to operations in the West Indies. This last expedition was the special brain-child of Henry Dundas, who believed that the French were heavily dependent on trade with their rich Caribbean sugar islands.

The 6,500-man West Indian expedition, jointly commanded by Major General Sir Charles Grey and Rear Admiral Sir John Jervis, arrived at Barba-dos in January 1794 and in a three-month campaign brought all the French West Indies except Haiti into British possession. Then yellow fever began to take a heavy toll among the invaders, and republi-can troops from France joined native and colonial militia in a counterattack on Guadeloupe. Under the leadership of the able and ruthless mulatto Victor Hugues, the French–West Indian forces quickly surrounded the British garrison. Jervis, down with the fever like many of his seamen and the majority of the troops ashore, was unable to cope with an enemy who had no visible com-munications and relied on infiltration from scat-tered points. Obliged to surrender Guadeloupe and evacuate the British troops, he and Grey re-turned to England in November, worn with fatigue and illness. Hugues's followers, stirring up revolt as they advanced, at length drove the British out of all the Antilles except Jamaica and Barbados.

The Glorious First of June, 1794

A food shortage in southern France, resulting from bad weather and the injudicious conscription of peasants, was threatening to bring on civil war. To relieve this situation the French government

purchased in the United States a large quantity of grain. It was loaded into American vessels at Nor-folk and Baltimore, but getting it to France pre-sented a problem because the British had declared grain contraband. Also in the Chesapeake Bay area a large number of French Indiamen were carrying revenue-producing sugar and coffee. In a hazard-ous attempt to get all these vessels safely across the Atlantic at one time, the French government had them assembled into a large convoy of 130 sail and sent two ships of the line and two frigates to escort them to France. They departed the Chesapeake on 11 April 1794.

The British had obtained information of the great Franco–American convoy, and Lord Howe, in his flagship the *Queen Charlotte*, put to sea with the Channel fleet to make sure that it never reached France. On 19 May he looked into Brest and was shocked to find the roads empty. The Brest fleet had evidently slipped out during foggy weather past his sentry frigates. Neutral merchant-men, however, soon put Howe in the French fleet's wake. It was his intention to overtake and shatter it as quickly as possible and then round up the convoy at his leisure.

Compared to the experienced British, the officers of the French warships were amateurs. The fleet commander, Louis de Villaret-Joyeuse, had fought under Suffren in the preceding war, but he was new to his post, having been promoted to rear admiral and put in command of the Brest fleet specifically to escort the grain convoy from the Atlantic to France's Biscay ports. Only one of his captains had commanded a ship of the line before 1789. The rest had been lieutenants, merchant skippers, and dockyard officers, and one was a former seaman from below decks. But what France's Republican navy lacked in experience it made up for in revolutionary fervor, reflected in the new names given its ships: *Patriote, Révolu-tionnaire, Tyrannicide, Vengeur du Peuple*.

On learning that Howe was at sea, the Commit-tee of Public Safety had peremptorily ordered Vil-laret out of port to the rescue of the convoy, further directing him to save his own ships and to avoid battle if possible. Robespierre himself added the grim warning that if the convoy were captured, Villaret should pay with his life—a threat not to be taken lightly at the height of France's Reign of Terror.

Villaret sped to the west and began cruising anxiously in the rendezvous area. The convoy was overdue. At last at dawn on 28 May he was relieved to see a sweep of sail on the squally horizon to his lee in the northwest. A little later he was startled to

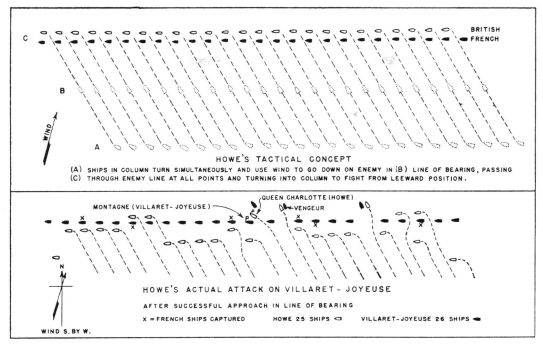

HOWE'S TACTICAL CONCEPT
(A) SHIPS IN COLUMN TURN SIMULTANEOUSLY AND USE WIND TO GO DOWN ON ENEMY IN (B) LINE OF BEARING, PASSING
(C) THROUGH ENEMY LINE AT ALL POINTS AND TURNING INTO COLUMN TO FIGHT FROM LEEWARD POSITION.

HOWE'S ACTUAL ATTACK ON VILLARET-JOYEUSE
AFTER SUCCESSFUL APPROACH IN LINE OF BEARING
X = FRENCH SHIPS CAPTURED   HOWE 25 SHIPS ◁   VILLARET-JOYEUSE 26 SHIPS ◄

Battle of the First of June, 1794

recognize that it was not the convoy but Howe's Channel fleet. A count of ships, however, revealed that they were at least equal in number, 26 to a side.

Villaret promptly hauled into the wind and led Howe away from the rendezvous area. The chase continued through the 28th and 29th, with elaborate maneuvering and partial engagements, in which Howe forced the withdrawal to port of four of Villaret's ships, heavily damaged, with a similar departure of only one of his own. Having seized the weather gage, Howe intended to engage at the first opportunity. But during the next two days thick weather and a succession of gales hampered maneuvering and kept the fleets from closing. Meanwhile, French fortunes were improving as four fresh ships arrived to reinforce Villaret, giving him 26 ships to Howe's 25.

The fifth day of contact, 1 June, dawned cloudy with strong breezes, but visibility was good. The fleets lay about four miles apart, the French to leeward, leading the British on a northwest course. Shortly after seven, Howe ordered his fleet to form line of battle, and ten minutes later indicated his tactical plan by hoisting Signal 34, which required each of his captains to pass astern of his opposite in the enemy line and then to fight from the leeward position. It appeared that the British admiral was about to throw away the wind advantage he had

won in two days of maneuver, but Howe probably expected only a few of his ships to penetrate the enemy's column—enough to prevent him from falling off downwind and retreating. In fact, an escape clause appended to Signal 34 stated that "captains . . . not being able to effect the specified intention . . . are at liberty to act as circumstances require." Howe meant no doubt to force a decision by bringing on a melee, in which superior British gunnery at close range would give him the advantage. Besides being a superb shock tactic, the maneuver would enable ships that penetrated the enemy column to rake opponents on either hand while passing through, and to reap the advantage of tactical surprise, for the French lee batteries and gunports might be expected, and in fact were found, to be secured.

When Howe had closed his line to his satisfaction, he made hoist shortly before 8 a.m. "to engage the enemy." Ten minutes later a signal gun was fired, the preparatory flag was hauled down, and each British captain put his ship's helm to the wind and ran down to engage his opposite number. The 68-year-old admiral, who had been sleepless for four days save for an occasional armchair doze, was haggard from fatigue but still vigorous. Closing his pocket signal book, he turned to his staff with the remark, "Now, gentlemen, no more book, no more signals. I look to you to do the duty of the *Queen*

Charlotte. I don't want the ships to be bilge to bilge, but if you can lock the yardarms, so much the better; the battle will be the quicker decided."

Only seven of Howe's ships, including his flagship, penetrated the French line; the rest came round to engage in the traditional manner on the windward side. The *Queen Charlotte,* in passing through the enemy line just astern of Villaret's *Montagne,* fired a raking broadside that struck down 200 Frenchmen.

Howe's attack shattered both formations, bringing about the first intentionally produced melee since the adoption of the Permanent Fighting Instructions. At close range, French valor and the doctrine of shooting at rigging were unequal to British valor and the doctrine of shooting at hulls. Exploding gunpowder blackened the air, so that neither admiral had a clear view of the four-mile-long battle or the means of directing ships. The outcome had been placed in the hands of subordinates, among whom the inroads of the Revolution became evident. The French had the spirit, but not the skill, to conquer.

The battle was heavy in the center and rear, but the French van was largely untouched. Amid the confusion, the captains of the van reverted to French practice. Falling off the wind, they formed a reserve to leeward. Villaret, ever thinking of the convoy, was endeavoring to break off action and retreat. Observing the self-appointed reserve to leeward, he joined it with all the French ships able to follow his example. Forming a 16-ship column, he sent in frigates to tow three of his dismasted ships to its shelter. He then bore up and cleared the battle area, abandoning the French ships he had little chance of rescuing. Howe made no attempt to pursue, then or later.

Of the seven ships Villaret left behind, the fiercest battle was fought by the *Vengeur du Peuple.* She became locked together with the *Brunswick,* whose anchors caught in the *Vengeur's* forechannels. Thus clamped in deadly embrace, the French ship swept the *Brunswick's* upper decks with langrage, but the British, blowing out their own gunports, hulled their opponent till she went down, carrying 300 men, some of whom shouted *"Vive la République!"* before the waters closed over them.

Howe took the other six ships to England as prizes of war. On 3 June, the convoy passed over the battle site without raising a sail and proceeded unhindered to its dispersal point, giving the National Convention occasion to proclaim victory. Villaret excused his abandonment of seven ships with the explanation that "while the admiral

amused himself refitting his prizes, I saved my convoy, and I saved my head."

Howe's physical exhaustion had saved Villaret's fleet from annihilation, but in England, which had waited 18 months for its first success against the French fleet, his relatively modest victory was hailed as the "Glorious First of June." The victors were voted medals and prize money to the accompaniment of a generous award of titles, Howe himself receiving an earldom.

Breakup of the First Coalition

The British Mediterranean fleet, deprived of Toulon, found itself again blockading the port and seeking adequate base facilities. Spain's increasing coolness made Minorca unavailable, and Gibraltar was too far away to provide support. Lord Hood, in his last campaign before retirement, set out to remedy this situation by occupying Corsica, where patriot partisans were revolting against the French. For lack of sufficient soldiers, British seamen and naval officers did much of the fighting ashore, in the course of which Captain Horatio Nelson was wounded in the face, losing the sight of his right eye. By June 1794 Corsica was in the hands of the British, providing them with a useful base.

In November 1795, John Jervis, promoted to vice admiral, took command of the British Mediterranean fleet. He could hardly have arrived at a time less favorable to allied fortunes. Prussia had liquidated an unsuccessful campaign on the Rhine and made peace the preceding May. Occupied Holland had then formally joined France as an ally, and Spain retired from the war in July. The British responded by seizing the Cape of Good Hope, Ceylon, and other Dutch holdings—in India and the West Indies. They also put a North Sea fleet off Texel under Vice Admiral Adam Duncan to watch the Dutch navy and to interdict the passage of Baltic timber and hemp to France. On balance, however, the end of 1795 saw the French military position immensely improved and the first coalition reduced to only two major powers—Britain and Austria.

The five-man Directory, recently made the French national executive, resolved to obtain a military decision by striking simultaneously at both remaining enemies. To command this dual attack they appointed France's two most brilliant young generals, Napoleon Bonaparte to command the Army of Italy and the anglophobic Lazare Hoche to head the Army of England. Bonaparte was to drive across Lombardy, with Vienna as his objective.

Hoche was to launch an amphibious thrust into the British Isles, directed at London.

General Bonaparte took command of the Army of Italy in March 1796 and in a dazzling six-weeks' campaign cleared the Austrians from Lombardy. In mid-December of the same year, General Hoche put to sea and headed for Bantry Bay, Ireland, his army of 14,000 embarked in transports escorted by the Brest fleet, including 17 of the line. Incompetence and bad weather spoiled the operation. Gale after gale scattered the invasion armada, which straggled back piecemeal into French ports. Not a soldier had managed to land, but Hoche could count himself lucky—the storms that spoiled his plans had also saved him from Britain's Channel fleet.

Spain had declared war against Great Britain the preceding August. The Spanish ships, in design and sailing qualities, were unexcelled, but their conscript crews were led by officers who disdained professional study and training in their reliance on raw physical courage. The British cabinet, counting numbers rather than quality, ordered Corsica evacuted. Jervis shifted his fleet to Gibraltar and then to Lisbon, where he arrived in December 1796.

From Paris early the following year came demands that the Spanish fleet leave the Mediterranean and proceed to Cadiz. This was to be the first step in a move to Brest for a renewal of Hoche's invasion attempt, to be supported this time by the combined fleets of Holland, France, and Spain. Complying with the French demand, Admiral Don José de Córdoba left Cartagena on 1 February 1797, and passed into the Atlantic with 24 ships and a Cadiz-bound convoy.

The Battle of Cape St. Vincent, 14 February 1797

When Jervis learned of Córdoba's departure, he immediately put to sea from Lisbon and, with his ten available ships, proceeded to Cape St. Vincent to watch the Straits. Here on 6 February he welcomed the arrival of a reinforcement of five more of the line. Easterly winds then drove him from the coast. A week later he was regaining his position when a frigate reported an enemy contact to the southwest. This was the Spanish fleet, which had also been blown out into the Atlantic and was now taking advantage of the westerly wind to bear up for Cadiz.

When the mist lifted the next morning, 14

February, the British battle fleet sighted the Spaniards running before the wind in some disorder. The British approached close-hauled, and at 11 a.m. Jervis brought his 15 ships into line of battle, with Thomas Troubridge in the *Culloden* leading and Jervis's flagship *Victory* at the center. Heading for a gap in the Spanish formation, Jervis signaled, "A victory is very essential to England at this moment," and then, "Pass through the enemy line."

Córdoba, in something like panic, strove to close the gap, ordering his main body to spread more sail and recalling Rear Admiral Moreno, who commanded his van division. He was too late. The *Culloden* broke through, leaving 7 ships with Moreno to leeward and a main body of 17 under Córdoba's direct command to windward.

The Spanish main body, to avoid colliding with the British or among themselves, swung north in a ragged line, exchanging fire with their opponents. Moreno tried to break through the British formation, but a few broadsides turned him away—one of his ships running the length of the British line to cross over its rear, the others wearing about to rejoin Córdoba by doubling around the British van.

When the leading British ships had passed out of range of the enemy, Jervis hoisted the signal "Tack in succession." Troubridge, who had been impatiently awaiting something of the sort, promptly reversed course and headed for the retreating main body. Thereafter, each British ship, in conformity with Jervis's signal, was expected to advance to the point where the *Culloden* had turned, come about, and follow the *Culloden* back toward the Spaniards. In the circumstances, this was a dubious tactic. Had all the British ships reversed course *simultaneously*, all would have had continuous use of their guns and also held the Spanish main and lee divisions apart. By turning in succession, they masked part of their own fire and at the same time presented Córdoba an opportunity to escape, join Moreno, and head for Cadiz.

All this was abundantly clear to Horatio Nelson in the 74-gun *Captain*, third ship from the British rear. He had no stomach for following uselessly down to the turning point, particularly when he perceived that Córdoba's leading ships were putting their helms over to run across the British rear. In defiance of Jervis's signal and the sternest of naval regulations, he took his ship out of the line of battle, wore around, cut between the two British rear ships, and headed to block the advance of Córdoba's 17 men-of-war, led by the 130-gun flagship *Santisima Trinidad*, the biggest warship in the world. Engaging this mighty four-decker, he

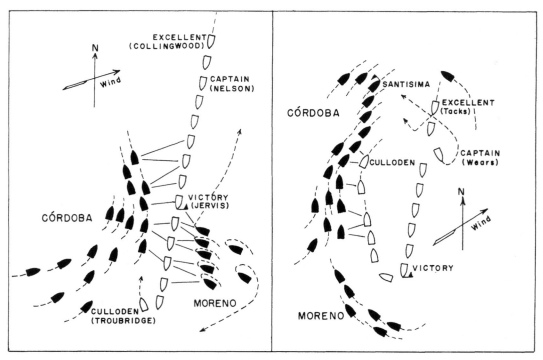

Battle of Cape St. Vincent, 14 February 1797

forced her into the wind. Other Spanish ships were soon swarming about the *Captain*, pouring in shot.

Luckily for Nelson, the *Culloden* and the rest of the British van ships were fast approaching. Also Cuthbert Collingwood in the *Excellent*, 74, in response to a signal from Jervis, had left his position at the rear of the line and soon steered between the now heavily damaged *Captain* and the *San Nicolas*, 80, his broadsides driving the Spanish seamen from their guns. The *San Nicolas* luffed, only to fall afoul of the *San Josef*, 112, while the *Captain* fetched up on her quarter, grinding bulwarks into her quarter galleries.

Nelson now called away boarders, and himself went into the *San Nicolas* through a stern window. After a scuffle in the cabin, he reached the deck, where he found shipmates pausing to haul down the Spanish colors before going up the chains of the adjacent *San Josef*. Shouting "Westminster Abbey or victory!" Nelson boarded the second enemy. Soon afterward he received the formal surrender of both ships.

Five ships of the Spanish main body had now struck. The action, however, increased in intensity as Spanish reinforcements closed in. Moreno completed his circuit of the British fleet, and ships of the Spanish rear were entering the battle. These developments distracted the British from taking

possession of the surrendered *Santisima* and enabled Córdoba to gain the shelter of his reinforcements. As sunset approached, Jervis grew anxious to cover his remaining four prizes. He wore the *Victory* at 5:45 and signaled close order of battle.

Jervis's signal caused the British to disengage, and permitted Córdoba to haul off to the north. His ships made a leisurely return to Cadiz, on which Jervis, in compliance with the First Lord's instructions "never if possible to suffer the main body of the fleet of Spain to be between you and us," soon clapped a blockade.

For his victory, which lifted the spirits of all Englishmen at a time of profound depression and near bankruptcy, Jervis was created Earl of St. Vincent and granted a generous annual pension. Nelson was made a Knight of the Bath, and each captain of the fleet received a medal.[1]

The main tactical significance of the Battle of Cape St. Vincent lies in the manner in which Nelson's and Collingwood's single ships and the rest of the British ships independently closed in on a portion of the Spanish fleet, crushing it before the rest of the enemy ships could arrive to lend support.

[1]A few days after the battle, Nelson learned that since 2 February he had been a rear admiral, a rank he had attained by seniority.

The battle thus introduced a new principle into naval warfare, that of dividing one's own force in order to move each segment with the greatest facility to the point where it is most needed. Nelson further developed this principle in his victorious battles of the Nile and of Trafalgar, which became the study of later generations of naval officers.

The Cape St. Vincent battle brought Nelson fame. The British public acclaimed his daring in leading boarders over the heavily armed *San Nicolas* ("Nelson's Patent Bridge for Boarding First Rates") to capture the still stronger *San Josef*. Within the Royal Navy, however, Nelson had his critics. Had he not abandoned the line without orders? But Jervis praised his initiative, which, had it failed, would have been insubordination. When Jervis's fleet captain, Robert Calder, pointed out that Nelson had disregarded signals, the admiral snapped, "It certainly was so, and if ever you commit such a breach of your orders, I will forgive you also."

Córdoba's defeat cost him his command and destroyed the morale of the Spanish navy. There would be no Spanish support for any further French invasion schemes—at least not for several years. But this advantage, from the British point of view, was quickly offset by the victories of General Bonaparte. On 2 February he had captured Mantua. On 23 March he led his triumphant troops into Trieste. On 18 April he took Austria out of the war by forcing on her the Truce of Leoben, a preliminary to the Treaty of Campo Formio. England now stood virtually alone against the Atlantic alliance of France, Holland, and Spain. Her only remaining ally was Portugal, whose sole contribution was permission to use Lisbon as a base for blockading Cadiz.

The British Naval Mutinies, 1797

Four days before the peace at Leoben, the seamen of the Channel fleet refused to go to sea. During the next month the mutiny spread to the Nore and the fleets off Texel and Cadiz.

Inadequate pay was foremost among the sailors' grievances. For able-bodied seamen it had stood at 22s. 6d. a month since the reign of Charles II, and it was but a fraction of current wages in the merchant marine. The men were paid only in home ports and at six-month intervals. Even then the payment was by warrant, a form of check that could be cashed at face value only in naval offices. Particularly galling was the fact that all pay ceased during any period of disability from duty—even that resulting from wounds incurred in combat. Prize money proved

an irregular source of income, and the share allocated to seamen was disproportionately small.

Food on board men-of-war was both scanty and bad. Rations were reduced by use of 14-ounce ("purser's") pounds to allow for mythical "leakage." The generally poor quality of provisions was hardly compensated by the daily issue to every member of the ship's company of one gallon of beer and a half pint of rum, which when watered was called "grog." Despite experiments with fresh vegetables, which had kept West Indies squadrons healthy, the Admiralty issued only flour, dried peas and beans, and salted meat. Hence even Duncan's officers and crews, operating close to home, suffered from scurvy.

A principal complaint concerned inadequate shore leave. During hostilities liberty was curtailed at home and abroad, being confined to dockyard precincts. Though in home ports women and families were usually permitted to live on the berth decks, the men themselves might spend years without setting foot on shore. The system amounted to virtual imprisonment.

It is significant that the seamen made no demand for mitigating flogging and other brutal punishments—the threat of the cat at sea was after all no more terrifying than the harsh laws ashore. Among British naval officers there were a few brutes and sadists, whose misdeeds have somewhat obscured the work of such officers as Nelson, Collingwood, Howe, St. Vincent, and many others who without relaxing discipline spared no pains to see that their men received justice and got decent food.

After three weeks of parleying, the Admiralty commissioners gave way on all important points and agreed to a seamen's pay raise of 5s. 6d. The Spithead mutiny formally ended on 15 May.

Though the concessions applied to the navy generally, the Admiralty had scarcely begun to implement them when a more serious mutiny broke out at the Nore, an anchorage at the mouth of the Thames estuary. From here it spread to Duncan's North Sea fleet. The spirit was markedly different from that at Spithead. At the Nore the mutineers ran up the red flag and established contacts with the pro-French republican societies in London.

For leader and spokesman, the Nore mutineers chose Richard Parker, a former naval officer but a natural rebel. Cashiered for insubordination, he had later been thrown into jail for debt, whence he had been conscripted back into the navy as a seaman. Some of the demands made by Parker and his followers were reasonable, but many were not, and the mutineers alienated public sympathy by block-ading the Thames. At Spithead the leaders had announced that they would return to duty should an enemy put to sea; Parker's followers threatened to carry the fleet to France.

In the North Sea, Duncan's personal influence steadied the crews of the *Adamant* and his flagship *Venerable*. A huge man, still powerful at 66, Dun-can quelled mutiny in the *Adamant* by dangling the leader over the side by one arm. With his two ships and a frigate, he maintained the blockade of the Dutch squadrons by means of a ruse. Signals he made to his frigate, stationed on the horizon, were transmitted on to imaginary forces beyond. Thus deceived, the Dutch continued to swing at their anchors the three weeks it took the British govern-ment to suppress the Nore mutiny and hang Parker and 13 of his associates.

Lord St. Vincent, off Cadiz, repressed incipient mutiny with an iron hand. In one famous incident he forced the seamen of a mutinous ship to hang their leader by threatening to sink the vessel with gunfire, crew and all. But, balancing severity with humanity, he was ever watchful to see that his men were well fed, justly treated, and kept busy. As diversions in the touchy summer of 1797 he twice bombarded Cadiz and, in a moment of lapsed judg-ment, consented to a scheme of Nelson's and Troubridge's for capturing a cargo of Manila silver rumored to be at Santa Cruz in the Canary Islands. The Santa Cruz expedition was a complete fiasco—200 Englishmen were killed, and Nelson lost his right arm.

The Battle of Camperdown, 11 October 1797

By midsummer Duncan was again blockading in full strength. In early October, however, being low in stores, he put back to Yarmouth Roads with the bulk of his ships to revictual. Admiral Jan de Win-ter seized the opportunity to take the Dutch fleet out for a shakedown cruise. On the 8th he put to sea via the Texel channel and headed south along the coast. His ships were sighted by British patrols, and a fast cutter carried the report to Yarmouth. Duncan received the word next morning. By noon he was steering for the Dutch coast.

Numerically the opposing fleets were equal, 16 ships in each, with accompanying frigates and smal-ler craft. The British, however, were superior in guns and tonnage, with seven 74s, seven 64s, and two 50s to their opponents' four, seven, and five respectively, the smallest of the Dutch ships actually carrying 54 guns. On the other hand, the shallow draft of de Winter's vessels, a handicap in

the open sea, had obvious advantages with shoal water hard by. The wind being from the northwest, the Dutch admiral could avoid battle merely by falling off downwind, or he could accept battle and then withdraw safely when hard pressed.

British scouts at 9 a.m. on 11 October signaled "enemy to leeward," at which Duncan ordered general chase, for he was determined not to let the Dutch gain the security of the shoals. His fleet came down in two divisions from the northwest. With all sails set, his ships fell into increasing dis-order as the swifter ships took the lead. After two hours Duncan sighted his opponent some nine miles off the coastal town of Camperdown. Observ-ing that de Winter had backed his topsails and was preparing to make a stand, he ordered his ships to shorten sail and re-form the line. To ensure that the battle should be orthodox, he made the general signal for each ship to attack its opposite number. Before he could get his ships back in column, however, the Dutch began edging toward the shoals. Noting this, Duncan threw formalism to the winds and ordered all ships to up helm and run down to engage the enemy rear and center. This decision was crucial. As de Winter told him later, "Your not waiting to form line ruined me. If I had got nearer to the shore and you had attacked, I should probably have drawn both fleets on to it, and it would have been a victory to me, being on my own coast."

To grapple the enemy effectively and prevent him from passing into shoal water, Duncan next hoisted the signal (Howe's No. 34) to pass through the enemy line. Then, suspecting that the signal might not be understood or that his disordered squadrons might find it impossible to execute, he signaled for close action. Though the numerous hoists had bewildered most of Duncan's captains, not one had any thought of not engaging the enemy closely. Typical was the reaction of one captain, a

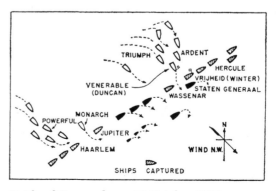

Battle of Camperdown, 11 October 1797

fellow Scot, who hurled the signal book to the deck with an oath. "Up wi' the hel-lem," he roared to the master, "and gang into the middle o't!"

In the same spirit most of the other British ships kept on through raking fire and sought an opponent where the action was thickest. But Vice Admiral Richard Onslow, commanding the British rear squadron, correctly executed Signal 34, taking the *Monarch* through the enemy line and luffing up to leeward of the *Jupiter*, flagship of the Dutch rear. A few minutes later, Duncan brought the *Venerable* through astern of de Winter's *Vrijheid* and engaged her from leeward. These penetrations, at van and rear, effectively gripped the whole fleet, for the rest of the Dutch vessels could not honorably desert their flagships.

As units of both fleets maneuvered in support of their admirals, the action developed into two melees. Unlike the French and Spanish, the Dutch followed the British example of firing at hulls; scarcely a mast or spar of the North Sea fleet was damaged, but casualties of men and guns mounted rapidly on both sides. One English ship was hulled 98 times; most of the Dutch vessels in the two centers of action were so badly shattered as to be worthless for further service.

Englishmen had not met such stubborn antagonists in any fleet battle since the Anglo–Dutch wars. It was only a matter of time, however, before weight of British shot and larger British hulls prevailed. When both Dutch flagships struck, seven of their line—mostly from the center squadron, which had not been heavily engaged—slipped away into shoal water out of British reach. The other nine, with two frigates in addition, were prizes of war.

The battle cost the North Sea fleet some 200 killed and more than 600 wounded—about 10 percent of its complement. The smaller Dutch fleet had as many wounded and nearly double the number killed. "It is a matter of marvel," said de Winter, a huge man like his opponent, "that two such gigantic objects as Admiral Duncan and myself should have escaped the general carnage of this day."

Following hard upon the crisis of the mutinies, the victory over the Dutch served to renew public confidence in the Royal Navy. Bonfires and oratory blazed from Scotland to Devon, and in the general enthusiasm the fleet commander became Viscount Duncan of Camperdown.

Chapter 7
Nelson and Bonaparte

Neither the defeat of the Spanish fleet off Cape St. Vincent in February 1797 nor the shattering of the Dutch fleet off Camperdown the following October deterred the French Directory from its plan of invading the British Isles. Troops made available by the cessation of hostilities on the Continent were shifted into a new and more formidable Army of England. General Hoche, the architect of the invasion plan, was now dead, but the Treaty of Campo Formio had made General Bonaparte available. Into his hands the Directors placed their cherished project, with orders to prepare for a full-scale cross-Channel attack.

Arriving in Paris early in December 1797, Bonaparte soon plunged into his new assignment, energetically inspecting the Channel coast. But the more he studied the problem of conquering Britain by frontal assault, the less he liked it. Besides, his thoughts were elsewhere. Having played Caesar in Italy, he now dreamed of playing Alexander in the East. While going through the routine of preparing to invade England, he was secretly planning to invade Egypt. His personal reasons were mainly romantic and egotistical, the desire for exotically named victories to crown his fame and to enhance his drive to power, but the reasons he adduced to the Directors were of another sort and won their grudging support.

Bonaparte spoke, on the one hand, of commercial advantages, of an eventual expedition against India. On the other, he assured the Directors that it would be impossible to invade England before the following autumn, that by then he would have completed his conquest of Egypt and returned to France. The expedition would thus serve as a giant diversion, attracting British warships to the defense of India and thereby simplifying the problems of the cross-Channel assault, which might be impossible with the Royal Navy concentrated in European waters. He scouted the Directors' fears that the invasion would make an enemy of Turkey, pointing out that not the sultan but the military caste of Mamluks controlled Egypt. Doubtless the sultan would prefer sharing control with France to remaining deprived of all authority in Egypt by the arrogant Mamluks.

The Egyptian Campaign

With some reluctance the Directory finally approved Bonaparte's proposal. Though the immense preparations that were immediately set afoot could not be concealed, their purpose was a well-guarded secret. All Europe soon knew that a great seaborne expedition was in the making, but few besides Bonaparte and the five Directors were aware that its destination was Egypt. Bonaparte seemed tireless, his enthusiasm without bounds. Working night and day, he alerted Vice Admiral François Paul Brueys's fleet at Toulon, contracted for French and Italian merchantmen to serve as transports, collected artillery and cavalry, and out of his Army of Italy assembled an Army of the East, which as a subterfuge he temporarily labeled "the left wing of the Army of England."

Escorted by Brueys's fleet, the convoy departed Toulon on 19 May 1798. On the following night a gale threatened to wreck the enterprise at the outset. But Bonaparte's famous luck held; not a ship was lost. In the ensuing days the expedition picked up contingents from Italian ports until the armada comprised 280 transports, escorted by 13 sail of the line, 7 frigates, and 35 lighter vessels. On board were more than 50,000 men, including the cream of the French army, with Bonaparte in command. On 9 June the armada put in at Malta, which quickly capitulated after a token show of resistance. Bonaparte thereupon turned over the island base to an occupation force of 4,000 French troops and on 19 June set out for Alexandria.

In retrospect, Bonaparte's Egyptian expedition appears even more quixotic than Medina Sidonia's Spanish Armada against England two centuries earlier. A man less supremely confident of his invincibility would have been appalled at the risks. He was undertaking to transport an army across a sea he did not control to a hostile coast where he had no base. His escorting fleet of warships was far too weak to support his landing and at the same time afford cover against attack from an enemy fleet. By secrecy and evasive routing he hoped to attain the surprise that alone could bring success. He succeeded by the narrowest of margins, for just over the horizon sailed a British fleet under Rear Admiral Sir Horatio Nelson, a name Bonaparte would come to respect and fear.

Nelson, back at sea after months ashore convalescing from the loss of his arm, had been ordered by Lord St. Vincent to take three 74s and three frigates to reconnoiter Toulon and gain intelligence of the immense French expedition there assembled. The severe gale of 20 May that had threatened Bonaparte's enterprise hit Nelson's little observation squadron with full force. His flagship *Vanguard* was partially dismasted, and his frigates were so scattered that they retired to Gibraltar. In the lee of Sardinia he succeeded by prodigious efforts in repairing the damaged flagship in four days. On 28 May he learned from a passing merchantman that the French armada had sailed, whereupon he hastened to the appointed rendezvous off the French coast in the hope of finding his frigates. Instead he found a contingent of ten of the line, a 50, and a brig, under Rear Admiral Sir Thomas Troubridge, sent by St. Vincent to give Nelson a force sufficient to handle the French, wherever they might be. Unfortunately Nelson's new force had no frigates either.

Thus reinforced to 13 of the line, Nelson headed east around Corsica to the coast of Italy, lamenting his lack of frigates, without which he was almost fatally hampered in search and scouting operations. Off Naples on 17 June, he learned that the French had attacked Malta. Thither he proceeded by the shortest route, through the Straits of Messina.

Nelson reached Cape Pessaro, Sicily on 22 June. Here a passing brig informed him that Malta had fallen and that the French armada had sailed again on the 16th. This was to prove a fateful piece of misinformation. On that date, as we have noted, Bonaparte was still at Malta, not sailing for Egypt until the 19th. The steady wind from the northwest convinced Nelson that the only likely goal of the French was Alexandria, and thither he promptly shaped his own course. Unhampered by wallowing transports and anticipating early action, he formed his fleet into three parallel columns, on the principle—afterward written into his famous Trafalgar Memorandum—that the order of sailing should be the order of battle. Two of his columns were to attack the French men-of-war; the third would pursue the transports.

Bonaparte was heading almost due east for the southern coast of Crete, whence he intended to cross the Mediterranean narrows and then move along the African coast to Alexandria. As Nelson's compact formation and Bonaparte's tight convoy moved on converging courses, the mists thickened unseasonably. In the evening of 22 June the two forces actually crossed paths within what in clearer weather would have been visual range. That night Brueys was alarmed to hear British signal guns in the distance.

Nelson, taking a direct route, reached Alexandria first, on 28 June. Finding no French ships in the harbor, he bitterly concluded that he must have guessed wrong. Still laboring under the misapprehension that Bonaparte had departed Malta on the 16th, he could not believe that he had outsped the French by six days. His impatience and restless energy now betrayed him into a false move. Scarcely pausing, he set sail to find the enemy wherever he might be. From the Pharos outside the harbor of Alexandria, lookouts within a few hours saw the last of Nelson's sails disappearing northward over the horizon as they caught their first glimpse of French sails arriving from the west.

Reaching Alexandria on 1 July, Bonaparte received from the French consul the electrifying information that Nelson had touched there only three days before. In the circumstances a lesser man might have withdrawn, at least temporarily, but Bonaparte characteristically chose the bold course of landing at once, even though the hour was late and the sea heavy. Moving westward some miles along the coast, the transports began hoisting out boats, while Brueys gave cover. Despite the perils of collision and foaming reefs, some 4,000 troops managed to struggle onto the beach that evening, and at the head of these Bonaparte marched through the night upon Alexandria, which fell the next day. The transports thereupon entered the harbor, while Brueys anchored his 13 of the line and 4 frigates in the deeper water of Aboukir Bay, some 12 miles northeast of the city.

Bonaparte, leaving 3,000 soldiers behind to garrison Alexandria, ascended the west bank of the Nile with 30,000, followed by a flotilla bringing supplies and artillery. After three weeks he reached a position opposite Cairo and almost in the shadow of the Pyramids. Here 10,000 mounted Mamluks backed by 24,000 foot were drawn up in gorgeous array to contest his advance. The French held their fire in the face of the impetuous charge of the Egyptian cavalry. Then at point-blank range they opened with musketry and grape. That volley broke the power of the Mamluks and made Bonaparte master of lower Egypt. Two days later, on 23 July, he entered Cairo.

Nelson meanwhile had been combing the Mediterranean in an agony of frustration and apprehension. From Alexandria he steered north to the coast of Asia Minor. Gleaning no information

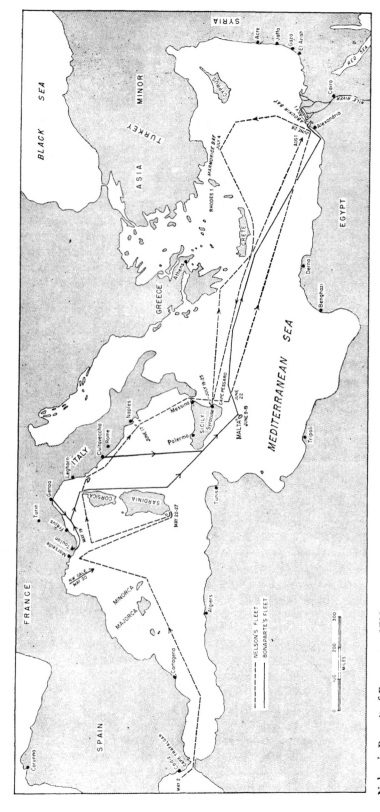

Nelson's Pursuit of Bonaparte, 1798

there, he began beating back toward Sicily and put into Syracuse on 19 July. The almost intolerable tension was somewhat relieved by the news that the French had not attacked Sicily or Naples, but beyond that he could learn nothing. "If they are above water, I will find them out," he said grimly, "and if possible bring them to battle." Pausing only long enough to take on provisions, Nelson was again at sea on the 25th, steering eastward. Off Greece he at last picked up a piece of useful information. The French armada had been seen four weeks earlier off Crete steering southeast. On this intelligence, Nelson at once shaped course again for Alexandria.

The month-long search, while trying Nelson's nerves to the utmost, was by no means wasted time. Unlike many naval commanders of his day, he refused to hold himself aloof. Scarcely a calm day passed that he did not have one or more of his captains on board the *Vanguard* to share his meals and, more important, his views. Every conceivable circumstance was reviewed—combats at sea and at anchor, by day or by night. Nelson never relinquished his command or his responsibilities, but his leadership and his professional judgment so unified his captains that their minds became extensions of his own, his decisions theirs. "I had the happiness," Nelson later wrote, "to command a Band of Brothers."

The passage of time had served the French admiral quite otherwise. As the days went by with no signs of the British, he gradually relaxed his precautions. Anchored in the open roadstead, he allowed his men to forage ashore, permitted his frigates to neglect picket duty, and left off the regular drill needed to keep his gunners combat-ready. He did make a battle plan, but it was perfunctory, based on habit rather than expectation of attack. Assuming a fortress mentality, he proposed to meet any possible British onslaught at anchor in the treacherous waters of Aboukir Bay, where the British superiority in seamanship would be nullified by a static battle. He drew up his fleet in a north–northwest, south–southeast line hugging a shoal on the westward side. Believing that the puny battery on Aboukir Island a mile and a half away to the northeast would protect his van, he stationed his strongest ships in the center and rear out of respect to the British custom of massing on these divisions. He forgot that such a practice was employed by the British in actions *at sea*, since it was difficult for the van to succor the rear against the wind that gave the fleet headway. At anchor it was a different story.

His situation was in several respects fatally weak. His ships were anchored by the bows only, with excessive intervals between ships, an obvious defect he planned to remedy in the event of impending attack by rigging stern anchors and springs[1] and passing cables between ships. The most serious flaw in Brueys's disposition was that it depended for defensive strength mainly on an offshore wind blowing into the teeth of any approaching enemy. But winds in the Mediterranean are not readily predictable. In fact, when Nelson again reached Egypt, a stiff breeze was blowing directly down the French line, van to rear, permitting the British to attack as they chose and preventing French ships from moving forward to assist their neighbors ahead. Brueys, in short, through negligence, miscalculation, and inadequate understanding of tactics, had made his fleet extraordinarily vulnerable to attack by seamen who knew their business—and Nelson and his captains knew their business.

The Battle of the Nile, 1 August 1798

The British fleet passed the transport-filled harbor of Alexandria in the early afternoon of 1 August and steered for the French men-of-war, whose masts were visible in the distance across the coastal flats. Despite the presence of the 120-gun flagship *Orient* and three 80s in the French line, the hazards of entering an unfamiliar roadstead without dependable charts, and the lateness of the hour, Nelson decided to attack without delay.

The French fleet meanwhile was all confusion. Brueys, appalled by the celerity of the British approach despite unfamiliar shoals and oncoming darkness, wavered between remaining at anchor and flight. He cleared for action, but only on the seaward side, and he failed to get stern anchors out or to rig springs and cables before the enemy was upon him.

Nelson's plan, with which his captains were perfectly familiar, was for each British ship to anchor by the stern as it came alongside the French line. The following British ship would pass on the disengaged side of the first one and anchor next ahead, so that the first fire from each French broadside would be met by first fire from a fresh British broadside. One British ship would take station off

---

[1]The term spring, as used here, refers to a cable run from the anchor through a stern or quarter port to the capstan. Taking up or paying out on this cable enabled a ship to be turned to direct her broadsides wherever desired.

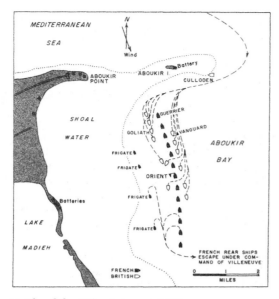

Battle of the Nile, 1 August 1798

the bow and another off the quarter of each of the leading French ships, giving the British a two-to-one advantage in the sector under attack. From these positions the English men-of-war would be in small danger of broadsides from the uncontrollably swinging enemy ships, while by use of their springs they could direct their own broadsides where they willed.

Nelson probably expected all his captains to anchor along the seaward side of the enemy van and center, since he must have assumed that Brueys would take the elementary precaution of anchoring so close to the shoal that no ship could pass on his landward side. But Captain Thomas Foley, from his position in the leading British ship *Goliath*, saw an opportunity for an even better method of attack. Noting that the French ships were swinging freely at their bow anchors, without a moment's hesitation he crossed the bows of the *Guerrier* at the exposed head of the enemy column. Delivering a murderous raking fire, he came to anchor on the landward side of the French line. Four more British ships followed.

Foley's instant decision was probably based on Nelson's remark that "wherever an enemy ship can swing, one of ours may anchor." Nelson, at any rate, tacitly applauded his subordinate's initiative by carrying out its tactical counterpart. Arriving sixth in the *Vanguard*, he anchored *outside* the enemy line, and so did the next few arrivals. The British thus doubled the weak French van and part of the center, placing them between two fires, while the rest of the French line, held by the wind,

looked on helpless. Soon after seeing his fleet in position, Nelson was struck on the forehead by a piece of langrage and was out of the battle for some hours. But his task was done—he had brought his fleet to action; his Band of Brothers could carry on.

Nightfall threw the baffled French into increasing confusion without greatly incommoding the English, who by Nelson's prior direction had lighted recognition lanterns in the tops. Three British stragglers at last reached the bay, led by Troubridge's *Culloden*, but Troubridge, ardent for battle, cut the reef too closely and grounded hard. While the captain and crew raged in frustration the *Culloden* tamely served as a buoy to guide the last two ships safely. These, arriving as a timely reserve, advanced to the relief of two English 74s opposite the French center, where they were taking heavy punishment from the huge *Orient* and an 80-gun ship next astern.

As the ships of the French van, shattered by overwhelming gunfire, surrendered one at a time, Nelson's ships moved methodically down both sides of the enemy line, enveloping the center and part of the rear. The *Orient*, under fire from several directions, burst into flames which crackled up her rigging and slowly ate into her hull. At ten o'clock, as the fire reached her magazines, the great flagship blew up with a force that opened the seams of nearby vessels. Awestruck by this appalling spectacle, battle-hardened seamen left off working their guns, and dead silence reigned for many minutes. Then the roar of battle resumed, and ships of the French center and rear began to strike their colors.

Dawn of 2 August 1798 revealed an unparalleled scene of triumph on the one hand and of devastation on the other. The British had not lost a single ship, and while their casualties amounted to nearly 900 men, French losses were almost six times as great. All the French ships except the three at the rear of the line had been taken or destroyed. Of these, one was deliberately grounded and burned by her crew. With the other two and the two remaining French frigates, Rear Admiral Pierre Villeneuve managed to slip out of the bay and escape to Malta.

From the quarterdeck of the *Vanguard*, Nelson surveyed his nine prizes with satisfaction. "Victory," said he, "is not a name strong enough for such a scene." The night's work had destroyed France's Toulon fleet, given Britain uncontested command of the Mediterranean, and isolated Bonaparte and his army in hostile Egypt. Even those who escaped in the fleeing ships were psychologically beaten men; the "horror of the

Nile" was to cloud their judgment and to fill them with premonitions of defeat in future engagements with the British. Bonaparte himself was chastened by his first contact with triumphant sea power, and though he was never fully to grasp the significance of naval operations, the tall ships of England had won his lasting respect and would influence all his future campaigns.

Tactically Nelson's Nile victory was unique in that he had found a solution to a problem over which naval theorists had been puzzling since the earliest days of the formalist–meleeist controversy—how to mass on part of the enemy force while containing the rest; in short, how to attain tactical concentration. While Brueys's faulty disposition had provided the British with the opportunity of massing on his van and center, and a fortuitous wind had held the French rear out of action, Nelson deserves credit for instantly perceiving the possibilities and acting upon them. When at Trafalgar he again met a French fleet in battle, he would demonstrate that he could work the same combination with no special advantages of wind or shoals.

More significant than its tactical implications were the strategic results of the battle. Like all decisive naval victories, it exercised a powerful influence far beyond the scene of action.

The Second Coalition

Nelson's victory reignited the war in Europe. Heartened by the isolation of Bonaparte, France's enemies were soon again on the march. William Pitt the Younger was at last able to achieve his Second Coalition. The British and their allies lost no time in exploiting their newly won command of the Mediterranean. Russo–Turkish forces recaptured the Ionian Islands. A British squadron detached by Lord St. Vincent from the Cadiz blockade reconquered Minorca.

By January 1799, Russia, Turkey, Portugal, Austria, the Papal States, and the Kingdom of the Two Sicilies[2] had joined England in the new coalition. An Austro–Russian army invaded Italy and by mid-July had expelled the French from all of the peninsula except the area around Genoa. At the same time France faced peril in central Europe, where allied armies outnumbered the French. At home, civil war threatened. The prestige of the Directory reached its nadir.

Following the Battle of the Nile, Nelson based his fleet on Naples, where he was received with

public adulation. Accepting the hospitality of British Ambassador Sir William Hamilton, he soon succumbed to the charms of Emma, Lady Hamilton. This passionate liaison lasted until the end of Nelson's life, to the scandal of his friends, the wreck of his marriage, and the near-ruin of his career.

Emma Hamilton, a close friend of Queen Maria Carolina, soon enlisted Nelson in her majesty's cause. When the French in the adjoining Papal States threatened Naples, Nelson spirited the royal family on board his flagship and took them and the Hamiltons to Palermo, Sicily. Because Nelson thereafter divided his time between Naples and Palermo, it sometimes seemed to his fellow officers that he was more interested in Emma Hamilton than in his duty. But Nelson recognized that the Kingdom of the Two Sicilies afforded the only places in the Mediterranean where the Royal Navy might expect to find support.

When an ailing Lord St. Vincent was relieved from command of the Mediterranean fleet by Admiral Lord Keith, Nelson was deeply embittered, believing that he and not Keith should have received the appointment. Nelson was further galled when Keith, in ordering him to blockade Malta, stipulated that he was to base his squadron on Syracuse or some other port on the east coast of Sicily. Keith's intention, as Nelson suspected, was in part to keep him away from the influence of the Hamiltons and the queen.

Keith's well-meaning plan did not succeed, for Nelson, whose complex personality combined the sensitive artist with the fearless warrior, simply went to pieces with frustration and resentment. His health became so affected that he asked and received permission to return to England. He and the Hamiltons journeyed to great acclaim through Northern Italy, Austria, and the German states and so back home, landing at Yarmouth. The people of England received the hero of the Nile with demonstrations of enthusiasm, but in society Nelson experienced a certain coldness, occasioned by his continued open association with Lady Hamilton.

Meanwhile, the bright prospects of the Allies in the summer of 1799, when victory over France seemed at hand, had suddenly faded as jealousy among the near-victors led to suspicion, suspicion to blunder, and blunder to disaster. When half-mad Czar Paul detached his army from the Austrians in Italy, the Archduke Charles withdrew his Austrians from the Russians in Switzerland. Before the detached Russian armies could unite, the French defeated them both and also compelled an Anglo–Russian invasion force in Holland to withdraw with heavy losses. The czar thereupon served

---

[2]Southern Italy and the island of Sicily. The mainland portion was called the Kingdom of Naples.

notice that he was quitting the alliance and recalled his armies to Russia. Thus the Second Coalition fell asunder. On all fronts save in Italy the French had hurled back their enemies.

Almost as though on signal, there arrived the man who could restore to France the grandeur she had lost. On 9 August 1799, at Fréjus on France's Mediterranean coast, Napoleon Bonaparte came ashore.

Abandoning his army in Egypt, he had sailed from Alexandria with two swift frigates and two smaller vessels and slipped undetected through the Royal Navy's inadequate screen.

On arriving in Paris, Bonaparte found himself the man of the hour. His amazing luck had brought him home at precisely the right moment to attain his ends. France was no longer in serious danger, but to most Frenchmen it was not apparent that the crisis had passed. They saw only that the Directors had thrown away Bonaparte's brilliant, peace-crowned victories of 1797 and plunged the country into a disastrous war.

With the assistance of his brother Lucien, Bonaparte engineered a series of decrees that cleared the way for a coup d'état. Sensing that after ten years of internal strife France would gladly accept a strong executive, he drafted a new constitution that provided for a head of state with extraordinary powers. It was overwhelmingly accepted in a plebescite on 15 December 1799, and Bonaparte, then 30 years old, was acclaimed First Consul. As such he was virtual dictator of France.

In order to establish himself among his war-weary people as a man of peace, Bonaparte offered England and Austria terms that he knew they would reject. While his captive newspapers were creating propaganda out of this situation, he set about with considerable success shoring up the national finances. At the same time he took the French army and navy under his direct command. By spring he felt ready to deal militarily with the remnants of the Second Coalition.

Bonaparte elected to act first against Austria, as the most accessible adversary. In May 1800 he led an army across the Alps, dragging his guns through the snow over the difficult Great St. Bernard Pass, and descended into Italy. The main Austrian army, its communications cut, abandoned its strong position on the French border and marched hastily eastward, only to be overwhelmed by Bonaparte's forces in mid-June at the Battle of Marengo. Six months later General Jean Victor Moreau decisively defeated the Austrians at Hohenlinden in Germany, whereupon the War of the Second Coalition collapsed as Austria accepted the Peace of Lunéville.

The Copenhagen Campaign

To counter Britain's sea power, Bonaparte set out by devious means to stir up trouble in the Baltic. Playing on the vanity of the addled czar and on the economic interests of Sweden and Denmark, he eventually induced them, together with Prussia, to form a new Armed Neutrality of the North. The objective of the Armed Neutrality was to exclude British trade from the Baltic Sea and to undermine the Royal Navy by depriving Britain of masts, spars, and other vital naval stores. To forestall such an intolerable situation, the British government acted quickly, assembling a fleet at Yarmouth for operations in the Baltic.

Assuming command at Yarmouth in February 1801 was Admiral Sir Hyde Parker, age 62, a man long on seniority but short on experience. Parker had been selected because the Ministry thought the Danes might be persuaded to withdraw from the League without fighting. As second-in-command the Admiralty named Baron Nelson of the Nile, apparently in order to have a fighting admiral on the scene should fighting be necessary. No one stopped to consider the difficulties this arrangement would raise for both admirals, or Nelson's record of noncooperation with less talented superiors. Nelson would in event of hostilities have to persuade Parker to let himself be superseded by an officer 20 years his junior. Remarkably enough, that is exactly what happened.

At the beginning, however, the command situation was tense. While Nelson fretted at the delay, Parker swung placidly at anchor, simply ignoring his second-in-command. But time was not to be wasted, for the coming of spring would soon free the Baltic ports of ice, permitting the Northern Allies to combine their fleets. At length Nelson, more aware than most men of the importance of time, seems to have dropped a hint to his old friend St. Vincent, who had just taken over as First Lord of the Admiralty. At any rate, the force suddenly sailed on 12 March, with relations between the two admirals something less than cordial.

The fleet that arrived off the Skaw on 19 March included 23 sail of the line, with Parker's flag in the *London*, 98, and Nelson's in the *St. George*, 98. Besides these three-deckers, there were fourteen 74s, five 64s, and one 50, plus 11 frigates and 23 smaller vessels. Parker sent a frigate ahead carrying the British envoy, Nicholas Vansittart, with an ultimatum to the Danes to withdraw from the League forthwith. The fleet followed slowly, much to the annoyance of Nelson, who wanted to back up the ultimatum with ships of the line, which he called "the best negotiators in Europe," before the Danes had time to strengthen their defenses. But, Parker deeming otherwise, the fleet on 20 March anchored north of the Island of Zealand to await Vansittart's return. When the envoy arrived on 23 March bearing a negative reply, Parker at last summoned Nelson. "Now we are sure of fighting," Nelson wrote to Lady Hamilton, "I am sent for."

Arriving on board the *London*, Nelson found a council of war steeped in gloom. The Danish defenses, Vansittart reported, were much more formidable than had been supposed. Most of the council favored waiting for the united Baltic squadrons to emerge to do battle. To Nelson this was the height of folly, for it would leave the Baltic closed to British trade and at the same time give the Allies the initiative to attack when they chose. Eager to hit at Russia, the heart of the coalition, Nelson proposed slipping around south of Zealand, via the Great Belt, and descending on the Russian fleet at Reval before melting ice permitted it to retire to the strong defenses of Kronstadt. This course had the "Nelson touch" of striking where the enemy least expected. It would permit the British to defeat the Allied fleets in detail.

This plan proving too bold for the unimaginative Parker, Nelson proposed an attack on Copenhagen. The city's defenses, according to Vansittart, were oriented to the north, with the harbor entrance protected by the powerful Trekroner Battery. Nelson therefore recommended an attack from the south. As he talked, his enthusiasm began to infect the council, which at length adopted his general plan.

Parker at first intended to reach Copenhagen from the south by going west around Zealand, but learning more of the intricacies of the Great Belt route, he decided to brave the narrow gauntlet between Zealand and Sweden. (See map, p. 14.) This he did on 30 March, hugging the eastern shore to avoid the fire of Danish batteries, and anchored five miles northeast of Copenhagen in the body of water known as the Sound. Nelson now led a boat party to examine the Danish defenses.

East of the Trekroner Battery, the Sound was divided by the Middle Ground Shoal into two roughly north–south channels. In the western passage, King's Channel, the Danes had anchored a row of blockships to cover the southern approaches to the city. These comprised ten dismasted ships

and ten lighter floating batteries. All mounted powerful guns, and the more heavily armed vessels were distributed fairly evenly along the line. On the shore, some distance away, were additional batteries. Nelson's inspection confirmed him in his conviction that the city should be attacked from the south, not directly into the guns of the Trekroner—which, as he expressed it, would be "taking the bull by the horns"—but via King's Channel and the line of blockships. This opinion he reported to a second council of war, meeting that evening on board the *London*.

Nelson found that in his absence pessimism had once again set in, but again his enthusiasm carried the day. He urged the attack from the southern end of the line of blockships to be made by ten of the lightest draft ships of the line and volunteered to lead it himself. Meanwhile Parker with the rest of the force would demonstrate to the north of Copenhagen to hold the Danes from reinforcing the southern extremity of their defenses. Once the blockships had been destroyed, bomb ketches could be placed in position to bombard the city. Parker allowed himself to be persuaded to accept this course of action and, on an impulse of generosity, gave Nelson 12 ships instead of the 10 he asked for.

Nelson first shifted his flag from the *St. George* to the lighter draft *Elephant*, 74. Then, in contrast to the Nile, where he gave his captains only general instructions, he made the most careful preparations. Moving his fleet to a position southeast of the lower end of the blockship line, he studied the situation minutely. In his orders he listed the 20 vessels opposing him, giving the estimated number of guns in each. To each of his own ships he assigned one or more Danish ships as targets. Because the blockships were backed by shore batteries and were anchored bow and stern on the very edge of shoal water, he made no plans to double as he had done at the Nile. Nor did he expect to mass on the southern end of the enemy line, for this would permit the carefully prepared Danish vessels to use their springs to swing ship and rake the British. This possibility Nelson planned to counter by a nearly simultaneous engagement of the entire line, relying on sheer gun power to crush the enemy. He so arranged his own line as to bring a superior number of guns against nearly every Danish ship or combination. Meanwhile, frigates under Captain Edward Riou were to demonstrate to the north of the line, and Parker's remaining force was to stand toward Copenhagen to be available as a mobile reserve.

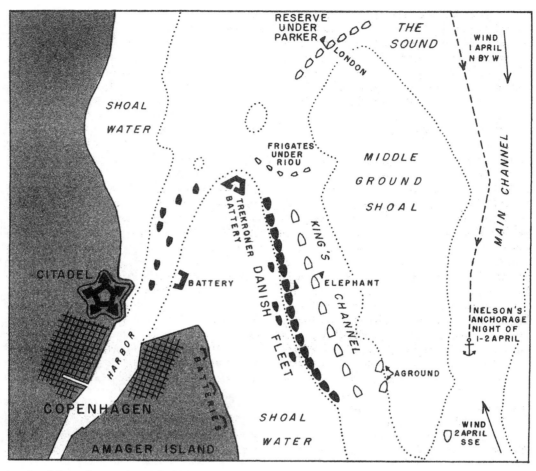

Battle of Copenhagen, 2 April 1801

The Battle of Copenhagen, 2 April 1801

During the night of 1–2 April, as Nelson expected, the wind shifted to the south–southeast, and all was in readiness for the attack. At 7:30 the following morning he held a final conference. Between 9:45 and 10:15 all ships were under way and forming into line of battle in close order at 300 yards distance. As the fleet began the approach for the attack, the Baltic pilots became panicky at the prospect of coming under fire and refused to conn the ships. One of the sailing masters of the fleet volunteered to lead the column, but while confusion still reigned, two British ships went aground. A third found herself unable to weather the Middle Ground Shoal. Thus at the outset Nelson's force was reduced by a quarter, and his gun superiority was cut down from 6 to 5 to an inferiority of 5 to 5½. Undaunted, the British advanced in silence as was their custom when standing into battle. To the north Parker's force was able to make little headway against the wind, but Riou got his frigates into

position northeast of the Trekroner, where he heavily damaged the northernmost ship of the Danish line.

The loss of the three ships required a last-minute revision of Nelson's plans. The *Edgar* now led the line in, and then each ship passed outboard of her leader and anchored ahead of her, so that the order of the line was reversed. Thus no British ship had to take the fire of the whole enemy line and, as at the Nile, the first fire of each enemy ship was met by the first fire of each British ship. The firing, opened by the Danes, reached a bloody climax by 11:30 a.m. and continued with little abatement until 2:00 in the afternoon. "Here," Nelson wrote, "was no maneuvering: it was downright fighting."

Watching the mutual slaughter from the *London*, Parker became increasingly alarmed and discussed with Captain Otway, his flag captain, whether he should call off the action. Captain Otway strongly opposed any such move and volunteered to go by boat to consult Nelson before a decision was made. To this Parker agreed. Yet before Otway had time to reach the *Elephant*, Parker at 1:30 hoisted the signal "Discontinue the action." Nelson at first appeared to take no notice of it, and then directed that a mere acknowledgement be sent and inquired whether his own for close action was still flying. Assured that it was, Nelson put his telescope to his blind eye, remarking to the *Elephant*'s captain, "You know, Foley, I have only one eye—I have a right to be blind sometimes. I really do not see the signal." None of the ships in Nelson's line either repeated or obeyed Parker's signaled order. To the north, Riou, exercising a semi-detached command, felt obliged to obey and regretfully began to withdraw, saying, "What will Nelson think of us?" A moment later a cannon ball cut him in two.

In the circumstances, Nelson had every right to be blind. It would have been physically impossible for his ships to retreat the way they had come, for in that direction the wind was dead foul. The only way out was past the entire blockship line and the Trekroner battery, considered by all too dangerous to attack. Nelson's force was thus in a position from which only victory could extricate it.

At about two o'clock the Danish fire began to slacken, and soon thereafter Nelson sent an ultimatum ashore: "To the Brothers of Englishmen, The Danes. Lord Nelson has directions to spare Denmark, when no longer resisting; but if the firing is continued on the part of Denmark, Lord Nelson will be obliged to set on fire all the Floating-batteries he has taken, without having the power of saving the brave Danes who have defended them." To the preparation of this note, Nelson gave great care, even sealing it with his own signet—rather than a wafer, which would have implied haste. Although his antagonists were by no means in the hopeless position the note suggested, Nelson's bluff worked—perhaps because the Danes had just received news of the assassination of Czar Paul and realized that Russia might soon be pulling out of the Armed Neutrality. The Danes agreed to supply the British fleet for 14 weeks, during which time they would not ready any ships for sea. They also agreed to quit the Armed Neutrality.

Nelson urged Parker to proceed at once against the Russian ships at Reval. He even offered to take a small detachment to seek out the Russian and Swedish fleets. It was to no avail. All enterprise seemed to have gone out of Parker, who insisted on waiting for additional instructions from England. At length the frustrated Nelson applied for leave to return home. Parker gladly consented, relieved at the prospect of ridding himself of his uncomfortably demanding subordinate. Then on 5 May, a month after the battle, the new instructions came.

Both admirals were thunderstruck. Parker was recalled to England, and Nelson was left in command in the Baltic.

The next day Nelson sailed for Reval. But Parker's delay had spoiled his opportunity. The ice had gone out three days before, and the Russians reached Kronstadt in safety.

The Peace of Amiens

Although Nelson's move against the Russians came too late for the destruction of the Russian fleet, it did not much matter. With the new czar, Alexander I, Russian sympathies changed, and the Armed Neutrality was dead. When Nelson went ashore at Reval, he was welcomed as the "young Suvorov," and on his return to England, he was again the hero of the hour, being raised a degree in peerage to become Viscount Nelson.

With the collapse of the Armed Neutrality, England once again blocked Bonaparte. He had lost the initiative, and Britain's sea power had grown ever stronger. At the opening of the war, the Royal Navy had 15,000 men enrolled; at the end of 1801, 133,000 manned its ships. The navy had grown from 135 to 202 ships of the line and from 133 to 277 frigates. At the same time, the French navy had been reduced by more than 50 percent, and few of the remaining ships were fit to take to sea. The impact of the war had wrought profound changes in the economic life of both countries. In many places in England, the people were in want. Almost everyone was heartily tired of war. Henry Addington's new ministry was eager to consummate a peace, having no idea how a continuation of the war might lead to ultimate victory.

Bonaparte was equally anxious for peace, but for other reasons. He hoped to gain at the conference table what he had been unable to win by force of arms. Thus, when Britain's secret overtures came to his attention, he was ready to receive them. Like a good negotiator, however, he exploited his enemy's weaknesses while concealing his own— the First Consul proved as adept in diplomacy as in commanding armies. After a preliminary agreement was signed on 1 October 1801, the British began speedily disarming. In later negotiations Bonaparte blandly denied verbal agreements made in former discussions. As a result, Britain, having lost her bargaining power by her too hasty disarmament, had to restore many of her hard-won overseas conquests. While wits might quip about "the peace which passeth understanding," the general rejoicing drowned the voices of the Jeremiahs. Englishmen returning to the joys of peaceful living had no use for "Ancestral voices prophesying war."

Chapter 8
The War of the French Empire

Englishmen rejoiced at the treaty signed in Amiens in the spring of 1802, ending the nine-year-old war with France. It soon appeared, however, that Bonaparte regarded the peace as merely an opportunity for further French aggrandizement. His armies remained intact. His shipyards hummed with activity. He maintained troops in Holland, intervened in German affairs, invaded Switzerland, and annexed Piedmont.

Alarmed at Bonaparte's open contempt for the peace treaty, the English concluded that they had no alternative to breaking it themselves. They had returned Minorca to France, but they refused to give up Malta, their only remaining base in the Mediterranean. Bonaparte, with much bluster, threatened to renew hostilities. On 18 May 1803, Britain called his bluff by declaring war on France.

The Addington ministry had no plans for the strategic direction of the new war. It had come to power to conclude a peace, and when events again forced war, its program collapsed. Yet there was one thing that any British cabinet would do almost automatically: it issued orders for the Royal Navy to reestablish the blockade of French ports. Upon the declaration of war, five of the line sailed from Tor Bay under veteran Vice Admiral Sir William Cornwallis. Three days later they appeared at their old station off Ushant. Also on the 18th Keith hoisted his flag at the Nore, and that same evening Nelson boarded the *Victory* at Portsmouth and was quickly away to take command of a new British Mediterranean fleet.

Napoleon's Invasion Plans

Incensed at the British declaration of war, Bonaparte determined at last to invade England. A blow at Britain's very heart was the proper reply to Perfidious Albion, and this could be achieved only by crossing the Channel. "They want us to jump the ditch, and we *will* jump it!" he vowed.

On Bonaparte's orders, French shipwrights at every Channel port and in many inland towns toiled at building the invasion flotilla of some 2,000 craft. Designed to carry the maximum load without regard to sea-keeping qualities, they were general-ly flat-bottomed, so that in a tideway they became unmanageable. The preparations were so frenzied that in England everyone hourly expected Bonaparte to make the attempt. Yet summer, fall, and winter dragged on, and he still did not come.

Several things stood in his way. The harbor at the Boulogne assembly and staging area needed extensive dredging and enlarging. This being accomplished at tremendous cost in time and effort, it was found impossible to effect a sortie of the whole flotilla on a single tide. Thus something over 12 hours would elapse before the second segment could follow the first, a delay that would facilitate piecemeal destruction by British forces of the barges crowded with the seasick victors of Marengo.

Meanwhile, the Addison government, obsessed with fear of Bonaparte, made no plans at all for the offensive, instead directing its energies toward repelling the French legions in the Kentish and Sussex meadows. Ill-considered directives went out urging men to enlist in the Volunteers, but the chief result was to dry up the source of men for the regular army, the only force that could be used abroad. Pitt, concluding at length that Addington's policies gave no prospect of victory, denounced them in Commons. Addington resigned, and on 7 May 1804, the king sent for Pitt. On the same day that Pitt undertook his duties, Napoleon had himself declared Emperor of the French.

All summer Pitt worked to create a new coalition against Napoleon. By November Russia and Austria were prepared to sign a treaty for an Armed League, to be led by Russia but paid for by Britain. The League was to insist on the evacuation of French forces from Italy, Germany, and Holland. In return for this support on the Continent, Russia demanded that Britain make a show of force in the Mediterranean—one comprehensible to the land-minded rulers of Europe. Accordingly, Pitt began preparing for an army to be sent to that area.

As French ships returned from the Caribbean and took refuge in the neutral Spanish port of Ferrol, British warships sealed them in. When Spain joined France in the war, the British blockade was extended to cover Cadiz and Cartagena. Thus English men-of-war checked Napoleon's every move at sea. In Mahan's words, "Those far distant, storm-beaten ships upon which the Grand Army never looked stood between it and the dominion of the world."

Napoleon at last came to realize that he could not cross the Channel with barges alone. Hence he conceived the notion of massing ships in the English Channel to drive off or destroy the blockading fleets. The weakness of such a plan was that in the unlikely event the French and Spanish ships managed to escape the British blockaders and massed in the Channel, the commander of the combined fleet would find himself in the position of Medina Sidonia 216 years before—too busy fighting for his life to protect the invasion flotilla.

Turning his eyes on Britain's colonial possessions, Napoleon directed Admiral Comte de Missiessy, in command of the French fleet at Rochefort, and Admiral Pierre Villeneuve, the refugee from the Battle of the Nile, now commanding the Toulon fleet, to raid British colonies and commerce in the West Indies. In January 1805, in the temporary absence of the Rochefort blockading squadron of Sir Thomas Graves, Missiessy with five of the line and five frigates sailed for Martinique. Villeneuve attempted to depart Toulon but was driven back by weather.

As Missiessy approached the West Indies, Napoleon's fertile brain produced a new invasion scheme. He now conceived what he called his Grand Design, a plan that was to work as follows: Villeneuve was to break loose from Toulon and, sailing westward, release the Spanish ships at Cartagena. Then, passing Gibraltar, he was to liberate Rear Admiral Federico Gravina's squadron at Cadiz. Commanding the combined force, he was to sail for the West Indies, where he would join Missiessy and wait 40 days for the Brest fleet. On its arrival, the combined fleet would sail for the Channel to cover the crossing of Napoleon's flotilla. It was assumed that the British squadrons, alarmed for their colonies, would abandon European waters and speed to their protection.

Such was the Grand Design. It failed for many reasons, but its inherent weakness was that it did not appreciate a fact the British understood well: that the English Channel was Britain's strategic center, and that whatever other dispositions they might make, the British would never fail to make provisions for the control of those waters.

Nelson's Pursuit of Villeneuve

Orders to implement the Grand Design went forth from Paris to the various commanders concerned.

Taking advantage of Nelson's intentionally loose blockade, Villeneuve with 11 of the line sailed from Toulon on 30 March 1805.

Nelson's shortage of scouting frigates left him in the dark as to his enemy's movements. He could not be sure whether Villeneuve's destination lay to the east or to the west. His mission called for protection of the Mediterranean station, and he knew that the most vulnerable points lay to the east—Naples, Malta, and Egypt. Additionally, he knew that Pitt planned operations in the central Mediterranean. Accordingly he took station off the island of Ustica, in position to guard the approaches to both the Straits of Messina and the Sicilian Channel.

Meanwhile Villeneuve made his way westward. On 7 April he was off Cartagena. He signaled the Spanish ships in port to join him, but they were not ready for sea, and the specter of Nelson would not allow him to wait. The next day he passed through the Straits of Gibraltar, rounded Cape Trafalgar, and set his course for Cadiz. There he was joined by eight Spanish ships under Admiral Gravina. Together that night they set sail for the West Indies. At the same time Missiessy with the Rochefort squadron was heading back toward France on the false assumption that Villeneuve had abandoned the West Indies operation. Already the machinery of the Grand Design was beginning to creak.

Villeneuve's passage by Gibraltar had not gone unobserved. It was reported to Admiral Sir John Orde, who, heavily outnumbered, set out for the Channel to warn the Brest blockade and the Admiralty. On the way he looked into Cadiz and found it empty. Villeneuve, with Gravina, had disappeared into the Atlantic.

From Gibraltar to London the news of Villeneuve's disappearance was received with dismay. A southbound convoy en route to Malta with 6,000 troops under General Sir James Craig—the British contingent Russia had demanded as her price for entering the Third Coalition—might easily fall victim. An administrative shakeup had recently brought to the office of First Lord of the Admiralty a 78-year-old former naval officer, Admiral Lord Barham. The new First Lord promptly issued necessary orders to ensure the safety of Craig's troops, to maintain sufficient naval force in the Channel, and to transfer ships to the West Indies in event Villeneuve had gone there.

Nelson in the meantime was fuming at his station near Ustica. With every passing day it became more evident that Villeneuve had designs to the west, not the east. On 10 April Nelson began to

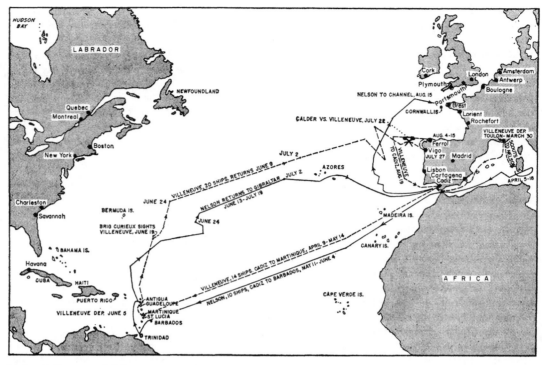

Nelson's Pursuit of Villeneuve, 1805

beat his way westward against head winds. When he finally arrived at Gibraltar on 8 May, he learned to his relief that Craig's expedition had taken shelter in Lisbon, and Nelson detached one of his own ships to strengthen its escort. Next, he was informed by a frigate out of England that Villeneuve had not been reported to the north. He was now convinced that the French admiral's destination must be the West Indies. On the 11th Nelson, more than a month behind his enemy, set out in pursuit.

On 4 June, 21 days after Villeneuve's arrival at Martinique, Nelson was at Barbados. It was almost as though the ships had responded to their commander's eagerness, for they had made an almost record crossing of 24 days. Villeneuve, ordered to raid the British colonies, was en route to Antigua when he learned the alarming news that Nelson was on his heels. He made up his mind at once. Gone was any idea of waiting for a concentration in the West Indies. In disregard of orders, he set sail for Ferrol.

As soon as Nelson learned of Villeneuve's departure from the West Indies, he dispatched the fast brig *Curieux* to England with a warning that the Combined Fleet apparently was heading for Europe. On 13 June, having spent a little more

than a week in the West Indies, he set course for Gibraltar.

By a stroke of luck, the *Curieux* sighted Villeneuve at sea, inferred from his position and course that he was headed for Ferrol, and hastened with the word to Plymouth. Lord Barham lost no time in sending a warning and a reinforcement of eight ships to Sir Robert Calder on the Ferrol station. The junction was none too soon. On 22 July, in heavy mist, Calder's lookouts discerned strange sails to westward. It was the Combined Fleet. Calder had been presented with the opportunity Nelson had twice crossed the ocean to attain.

Although the fleets sighted each other about noon, neither was able to make out much about the other for nearly two hours. Then Villeneuve formed line of battle in a single column. Calder maneuvered to get between Ferrol and the enemy to mass on the enemy's center and rear; unlike Nelson, in the forthcoming Battle of Trafalgar, he made no provision to contain the van. Before Calder could engage, the commander of his van division saw ships of the enemy van looming out of the mists ahead. To block the way to Ferrol, he tacked and led the British fleet around to a parallel course, thereby committing it to a formal battle. Calder, not one to force a melee, accepted the situation. In the thickening mist, gunners fired at flashes and the sound of guns. Darkness ended the action. The British had captured two Spanish ships and had one of their own disabled.

Thereafter neither Villeneuve nor Calder made any serious attempt to renew the battle. As the weather worsened, the French admiral decided to make a run for Vigo, which he reached on 28 July. After detaching three damaged ships and 1,200 sick men, he crept along the coast to Ferrol, where he added 14 French and Spanish ships to his fleet.

On learning that the Combined Fleet had reached northern Spain, Napoleon, at Boulogne, believed that the time was ripe for the crossing. To Villeneuve he sent peremptory orders to proceed to Brest, free the Brest fleet from Cornwallis's blockade, and with it seize control of the Channel. He concluded grandly: "I count on your zeal in my service, your love of your country, and your hatred of that nation which has oppressed us for 40 generations, and which a little perseverance on your part will now cause to reenter forever the ranks of petty powers." To Admiral Honoré Ganteaume, commanding the Brest fleet, he wrote: "Never will my soldiers of the land and sea risk their lives for a greater goal."

As Villeneuve, in compliance with the imperial order, was leaving Ferrol with 29 ships, the Royal Navy was concentrating, true to the reflex action of centuries, at the mouth of the Channel. Calder, finding his station vacant, raised his blockade and headed for Brest, joining Cornwallis with ten ships a few hours after the arrival of the seven ships of the Rochefort blockade. Nelson, who had learned at Gibraltar that the Combined Fleet had not been sighted in that area, headed north also and added his 12 ships to the Brest blockade, making a total strength of 39 ships of the line. This was the outcome of Napoleon's plan to disperse the British fleet.

After leaving Ferrol, Villeneuve held on to the northwest, as though to gain westing for the run to the Channel. After two days of desultory movements, of shying at the sight of every strange sail, he lost heart. On the evening of 15 August he gave the order that put his fleet on course, not for the Channel but for Cadiz.

Cornwallis must have guessed that Villeneuve would never reach the Channel, for on 16 August he sent Calder with 18 of the line back to Ferrol. At the same time he detached Nelson in the *Victory* to proceed to England where he would enjoy a brief leave, his first after two years at sea.

On 20 August, Villeneuve entered Cadiz. This ended once and for all Napoleon's Grand Design.

At first the port could scarcely be said to be blockaded, for Collingwood had only 4 ships to watch Villeneuve's 27. But Calder, finding Ferrol empty, sailed on and joined Collingwood off Cadiz on 29 August.

For two days Napoleon had kept an anxious eye on the waters of the Channel. Then came a letter from his naval minister expressing the conviction that Villeneuve had gone to Cadiz. In a rage, Napoleon canceled his plan for invading England, at least for the time being. In its place, he substituted an alternate plan, already worked out in some detail. His Grand Army, instead of crossing the Channel, would march against Austria in a move to break up the Third Coalition. When Napoleon received Villeneuve's report that he was in fact at Cadiz, he ordered him to enter the Mediterranean to support the Austrian campaign by attacking Naples. At the same time, having had enough of Villeneuve's irresoluteness, he secretly dispatched Admiral François Rosily to relieve him.

The Battle of Trafalgar, 21 October 1805

As Napoleon was setting his face toward Austria, Nelson was taking leave of his friends in London before departing to resume his old command. On 13 September, after saying farewell to his beloved Emma, he proceeded to Spithead where he was met by cheering crowds. Many wept, and not a few knelt and blessed him as he passed. That afternoon he once more hoisted his flag in the *Victory*, which sailed the next morning in company with a frigate. Off Lisbon he sent the frigate ahead with a message ordering Collingwood not to disclose his coming, for, as he wrote, "I hope to see the enemy at sea." As a result, when, on 28 September, the *Victory* joined Collingwood's fleet, not a gun saluted, and not a flag was broken.

Nelson regretfully brought orders from the Admiralty for Calder to return to England to face court-martial for "not having done his utmost" to destroy the Combined Fleet. In a spirit of generosity and courtesy to a fellow officer, Nelson allowed him to go home in his own flagship, the 98-gun *Prince of Wales*, thereby depriving himself of a three-decker on the eve of action.

On taking command off Cadiz, Nelson had as his primary objective luring Villeneuve to sea so that he might destroy him. To this end he adopted his usual loose blockade. Watchful frigates kept Cadiz under observation while the main fleet cruised some distance to westward.

Knowing that Villeneuve could command from 30 to 35 of the line, and realizing that it might be a long wait before he emerged, Nelson arranged for provisioning his fleet in relays while still remaining at all times ready to fight. He began by dispatching Rear Admiral Thomas Louis with five ships to Morocco to replenish.

Having no opportunity for the informal discussions with his captains that had preceded the Battle of the Nile, Nelson set down his ideas on paper as a guide. The Memorandum is worth quoting in part, as an example of Nelson's tactical thinking and of his trust and confidence in subordinates.

> Thinking it almost impossible to bring a fleet of forty sail of the line into line of battle in variable winds thick weather and other circumstances which must occur, without such a loss of time that the opportunity would probably be lost of bringing the enemy to battle in such a manner as to make the business decisive—
>
> I have therefore made up my mind . . . that the order of sailing is to be the order of battle. . . .
>
> The second in command will after my intentions are made known to him have the entire direction of his line to make the attack upon the enemy and to follow up the blow until they are captured or destroyed.
>
> The whole impression of the British fleet must be to overpower from two or three ships ahead of their commander-in-chief, supposed to be in the centre, to the rear of their fleet. . . . Something must be left to chance; nothing is sure in a sea fight beyond all others. Shot will carry away the masts and yards of friends as well as foes but I look with confidence to a victory before the van of the enemy could succour their rear. . . .
>
> The second in command will in all possible things direct the movements of his line by keeping them as compact as the nature of the circumstances will admit. Captains are to look to their particular line as their rallying point. But in case signals can neither be seen or perfectly understood no captain can do very wrong if he places his ship alongside that of an enemy.

The Memorandum is noteworthy for its spirit of aggressiveness, its trust in subordinates, its simplicity, and its confidence in victory. While it in no way diminished the fleet commander's control of his ships, it left complete initiative to Collingwood "after my intentions are made known to him." It provided for flexibility and for the greatest freedom of action on the part of each captain.

Briefly, Nelson's plan was to divide his fleet into three divisions, Collingwood's to leeward to deliver the principal thrust on the enemy rear and Nelson's own division to windward to contain the van and then strike at the center and force a decision before the enemy van could get back to take part in the battle, with his third division to be a reserve of eight ships to give support as needed.

On the morning of 19 October 1805, the inshore frigate signaled, "The enemy's ships are coming out of port." The opportunity Nelson had worked so long for had arrived.

Villeneuve was complying with Napoleon's order to proceed to Naples, but sooner than he had at first intended, for he had learned two days before that Rosily was on his way to take command of the Combined Fleet. Rather than endure the disgrace of being relieved under conditions that suggested cowardice, he would try to make the Straits of Gibraltar before he was intercepted. If not, well then, death with honor was preferable to the alternative.

When Nelson heard of Villeneuve's sortie, he guessed it could mean only that the latter was bound for the Straits, and he took a course to intercept. On the night of the 20th Nelson invited several midshipmen to dinner, promising them that the morrow would bring something for them to talk about all the rest of their lives.

The whole Combined Fleet was by then at sea, between Cadiz and Cape Trafalgar. Despite Nelson's precautions, Villeneuve knew that he was in the area. Hence the French admiral scarcely expected to make it to the Straits without a fight, but he was determined to press on. During the night he held on course, expecting to receive at any moment the smashing broadsides of the *fougueux amiral*, as the French called Nelson. Out of the dark he had struck at the Nile, and out of the dark he might strike again. But the night passed without incident. Nelson, who had come within 25 miles of Cadiz, had opened out toward the southwest during the hours of darkness to allow the Allies to gain sea room, but more especially to keep them from running back to Cadiz before he could force an engagement.

As dawn broke on 21 October 1805, the sea was smooth, with a gentle breeze from the west–northwest. The British fleet was about 20 miles west of Cape Trafalgar. First light revealed to its anxious lookouts the welcome sight of white patches of canvas on the eastern horizon. A little after 6 a.m., Nelson began to implement his Memorandum. Because of the absence of Admiral Louis's ships, he discarded the idea of a reserve division and sent a signal for his fleet of 27 sail to form two columns on an easterly course. He, in the *Victory*, led the northern or windward column, while Collingwood in the *Royal Sovereign* headed the southern or leeward column, as planned.

About this time Villeneuve, realizing that he could not reach the Straits without engagement, gave the command to wear together and form column of battle in reverse order. This had the effect of turning the Combined Fleet into a single line on a northerly course, the third squadron under Rear Admiral Pierre Dumanoir leading. But the order came too late for the Allies to retreat to Cadiz. There was no hope of avoiding engagement. One of the Spanish captains, as he grasped the situation, snapped his telescope shut, exclaiming "Perdidos!"

As Villeneuve's ships made their turn, the line became slightly bowed, concave toward the British. The handier Allied ships were forced to back sail to wait for the laggardly ones. Thus for nearly two hours the Combined Fleet made good no distance at all, while the British, their two columns at an oblique angle to the Franco–Spanish line, advanced with all sails set, including studding sails.

Collingwood, in compliance with the Memorandum, was heading to cut the Allied line at the twelfth ship from the rear, while Nelson was on a course for a point two miles ahead of the enemy van. The relative movement put the *Victory* on a collision course with the *Neptuno*, now Villeneuve's leading ship.

The psychological pressure on the waiting French and Spanish was intense. No one could tell where the blow would fall. So long as Nelson held his course, the Allied van had to brace to receive the onslaught of Nelson's 12 juggernauts. Yet by simply putting the helm over, Nelson could deliver his thrust at Villeneuve's center, with the van held out of action by the lightness of the wind and by the necessity of reversing course.

Assigning a double role to his own squadron was Nelson's most novel concept. Where Calder had failed to hold the Allied van until he could force a decision, Nelson, by his understanding of the enemy's psychology and by his threat to the van, ensured that it would be out of action while he and Collingwood disposed of the center and rear.

As the morning wore on, the British continued their implacable closing on the Allies. The two British columns, their black and yellow hulls somber under their clouds of canvas, their guns run out and double-shotted, were forbidding indeed. Anticipating that his van ships might be in action before the rearmost ones could catch up, Nelson had headed each column with his heaviest ships. Leading his own were three-deckers, the *Victory*, 100 guns, and the *Téméraire* and *Neptune*, 98 guns each. Heading Collingwood's squadron were the *Royal Sovereign*, 100, and the *Prince*, 98. As the fleets neared one another, several of Nelson's officers pleaded with him to allow a different ship to take the lead lest Nelson himself be uselessly killed or disabled. Nelson appeared to acquiesce, and signals were made for the *Téméraire* to take the lead. But when the *Téméraire*, slightly handier than the *Victory*, began to edge forward, Nelson ordered her back into second position in line.

About 11 a.m., when it seemed battle would be joined in another hour, Nelson went below to his cabin. Here he added a codicil to his will and composed a prayer, which he left as a legacy to his country:

> May the great God whom I worship grant to my country, and for the benefit of Europe in general, a great and glorious victory; and may no misconduct of anyone tarnish it; and may humanity after victory be the predominant feature of the British fleet. For myself, individually, I commit my life to Him who made me, and may his blessing light upon my endeavours for serving my country faithfully. To Him I resign myself and the just cause which it is entrusted to me to defend.

After he returned to the deck, Nelson was informed that Cape Trafalgar had been sighted. He then composed his most famous signal. At 11:35 there rose to the *Victory*'s yardarm: "England expects that every man will do his duty." There fol-

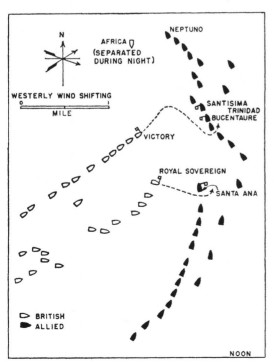

Battle of Trafalgar, 21 October 1805

lowed another, which remained flying until it was shot away: "Engage the enemy more closely."

The moment was at hand. About noon, while the *Victory* was still out of range and still relentlessly steering for the Allied van, Collingwood's division began the action. Instead of steering, as the Memorandum directed, to isolate the last 12 ships in the Allied line, Collingwood decided to cut off the last 16, thus opposing his 15 ships to a greater number. But he relied on superior British seamanship and gunnery, and in these expectations he was not disappointed. Nelson apparently approved, for as Collingwood bore down on the *Santa Ana*, he exclaimed, "See how that noble fellow Collingwood carries his ship into action!"

Collingwood's division by this time was no longer in column, but in line of bearing to the southwest. As the enemy's rear was curved toward the southwest, it made the two lines nearly parallel and brought Collingwood's ships into action much more rapidly than was possible for Nelson's, still in column. Within 15 minutes, eight of Collingwood's ships had broken through the Allied rear, and soon all were furiously engaging the enemy.

Meanwhile the French and Spanish admirals had broken their colors. Satisfied that his feint toward the van had prevented Villeneuve from interfering with Collingwood, and that it was too late for Dumanoir to counter his own attack, Nelson directed Thomas Hardy, captain of the *Victory*, to turn to starboard and make for the *Bucentaure*, Villeneuve's flagship. About 12:30, the *Victory* put her helm over and bore down. As she passed astern of the *Bucentaure*, she discharged her port broadside, causing a hundred casualties and unnerving Villeneuve. Behind the *Victory* in quick succession followed the *Téméraire, Neptune, Leviathan, Conqueror, Britannia, Ajax*, and *Agamemnon*.

Nelson, having successfully brought his fleet into action, quietly walked the quarterdeck of the *Victory* with his old friend Hardy. As was his custom in battle, Nelson wore his medals, making himself a conspicuous target. All around were scenes of horror and destruction. Blood flowed across the white decks and collected in streams in the scuppers. Nelson's secretary, standing near him, was struck and killed by a cannonball. "This is too warm work, Hardy," Nelson remarked, "to last long."

As they continued their stroll, Hardy suddenly noticed that he was alone. Turning, he saw Nelson collapsing on the deck. "They have done for me at last, Hardy," Nelson murmured. As he was borne below, he covered his face and medals with his handkerchief so that the men might not recognize

him and be disheartened. In the cockpit the surgeon could only confirm Nelson's diagnosis. A sharpshooter in the rigging of the *Redoutable* had picked him off, the ball passing through his shoulder, lung, and spine, and lodging in the muscles of his back. Five minutes later Villeneuve surrendered the *Bucentaure*. By such a narrow margin was Nelson deprived of receiving the submission of his rival.

While the action continued, Nelson in the *Victory*'s cockpit was kept informed of the progress of the battle. By a little after two the action in the center was nearly over. Eight French and Spanish ships had surrendered. In another hour Collingwood's division had won out in the rear, and Hardy hastened below to inform his dying leader. "I hope that none of our ships have struck," Nelson said.

"No, my Lord, there is no fear of that."

Then Hardy was summoned back to the quarterdeck to repulse the counterattack of Dumanoir, who by almost superhuman efforts, using his ships' boats as tugs to help him around, had come down from the van. Within 20 minutes this attack had failed, and Hardy went below to report to Nelson that 14 or 15 of the enemy had struck. "That is well," whispered Nelson, "but I had bargained for 20." Then Nelson's seaman's instinct came to the fore. He could feel from the motion of the vessel that the wind was freshening, and mindful of the crippled condition of the ships, friend and foe alike, and of the proximity of the dangerous lee shore of Trafalgar, he gave his last order: "Anchor, Hardy, anchor!"[1] Then growing weaker, he begged Hardy not to throw his body overboard, and with some flash of childhood's affection, asked Hardy to kiss him. Shortly afterward he murmured, "Thank God, I have done my duty. God and my Country." A moment later he was dead.

About the same time Dumanoir with four ships, and the mortally wounded Gravina with ten, pulled out of the fight, leaving the remainder as prizes to the British. The Battle of Trafalgar was over.

Napoleon's Continental System

Nelson's victory ended Napoleon's threat to invade England. The victory forever denied Napoleon the use of the sea; all his later campaigns were landbound. Without naval protection French overseas trade slackened to a virtual standstill while Britain's was free to expand. Britain now had the initiative to project her power via the sea to strike at any point

[1]Collingwood did not see fit to carry out this order. As a result all but five of the prizes were lost in the gale that sprang up after the battle.

on the coast of Europe where Napoleon might be vulnerable.

Napoleon, for his part, set out to make himself invulnerable and also to ruin England by bringing all continental Europe and all European trade under his control. A month after Trafalgar, his Grand Army crushed the Russian and Austrian armies at Austerlitz, thereby shattering the Third Coalition. Napoleon then went on to conquer southern Italy, rout the Prussian army, and defeat the Russians twice again. Instead of humbling the czar, he joined him in the Treaty of Tilsit, whereby France and Russia agreed to carve up Europe between them. He required Prussia, Austria, Denmark, and Portugal to align themselves with France.

In his Berlin Decree of November 1806, Napoleon set forth the essence of his Continental System for excluding England from European markets. The Decree declared the British Isles blockaded, closed every port under Napoleon's control to British vessels, and ordered all goods of British origin seized. Without the capability of keeping a fleet at sea, Napoleon defied the principle of international law that to be legal a blockade must be effective.

To contest this new form of economic warfare, Britain retaliated with Orders in Council declaring all French-controlled ports blockaded and permitting neutrals to trade through them only by calling first at an English port and paying duty on their cargoes and buying licenses before going on to their destinations. Thus the practical British made their economic war a paying proposition.

Napoleon's hope of starving the British Isles through the Berlin Decree proved futile. The effect of the Decree was to lend respectability to smuggling. Even the emperor was obliged to supply his soldiers with English overcoats and boots. Yet, refusing to abandon the blockade, in December 1807 he issued the Milan Decree, outlawing any neutral ships that submitted to British search or complied with the Order in Council by paying duties to Britain. All such ships were, he declared, lawful prize for his ever-increasing swarm of privateers. Napoleon's Continental System had become a contest of endurance—whether continental Europe could stand the strain of commercial isolation long enough to bring about the ruin of England.

British products began to pile up in British warehouses, and many British businesses failed, but development of new overseas markets prevented national bankruptcy. As time passed, the new markets—in Asia, Australia, New Zealand, South America, and the Caribbean—more than offset the losses resulting from the stoppage of trade with the Continent. Napoleon's blockade thus had the long-term effect of actually increasing British prosperity.

On the other hand, the Continental System ruined Napoleon. The countries of Europe, geared to the British economy, were impoverished without British trade. The good will Napoleon had garnered as the self-styled defender of the rights of man was dissipated as his decrees denied the Europeans the necessities of life. Attempts to enforce his System brought him into wars in the Iberian Peninsula and on the plains of Russia that swallowed up his armies. His attempts also provided the British Whale the opportunity to come ashore in the guise of a Lion.

The Peninsular War

Preparatory to closing the ports of Portugal, which provided a gap in his Continental System, Napoleon seized control of Spain, replacing the king with his brother Joseph. He thereby set off a rebellion that he was never able to subdue. Britain, responding to pleas of the Spaniards and the Portuguese, in August 1808 sent by sea to Portugal an army that quickly ousted the occupying French from that country. In October, 20,000 British soldiers under Lieutenant General Sir John Moore advanced from Portugal into Spain to join the Spaniards, who had forced the French occupying forces back to the River Ebro.

Napoleon reacted swiftly. He crossed the Pyrenees with heavy reinforcements, determined to chastise Spain, regain Lisbon, and drive the British into the sea. He scattered the Spaniards at Burgos and occupied Valladolid. When Moore arrived at Ciudad Rodrigo, he learned the appalling news that Napoleon's army, far outnumbering his own, stood between him and Burgos, his objective. Like other British generals who found themselves in hopeless situations, Moore, pursued by a French army of 50,000, raced with his forces to the nearest port, in this case Coruña, and called for support by the Royal Navy. In a brilliant rearguard action, Moore lost his life, but he got most of his troops on board transports and safely out to sea. Once again sea power had taken troops to the scene of action and pulled them out when they had to be evacuated.

Britain, having secured the means of coming to grips with Napoleon, had no intention of remaining out of the Iberian Peninsula. In April 1809, Lieutenant General Arthur Wellesley landed at Lisbon with 20,000 British troops, bolstered by

3,000 Hanoverians. Napoleon had now quitted Spain to deal with Austria, which had reentered the war against him, but in various parts of the peninsula there were more than 250,000 French troops.

As Wellesley took stock of the situation, he realized that the terrain of the peninsula favored a strategy based on the exploitation of sea power. His own army could be supplied and reinforced by sea far more easily than could the French by land through the rugged mountains (and rebellious population) of Spain.

Since the army he commanded was too weak to force a decision, Wellesley (newly created Viscount Wellington) concluded that he must make his base at Lisbon secure from any French attack. To that end he directed thousands of Portuguese workmen in constructing the celebrated lines of Torres Vedras—some 50 miles of trenches, breastworks, and redoubts across the approaches to the city. He then advanced to the Spanish border with an army of 18,000 British and 14,000 Portuguese.

As he had anticipated, Marshal André Masséna, with 65,000 French, took the field against him. Wellington fell back, over utterly scorched earth, to his prepared position behind the lines of Torres Vedras. One probing attack convinced Masséna that a serious attempt at penetrating the lines could only result in the slaughter of his troops. So he settled down to a siege—in a countryside that had been stripped of sustenance. As Masséna's men ate their pack animals, Wellington's army grew stronger, amply supplied by regular convoys from England. Sea power enabled one army to wax strong while another, almost within eyesight, starved to impotence.

Sheer hunger at last obliged the French to fall back, again traversing the scorched earth, with Wellington's army following. Masséna's fruitless campaign had cost him 25,000 men. The moral effect of his defeat spread throughout Europe and gave Wellington's men a psychological ascendancy they never lost. Their renewed advance was the beginning of a two-year march through Spain to France itself.

Napoleon's Russian Campaign

Since France could not supply the manufactured goods the Russians needed, they had to look elsewhere. Czar Alexander began to wink at the smuggling of British goods and freely allowed neutral ships to bring in British colonial products. Napoleon, rather than see his Continental System thus ignored, threatened Russia with war. An uneasy truce continued through 1811, with neither side

willing to back down. The czar, encouraged by Wellington's successes in the peninsula, remained defiant. Napoleon made up his mind accordingly to turn the power of his seven kingdoms and 30 principalities on Russia. On 23 June 1812, the vanguard of his Grand Army crossed the Nieman River, Russia's boundary with Poland. In all, some 600,000 men plunged into the vastness of the Russian plains.

The czar's generals counseled a policy of retreat and scorched earth. At last, in early September, the Russians took a stand at Borodino, 500 miles from the frontier and only 70 miles short of Moscow. In the bloodiest contest of the war, the Battle of Borodino, the Grand Army forced the Russians to retreat, but the fight had cost Napoleon 30,000 men.

Napoleon pressed on to Moscow, expecting that its capture would induce the Russians to ask for terms. Nothing of the sort happened. He found the city empty, and soon it was ablaze, ignited by unseen hands. The fire lasted several days, leaving Moscow a gutted shell.

After waiting five weeks for a surrender that never came, Napoleon on 18 October gave the order for the fatal retreat. The Grand Army, heading back toward western Europe, was shortly overwhelmed—partly by winter weather, partly by the Russian army, which raided but would not commit itself to pitched battle, partly by its own indiscipline in retreat, but most of all by lack of food for the soldiers and of fodder for the horses. Both men and animals faced starvation, and the losses were appalling. Large-scale straggling and a spirit of *sauve qui peut* destroyed all organization as the army vainly sought to live off the denuded countryside.

The Russian campaign ended in mid-December 1812. Of the 600,000 men who had invaded Russia in June, only 20,000 half-frozen scarecrows stumbled back across the Nieman.

The Defeat of Napoleon

Napoleon, having returned to Paris after a second time deserting an army in the East, worked miracles in raising new levies. Meanwhile, his setbacks in Spain and Russia encouraged Prussia, Sweden, and Austria to join Russia and Britain in a Fourth Coalition. The new coalition, at last realizing the necessity, achieved the coordination and unity of objective so conspicuously wanting in the earlier anti-French alliances. At Leipzig in October 1813, Napoleon turned upon his adversaries and in the Battle of the Nations suffered a resounding defeat.

With his shattered army he fell back into France. Outnumbered two to one, he could no longer replace losses. In the spring of 1814, the armies of Russia, Prussia, and Austria closed on Paris as Wellington entered Toulouse in southern France. Napoleon, exhausted in resource, in body, and in spirit, abdicated on 6 April 1814, and was exiled to the Island of Elba.

Less than a year later, owing to the follies of the restored Bourbons, Napoleon was able to slip back into France, rally an army of 200,000, and turn on the divided allies. He marched first toward Belgium to cut Wellington (now the duke of Wellington) off from the Prussians under Blücher. Wellington held his thin lines firm until they had broken the massed French troops. Blücher arrived in time to complete the rout. In Wellington, Napoleon had at last found his master. The Battle of Waterloo, 18 June 1815, saved Europe from further bloodshed. The end of the "Hundred Days" found the ex-emperor prostrate once again.

A month later, the man who had held Europe at his feet, but who had never understood sea power, surrendered, appropriately enough, to a unit of the force that had made his defeat possible. Boarding HMS *Bellerophon* off the Isle of Aix, he was received with no ceremony. "General Bonaparte" gave himself into the hands of the one nation that had opposed him throughout. This time there would be no return. His new place of exile was St. Helena, a small island in the South Atlantic. There, on 5 May 1821, he died, uncomprehending to the last how he, the greatest military genius Europe had ever produced, leading the largest armies the world had ever seen, had been defeated by "the nation of shopkeepers," whose strength lay in their ability to use the sea.

Summary

In the wars of the French Revolution and Empire, the British government, headed by William Pitt the Younger, returned to the Plan of the elder Pitt, that of acquiring and, if necessary, subsidizing allies on the Continent and using the Royal Navy to blockade and destroy the enemy's fleets and seaborne commerce, to attack the enemy's colonies, and to cooperate with allies by strikes around the enemy's periphery. In the course of the 22-year conflict, England formed four major coalitions (temporary alliances) with continental powers.

In the War of the First Coalition (1793–97), the Royal Navy demonstrated its superiority by blockading France and by defeating the French Brest fleet in the Battle of the First of June (1794).

France, by forming an alliance with Spain (1796) and by forcing Austria out of the war (1797), broke up the First Coalition; but a French plan to invade England was foiled by Jervis's victory over the Spanish fleet in the Battle of Cape St. Vincent (February 1797) and Duncan's victory over the Dutch fleet in the Battle of Camperdown (October 1797).

The War of the Second Coalition (1798–1800) was brought about by the failure of a renewed French attempt to come to grips with Britain. Bonaparte, entrusted with the project, chose to strike at the British Empire by leading an army against India via Egypt. The attempt, requiring him to use the sea, proved disastrous, for Nelson shattered the Toulon fleet in the Battle of the Nile (August 1798), thereby isolating Bonaparte and his army in Egypt, and encouraging Austria, Russia, and other powers to join Britain in a Second Coalition. In October 1799, however, Russia, suspicious of her allies, withdrew from the war. That same month Bonaparte returned secretly to France, where he quickly assumed control as First Consul. In 1800 his armies decisively defeated the Austrians at Marengo and Hohenlinden, forcing Austria out of the war and breaking up the Second Coalition.

Nelson, in sharp reaction to Bonaparte's attempt to undermine British sea power through the Armed Neutrality of Baltic nations, destroyed the Danish fleet in the Battle of Copenhagen (1801). Such British blows, however, were as indecisive as French efforts to dominate Britain. Deciding that the problem of the Elephant and the Whale was insoluble, Britain and France in March 1802 concluded the short-lived Peace of Amiens.

When it became apparent that Bonaparte had no intention of abiding by the terms of Amiens, Britain in 1803 declared war on France. The reaction of Bonaparte, now the Emperor Napoleon, was to make all-out preparations for a cross-Channel invasion of England. Complying with Napoleon's Grand Design, Villeneuve, commanding the Toulon fleet, eluded Nelson's blockade, picked up Spanish ships at Cadiz and, in an endeavor to attract British ships away from the Channel, crossed to the West Indies. The approach of Nelson in pursuit, however, induced Villeneuve to head back for Europe. Instead of going to the Channel, as Napoleon commanded, Villeneuve retired to Cadiz. When Napoleon ordered him out again, Nelson, on 21 October 1805, smashed his Combined Fleet in the Battle of Trafalgar.

Napoleon, using the army he had assembled to invade England, now struck at the Third Coalition, recently organized by Pitt. Following victories over the armies of Austria, Naples, Prussia, and Russia, he induced the czar to sign the Treaty of Tilsit, whereby France and Russia agreed to carve up Europe between them. Napoleon was now able to strike at Britain by putting greater emphasis on economic warfare. Through his Continental System, he undertook to exclude Britain from the trade of the Continent by closing all ports under his control to British goods and ordering all goods of British origin seized. To close the gaps in his System, he went to war with Spain and Portugal and, later, Russia. The war in the Iberian Peninsula contained a quarter million of his veteran troops and opened the way for a British army under Wellington to attack Napoleon's main forces and ultimately to invade France. Napoleon's invasion of Russia and his winter retreat from Moscow cost most of the 600,000-man army he had assembled in western Europe.

In the War of the Fourth Coalition (1813–15), Prussia, Sweden, and Austria joined Russia and Britain in defeating Napoleon's weakened forces and obliging him to abdicate. When he returned from exile on Elba, he was finally defeated in the Battle of Waterloo by the armies of Britain and Prussia and again exiled, this time under guard on the island of St. Helena in the South Atlantic.

In the Wars of the French Revolution and Empire the Royal Navy attained maturity in tactics under sail. Freed at last from the shackles of the Fighting Instructions, British commanders passed their ships through the enemy's line to break it up and bring on a melee. This was to their advantage because British gunnery reforms gave them not only a faster rate of fire but, by reducing the number of men required to work each gun, enabled them to fight port and starboard broadsides simultaneously. The melee, moreover, put a premium upon close-range fire and mutual support among ships, in both of which British captains were especially indoctrinated.

In the First of June and Camperdown battles, British penetration of the enemy's line served to cut off his retreat. In the Cape St. Vincent battle, the British achieved an advantage over the enemy by dividing their own fleet and moving each segment to the point where it was most needed. In the Battle of the Nile, Nelson made use of the wind to hold part of the enemy line out of battle while he concentrated his attack on another part. In the Battle of Trafalgar, Nelson had one division of his fleet attack the enemy rear while his other division feinted at the enemy van to hold it out of the battle and then attacked the enemy center.

Chapter 9
The Beginnings of the U. S. Navy

At the end of the War of the American Revolution, the weak central government of the United States had to deal with the problems of debt and depression without having the power to tax. In the circumstances Congress concluded that the Continental Navy was an expendable luxury and ordered it disbanded. By 1785 all U. S. warships had been sold or otherwise disposed of.

Officers and men of the Continental Navy returned to their peacetime pursuits in merchant shipping, but they soon found that in gaining independence they had forfeited privileges they had enjoyed as British subjects. The London government, applying the Navigation Acts to the United States, issued Orders in Council that barred Americans from the lucrative British West Indies trade and limited British imports from the United States to raw materials and naval stores.

To survive, the U. S. merchant marine had to search out new markets. A few hardy Yankee skippers early found their way to China. Others sought new European contacts. On the high seas the Americans learned what it meant to be no longer under the protection of the British flag. The China trade proved financially hazardous but not nearly so dangerous as commerce with southern Europe. For in the Mediterranean and outside the Straits of Gibraltar, U. S. merchant vessels had now become fair game for the seagoing Barbary cutthroats operating off the North African coast.

Capture of merchantmen was part of the notorious Barbary System, which extended back to medieval times. In the eighteenth century the Barbary States—Morocco, Algiers, Tunis, and Tripoli—were ruled by petty despots, and all but Morocco were held in the Ottoman Empire by a kind of feudal allegiance. For all of them, seizure of ships, ransom of captives, and tribute money were major sources of income. Seafaring nations could purchase immunity for their merchantmen by paying monetary tribute. Even Britain, France, and Holland, with navies powerful enough to smash the robbers' nests, paid the required protection money, partly because it was cheaper than convoy or going to war and partly because the System hampered commercial rivals. Ships of na-

tions too poor to pay, and lacking power to retaliate, were liable to capture whenever they entered waters patrolled by the Barbary corsairs.

In 1784 the Moroccans seized an American ship. The following year the Algerians captured two more and enslaved the crews. Morocco in 1786 sold the United States a treaty of immunity for the bargain price of $10,000, but Algiers could not be bought off so cheaply. Cynical London merchants were only too happy to see growing American competition thus checked. "If there were no Algiers," Benjamin Franklin reported one of them as saying, "it would be worth England's while to build one."

The desire for naval protection, particularly among the influential commercial classes, had a perceptible effect on the adoption of the U. S. Constitution in 1789. Though under the Constitution Congress was authorized "to provide and maintain a navy" and at last had the power to finance it through taxation, naval appropriations had to await the settling of more pressing problems, particularly the national debt. Political pressure for a fleet had diminished, moreover, because war between Portugal and Algiers had sealed the corsairs inside the Mediterranean.

Congress could and did favor American shipping by means of preferential tariffs and harbor duties. At the same time British West Indian planters, who had seen their slaves starve when American cattle, fish, and grain had been cut off, welcomed brigs and schooners from the United States that arrived in defiance of the Orders in Council. Even the London government, perceiving the necessity, chose to wink at this profitable smuggling. Thus encouraged, American shipping and shipbuilding boomed. In the first five years under the Constitution, U. S. merchant tonnage rose from 124,000 to 439,000.

Under the new government, naval affairs were administered by President Washington's secretary of war, General Henry Knox. As early as 1790 Knox, citing the continued enslavement of Americans by Algiers, requested the first estimates for a seagoing navy. Opposition in Congress, however, forced a suspension of all naval shipbuilding plans until 1793. Two events that year put an entirely new complexion on the matter. A truce between Portugal and Algiers permitted a corsair fleet to sail out into the Atlantic, where it promptly captured 11 American ships. France's declaration of war on Britain resulted in increasingly severe restrictions on neutral carriers. New British Orders in Council authorized stopping all neutral ships taking foodstuffs to France and all ships trading with the French West Indies, which had recently been thrown open to American trade. Retaliatory measures by the French government and captures by French privateers of American merchantmen trading with England or her possessions aggravated the situation. Thus spurred, the U. S. Congress turned to serious consideration of establishing a navy.

The Navy Act of 1794

Favoring the creation of a U. S. navy were the Federalists, led by President Washington's secretary of the treasury, Alexander Hamilton, and representing mainly the commercial interests of the Northeast. They were willing and anxious to protect their lucrative trade with the use of armed force.

Opposing the Federalists were the Republicans,[1] representing the artisans and landholders of the South and inland districts and headed by Secretary of State Thomas Jefferson. To them a navy was aristocratic, imperialistic, and prohibitively expensive. They argued, moreover, that the creation of a navy would mean taxing the whole country for the benefit of New England merchants and shippers.

With lines sharply drawn and debate raging in and out of Congress, the best legislation the Federalists could get passed was embodied in the Navy Act of 27 May 1794, which provided for the purchase or building of six frigates. It carried a cancellation clause in event of peace with Algiers. Inadequate as the Act was in the opinion of most Federalists, it established the U. S. Navy.

Knox, after consultation with naval officers and shipbuilders of the American Revolution, had decided to interpret the word "frigate" loosely. With the Algerians in mind, he planned to build outsize 44s, able to overmatch any Barbary frigate. What he intended was, in fact, a new type of warship, as long as a ship of the line but less broad of beam, more heavily armed than any standard frigate—capable of outrunning the one and of defeating the

other. Congress approved construction of only three of this class, however, specifying that the other three should be 36s.[2]

In 1796, when work on the frigates was well under way, the United States succeeded in getting a treaty from the Algerian ruler, at a cost of $525,000 in ransoms, a 36-gun frigate, and a $21,000 annual tribute in the form of naval stores. Congress nevertheless permitted completion of the *United States*, 44, the *Constellation*, 36, and the *Constitution*, 44. All were launched in 1797. The new 44-gun ships incorporated the theories and practices of many men, but because the final designs were completed under the direction of Joshua Humphreys, a Pennsylvania shipbuilder, they are often called "Humphreys frigates."

". . . not one cent for tribute!"

To the British it had become clear that they, as well as the French, were going to become increasingly dependent on American foodstuffs and American shipping to feed themselves and their colonies. Hence the London government began to take a more conciliatory attitude, opening the British West Indies to American trade, avoiding outright seizure of neutral vessels, and limiting seizure of cargoes to French property or goods the British considered contraband. They even permitted neutrals to ship goods between French possessions and French ports, provided such trade had been normal before the war and merchantmen engaged in the trade stopped at a neutral port and paid duty. The British thus limited and slowed down supplies to their enemy without attempting to halt them altogether. Toward the end of 1797 the United States and Great Britain codified their maritime relations in Jay's Treaty. The treaty provided no important concessions to U. S. maritime rights, but by providing for the elimination of old grievances on both sides it had the important effect of postponing warfare between the United States and Britain.

The French denounced the treaty as violating the 1778 Franco–American treaties of commerce and alliance. They were particularly incensed at the acknowledgment of foodstuffs as seizable contraband—at a time when a series of poor harvests had made France heavily dependent on the United States for grain.[3] In retaliation, the Directory contemptuously refused to receive the American

---

[1] Not to be confused with the present Republican Party of the United States, which is a lineal descendant of Hamilton's Federalist Party.

[2] It was the usual practice for a ship of war to carry more guns than her official "rate."

[3] The Battle of the First of June (1794), it will be recalled, resulted from French efforts to safeguard a large grain convoy en route from the Chesapeake.

minister to France, ordering him to leave the country, and issued a series of decrees of increasing harshness. These culminated in the decree of 18 January 1798, which stated: "Every vessel found at sea laden in whole or in part with merchandize coming from England or her possessions shall be declared good prize." As paraphrased by a French politician, "If a handkerchief of English origin is found on board a neutral vessel, both the rest of the cargo and the ship itself are subject to condemnation."

The decree made most American shipping fair and very profitable game for French privateers that swarmed in the West Indies, whence they cruised the U. S. Atlantic coast seeking victims. In a single year they seized more than 300 American merchant ships.

The insult to America's representative, the decrees, and the resultant seizures of American vessels were ample justification for war. But what really aroused the U. S. public to a fighting pitch was the notorious X Y Z Affair. In an attempt to head off war, President Adams in the fall of 1797 sent to Paris three commissioners with instructions to secure a treaty—a French version of Jay's Treaty. The American envoys, never officially recognized, were met by anonymous go-betweens (Messrs. X, Y, and Z) from French foreign minister Talleyrand. These proxies demanded bribes and "loans" amounting to several million dollars as the price for opening negotiations. When this piece of effrontery became known in the United States, all but the most ardent Francophiles were disillusioned. Popular indignation was expressed in the slogan "Millions for defense, but not one cent for tribute," which caught the public's fancy in an outburst of patriotic fervor that swept Congress and country.[4]

The United States was now in a mood to take positive action. Early in 1798 Congress voted to complete the frigates *President*, 44, *Congress*, 36, and *Chesapeake*, 36, on which work had been stopped. On 30 April, Congress created the Navy Department. In May it authorized the seizure of "armed vessels under authority or pretense of authority from the Republic of France" in American coastal waters. In July it extended authorization of American warships or privateers to "subdue, seize and take any armed French vessel" anywhere on the high seas. Thus the United States was launched

into a limited, undeclared war—the Quasi-War with France.

As first secretary of the navy, President Adams selected Benjamin Stoddert, a 47-year-old merchant shipper of Georgetown, Maryland, who had served in the War of the American Revolution and in the Continental Congress. Given control over administration, logistics, and operations, Stoddert performed with distinction throughout the Quasi-War. His first task was to put the Navy on a wartime footing. His second was to build up the fleet, to obtain more ships to fight the war and the crews to man them. His chief source for both was the merchant marine. By the war's end he had a fleet of 50 vessels, obtained through purchase, new construction, gifts from the states, and cooperation of the Treasury Department's revenue cutters.[5] By that time there were in the Navy 154 commissioned officers, more than 350 midshipmen, and some 6,000 seamen. The Marine Corps, reestablished in 1798, numbered nearly 1,100.

Operations of the Quasi-War, 1798–1800

Shortly after the original congressional authorization, Stoddert had his warships out patrolling the Atlantic coast. The first American prize was the privateer *Croyable*, 12, captured in July 1798 off New Jersey by the ex–merchant ship *Delaware*, 20, whose commanding officer was Captain Stephen Decatur, father of the more famous son of the same name, who was then serving as a midshipman on board another American vessel. The *Croyable* was taken into the U. S. Navy as the schooner *Retaliation*, 14.

Following the July authorization by Congress to extend operations and to capture French warships, Stoddert sent a series of expeditions to the West Indies, where most of the privateers were based. The first expedition, commanded by Commodore[6] John Barry, senior officer of the new navy, comprised the *United States* and the *Delaware*. The expedition captured only a couple of privateers, not through lack of zeal, but because there were no French warships present and most of the privateers were shallow-draft vessels that skipped away into shoal water to elude capture.

The second expedition, arriving in the West Indies in the fall of 1798, included the *Retaliation* (ex-*Croyable*), commanded by Lieutenant William

---

[4]Bribery was much practiced in eighteenth-century diplomacy and international relations. While the American public was crying, "Not one cent for tribute," the U. S. government was paying tribute to all four Barbary powers.

[5]Ancestor of the U. S. Coast Guard, which normally serves with the U. S. Navy in time of war.

[6]Barry was a captain, the highest rank in the U. S. Navy until the Civil War. *Commodore* was an honorary title, assumed by an officer commanding a company of ships.

Bainbridge, an officer destined to suffer more than his share of hard luck. Sent to investigate strange sails off Guadeloupe, his vessel was captured by a pair of French frigates, the *Insurgente*, 36, and the *Volontaire*, 44. Overwhelmingly outgunned, Bainbridge had no choice but to surrender. The *Retaliation* was the only U. S. warship taken by the enemy during the war. The following year the Americans had the satisfaction of capturing her again from the French.

When American coastal waters had been swept clear of raiders, Stoddert sent the greater part of his forces, some 21 ships organized in four squadrons, to operate in the West Indies. Here they had an enormous advantage over the French, because British victories in the battles of Cape St. Vincent, Camperdown, and the Nile had left France and her allies cut off from the New World colonies. The only French men-of-war of any consequence to elude British vigilance and reach American waters were occasional fast frigates maintaining uncertain communications between France and her remaining West Indies possessions.

The American squadrons had the free use of numerous British ports and bases and the full support and cooperation of the Royal Navy. They also had the inestimable benefit, for a fledgling fleet, of serving with the finest navy in the world when it was at the height of its readiness. From this period of friendly contact with the British fleet, the U. S. Navy acquired its basic signal systems, its general plan of maneuver in formation, and the beginnings of a professional attitude.

The most influential of the American commodores was Thomas Truxtun, a stern and tireless drillmaster who sought to mold his own navy on the British model. A master of his profession, he had published a manual of celestial navigation and the first complete signal book in the U. S. Navy. In his frigate *Constellation* he fought the two most famous actions of the Quasi-War.

On taking command of his squadron, based on St. Kitts, Truxtun ordered all ships to patrol independently when not engaged in convoy escort. It was while on independent patrol with the *Constellation* off Nevis in February 1799 that he made the contact that led to the first of his famous battles. (See map, p. 44.)

Sighting a sail 15 miles to leeward in a strong northwest wind, Truxtun took a converging course in order to close and investigate. The stranger was at length seen to be a frigate. She was in fact the *Insurgente*, one of the captors of Bainbridge's *Retaliation*. Considered the fastest frigate in the French navy, she might have made good her escape but for an untimely accident. The wind suddenly rising to gale force, the *Constellation* managed to shorten sail in time, but the *Insurgente* lost her main topmast. The American frigate now closed rapidly. With his vessel heeling far over under her spread of canvas, Truxtun chose the leeward position in order to have continuous use of his main battery of 24-pounders. Bringing the *Constellation* up on the lee quarter of the *Insurgente*, he fired a double-shotted broadside into her hull.

The French frigate quickly returned the *Constellation*'s fire, aiming high but doing only moderate damage to her rigging—and almost none to her hull. The *Insurgente* presently wore in an attempt to board, but the *Constellation* forged ahead and across her bow, delivering a raking fire. After a running cannonade on parallel courses, the *Constellation* once more crossed her opponent's bow and raked again. Then, falling off, she crossed her stern, ready for a third rake. At that, the French captain, observing his situation to be hopeless, his decks littered with dead and wounded, hauled down his colors.

The French had suffered 29 killed and 41 wounded. Three Americans were wounded and one was killed, not by the enemy but by his own division officer for deserting his gun. The *Constellation* had a greater weight of broadside than her opponent, and the French captain blamed his defeat on this disadvantage and the early loss of his topmast. The fact remains, however, that the Americans clearly outsailed, outmaneuvered, and outfought their enemy. The *Insurgente* carried nearly a hundred more men than the *Constellation*, but she could never make full use of them, because Truxtun saw to it that they had no opportunity for boarding.

Almost exactly a year later, Truxtun fought his second battle in the *Constellation*. He was cruising off Guadeloupe when he sighted a large vessel and gave chase. She proved to be the 50-gun frigate *Vengeance*, bound for France with passengers and specie and anxious to avoid battle. After a day-long pursuit, Truxtun in darkness worked the *Constellation* up to his enemy's weather quarter and commenced, as he described it, "as close and as sharp an action as ever was fought between two frigates," an action lasting nearly five hours.

In a fruitless attempt to escape, the Frenchmen fired at the *Constellation*'s spars and rigging. The Americans fired low, penetrating the hull of the *Vengeance* with more than 200 shot. A hundred of her ship's company were killed or wounded, and her hull began filling with water. Her captain tried desperately to surrender, but in the darkness and amid the roar of battle the Americans neither saw his flag nor heard his hail.

When toward 1 a.m. the French fire was completely silenced, the American frigate was almost stripped of rigging, and 40 of her crew were casualties. Before she could move in to take her prize, her mainmast, all shrouds and stays cut, snapped off at the deck. Midshipman James Jarvis, commanding the main top, had been warned of his danger but refused to leave his post without orders, remarking to the topmen that if the mast went they must go with it—and so they did, only one man being saved.

By the time the wreckage on the *Constellation* had been cleared away, the *Vengeance* was nowhere to be seen, and Truxtun conjectured she had sunk. But she had merely drifted off in the darkness, her crew and passengers desperately pumping and bailing in order to stay afloat. With only the stumps of her mizzen and foremast standing, she arrived at Curaçao five days later and ran her riddled hull aground to avoid sinking. Her captain reported that he had engaged a ship of the line.

Busiest of all the American warships in the undeclared war was the "lucky little *Enterprise*." Built specifically for her task, this swift, shallow-draft, 12-gun schooner outdid the frigates in protecting trade and capturing enemy ships. During one cruise she took 5 privateers (one a 12-gun brig), dismasted a 12-gun lugger, and freed 11 captured American merchant vessels.

The most far-ranging of the American men-of-war was the frigate *Essex*, 32, Captain Edward Preble, which proceeded via the Cape of Good Hope to the East Indies. Here she recaptured several American merchantmen before escorting a merchant convoy back home.

The last battle of the Quasi-War was fought after U. S. and French representatives had concluded a convention of peace. On 12 October 1800, some 600 miles northeast of Guadeloupe, the U. S. frigate *Boston*, 28, unaware that the war was over, attacked the corvette *Berceau*, 24, which was equally uninformed, and forced her to surrender.

Throughout the war, President Adams had disappointed his more hotheaded supporters by continuing to seek agreement with France. Talleyrand was equally anxious to come to terms, having no desire to drive the United States into further concert with the British. Moreover, blockaded France desperately needed the cooperation of American shipping to maintain the economy of her West Indies possessions.

Opposition within the United States delayed the sending of a commission during the period when Bonaparte was stranded in Egypt and France was on the verge of collapse. When the commissioners finally reached Paris in March of 1800, Bonaparte was in power as First Consul, and shortly afterward he gave the death blow to the Second Coalition by defeating the Austrians at Marengo. In this atmosphere, the best terms the commissioners were able to obtain in the Convention of Peace were less than satisfactory to most Americans. As finally ratified in July 1801, the agreement annulled the embarrassing Franco-American treaties of 1778 and the obnoxious French decree of 1798, but the price was high—nothing less than cancellation of all claims against France for spoliations of American commerce.

Announcement of the terms of the Convention, coming on the eve of the 1800 national elections, cost Adams the presidency. Jefferson and his Republicans took over the administration and won a substantial majority in Congress.

Nevertheless, a great deal had been accomplished. Hostilities were ended. The French government had promised to remain within the bounds of prize law. American warships, by defeating their equals and capturing more than 80 French vessels had given the world a convincing demonstration that the U. S. Navy was a force to be reckoned with. And the way was opened for the purchase of Louisiana by the United States in 1803. Part of the price to France was the assumption by the U. S. government of the $7,000,000 in French debts to American citizens acknowledged by the unpopular 1800 convention.

The War with Tripoli, 1801–5

Congress now voted to reduce the Navy to a peacetime establishment, and President Jefferson willingly carried out the reduction. All the American warships were sold except the *Enterprise* and 13 frigates, and 7 of the latter were laid up in reserve. The naval officer corps was correspondingly reduced, and the officers remaining on duty had their pay cut sharply.

But the Barbary powers, by their demands and insolence, once more saved the Navy. The rulers of Tripoli and Tunis demanded more tribute. When the U. S. frigate *George Washington* arrived at Algiers to deliver the annual tribute and lay under the guns of the Algerian forts, the dey pressed her temporarily into his own service. By threatening to sink the ship and enslave the crew, he induced her captain, that hard-luck officer William Bainbridge, to sail under Algerian colors, carrying to Constantinople 200 passengers, as many animals, and a million dollars' worth of gifts—the dey's own tribute to his suzerain, the sultan.

When the increased tribute demanded by the pasha of Tripoli was not forthcoming, he declared war Barbary-style by having his men chop down the American consul's flagpole. Jefferson recognized the futility of trying to meet the escalating Barbary demands. To protect American shipping, he sent to the Mediterranean in the spring of 1801 a squadron consisting of the frigates *President, Philadelphia,* and *Essex* and the schooner *Enterprise,* under the command of Richard Dale, who had been John Paul Jones's first lieutenant in the *Bonhomme Richard.*

Making his base at Gibraltar with the permission of the British governor, Dale visited Algiers and Tunis for a display of force, and late in July 1801 blockaded the port of Tripoli. After 18 days, however, he was obliged to lift his blockade and retire to Malta for water.

En route, the 12-gun *Enterprise* encountered a Tripolitan corsair, the *Tripoli,* 14. In a close engagement, the *Enterprise* nimbly sidestepped enemy attempts at boarding and several times raked her opponent. After three hours the *Tripoli* was helpless, her crew begging for mercy. Twenty of them had been killed, 30 wounded. Not a man on board the *Enterprise* was injured, and the lucky little schooner had suffered no material damage to hull or rigging. Lieutenant Andrew Sterrett, captain of the *Enterprise,* having no authority to take prizes, ordered the *Tripoli* stripped to a single spar and a rag of sail and cast adrift.

Congress, deciding to push the war with greater vigor, in 1801 appropriated funds for fitting out a larger Mediterranean squadron. Thomas Truxtun was offered the new command but refused it because he was denied the normal and sensible arrangement of having a captain to command his flagship. Secretary of the Navy Robert Smith chose to interpret Truxtun's refusal as resignation from the service, thereby discarding an officer who had done more than most to mold the U. S. Navy into a professional team.

In Truxtun's place Smith appointed Richard Morris, who arrived in the Mediterranean in the spring of 1802 with five frigates and some smaller vessels. He blockaded Tripoli, but with indifferent success, because he lacked shallow-draft vessels that could attack the small, shoal-hugging Tripolitan freighters. His squadron did, however, capture one Tripolitan corsair, destroyed another with gunfire, and burned some beached coasting vessels. Then Morris, thinking he had done well enough, lifted the blockade and went off to watch

the other Barbary powers. He had failed to induce the pasha of Tripoli to lower his price for peace: $200,000 and reimbursement for all costs of the war. Before the summer was over, Secretary Smith curtly ordered Morris back to the United States for his "inactive and dilatory conduct," and President Jefferson dismissed him from the service.

The third squadron, sent to the Mediterranean in 1803, included only two frigates, the *Constitution* and the *Philadelphia,* which were intended mainly to back up the work of five shallow-draft brigs and schooners. For commodore of the new squadron Secretary Smith selected a very junior captain, 42-year-old Edward Preble.

A hot-tempered down-Mainer, Preble was a taut disciplinarian. He was scarcely known to his officers, for they were mostly from the central and southern states, and Preble, as we have noted, spent the Quasi-War cruising in the *Essex* to the Far East and back, a voyage that had impaired his health and done nothing to improve his temper. After experiencing the rough side of Preble's tongue, most of his officers took a strong dislike to their commodore. Preble, for his part, was dismayed to find that not one of his commanding officers was as much as 30 years old. "They have given me nothing but a bunch of boys!" he was reported as saying.

In mid-August 1803 Preble sailed for the Mediterranean in the *Constitution.* The crossing was uneventful, but one night as the frigate was approaching the Straits of Gibraltar a display of spirit by the new commodore won him the respect of every officer in his squadron. Observing a strange vessel looming through the darkness, Preble had his crew silently brought to quarters and then gave a routine hail, "What ship is that?" After repeatedly failing to get a satisfactory answer, Preble threatened to open fire, whereupon the stranger announced disdainfully: "This is His Britannic Majesty's ship *Donegal,* 84 guns, Sir Richard Strachan, an English commodore. Send your boat on board!"

Replied Preble, leaping upon the nettings: "This is the United States ship *Constitution,* 44 guns, Edward Preble, an American commodore, who will be damned before he sends his boat on board of any vessel! Blow your matches, boys."

The strange vessel, which turned out to be a 32-gun British frigate, now quickly sent a boat with an apology and the explanation that her captain had been stalling for time to bring his men to quarters. That settled the matter amicably and the frigates soon drew apart, but the crew of the *Constitution* was deeply impressed that their commodore had been perfectly willing to attack a ship of the line. This incident marked a turning point in Preble's relations with his subordinates. They gradually realized that he was a sick man, driving himself by almost superhuman will to carry out his orders. His young officers were soon proud to be known as "Preble's boys," a title they carried into the War of 1812, in which nearly every one of them made a distinguished name for himself.

On arriving at Gibraltar, Preble found the *Philadelphia* with a Moroccan corsair that she had taken at sea together with a captured American merchantman. Evidently Morocco, in violation of treaty commitments to the United States, was again preying on American vessels. Commodore Preble at once took countermeasures. Sending the *Philadelphia* and the schooner *Vixen* on ahead under Captain Bainbridge to blockade Tripoli, he appeared before the Moroccan port of Tangier with a powerful force, including frigates of the squadron he was relieving. The emperor of Morocco, impressed by this display of strength, disavowed the capture and reaffirmed his treaty with the United States without further payment. Preble, having thus assured the safety of his supply ships arriving from across the Atlantic, proceeded to cruise in the Mediterranean.

Meanwhile, "Hard Luck Bill" Bainbridge got into trouble again.

Preble had sent the *Vixen* along with the *Philadelphia* not only for inshore work but also for mutual support. But Bainbridge, learning that a pair of Tripolitan corsairs were out cruising, made the mistake of detaching the *Vixen* to look for them while he remained in the *Philadelphia* off Tripoli. Subsequently he caught sight of one of the corsairs trying to slip into the harbor and gave chase. But the corsair hugged the shallows where the frigate could not follow and made her way to safety.

Turning back toward open water, the *Philadelphia* drove hard onto an uncharted reef at such an angle of heel that neither of her broadsides could be brought to bear on the Tripolitan gunboats that soon swarmed around her. With the *Vixen* gone, the *Philadelphia* was helpless. Bainbridge and his men tried various means to work their ship loose— setting a heavy press of sail, pulling on anchors, and finally heaving overboard guns and chopping down the foremast in a vain attempt to escape by lightening ship.

Luckily for them, the Tripolitans restricted their fire mainly to the frigate's masts and rigging— to prevent her escape, to capture the Americans alive to hold for ransom, and to secure the frigate undamaged for their fleet. But Bainbridge was una-

ware that his ship's company was in little danger of being killed. Observing reinforcements, including the ketch *Mastico*, coming out from Tripoli, he had his signal books and ammunition thrown overboard and then struck his colors. That evening he and his crew were led triumphantly into the city to begin a long imprisonment. Two days later, high water during a gale enabled the Tripolitans to free the *Philadelphia* from her reef. They also fished up and remounted all her guns.

Preble learned the bad news from a passing frigate while cruising off Sardinia in late November. It was a staggering blow. Possession of the *Philadelphia* gave the Tripolitans a naval force at least as great as his own, but Preble did not even consider falling back on Gibraltar to await reinforcements. Instead he established himself at Syracuse, Sicily, a central position from which he could both police the Mediterranean and maintain his blockade.

In December Preble sailed with the *Constitution* and the *Enterprise* to reconnoiter. On making landfall off the African coast, his lookouts sighted the *Mastico*, just out of Tripoli. The *Enterprise* gave chase and took possession. When the Americans were informed that the ketch had participated in the capture of the *Philadelphia*, they declared her lawful prize and took her into the U. S. Navy as the *Intrepid*.

From outside the reef off Tripoli harbor, Preble observed that the *Philadelphia* lay under the guns of the pasha's castle and within easy range of shore batteries and nearby armed vessels. He concluded that it would not be possible to recapture her, but there was a chance she could be destroyed. Lieutenant Stephen Decatur, Jr., the youthful captain of the *Enterprise*, agreed and volunteered to lead an expedition to do the destroying. Preble accepted Decatur's offer and also his suggestion that he use the *Intrepid* (ex-*Mastico*) because her Mediterranean rig would serve as a passport into Tripoli harbor. The plunderer of the *Philadelphia* was thus to be the instrument of her destruction.

On the evening of 16 February 1804, the *Intrepid*, to all outward appearances a native ketch, coasted into Tripoli harbor on a dying wind. At the helm was Salvador Catalano, a Sicilian pilot who knew the roadstead and could speak Arabic. Decatur, in Maltese garb, stood at his side. All but a half dozen of the volunteer crew were concealed below decks. Presently the hull of the *Philadelphia* became visible in the dim light of a crescent moon. Hailed and warned to keep off, Catalano, at Decatur's dictation, stated that his vessel had lost her anchors in a storm and requested permission to tie up alongside for the night. The request being granted, the lines were being passed when something aroused the Tripolitans' suspicion. As the vessels touched there was a cry of "Americanos!"

"Board!" shouted Decatur, and 60 Americans swarmed onto the *Philadelphia*. There were too few guards on board the frigate to put up a fight. Decatur and his men, using sabers and battle-axes, killed four or five and drove the rest overboard. Meanwhile, demolition parties were bringing combustibles from the *Intrepid*. These they distributed about the *Philadelphia* and ignited. The frigate, sunbaked in Tripoli harbor, caught fire and burned like tinder. Some of the demolition teams deep in the hold barely made it back up the ladders, but all boarders at length regained the *Intrepid*. Decatur himself, last to get off the blazing ship, leaped into the rigging of the ketch as she pulled away.

By towing with boats and using sweeps, the crew managed to extricate the *Intrepid*, her sails barely drawing in the light offshore breeze and her path lighted by the great torch of the burning *Philadelphia*. The Tripolitan warships and shore batteries opened a wild and erratic fire, but the *Intrepid* slipped out the way she had come. The *Philadelphia* burned to the waterline, went adrift, and sank. Decatur's exploit won him a captain's commission and fame at home and abroad. At 25 he became the youngest captain in the history of the U. S. Navy. The crew of the *Intrepid* received two months' extra pay.

The following summer, Preble borrowed gunboats and mortar boats from the Kingdom of Naples, which was also at war with Tripoli, and undertook to bombard the enemy into submission. At the first attack in early August, the U. S. squadron took the forts, batteries, and fleet under fire, while the mortars lobbed shells into the walled city. At the same time the borrowed gunboats, with Neapolitan crews and American boarding parties, approached the reef, outside of which a line of Tripolitan boats was on guard. Eleven of the enemy boats advanced and ganged up on four boats led by Stephen Decatur. The Tripolitans, scimitar in hand, were poised to board and fight hand to hand across decks, a style of warfare at which they were experienced and for which they were justly feared.

But this time it was their opponents who did the boarding. The Tripolitans had never seen anything like it. Even before the boats touched, the Americans, whooping like Indians, were leaping across, firing pistols, poking with boarding pikes, or swinging cutlasses and battle-axes.

From Stephen Decatur's boat 19 Americans leaped into an enemy boat and quickly subdued the 19 defenders. Decatur had a narrow escape when he broke off the blade of his cutlass against the pike of a big Tripolitan. He then seized the pike and wrestled the big fellow to the deck, whereupon another Tripolitan swung a scimitar at Decatur's head. A seaman, Daniel Frazier, too wounded in the arms to hold a weapon, warded off the blow by thrusting his own head under the descending scimitar. The Tripolitan grappling with Decatur now rolled him under and drew a knife. Decatur managed to hold his opponent's knife hand with his own left, while drawing from an inside pocket a pistol, which he fired into the fellow's back.

At length Preble signaled recall, and as the *Constitution* advanced to cover the gunboats' retirement, the Tripolitans fled back through the reef, leaving three of their boats in American hands. In the captured boats were 47 dead Tripolitans, and of the 49 prisoners taken about half were wounded. Only four Americans, including Frazier, were seriously wounded, and the only American killed was Stephen Decatur's younger brother James, who was treacherously shot in the head when he came to take possession of an enemy boat that had hauled down its flag in the face of heavy American musket fire.

Following this attack, the pasha offered to settle for $150,000 in ransom money and no further tribute. This was a far better offer than the first or second Mediterranean squadrons had been able to exact, but it was not good enough for Preble. He ordered the attacks resumed, specifying, in view of the Tripolitan treachery in killing James Decatur, that in hand-to-hand fighting there was to be no granting of quarter. The specification was unnecessary. During the next few weeks, the Americans made four more attacks, but the enemy gunboats never again came from behind their reef. On the other hand, the pasha refused to lower his price.

As a last resort, before the season of bad weather drove the squadron from before Tripoli, Preble employed a bomb vessel to blow up the remnant of Tripoli's naval and commercial shipping and possibly blast in the city wall. The *Intrepid*, again selected, was loaded with five tons of bulk powder and sent in on the evening of 4 September manned by Lieutenant Richard Somers, Midshipmen Henry Wadsworth and Joseph Israel, and ten seaman volunteers. These men were to place the ketch near the pasha's castle, light a fuse, board two small boats, and row rapidly away. The ketch blew up prematurely, killing her crew and doing little damage to the enemy. The cause is unknown, but the three officers had declared that rather than have the powder captured by the Tripolitans they would blow up the *Intrepid* with all hands.

With Preble's vigorous prosecution of hostilities, the long-drawn-out war had gained stature in American opinion. A final heavy thrust might now win a victory, restore peace, and end the payment of tribute—not only to Tripoli but also to the other Barbary states, which presumably would be over-awed. To that end the most powerful American naval force yet assembled began arriving in the Mediterranean: the frigates *John Adams, President,* and *Constellation* and smaller vessels, with more to follow.

On board the *President* was Captain Samuel Barron, considerably Preble's senior. The secretary of the navy sent Preble a letter praising his services but pointing out that seniority must prevail. Preble was ordered back to the United States, where President Jefferson received him with warmth and distinction. At Preble's urging the government accelerated the construction of gunboats for inshore work against Tripoli. That was his last service to his country. His health further declining, he died in August 1807 at the age of 46.

Neither Barron nor his successor, John Rodgers, improved upon Preble's efforts, other than to countenance and assist in a political venture to unseat the pasha, who had usurped the throne from his elder brother Hamet. A firebrand named William Eaton, who had come out as Navy Agent to the Barbary States, located Hamet and his followers and readily induced them to invade Tripolitan territory. In early March 1805 a ragtag army of 400 set out from Alexandria under "General" Eaton. Spearheading the force were a midshipman, a noncommissioned officer, and seven marines under Lieutenant Presley O'Bannon—all from the brig *Argus*, which had brought Eaton to Egypt.

In a trouble-filled, 600-mile march across the Libyan desert, Hamet's army was gradually swelled by adherence of desert tribesmen to more than 700 fighting men and 500 camp followers, including women and children. Toward the end of April this motley horde reached the Tripolitan coastal town of Derna, which they captured in joint operations with two brigs and a schooner from Barron's squadron. They held this position for several weeks and had beaten off a number of counterattacks when word came that the war was over.

The pasha, trembling for his throne, had at last capitulated. In return for American withdrawal of support for Hamet, he agreed to abandon his pretensions to tribute, and release Bainbridge and his

crew for a mere $60,000 ransom. When Eaton protested, it was pointed out to him that no nation had ever obtained more favorable terms from a Barbary power, and that the pasha, if forced to relinquish his crown, would doubtless exact advance vengeance by massacring his American prisoners.

Jefferson's Gunboat Navy

President Jefferson and his Republican Party wished to remain aloof from Old World quarrels. A navy that displayed offensive potentialities made the Republicans uneasy. A navy capable only of defending the American coastline could offend no one, and so Jefferson turned his back on the blue-water concept. In early 1803, fifteen small gunboats were authorized, each to carry one or two guns. In 1805, twenty-five more were authorized. Since this was the only American naval construction during the war period, Jefferson's pacific intentions were advertised to the world.

In time of peace most of the gunboats would be laid up. At outbreak of hostilities they would be distributed along the coast from Maine to Louisiana. To repel an invasion they would cooperate with stationary land fortifications, artillery, and floating batteries.

History has shown that such passive defense is almost useless against a determined invader backed by naval firepower and able to pick his point of assault. Even supposing the scattered gunboats could be brought together quickly enough to oppose an invasion, they were defensively too weak to stand up against thick-sided frigates or ships of the line. Moreover, the gunboat policy made no provision for carrying out such vital functions as backing up foreign policy, breaking a blockade, or protecting maritime commerce. It thus ignored the lessons of the Revolution and of subsequent American experience. Yet this fatuous policy reached its height just when the Americans had become virtually the only neutral traders on the high seas and when Britain and the French Empire, in their final struggle for survival, were each taking drastic steps to isolate the other from the rest of the world.

Summary

The U. S. Navy, established ten years after the American Revolution, came into being to protect America's expanding maritime trade. The enabling legislation, the Navy Act of 1794, was passed ostensibly to protect American merchantmen and their crews from capture by the North African corsairs. But the immediate justification was the outbreak of war between Britain and France and the operations of each to curtail American trade with the other. Supporting the establishment of a seagoing Navy was the Federalist Party, led by Hamilton and representing the commercial interests of the East. Opposing it was the Republican Party, led by Jefferson and representing the agrarian interests of the South and West.

As difficulties with the North African states subsided, the building of six frigates as provided by the 1794 Act was to be discontinued, but in response to mounting interference with American shipping by Britain and France, Congress permitted the completion of three. The United States came to terms with Britain in Jay's Treaty, but this agreement served only to inflame the French government, which insulted American representatives and began confiscating American ships carrying goods of British origin. As a result, Congress in 1798 resumed naval construction, established the Navy Department, and launched the Navy on an undeclared war against armed French vessels—the Quasi-War with France (1798–1801), fought mainly in the West Indies.

The victories of the Quasi-War, particularly those of Truxtun in the *Constellation*, aroused the pride of the American public in the new navy and assured the permanence of the Navy Department. But the pro-Navy and anti-Navy factions drew different conclusions from the war. The Federalists were aware that the Navy's moderate successes had been made possible by the overseas victories of Britain's ships of the line, which isolated France from her colonies. They agreed with Secretary Stoddert that the United States needed a bigger navy. From the Republican point of view, the war proved the sufficiency of a small, cruiser navy. The Republicans, in office at the conclusion of peace, forthwith stripped the Navy down to minimum size.

The pasha of Tripoli's declaration of war forced President Jefferson to send a series of naval squadrons to the Mediterranean. Here hostilities dragged out over four years (1801–5), partly because of temporizing and misplaced economizing by the Republican government and partly through lack of aggressiveness by the early squadron commanders. The war took on a new vigor in 1803 when Preble arrived in the Mediterranean. The burning of the captured *Philadelphia* in the teeth of Tripolitan defenses aroused the enthusiasm of the American public. Assisted by ardent young officers like Decatur, Preble established a base at Syracuse and in 1804 clapped a tight blockade on Tripoli and staged a series of naval assaults against the city, fortifications, and shipping. The U. S. administration, stimulated at last into action, finally sent adequate naval forces to the Mediterranean. Though Preble was superseded, he had paved the way for a treaty requiring no further payment of tribute to Tripoli.

The Republicans, still in office at the conclusion of the Tripolitan War, drew from it the astonishing conclusion that the United States and American interests could be adequately defended by gunboats operating in cooperation with artillery and fortifications ashore. For the next few years all appropriations for naval construction were diverted to the building of more and more gunboats. At the same time Napoleon was issuing new decrees and the British were putting forth new Orders in Council so severely restrictive to neutral shipping that the U. S. Navy would soon be forced into a war for which it was materially unprepared.

Yet, despite the crippling Republican policies, the U. S. Navy preserved two advantages that were to make American naval operations in the War of 1812 among the most memorable in the nation's history: first, the finest ships of their type in the world, notably the *Constitution*-class frigates, and, second, a corps of skilled officers, thoroughly imbued with the ideals and attitudes of a professional service.

Chapter 10
The War of 1812

In the post-Trafalgar period the intensifying commerce warfare between Britain and France left the United States the only major neutral trader on the high seas. American merchant shippers enjoyed unprecedented prosperity both in the general carrying trade and as exporters of American wheat, tobacco, and cotton. At the same time U. S. merchantmen and even naval vessels, caught between Britain's Orders in Council and Napoleon's retaliatory decrees, were subjected to increasing interference that eventually grew intolerable. When at last in 1812 the people of the United States again took up arms in defense of their neutral rights, they chose Britain as their antagonist because French ships had been virtually driven from the seas. The declaration of war itself was the result of no specific new incident. It was rather an explosive reaction to tensions built up through years of friction with the Royal Navy and of bitter feelings aggravated by British support of marauding Indian tribes in America.

Warships of the Royal Navy, constantly in and out of American harbors to victual and to gather information on French privateers or merchant ship movements, flaunted their power. Most galling was their practice of pressing seamen from American ships. British naval officers, operating with undermanned crews that were further depleted by desertions, insisted on the right to search neutral vessels for British subjects. In their desperate need for men, they were likely to consider as an Englishman anybody who understood the English language.

In June 1807, the notorious *Chesapeake–Leopard* affair gave credence to the most extreme stories of British abuses. Commodore James Barron in the frigate *Chesapeake*, 36, left Hampton Roads en route to take command of the U. S. Mediterranean Squadron, which his brother Samuel had commanded during the War with Tripoli. Putting out to sea at the same time was H.M. frigate *Leopard*, 44. When the two frigates, on converging courses, were some ten miles outside the Virginia Capes, the captain of the *Leopard*

hailed and sent over to the *Chesapeake* a boat with a lieutenant bearing a written demand that the Americans submit to search for deserters from the Royal Navy. When Barron sent back a refusal, the *Leopard* opened fire, killing three Americans and wounding a dozen more. Utterly unprepared for battle, the *Chesapeake* was forced to strike her colors. A party from the *Leopard* then boarded her and carried off four men, only one of whom proved in fact to be a British deserter. He was hanged.

The American public reacted violently to this outrage. Impressment of merchant seamen was bad enough, but removing sailors by force from an American warship was an act of extreme provocation. The incidental slaughter of other Americans was indefensible under any circumstances short of war. "Never since the Battle of Lexington," President Jefferson said, "have I seen this country in such a state of exasperation."

In the heated atmosphere, Jefferson was able to push through Congress an embargo on all exports. But, although the embargo was designed as economic retaliation short of war, during the 15 months it was in effect it created greater hardships at home than abroad. In 1809, in response to popular protests, Congress repealed the embargo, replacing it with a nonintercourse act, which permitted trade with all ports except those under British or French control. American commerce quickly revived, accompanied by a resumption of spoliations of American merchantmen by warships of Britain and France. By 1810 the British had seized nearly a thousand American ships; the French and their allies, about 800.

The question of neutral rights on the high seas, though always in the background, did not itself actually bring on the War of 1812. The northeastern states, with the strongest maritime interests, were definitely against war. Prospering in spite of losses and humiliations, they demanded an enlarged navy to protect commerce. But they opposed retaliatory measures that could bring on an armed conflict with Britain and thereby disrupt American seaborne commerce altogether. The impetus that eventually brought about war came not from the eastern seaboard but from the agricultural and pioneer South and West.

In 1809 James Madison succeeded Thomas Jefferson as president, thereby continuing Republican control. The congressional election of the following year swept in a younger generation of Republican "War Hawks," led by Henry Clay of Kentucky and John C. Calhoun of South Carolina. These fiery young statesmen reflected the pioneers' insatiable land hunger. To them the national destiny required the seizure of Spanish Florida and British Canada. From the former, Creek and Seminole Indians periodically raided into the Deep South. In the Northwest the Indians had been formed into a confederacy under Chief Tecumseh, partly to oppose the westward advance of American pioneers. The Indians in both areas were widely believed to have been armed and encouraged by the British. Tecumseh's repulse in November 1811 in the Battle of Tippecanoe convinced the War Hawks that the trans-Ohio pioneer could be safeguarded only through the conquest of Canada.

Knowing little about maritime matters and caring less, the ultranationalist War Hawks nevertheless denounced impressment and loudly condemned trade restrictions, particularly when they hurt commerce originating in the Mississippi Valley. Yet they voted consistently against every measure to strengthen the U. S. Navy for a sea war against Britain. The way to get at Britain and her feeble ally Spain, they insisted, was to strike at their possessions in America. "On to Canada!" became their monotonous cry. Capture of Canada, wrote Jefferson, would be "a mere matter of marching." Clay insisted that if necessary the Kentucky militia could capture it all by themselves.

Britain's difficulties and Napoleon's continuing successes encouraged the War Hawks to spur President Madison into action. In April 1812, Congress, under their leadership, authorized the president to reimpose the embargo and call up the militia. On 1 June Madison presented his war message, drawing particular attention to impressment, neutral rights, and Indian affairs. In Congress the War Hawks rode down the opposition of congressmen from the Northeast. The House of Representatives decided for war by a vote of 79 to 49; the Senate, by a vote of 19 to 13. On 18 June 1812, the United States, with defense forces consisting of a 6,700-man army, a total of 18 seagoing warships, and a scattering of gunboats, mostly out of commission, formally declared war on the Mistress of the Seas.

The War at Sea, 1812

At New York Commodore John Rodgers was holding in readiness a squadron comprising three frigates, a sloop, and a brig. Upon receiving news of the expected declaration of war, he promptly and eagerly put to sea. His objective was a lightly escorted 110-ship convoy from Jamaica reported to be riding the Gulf Stream en route to England, a course that would bring it within 450 miles of New York harbor. To Rodgers's sailors the big convoy seemed as good as captured. They could almost hear the prize money jingling in their pockets.

On the morning of the second day out, American lookouts sighted a British frigate. She was the *Belvidera*, bound for Halifax. Rodgers, considering destruction of enemy warships his overriding duty, reluctantly abandoned the search for the convoy and went after the frigate. By midafternoon he had drawn close enough to open fire—the first shots of the War of 1812. The crew of the British frigate in desperation now lightened ship by jettisoning anchors, spars, and boats and pumping out drinking water—measures that Rodgers dared not adopt at the beginning of a long cruise. That night the *Belvidera* made good her escape.

Rodgers turned back and pursued the convoy almost to within sight of England but could never overtake it. In the approaches to the English Channel, he turned and headed south, to the latitude of Madeira, in order to capture British merchantmen in the easterly trade winds. At the end of August 1812 he put into Boston with seven rather insignificant prizes.

Rodgers's cruise was accounted a failure, even by himself. His lack of success supported the view, soon officially adopted, that American men-of-war should operate not in squadrons but singly or in pairs, as commerce raiders. Rodgers's squadron had taken few prizes, but it had nevertheless performed an invaluable service—nothing less than saving the U. S. merchant marine.

American merchant ships, in anticipation of war, had sped abroad to make what might be their last delivery and to pick up cargo. Vice Admiral Herbert Sawyer, commanding the Halifax station, planned to place a ship before each major U. S. port in order to snap them up when they came back to America. But when the *Belvidera* reached Halifax with news that hostilities had begun and that the New York–based squadron was at sea, Admiral Sawyer canceled his original plan and sent the entire Halifax squadron to cruise off New York with the object of capturing Rodgers's ships on their return. As a result, hundreds of American merchant vessels that raced for home on news of the war were able to make it safely into port.

At New York, the U. S. brig *Nautilus*, 14, apprised of the approach of the ships from Halifax, darted out to sea with the aim of seeking out and warning Rodgers. Instead, off Sandy Hook she ran into the British squadron, which, after a six-hour chase, forced her to surrender. The following week, the squadron chased and very nearly captured the U. S. frigate *Constitution*.

The *Constitution* had not been able to join Rodgers's ships before the outbreak of war because she was at Annapolis recruiting and fitting out. In mid-July her new commanding officer, "Preble's Boy" Captain Isaac Hull, now a portly 39, at last left the Chesapeake and headed up the coast for New York. Off New Jersey he sighted the British squadron, which he mistook for that of Rodgers. Recognizing his mistake barely in time, he hauled off to the southeast. During the persistent calms of the next two days, his crew kept the *Constitution* out of range of the pursuing British only by towing with the ships' boats or by the backbreaking device of kedging—repeatedly sending forward by boat an anchor at the end of a long line, and then, when the anchor had been dropped, heaving on the line to draw the ship up to it. On the third day, when a sudden squall concealed the *Constitution* from the British, Hull changed course and made good his escape.

Cut off from New York, Hull steered for Boston. Here he remained only long enough to take on supplies. Departing on a raiding cruise, he captured several merchantmen and sent them into port with prize crews. On the afternoon of 19 August, when about 700 miles due east of Boston, the *Constitution* sighted a sail and stood down as usual to investigate. The stranger proved to be not another merchant vessel but H.M. frigate *Guerrière*, 44, which had been detached from the British squadron off New York and was proceeding to Halifax for refit.

The British commanding officer, Captain James Dacres, knew that the *Constitution*'s weight of broadside was heavier than his own, but he scorned the odds. The Royal Navy was accustomed to victories over stronger opponents. At the outbreak of war, Dacres, then off New York, had sent a challenge to Commodore Rodgers, stating that he would be "very happy to meet the *President*, or any other American frigate of equal force . . . for the purpose of having a few minutes' tête-à-tête." Now the *Constitution*, sister ship of the *President*, was approaching as if to accept the challenge.

Both captains stripped their ships to battle canvas—topsails and jibs. Then, as the American frigate came down before the wind, the *Guerrière* wore three times, firing broadsides as she crossed the *Constitution*'s bow. Hull, conforming to Dacre's movements, swung his bow right and left to avoid raking fire. Such shot as struck the *Constitution*'s thick hull bounced off harmlessly, winning her the nickname "Old Ironsides."

Dacres now settled on a course before the wind, inviting close combat. Hull set his maintopgallant sail and foresail for greater speed and surged up alongside his opponent, coolly withholding fire. When at last the *Constitution* was within half pistol shot of the *Guerrière* with all guns of her starboard battery bearing, Hull shouted, "Pour in the whole broadside!"

Flames leapt from the hull of the *Constitution* as her starboard guns, double-shotted with round and grape, opened fire. The *Guerrière*'s port guns replied but had little effect on her opponent's tough side timbers. On the other hand, the American round shot repeatedly pierced the hull of the British frigate, hurling clouds of lethal splinters, and the *Constitution*'s grape shot ripped through her sails and rigging. Under the bombardment, the *Guerrière*'s mizzenmast began to creak and sway and presently crashed over the side, causing her to slow down and turn into the wind. The *Constitution* now forged ahead and crossed her bow, delivering raking fire the length of her deck.

As the *Constitution* wore to avoid being raked from astern, the *Guerrière*'s bowsprit thrust into the American frigate's mizzen rigging. Both captains now called boarders away, and as the sailors left their guns and crowded at the point of contact, sharpshooters in the tops inflicted heavy casualties, especially on the *Guerrière*, where Captain Dacres was among the wounded. Before either crew could board, the frigates wrenched apart with much snapping of lines, and the *Guerrière*'s fore- and mainmast went over the side, leaving her rolling helplessly in the heavy seas. With no flag remaining to strike, the *Guerrière* fired a gun to leeward in token of surrender. The next day, after the prisoners had been removed, the shattered hulk was burned. American losses were 7 killed and 7 wounded; the British, 15 killed and 63 wounded.

In Boston, where "Mr. Madison's war" had hitherto had little popular support, the victorious *Constitution* was welcomed back with wild acclaim. Hull's victory raised the spirits of the whole nation, distressed by recent news of defeats near the Canadian border. Here Jefferson's "mere

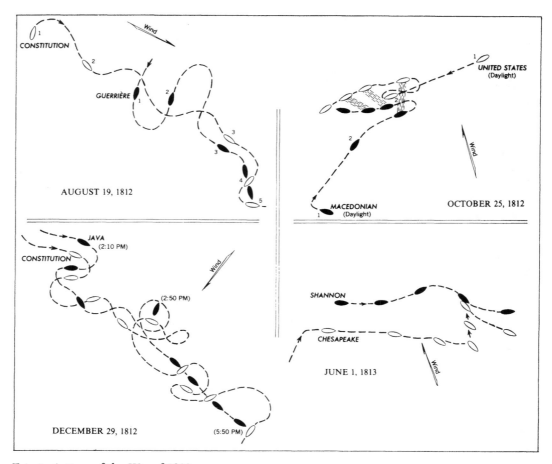

AUGUST 19, 1812

OCTOBER 25, 1812

DECEMBER 29, 1812

JUNE 1, 1813

Frigate Actions of the War of 1812

matter of marching" had got off to a wretched start. Indians had captured Fort Dearborn (Chicago) and massacred the American defenders. A small British raiding party had seized the U. S. post on Mackinac Island. General William Hull, Captain Isaac Hull's irresolute and aging uncle, had ignominiously surrendered Detroit to the British without firing a shot. There was real apprehension among the Americans that the United States was about to have its Northwest Territory wrested away. The victory of the *Constitution* went far toward uniting a bitterly divided country in a resolution to push the war more vigorously.

As if to demonstrate that the American victory over the *Guerrière* might have resulted from something more than heavier weight of broadside, the U. S. sloop-of-war *Wasp*, 20, commanded by Master Commandant Jacob Jones, in October 1812 defeated the British brig *Frolic*, 20. Exercising superior gunnery, the Americans silenced the brig's guns and also cut away her head braces so that her after sails swung her bow to port, enabling

the *Wasp* to sweep her deck with raking fire. When the victorious Americans boarded, they found that of the *Frolic*'s crew of 110, ninety were casualties. Before the *Wasp* and her prize could complete rerigging, a British ship of the line appeared on the scene and captured both. The *Frolic* was burned, too wrecked to be worth saving.

October also saw the second of the American frigate victories. Commodore Stephen Decatur in the *United States*, 44, was off Africa plying the southern, westbound transatlantic route when he encountered the British frigate *Macedonian*, 38, fresh out of refit, bound for the West Indies. The *Macedonian* was a fast ship, but her heaviest guns were only 18-pounders. The 24-pounder long guns and 42-pounder carronades of the American frigate held the advantage in range and an almost 2-to-1 advantage in weight of broadside, but the *United States* was notoriously slow.

The British captain, John S. Carden, a very senior frigate commander, itching for a fight but grossly underestimating the quality of his opponent, believed he could close with and outfight the lumbering American frigate. Decatur, the youthful firebrand of the Tripolitan War, now at age 33 fought with caution, restraint, and shrewdness. Though the British had the weather gage, Decatur maneuvered to keep the *Macedonian* from closing too fast. While the *United States* remained beyond the reach of the British 18-pounders, her 24-pounders riddled the *Macedonian's* hull, knocked over her mizzenmast, stripped her of her remaining topmasts, dismounted many of her guns, and turned her decks into such slaughterhouses that the survivors, in order to have room to work what was left of her battery, tossed overboard the piled up dead and mortally wounded. During the entire engagement Carden never got within a hundred yards of the *United States*. At the end, Decatur mercifully declined an opportunity to rake. Carden surrendered, and the *Macedonian* was taken into the U. S. Navy. The British had suffered more than a hundred casualties; the Americans, only a dozen.

In December the Americans won their third successive frigate victory. Off Salvador, Brazil, the *Constitution*, now commanded by Commodore William Bainbridge, met the *Java*, Captain Henry Lambert, in one of the hardest-fought frigate battles of all time. The two ships were superficially well matched, each nominally a 44. The American, however, was heavier and had a somewhat heavier weight of broadside and a slightly larger crew. But the crucial difference lay in the comparative state of training of their crews. The *Java* had drilled with the great guns only once since leaving England. The Americans, as was their custom, had been in continual practice with both guns and musketry.

Engaging, the two frigates for almost two hours pounded hulls, tore up rigging, and bloodied decks while circling about, attempting to rake and to avoid being raked. At length the *Java*, her bowsprit and foremast shot away, missed her tack and was caught in stays. While she thus hung motionless, unable to turn in either direction, the *Constitution* swept across her stern, delivering a murderous raking fire. In desperation, Captain Lambert attempted to ram the American frigate and board her, but the attempt merely gave Bainbridge an opportunity to cut across the *Java's* bows and pour in another terrible raking broadside. Down came her masts. Lambert was killed by a shot from the *Constitution's* maintop. The *Java*, helpless, ceased fire, whereupon the *Constitution* withdrew briefly to make repairs. Bainbridge, twice wounded but still in command, presently returned and placed his ship in a raking position across the *Java's* bows, whereupon the British struck their colors. The in-

adequately trained British crew had suffered 122 casualties; the Americans, 34. The *Java*, wrecked beyond salvage, was burned the next day. The *Constitution* returned to Boston for repairs. "Hard Luck Bill" Bainbridge, who had surrendered the *Retaliation* and the *Philadelphia* and been humiliated in the *George Washington*, had at last completely justified the Navy's faith in him.

The series of American victories over British ships shocked and dumfounded the people of England; not in almost a decade had a captain of the Royal Navy struck his colors. The few British victories over American ships had been achieved only by immensely superior force: the whole Halifax squadron against the *Nautilus*, 14; HMS *Barbados*, 28, against the USS *James Madison*, 14; HMS *Poictiers*, 74, against the USS *Wasp*, 20; HMS *Southampton*, 32, against the USS *Vixen*, 14. On the other hand, all the defeated British commanding officers except the captain of the *Frolic* had been conquered by bigger ships with superior weight of broadside. But the British were victims of their own negligence too, for the American crews they fought were better trained. Since Trafalgar, ships of the Royal Navy, encountering few enemies at sea, had neglected drill with the great guns.

The Americans were elated by their string of conquests. Congress, after piling honors on the victors, enthusiastically voted funds for six additional frigates and four ships of the line. But, gratifying though the victories were to the American people, they had little effect on the outcome of the war. The U. S. Navy was too tiny, compared to its adversary, to guard American seaborne commerce or seriously disrupt British commerce, protected as the latter was by a well-organized convoy system. Much more effective was the swarm of privateers that sailed from American ports.

The War at Sea, 1813

In early 1813 no officer in the U. S. Navy was more renowned than Master Commandant James Lawrence, then only 32 years old. Idolized by the public, he was a favorite of his fellow officers. He had early won fame as Decatur's second-in-command at the burning of the *Philadelphia*. In the first few weeks of 1813, he added to his reputation by gallant actions off the Brazilian coast, where he had remained in command of the U. S. sloop *Hornet* after the *Constitution* had gone home following her victory over the *Java*. Eluding a British 74, Lawrence captured a merchant brig with $23,000 in coins on board and shortly afterward sank H.M. sloop *Peacock* in a brief, bloody battle. He was rewarded by promotion to captain and given command of the U. S. frigate *Chesapeake*, then lying in Boston harbor under the surveillance of two British frigates.

Captain Lawrence took command of the *Chesapeake* in May, with orders to prepare her for a raid on shipping in the Gulf of St. Lawrence. His immediate problem was to obtain an adequate crew. Since American seamen signed on men-of-war for a cruise only, the best professional sailors in the Boston area, tempted by tales of riches to be won, were by this time at sea in privateers. Hence Lawrence had to man his ship with a large infusion of raw recruits.

Under the circumstances, Lawrence should have refused to fight another frigate until he had trained his men. But when Captain Philip Broke of H.M. frigate *Shannon* pointedly dismissed his other blockading frigate and paraded back and forth before Boston harbor, the ardent young Lawrence could not resist the implied challenge. On 1 June, even before Broke's written challenge reached him, he put to sea. He was taking out the ill-manned *Chesapeake* against a formidable antagonist. The ships themselves were very nearly of equal strength, each rated at 38 guns and in fact carrying about 50. But the *Shannon* was in several respects the crack frigate of the Royal Navy. Broke, a gunnery expert, had commanded her for seven years. He had contrived novel devices for control and accuracy of fire, and, in a period when most British naval officers neglected gunnery practice, he drilled his men at the guns twice a day, five days a week.

The result was what might have been expected. Broke led the way out to sea and hove to, awaiting his opponent. This was to be no battle of maneuver. The *Chesapeake*, coming up on the *Shannon's* weather quarter, had her headsails shot away and her helmsman killed. Out of control, she turned into the wind, was taken aback, and, with sternway on, drifted down into Broke's raking broadsides. British boarders, led by their captain, swarmed on board the American frigate. By this time, most of the American officers were casualties and Lawrence himself, mortally wounded by a musket shot from the tops, had been carried below, repeatedly crying, "Don't give up the ship!" The British quickly overwhelmed the leaderless American crew. The battle had lasted just 15 minutes. In that quarter hour, 62 Americans were killed and 73 wounded. The British suffered almost as severely: 43 killed, 39 wounded. The victors took the *Chesapeake* and their American prisoners of war to Hali-

fax. Lawrence died en route, deliriously repeating, it was said, "Don't give up the ship."

Despite a tightening blockade, some of the U. S. Navy's smaller vessels, sloops and brigs, and many American privateers managed to get to sea and raid British maritime commerce, not in the regular sea lanes of trade, where merchantmen moved in well-escorted convoys, but in coastal waters, including those surrounding the British Isles. When the small American warships met their Royal Navy counterparts, they did not hesitate to attack. The sole U. S. defeat of the war, in such sloop and brig duels, occurred in August 1813 when the American brig *Argus*, 18, after capturing 19 prizes in British waters, was herself defeated and captured by H.M. brig *Pelican*, 18, off the coast of Wales. The following month off the Maine coast the "lucky little *Enterprise*," now converted into a 14-gun brig, in a fierce engagement defeated H.M. brig *Boxer*, 18. Both commanding officers were killed in the battle, and they were buried side by side in a Portland cemetery.

Operations on the Great Lakes

The British, in occupying Detroit, threatened to carry out their plan of converting the vast American Northwest Territory into an Indian buffer state between the United States and Canada. But their hold on Detroit was somewhat tenuous because the British troops and their Indian allies depended for provisions, munitions, and other supplies on transportation via the St. Lawrence River and the Great Lakes. Accordingly, a major American objective was to cut their water communication line. A drive to capture Montreal and thereby block the St. Lawrence failed when New York militia refused to cross the border into Canada.

On Lake Ontario a joint American army–navy force raided York (now Toronto), the capital of Upper Canada, set fire to the parliament building there, and then captured Fort George on the Canadian side of the Niagara River. But neither the Americans nor the British ever gained control of the lake itself. The opposing naval commands under U. S. Commodore Isaac Chauncey and his British counterpart, Commodore Sir James Yeo, engaged in a fruitless shipbuilding race. When occasional skirmishes left the rivals' relative strength about the same as before, the campaign degenerated into a battle of adz, hammer, and chisel that eventually produced great 100-gun ships destined never to fire a shot in battle.

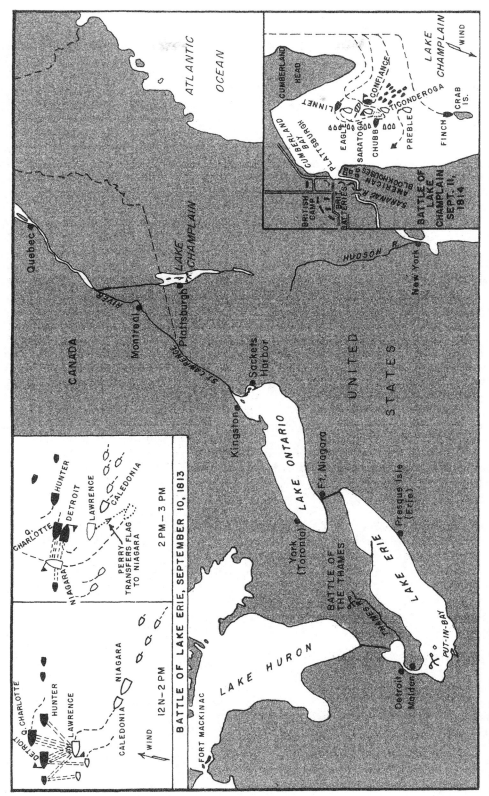

Lake Battles of the War of 1812

Inset (upper right):

LAKE CHAMPLAIN

CUMBERLAND HEAD

WIND

LINNET
CONFIANCE
TICONDEROGA
EAGLE
SARATOGA
CHUBB
PREBLE
FINCH
CRAB IS.

CUMBERLAND BAY

PLATTSBURGH

HUDSON R.

SARANAC R.

AMERICAN BLOCKHOUSES

BRIT. BATTERIES

BRITISH CAMP

BATTLE OF LAKE CHAMPLAIN SEPT. II, 1814

Main map labels:

ATLANTIC OCEAN

Quebec

CANADA

Montreal

ST. LAWRENCE RIVER

Plattsburgh

LAKE CHAMPLAIN

New York

Sackets Harbor

Kingston

LAKE ONTARIO

UNITED STATES

Ft. Niagara

York (Toronto)

BATTLE OF THE THAMES

THAMES R.

LAKE ERIE

Presque Isle (Erie)

PUT-IN-BAY

Detroit
Malden

LAKE HURON

FORT MACKINAC

Inset (lower left):

BATTLE OF LAKE ERIE, SEPTEMBER 10, 1813

2 PM – 3 PM

HUNTER
Q. CHARLOTTE
DETROIT
LAWRENCE
CALEDONIA
NIAGARA
PERRY TRANSFERS FLAG TO NIAGARA

12 N – 2 PM

Q. CHARLOTTE
HUNTER
DETROIT
LAWRENCE
CALEDONIA
NIAGARA
WIND

At the outbreak of war, the British had on Lake Erie a small squadron of armed vessels; the Americans had no warships there at all. Following General Hull's abject surrender of Detroit, the U. S. secretary of the navy sent Sailing Master Daniel Dobbin with a contingent of shipwrights to Lake Erie to choose a base and begin building an American squadron. Dobbin chose Presque Isle (Erie) and began work on four schooners. At about the same time Commodore Chauncey, unaware of Dobbin's operations, sent Lieutenant Jesse Elliott to Lake Erie for the same purpose. Elliott selected Black Rock on the Niagara River and began his operation with conspicuous success by capturing the British armed merchant brig *Caledonia*. Then, after purchasing four schooners, he returned to Lake Ontario.

On the first day of 1813, Chauncey, visiting Presque Isle, decided that Dobbin's schooners were too small to be of much use in battle and ordered work begun on two 20-gun brigs. The following month he appointed to command the growing U. S. Lake Erie squadron 27-year-old Master Commandant Oliver Hazard Perry, who volunteered for duty on fresh water to escape the boredom of a blockaded seagoing navy. Noting that Black Rock could be reached by British guns, Chauncey canceled it as a naval base.

Perry arrived at Presque Isle at the end of March and set to work with immense energy to expedite the completion of the two brigs—procuring more shipwrights, overseeing the cutting of timber, combing the area for scrap iron and blacksmiths, obtaining supplies via Pittsburgh, and recruiting militia to guard the base.

One of the brigs Perry named the *Niagara*; the other, which was to be his flagship, he named the *Lawrence*, for his late friend, the captain of the ill-fated *Chesapeake*. These vessels, mounting eighteen 32-pounder carronades and two long 12-pounders, would be the most powerful men-of-war on the lake.

Watching this building program was General William H. Harrison, who, with an army of Kentuckians, was in northern Ohio waiting for the Americans to seize control of Lake Erie so that he could march on Detroit. Also keeping track of the building were the British, who began construction of a new ship, the *Detroit*, at their base at Fort Malden. In May 1813 Commodore Yeo sent Commander Robert H. Barclay, a distinguished veteran of Trafalgar, to command the British Lake Erie squadron. Barclay's orders were to see that the two segments of the U. S. squadron did not get together

and that the two brigs building at Presque Isle never got out of port.

By mid-June Barclay was cruising between Presque Isle and the Niagara River, endeavoring to keep each blockaded. At that time the British army, following the American capture of Fort George, had temporarily withdrawn from the Niagara peninsula. Perry, taking advantage of this situation, withdrew the *Caledonia* and the schooners from Black Rock and had them towed by oxen against the swift river current to Lake Erie. Then, hugging the shore, he slipped with them past Barclay in a fog, to the safety of Presque Isle Bay.

On 23 July, despite shortages of materials and skilled craftsmen and the backbreaking labor of transporting guns, ammunition, and stores from Pittsburgh via river and barely passable road, the two brigs at Presque Isle were completed. On 2 August, while Barclay was off station, evidently for replenishment, Perry, with the aid of pontoons, succeeded in dragging the *Lawrence* and the *Niagara* unarmed over the bar into the open lake and then installed their guns—a feat he could never have accomplished had Barclay's squadron been present.

Shortly afterward Elliott, now a master commandant, arrived from Lake Ontario with a final contingent of 101 officers and men, and General Harrison lent Perry a hundred marksmen to serve as sharpshooters in the tops. Perry appointed Elliott his second-in-command and put him in charge of the *Niagara*. Elliott, however, was not entirely mollified. He considered that he, as captor of the *Caledonia*, and not the newcomer Perry, should have been given the Lake Erie command.

When Barclay, returning to blockade Presque Isle, caught sight of Perry's squadron on the lake, he beat a hasty retreat to his base at Malden to await completion of the *Detroit*, which was to be his new flagship. Perry meanwhile moved up the lake and established himself at a base at Put-in Bay in a group of islands opposite Malden.

In early September the *Detroit* was completed but unarmed. By this time provisions at Malden were almost exhausted, and the 14,000 Indians there, counting women and children, were consuming what was left at a great rate. To avoid starvation it was imperative that the British promptly regain control of lake communications and bring in supplies. So Barclay armed his ships with a conglomeration of guns from Fort Malden— 17 long guns of mixed caliber and 2 carronades. On the morning of 10 September, deeply discouraged, aware that he was going out to meet a more powerfully armed foe, Barclay set out to challenge his opponent. Besides the *Detroit*, he had the ship *Queen Charlotte*, armed with three long 12-pounders and 14 carronades, the schooner *Lady Prevost*, 13, the brig *Hunter*, 10, and two smaller craft.

The Battle of Lake Erie, 10 September 1813

Sighting the British, the American squadron came down before the wind and approached the enemy on a slanting course. Flying from the main-royal masthead of the *Lawrence* was Perry's battle flag, blue with Captain Lawrence's words sewn on it in white muslin: DONT GIVE UP THE SHIP.

Perry's orders for combat, issued earlier, specified that his flagship *Lawrence* was to pair off against the British flagship *Detroit* and his brig *Niagara* against Barclay's other heavy, the *Queen Charlotte*. Perry expected little of his other vessels: five schooners and a sloop, armed with one or two guns each, and the *Caledonia*, armed with three. But his two brigs could hurl a weight of broadside about 40 percent greater than that of their opponents. Hence he directed his vessels to move rapidly to within pistol shot of the enemy in order to make optimum use of their sharpshooters and their short-range carronades. To emphasize this point, he concluded with a paraphrase of Nelson's famous words in the Memorandum: "If you lay your enemy alongside, you cannot be out of your place."

Coming down before the wind, the *Lawrence* began taking heavy punishment from the *Detroit*'s long guns. Perry pushed grimly on, however, withholding fire from his carronades until they bore. At close range the *Lawrence* then fired a broadside that killed or wounded a good many of the *Detroit*'s crew and left her deck a mass of broken spars and lines, but her guns continued to fire.

The *Niagara* meanwhile lay to windward some distance away behind the sluggish *Caledonia*, despite Perry's signals to close and engage. The *Queen Charlotte*, unable to reach the *Niagara* with her carronades, joined the *Detroit* and other British vessels in firing into the *Lawrence*. The American flagship, in two hours of fighting against such odds, was gradually reduced to a wreck with more than half her ship's company dead or wounded. At last the purser, the chaplain, and Perry himself fired her last serviceable gun. Leaving the national ensign still flying on the shattered *Lawrence*, Perry now embarked in his only usable small boat, carrying his commodore's pennant and his blue battle flag. With solid shot from the British guns splashing around him, he had himself rowed to the *Niagara*, which, in the freshening breeze, had just passed to windward of the *Caledonia*. As Perry boarded his fresh brig, the national ensign was lowered on the *Lawrence*.

Ordering Elliott into his boat to go to urge forward the lagging rear schooners and sloop, Perry took command of the *Niagara*, which on his orders forged ahead and bore up as if to break through the British line just ahead of the *Detroit*. To avoid being raked and also to bring a fresh broadside to bear, the *Detroit* wore. In doing so she collided with the *Queen Charlotte*, which was ranging ahead to leeward. As the two British ships lay fouled, Perry sailed the *Niagara* athwart the bows of one and the stern of the other, his starboard guns sending double-shotted raking fire the length of their decks. At the same time his port guns fired salvos at small British ships off to port.

Shortly afterward the *Detroit* and the *Queen Charlotte*, reduced to helplessness, lowered their flags, and the smaller British vessels followed suit. American casualties numbered 123, two-thirds of them in the *Lawrence*. British casualties numbered 135.

Taking an old letter from his pocket, Perry scribbled across the back his report to General Harrison:

> Dear Gen'l:—We have met the enemy and they are ours:
> Two Ships, two Brigs, one schooner & one Sloop.
>   Yours, with great respect and esteem
>   O. H. Perry

By the end of the month, sooner than the enemy believed possible, Perry had repaired his ships and transported General Harrison's army across the lake. The British, promptly evacuating Malden and Detroit, retreated up the Thames river valley with their Indian allies, but Harrison's forces overtook and dispersed them. In this encounter, known as the Battle of the Thames, the Indian leader Tecumseh was killed. With his death, Indian opposition to the Americans collapsed. The Northwest Territory rested securely in American hands, assuring the United States the integrity of the states of Ohio, Indiana, Illinois, Michigan, and Wisconsin as part of the Federal Union.

Porter and the *Essex*

In late 1812, before the British blockade seriously restricted the U. S. Navy, Captain David Porter put to sea in the U. S. frigate *Essex*. He missed a

South Atlantic rendezvous with Bainbridge and Lawrence and proceeded independently around Cape Horn. For a full year the *Essex* cruised the Pacific, raiding enemy commerce. Her most damaging stroke was ruining Britain's whaling industry by capturing a dozen of her whalers and driving the rest to cover. From captured vessels, whalers and merchantmen, all well-supplied for distant cruising, Porter took care of his own crew's needs. One fine whaler, armed with ten 6-pounders and ten 18-pounders, he chose as a consort for the *Essex*, renaming her *Essex Junior*. So numerous were his captures that he had difficulty providing prize crews from his small ship's company. To serve as prizemaster of a recaptured American whaler he was obliged to appoint his youngest midshipman, who was also his foster son: David Glasgow Farragut, the future admiral, then just 12 years old.

Learning that British warships were in pursuit of him, Porter retired to the Marquesas Islands for a thorough refit. Then, instead of continuing around the world, and so back home, he could not resist the challenge of British naval units in the Pacific. He returned to the South American coast, reaching Valparaiso on 3 February 1814. Five days later, two British warships arrived at the port: H.M. frigate *Phoebe*, 38, Captain James Hillyar, and H.M. sloop-of-war *Cherub*, 20.

Porter realized that he was in a precarious situation. His fire power was short-range, concentrated in a main battery of forty 32-pounder carronades. The *Essex Junior* was too lightly built and armed for combat. The *Phoebe* and *Cherub* outranged him with their long guns, and their combined weight of broadside was heavier than his. Porter hoped to get to sea, separate the British vessels, and defeat them one at a time. But Hillyar was vigilant. He cruised back and forth at the seaward end of the roadstead prepared to intercept any move the *Essex* might make. He scoffed at Porter's challenge to meet him in single combat, with the *Phoebe* alone.

Porter waited in vain more than six weeks to catch Hillyar napping. Then on 28 March under the strain of a gusty south wind, one of the *Essex's* anchor cables parted. When the second anchor failed to hold, the crew cut its cable also, and the *Essex* went adrift. Close-hauled, she ran to windward of the *Phoebe* and the *Cherub* and reached the open sea. With escape in sight, she was hit by a violent squall, and her maintopmast went overboard. Unable now to outspeed the British ships, Porter tried to regain the safety of the harbor. Failing this, he put in toward the coast and anchored in neutral waters a few miles north of Valparaiso.

The British ships, ignoring Chile's neutrality, closed in to attack and opened fire a little before 4 p.m. Standing off beyond range of Porter's carronades, they simply battered the *Essex* into helplessness with their combined battery of 30 long 18-pounders and two long 9s. The only hits Porter attained were with three long 12-pounders firing through the *Essex's* stern ports. Seeing his officers and men going down in great numbers, he tried to run his ship aground and destroy her rather than see her captured, but the wind failed him. He then authorized all who wished to do so to swim ashore to avoid being taken prisoner. At 6:20, when the swimmers were near the beach, Porter struck his flag. The *Essex* had suffered 58 killed and 65 wounded, more than half her crew, while the *Phoebe* and the *Cherub* together had only 15 casualties. Porter had made the common error of a naval commerce raider in seeking battle instead of pursuing his strategic objective, the enemy's merchantmen.

Operations in America, 1814

In late June 1812, before the news of the American declaration of war reached London, the British government revoked the Orders in Council, insofar as they applied to the United States, forbidding trade with ports controlled by Napoleon. It thus removed a major cause of American complaints. Upon the arrival of the declaration in England, the Cabinet decided to await the American reaction to the revocation of the Orders, hoping that "the accustomed relations of peace and amity between the two countries may yet be restored."[1] When peace efforts failed—over the issue of impressment, which the British insisted upon treating as a purely domestic matter—the Royal Navy began to build up its squadrons at Halifax and in the West Indies.

In December 1812 the news reached London of the virtual annihilation of Napoleon's armies in Russia. The need to come to terms with the United States now appeared less urgent. A few days later the British government announced a commercial blockade of the Delaware and Chesapeake bays, a measure intended to weaken the U. S. government by sowing discontent, while sparing the merchants

[1] In the king's speech from the throne on the opening of Parliament, 30 July 1812.

of New York and New England, where antiwar sentiment was known to be strong.

Napoleon's defeat at Leipzig in October 1813 and his abdication in April of the following year freed more and more British power for employment in the war against America. Finally, at the end of May 1814, the blockade included "all the ports, harbors, bays, creeks, rivers, inlets, outlets, islands, and seacoasts of the United States." The total blockade of 1814 cut American merchant traffic to 11 percent of the 1811 figure. The practical cessation of coastal traffic, moreover, seriously disrupted the internal economy. A host of wagoners, taking up this domestic carrying trade, were able to move only a fraction of the accumulated tonnage.

Under conditions of growing commercial paralysis along the seaboard, America's most popular, as well as most effective, means of maritime reprisal continued to be privateering. The skippers of close-winded schooners, who with intimate knowledge of local waters might skim out of shallow passages, gambled that they could outsail the British watchdogs. Of 526 privateers registered, 200 actually made one or more cruises, taking more than 1,300 prizes. Their pinpricks, by annoying Britain's politically powerful merchant class, contributed to the unpopularity of the war in England and, consequently, to the negotiated peace.

Negotiations of one sort or another for ending hostilities had begun almost with the declaration. Following the defeat of Napoleon, President Madison accepted a specific proposal of the British prime minister—that delegates from their two nations enter into negotiation at Ghent, in Flanders, with a view to bringing the struggle to an end. Britain, mindful that victories in the field would strengthen her position at the conference table, began sending Wellington's veterans of the Peninsular War to launch a series of campaigns in the United States. The British planned to invade from the north in order to establish a claim for transferring a portion of northeastern United States to Canada. To distract the Americans and induce them to make concessions in that quarter, they also planned amphibious assaults from the Chesapeake Bay and the Gulf of Mexico.

In the summer of 1814, ships of the Royal Navy entered the Chesapeake and landed 4,000 seasoned troops without opposition on the west bank of the Patuxent River. The British warships chased American gunboats up the river, and the invaders marched on Washington, routing the hastily formed militiamen who stood between them and the city. After government officials, including President Madison, had fled in panic, the enemy troops, in reprisal for the burning of the parliament building at York, set fire to the White House, the Capitol, and other public buildings.

A small British squadron meanwhile had worked its way up the Potomac River, partly by kedging. It forced the capitulation of Alexandria, on the Potomac opposite Washington, and seized American shipping there. Under the double threat of enemy troops and ships, U. S. authorities ordered a sloop and a frigate at the Washington Navy Yard burned to keep them from falling into the enemy's hands.

Retiring from the Washington area, the British fleet and army moved up the bay for a raid on Baltimore. The troops were landed on the approaches to the city, but the attack was thwarted by the British fleet's inability to force its way past Fort McHenry into the harbor. On the night of 13–14 September, Francis Scott Key, an American civilian held on board one of the British ships, witnessed the unsuccessful bombardment of the fort. To memorialize the fort's spirited and spectacular defense, he wrote "The Star-Spangled Banner."

The Battle of Lake Champlain, 11 September 1814

In the Montreal area, in the summer of 1814, Sir George Prevost, governor-general of Canada, had 12,000 troops, including four brigades of Wellington's veterans, poised to advance into the United States via the old Lake Champlain invasion route. To block the proposed British invasion, the United States had available in the area only 1,500 troops. These men, commanded by Brigadier General Alexander Macomb, stationed themselves at Plattsburgh on the western shore of the lake.

Prevost delayed his invasion, not out of respect for Macomb's puny army but because, like Sir Guy Carleton 38 years earlier, he had to wait until the British seized control of Lake Champlain. The British squadron on the lake would have to defeat the American lake squadron. Otherwise American naval guns would be able to dominate the lakeside road that Prevost had to use and could prevent British use of the lake for hauling supplies forward.

The American lake squadron, built and commanded by Master Commandant Thomas Macdonough, another "Preble's boy," consisted of the corvette *Saratoga*, flagship, armed with 27 guns; the brig *Eagle*, 20; the schooner *Ticonderoga*, 17;

the sloop *Preble*, 7; and ten row galleys mounting one or two guns each.

The smaller British squadron, at the northern end of the lake, comprised the brig *Linnet*, 16 guns; the schooners *Chubb* and *Finch*, 11 each; and a dozen one-gun row galleys. The British, however, had under construction a 37-gun frigate, the *Confiance*, destined to be the new flagship. She would be by far the most powerful single man-of-war on the lake, capable, the British boasted, of defeating the entire American squadron.

The *Confiance* was launched on 25 August. As soon as Prevost heard the news, he ordered the invasion to begin, apparently ignorant that vessels are launched before construction is completed or that a newly launched warship is far from ready for combat.

Now that their country was invaded, volunteers from New York and Vermont flocked to Plattsburgh to strengthen Macomb. Macdonough brought his squadron into Plattsburgh Bay to cover Macomb's flank from attack by the British squadron. He anchored his four major vessels in a roughly north–south line between the mainland and Cumberland Head. Thus there would be no sail handling; each vessel would be a steady gun platform with maximum gun crews.

As the British regulars occupied Plattsburgh on 6 September, Macomb withdrew across the Saranac River into a prepared defensive position, destroying the bridges behind him. Prevost now began goading Captain George Downie, the newly arrived commodore of the British squadron, to bring his force out for an immediate joint attack. Downie, against his better judgment, at last gave in. At the first north wind, needed to carry his squadron up the lake, he set sail. Workmen were still engaged on board the *Confiance*, and her new crew had had no opportunity to test her sailing qualities or drill with her guns.

On the morning of 11 September, with his ships off Cumberland Head, Downie had himself rowed around the point to size up the American disposition. Both Downie and Macdonough, like all naval officers of their day, had carefully studied Nelson's battles. Neither could have failed to note the similarity of Macdonough's disposition to that of Brueys in the Battle of the Nile—at anchor with the wind blowing down his column from van to rear and his van blocked from forward movement by a peninsula. Downie decided to do exactly what Nelson had done in 1798—mass his fire initially on the American van and then work on down the column.

But Macdonough had seen to it that there were three vital differences between his disposition and

that of Brueys. The tip of Cumberland Head was south of Macdonough's van; to reach his van the British vessels would have to come more closely into the wind than most of them were capable of doing. Cumberland Head was hilly; it would probably kill whatever wind from the north there was. Unlike Brueys, Macdonough had rigged spring lines in order to be able to turn his vessels and redirect their broadside fire. When he learned that the British squadron was outside Plattsburgh Bay, he beat to quarters and, paraphrasing Nelson's Trafalgar signal, hoisted a message to his fleet: IMPRESSED SEAMEN CALL ON EVERY MAN TO DO HIS DUTY.

Downie returned to his squadron, which then advanced southward, formed line abreast, and with drums rolling advanced on the American fleet. The topsails of the tall-masted *Confiance*, catching the breeze over Cumberland Head, drew the flagship ahead until she was receiving concentrated fire from the entire American line. Wheeling to starboard alongside the *Saratoga*, she fired a double-shotted broadside that swept down 40 of the American flagship's crew. Return fire from the *Saratoga* cracked masts of the *Confiance* and dismounted one of her guns. It rumbled across the deck and crushed Downie.

The smaller vessels on both sides were quickly out of the main battle. The *Chubb* struck her colors. The *Finch*, becalmed, drifted off to the south. The *Preble*, disabled by fire from the British galleys, took refuge under Macomb's batteries. The *Ticonderoga* joined the galley battle.

Meanwhile, the four larger vessels fought the decisive action. The *Eagle* came under intense fire from the forward guns of the *Confiance* and from the port broadside of the *Linnet*, which had come alongside her. When most of her starboard guns had been knocked out, the *Eagle* cut her cables and reanchored astern of the *Saratoga*. This move permitted the *Linnet* to take a raking position across the *Saratoga*'s bow. In half an hour of gradually slackening fire, all four vessels were stripped of masts and wrecked beyond repair.

When the engaged broadsides of both flagships were about smashed into silence, Macdonough wound ship 180 degrees, thereby bringing a fresh broadside to bear on the *Confiance*. The latter, attempting a like maneuver, managed to turn only half way and thus took the raking blasts of the *Saratoga*'s fresh guns. With rising water below threatening to drown her wounded, the British flagship surrendered. The *Saratoga* then turned her fresh broadside on the *Linnet*, which quickly surrendered, as did the *Finch*, now grounded on

Crab Island. A few of the British galleys avoided capture by rowing away. Two hours and 20 minutes of close fighting had cost 200 American and 300 British casualties.

Macdonough's victory was in every sense decisive, for the battle, for the campaign, and for the war. Prevost, his logistics endangered, beat a hasty retreat into Canada, abandoning his heavy artillery and supplies. As a consequence of his failure, the British government restudied its position and accepted Wellington's estimate that the cost of a new offensive would outweigh the probable gains. The British therefore dropped their demand for territorial concessions and so notified the delegates at Ghent, thereby paving the way for conclusion of peace before the end of the year.

Operations of 1815

In the interval between the signing of the treaty at Ghent, 24 December 1814, and communicating cease-fire orders to the scattered naval and military units, several bloody battles were fought. On land, the most famous was Major General Andrew Jackson's repulse of the British attack on New Orleans. Aside from the fact that the Royal Navy's command of the sea made the landing of troops possible, the naval aspects of this battle are fairly incidental. Five American gunboats under the command of Lieutenant Thomas ap Catesby Jones tried to deny the British access to Lake Borgne, but 40 armed ships' launches and brigs brushed them aside. Jackson took up a position on the left bank of the Mississippi, his right flank protected by the river and his left by a swamp. Two little American schooners, the *Carolina* and the *Louisiana*, contributed effective fire support from the river. After the *Carolina* was burned by hot British shot, her crew served guns ashore. On 8 January several thousand veterans of the Peninsular War, under Major General Sir Edward Pakenham, made a frontal assault on Jackson's well-entrenched sharpshooters. When the smoke of the rifles lifted, Pakenham and more than 2,000 of his troops lay dead, and the rest were in flight. American losses were 71. The American victory, won two weeks after peace had been signed, had of course no effect on the war, but it set Jackson's feet on the road to the White House.

On the seas, the heavy frigate *President*, under command of Captain Stephen Decatur, was captured in mid-January 1815 while trying to elude the British blockading squadron off New York harbor. The lucky *Constitution*, under Captain Charles Stewart, had meanwhile made good her escape from Boston, and late in February 1815 in a single action captured sloops *Cyane*, 20, and *Levant*, 18. Usually, when two British vessels attacked one enemy, one of them engaged the opponent while the other maneuvered into raking position. But on this occasion Stewart handled Old Ironsides with such consummate seamanship that she was never raked during the action.

The Treaty of Ghent said nothing about impressment or neutral rights, but with Napoleon presumably safely exiled on Elba these matters no longer presented a problem. The treaty provided merely for an end to fighting and the *status quo ante bellum*, mutual restoration of territory. But news of the treaty and of the Battle of New Orleans arriving at the same time led many Americans to believe that the United States had defeated Britain and had imposed a victor's terms. The United States had at any rate achieved an undisputed boundary with Canada, which eventually by mutual agreement was disarmed and became the world's longest undefended frontier. The Americans soon forgot the blockade, the burning of Washington, and the blunders of their army. But they remembered their naval victories and acquired an enhanced sense of national unity.

Summary

From the British point of view, the War of 1812 was a limited war, concluded by a negotiated peace—a war in which England became reluctantly involved while using her control of the seas to help bring about the defeat of Napoleon. From the American point of view, the War of 1812 was a struggle to end British-inspired Indian forays, to acquire Canada, and to assert the nation's rights as a neutral against British interference at sea.

On the Atlantic the war consisted mainly of blockade of U. S. ports and waterways by the Royal Navy and of raids on British maritime commerce by U. S. naval vessels and privateers. On the northern front victory hinged on control of waterborne logistic transport. European events determined the tempo. The shorthanded British were on the defensive in 1812, unwilling to devote more than minor resources to the North American theater. In 1813 they remained on the defensive in Canada while extending the coastal blockade. In 1814, the British extended their blockade to the entire U. S. coast and, with Wellington's veterans available, made a successful raid on Washington, an unsuccessful raid on Baltimore, and an abortive invasion of New York state along the old Lake Champlain invasion route.

United States naval commerce-raiding operations led to more than a score of small-scale battles in the Atlantic and one in the Pacific. To the astonished exasperation of the British and the delighted surprise of the Americans, in single-ship duels Americans won three out of four frigate battles and seven out of eight sloop and brig battles. On the oceans there were during the war 25 engagements between British and American men-of-war; of these the Americans won 13. The side with the heavier fire power won in all instances but two. The exceptions were the victory of the American sloop-of-war *Wasp* over the British brig *Frolic* and the victory of the *Shannon* over the *Chesapeake*. The engagements proved that the U. S. Navy produced sea fighters at least as good as those in the Royal Navy, but the ocean battles had no effect on the outcome of the war. Great Britain's overwhelming numerical superiority in warships of all types enabled her to blockade the American coast and conduct amphibious raids almost at will. Inconclusive American commerce raiding, whether by ships of the U. S. Navy or by privateers, constituted the only seaborne reprisal possible to the United States. For Americans, the crowning indignity, which established beyond doubt the bankruptcy of the gunboat defense policy and the failure of a militia system for national defense, was the burning of Washington.

On the Canadian border, the failure of the United States to attain its initial objectives derived from haphazard planning, inadequate leadership, and, once again, the weakness of the militia system. Frustration might well have given place to catastrophe had it not been for the two decisive victories of the American lake squadrons. Perry's victory on Lake Erie made possible another victory in the Battle of the Thames that followed. These two victories removed the threat of the conversion of the U. S. Northwest Territory into an Indian buffer state. Macdonough's victory on Lake Champlain is of equal or even greater significance in that it averted cession of U. S. territory (in Maine at least) to Canada. It is only conjecture what course the war might have taken had Downie won and Prevost continued south, but Macdonough's victory brought about a British reconsideration of the war strategy and thus contributed directly to the successful compromise of the peace negotiations.

Chapter 11
Navies in Transition, 1815–60

Naval development in the period 1815–60 reflected the industrial and scientific revolution that transformed the United States and western Europe. The major navies of the world began to shift from sail to steam, from wood to iron, and from solid shot to shell. As a result, the appearance and handling of warships and their armament changed more drastically than in the preceding three centuries. Though there were a few minor wars during the period, the strange new navies were never put to the test of battle between fleets at sea.

The U. S. Navy: Operations

Following the War of 1812 there was no such slashing of U. S. naval forces as had occurred after previous wars. One reason was national pride in the Navy's accomplishments. A more important reason was the need to protect a skyrocketing foreign trade. Laid down during the war and launched not long after the return of peace were the 74-gun ships of the line *Independence, Washington*, and *Franklin*. Subsequently nine more ships of the line were authorized—all, of course, wooden sailing ships. Though this ambitious building program was eventually cut back, the United States acquired a respectable, if somewhat outdated, fleet. In line with the American policy of building outsize versions of each type, the standard armament of the capital ships completed after 1820 was 86 guns. One, the gigantic *Pennsylvania*, was armed with 120 guns and was at the time of her launching the largest warship in the world.

Such an expanding navy was too much for an inexperienced, civilian secretary of the navy to administer. During the war, Secretary William Jones, overwhelmed with paper work, had urged Congress to establish a three-officer Board of Navy Commissioners to advise him and help him in his tasks. Congress established such a board in early 1815, too late to be of use to Jones but of great value to his successor, Benjamin Crowninshield. President Madison nominated as commissioners Captains John Rodgers, Isaac Hull, and David Porter. Other early commissioners were Captains William Bainbridge and Stephen Decatur.

The enlarged U. S. Navy was early formed into semipermanent squadrons and sent to various quarters of the world, wherever needed, mainly to protect trade. The Mediterranean Squadron was revived to carry out the work of earlier squadrons sent to that area—to deal with the perennial nuisance of the Barbary corsairs. Because by 1807 the United States had fallen behind in tribute payments to Algiers, the dey had ordered his corsairs to resume captures of American merchantmen. Following the War of 1812, Congress declared war on Algiers and the president sent Stephen Decatur to the Mediterranean with a squadron of nine vessels, including three frigates. His orders were to exact satisfaction from all the Barbary powers for unneutral and unfriendly acts, and to cancel the treaty requiring tribute to Algiers.

En route, as if to signal ahead the seriousness of his mission, Decatur captured two Algerian warships. On arrival at Algiers, he laid before the dey a new treaty in which the latter was to agree to capture no more American vessels and to require no more tribute. Decatur ordered the Algerian ruler to sign the treaty and stick to its terms or expect to see the rest of his fleet captured or destroyed. The dey signed.

Decatur then proceeded to Tunis and Tripoli, where he demanded and received indemnity for prizes American privateers had sent to these ports during the War of 1812 and which had been turned over to the British. "Why," grumbled the pasha of Tripoli, "do they send wild young men to treat for peace with old powers?" Decatur's visit was followed by that of another, more powerful squadron, including the new 74-gun *Independence*, to impress upon the Barbary states that the United States had entered the ranks of major sea powers and was no longer subject to their piratical system.

The U. S. Navy maintained its Mediterranean Squadron regularly until the American Civil War, using leased facilities at Port Mahon, Minorca. In the 1820s the squadron had its hands full in the eastern Mediterranean combating piracy growing out of the ten-year-old Greek War of Independence.

The U. S. West Indies Squadron was established to protect American shipping in another hotbed of piracy. By the latter part of the eighteenth century, buccaneering had been largely suppressed in American waters. During the Wars of the French Revolution and Empire, it flourished anew, and nowhere was it more prevalent or conducted with greater ferocity than in the Caribbean Sea and the Gulf of Mexico. The situation became intolerable after 1810, when Venezuela, Colombia, and Mexico, revolting against Spanish rule, and Cuba and Puerto Rico, remaining loyal to Spain, sent against each other's shipping swarms of privateers that readily turned to piracy, attacking friend and foe alike.

A chief target of the pirates was shipping in and out of New Orleans, principal outlet for the Mississippi Valley. With heavy western migration, it became the second busiest port in the United States, surpassed only by New York. In 1819 the secretary of the navy sent Captain Oliver Hazard Perry to persuade the government of Venezuela to stop its wholesale issuing of letters of marque, which proved in effect to be mere licenses for piracy. Perry completed his mission, but succumbed to yellow fever on the return voyage.

Perry's mission helped a little, but it was evident that more direct methods were needed. In 1822 the U. S. Navy established its West Indies Squadron, which for several years was fully occupied in running down pirate craft and extirpating the hundreds of pirate nests infesting the Caribbean islands and even the Gulf coast of the United States.

Commodore James Biddle, first commander of the West Indies Squadron, found himself hampered by lack of small craft to get at the pirate hideaways. Even when he captured a gang of pirates, American courts were likely to release them for lack of evidence. Biddle's successor, Commodore David Porter, was more successful because he demanded and got enough light-draft vessels for the work at hand. Most valuable for operating in calms and penetrating shallow bays and inlets was the ex–Long Island Sound ferryboat *Sea Gull*, an armed steam sidewheeler in which Porter often wore his flag. When he caught a pirate, he usually found legal justifications for turning him over to the British pirate hunters in the area, who promptly hanged him without recourse to civilian courts. But the bellicose Porter overreached himself at Fajardo in Puerto Rico. One of his officers having been briefly imprisoned there, Porter landed with a force of 200 men and gave the mayor a choice between publicly apologizing or seeing his town

blown off the map. When word of this high-handed action reached Washington, Porter was called home to face a court-martial, which suspended him for six months. At that he resigned from the service in disgust and accepted a commission as commander in chief of Mexico's navy. In 1841, the West Indies Squadron, having successfully completed its mission, was absorbed into a new Home Squadron.

By the 1830s expanding American trade with the Orient required more protection than could be afforded by the occasional visit of a man-of-war. The need was made evident in 1831 when the inhabitants of Quallah Battoo on the coast of Sumatra plundered an American merchantman and slaughtered a number of her crew. The following year a U. S. frigate put ashore a landing party that stormed the fortifications and burned the town.

The U. S. East India Squadron, established in 1835, not only protected American commercial interests from China to Arabia but also supported some of the most fruitful diplomacy of the century. Commodore Lawrence Kearny, its commander from 1840 to 1842, by alternating courtesy and tact with a show of force, paved the way for negotiations that opened American trade with China on the same "most-favored-nation" basis that Britain had been able to extract only through warfare.

Other U. S. squadrons operated off Brazil, in the Pacific, and off West Africa. The African Squadron was established to fulfill an agreement with Britain to assist in suppressing the slave trade, which Congress in 1819 had branded a form of piracy. Almost from the beginning, the U. S. squadron was distracted by its efforts in the founding and protection of the Republic of Liberia, where former American slaves were being repatriated. It was withdrawn altogether in 1824 in a dispute with the British over the right to visit and search suspected slavers flying an American flag—a matter about which the United States was understandably touchy. Thereafter for many years slave ships from various nations, some so foul that they could be smelled before being sighted, brazenly plied the Atlantic under the unauthorized protection of the Stars and Stripes. By the terms of the U. S.–British Webster-Ashburton Treaty of 1842, the United States agreed to return a squadron of at least 80 guns to the African coast, with the understanding that only American ships would intercept and search vessels flying the American flag.

Closely related to the Navy's trade-protecting function were important contributions to exploration, survey, and research made by American naval personnel. No voyage of the first half of the nineteenth century aroused wider interest than that of the United States Exploring Expedition of 1838–42, and none added more to man's knowledge of the Pacific Ocean area. Carrying scientists with elaborate equipment, the squadron of six vessels, commanded by Lieutenant Charles Wilkes, USN, skirted Antarctica, touched at the Tuamotu, Society, and Fiji islands, and surveyed what is now the west coast of the United States. Wilkes's book about the expedition became a best seller and brought the Navy much favorable publicity.

The contributions of Lieutenant Matthew Fontaine Maury, USN, to the science of oceanography were unique, justly earning him the title Pathfinder of the Seas. In charge of the Depot of Charts and Instruments (the antecedent of the U. S. Naval Observatory and Hydrographic Office), Maury studied old log books. In them he found his first clues to the habits of wind, weather, current, temperature, and barometric pressure from season to season and from area to area in the world's oceans. Aided by information supplied by mariners of many nations, Maury prepared charts showing the best whaling grounds and the prevalent temperatures, winds, currents, and weather conditions in all seasons. These charts and their accompanying *Explanations and Sailing Directions*, which appeared as a ten-page pamphlet in 1848 but rapidly expanded in succeeding editions to more than a thousand pages, indicated the best sea routes for maximum speed and optimum conditions. Maury's charts and *Explanations* enabled mariners to cut the average sailing time from New York to California, for example, by 47 days, at a saving of $2,000,000 a year.

The U. S. Navy: Problems

Despite these solid contributions, all was not well with the U. S. Navy. The sailors were, in general, ignorant, often rascally fellows, recruited from the dregs of port cities around the world. The polyglot crews thus formed were often unable to communicate with one another and were capable, for the most part, of only simple labor. Dealing with steam propulsion, when it was adopted by the Navy, was quite beyond most of them. They were disciplined by fear, mainly of the lash. Flogging was the usual, and frequently applied, punishment in the U. S. Navy, as in other navies. The chief reward was "grog," which in the U. S. Navy after the War of 1812 was a daily allowance of half a pint of whisky for each man.

Among the U. S. naval officers who fought in the War of 1812 were many men of ability and charac-

ter. They were all subject, however, to the baneful custom of fighting duels over the slightest reflection, or supposed reflection, on their honor. The Navy lost some good officers through this practice, including the most honored and widely beloved of its captains, Stephen Decatur. In 1820 in a duel fought at Bladensburg, near Washington, Decatur was killed by James Barron—the end result of an old grudge that began when Decatur presided over the court-martial that suspended Barron for unreadiness in the *Chesapeake–Leopard* affair. The 1837 Navy Regulations, making dueling a court-martial offense, discouraged without entirely stopping the practice.

More serious in its long-term effect was the usual postwar logjam in promotions. The situation was aggravated following the War of 1812 by the fact that the young U. S. Navy had been led for the most part by young officers. These regulars, remaining in the naval service, monopolized the higher ranks through the ensuing long period of peace. The result was stagnation in the rank structure, which Congress intensified by refusing to establish any higher naval rank than captain, with "commodore" as a courtesy title (without increase in pay) for squadron commanders.

Because there were so many lieutenants, midshipmen of 30 became a commonplace, and at least one reached the age of 50 without being promoted. The naval hierarchy became divided into a large body of very junior officers and a comparatively small body of lieutenants, commanders, and captains. The aging midshipmen were in fact scarcely officers at all. They messed with the crew and had little association with their seniors. Their education, carried out generally at sea, was entrusted to chaplains and to politically appointed schoolmasters.

At the other end of the scale, the aging heroes of 1812–15 squatted on their rank. These veterans took turns on the Board of Navy Commissioners, which for 20 years was dominated by Commodore John Rodgers. Misreading the history of the American Revolution and the War of 1812, they accepted the view widely held in political and military circles that national security should be based on a strategy of coast defense and commerce raiding. Coast defense was to be a function mainly of the Army, using elaborate fortifications. Few remembered that the Navy's *guerre de course* in the two wars against England, while producing some brilliant exploits, had been wholly ineffective against strongly defended convoys.

But while the Navy languished strategically, it became increasingly receptive to new technological ideas. This was the result mainly of the enterprise of a few officers with the intellectual flexibility to realize that naval weapons had to keep pace with the new scientific revolution. Outstanding among these men were Matthew Calbraith Perry, brother of the victor of Lake Erie, and the officer-politician Robert F. Stockton, both veterans of the War of 1812; and John A. Dahlgren, the ordnance expert, who by sheer merit broke through the promotion deadlock.

To men of this caliber it was apparent that a better system of recruiting and training seamen and of educating officers was needed. Perry was at the forefront of those who advocated changes in the current system. With regard to enlisted men, Perry as early as 1824 recommended to the secretary of the navy the adoption of an apprentice system and school ships to attract into the Navy and train American boys of good character. Not until 1842 did Perry have his way. Then the new U. S. brig *Somers*, with 74 selected apprentice boys on board, was placed under his general supervision for an experimental schoolship cruise.

To command the *Somers* Perry selected his brother-in-law, Commander Alexander Slidell Mackenzie, who, like himself, had been agitating for the apprentice plan and was eager to make it work. Perry appointed one of his sons, a lieutenant, acting master, and another son and a nephew served as midshipmen. It was thus somewhat of a family enterprise.

A fatal assignment was that of Midshipman Philip Spencer, son of the secretary of war. Spencer had a bad reputation, but Perry appointed him nevertheless, possibly to demonstrate the reforming effect of this system, possibly to curry favor with the Tyler administration. On the return from a voyage to West Africa, a steward informed Mackenzie that Spencer was inciting his shipmates to mutiny, with the purpose of murdering the officers, seizing the ship, and setting up business as a West Indies pirate. Spencer may well have been mentally unbalanced, but Mackenzie's reaction suggests that he was not particularly stable himself. Even after clapping Spencer and two other supposed mutineers into irons, Mackenzie managed to convince himself, on the basis of some curious evidence, that it was necessary for the safety of the ship to hang Spencer and the two enlisted men at the yardarm. This he presently did. The story, when it reached the public, created a national sensation. Mackenzie was tried by court-martial and acquitted, but the apprentice-and-schoolship plan was quietly dropped, not to be revived till 1864. Meanwhile, Congress in 1850 abolished

flogging of seamen and in 1862 put an end to the spirit ration.

Though the United States Military Academy at West Point, founded in 1802, had proved its worth by the success of its graduates in the War of 1812, Congress repeatedly turned down recommendations that a similar academy be established for the training and education of midshipmen. In such opposition the legislators were supported by some distinguished naval officers who argued that trying to teach sailors ashore was like "teaching ducks to swim in a garret." It was only necessary, they said, for the aspiring young officer to "keep his eyes open," and they pointed to the example of such successful and cultured officers as John Paul Jones, Stephen Decatur, and Oliver H. Perry, all virtually self-educated.

To officers of the caliber of Maury and M. C. Perry, it was apparent that in a changing navy officers succeeding to positions of command were all too frequently ill prepared for their responsibilities. Maury and Perry continued to advocate a school ashore to provide midshipmen with a complete, uninterrupted education. The example of Philip Spencer provided them with an additional argument. Midshipman Spencer apparently was a product of the Congressmen's habit of appointing midshipmen as a form of political patronage, which influential constituents sometimes used as a means of getting rid of family blacksheep and other undesirables. Perry pointed out that a period of education ashore would provide a safe way to check up on the appointees and get rid of the unworthy and incompetent before they were sent to sea.

The first naval schools ashore came about through the stiffening of examinations that midshipmen had to take to become "passed midshipmen," a title they held until openings became available for them to assume the rank and duties of lieutenants. To assist the midshipmen in preparing for their examinations, coaching schools were set up in the navy yards. In the 1840s the school at Philadelphia began to acquire an outstanding reputation, chiefly through the efforts of Professor William Chauvenet, a recent honor graduate of Yale. Chauvenet's school became so popular with the midshipmen that the Navy began to phase out the other preparatory schools. When the Navy Department permitted Chauvenet to extend his course to a full year, the Philadelphia school soon outgrew its quarters in a building it shared with a home for old sailors.

George Bancroft, historian and educator, on becoming secretary of the navy in 1845, set about getting for the school a more spacious and desirable location. He found what he sought in the buildings and grounds of an army post that had outlived its usefulness: Fort Severn, at Annapolis, Maryland, near where the Severn River empties into Chesapeake Bay. From the secretary of war he received assurance that the Army would be willing to transfer its obsolete post to the Navy. When an examining board of senior naval officers, including M. C. Perry, met at the Philadelphia school, Bancroft recommended removing the school to Annapolis, and the board concurred.

On 10 October 1845, the Naval School, with an enlarged faculty and student body, opened at Annapolis under the stern but fair superintendency of Commander Franklin Buchanan. Following the example of West Point, the superintendent set up an Academic Board of officer and civilian members of the faculty to "decide on the merits of the midshipmen, report on the system of instruction, and suggest any . . . alterations which their experience may dictate." On the recommendation of the Academic Board, the course of instruction was lengthened in 1850 to four years, and the Naval School was renamed the United States Naval Academy. A further change, instituted in 1851, made the four years consecutive, with summer practice cruises at sea.

The Mexican War, 1846–48

By 1845 Texas, into which many Americans had immigrated, had enjoyed de facto independence from Mexico for nine years, and the Mexican army had not managed to make any serious attempt at reconquest. California, where armed revolt had driven out the central government's representatives, was almost equally free of Mexican control. The two chief officials were Californians, virtually self-appointed to office. The civil governor ruled southern California from Los Angeles; the military commandant maintained his capital at Monterey. Antagonism between these two leaders, plus factional strife between the natives and American settlers, so complicated the governmental situation that intervention by the United States probably prevented civil war.

On 1 March 1845, President Tyler, as almost his last official act, signed a joint congressional resolution by which Texas, at the request of the Texans, was annexed to the United States. President Polk's incoming administration, anticipating war with Mexico, began to deploy its armed forces for maximum effectiveness. George Bancroft issued most of the key orders. As secretary of the navy, he ordered Commodore John Sloat's Pacific Squadron

to prepare to seize San Francisco and such other California ports as he could. As acting secretary of war, he ordered General Zachary Taylor to advance into Texas and take position near the Rio Grande—in territory in dispute between Texas and Mexico. As secretary of the navy, he ordered Commodore David Conner's Home Squadron to support Taylor by transporting troops, convoying supply ships, and protecting Taylor's bases. Informally, he arranged for a small "exploring expedition" of frontiersmen and scouts under Brevet Captain John C. Frémont to enter California. Later a column of soldiers under Brevet Brigadier General Stephen W. Kearny set out from Fort Leavenworth, Kansas, for New Mexico.

Taylor's advance to the Rio Grande in the spring of 1846 met with resistance by Mexican troops. In a series of skirmishes they killed several Americans, whereupon the United States declared war on Mexico. Commodore Sloat then moved his squadron of four sailing vessels, including a frigate, from his temporary base at Mazatlan, Mexico, to the California coast. In July he hoisted the American flag without opposition in both Monterey and San Francisco. Sloat then fell ill and was relieved by Commodore Robert Stockton, who had arrived in the frigate *Congress*.

Stockton formed his sailors and marines into a small army, to which he attached Frémont's group, now including American settlers, and Kearny's soldiers, who en route to California had captured Santa Fe and annexed New Mexico. The small combined force proceeded to take Los Angeles, San Diego, Santa Barbara, and other California towns. Early in 1847 representatives of the weak Mexican defense forces signed the treaty of Cahuenga, which ceded California to the United States and ended the war on the Pacific coast.

The central government at Mexico City neither acknowledged defeat nor recognized U. S. annexation of New Mexico or California. To bring the Mexicans to terms, the United States planned to occupy their capital. That was General Taylor's assignment, but, though he had penetrated far into Mexico, he was still too far north to offer much of a threat. So President Polk dispatched an army of some 12,000 troops under Lieutenant General Winfield Scott to land at Veracruz and march directly inland to Mexico City.

By the time Scott's expedition got under way, Conner's blockade of Mexico's east coast was very nearly impenetrable, and his Home Squadron had undisputed command of the Gulf. In early March 1847 Scott's transports joined the Home Squadron at its anchorage in the roadstead of Antón Lizardo,

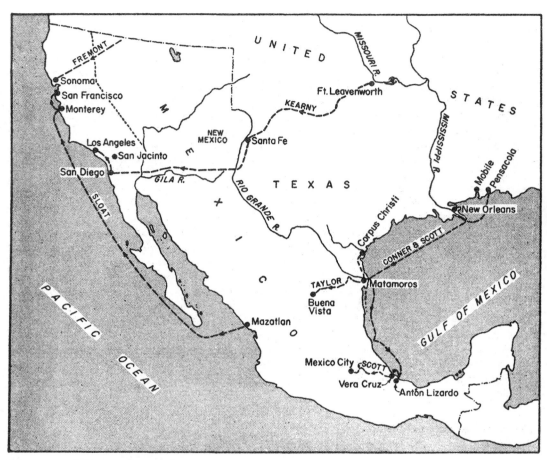

Campaigns of the Mexican War

13 miles south of Veracruz. Present were nearly a hundred vessels, including a good many steamers. This was to be full-scale amphibious invasion, not to be surpassed in numbers of American ships involved and numbers of American troops landed until World War II.

Reconnoitering the Mexican coastline in a small steamer, Scott, Conner, and their staffs decided to land the troops on a strip of beach three miles south of Veracruz. At the Antón Lizardo anchorage the landing force early on 9 March transferred from nonparticipating transports to the ships assigned to support the landing. These vessels proceeded up the coast towing the 65 surf boats that were to serve as landing craft.

In the early afternoon the transporting vessels, most of which were to serve also as fire-support ships, came to anchor off the beachhead, and sailors in the surf boats cast off their tow lines and rowed to the ships that were designated to fill them with troops. Each division of boats was commanded by a naval lieutenant, and each boat was commanded by a midshipman or petty officer. When Mexican cavalry appeared on dunes behind the beach, the invaders assumed that they would have to fight their way ashore, but the cavalry commander, perceiving the odds against him, withdrew his force into the city.

To provide close fire support, six light-draft gunboats, armed mainly with 32-pounder shell guns, took station 90 yards from the beach. When the landing craft were filled, they advanced to a line of departure, marked by a steamer 40 yards offshore. On signal from General Scott's command ship, the boats headed toward the beach. The first wave of invaders splashed ashore almost simultaneously, not under fire but to the accompaniment of cheers from the fleet. As a soldier planted an American flag on the sand dunes, bands on board several ships struck up "The Star-Spangled Banner."

Promptly upon discharging their passengers, the landing boats hurried back to the transports to pick up a second wave. By 10 p.m., 10,000 Americans were on the beach. The rest came ashore at leisure the next morning.

As Army and Navy were preparing for joint operations against the city of Veracruz itself, Commodore M. C. Perry relieved the ailing Conner in command of the Home Squadron. After a three-day bombardment by naval guns afloat and army and naval guns ashore had breached the city's walls in several places, the defenders capitulated.

While Scott's army marched inland toward Mexico City, Perry's squadron tightened the blockade and captured several ports. The commodore permitted exports and nonmilitary imports, but he ordered customs duties to be collected to help defray the costs of war.

Accompanying Scott's army were 300 U. S. marines, who at Chapultepec fought the first inland battle in U. S. Marine Corps history. When Mexico City fell, Scott, desiring to impress the populace, selected the brightly uniformed marines to mount guard in the halls of Montezuma.

By the terms of the subsequent Treaty of Guadalupe Hidalgo, Mexico ceded California and New Mexico to the United States and recognized U. S. sovereignty in Texas all the way to the Rio Grande. The ceded area provided territory that became the states of California, Nevada, and Utah, most of Arizona, and parts of New Mexico, Colorado, and Wyoming. For it the United States paid Mexico $15,000,000.

Other Navies

Decatur's operation against the Barbary states failed to put the corsairs out of business. The following year, 1816, an international commission appointed by the Congress of Vienna authorized Britain to end the nuisance. Lord Exmouth took five ships of the line to Algiers and attacked the port and its defenses, afloat and ashore. The dey, after seeing his shipping burned, his capital bombarded, and his coastal fortifications battered out of action, accepted the British terms.

Exmouth's attack ended the formal system of protection money, but the profits from seizing ships were too rich a temptation for the Barbary monarchs to resist for long. European and American squadrons were obliged to make periodic visits to the Barbary coast, until France in the 1830s conquered Algeria, citing as justification the necessity of abolishing the system.

In 1821 clandestine resistance of the Greeks to their Turkish masters turned into open revolt. The sultan, unable to suppress the insurrection, in 1825

called on the viceroy of Egypt for troops and ships. By 1827 the Egyptians had reconquered Athens, and the Greek insurgents were apparently facing defeat. At this point, Britain, France, and Russia sent an international fleet, including ten of the line, under British Vice Admiral Sir Edward Codrington, to intervene. Codrington was under orders to limit his operations to blockade, while the allied powers tried to induce the sultan to accept mediation of the conflict.

To put additional pressure on the Turks, Codrington, on 20 April 1827, exceeded his instructions by taking his combined fleet into the Greek harbor of Navarino and anchoring alongside the Turco–Egyptian fleet. In the tense situation, an exchange of small-arms fire developed into a general engagement—the Battle of Navarino, the last fleet engagement fought entirely under sail. Though the Muslim manpower and firepower far exceeded that of the Europeans, the superior training of the latter enabled them in a confused melee to destroy the Turco–Egyptian fleet. As a result, the Egyptians withdrew their army, and the Russian czar was encouraged to intervene openly as a "defender of the faith." In 1830 the sultan was forced to acknowledge Greek independence.

In the next quarter century, Europe's navies engaged in no important campaigns. Operating on decreased budgets, uncertain whether the future of naval warfare lay with sail or steam propulsion, with solid shot or shell, the sea services nevertheless kept busy. They protected commerce, looked after imperial interests, conducted voyages of exploration and scientific research, and, in the language of the day, "showed the flag" and "chastised native insolence."

The scientific expedition of the greatest long-range influence was that taken by a tiny surveying vessel, HMS *Beagle*, in the early 1830s. While the *Beagle* was exploring the coast of Patagonia, the Falkland Islands, the Galapagos Islands, and the west coast of South America, Charles Darwin, a civilian naturalist attached to the expedition, was collecting many of the specimens and data on which he later based his theory of biological evolution.

Around 1840, the French and British navies took part in military expeditions, all trifling so far as fleet operations were concerned. In reprisal for the riotous looting of a French bakery in Veracruz, Mexico, French warships, in the so-called Pastry War, turned their new shell guns on the harbor fortress, which soon surrendered. In the Opium Wars with China, both Royal Navy and British East India Company warships participated. The main long-term effect of these operations was that they convinced a few naval officers of the value of shell-fire, iron hulls, and steam propulsion.

The Crimean War, 1854–56

In 1853 a Russian army violated Turkish territory and brought on hostilities by marching into what is now Romania. To prevent any sudden Russian descent on Constantinople, Britain and France dispatched strong naval squadrons to the Sea of Marmara.

Russia's Vice Admiral P. S. Nakhimov, far from being awed into inactivity, cruised freely in the Black Sea in search of Turkish ships, In November 1853 he discovered a squadron of seven frigates off the ill-fortified Turkish port of Sinop. With six ships of the line Nakhimov entered the roadstead and, using 68-pounder shell guns, sank all seven of the frigates, silenced the shore batteries, and set fire to the town. At a cost of fewer than 40 fatalities, he had killed nearly 3,000 Turks.

Western Europe was shocked by the ruthlessness of the Russians, who turned their guns indiscriminately on vessels trying to surrender, on boats, and on men struggling in the water. The British and French admiralties, which still preferred shot to shell and wooden hulls to iron, were jarred into reappraising their naval weapons. Evidently unarmored wooden hulls had been rendered obsolete by the shell gun, which not only shattered them but set them afire.

Since Britain and France had informally undertaken to protect Turkey, the Battle of Sinop practically obliged them to declare war on Russia. In June 1854 an Anglo–French fleet entered the Black Sea and landed 60,000 British and French troops at Varna, thereby taking the pressure off the Turkish

army and inducing the Russians to withdraw across the Danube.

The Allies had thus attained their minimum aim without fighting, but their governments believed it was important to achieve something more tangible, if only to gratify public opinion. Both Britain and France sent fleets, and France sent troops to attack Russia via the Baltic Sea, but the only lasting advantage the allies attained by this northern operation was to hold Russian defense forces that otherwise might have been shifted to the Black Sea area.

In the South the allied leaders were directed to transport their troops from Varna across the Black Sea to the Crimean Peninsula and seize the Russian naval base of Sevastopol. They would thus avenge Sinop, humiliate Russia, and possibly bring the war to a close before winter, 1854.

The passage across to the Crimea was unopposed, the outnumbered Russian Black Sea fleet choosing to remain at Sevastopol. The Russian restraint was fortunate for the Allies because the French warships were so crowded with troops that they could hardly have fired a shot in self-defense.

Chosen for the Crimean landing was a place marked "Old Fort" on the charts, some 30 miles north of Sevastopol. The ground here was flat and hence favorable for advance, but the beachhead proved a logistic nightmare. There was little or nothing to forage in the area, and except for a single spring all available water was salt or brackish. Because there was no harbor at or near the invasion beach, it could not possibly serve as a base of operations.

To counter opposition to the landing, which never appeared, the French drew up a line of rocket-firing boats. To bring artillery ashore they used specially constructed landing craft, and the British did almost as well with small steam paddle launches and decked-over pairs of boats. Yet dilatoriness and indecision which had hampered the expedition from the beginning, were nowhere so apparent as at the beachhead, where of all places movement should be well planned, swift, and decisive. Merely getting the men and their equipment ashore took from 14 to 18 September, and the British troops waited through rain and blazing sun for nearly three days before their tents were disembarked. Lacking adequate medical facilities, hundreds of men died of cholera and dysentery. Materials moved back and forth between fleet and shore, while the commanders tried to make up their minds about just what equipment the troops really needed.

The British and French soldiers, ill-led but

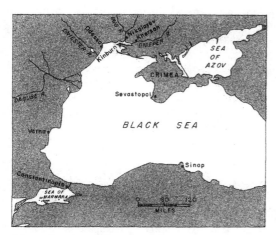

Main Theater of the Crimean War

courageous, in a month's time fought their way around south of Sevastopol. In this area were harbors, none really good, but capable in a pinch of serving as logistic bases. Meanwhile, inside the Russian base engineers, sailors, and civilians, including women, rapidly repaired neglected fortifications.

In mid-October 1854 the Allies at length began offensive operations with a bombardment in which both fleet guns and shore artillery participated. It was a waste of time because, though Sevastopol's southern defenses were wrecked, the cannonade was not followed by an assault. The operation did, however, have a measurable influence on the history of naval warfare by demonstrating the advantages of steam propulsion. The sailing ships of the line, virtually becalmed, had to be pushed and towed into position by small steamers. Even then they were too far out to be effective. Unable to maneuver, they were mere stationary targets for the Russian shore batteries, which inflicted great damage. By contrast, two screw-ships, moving in close to the shore, knocked out some of the batteries and then sped nimbly out of harm's way.

The failure of the Allies to assault when assault was relatively easy turned the operation against Sevastopol into a siege and doomed the British and French to spend the winter in the Crimea. Sevastopol fell at last on 9 September 1855, a year almost to the day after the initial allied landings at Old Fort beachhead.

While engineers set about demolishing Sevastopol's dockyards and fortifications, an Anglo–French expeditionary force including some 9,000 troops proceeded by sea to Kinburn. Here at the end of a long spit of land three forts guarded the entrance to an estuary into which flowed the Bug, the Ingul, and the Dnieper rivers. Capture of the Kinburn forts would permit the Allies to close all three rivers, thereby cutting off from the Black Sea the naval base and arsenal at Nikolayev and the rich commercial city of Kherson. The expeditionary force isolated the forts by landing troops on the spit above them. Two days later, after a bombardment from land and sea, the Russian garrisons surrendered.

Chiefly responsible for this quick victory were three ungainly little armored floating batteries, the *Tonnante*, the *Dévastation*, and the *Lave*. Hurriedly built by the French in reaction to the Battle of Sinop, they were the world's first ironclads to go into action. With sufficient steam power for maneuvering, but not for cruising, they had 17-inch-thick wooden hulls covered above the waterline with 4½-inch-thick iron plates. As they battered the forts from a range of less than a thousand yards, solid shot merely bounced off their plates, and shells burst on impact, doing no damage at all. The fall of Kinburn had little effect on the outcome of the war, but the bombardment of the forts, viewed by officers of several nations, ushered in the age of naval armor.

The Russians, constrained at last to capitulate, were obliged to leave Sevastopol dismantled, but they received credit for an effective defense. The Allies won the war but sullied their military reputations.

Technological Developments

Naval officers, despite unhappy experiences with calms and contrary winds, were not at first generally receptive to the idea of steam propulsion for fleets. Steam in the early nineteenth century was even less efficient than sail propulsion; early engines were liable to breakdowns that could be fatal in action. Use of steam drastically cut down on a ship's cruising radius; an early steamer would burn up all her fuel in less than a hundred miles. The paddle wheel masked as much as a third of the broadside and, while the superior mobility of the steamer was certainly an advantage in battle, one lucky shot could disable her paddle wheel or engine and leave her outsailed and outgunned. Hence naval officers preferred to let commercial vessels make the trial-and-error experiments that at length produced dependable, high-speed steam engines that were economical of fuel.

There was, to be sure, one early experiment in naval steam propulsion. The U. S. Navy, exasperated by the British blockade in the War of 1812, had Robert Fulton, the famed steamboat builder, design and build a steam-propelled blockade breaker. This was the *Demologos* (later renamed *Fulton*), the world's first steam warship. Constructed with sides five feet thick, carrying her boiler and engine low in twin hulls with the single paddle wheel in between, she was nearly invulnerable to contemporary ordnance. Before the *Demologos* was ready for action, however, the war ended. She was tied up as a receiving ship at the Brooklyn Navy Yard and subsequently destroyed by fire.

The British and French navies took to the use of steam very tentatively, at first applying it only to auxiliary vessels—tugs, dispatch boats, and such. In the 1830s, they at last commenced building small steamers especially for use in combat. The U. S. Navy was even more hesitant. Two decades after the War of 1812 it had not built a single steamer of any sort.

At last, in 1837, the U.S. Navy launched its second steam warship, the *Fulton II*. A 700-ton sidewheeler, she was 180 feet long and carried four tall stacks and three masts. Matthew C. Perry, long an outspoken advocate of steam propulsion, superintended her building and served as her first commanding officer. Acceptance by the Navy Commissioners of his plan for hiring, paying, and ranking men to fire his boilers and run his machinery practically established the U. S. Navy's engineer corps.

Because of the *Fulton's* limited coal capacity and other defects, she could not be considered a seagoing vessel, but Perry managed to get her from New York to Washington, where he showed her off to President Van Buren and members of Congress, convincing them of the practicality of a steam navy. Partly as a result, the U. S. Navy in 1842 took a strong, if temporary, lead over the rest of the world's navies by launching the 3,220-ton sidewheelers *Mississippi* and *Missouri*. The *Missouri* was consumed by fire the following year, but the *Mississippi* enjoyed a distinguished career, participating in the Mexican War and the opening of Japan. She was at last destroyed in the American Civil War in the river for which she was named.

The widespread reluctance to adopt steam for combat vessels was eventually overcome by the development of a practical screw propeller. This was achieved independently in England by Francis Pettit Smith, a farmer with no engineering training, and by the Swedish inventive genius John Ericsson. The screw had none of the objectionable features of the paddle wheel, but the British Admiralty could not at first be convinced that a screw-propelled vessel could be steered. Rebuffed in England, Ericsson was easily persuaded by Captain Robert Stockton to come to the United States. Here Stockton, through his insistence and political influence, induced the Navy in 1842 to authorize the building of a screw steamer to Ericsson's specifications. This was the sloop-of-war *Princeton*, the first screw-propelled naval steamer. She was also the first warship to have all her machinery below the waterline and thus out of reach of shot.

The Royal Navy, at length convinced of the merits of the screw, launched the screw-sloop *Rattler* shortly after the appearance of the *Princeton*. The *Rattler*, by triumphing over a paddle-wheeler of the same horsepower in a tug-of-war and in several speed trials, firmly established screw propulsion. In the next few years Britain converted a number of her old veterans of the Napoleonic wars to steam and screw. France in 1850 launched her first screw ship of the line, the *Napoléon*. Two years later Britain followed suit with the *Agamemnon*.

During the mid-1850s the United States began launching the *Merrimack* class of fast screw frigates that were to play an important role in the coming American Civil War.

In the first Opium War the British East India Company used a pair of iron-hulled steam gunboats, and by 1844 Britain and the United States each had an iron-hulled naval steamer on the Great Lakes. The Royal Navy began ordering iron frigates, but just when it appeared that iron was about to be universally adopted for naval hulls, a series of tests convinced the British Admiralty that iron, in its current state of metallurgical development, was more vulnerable than oak. The Royal Navy thereupon converted its new iron frigates into troop transports, and iron construction of naval vessels was virtually abandoned for several years. No iron ships fought in the Crimean War.

Navies were slow to adopt the explosive shell for general use although naval officers recognized the inadequacy of solid shot as a ship destroyer, a fact demonstrated in the Battle of Trafalgar, when thousands of shot were fired at close range without sinking a single ship. For centuries small mortar boats and bomb ketches had been lobbing explosive-filled projectiles into fortifications with deadly effect, but officers considered shells too great a fire hazard to be carried about and fired in the main fleet, and at any rate those that could be fired from the standard 24- and 32-pounders were too small to be effective.

Following the Napoleonic Wars, a French artillery officer, Henri-Joseph Paixhans, designed a shell gun, shorter, lighter, using smaller charges than guns of the same caliber designed for solid shot, and in 1824 demonstrated its potentiality by splintering an old two-decker. Though both the French and the British navies in the late 1830s adopted the Paixhans gun, it was regarded as a special-purpose weapon, secondary to solid-shot ordnance.

The annihilation of the Turkish fleet at Sinop convinced the naval powers that the shell had come to stay. It also led to the protection of hulls, wood or iron, with thick iron plates, thus producing the ironclad. Both the British and the French hurriedly built ironclads to participate in the Crimean War. Following the war, the French built the *Gloire*, the first seagoing ironclad. She was a 5,600-ton wooden frigate armored with iron plates 4¾ inches thick. The Royal Navy countered by contracting for its first battleship, HMS *Warrior*. The *Warrior*, launched in 1860, was 380 feet long, displaced 9,000 tons, and had a 4½-inch armor belt backed with 18 inches of teak. No wooden hull could have stood the strain of such length or carried the weight of her armor, her necessarily powerful engines, and her 40 guns, all immensely heavier than any regularly used afloat in the age of sail. Recognizing this, her architects made her hull completely of iron.

The launching of the *Warrior* ended the era of wooden warships. There remained of course numerous veterans of earlier years that were to see some service. Wooden steam sloops and frigates, for example, were to play a major role in the impending American Civil War. But after 1860 Britain built warships only of iron or, later, steel. And though there was some backtracking in other navies, all eventually followed Britain's example.

At the end of the Napoleonic wars, naval guns were little different in construction and performance from those used in the Spanish Armada campaign. There had been some improvements in loading and aiming, and better carriages had been devised, but the gun itself was still the cast-iron, smoothbore, solid-shot-firing muzzle-loader used of old. Ranges were about the same, averaging 300 yards point-blank and 2,500 yards extreme. Attempts at improving accuracy were largely nullified by the fact that the solid shot, partly because of rust, were rarely perfectly spherical. Hence there had to be considerable "windage"—space between the shot and the surface of the bore—to avoid wedging. Thus much of the propulsive force of the exploding charge was lost, and the ball went bouncing from side to side along the bore and emerged at unpredictable angles.

The introduction of the paddle wheel, by cutting down the number of guns a vessel could carry, stimulated experiments toward developing more effective gunfire with fewer guns. One answer was the pivot gun, which could be swung about to strengthen either broadside. A more satisfactory answer was bigger guns, but they would have to be stronger guns, because charges needed to propel shot of more than 32 pounds were likely to burst brittle cast-iron barrels, wounding or killing the gun crews.

In the early 1840s Ericsson and Stockton each designed a huge 12-inch wrought-iron gun for installation on board the *Princeton*. When Ericsson's gun, which he named the Oregon, developed cracks near the butt during test firing, the inventor strengthened the breech with heavy wrought-iron bands. Stockton built his similar gun, called the Peacemaker, with thicker metal but without any reinforcing breech bands. During demonstration firing, the Peacemaker blew up, killing an officer, two congressmen, the secretary of the navy, and

the secretary of state. The U. S. Navy thereupon barred further use of wrought-iron guns, and ordnance experts everywhere viewed them with suspicion.

In the early 1850s Commander John A. Dahlgren, USN, designed a bottle-shaped gun, thick at the breech with considerable taper toward the muzzle, where the pressure of the exploding gases was less intense. An obvious improvement over the ordnance then in use, the Dahlgren gun was quickly adopted by the U. S. Navy.

The Dahlgren gun was outmoded at last by the built-up gun, in which the barrel consisted of two or more concentric tubes, the outer being slipped over the inner while glowing hot and left to shrink firmly into position. In the British-designed Armstrong gun, the inner tube was a wrought-iron bar, coiled and welded into tubular form. Thus the metal received the stresses of firing along its length instead of across its width.

To lend some protection to the pivoting big guns and their gunners, which at first were exposed on the weather deck, John Ericsson and Captain Cowper Coles of the Royal Navy each independently developed the naval gun turret. The turreted ship first completed was Ericsson's *Monitor*, which fought the *Virginia* in the Battle of Hampton Roads in 1862.

Until the middle of the nineteenth century, shells as well as solid shot were spherical. The fuse was a hollow cylinder filled with hardened gunpowder. Cut to burn for a period of time corresponding to the range of the target, the fuse was pounded or screwed into a hole in the shell until the after end was flush with the outer surface. The shell was then inserted through the muzzle into the barrel of the gun, where it was held in place, fuse pointed outward, by a collar called a sabot. When the gun was fired, the flames flashed around the shell and ignited the fuse as the projectile passed along the barrel.

Understandably, such time-fused shells tended to explode too soon or too late.[1] The alternative was the percussion fuse, to set off the explosion on impact, but the projectile would have to strike fuse-first, and that was impossible to control with spherical shells. An elongated shell tended to tumble end over end—unless it were made to rotate on its long axis. Such rotation could be imparted by rifling the gun barrels, as makers of small arms had

---

[1]Francis Scott Key's "bombs bursting in air" of "The Star-Spangled Banner" evidently had fuses that were too short.

long since demonstrated. But for the rifling to be effective, the shell would have to fit snugly in the barrel, thereby building up pressures that could burst early nineteenth-century ordnance.

Before the development of the sturdy built-up gun, British ordnance experts sought to achieve the effect of rifling while preserving windage. The result was the Lancaster gun, which fired an elliptical shell from a twisted elliptical bore; and the Whitworth gun, which fired a hexagonal shell from a twisted hexagonal bore. Such makeshifts proved not good enough. The first gun in general use that could safely withstand the pressures produced by rifling was the built-up Armstrong. It fired elongated projectiles coated with lead that engaged the rifling as they passed out along the bore.

The U. S. Navy long resisted the trend toward rifling. Throughout the Civil War and for 20 years thereafter, the smoothbore Dahlgren was standard on board American naval vessels. There were good reasons. Dahlgrens, with their round shot and heavy charges, were better at penetrating armor than contemporary guns using smaller-caliber elongated projectiles. The greater range conferred by rifling was considered a standing temptation to shoot off one's ammunition before closing with the enemy. American naval officers were confirmed in their prejudice by their experience with the rifled Parrott gun. It had a heavy wrought-iron band shrunk around the breech, but lacking reinforcement along the whole length of the barrel, it had a notorious tendency to blow off its own muzzle.

Administrative Changes

It was early evident that the naval organization of the age of sail was inadequate to deal with the problems posed by the new technology. To meet the challenge, the leading navies made major changes in administration and command. Because the period was one of comparative peace, the emphasis everywhere was on logistics; little was done to improve overall operational command. Changes made in the navies of Britain and the United States illustrate the trend.

The British Admiralty was completely reorganized in 1832, when Sir James Graham, then First Lord, broke up and redistributed the top administrative commands. In the new organization, five sea lords, all officers, reported to him directly in the Board of Admiralty. Each of the sea lords superintended the work of one of five civil departments of the Admiralty. Each department was headed by an executive officer who reported to the cognizant sea lord. The executive officers bore the titles Sur-

veyor of the Navy, in charge of materials and design; Accountant-General, or treasurer; Storekeeper-General; Controller of Victualling; and Physician-General.

Ten years later the U. S. Navy replaced the Board of Navy Commissioners with a similar departmental system, which was even more closely adapted to the navy of iron and steam. The organization set up in 1842 provided for five bureaus, each headed by an officer: Navy-Yards and Docks; Construction, Equipment, and Repairs; Provisions and Clothing; Ordnance and Hydrography; and Medicine and Surgery.

The only means of coordinating the new departments and bureaus was, in the Royal Navy, through the First Lord of the Admiralty; in the U. S. Navy, through the secretary of the navy. Both were political appointees and members of the cabinet. In the United States the secretary of the navy has traditionally been a civilian. Since the incumbency of Lord Barham, of Trafalgar days, this has been true also of the First Lord, though a few retired officers have held the position. Neither navy had an officer in overall command of operations, and the British sea lords and the American bureau chiefs were too involved in logistics to advise the civilian head of the navy on the conduct of war. Except for certain temporary, makeshift arrangements, this was the situation until the end of the century.

On the operational level, changes were equally necessary to meet the new challenge. Hence in 1837 the engineer officer appeared in both the Royal Navy and the U. S. Navy. But there was a difference. In the U. S. Navy the engineer was from the beginning a commissioned officer, albeit a staff officer, not absorbed into the line until the end of the century. In the Royal Navy aristocratic tradition, which put the warrior on a higher plane than the ship handler, kept the engineer in the status of warrant officer for ten years. When in 1847 senior British naval engineers received commissions, they assumed the curious title "inspector of machinery afloat."

Summary

The years 1815–60 were a period of minor military operations. The American and British navies, to be sure, humbled Algiers. British and French fleet units were involved in imperialistic wars against China. The United States Pacific and Home squadrons participated in the Mexican War of 1846–48. The Royal Navy and the French *Marine* operated in both the Baltic and the Black seas during the Crimean War of 1854–56. None of these wars, however, was a major conflict, and none produced fleet battles at sea.

The period nevertheless was momentous in naval history. After 2,000 years of oar propulsion and 300 years of sail propulsion, the navies of the world made their great shift—to steam propulsion. At the same time they began adopting armor; the iron hull; rifled, built-up guns; and the percussion-fused shell. The world's armies, while not so completely revolutionized by the new technology, also found themselves with an arsenal of new weapons.

No one doubted that the technological changes would have a great impact upon the nature of warfare. Armchair tacticians filled the military journals with their theories. But in 1860, when HMS *Warrior* was launched, few of the new weapons and few of the new theories had been put to the test of combat. Hence the outbreak of civil war in the United States the following year drew the prompt attention of military thinkers all over the world. As the war developed into a major conflict, various governments sent observers to report how the new weapons performed under fire. The American Civil War thus became, among other things, a testing ground for the new military technology.

Chapter 12
The American Civil War: The Blockade and the Cruisers

Though slighted by many military historians, the role of the U. S. Navy in the American Civil War was crucial. The Navy's basic strategy of blockade, supplemented by the investing and capture of Confederate ports and by riverine warfare in the West, was an essential precondition to the victories of the Union armies. The seceding states east of the Mississippi depended on the production and export of cotton. The Confederacy as a whole lacked an industrial base, and the eastern portion was not self-sustaining, even in foodstuffs. Though the Union navy was initially small and ill-equipped for its task—sealing off some 3,500 miles of enemy coastline and patrolling nearly 200 harbors and navigable rivers—between 1861 and 1865 it grew exponentially under the able leadership of Secretary of the Navy Gideon Welles. In conjunction with the Union army, it successfully carried out a policy aptly termed the "Anaconda." Like a giant anaconda, the joint force gradually tightened its coils until the trade and commercial life of the South were almost totally extinguished. In the latter years of the war, appalling shortages of consumer goods of all types coupled with unbacked banknotes to create a printing press inflation. By the fall of 1864, one gold dollar was worth $2,000 in Confederate currency.

Surrender of Fort Sumter

After declaring its independence, the Confederate States of America claimed by right of eminent domain all Federal installations within its borders—intending to make monetary recompense after suitable negotiations. In the seven states that first seceded there were the Pensacola Navy Yard, 15 forts guarding harbors, 6 Federal arsenals, and in Texas, 18 military posts, all with quantities of weapons. After Virginia joined the Confederacy, there was the most valuable prize of all, the Norfolk Navy Yard. The Southern governments, unable to produce even small arms in the amount necessary should war break out, sought the Union properties as much for their weaponry as for their real estate value.

When the Confederacy was first established in February 1861, the vacillating James Buchanan was still the lame duck president of the United States. Capitalizing on his hesitation and on the weakness of the garrisons in most of the forts, the South took over most of these properties without conflict. Because of their remoteness and strength, Fort Pickens at Pensacola, Fort Taylor at Key West, and Fort Jefferson in the Tortugas remained in Federal hands. So too did Fortress Monroe in Virginia, and for a brief time the forts in Charleston harbor.

Because of South Carolina's primacy in the secessionist movement, the forts at Charleston had a symbolic significance for both North and South. Of the three stonework fortifications, only Fort Moultrie, on the mainland north of the harbor entrance, was garrisoned. Concerned by the possibility of a surprise attack, Major Robert Anderson, USA, prudently shifted his little command of 83 men to the more defensible Fort Sumter, located on a man-made island athwart the harbor entrance. South Carolina militia thereupon occupied Fort Moultrie and the smaller Castle Pinckney.

On 9 January 1861, a merchant vessel under army charter, the *Star of the West*, attempted to run in supplies and reinforcements to Sumter. She was fired on by new Confederate batteries on Morris Island, just south of the harbor entrance—the first shots of the Civil War. Unarmed, the relief ship withdrew.

After months of tacit truce, Confederate General Pierre Beauregard, former engineering officer in the U. S. Army, had his attack plan prepared and his batteries emplaced. At dawn on 12 April 1861, the bombardment of Fort Sumter began, rendering inevitable the war that was to prove the bloodiest in American history.

With its full garrison and all of its guns, the fort would have been nearly impregnable. But with only a third of its proper battery and about an eighth of its full garrison, Anderson was able to make only a token resistance. After a three-day exchange of spirited fire with the Confederate batteries, he acknowledged the hopelessness of his position and surrendered.

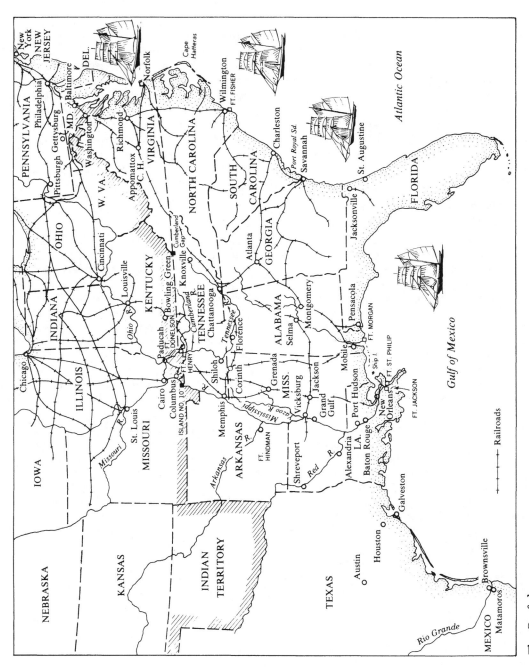

The Confederacy

Meanwhile, a small relief expedition with 200 reinforcements, which had been sent by the U. S. Navy, stood off Charleston harbor impotent to intervene. Accomplishment of its mission depended on the presence of the guns of the paddlewheel sloop *Powhatan*. But unknown to the Navy, the big sloop had been diverted by order of President Lincoln to a secret expedition for the relief of Fort Pickens. The otherwise fruitless relief force off Charleston was allowed to carry away the paroled soldiers of Anderson's command.

Lincoln's response was immediate: on 15 April he called 75,000 state militia to Federal service. This threat of coercive action prompted Virginia, North Carolina, Arkansas, and Tennessee to join the seven states already seceded.

Loss of the Norfolk Navy Yard

The Norfolk Navy Yard, biggest in the country, had one of the two large naval drydocks and was the storage arsenal for 300-odd Dahlgren guns, 50 or more of which were 9-inch weapons of the latest design. Here too were several vessels under repair, including the 50-gun screw frigate *Merrimack*.

Well aware of secessionist sentiment in Virginia, Secretary Welles warned the commandant of the yard, Commodore C. S. McCauley, to exercise "great vigilance." On 12 April, the secretary ordered Engineer in Chief Benjamin F. Isherwood, USN, to Norfolk to supervise engine repairs on the *Merrimack* so that she could be shifted to Philadelphia. When Virginia seceded, Commodore Hiram Paulding was immediately sent to relieve McCauley, who for fear of provoking the Virginia militia hesitated to take appropriate action. Paulding's orders were to evacuate or destroy all naval material and shipping at Norfolk.

When Paulding in the USS *Pawnee* reached Norfolk on 20 April, he found that the *Merrimack* and three other vessels had been scuttled by McCauley's orders. In spite of reinforcements from Fortress Monroe, Paulding lacked the force to withstand an unexpected attack. Working through the night, bluejackets and marines from the *Pawnee* mined the drydock, spread combustibles around the buildings and tophamper of the partially submerged ships, and tried unsuccessfully to sledge off the trunnions of the big guns. A little before dawn the powder trains were ignited. As the firing parties rowed away, the yard turned into a sheet of flame. When the fires burned themselves out, the Confederates found undamaged the largest cache of modern ordnance in North America—the guns that would later arm the newly constructed forts defending Southern harbors.

Proclamation of the Blockade

In view of the overwhelming preponderance of Union industrial superiority, it was evident to everyone that the South could never match the Northern navy ship-for-ship. President Jefferson Davis, of the Confederate States of America, accepted the traditional role of the weaker power at sea, commerce raiding, and by proclamation offered letters of marque and reprisal to armed privateers. Two days later Lincoln proclaimed a blockade of the Southern ports.

Since, under international law, neutrals are not bound by a "paper blockade," it behooved the U. S. Navy to make the blockade an effective one as soon as possible. With its 7,600 men, and only 42 ships in commission (many of them on distant stations), the Navy appeared to be facing an impossible task.

But with a merchant marine and a large seafaring population to draw on, with abundant yards and machine works, and with the dedication and drive of Secretary Welles and his principal administrative aide, Gustavus V. Fox, the assistant secretary, the sea service expanded explosively. Counting converted grain barges and ferryboats—anything stable enough for a gun platform—there were 264 vessels in commission by December of 1861. Thousands of new "naval volunteers" may have lacked the smartness of the Old Navy but, drawn mainly from the fishing fleets and the merchant marine, they already knew their seamanship.

Once the blockade was initiated, it became obvious that its full implementation would require logistic support of a scale and variety not previously contemplated. The inshore patrol would be steam-propelled; hence colliers and coaling stations, preferably near the blockading stations, would be required. As more ships joined the squadrons, more and larger base facilities would be necessary. Though there were adequate bases in the North, there was an evident need for others close to the Southern ports the Navy was attempting to seal. Possession of a base near Charleston and Savannah, for example, would greatly increase the number of Federal ships on station by eliminating the need for individual blockade vessels to return periodically to Washington or Philadelphia for upkeep. Furthermore, ships taking on coal or undergoing repairs at such an advanced base would always remain available as a ready reserve for speedy reinforcement of the ships on patrol.

So the Navy planned to capture strategic sites for advanced bases as soon as adequate amphibious forces could be assembled. With the ships and troops available in 1861, any attempt to seize fortified ports such as Charleston, Savannah, or Wilmington, North Carolina, was out of the question. Yet the sites to be occupied would have to provide good, deep anchorages and the possibility of developing docking facilities. Furthermore, they had to be near the Confederacy's major ports and at the same time be easily defensible from the landward side. Luckily, the length and convoluted nature of the Southern coastline, which made blockade so difficult, facilitated capture of the sort of bases the Navy required. With thousands of miles of coast and almost 200 harbors, the Confederacy could hardly manage to fortify in advance every place the Navy might strike.

Port Royal

As soon as the ships and men became available, the Union set about seizing bases along the Confederacy's coastline. The first important operation was that against Port Royal, midway between Charleston and Savannah, undertaken by Commodore Samuel F. Du Pont in November 1861. Port Royal was defended by two earthwork fortifications, on opposite sides of the harbor entrance—Fort Walker, on Hilton Head, and Fort Beauregard, on Bay Point.

The U. S. Navy lacked experience in fighting forts with steam vessels. At this time it was an open question whether their superior maneuverability compensated for the danger of having enemy shot rupture their steam lines or pierce their boilers. Consequently, Du Pont demanded a formidable flotilla. Besides a supply convoy sailing separately, the striking force comprised 11 large warships, 36 transports carrying 13,000 army troops, and several new "90-day gunboats." The armada had a 5-to-1 fire superiority over the guns of both forts together.

Loss of ships' boats in a storm off the Carolina coast dictated a change from the original plan of amphibious attack to a purely naval operation. After reconnaissance and soundings, Du Pont left his troop carriers at anchor well offshore, and took his fighting ships in to bombard Fort Walker. Heavily gunned on its seaward side, the fort had only two guns bearing on its northern flank. It was the commodore's plan to pass the fort into the sound with his whole force, then to detach his starboard division of gunboats to deliver enfilading fire on the weak northern flank while his big ships steamed on

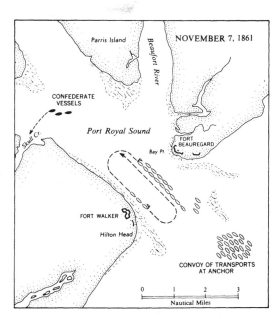

The Attack on Port Royal, South Carolina

an elliptical course and dueled the main Confederate batteries.

But when the flagship, the 46-gun steam frigate *Wabash*, turned to port to lead back past the fort at short range, only two other vessels of his column of nine actually followed. The others joined the gunboats in pounding the north flank of the fort. The three ships with Du Pont completed two ellipses and began a third. The awkwardness or insubordination of the other captains turned out to be of little consequence, for the combined volume of naval firepower soon smothered the defenses, and the fort was abandoned. The weaker Fort Beauregard was now deemed indefensible, and the Confederates abandoned that also. The Federal troops were now able to come ashore at their leisure without firing a shot. Port Royal would be a major base for the blockaders for the rest of the war.

In many respects the Port Royal action exemplifies the type of operation the Union navy mainly engaged in. Some were unopposed; others involved extensive campaigning by troops ashore. Hatteras Inlet, Roanoke Island, Elizabeth City, New Bern, Amelia Island, Jacksonville, Ship Island, and Pensacola were all invested in their turn. Union recovery of St. Augustine and Norfolk soon reduced the Confederacy's control of its Atlantic seaboard to the port of Savannah and the stretch of blockaded coast between Charleston, South Carolina, and Wilmington, North Carolina.

The *Trent* Affair

The fundamental grand strategy of the South was to defend its territory and count on simple war weariness in the North ultimately to bring peace. Southern leaders, however, were also convinced that a protracted war and an effective blockade would compel England and perhaps France to intervene to secure the raw cotton required for their mills. This "King Cotton" myth was exploded by a number of factors: the existence in Europe of a very large cotton inventory, rapid development of Egyptian and Indian cotton culture, and the effective propaganda of Northern abolitionists in England.

England in fact once came close to intervention, but not for economic reasons. The South, seeking diplomatic recognition abroad, dispatched two former U. S. senators, James M. Mason and John Slidell, as its plenipotentiaries in Europe. The emissaries, with families and staff, ran the blockade to Havana, where they embarked in the British mail-packet *Trent*. Apprised of this, Captain Charles Wilkes, USN, commanding the screw sloop *San Jacinto*, on 8 November 1861 intercepted the *Trent* at sea, boarded her, and took off the distinguished passengers as prisoners. This was strictly Captain Wilkes's own idea, but it nearly brought war with England.

In legalistic terms, Wilkes's action violated the principle of neutral rights that dictates that the flag conveys its nationality to the ship that flies it—a doctrine the United States had gone to war for in 1812. In Britain, an aroused public and a hostile press damned the act as an insult to the honor of their flag. But Lincoln pointedly stressed the lack of government sanction, Secretary of State Seward sent a note of apology and conciliation to the British envoy in Washington, and Mason and Slidell were released from their dungeon in Boston harbor.

The Ironclads

The agrarian economy of the South obviously could not begin to build in competition with the Northern shipyards. But the 1860s were an era of invention and of rapid improvements in engineering and weaponry. Perhaps by quality and innovation the Confederacy could with a very few superior ships cancel out the North's advantage in numbers. Stephen R. Mallory, secretary of the Confederate Navy, had earlier been chairman of the Naval Affairs Committee in the U. S. Senate. Well aware of the nascent technological revolution in naval vessels, he sought to produce armored warships long before Secretary Welles proposed an Ironclad Board for the Union navy.

For speedy results, the most promising project would be to convert ships already built. The sunken hulk of the *Merrimack* at the Norfolk Navy Yard looked especially suitable. About 260 feet long, displacing 4,500 tons, powered by two 600-horsepower engines, she had a mounted battery of 40 Dahlgren guns. In early July 1861, Mallory ordered her conversion to an ironclad. She was raised, her burned-out superstructure cleared away, and her power plant repaired.

The engineers in charge of the *Merrimack* project were handicapped by the lack of industry in the South. There was only one rolling mill in the Confederacy capable of turning out the two-inch slabs for side armor. With no steel production to draw from, the mill had to use old railroad rails for feedstock. But as the months went by, the makeshift conversion—rechristened the CSS *Virginia*—took shape. Her essential innovation was her casemate, 178 feet long, armored with two layers of iron plate, and with sides sloping about 35 degrees from the vertical. The casemate was pierced for seven guns of from 6 to 9 inches in bore, four of them rifled. The top of the casemate was a heavy iron grating for ventilation. In addition, a stout iron ram was fixed to her bow. The unarmored portion of her hull, bow and stern, had only a foot or so of freeboard, and would be awash, or nearly so, when she was under way.

It was Mallory's hope that the *Virginia*, when operational, would at the very least be able to destroy the wooden warships of the Union navy blockading the lower Chesapeake, and cut off the Union forces in Fortress Monroe from waterborne supplies and reinforcements. In addition, the Confederacy had reliable intelligence that General George McClellan, USA, intended to move on Richmond from its Chesapeake Bay flank, via the Yorktown Peninsula. Union loss of naval control in the Hampton Roads area would vitiate this plan.

The threat was real enough for Secretary Welles to seek a counter to the *Virginia*. The Ironclad Board, convened on his order in August 1861, reviewed more than a hundred ironclad proposals and reported that, though armored vessels were impractical for deep-water operations, they would be invaluable for inshore and riverine war. They recommended three contracts: the *Galena*, a lightly protected gunboat; the *New Ironsides*, a broadside type, which was to do good work at

Charleston; and the *Monitor*, a radically innovative design by John Ericsson.

The *Monitor* may well have been the most original design in the history of naval architecture. In mid-September, on the mere promise of a contract, Ericsson began work. With talent, dedication, and drive, and constant daily supervision, he had the vessel afloat in 101 working days. There was never a comprehensive design or scale model. While construction was in progress, Ericsson himself dashed off a hundred detailed drawings as needed. The first engineer of the *Monitor* estimated that the ship contained more than 40 patentable inventions.

The *Monitor*, and successive vessels like her, were designed to carry heavy armor over a small battery of the largest caliber guns. With minimal reserve buoyancy, they had little freeboard; their well-protected turrets offered the only targets to enemy fire. All nonessential tophamper was avoided.

The finished *Monitor* had a hull 124 feet long, on which was riveted a raftlike deck 172 feet by 41½ feet, the vertical sides of which carried 4½-inch iron armor backed by oak. This deck was protected from plunging fire by one-inch armor on its horizontal surface. The 9-foot-high turret, 20 feet in diameter, was set on a brass ring laid into the deck. Eight layers of one-inch rolled iron plates made up the laminated sidewalls of the cylindrical turret. The turret cover was a grating of railroad rails. The 140-ton turret rested on a spindle which extended down to the keel. This spindle was cogged to a steam auxiliary engine that could turn the turret through a complete 360-degree revolution.

The battery consisted of two 11-inch Dahlgren smoothbores. When their muzzles were inboard of the ports (as for cleaning and loading), the ports were automatically shielded by heavy iron "port stoppers" that swung over like pendulums. It was Ericsson's opinion that the turret should be revolved to bring the enemy under fire only an instant before actual firing, so that the exposure of the gun crews in opening the ports would be kept to a minimum.

The engine was of the then conventional double-trunk type with its 36-inch cylinders bored in a single casting. There were two return-tube box boilers. The *Monitor*'s first commanding officer was Lieutenant John L. Worden, USN—a brave man and a beloved leader, though rather lacking in the technical background this novel type of ship was to demand. The *Monitor* was commissioned on 25 February 1862 and after brief testing was ordered to Hampton Roads.

The Battle of Hampton Roads

The anchorage of Hampton Roads is the estuary of the James River, here broadened to six miles. The north shore was held by Union troops, in Fortress Monroe on Old Point Comfort and in newly emplaced batteries at Newport News. The Confederates, holding the south shore, had fortifications at Sewell's Point and at Pig Point to the west. Flag Officer Louis M. Goldsborough, commanding the North Atlantic Blockading Squadron, had an apparently indomitable force—the 50-gun screw frigates *Minnesota* and *Roanoke*, the sailing frigates *St. Lawrence* and *Congress*, both 44s, and the sailing sloop *Cumberland*, 24, as well as tugs and auxiliaries. Mindful of the threat posed by the *Virginia*, the Union commander hoped to destroy her by ramming if she ventured out of the Elizabeth River.

On 8 March 1862, Flag Officer Franklin Buchanan, now in Confederate service, took the *Virginia*, his new command, out into Hampton Roads. There would be no shakedown, no engine run-ups, no gunnery drills. This trial run would be directly into action. Under her own steam in deep water the hybrid vessel quickly manifested her deficiencies. In calm water she could make at best five knots. She answered the helm so sluggishly that it took more than half an hour to turn her around.

To free some small Confederate gunboats blockaded up the James, Buchanan headed first toward the *Congress* and the *Cumberland*, anchored off Newport News. The Union vessels hastily cleared for action, and the *Congress* and the *Virginia* ex-

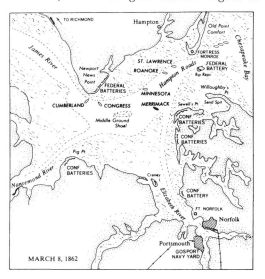

The Battle of Hampton Roads

changed broadsides as the latter ponderously charged the *Cumberland*. While heavy solid shot ricocheted harmlessly off her tallow-drenched casemate, the *Virginia* ploughed her ram deep into the *Cumberland*'s starboard bow—barely avoiding being drawn down with her rapidly settling prey. Fortunately for the ironclad, her ram structure broke off, and she managed to back clear. Buchanan then proceeded to rake the sinking vessel, whose guns not yet submerged continued to fire. She at length came to rest on the shallow bottom with her flag still at her peak above water.

Supported by the armed tugs *Beaufort* and *Raleigh*, the *Virginia* turned on the *Congress* and set her aflame with shellfire. The burning frigate struck her colors. During this operation, Buchanan, who had gone topside for a better view, was wounded by a Union musket fired from the shore. Lieutenant Catesby ap Roger Jones thereupon succeeded to command.

Meanwhile the *Minnesota*, straining to reach a closer support position to her outmatched consorts, went hard aground. The burning *Congress* at length blew up as the flames reached her magazine.

After the 23-foot draft of the *Virginia* frustrated Jones's efforts to get closer than 2,000 yards to the stranded *Minnesota*, he finally withdrew to an anchorage near Sewell's Point. Except for the loss of her ram, some damage to her topsides, and the smashed muzzles of two of her guns, the *Virginia* had survived her baptism of fire very well. Her armor had proved impenetrable, and she was ready for action the following day. At the cost of 21 casualties, the ironclad and her tiny escorts had sunk a large sloop-of-war and set a heavy frigate fatally ablaze, killing or drowning 250 Union sailors.

Yet even while the *Virginia* was gaining her one-sided victory, the *Monitor* was arriving on the scene. Towed by a tug, she had labored down the coast from New York. For the crew, it had been a nightmarish voyage. Rough weather off the Delaware Capes caused water to surge through badly stopped hawse pipes, flooding out the exhaust blowers and the engine. The wheel-ropes jammed, so that the safety of the ship depended solely on the tightly drawn hawser connecting her to the tug. About 4 p.m. on 8 March she reached Cape Charles, and in the calmer waters of the Chesapeake was able to get under way in the direction of the sound of cannonading off Norfolk. Reporting to Captain John Marston, the senior officer present, in the *Roanoke*, the *Monitor*'s commanding officer, Lieutenant Worden, was ordered to cover the grounded *Minnesota*. He anchored just west of her.

The following morning, when the *Virginia* came back to finish off the *Minnesota*, still stuck fast, the *Monitor* moved out to challenge her. Coming into close range, the adversaries exchanged fire without perceptible damage from the numerous hits. Like a terrier baiting a bull, the much more maneuverable *Monitor* kept close to her enemy, so that at times the *Virginia* could hardly get a gun to bear. The mere 12-foot draft of the Union vessel, moreover, provided her with considerably more working room in the shallows of the Roads. When, after two hours of dueling at pistol ranges, Jones tried to ram the *Monitor*, she turned so nimbly that the blow was a glancing one, damaging the *Monitor* not at all, and springing another leak in the *Virginia*'s damaged bow. The frustrated Confederate commander tried to come alongside for boarding, but the well-conned *Monitor* demonstrated that she could maintain a distance and line of bearing of her own choosing. Then the *Virginia*, seeking at least to destroy the grounded *Minnesota*, maneuvered for a nearer and more effective vantage point and also went hard aground.

With both the *Minnesota* and the *Monitor* pounding the *Virginia* at close range, it seemed inevitable that her armor plates would be battered off, even if they could not be penetrated. Then, at the moment of an apparent Union victory, when the *Monitor* at 10 or 15 yards' range was about to deliver the coup de grace with her 11-inch guns, a Confederate shell struck the narrow eyeslit of the *Monitor*'s pilothouse. Thus lucky hit, wounding and temporarily blinding Lieutenant Worden, left the Union vessel without effective command for 20 minutes. Because Lieutenant Samuel D. Greene, the *Monitor*'s executive officer, was busy with the guns in the turret, he did not assume the conn until after the helmsman had sheered off out of effective range.

Meanwhile, the alert Confederate commanding officer had his boats out and managed to kedge his ship out of the shallows. With the tide falling and the water from leaks rising in the *Virginia*'s bilges, Jones prudently withdrew. Greene, belatedly taking command, brought the *Monitor* back to the *Minnesota*, throwing two or three shots after the departing *Virginia*. Thus ended the Battle of Hampton Roads.

Except for minor damage to her pilot house, the *Monitor* was intact. The *Virginia*'s casemate had been unpierced, but many of her plates were cracked, and the stout oak backing was fractured. Her superstructure was thus wrecked, and her hull damage required dry-docking. There is little doubt that if the new Dahlgrens of the *Monitor*'s battery had not been restricted by Bureau of Ordnance order to 15-pound charges, as opposed to the 25- and even 30-pound charges later found to be safe, the *Monitor*'s guns would have speedily defeated the armor of the *Virginia*.

As it was, however, the Confederate ram remained at Norfolk for two months, a kind of one-ship fleet in being. After repairs, she reappeared in the Roads on 11 April, 8 May, and 9 May. But substantial reinforcements to Goldsborough's command, including the ironclads *Galena* and *Naugatuck*, made any further offensive move by the *Virginia* suicidal. The blockade was preserved, and as early as 5 April McClellan was able to move 121,500 soldiers of the Army of the Potomac to the Yorktown Peninsula, as planned.

In spite of tactical Union victory in some bitter battles, McClellan's advance on Richmond was halted by the Army of Northern Virginia. However, with Union Major General Ambrose Burnside's troops toiling north from North Carolina and McClellan's army at their doorstep, the Confederate command decided that Norfolk could not be held. On 10 May they abandoned the city and its invaluable navy yard. The undependability of the *Virginia*'s engines and her general lack of seaworthiness made it quixotic for her to try to fight her way out to deep water. Regretfully, the Confederate Navy blew up its most historic vessel. The *Monitor*, none too seaworthy herself, foundered off the Carolina capes later that same year.

Confederate Mines and Submarines

The *Virginia* was the only Confederate armored vessel that might have made a significant impact on the outcome of the war. Although a number of other Southern ironclads were built at various places, and some had small local successes, they were never a match for the improved *Monitors*, which the North built in quantity.

As the weaker naval power, the South naturally turned to other technological innovations. By far the most successful was the mine or, as then designated, the "torpedo," a stationary underwater charge fired by either contact fuse or shore-directed electrical impulse. Matthew Fontaine Maury resigned his U. S. naval commission to become chief of the Confederacy's Submarine Battery Service, and in the face of enormous obstacles, including a vexing dearth of copper wire in the South, he managed to mine the principal ports and harbor entrances of the Confederacy. Thirty-one Union vessels were lost to mines—more than to any other cause.

The Confederates also experimented with a curious hybrid small attack craft called a "David," steam-propelled and carrying a contact mine at the end of a long spar ahead of the bow. It cruised wholly submerged except for hatch and funnel. It was hoped that under cover of darkness such a vessel could be eased up to a ship at anchor without detection. In 1863 at Charleston a David did attack the *New Ironsides*. It caused some damage but failed to sink the powerful Union ship.

A true submarine was also developed, at Mobile, the CSS *Hunley*, a tiny, hand-powered metal cigar, carrying a crew of nine. After it had drowned two successive crews on trials, General Beauregard in exasperation ordered that it not be submerged again. Operating as a David, it did, however, later sink the screw sloop USS *Housatonic*, drowning a third crew in the process.[1]

Commerce Warfare

Apart from long-shot gambles on radically new weapons—doomed to failure by the puny industrial base of the South—the only feasible offensive strategy for the Confederate Navy was commerce warfare, the classic expedient of the weaker naval power. The leadership of the South, recognizing its lack of a native merchant marine to draw on, hoped that President Davis's proclamation of April 1862, authorizing letters of marque and reprisal, would attract foreign adventurers and European ships to employment as privateers. By establishing legal sanction to freebooting and offering the protection of its flag, the South hoped not only to strike at the source of Northern economic strength but also to vitiate the blockade's effectiveness by compelling the Union to scatter its naval vessels in high-seas search for the privateers. Once Confederate sovereignty was fully recognized abroad, consular prize courts could be set up in foreign ports and prizes sold off far from the harbors of the Confederacy.

This policy seemed in accord with American naval tradition, for, as we have seen, in both the American Revolution and the War of 1812, pri-

---

[1] The first submarine to participate in naval warfare was the *Turtle*, built during the American Revolution, mostly of oak, by David Bushnell of Connecticut. It was so named because it resembled a turtle, moving sidewise, tail down, with a brass conning tower for a head. For horizontal and vertical motion, the one-man operator turned screw propellers by hand. The *Turtle* made one unsuccessful attack, on a British warship in New York harbor. In 1800 Robert Fulton built a more practical submarine, the *Nautilus*, but was unable to find a sponsor.

vateering had been the principal U. S. offensive strategy on the high seas. But the drift of world opinion had changed since then. Though the United States had not acceded to the pact, the Declaration of Paris of 1856 (which Britain and France had signed) outlawed captures by armed private vessels. England, in fact, refused to allow prize courts anywhere in her far-flung territories, and France followed her lead. In the circumstances, foreigners viewed the prospects of reward incommensurate with the risks and were not attracted.

However, the Confederacy itself, and also certain of its member states as individual sovereignties, did commission a number of privateers early in the war, mostly small, ill-armed ships. But after the first few weeks, it began to be increasingly difficult to get prizes in through the blockade, and by mid-1862 privateering had virtually disappeared. Even so, the depredations of the 30 or so privateers sent out were for a brief time worrisome and costly to the Union. For example, the brig *Jefferson Davis*, 5 guns, 74 men, 230 tons, in one seven-week cruise ranging from Cape Cod to Trinidad captured 10 Union merchantmen. At one period the Union navy had 8 vessels assigned to running her down—suggesting that enough like her would have materially reduced the effectiveness of the blockade and other naval operations. Few as they were, in the first five months of the war Confederate privateers captured between 50 and 60 merchantmen, with the loss of only 2 of their number. Marine insurance rates for American merchant vessels went up, and transfers to foreign registry of private U. S. vessels became common.

But as the rate of captures went up steadily, no new privateers appeared. Anyone with the necessary capital and taste for speculative adventure was drawn to the somewhat less hazardous and distinctly more profitable business of blockade-running.

The South had not run out of expedients, however. If privateering yielded disappointing results, then national cruisers, regular naval vessels, might do the job. These ships—mainly foreign-built and foreign-manned, though officered by Southerners—were in fact to inflict enormous injury on the merchant marine of the North. Some notion of the "direct damage" done is provided by the fact that the Geneva Tribunal adjudicating the *Alabama* Claims after the war awarded the United States $15,500,000 for merchantmen destroyed by cruisers built in British yards.[2]

Moreover, the indirect costs occasioned by the raiders were vastly greater. Marine insurance costs were of course much raised. American shipping firms sold many of their vessels, some even abandoning the business altogether. One hundred twenty-six U. S. ships were transferred to foreign registry in 1861, 135 in 1862, and 348 in 1863, when the cruiser *Alabama* was at the height of her depredations.

Of greater importance to the Southern cause was the large number of Union naval vessels diverted from the blockade and scattered over the oceans in "needle in a haystack" searches for the elusive commerce-destroyers. The *Alabama*, for example, had a squadron of seven vessels looking for her in the Caribbean alone. Inasmuch as some ocean-going cruising by the U. S. Navy would have been necessary in any event, it is impossible to cite a precise figure for the number of ships pulled off the Southern coasts and away from inshore operations by the necessity of tracking down Confederate raiders. But it can be no exaggeration to say that the Confederate cruisers, few in number as they were, so diverted at least ten times their own tonnage.

The first of the regularly commissioned naval vessels to undertake commerce-raiding was the *Sumter*, a screw steamer of 500 tons converted from a peacetime packet. Bought by the Confederate government from a New Orleans shipping firm, she was refitted for war and armed with an 8-inch pivot and four short 24-pounders in broadside.

Captain Raphael Semmes took her down the lower Mississippi in June 1861 and played hide-and-seek with the blockading *Brooklyn*, whose draft was too deep to get over the bar. The favorable moment for escape finally came when the *Brooklyn* went off on a local chase. The *Sumter* made a dash for it and outdistanced the *Brooklyn* when the latter attempted to retrieve her lapse. Cruising in the Caribbean and off the coasts of Spain and Portugal, the *Sumter* took 17 prizes, of which six were burned, two recaptured, and two ransomed. Seven that had been sent to Cuban ports for disposition were seized by the Spanish authorities and later released to their Northern owners.

After the *Sumter*'s escape from the *Brooklyn*, the *Niagara* and the *Powhatan* were detached from the Gulf Squadron, and joined the *San Jacinto*, the *Iroquois*, the *Richmond*, and the *Keystone State* to

---

[2]Inflation has rendered it difficult to appreciate the magnitude of this figure in terms of the 1865 monetary

situation. The modern reader should bear in mind that the average annual *total receipts* of the U. S. government for the period 1861–65 was $161,000,000. A comparable award today would run into hundreds of millions.

scour the Caribbean in what proved a fruitless search. In January 1862 the *Sumter* was finally run to earth at Gibraltar by the USS *Tuscarora*, which was presently joined by the *Kearsarge* and the *Ino*. Apart from the obvious danger of being blown out of the water if he ventured forth from his neutral sanctuary, Captain Semmes was bedeviled by a number of other problems. He could get no coal at Gibraltar, his boilers were rusted through, and his engines needed repairs. So Semmes had the *Sumter* surveyed and sold. But she continued to work for the Confederacy, for her British owners converted her into a blockade-runner.

The brief career of the *Sumter* as a raider is fairly typical of other cruisers. Her principal significance is that she was the apprenticeship of the master-raider of them all, the redoubtable Raphael Semmes. From the cruise of the *Sumter*, Semmes learned to avoid such frequented roadsteads as Gibraltar, and to destroy his prizes rather than risk losing by diplomacy in neutral ports what his guns had captured. And he so perfected the timing of his cruises that he was for a long time able to anticipate every move of his pursuers.

The *Sumter* was unusual in being a Southern-owned steamer converted to a war vessel. Lacking facilities for building ships, the South was obliged to rely largely on the efforts of its agents abroad in purchasing vessels and in having them built. Shortly after the firing on Fort Sumter, the Confederate Congress authorized the purchase of, and made appropriations for, six sail–steam cruisers to cost $165,000 each, and two million-dollar ironclad rams. James D. Bulloch and James H. North, both former officers in the U. S. Navy, were sent to England to try to procure these vessels. This assignment was to involve a great deal of intrigue and peculiarly British red tape, problems with which the able and persistent Bulloch proved quite capable of coping. The American minister to Britain, Charles Francis Adams, and the American consuls in the British shipbuilding ports attempted by every possible expedient of diplomacy and British law to circumvent the Confederate agents' efforts.

The British neutrality laws, like those of all civilized nations in 1861, specifically forbade the "equipping, furnishing, fitting out, or arming" of a ship intended for making war on a friendly state. The manufacture and sale of arms or other contraband to either belligerent was permitted, though this could be done only at the subject's own risk. As far as the courts of England were concerned, proof of the vessel's warlike character had to be established to warrant seizure of the vessel. This provision opened the possibility that commerce raiders could be constructed in British yards, then as unarmored vessels be cleared to a dummy foreign purchaser. The Confederacy had agents in many European and Caribbean ports, some of them foreign nationals. Meanwhile ordnance could be manufactured in England and transported to a previously agreed-on rendezvous. There the raider would be armed and commissioned. She need never have seen a Confederate port from first to last. Guided at every step by British legal counsel, Bulloch successfully followed this procedure to the end of the war, sending forth the *Florida*, the *Alabama*, and the *Shenandoah*, among others.

The purchase of British-built ironclads was another matter, since the warlike purpose of such vessels would be established by the details of their construction. Even the ingenuity of Bulloch proved unavailing. The firm of Lairds of Birkenhead contracted to build two "rams" carrying a battery of 9-inch rifles, ostensibly for the French government, later for the pasha of Egypt, then for a French private firm. Lord Russell, British Foreign Secretary, ordered them seized in 1863 shortly before their completion. Had they actually been delivered to the Confederacy, they would have posed a severe problem for the Union navy.

The *Florida* was completed in March 1862. She sailed to Nassau, where through the connivance of the colonial authorities she was armed with two 7-inch and six 6-inch rifles, and commissioned under the command of Commander John N. Maffitt, CSN. She had an eventful and successful career, being finally captured in October 1864 by the USS *Wachusett* in the harbor of Bahia, Brazil. This barefaced violation of Brazilian neutrality was later apologized for very handsomely by the United States. But the *Florida* herself was sunk in an "unforeseen accident" at Hampton Roads before she could be delivered back to Brazil.

The *Alabama*

The *Alabama* was justly the most famous of the Confederate raiders. Barkentine-rigged, she was 230 by 32 feet; loaded she drew 15 feet. Her 300-horsepower engine gave her a trial speed of 13.5 knots. While cruising she normally depended on her sails to conserve coal.

To avoid possible seizure by the British authorities, the *Alabama*, once she was launched, simply never returned from her trial run, proceeding rather to a rendezvous in the Azores where arms, coal, and her prospective officers were sent by Bulloch to fit her out. While the Portugese port officials in Porto Praya were encouraged to believe that the *"Enrica"* was merely coaling from the chartered *Agrippina*, a battery consisting of six long 32-pounders in broadside, a rifled 100-pounder, and an 8-inch shell gun were winched into place in the cruiser. Eighty-three of the sailors who had brought the ship from England, mostly English and Irish adventurers from the Liverpool waterfront, volunteered as a skeleton crew to be filled out with volunteer recruits from prizes. Raphael Semmes took his ship outside territorial waters to perform the commissioning ceremony: mustering the crew, reading his orders, and raising the Confederate ensign. The *Alabama* was past her period of masquerade. She was a ship-of-war, ready to fulfill her mission.

Semmes was a stern and able disciplinarian; no lesser man could have handled his crew of Liverpool toughs. He spent the first two months in the North Atlantic, making 20 captures. Profiting from his experience in the *Sumter*, he took what he wanted from the prizes, then put them to the torch. When the accumulation of prisoners on board the *Alabama* became too great a problem, Semmes stripped a captured vessel and made a cartel ship of her, on which the superfluous passengers could make their way to land.

After cruising as far as the Grand Banks, the *Alabama*, her coal nearly exhausted, made for Fort de France, Martinique, a previously arranged fueling rendezvous. The *Agrippina* awaited her, but before coaling could be accomplished the USS *San Jacinto* appeared and began patrolling just outside the three-mile limit. Sending his tender ahead, Semmes slipped past the *San Jacinto* at night and completed coaling in an obscure little port of Venezuela.

Semmes now cruised in the Caribbean, hoping to intercept one of the "treasure steamers" on the run from Colon to New York with California gold in her cargo. The captured gold would enable him to pay the long-overdue wages of his crew, which had already attempted mutiny. He had no such luck. Of a number of captures in this area, the most valuable was a large passenger liner outbound from New York, which yielded less than $10,000 in silver dollars and U. S. Treasury notes.

Semmes next moved into the Gulf of Mexico with the object of interfering with an expected amphibious operation against the Texas coast. Off Galveston, which a Union squadron was bombarding, the *Alabama* steamed slowly, inviting the attention of a Federal man-of-war. Presently the gunboat conversion USS *Hatteras* came out to investigate. Twenty miles away from the support of the rest of the squadron, the *Hatteras* hailed the *Alabama*, which first identified herself as a British

ship. But when the Union vessel sent off a boarding party to inspect her papers, her first lieutenant bellowed, "This is the Confederate States steamer *Alabama*!" and Semmes immediately ordered a broadside. The superior armament of the *Alabama* made short work of the Union gunboat. In a sinking condition, the *Hatteras* fired a gun to leeward to signify surrender. Semmes quickly transferred the surviving members of her crew to his own ship, and a few minutes later the *Hatteras* sank. The *Alabama* then made a quick run to Kingston, Jamaica, to put her prisoners ashore on parole before the alarm was spread.

For another 18 months Semmes played cat-and-mouse with the Union cruisers scouring the sea lanes of the world in fruitless pursuit. Operating successively in the Caribbean, the South Atlantic, the Indian Ocean, Sunda Strait, the South China Sea, and the Bay of Bengal, the *Alabama* gradually became the victim of her own successes. As Semmes worked farther and farther afield, he found progressively fewer Northern merchantmen. Doubling back to the South Atlantic again, the *Alabama* made two final captures as she cruised north to Europe to refit. On 11 June 1864 Semmes took his ship in to the port of Cherbourg and requested docking facilities from the French government.

While operating earlier in the broad oceans, Semmes had been able to forestall pursuit by timing his moves to anticipate Union vessels sent out to intercept him. Because there were no transoceanic cables, he normally had several days or even weeks of leeway. But when the *Alabama* anchored in Cherbourg, the U. S. consul was able to telegraph Captain John A. Winslow of the U. S. screw sloop *Kearsarge*, anchored off Flushing on the Dutch coast. Three days later the Union warship appeared off Cherbourg. Without anchoring, the *Kearsarge* took up a patrol station just outside the port.

It had been Semmes's plan to dock his vessel and send his crew off on a well-deserved leave. But it soon became apparent that he was unlikely to be granted the dock facilities he had requested, and the practical alternatives open to him were to accept internment in Cherbourg or to go out and fight. Because the *Alabama* and the *Kearsarge* appeared to be evenly matched, Semmes allowed his temperamental bias in favor of the bold course to have its way. Through the U. S. consul he challenged Winslow to a single-ship duel as soon as the *Alabama* had refueled.

On the morning of 19 June the *Alabama* headed out to sea. The *Kearsarge* steamed ahead to clear territorial waters. The new French ironclad *Couronne* followed and anchored at the three-mile limit. The private yacht *Deerhound*, of British registry, hovered about to witness the impending action. Thousands of spectators lined the shore.

When about seven miles from the coast, the *Kearsarge* reversed course and bore directly down on the *Alabama*, which sheered off to port in order to present her starboard battery. The *Alabama* fired the first broadside at 2,000 yards. Most of her shot fell short, but one or two cut into the *Kearsarge*'s top-hamper. Winslow held his fire as his ship bore down on his opponent. Quickly reloading, the Confederate got off another broadside at 1,000 yards. Only then did the *Kearsarge* in turn sheer off to port, present her starboard battery, and begin firing.

In the ensuing action, the two ships turned in a clockwise direction on opposite sides of a circle a half mile in diameter. This maneuver was the result of both ships keeping starboard batteries bearing while on opposite courses, and of each endeavoring to achieve a raking position on her adversary. A three-knot tidal current gradually set the rotating vessels down toward the coast west of Cherbourg.

It soon appeared that the antagonists were not evenly matched after all. The tired machinery of the *Alabama* could not keep up with her opponent's speed. To conserve ammunition, the Confederate gunners had neglected drill. The *Alabama*'s powder and shells had deteriorated. The *Kearsarge*, on the contrary, was freshly refitted and battle-ready. Moreover, Winslow had protected her engines and boiler spaces by hanging chains down her sides and sheathing them over with boards, both to conceal them and to hold them secure. After an hour of battle, and seven rotations, the *Alabama* was in a sinking condition while the *Kearsarge* was only slightly damaged. Semmes now attempted to beach the *Alabama* on the coast, but water rushing in through her riddled hull extinguished her furnace and left her helpless. The *Kearsarge* now cut across her bow and raked her, whereupon Semmes struck his colors.

As the stricken *Alabama* began to sink, both victor and vanquished quickly launched boats, and the *Deerhound* came up to help in the work of rescue. Semmes flung his sword into the sea and then plunged overboard. Twenty minutes after her surrender, the bow of the *Alabama* rose perpendicularly in the air as she sank stern first. Semmes, together with 40 of his ship's complement, was picked up by the *Deerhound* and taken to England. In Union eyes this avoidance of capture was the only flaw in the news of the victory. Winslow received the thanks of Congress and was promoted to commodore.

Between 5 September 1862 and 27 April 1864, the *Alabama* had captured 68 Union vessels, destroying most of them at sea. Semmes's epic cruise is by all odds the most successful in the history of commerce raiding. Besides the direct damage inflicted, the *Alabama* caused enormous indirect losses to Union shipowners—higher marine insurance premiums, delays and cancellations of sailings, and spoilage of cargoes.

To take the place of the *Alabama*, Bulloch purchased the *Shenandoah*, which was armed in the Madeira Islands by a tender in October 1864. The *Shenandoah* sailed at once for the Pacific, where she began her depredations the following month. Operating chiefly around the Aleutian Islands, she captured a total of 36 vessels, mostly whalers, and gave the American whaling industry a blow from which it never recovered. Because news of the Confederate surrender did not reach Captain Waddell until 2 August 1865, two-thirds of the *Shenandoah*'s captures were made after the end of the war. The destructiveness of the *Shenandoah*'s cruise was second only to that of the *Alabama*.

Blockade-Running

Up to the time of the fall of New Orleans, blockade-running was not unduly hazardous. Vessels of all types were loaded with cotton bales to make the run to Havana, Nassau, Bermuda, or St. Thomas. As the blockaders grew more efficient and more numerous, it became no longer feasible to run through in small sailing vessels. Only fast steamers were left in the business. Even so, the risks of capture became progressively greater as the war went on. By the summer of 1863, the Union navy had captured 850-odd blockade-runners, and already specially built craft were being employed.

The more efficient the blockade became, the greater were the rewards to those who could run goods through. Joint-stock companies were found in Britain; Clyde-built ships especially adapted to blockade-running and commanded by British officers were sent out to Nassau and Bermuda.

These blockade-runners were fast, wooden-hulled, shoal-draft vessels of about 450 tons. For the most part they were paddle-wheelers, burning anthracite to avoid smoking. They had fine lines, a length–beam ratio of eight or nine to one being common. They were, above everything, fast. Some could make 17 knots or better. Many of them had telescopic stacks; there was little top-hamper; the masts were mere sticks. Painted gray, low in freeboard, proceeding "blacked out" at night, they were nearly invisible.

In a typical run, the blockade-runner would load at St. George's, Bermuda, be piloted out the intricate channel at nightfall, and dodge the Union vessels lying in wait outside the reefs. Through the night she would steam at something less than her best speed, maintaining a sharp lookout for Union cruisers. Navigating carefully, she would try to make a precise landfall two days later in the early evening, at, for example, Savannah. She would make her approach after dark, hugging the shore, and exchanging light recognition signals with the coast stations and the forts. Then came the final dash at top speed, past the "inshore blockade." At the pier the crated munitions and such luxuries as liquors, Paris gowns, linens, laces, corsetry, tea, and coffee were quickly unloaded, and the company's agent took charge of speedily moving them to a warehouse. Without delay, bales of cotton were stacked in the hold and tiered on deck, with a few extra bales on top on the captain's personal account. The ship would then be fumigated with sulfur to smoke out any stowaways. At nightfall, the ship's officers got a fix on any blockaders visible and plotted them on their chart. Since the blockaders usually anchored at night, it was sometimes not too difficult to steam silently between them in the dark. Strict silence on board the blockade-runner was of course the rule, and sometimes the outward dash was altogether undetected. If discovered, the blockade-runner could still rely on her superior speed.

Even after escaping the inshore blockade, there was still the chance of being sighted by one of the faster Union ships at sea. But on any one given voyage, the odds favored the blockade-runner as long as there was a port in Confederate hands to run to. Up to January 1865, 84 specially built steamers had been regularly employed in blockade-running. Of this number, 37 were captured, 25 were lost by grounding, collision, and accident, and 22 survived the war.

In the period 1863–64, the profits of blockade-running were so large that two or three successful round trips, which might be accomplished in as many weeks, would more than pay off the cost of the ship. Coffee, for example, worth 12¢ a pound in Nassau, brought $2.75 (in gold) in Richmond. As early as December 1862, the accepted freight rate from Nassau to Savannah was $500 a ton. Owners of a single lucky ship could easily clear over a million dollars a year. As the risks multiplied, even the officers and crews came to enjoy what were then deemed fabulous returns. A merchant skipper who in 1860 earned perhaps $140 to $160 a month received $5,000 a month for commanding a blockade-runner—and this was supplemented by opportunity for private speculation. Ordinary seamen received base pay of $100 a month and a bonus of $50 for each successful round trip.

It must not be supposed that the blockade-runners in any significant sense defeated the strategy of blockade. Indeed by draining off the South's slender supply of trained seamen, by attracting capital that might otherwise have gone into further development of the South's war industries, and by stimulating the gold flow out of the country and hence further debasing the currency, the blockade-runners may well have weakened the South more than they aided.[3] Their total carrying capacity was inadequate to move any but a small fraction of the cotton grown, and the higher profits in carrying expensive luxuries made a disproportionate share of the incoming cargoes frivolous items of no possible benefit to the war effort. The "blockade auctions" featured bolts of silk, jewelry, and French brandy while industry was in desperate need of chemicals and boiler iron, and while the hospitals utterly lacked opiates and other drugs. The resentment stirred by the speculative few who amassed fortunes while the Army of Northern Virginia fought in rags compelled the Confederate Congress to pass an act (1 March 1864) that forbade the importation of luxuries. This law was apparently not generally enforced, however, since editorial denunciations of the "speculators" were as frequent in the Southern press afterward as before.

---

[3] It is of interest that the Confederate government itself entered this field of unrestricted "private enterprise," being the secret owner of four blockade-runners, and having a part interest in a number of others.

Chapter 13
The War in the West

From the very beginning it was obvious to Lincoln and his military advisers that seizing control of the Mississippi River and its tributaries was absolutely essential to Northern victory. Economically the rivers were the natural water highways for the produce of the loyal states of the Midwest. Navigable waterways, moreover, were the most secure and dependable lines of communication for the supply needs of the large armies destined to fight in the trans-Appalachian region. Effective command of the Mississippi would split off Texas, Arkansas, and Louisiana from the rest of the Confederacy and thus deprive the eastern armies of the South of much of their food supplies. Foreign imports transshipped via Mexico would be cut off. To deny the Mississippi to the Confederacy was thus a logical extension of the blockade principle to the interior of the continent.

The Southern leadership also recognized the importance of the western rivers and made major effects to thwart Union offensives. It would cost the North two years of combat and the lives of tens of thousands of men to achieve control of the Mississippi and its major tributaries.

When Kentucky finally declared for the Union, the South lost the potential of the Ohio River as a main line of defense. The Tennessee and the Cumberland rivers, flowing out of Tennessee into the Ohio, became in fact avenues of invasion. The Union speedily put together a riverboat navy, at first consisting mainly of gunboats converted from river steamers but soon reinforced by the Eads gunboats, most of which were built as war vessels from the keel up. These vessels, named for their designer and builder, carried 13 pieces of heavy ordnance and were protected by 2½-inch cast-iron plates. With a part of this force, Flag Officer Andrew Hull Foote, USN, undertook to cooperate with a young brigadier general recently recalled to the regular army from civilian life—Ulysses S. Grant, who had about 17,000 troops at his disposal.

The first Union objective was Fort Henry, an improvised Confederate fortification 60 miles up the Tennessee River from the Union base at Paducah. On 6 February 1862, with seven gunboats, Foote simply closed in to within 600 yards range

and blasted the Confederate defenses into submission. Grant's army, marching overland, had not even reached the scene, and hence merely supplied a garrison for the conquered strongpoint.

Confederate Fort Donelson on the Cumberland River was not so easily vanquished. It was a naturally much stronger position on high ground on the west bank, and here Brigadier General Gideon J. Pillow, CSA, and his 15,000 men elected to put up a stout resistance. By 13 February, Grant had his siege lines out. The following day, Foote took his squadron close in to duel the guns of the fort, while Grant maneuvered to cut the last land route of escape for the trapped garrison. The Union ships were sorely punished, three of them forced out of action. Foote himself received a wound whose complications ultimately would prove fatal. But Grant's men blocked the only connecting road, and the Confederate garrison was trapped. General Pillow with a small force escaped upriver by steamer, and Colonel Nathan B. Forrest's cavalry detachment slipped away over the frozen marshes. But on the 16th the 10,000 Confederate survivors in the fort reluctantly accepted Grant's demand for unconditional surrender. So was a national reputation born. The Northern press at last had an authentic hero in "Unconditional Surrender" Grant.

The loss of forts Henry and Donelson and defeats in Missouri induced the Confederates to withdraw on both sides of the Mississippi to a point 60 miles south of Columbus, where the river makes a pair of 180-degree bends. Here was defensible high ground, and here was low-lying Island Number 10, the tenth island downriver from Cairo. At this point a Confederate force of nearly 10,000 men, with ample artillery and a six-ship gunboat flotilla, opposed an attack force of 20,000 under Brigadier General John Pope, USA, and a Union gunboat flotilla.

Swampland on both banks of the river made land attack or siege impossible unless Pope could somehow get his forces, properly supported, downriver from the Confederate positions. His army occupied New Madrid, which was below Island Number 10, and for direct waterborne supply his troops cut a canal through a drowned forest to

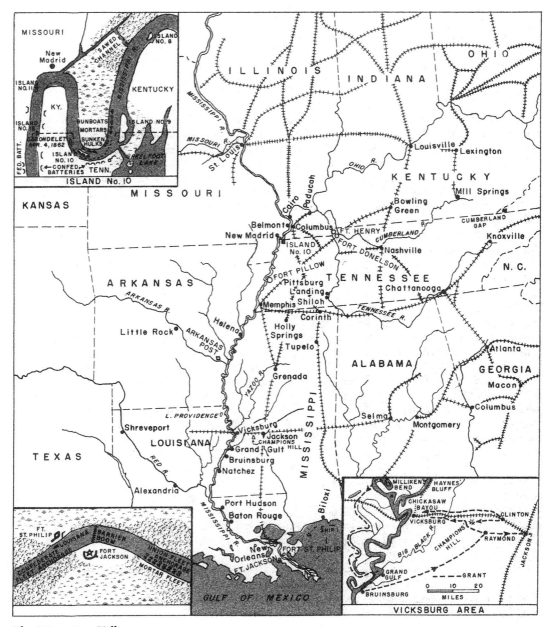

The Mississippi Valley

the river above Number 10. The canal, however, was not deep enough for the Union fighting vessels, which were needed downriver to cope with the Confederate gunboats. Captain Henry Walke, of the *Carondelet*, volunteered to run the gauntlet of the Southern batteries.

Walke prepared carefully, faking down anchor chain on deck as protection against plunging shot, and lashing a coal barge to his exposed side. On the night of 4 April in a furious thunderstorm, the *Carondelet* steamed slowly downriver. Reinforced by a company of army sharpshooters on board, the crew stood by with cutlasses in hand as the shielded Union gunboat swept past the water batteries. She made it without casualty. Two nights later the *Pittsburg* duplicated her feat, also in a timely thunderstorm.

After the Union armored vessels had chased the wooden Confederate gunboats downriver, Pope moved his force across from Missouri without opposition. Checkmate. The Confederate garrison with all its heavy artillery surrendered without inflicting a casualty.

Meanwhile, Grant was planning to lead his newly formed Army of the Tennessee against the strategic center of Corinth. For this operation he was to be reinforced by a contingent of 20,000 men from Brigadier General Don Carlos Buell's Army of the Ohio. Naval control of the Tennessee River enabled General Grant to move within striking distance of Corinth by water, and he established his main force of 33,000 at Pittsburg Landing to await Buell's men. General Albert Sydney Johnston, CSA, rapidly concentrated a force of 45,000 at Corinth and flung this army on Grant. The ensuing Battle of Shiloh, 6–7 April 1862, was one of the worst bloodlettings of the war, with combined casualties of 20,000 or more. A tactical draw, it might have been a Union defeat except for the expeditious arrival of Buell's troops by riverboat and the timely fire support of the gunboats *Tyler* and *Lexington* for Grant's beleaguered men late in the critical first day of the battle. By this battle, the South temporarily blunted the Northern army offensive, but only at the cost of fatally weakening Confederate defenses elsewhere—notably at New Orleans.

New Orleans

Great entrepôt of the Mississippi Valley, New Orleans was the largest and richest city in the South. Located a hundred miles upriver from the Head of the Passes, where the river divided to enter the Gulf through three separate major channels, New Orleans before the war had been the number one cotton port, and second only to New York in exports. Its capture by Northern forces would be a great prize in itself and also, of course, a necessary adjunct to controlling the whole river. As early as September 1861, the Union navy had seized Ship Island, lying off the coast east of the delta. This became a major advance base for the blockaders.

In spite of a small local success by the little turtle-shaped Southern ironclad *Manassas* in driving off a Union attempt to seal the Head of the Passes, and in spite of successful running of the blockade by small ships that could slip out through the many minor channels from the river to deep water, the Union navy soon made its weight felt in New Orleans. The city's prewar stream of trade was choked off to a trickle.

For defense against direct assault from the Gulf, New Orleans relied mainly on fortifications and a stout log barrier at Plaquemine Bend, 90 miles downriver from the city. Fort Jackson, a star-shaped, masonry structure on the right bank, was armed with 16 guns in casemate and 74 *en barbette*. Slightly upstream on the left bank stood Fort St. Philip with 52 guns, none casemated. The river at this point narrows to 700 feet, and there is commonly a four-knot current. The Confederates had constructed, directly under the guns of Fort Jackson, a great, floating boom of cypress logs, held a few feet apart and parallel to the current by large crosswise beams and heavy anchor chain. A couple of dozen 3,000-pound anchors secured the barrier to the bed of the river. Formidable as it was, this obstacle was breached by nature in the late winter floods of 1861, when floating debris from upriver broke through the boom in one place. Improvised repairs were speedily made in the form of dismasted schooners chained together. The defenders also had at hand the *Manassas*, armed with a single 32-pounder, and a dozen small wooden gunboats. There were building in New Orleans two potentially formidable ironclads, the *Louisiana* and the *Mississippi*, but they would be unfinished in the South's time of need.

Meanwhile, General Johnston, hoping to block General Grant's advance on Corinth, had drained off to the north most of the soldiers who might have defended New Orleans. Major General Mansfield Lovell, commander of New Orleans's defenses, had fewer than 1,500 men to garrison the forts and in the city only some 3,000 ill-armed militia. The Confederate leadership, however, was not greatly worried by possibilities of a naval assault from the Gulf. The real danger, they thought, would come from upriver, and could best be nullified by Confederate victories in that quarter.

The Union army was at first disposed to postpone any operation against New Orleans, believing it would require a major campaign with 50,000 men and full naval support. But Assistant Secretary of the Navy Gustavus Fox, strongly seconded by Commander David Dixon Porter, believed a wholly naval campaign might succeed, with troops required only to occupy the city after surrender. Porter argued that a fleet of mortar boats could wreck forts Jackson and St. Philip to the point where deep-draft naval vessels could pass upriver and threaten the city.

Once decided on, the expedition was put together with dispatch. Captain David Glasgow Farragut was designated Commander of the Western Blockading Squadron and commodore of the push against New Orleans. By late February 1862, Farragut was assembling his assault fleet at Ship

Island—four first-class steam sloops, the *Hartford* (flag), *Richmond*, *Pensacola*, and *Brooklyn*; the big veteran sidewheeler *Mississippi*; and 12 gunboats. The *Hartford* was almost new, 225 feet long, displacing 2,900 tons loaded, and capable of eight knots under power alone. Her armament was 22 nine-inch Dahlgrens in battery and two rifled 30-pounders fore and aft. The other first-class sloops were similar. Three of the smaller vessels were of 1,000 tons, the rest 500.

Porter's 21 mortar boats, small converted schooners, each armed with 13-inch mortars newly manufactured in Pittsburgh, soon joined the commodore's command, and the expedition got under way. Unhappily the surprise Farragut counted on was lost when he discovered that the undredged channel of the principal mouth of the Mississippi had silted up so that the heavier vessels grounded on the bars, even at high spring tides. Lightening ship at Ship Island and then butting a channel through the mud finally enabled the ships to get across the bar, but a whole month was lost, and the entire Confederacy had wind of the threat.

Farragut, however, characteristically had made good use of the time during this exasperating delay. He carefully analyzed the intelligence reports that were coming in, brought up to date the voluminous paperwork incident to administering and supplying the blockading force, and acquainted his captains in detail with his plans.

On 17 April 1862, Porter's mortar boats moved up to positions about two miles downstream from Fort Jackson. Fifteen of them, hugging the right bank, concentrated on that fort. The other six, anchored in the stream, fired at Fort St. Philip. The fused mortar shells, coming in at one a minute, soon burned out the wooden structures in the parade of the forts and at one time threatened the magazines in Fort Jackson. But Confederate fire at the more exposed Union vessels scored hits and sank one. After a week of sustained bombardment, the sleepless garrisons in the forts were low in morale. During the night of 20 April, the gunboats *Itasca* and *Pinola*, working for some hours under Confederate fire, succeeded in breaching the boom barrier, effecting a channel wide enough for Farragut's vessels to pass through, one at a time.

Farragut meanwhile was readying his big ships to fight past the Confederate positions. Anchor chain was faked over vulnerable midsections; sandbags were piled around machinery spaces; splinter nets were spread; decks were painted white to assist in blacked-out shiphandling. All ships were trimmed by the bow; if grounded, they would be able to back off with the aid of the current. At 2

a.m., 24 April, the *Hartford* signaled: Get Under Way.

Supported by continuous covering fire from Porter's mortar boats, the little gunboat *Cayuga* led Farragut's first division through the narrow gap in the log-and-schooner boom. As the forts opened fire, the ships blasted away with grape and cannister at the Confederate gunflashes. The *Mississippi*, number three in the line, was struck a glancing blow by the *Manassas*, without injury, and all eight vessels of the first division steamed out of range upriver. The *Hartford*, leading the second division, had a narrow escape off Fort St. Philip when a Confederate tug managed to jam a flaming raft against her side. But shells rolled from the deck of the flagship destroyed the raft, and timely damage control saved the ship. Of the larger vessels, the *Brooklyn* suffered most severely. She was damaged in a collision with the *Kineo* while trying to pass through the boom; then off Fort St. Philip she was nearly sunk by the ram of the plucky little *Manassas*. The *Iroquois* collided with the stationary *Louisiana*, inoperative as a ship, but serving as a battery to add to the firepower of Fort St. Philip. The *Iroquois* suffered severe casualties before she could back off and proceed upstream. Only three of Farragut's gunboats were too damaged to pass the forts. Though all the Union vessels were hit, many repeatedly, the hour's action cost the Union no ships, and casualties overall were moderate.

There were mopping-up actions early next day. The big *Mississippi* chased the *Manassas* ashore, where she was abandoned. The Northern gunboats sprinted upriver to finish off their outgunned opponents. Only the *Varuna*, raked by the Confederate *Governor Moore*, was lost. The Union navy had swept the river.

At Chalmette, where Jackson's forces held fast in the War of 1812, the Confederates had improvised a heavy battery, which they counted on to be New Orleans's inner line of defense. But the Union fleet, with its much superior gunpower, quickly smothered this last vestige of opposition and came to anchor off the city.

Forts Jackson and St. Philip, cut off from supplies and reinforcements, surrendered on 28 April. Major General Benjamin F. Butler's occupation troops arrived at New Orleans on 1 May. The North had secured a great victory at moderate cost.

On to Vicksburg

Hindsight suggests that now the best employment of Farragut's deep water ships would have been an immediate move on Mobile, still inadequately defended. Success here would have effectively sealed off the whole Gulf Coast. But Lincoln and his advisers gave top priority to commanding the entire Mississippi and remained committed to using all available forces to this end. Hence Farragut, reluctantly and in exasperation, was obliged to carry out sustained and generally futile operations upriver. The basic objective was a simple one: The upriver gunboats, now under Commander Charles H. Davis, who had relieved Foote, were temporarily held up by Fort Pillow. They would fight their way down the Mississippi, and Farragut's fleet would fight its way up until the two could join—probably in the vicinity of Vicksburg.

The deep-draft, ocean-going sloops of Farragut's command were of course not designed for riverine operations. Repeated groundings on the shifting bars, damage from snags, and drifting debris took their toll. Yet one by one the river ports fell to the Union as Farragut's ships worked their way north—Baton Rouge on 8 May, Natchez on 18 May. On the 18th Farragut's advance agent, Commander S. P. Lee, was in the gunboat *Oneida* off Vicksburg demanding surrender—a proposition that the Confederate forces in that well-fortified position on the heights indignantly spurned.

Meanwhile, Davis's advance downriver was not an uninterrupted series of triumphs. Indeed, his succession to command from the wounded Flag Officer Foote began most ignominiously. On 10 May, the rams of the Confederate Defense Fleet pounced suddenly on Davis's force at Plum Bend, just above Fort Pillow. With minimal injury to themselves, they sank the Union ironclads *Cincinnati* and *Mound City*. Before the superior gunpowder of the Union force could be brought to bear, the Confederates withdrew to the protection of the fort's guns. Though the sunken Union vessels were soon raised and returned to service, the successful Confederate attack was a reminder to the Union navy of the need for vigilance.

This small Confederate success, however, did not save Fort Pillow. Occupation of Corinth by the Union army left the fort dangerously outflanked, and the garrison wisely abandoned it, after huddling for weeks under Davis's bombardment. The Union flotilla, now reinforced by four highly maneuverable wooden rams commanded by Colonel Charles Ellet of the Army Engineers, steamed down to Memphis, arriving on 6 June. Here the Confederate squadron of eight rams elected to make a desperate stand. While much of the population of Memphis looked on, the superior handling qualities of Ellet's vessels soon proved decisive. In an hour's melee, in which Colonel Ellet was mor-

tally wounded, the Union squadron sank or captured seven of the eight Southern ships. Only one escaped downstream. The Union army promptly occupied Memphis. Davis's ships had opened the river as far south as Vicksburg.

Operating below that city, Farragut realized that the guns on the heights of Vicksburg could not be effectively silenced by naval fire from the river. However, Major General Henry W. Halleck, in overall Union army command in the West, declined to provide the land forces necessary for a joint operation. Bound by his orders from Secretary Welles, Farragut resolved at least to take his fleet past the city. On 28 June he ran the Vicksburg batteries with eight of his ships, three more turning back more or less seriously damaged. The operation confirmed Farragut's conviction that fleet fire would not be effective against the well-emplaced Confederate guns on the hill crests.

Davis had brought his ships downriver, and the seagoing and freshwater navies joined forces just out of range above Vicksburg. It looked at the moment as if the Mississippi campaign were just about over. But in point of fact, it would be more than a year before Vicksburg would be in Union hands. Meanwhile it would be a bone in the throat to the Northern forces.

For the moment there was little the Union leaders in the Vicksburg area could do. Apart from the naval units, they had at hand only the 3,000 troops in Brigadier General Thomas Williams's command. Major General Earl Van Dorn, CSA, had 15,000 men constantly improving · Vicksburg's already strong defenses. For a time Porter's 16 mortar boats below the city and four of Davis's boats above lobbed 13-inch shells into the Vicksburg perimeter, doing some damage. But almost at once peremptory orders arrived from Washington transferring Porter and his boats to the aid of McClellan in Virginia. Williams's soldiers were put to work trying to bypass Vicksburg by digging a canal across the peninsula formed by the hairpin bend in the Mississippi opposite the city. The project proved infeasible. It also put a third of the troops on sick call from heat prostration and malaria. To cap Farragut's frustrations was the ignominy of having a Confederate ironclad run right through his whole fleet.

The Confederates had just completed an ironclad, the *Arkansas*, in an improvised yard at Yazoo City, on the Yazoo River north of Vicksburg. On 15 July the Union ironclad *Carondelet*, accompanied by a ram and a gunboat, quite by chance set out to reconnoiter the Yazoo just as the *Arkansas* was coming down. The Union ships turned tail and fled from their formidable-looking enemy. The Confederate ironclad chased the *Carondelet* hard aground and pursued the smaller vessels into the midst of the Union fleet. The *Arkansas*'s inadequate engines gave her bare steerageway in calm water, but with the aid of the current she swept through the anchorage, firing her guns as fast as they could be loaded. Broadsides from the Union ships rattled her railroad-rail-covered casemate, but she survived the gauntlet and chugged triumphantly to safety under the guns of Vicksburg. Because none of the startled captains of the Union ships had steam up, immediate pursuit was impossible.

Fearing for the safety of transports and mortar boats below Vicksburg, Farragut took his fleet downriver past the city that night, trying unsuccessfully as he did so to sink the *Arkansas* by concentrated fire. A few days later, he received permission to withdraw his big ships from the Vicksburg area. Concerned over the falling water level, he steamed downriver without delay, taking General Williams's troops with him. At New Orleans he received the welcome news that he had been promoted to rear admiral, the first officer of that rank in the U. S. Navy. Commander Davis presently took his freshwater navy 300 miles upstream to base at Helena, Arkansas. By default, 500 miles of the Mississippi was reopened to the Confederacy.

Van Dorn was thus able to reinforce the meager command of Major General John C. Breckenridge, CSA, who next proceeded to attempt the recapture of Baton Rouge. With the powerful support of naval gunfire, the Union garrison was able to repel this blow. The *Arkansas*, seeking to aid the Southern land forces, had engine trouble and was set afire by her crew to prevent her capture. The Union army decided to withdraw from Baton Rouge anyway, and the Confederates at this time began to fortify Port Hudson, just a few miles upstream.

Port Hudson, 150 miles downriver from Vicksburg, held a somewhat similar position—high ground commanding a sharp bend in the Mississippi. Its importance to the South was that if both Vicksburg and Port Hudson could be held, the Red River, which flows from the Southwest into the Mississippi between these positions, could continue to be an effective means of waterborne communication between the trans-Mississippi Confederate states and the rest of the South. Down the Red River came meat and grain for the Confederate armies, as well as European products shipped via Mexico. Heavy batteries on the heights at Port Hudson would also of course make any attempted

attack on Vicksburg from downriver a good deal more difficult.

Not until November did Grant have the forces to move on Vicksburg. Advancing from his supply base at Holly Springs with 40,000 men of the Army of the Tennessee, he hoped to pin the bulk of the Southern army in this theater in the vicinity of Grenada. Brigadier General William Tecumseh Sherman, meanwhile, with 32,000 men and the support of the freshwater navy (now commanded by Porter, back from Virginia), would attack the northern flank of the Vicksburg defenses. The timing would have to be nearly perfect, but the plan if successful promised to draw defense forces away from Vicksburg long enough for Sherman and Porter to capture the place. Sherman and Grant would then close in on the Confederate forces somewhere between Grenada and Jackson.

The 24,000 Confederate troops defending Grenada were by no means adequate to defeat Grant. But the weather was in their favor. December rains had made the unpaved roads impassable. The Union forces therefore advanced and the Confederates retreated along the Mississippi Central Railroad, the latter tearing up the rails and ties to slow down Grant's troops. Then Bedford Forrest's cavalry patrols slipped around behind the Union forces and wrecked more miles of the railroad, Grant's chief source of supply. They also cut the telegraph wires. Hence for a 12-day period, 19–30 December, Grant was unable to communicate with Sherman. Capping this mischief to the Union army, Van Dorn, now in command of the Confederate cavalry, led a force of 2,500 troopers on a surprise raid on Holly Springs, overwhelming its outnumbered garrison and totally destroying the immense supply dump. Stripped of logistic support, Grant ignominiously retreated 80 miles to Grand Junction, his men living hungrily off the land. His holding action thus collapsed, and much of the Confederate force that had faced him at Grenada shifted by rail via Jackson to Vicksburg. These reinforcements arrived in time to beef up the garrison of the Vicksburg perimeter before Sherman and Porter could strike.

Unaware of these setbacks, Sherman's transports, convoyed by Porter's gunboats, were coming downriver. The Navy's first task was to clear the lower reaches of the Yazoo River of Confederate mines, one of which sank the ironclad *Cairo*. Haynes's Bluff, eight miles up the Yazoo, would be the focus of the attack. Landing in the rain the day after Christmas, Sherman's men deployed for assault along the five paths that led through swamps to the Confederate fortifications on the bluff. The Navy furnished an effective curtain of artillery fire ahead of the advancing troops, but the blue columns, confined to narrow approaches, were raked by musketry and grapeshot. Repeated charges only added to an appalling casualty list. In this so-called Battle of Chickasaw Bluffs, Sherman's men suffered one of their rare defeats. The misery of this rainy winter campaign was further protracted while Sherman and Porter sought an alternative point of attack, but the rising water level in the rivers was turning the swampy shore itself into an impenetrable barrier. Porter grimly convoyed Sherman's army back upriver.

The Union command regretfully conceded that the capture of Vicksburg would have to wait, probably till after the spring floods receded. Various pursuits, however, kept the ships and troops busy during the winter. As a face-saving operation, a waterborne attack was mounted against Fort Hindman at Arkansas Post on the Arkansas River. The 5,000-man garrison was captured.

After Grant assumed personal command on the river, he established his combined forces at Milliken's Bend, just upriver from Vicksburg. With some skepticism, he authorized the Army Engineers to revive the canal project begun earlier by General Williams's men. If this bypass across the finger of land opposite Vicksburg could be made navigable, it would be a simple matter to shift the army south of the city, where Grant now expected to attack. Much work was done, but the spring freshets were to fill up the ditch with silt and debris and drown out the engineers' camp. Various predominantly naval attempts were made by the impatient Porter—all aimed at getting past Vicksburg or at gaining access to the upper reaches of the Yazoo. None was successful.

It thus appeared that for the time being the only profitable naval activity for the Union forces was to dispute control of the Mississippi between Vicksburg and Port Hudson and to raid the South's source of supply from the Red River. To that end the youthful Colonel Charles Rivers Ellet, son of the commander of the Union rams at Memphis, offered to run past the Vicksburg batteries with his late father's ram *Queen of the West*. Porter gave the project his blessing. Ellet planned to make the run before dawn on 2 February 1863, but a breakdown in his steering apparatus so delayed him that the sun had risen when he arrived off Vicksburg. The ram dashed past under heavy fire. Though hit repeatedly by shot and shell, she got by without a single casualty among her crew.

The *Queen of the West* had a brief but successful career as a raider, capturing a number of steamers laden with foodstuffs for the Southern armies. Then came disaster for the 19-year-old colonel. In the Red River he ran his ship aground. Before she could be worked off, Confederate soldiers swarmed on board, and all of her crew were killed or taken prisoner. The captured *Queen* then became the flagship of a little Confederate flotilla of converted riverboats and armed tugs.

On the night of 13 February, Porter, unaware of the *Queen's* fate, sent the ironclad *Indianola* past Vicksburg to support the ram. But the *Queen* and her consorts met and engaged the *Indianola* below the city, battering her badly and driving her hard aground. The Union ironclad too was captured.

With most of his armored vessels on detached duty far from Vicksburg, Porter was unable to exact prompt vengeance for this double humiliation by sending down a force adequate to deal with both of the captured vessels now in Confederate hands. But Porter was a man of salty, sardonic humor. Using a coal barge for a hull, he had his men construct a dummy monitor, with stacks simulated by barrels stacked atop one another, and formidable-looking log guns. Painted a sinister black, she looked, said Porter, a great deal handsomer than most of the genuine gunboats in his command. This synthetic monster was cast adrift at night and allowed to drift downriver past the Confederate batteries. News of her approach so panicked the Confederate working party trying to float the beached *Indianola* that they blew up their stranded prize. The *Queen of the West* hastily withdrew to the Louisiana waterways, where Farragut's gunboats later sank her.

Farragut did not share Porter's sense of humor. Exasperated by the stalemate at Vicksburg, and concerned over the growing strength of the Confederates at Port Hudson, he resolved to pass that position and at least blockade the Red River. He realized this would not be easy. His squadron would have to navigate against a five-knot current around a 150-degree bend in the river, while under the concentrated fire of 30 or more pieces of ordnance, all well entrenched. The Confederates, anticipating a night effort, had rigged locomotive headlights on the east bank to illuminate the river, and had piles of dry brush ready on the west bank. The latter were to be set afire as the ships approached, thereby providing sharp silhouettes for the gunners on the opposite shore. To offset total loss of power from a hit on a steam line or boiler, Farragut directed that each of his screw sloops have a gunboat lashed to her port side.

In the quiet darkness of the night of 14 March, Farragut led the way in the *Hartford*, which was paired with the gunboat *Albatross*. Once the *Hart-ford* grounded directly under the enemy guns. With the aid of the *Albatross* alongside, she managed to back off and continue upriver out of range. The *Richmond* and the *Monongahela*, much battered, gave up the attempt. The big sidewheeler *Mississippi*, steaming alone, grounded hard on the west bank, where she caught fire from enemy shelling. The next morning she blew up. Only the flagship and her little consort had succeeded in passing the batteries. However, as a two-ship fleet in being they were adequate to achieve Farragut's immediate objective of blocking the Red River traffic.

The Capture of Vicksburg

With the coming of spring, the falling level of the Mississippi finally made an overland route down the west bank available. In early April 1863, Grant marched most of his army to a point opposite Grand Gulf, the southern anchor of the Vicksburg perimeter. For the army to cross the river at this point would require the support of naval guns as well as naval transport.

Porter accordingly on the night of 16 April conducted seven of his ironclads and three supply-laden transports downstream past the Vicksburg batteries. Despite heavy fire from the shore, the fleet got by with the loss only of one of the transports. A week later six more transports tried their luck at passing this gauntlet of fire, and five made it. After a prolonged bombardment by the ironclads failed to silence the Confederate batteries at Grand Gulf, Porter and Grant simply moved downriver nine miles to Bruinsburg, where the fleet ferried the Union army across without opposition.

The crossing was facilitated by a feinted attack made simultaneously by Sherman's corps against Haynes's Bluff, at the opposite end of the Vicksburg defenses. So convincing was Sherman's fake assault that the Confederates thought it to be the main thrust and Grant's the diversionary move. Sherman, having thus fixed the northern flank of the Confederate defenses in position, then followed Grant with the bulk of his corps and joined the main body of the Union army near Grand Gulf, which the Confederates had evacuated.

Grant had already begun to apply the hard lessons of his December campaign against Vicksburg. Still smarting from the lessons he had learned from the Confederate cavalry, he dispatched Colonel Benjamin H. Grierson, USA, with a thousand hard-riding troopers, on a 600-mile ride around the heart of Mississippi. Between 17 April and 2 May

the Union cavalry tore down 60 miles of telegraph wire and ripped up rails of two railroads, thereby cutting off Confederate forces in Mississippi from communication with the rest of the Confederacy or the possibility of early reinforcement. The principal Confederate commanders thus isolated were Lieutenant General John C. Pemberton, who had 32,000 troops in the Vicksburg area, and General Joseph E. Johnston, overall Confederate commander in the West, who was in the early stages of assembling an army at Jackson, the Mississippi capital.

Applying another lesson he had learned, Grant daringly cut loose from his base on the river, ordering his men to live off the land. With his whole army of 44,000 he then marched on Jackson in order to place himself between the two Confederate armies. Johnston, driven out of Jackson by a part of Grant's army, ordered Pemberton to attack the Union force from behind. Instead, Pemberton probed southeast, hoping to cut the nonexistent Union supply line. Grant now wheeled about, defeated Pemberton at Champion's Hill, and chased him back to Vicksburg.

Johnston, retreating to the north, now ordered Pemberton to evacuate the city forthwith and join him. But Sherman, on Grant's right, cut off that avenue of escape by seizing Chickasaw and Haynes's bluffs north of the city. Union sailors, firing from gunboats on the river, watched Sherman's cavalry chasing the enemy from the bluffs whence his men had been bloodily repulsed the preceding December and toward which they had feinted just 18 days before.

Pemberton and his decimated army were now surrounded in Vicksburg, cut off from all supplies, while Grant's hungry men could once more be supplied by Porter's fleet. The Confederates were able to throw back an effort to take Vicksburg by storm, but the ensuing siege, with the city under ceaseless bombardment from land and river, could have only one conclusion. On 4 July 1863, just as the North was celebrating the victory at Gettysburg, Pemberton surrendered his starving army.

To Grant and Sherman, quite properly, goes the principal credit for the climactic phase of the Vicksburg campaign. But, as Grant himself generously conceded, it was the Navy that made the victory possible. The Union ships maintained the Army's single line of communication—the Mississippi River between Cairo and Vicksburg—at the end of which the Army was suspended like a Federal bucket in a Confederate well. Operating at once as mobile heavy artillery and as troop ferries, the gunboats ranged the whole navigable waterway system in the theater of operations, destroying Southern supplies, supporting Union garrisons under attack, convoying unarmed vessels, and cutting off all enemy waterborne traffic.

Meanwhile, Farragut's squadron had been performing similar services downstream. Urged on and closely supported by Farragut, Major General Nathaniel P. Banks, USA, in mid-May of 1863 began an offensive against Port Hudson. On the 27th Banks's troops made an unsuccessful effort to storm the fortifications, then settled down to bombardment and siege. News of the fall of Vicksburg made it evident to the garrison at Port Hudson that the Union could soon move overwhelming forces against them. In any event, the loss of Vicksburg largely destroyed the value of their own strategic position. On 8 July Port Hudson surrendered.

The Union now held undisputed control of the Mississippi. The Confederacy was split, in effect extending the "Anaconda" from the Gulf to Cairo. From this point on, the sliced-off western states of the Confederacy would be able to contribute little but moral support to the flagging fortunes of the South.

The Red River Campaign

The eminently successful Mississippi campaign was followed by the dismal Red River expedition, the greatest fiasco of the war. From a strictly military point of view, campaigning west of the Mississippi was now a needless dissipation of Union forces. But President Lincoln and Secretary of State Seward wished to establish a military presence in Texas as a restraint on the operations of a French army in Mexico. Northern businessmen backed the operation as a means of capturing thousands of bales of cotton reputed to be on the banks of the Red awaiting shipment.

The expedition, carried out in the spring of 1864, was conceived as a joint operation, with Porter's Mississippi gunboats supporting and supplying a 27,000-man army under General Banks. Porter, now a rear admiral, carried out his assignment with his usual zeal and efficiency, but his efforts were brought to nought by the stubbornness of the Confederates, who burned their cotton rather than see it fall into Union hands, and by the ineptitude of Banks.

A political general, Banks had proved himself a competent military governor in occupied New Orleans, but his performance in the field ranged from merely incompetent to disastrous.[1] The exercise of his command in the Red River expedition was not one of his finer achievements. Far short of the Texas border, he allowed his army, marching along a narrow road through heavily forested country, to become so strung out that a retreating Confederate force, seeing its opportunity, turned back and savagely attacked the isolated van. The rest of Banks's army fled in panic, leaving the gunboats to fend for themselves.

Under enemy fire, without army support, Porter returned down the Red River the way he had come. His difficulties were enormously aggravated by a falling water level, the result of an unusually dry winter. He was obliged to abandon and blow up his fine ironclad *Eastport*. He managed to get the rest of his boats past the Alexandria rapids only by the extraordinary measure of building dams to raise the level of the river.

[1]President Lincoln, for lack of skilled professional officers, used several politicians as generals in the U. S. Army. None of them proved particularly capable in the field.

Chapter 14
Closing the Confederate Ports

From the very beginning of the war, the North looked forward to the time when Fort Sumter would be recaptured and Charleston, hotbed of secession, occupied by Union troops. After the capture of Port Royal (November 1861) blockaders based on Hilton Head had made blockade-running from Charleston hazardous, but a trickle of traffic from Nassau and Havana continued to leak through. It was part of the Anaconda strategy to set about the capture of the important port cities of the South as soon as an adequate force could be mustered. Though possessing far less strategic value than New Orleans or Wilmington, Charleston had such symbolic value to both sides that it was inevitable that the North should attempt to occupy it at the first opportunity.

In anticipation of an eventual attack, both General Beauregard, commanding the military district, and Brigadier General Roswell S. Ripley, in local tactical command, exercised their considerable engineering skill in stiffening the defenses of the city. In addition to the original masonry forts—Fort Sumter, Fort Moultrie, and Castle Pinckney—Charleston acquired formidable new earthwork and sandbag-protected fortifications: Fort Wagner on Morris Island; Fort Beauregard and several smaller strong points on Sullivan's Island, to the north and east of the harbor channel; and Fort Ripley and a strengthened Fort Johnson, commanding the inner harbor. Collectively, these coast-defense installations mounted 149 guns of 9-inch caliber or larger and a much greater number of smaller weapons. Much of the ordnance was rifled, firing cored conical shot of great penetrating power. In addition, there were underwater obstacles of all varieties that human ingenuity could at that time devise—heavy piles driven into the bottom, log-and-chain booms, rope barriers designed to foul propellers, and quantities of mines, some of which could be exploded electrically from shore observation points.

Furthermore, Charleston harbor is a cul-de-sac; even if a Union squadron could fight past the outer forts and get into the anchorage, it would still be under heavy fire. There was no real analogy to the circumstances of Port Royal or the passing of the forts below New Orleans. A naval attack would be no matter of exposing the ships to an hour or so of hostile fire. To be successful it would have to overpower the enemy positions by long-sustained bombardment.

Rear Admiral Samuel F. Du Pont, commanding the South Atlantic Blockading Squadron, did not underestimate the problem. But when, in early 1863, the *New Ironsides* and the *Passaic* and *Nahant*—the latter two formidable new monitors of improved design—joined Du Pont's fleet, the Navy Department began to pressure the admiral to consider a purely naval attack on Charleston. As other newly commissioned armored vessels became available, Du Pont prepared to put to trial the moot question of whether armored ships could successfully duel equally well-armed land forts.

The grand attack was scheduled for 7 April 1863. The plan was simple. The nine Union ironclads would proceed in column up the main ship channel till they were within 600 to 800 yards of Fort Sumter, which they were to take as their primary objective and, if possible, reduce by deliberate, aimed fire. When and if this was accomplished, the second objective would be the destruction of the Morris Island batteries. The problem of mines and obstructions was to be met by an improvisation of Ericsson's—a V-shaped raft with trailing grapnels to foul the anchor lines of the "torpedoes," an awkward device designed to fit around the bow of a monitor. The lead vessel, the *Weehawken*, had the dubious honor of managing this invention in battle.

The advance started inauspiciously with the *Weehawken* getting the grapnels of her minesweep fouled in her own anchor chain. The other ironclads consumed an hour getting under way. The cumbersome *New Ironsides* proved so awkward to handle in the narrow waters that she twice had to anchor to avoid running aground.

The head of the Union column did not reach the outer barrier of Fort Sumter until midafternoon. When the Northern ships had reached point-blank range, the presighted Confederate guns opened with a devastating blanket of fire, till then unparalleled in weight of metal and accuracy. Hundreds of rounds of heavy shot were fired at the Union iron-

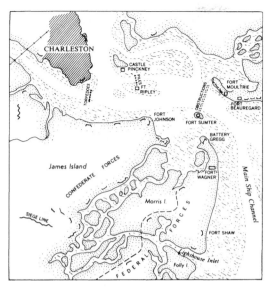

Charleston Harbor, 1863

clads, while the fleet, firing slowly, got off a total of only 139 shot, nearly all of which were directed against Fort Sumter. Fifty-five of these shot struck the walls and parapet, others falling inside the works. Considerable damage was done to the masonry, and the officers' quarters in the parade were demolished, but Sumter's fighting efficiency was not significantly impaired.

In order to get back over the bar before dark, Du Pont at 4:30 signaled recall and shepherded his battered line out once more into deep water. He had planned to renew the engagement the next day, but damage reports from his captains prompted reconsideration. Captain John Rodgers of the *Weehawken* reported 53 shot marks on his ship alone. The *Patapsco* had taken at least 47 hits. All the other Union vessels had been struck repeatedly. Worst hurt was the lightly armored *Keokuk*. Hit more than 90 times, she had been pierced at or just below the water line by 19 shot. Leaking like a sieve, she had barely managed to get away. She sank the following day.

The *Passaic* was sufficiently injured to require immediate yard overhaul. The other monitors had armor plates jarred loose, turret mechanisms jammed, and bolt heads sheared off, but had suffered surprisingly little structural damage. For what it was worth, Du Pont proved that well-armored ships could stand up to protected land batteries.

He had also proved that Charleston could not be taken by naval attack alone. He concurred with the unanimous judgment of his captains that further naval attack had no prospect of gain commensurate

with the risks involved. Not much later, at his own request, he was relieved as commanding officer.

The Siege of Charleston

With the arrival of Rear Admiral John A. Dahlgren as Du Pont's relief came a change in plans. Charleston would be invested by a regular siege. Brigadier General Quincy A. Gillmore of the Army Engineers would conduct the land phase, and the function of the fleet would be to support the operation.

Troops were moved to Folly Island in July 1863. Here Gillmore constructed batteries to command the Confederate works on the south end of nearby Morris Island. On 10 July he attacked across Lighthouse Inlet, strongly supported by the fire of four ironclads. These vessels paralleled the advance of the troops on the beach, laying down a barrage immediately ahead of them as they progressed to the outer defenses of Fort Wagner, which they reached after 14 hours. The *Catskill*, coming under severe fire during this support operation, was struck some 60 times by fire from Fort Wagner and considerably damaged. The other vessels were less severely treated.

The next day Gillmore's division tried to storm Fort Wagner, but was repulsed with considerable losses. Again on 18 July a more deliberate and carefully planned infantry assault was repulsed. The Navy served as mobile heavy artillery; joined by guns ashore it took Wagner under a ferocious crossfire that drove the Confederate gunners to their underground bombproofs. But as the attacking columns moved up, the Southerners rushed to the parapets once more and poured grapeshot and canister into the assault parties. This murderous action cost more than 1,500 Union soldiers killed and wounded. The 600 yards of sandy beach between the Union rifle pits and the walls of Wagner were so carpeted with blue-clad bodies that the fleet withheld fire on the fort until the wounded were removed.

After this, General Gillmore contented himself with establishing siege parallels and erecting heavy batteries on Morris Island—both to take Fort Wagner under fire and also to deliver fire on Fort Sumter and on the city of Charleston itself, five miles away. By mid-August the army had 60 heavy guns mounted, and periodically thereafter the fleet joined in the incessant barrage kept up on Forts Wagner and Sumter and Battery Gregg. As the bombardment reached a crescendo preparatory to an assault on Wagner planned for 7 September, the defenders evacuated both Wagner and Gregg and slipped away to the mainland by night. Gillmore then had the satisfaction of being able to turn a score of the Confederates' own guns on Charleston's remaining harbor defenses.

The pounding by army and fleet guns had by this time reduced Fort Sumter to ruins, with most of its guns dismounted. Making little effort to coordinate plans, both Dahlgren and Gillmore on the night of 8 September sent off boat parties to storm the fort. Five hundred naval and marine "boarders" initiated what was supposed to be a surprise attack. Two of the Union monitors moved quietly up for close support.

Though Fort Sumter's big guns had been silenced, the garrison was still full of fight. Probably forewarned by espionage, Major Stephen Elliot, CSA, commanding the fort, had every man on the alert. When the dark shapes of the boats appeared below them, the Confederates let loose a withering barrage of grenade and rifle fire. Almost at once, as if on signal, the guns of the surrounding Confederate forts and of the Southern ironclad *Chicora*, inside the harbor, opened up, all zeroed in at the base of Fort Sumter.

Most of the naval boats that had not already touched down hauled off, with or without orders. Gillmore's force of 700 soldiers had not come within range, and they prudently withdrew to Morris Island. The hundred or so Union soldiers and marines who got into the fort were promptly killed or captured. Instead of the easy victory Dahlgren had anticipated, the attackers had run into an ambush.

In October a joint effort was made to force evacuation of Sumter through sheer weight of gunfire. This also failed. Dahlgren and Gillmore settled down to a siege and continued bombardment. "Brave Charleston" was to hold out for another year.

Atlanta Threatened

After the simultaneous Union victories of Gettysburg and Vicksburg in July 1863, military activities came virtually to a standstill in the Virginia area and along the Mississippi; central Tennessee became for a time the principal theater of the Civil War. When General William S. Rosecrans, USA, forced General Braxton Bragg, CSA, below Chattanooga on the Georgia border, Lee detached Longstreet's corps and sent it by railroad to reinforce Bragg. At the same time Hooker entrained two Federal corps to reinforce Rosecrans. Longstreet arrived first, and at the Battle of Chickamauga (September 1863) the Confederates won a partial victory, forcing the

northern army back into Chattanooga. Grant, now given supreme command in the West, relieved Rosecrans and came in person to take charge. He succeeded in restoring the Federal line of communications, and in the Battle of Chattanooga (November 1863) chased Bragg from his entrenchments and into Georgia. Grant then left Sherman in command of the western army and proceeded to Washington to assume supreme command of the Union forces and to exercise direction in the field of the Army of the Potomac.

Now at last a unified land strategy was to be carried out. Grant would strike hard at Lee in Virginia, destroying or at least containing the Army of Northern Virginia, while Sherman headed into Georgia in a great flanking movement, the first major stage of which would be the investing and capture of Atlanta.

The advance on Atlanta gave a new sense of urgency to Farragut's long-cherished scheme to close the port of Mobile. For Sherman reasoned that if a demonstration were made against the Confederacy's only remaining Gulf port, the garrison of Mobile might be reinforced by detachments from the army of General Joseph E. Johnston (who had now replaced Bragg). In any event no assistance from Mobile would be available to the defenders of Atlanta. So in July 1864, the monitors Farragut had previously requested in vain were made available, and a troop contingent was provided to besiege and capture the forts.

The Mobile Campaign

Mobile, which was the last Gulf Coast port of any consequence left in Southern hands, is located at the head of Mobile Bay, 25 miles from the Gulf. Hence her defenses, like those of New Orleans earlier, consisted of forts distant from the city guarding the water approaches and supported insofar as possible by naval vessels. For deep-draft vessels, the only feasible channel ran between Fort Morgan, on Mobile Point, and Fort Gaines, on Dauphin Island. Fort Powell, to the northwest, guarded a shoaler approach. The Confederates had put down an impassable barrier of submerged piles two miles eastward from Dauphin Island to the channel. A triple line of moored torpedoes extended the barrier to a point 400 yards from the guns of Fort Morgan. The eastern end of the minefield was marked by a buoy. The unmined portion of the channel, left for the use of blockade-runners, was only 150 yards wide, and at pistol-shot range from Fort Morgan, a casemated masonry structure mounting 45 heavy guns.

In addition, the Confederates had inside the bay the new ironclad *Tennessee*, an improved version of the *Virginia* design. Her armament was two pivoted 7-inch rifled guns fore and aft, firing 110-pound shot, and two 6.4-inch rifles in each broadside. But she was underpowered and slow and by a defect of design had her steering chains exposed so that they could be severed by gunfire. She was supported by three light gunboats, the *Selma*, the *Gaines*, and the *Morgan*. All told, the little Confederate squadron had a total of 16 guns—to contest Farragut's battle force of 18 ships and 159 guns.

On 8 July 1864, the first of the Federal monitors, the *Manhattan*, reported at Pensacola; three more followed: the *Tecumseh* from the Atlantic, and the *Winnebago* and *Chickasaw* from the Mississippi. Then Admiral Farragut also learned that by the end of the month he could count on obtaining the cooperation of the troops under Major General Gordon Granger. Within a few days he developed his basic plan for the attack on Mobile Bay and its forts. He decided on an early morning assault on a day when he could count on a flood tide to help carry the ships past Fort Morgan into Mobile Bay and on a southwest wind to carry the smoke of battle away from the ships and into the fort. His wooden ships would be lashed together in pairs as at Port Hudson. The flagship *Hartford*, with the *Metacomet* on her port side, would lead the way through the open channel between the mine field and Fort Morgan. The *Brooklyn* and the *Octorara*, the *Richmond* and the *Port Royal*, the *Lackawanna* and the *Seminole*, the *Monongahela* and the *Kennebec*, the *Ossipee* and the *Itasca*, and the *Oneida* and the *Galena* would pair up and follow in that order.

The battle plan was later modified to include the four monitors, which were to proceed in a parallel column between the wooden ships and the fort. "The service that I look for from the ironclads," said Farragut, "is, first, to neutralize as much as possible the fire of the guns which rake our approach; next to look out for the [Confederate] ironclad when we are abreast of the forts; and, lastly, to occupy the attention of those batteries which would rake us while running up the bay." A second modification, which Farragut made with great reluctance, placed the *Brooklyn* and her consort in the lead, the *Hartford* in second place. This change, urged upon him because of the *Brooklyn*'s greater forward firepower and a torpedo–cowcatcher arrangement on her bows, he was to regret. The late arrival of the monitor *Tecumseh* caused a 24-hour postponement which prevented the fleet from making its attack simultaneously with the army's

landing on Dauphin Island to lay siege to Fort Gaines; otherwise the Union attack was launched according to plan.

The four monitors were well equipped for the role assigned them. The single-turreted *Tecumseh* and *Manhattan* were 1,000-ton craft armed with two 15-inch guns, which could throw a 440-pound steel-headed bolt as an armor-piercing projectile. The rotating turret was protected by 10-inch armor; superimposed on it was the pilot house, which could be entered only through the turret. The *Winnebago* and *Chickasaw* were shallow-draft, double-turreted river craft protected by 8½-inch armor and armed with four 11-inch guns apiece. They were no faster than the *Tennessee*, but they had heavier armor and larger guns.

At 5:30 on the morning of 5 August 1864 the Federal fleet got under way for the entrance to the channel. Every protective device that had proved valuable at New Orleans or Port Hudson was employed and, if possible, improved upon. The *Tecumseh* steamed slowly along the Fort Morgan side of the channel, somewhat in advance of the *Brooklyn* pair on a parallel course. The first shots were exchanged just after seven o'clock, the *Tecumseh* firing twice at the fort; she then reserved her fire for the *Tennessee*, which was discovered moving slowly into the bend in the channel beyond the Confederate minefield. While a general cannonading was joined behind him, Captain Craven of the *Tecumseh* devoted his attention exclusively to the Confederate ram. Her position and the narrowness of the channel between the minefield buoy and Fort Morgan made him doubt his orders from Farragut: "The vessels will take care to pass to the eastward of the easternmost

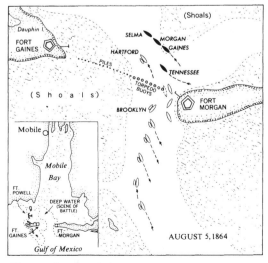

The Battle of Mobile Bay

buoy, which is clear of all obstruction." Craven turned his monitor to head for the *Tennessee* on a collision course, and passed about 300 yards ahead of the *Brooklyn*. With his 15-inch guns loaded with 60-pound charges and steel bolts, he bore down on his opponent. On board the Confederate ship the officers and crew braced themselves for the shock, for Admiral Buchanan ordered them to hold fire until the two ships actually came together. At this tense moment when they were little more than 100 yards apart, the *Tecumseh* ran upon a mine, which exploded and ripped out her bottom. The monitor sank bow first almost instantly, her stern rising out of the water so that her propeller was seen turning in the air as she plunged to the bottom. Of her complement of over 100, only 21 survived.

Fortunately for the Union attack, this catastrophe did not prevent the other monitors from maintaining their proper stations and carrying out their assigned duties, but a disastrous situation was rapidly developing among the wooden ships. The *Brooklyn's* captain, hearing a confused report of objects in the water ahead, stopped his ship and then backed her down against the current. Within a matter of minutes the *Brooklyn* and her consort lay across the channel, bows on and abreast the fort, while the other wooden ships bore down on them.

Farragut had sent his pilot into the maintop for a clear view above the smoke of the guns; he himself had taken a station in the port main rigging, climbing higher as the smoke rose and maintaining a position of easy communication with the pilot, with the captain of the *Metacomet* on the paddlebox of his ship alongside, and with the captain of the *Hartford*. When the *Tecumseh* sank, the admiral had ordered a boat from the *Metacomet* to rescue survivors in the water. Now, with the *Brooklyn* barring his way and threatening to congest his entire fleet where the channel passed close to Fort Morgan's guns, Farragut ordered the *Hartford* to pass to port around the stern of the *Brooklyn*, through the minefield, and into the channel again. It was on this occasion, according to certain postwar accounts, that Farragut shouted "Damn the torpedoes! Full steam ahead!"[1] Although her crew reported hearing the primers of the torpedoes snapping, the flagship passed through. As the admiral had suspected all along, most of the torpedoes were harmless through long immersion.

The *Hartford* proved too nimble for the clumsy

[1]Farragut himself records that he sought Divine guidance through prayer and heard an inner voice tell him to go forward. Eyewitnesses agree that the admiral did signal for full speed ahead.

Tennessee, which finally turned back to attack the other Union ships. The flagship meanwhile suffered casualties from the enfilading fire of the Confederate gunboats until she had room to maneuver and bring her guns to bear on them. Her broadsides then quickly repulsed the gunboats, and the *Metacomet* cut loose and went after them.

After blocking the rest of the Federal ships under the guns of Fort Morgan, the *Brooklyn* had at length got back on course and led the column through the minefield a mile behind the *Hartford*. Several vessels were hit by the fort's guns, but only the *Oneida*, at the end of the line, was disabled. Even she got past with the help of her escort and the flood tide. As the wooden vessels trailed into the bay, they were met by the *Tennessee*, which lumbered along and through the line, exchanging broadsides with ship after ship but seriously damaging none and in return receiving no injury worse than a perforated smokestack.

The *Metacomet*, fastest ship in the Union fleet, had no difficulty overtaking the Confederate gunboat *Selma*, which she forced to surrender. The other two gunboats meanwhile had come under fire by Farragut's battle line. The *Gaines*, in a sinking condition, was beached by her crew. Only the *Morgan* escaped; slightly damaged, she sought refuge under the guns of Fort Morgan, and eventually made her way to Mobile.

Four miles up the bay the *Hartford* anchored, and Farragut sent his crew to breakfast. The other Union ships soon anchored nearby. The captain of the flagship summed up the battle at that point by remarking to the admiral: "What we have done has been well done, sir; but it all counts for nothing so long as the *Tennessee* is there under the guns of Fort Morgan."

The Confederate admiral had decided to use his remaining six hours' fuel supply in an unexpected attack on Farragut's ships. After doing all the damage she could, the *Tennessee* might in his opinion serve as a floating battery in the defense of Fort Morgan. Characteristically, Buchanan wanted above all else to have another chance at the *Hartford*.

When Farragut was told that the *Tennessee* was returning, he could scarcely believe it. He had feared that the ram might attack the light ships he had left outside the bay, or wait to make a night attack on the fleet. Instead, Buchanan was playing directly into his hands—bringing his slow, awkward ram in broad daylight against 17 Federal warships, most of which could outmaneuver, outrun, and outgun him. "I did not think old Buck was such a fool," exclaimed Farragut.

What followed was a wild melee. First the *Monongahela* and then the *Lackawanna* rammed the Confederate, each attacker taking far greater damage than she inflicted. At last the two flagships came together obliquely, collided at the bow, and ground past each other port side to port side. The *Hartford*'s shot, fired at a ten-foot range, bounded off the *Tennessee*'s casemate, while the Confederate, plagued throughout the battle by bad primers, was able to fire only one shot, her last, into her opponent. Then the *Lackawanna*, steaming at full speed for the *Tennessee*, crashed instead into the circling *Hartford* near where Farragut was standing.

The monitors now moved in on the *Tennessee*. The *Chickasaw* followed close behind the ram almost as though being towed, her shot jamming port shutters, cutting the steering chains, and wounding Admiral Buchanan. The only shot that penetrated the ram's armor, however, was a steel bolt from a 15-inch gun of the *Manhattan*. One of the Confederate officers reported that it "admitted daylight through our side, where, before it struck us, there had been two feet of solid wood, covered with five inches of solid iron."

Almost dead in the water, three of her port shutters jammed, her steering gone, her stack shot away so that her gun-deck was filled with suffocating heat and fumes, the *Tennessee* was in a hopeless position. As the entire Union fleet was moving in for the kill and the Confederates could bring no guns to bear, Captain Johnston, with Admiral Buchanan's consent, climbed out onto the casemate top to show the white flag. It was then 10 a.m.

The Confederate naval forces had lost a total of 12 killed and 20 wounded in the entire battle, and only two were killed and nine wounded in the *Tennessee*. Union casualties for the battle were 52 killed and 170 wounded, not counting those lost when the *Tecumseh* sank. The *Hartford* alone had 25 killed and 28 wounded.

Fort Powell was evacuated and destroyed by its garrison on the night following the naval battle. The next day Fort Gaines surrendered. General Granger's troops were then transferred to Mobile Point, and Fort Morgan capitulated before the end of the month.

These victories brought to an end Mobile's traffic with the outside world. The city's military importance to the Union had already passed, for Mobile was no longer needed as a Union base for a land campaign. No serious attempt was directed against the city itself until the spring of 1865, when six Union ships and a launch were sunk by mines while the Navy was cooperating in siege operations

undertaken by the Army. With the fall of outlying fortifications, Mobile was finally occupied by Union troops on 12 April, three days after the surrender of Lee at Appomattox.

Sherman's March

In the meantime, Sherman had forced Johnston back on Atlanta. Using Fabian tactics, the weaker army of Johnston obliged Sherman to take 74 days to achieve a 100-mile advance. But President Davis, demanding action, replaced Johnston with Hood, who went on the offensive and was beaten three times in succession. Sherman now cut loose from his line of communications and circled Atlanta, severing rail lines and obliging Hood to evacuate the city to avoid being bottled up and captured. The near coincidence of the Battle of Mobile Bay and the fall of Atlanta (2 September 1864) marked the beginning of the end for the Confederacy.

Leaving General George H. Thomas in command of a force adequate to defeat Hood, Sherman himself set out with 60,000 men on his celebrated march to the sea. Living off the country, his army laid waste to a strip 60 miles wide through the one remaining major granary of the South. He emerged at Savannah in late December 1864, captured the city, and headed north into the Carolinas, where a small Confederate army under Johnston was unable to make effective resistance.

As word of Sherman's advance reached Dahlgren off Charleston harbor, the admiral formed a naval brigade equipped with two field howitzers, which did good service in General John G. Foster's command, campaigning between Savannah and Charleston. In addition, the Navy's shallow-draft gunboats were employed to advantage in providing logistic and gunfire support to Sherman's army as it marched north from Savannah. The doom of Charleston was sealed as Sherman's victorious Westerners closed in behind the city, which the Confederate garrison had to evacuate on 18 February 1865 in order to avoid capture. And so at long last the sailors of the fleet walked the nearly deserted streets of the city that had so long defied their guns.

The last act in the tragic drama of the Civil War was about to begin. Discounting Johnston's small force operating independently, Grant envisioned the final strategy as a pincers movement on Lee's army, tied to Richmond by the determination of the Confederate government to hold the capital at all costs. As Sherman's legions pushed inexorably north, Grant suddenly shifted the bulk of his forces to reinforce the Army of the James operating to the south and east of Richmond. Petersburg came under siege; the Petersburg–Richmond area became a gigantic fortress, covered by over 40 miles of entrenchments and dependent on rail connections to the south and west for supplies and reinforcements.

The First Fort Fisher Expedition, Christmas, 1864

As early as the winter of 1862, Secretary Welles had unsuccessfully petitioned the War Department to provide troops for a joint Army–Navy attack on the Confederate defenses at the mouth of the Cape Fear River in North Carolina. Wilmington, at the fall line of the river, was already a principal port for the blockade-runners. The dual approaches to the river mouth, the notoriously dangerous Frying Pan Shoals off Smith's Island, and the comparative remoteness from Union bases made the maintenance of a close blockade here especially difficult. The excellent rail connections between Wilmington and Richmond and other points in the interior of the Confederacy gave Wilmington a vital strategic importance—far greater than that of Mobile, second only to that of New Orleans. But with the multitude of demands for troops, Secretary of War Stanton for nearly three years could never seem to spare even the modest contingent required. Meanwhile the principal fortification at the mouth of the river, Fort Fisher, was gradually developed by the Southern command from a scantily manned "sand battery" to a very formidable complex of well-protected ordnance.

In September 1864 Secretary Welles renewed his proposal for an amphibious attack. Grant was interested in the operation as a step in isolating Lee from all outside supplies, and promised an adequate force by the first of October. Farragut, because of failing health and near exhaustion, declined the proffered naval command, but Admiral Porter, eager to regild his somewhat tarnished laurels after the fiasco of the Red River, embraced this new opportunity with his characteristic enthusiasm.

The plan of campaign as originally conceived was simple. A fleet mounting 150 guns would bombard Fort Fisher, which was known to be defended by some 800 men with about 75 pieces of ordnance. An army force to consist of not fewer than 8,000 troops would be landed under covering fire on the open beach north of the fort. This force would throw a trench line across to the Cape Fear River, thereby cutting off the fort from overland reinforcement and supply from the city. Capture of the fort by assault or siege could then be hazarded.

By mid-October a heterogeneous fleet of nearly a hundred vessels was mustered at Hampton Roads; it included everything from the latest screw frigates and ironclads down to makeshift gunboats converted from harbor ferries. In tonnage, it was the largest fleet to be assembled under the United States flag in the nineteenth century—not surpassed even by the ships supporting the U. S. assault on Veracruz in 1847.

Drilling of this awkwardly large and heterogeneous force in simple maneuver and gunnery presented an unusual command problem, which Porter cheerfully faced. He adopted an improved and more precise set of blockade instructions to govern interim operations off the mouths of the Cape Fear River, set about getting personally acquainted with all his captains, and prepared for general distribution a lithographed chart of the projected bombardment, showing the position of each of the 55 gunnery vessels to be employed.

A bombardment force of this size could be concentrated off Fort Fisher only by dint of pulling units off the blockade up and down the coast. Both Porter and Secretary Welles were eager to put the operation in train and to get these vessels back on their routine but important duties. The whole armada remained at anchor in Hampton Roads for five weeks, however, waiting for the dilatory General Benjamin F. Butler to bring his troops from Bermuda Hundred. With the Army and Navy serving as cooperating forces while lacking an overall operations commander, coordination required a high measure of compatability between the senior officers of the two services. This was notoriously lacking between Porter and Butler, another political general.

Porter was skeptical of the competence of political generals, and of Ben Butler in particular. His exasperation at what appeared to him needless delay was heightened when Butler finally arrived in late November, only to propose insistently that the fort be destroyed by a gigantic floating mine before any assault was attempted. Gathering the explosives to load this giant "torpedo" would mean yet more delay.

But the creator of the mortar flotilla relished innovative ideas. Informed by civilian scientists that the scheme might just work, he decided to give it a try. At least it would get the expedition under way. Once he made his decision, Porter set about the preparation of his floating firecracker with dispatch. The steamer *Louisiana*, weakened by dry rot and due for survey, was loaded with all the black

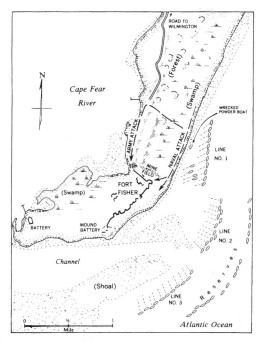

Second Attack on Fort Fisher, 13–15 January 1865

powder she could carry, about 215 tons of it. Fuse trains were laid about, and a clockwork device was improvised to set off the explosion after the volunteer crew had abandoned ship.

Time was lost procuring the explosives from various army and naval magazines up and down the coast. Protracted bad weather caused further delay. In mid-December the fleet at last cleared the Virginia capes. Another gale blew up just as the transports were making their rendezvous with the fleet. The naval ships merely anchored where they were, but the troop carriers scurried back to Beaufort. Not till 23 December were all the Union forces in position off Fort Fisher.

That night the *Louisiana* was towed by a tug to within 300 yards of the fort and there anchored. Her volunteer crew hastily set the clockwork mechanisms and lit candles, which would burn down to light fuses. Just to be sure, they also started a pine-knot fire in an after cabin. Though the night was dark and it was a blackout operation, there was some danger of fire from the fort igniting the explosives before the crew could get away. But all went well. The boatswain stationed at the rail quietly checked off by name each man as he slipped into the waiting boats. Presently the officer in charge gave the order to pull away to the tug, which was waiting at a discreet distance.

The rest is anticlimax. The clockwork exploder apparently failed to function. It was the fire that

finally set off the powder, 20 minutes after the scheduled time. The fireworks were impressive: a pillar of flame shot up to the sky, and four successive blasts were heard. But the shock wave was barely felt in the fleet. It is probable that the powder merely burned, rather than exploded.[2]

The Fort Fisher garrison had long known of the project and dreaded the coming blast. When it came, however, it did no damage, and some of the men slept through the night, unaware that it had occurred. Nobody in the fort assessed it for what it was. Colonel William Lamb, the commanding officer, concluded that a blockade-runner had run aground, set fire to herself, and blown up. A North Carolina enlisted man, standing sentry duty through the night, remarked to his relief the next morning, "Reckon one of them Yankee gunboats off thar done busted her biler."

At first light, the ships of the fleet stood in to their scheduled bombardment positions and laid a blanket of fire on the fort. About 115 shots a minute registered on or within the walls of the bastion. Two exposed magazines blew up, and the barracks and other wooden structures in the parade were quickly burned out. In little more than an hour the Confederates gave up even token resistance in this uneven gunnery duel, abandoning the parapets and seeking safety in underground bunkers. But silencing the fort was one thing; occupying it was quite another. The fleet kept up the bombardment till sundown, but no transports appeared.

The next morning, Christmas Day, the transports finally arrived. Porter dispatched 17 gunboats to cover the landing and provided a hundred ship's boats for putting troops ashore. At long last the assault was to be made.

Once more the fleet stood in and took the fort under slow, deliberate fire, while the soldiers were landed five miles to the north. Porter was delighted to see the blue-clad skirmish line reconnoitering and sharpshooting near the outer works of the fort.

Then came the incredible news that only some 2,200 of the 6,500 available troops had been landed and that these were being reembarked. Not knowing the circumstances of this decision, Porter assumed that the attack would be made the next day, and detailed the ironclads to keep the fort under fire through the night. But he presently received word from Butler that assaulting Fort Fisher was out of the question "as it was left sub-

[2]It is unlikely that even optimal performance of this floating mine would have seriously injured the earth-and-sandbag fortifications. If modern high explosives had been available, it would of course have been a different story.

stantially uninjured as a defensive work by the navy fire." Since Butler's orders specified that he was to conduct an assault, not a siege, and he now deemed an assault nothing short of suicidal, he firmly announced his decision to return with his troops to Hampton Roads.

Porter's exasperation at this turn of events was matched only by Grant's. At the latter's request, the secretary of war relieved Butler of his command and ordered him home to Massachusetts. Porter pressed for a renewal of the attack under a more resolute commander. Meanwhile, he took his fleet to Beaufort to replenish ammunition, victuals, and other supplies. From Grant he received a message: "Hold on if you please a few days longer, and I will send you more troops with a different general."

The Second Fort Fisher Expedition, 13–15 January 1865

Butler's decision was certainly open to question, but it had been based on reliable reconnaissance. The naval bombardment had in fact been appallingly ineffective. Of the 75 guns in Fort Fisher only 3 had been dismounted, and of the garrison of 800 men only 3 had been killed. The gunfire, for all its fury, had been largely unaimed, or if the gunners aimed at anything specific, it was the Confederate flag, which the garrison seems to have planted deliberately as a target to draw the Union fire away from themselves and their guns.

Porter, never one to admit failure, continued to point the finger of blame at Butler. Nevertheless, he sat down and completely rewrote his bombardment plan. There was to be no more unaimed area fire. Each ship was given specific targets. "The object," he wrote, "is to lodge the shell in the parapets, and tear away the traverses under which the bombproofs are located. A shell now and then exploding over a gun en barbette may have a good effect, but there is nothing like lodging the shell before it explodes." He forbade useless firing at flags. "These are generally placed at a point to entice us to fire at them," he noted, "and no harm is done by this kind of firing. Commanders are directed to strictly enjoin their officers and men never to fire at the flag or pole, but to pick out the guns; the stray shells will knock the flagstaff down."

In the evening of 12 January 1865, the second Fort Fisher expeditionary force arrived off the fort, accompanied by Porter's fleet, now increased to 62 vessels. The troops, commanded by tough, energetic Brigadier General Alfred H. Terry, consisted of the original landing force, now augmented to 8,000 men—the number the Navy had requested

in the first place. Toward dawn on the 13th, the fleet opened up with a thundering prelanding bombardment, with the *New Ironsides* and other ironclads approaching to within 700 yards of the beach.

At 8 a.m. Terry's men began going ashore. During the day they extended an entrenched line across the peninsula, thereby protecting their rear and cutting Fort Fisher off completely from the mainland. At sunset the wooden vessels ceased fire, but the ironclads kept up their bombardment through the night.

On the 14th the Federal troops brought field artillery ashore and pushed their outposts to within 500 yards of the fort's landward face. The fleet meanwhile hammered away at the seaward face. Conforming to Porter's revised instructions, the gunners were taking careful aim and gradually dismounting the Confederate ordnance. That night the Confederates brought reinforcements into the fort via the Cape Fear River, giving Colonel Lamb a total of some 1,500 men.

On the morning of the 15th, Porter sent ashore a force of 1,600 bluejackets and 400 marines to participate in the assault, scheduled for that afternoon. Sappers rapidly trenched their way through the sand to a point 200 yards from the fort's land face. Here they dug a row of rifle pits, which Porter's marines later occupied.

By noon naval gunfire had knocked out most of the guns on the seaward face of the fort. At 3 p.m. the fleet raised the curtain of fire to the upper batteries, and every ship blew her steam whistle. It was the signal for the attack. Led by division officers, the sailors, armed with revolvers and cutlasses, dashed along the beach toward the high waterside parapet at the eastern salient of the fort. The plan had been for the marines, in the rifle pits, to deliver covering small-arms fire, keeping the enemy from the tops. But in the confusion of the unrehearsed operation, the marine party was not properly stationed. Confederate troops stood up on the parapet and poured down a withering musketry fire into the advancing blue line. Three times the surviving officers rallied their men to try the assault again. A few of the sailors reached the parapet and climbed the rough wall, only to be clubbed and bayoneted by the defenders. In minutes the attack was over, an evident failure. More than 300 sailors had fallen. The survivors dug into the sand or retreated.

When the Confederate defenders on the parapets saw the sailors' attack break off, they paused to give three cheers—only to receive a volley of rifle fire in their backs. Terry's infantrymen, profiting from the distraction offered by the sailors' assault, had stormed their way into the fort at the opposite end of the land face. The defenders, despite their surprise, put up a desperate fight. They turned each of the traverses into a separate fort. But the Federal infantry stormed them one by one, while the fleet laid down a barrage of support fire just ahead of their advance. After dark the attackers reached and assaulted the formidable Mound Battery. The surviving Confederates fled down the beach toward the end of Federal Point. Their ammunition exhausted, they threw down their arms. At 10 p.m. General Terry arrived to accept their surrender. He ordered a rocket fired to announce the victory. The fleet responded with cheers, steam whistles, and rockets. General Lee's source of supply had been reduced to zero. The Navy's war was over.

In relation to numbers involved, the second attack on Fort Fisher was one of the bloodiest battles of the war. More than 700 Confederates had been killed or wounded. Union army losses were 691. The Navy lost 309. It was the only successful large-scale joint amphibious attack against a strongly fortified position in the whole course of the war. It demonstrated the effectiveness of heavy, aimed support fire from ships. It showed the feasibility of bold, well-coordinated assaults on even the strongest and best-engineered defenses. It thus foreshadowed the problems and successes of amphibious assaults in World War II.

General Butler, pausing on his way back home, was called to testify before the Congressional Committee on the Conduct of the War. He was maintaining that Fort Fisher was impregnable when word reached Washington that the fort had fallen.

The Finale

With his seemingly inexhaustible reinforcements and supplies, Grant was able at last to outflank the defenses of the Richmond–Petersburg bastion to the north and to the south. Striking in first one sector, then the other, he applied increasing pressure to the depleted Confederate forces. Lee was finally obliged to evacuate Richmond (2 April 1865) to avoid encirclement. As the Army of Northern Virginia headed west with the object of joining forces with Johnston in the mountains, Grant made his final, checkmating move. Shifting his main force parallel and to the south of Lee, Grant placed himself in an intercepting position. With Sheridan's cavalry directly athwart his line of retreat, Lee surrendered at Appomattox (9 April). A week later Johnston surrendered to Sherman. The Army's war was over. At the cost of nearly a million casualties, the Union was preserved and the institution of slavery destroyed.

Summary

The strategies of both the Union and the Confederacy were to a great extent dictated by the peculiar fact that the capitals of the opposing powers were on the periphery of their territories and only a hundred miles apart. In establishing its capital at Richmond, the Confederacy was obliged to tie up a mass army, the bulk of its military power, in Virginia. The Union placed a still larger army in Virginia, to defend Washington and attack Richmond, but the superior military skill of the Southern generals quickly turned the situation there into a stalemate. When it appeared that Robert E. Lee, commanding general of the Army of Northern Virginia, could not be defeated in battle, the Union used its surplus of military power in peripheral operations to cut off his sources of supply and starve his army into submission. The campaigns in Virginia were thus chiefly holding operations. The decisive campaigns were fought elsewhere.

As a first step in "shrinking Lee's logistic base," the Union set up a naval blockade to intercept supplies flowing from Europe to the Confederacy. To facilitate the blockade, Union forces seized bases near the main Confederate ports. The most important of the bases, Port Royal, between Charleston and Savannah, was captured in November 1861 by a fleet under Du Pont.

Endeavoring to break or weaken the blockade, the Confederates used ironclads, mines (called torpedoes), semisubmersibles, and a submarine. The first and most famous of the Confederate ironclads was the *Virginia* (ex-*Merrimack*). On 8 March 1862, she emerged from Norfolk into Hampton Roads, where she destroyed the sloop *Cumberland* and the frigate *Congress*. The next day she fought a four-hour drawn battle with the hastily constructed, newly arrived Union ironclad *Monitor*.

Mines destroyed 31 Union vessels, more than were sunk by any other means. At Charleston the Confederates attempted to break the blockade by the use of semisubmerged mine craft called Davids, one of which damaged the Union ironclad *New Ironsides*. The submarine, the CSS *Hunley*, was the first of her type to sink a warship in combat. After drowning two crews in trial, she drowned a third in the process of sinking the screw sloop *Housatonic*.

The Confederacy, with no navy of consequence to challenge the growing U. S. Navy, resorted to commerce raiding, not only to strike at an important source of Northern economic strength but also to weaken the blockade by inducing the Union to scatter its vessels in search of the raiders. The Confederates tried privateering with moderate success and then shifted to the use of regular naval vessels to do the raiding. The most famous of the Confederate raiders was the cruiser *Alabama*, commanded by Raphael Semmes. Built in England and armed and manned in the Azores, she never entered a Confederate port. In a two-year cruise that took her as far as the Indian Ocean and the South China Sea, she captured 68 Union vessels, most of which she destroyed.

Throughout the war blockade-running was a popular means of eluding the Union blockaders. As the blockaders became more numerous and more efficient, the commerce was largely limited to speedy, specially constructed steamers of low freeboard, generally built in England and not infrequently commanded by British naval officers, out of uniform and using false names.

A major means of "shrinking Lee's logistic base" was the Union capture of the Mississippi Valley, a conquest that cut off from the heart of the Confederacy the ample resources of the Confederate southwest and also goods flowing in from abroad via Mexico. The operation began in February 1862 when Grant's army and Foote's gunboats broke through the Confederate northwest defense line by capturing Fort Henry on the Tennessee River and Fort Donelson on the Cumberland River. Grant, supported by gunboats, then advanced up the Tennessee and repulsed an attack by the western Confederate army in the Battle of Shiloh (6–7 April).

The attempt to stop Grant drew Confederate forces from the South and left New Orleans underdefended. Farragut's Gulf fleet of screw sloops, gunboats, and a side-wheeler, supported by Porter's mortar schooners, ran up the Mississippi past the forts guarding the approaches to New Orleans and on 29 April forced the city's surrender.

Thereafter the gunboats advanced down the Mississippi from the north and the Gulf fleet proceeded up the river from the south, each overcoming resistance and capturing Confederate positions en route. The Confederates on the Mississippi, having the interior position, could shift forces north or south faster than the converging Union forces could shift strength the long way around, but so great was the Federal military predominance that the Union forces profited by their exterior position.

The two Union fleets came together near Vicksburg, which was located high on a bluff that ships' guns could not reach. In December 1862, Sherman with 32,000 Union troops, supported by Porter's gunboats, attempted to capture Vicksburg from the river. He was bloodily repulsed because Grant, coming south overland with 40,000 troops for a double envelopment (pincers), was obliged to retreat when the Confederates cut off his supplies.

The following year Grant marched his army down the Mississippi right bank and was ferried across south of Vicksburg by the Navy. He got between two Confederate armies and defeated first one, then the other. Finally, with support by Porter's gunboats, he laid siege to Vicksburg, which surrendered 4 July 1863. Four days later, Port Hudson, recently fortified by the Confederates, surrendered to General Banks, who had been supported and supplied by Farragut's fleet. The heart of the Confederacy was now surrounded—cut off from Europe by the Federal blockade and from the resources of the Southwest by the Union capture of the Mississippi Valley.

The Red River expedition of 1864, to capture cotton and to place the U. S. flag on Texas soil as a counter to French operations to control Mexico, proved a fiasco—notable chiefly for the extraordinary efforts to extricate Porter's river fleet from the receding waters.

Such was the success of the blockade-runners that the Union tried more effective means of sealing off the Confederate ports. Federal forces attempted without success to capture Charleston from the sea. In April 1863 a column of nine U. S. ironclads reached Charleston's inner harbor but was forced to retreat, severely battered, by gunfire from the surrounding forts. In August 1864 Farragut closed the port of Mobile by running his Gulf fleet past Fort Morgan into Mobile Bay and defeating the Confederate ironclad *Tennessee*.

In an extension of the Mississippi campaign, Sherman fought his way across Georgia, capturing Atlanta and Savannah, and marched up through the Carolinas, thereby outflanking Lee's army and cutting off its supplies from the deep South. As Sherman approached, the Confederate forces abandoned Charleston, which the Union navy promptly occupied. This left only one port, Wilmington, North Carolina, available to blockade-runners. To close this port, Porter pulled nearly a hundred vessels off blockade duty and joined the Army in an assault on sturdy Fort Fisher, which guarded the seaward approaches to Wilmington. The first attack, on Christmas Day 1864, was a failure, but the second, in mid-January 1865, put the fort in Union hands. With the port of Wilmington thus closed, Lee's logistic base was reduced to near-zero. His early defeat and the collapse of the Confederacy were inevitable.

Chapter 15
Naval Developments of the Late Nineteenth Century

At the end of the American Civil War, the U. S. Navy, with 700 ships mounting 5,000 guns and with 6,700 officers and 51,000 men on active duty, ranked in some respects first among the world's navies. Five years later its ironclad monitors had been laid up, its converted merchantmen sold or scrapped, and most of its riverine vessels decommissioned. By the end of 1870, only 52 ships mounting 500 guns were in full commission. This reduction of the U. S. Navy reflected postwar focusing of American interests on internal affairs— settlement of the West, industrialization of the Northeast, reconstruction of the South.

It was generally believed that American security was assured by the tensions within the European balance-of-power system and by the 3,000-mile breadth of the Atlantic. Most American leaders, including many naval officers, expected the United States to return to the defense policy of the early nineteenth century: coastal fortifications to protect the seaboard cities from naval attack and to deny an enemy any port through which an army could invade.

The U. S. Navy of the period was adequate for this plan. Its monitors could be hauled out of mothballs to assist in harbor defense and its cruisers could raid an enemy's commerce. Under construction for the latter service were two classes of steam-and-sail, wooden screw cruisers, laid down during the war to capture Confederate commerce-raiders and to seal off blockade-runners. Their slim hulls were designed along clipper-ship lines, and their engines—the first to employ superheated steam— were built under the supervision of the engineering genius Benjamin Franklin Isherwood, chief of the Navy's Bureau of Steam Engineering. In 1868 trials, the USS *Wampanoag*, the first of her class, achieved a speed of nearly 18 knots, absolutely unique for the times, and not attained by any other U. S. naval vessel until more than 21 years later. The *Wampanoag*s, like the 1812 frigates, could outrun anything they could not outfight. But the naval establishment of 1868 saw no great virtue in such speed, which used up an unconscionable amount of fuel. The *Wampanoag* and her sister ship were condemned for their poor sailing qualities,

the rest of the new cruisers were redesigned to carry more sail at the expense of steam power, and the secretary of the navy issued a general order requiring all vessels of the Navy except dispatch boats and tugs to be fitted with full sail power.

The underlying reason for the sail-power preference was economy. Between 1868 and 1883, Congress, with no prospect of war in sight, appropriated for the Navy barely enough funds to keep its existing ships manned and afloat. The tight budget imposed severe restrictions on operations and on the officer corps. Commanding officers were directed to use sail-power in all but the most exceptional circumstances. If they got up steam, they were ordered to enter their reasons in the log in red ink. As older ships were stricken without replacement, the Navy needed fewer officers. Promotions again stagnated; 35- and 40-year-old lieutenants became commonplace. Some years as few as ten midshipmen received commissions; the rest were turned loose by the Naval Academy with $1,000 "severance pay."

Even with obsolete ships and weapons, the U. S. Navy performed its traditional tasks, sometimes with a vigor that certain commentators a century later would brand "imperialist aggression." For example, in 1871 Rear Admiral John Rodgers, investigating the disappearance of an American trading schooner in Korean waters and receiving no acceptable explanation, ordered his sailors and marines ashore, where they destroyed several forts and killed 350 Koreans. United States sailors landed in Montevideo to protect American property threatened by riots; U. S. marines landed in Panama to keep open the trans-Isthmian railroad, threatened by rebel forces; U. S. marines joined British infantry in restoring order in Alexandria, Egypt. The U. S. Asiatic Squadron joined British and French vessels in a show of force to stop Chinese rioters from attacking Western property in Canton. From time to time U. S. marines were dispatched to protect American embassies and consulates at such widely separated points as Buenos Aires and Seoul.

Acting as diplomats, U. S. naval officers laid claim to uninhabited Midway Atoll, induced Japan to open additional ports to American commerce, obtained treaties of commerce and navigation with Korea, Tutuila in the Samoa Islands, and Madagascar, and arbitrated a border dispute in West Africa.

Several U. S. naval expeditions surveyed possible canal routes in Panama, Nicaragua, and Mexico. Other naval expeditions explored the Arctic. The most notable of the latter was the *Jeannette* Expedition of 1879, which ended in tragedy when the ship and all but one boat party were lost. Passed Assistant Engineer George Melville, leader of the boat party that survived, later participated in the Greely Relief expedition, which rescued Lieutenant A. W. Greely, USA, and the remnant of his exploring party from Ellesmere Island, where it had been marooned for nearly three years.

The Battle of Lissa, 20 July 1866

The Battle of Lissa, fought in the Adriatic Sea, is notable as the first battle between ironclad steam fleets. It was intensively studied by the world's navies for its lessons in tactics, armament, and ship construction.

In June 1866 Prussia and Italy attacked Austria in concert, the former, to unify Germany under Prussian leadership; the latter, to recover Venetia. The Italians, defeated on land, sought a naval victory to give them bargaining power at the peace table. Italy's navy was reputed the most powerful in the world. It had 12 ironclads, including the new steam frigates *Re d'Italia* and *Re di Portogallo* and the new turret-ram *Affondatore* ("Sinker"), all armed with large-caliber Armstrong rifles. It had moreover 16 wooden steamers. But the Italian sailors were ill trained, their officers lacked aggressiveness, and their commander in chief, Admiral Count Carlo di Persano, seems to have been ignorant of the elements of his profession.

To oppose Persano's dozen ironclads, the Austrians had only seven, all steam frigates, all somewhat antiquated. Their principal wooden ships were the *Kaiser*, a steamship of the line, five screw frigates, and a corvette. Only a few guns in each of the wooden ships were rifles. The Austrians had in fact less than half the firepower of the Italians, but they had an inestimable advantage in their fleet commander, Rear Admiral Baron Wilhelm von Tegetthoff, who had trained his crews well, and who possessed the aggressiveness and mastery of his craft so singularly lacking in the principal Italian commanders.

Persano, despite orders to "sweep the enemy from the Adriatic," merely engaged in useless maneuvers off his base at Ancona, during which he did

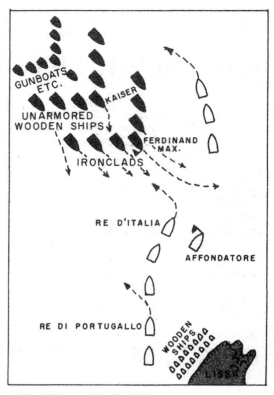

Battle of Lissa, 20 July 1866

not exercise his untrained gun crews. At length came a peremptory command from the king himself to "attempt against the hostile fortresses or fleet whatever operations may be thought likely to obtain a success." Persano, thus prodded, undertook to seize the small Austrian island of Lissa.

When Tegetthoff, with his fleet 165 miles away at the Austrian port of Pola, learned of the attack on Lissa, he at first assumed it was a mere feint. He could not believe the Italians would undertake so vulnerable an operation as an amphibious assault with no chance for surprise and without first securing control of the sea. At last, convinced by reports that the Italians were fully committed to the assault, Tegetthoff set sail. As he approached the vicinity of Lissa, he organized his fleet for battle. Aware of his gunfire inferiority, he chose a formation that facilitated ramming—three V-shaped divisions in column. In the first V were his seven ironclads led by his flagship, the *Ferdinand Maximilian*, at the point. The second V, comprising his wooden frigates and one corvette, was led by the big *Kaiser*. His remaining small vessels formed the third V.

For two days Persano's ships had been bombarding the forts on Lissa without being able to silence their 88 smaller-caliber guns. The fleet had suffered numerous personnel casualties, had an ironclad frigate put out of action, had shot away a large part of its ammunition, and had burned its fuel down to a two-day supply. Nevertheless, on the morning of 20 July Persano resumed his assault. He was bombarding the forts and about to land troops when lookouts reported the Austrian fleet steaming down from the northwest.

In something like panic, Persano hastily formed his ironclads in column and steered across the head of the oncoming Austrian formation. At this critical moment, for reasons never satisfactorily explained, Persano shifted his flag from the *Re d'Italia* to the *Affondatore*, which was outside the line of battle. As a result, a wide gap opened between the first three Italian ships and the rest of the column. Tegetthoff responded by leading his van division of ironclads through the opening. His wooden ships engaged Persano's wooden ships and rear ironclads.

The battle quickly became a melee, in which the movements of ships were partly obscured by fog and smoke. Twice the *Affondatore* tried unsuccessfully to ram the wooden *Kaiser*. The *Kaiser* struck the *Re di Portogallo* a glancing blow but was set aflame by her gunfire and was subsequently forced out of battle by the *Affondatore*. At the same time Austrian shellfire set an ironclad Italian gunboat fatally ablaze.

The most spectacular action of the battle was the ramming of the *Re d'Italia* by Tegetthoff's flagship. As the *Ferdinand Maximilian* groped about in the murk of battle, she came upon the *Re d'Italia* broadside to. The Italian ship had lost rudder control and was barred from going ahead by another Austrian ship. Backing down, she was dead in the water when the *Maximilian* at full speed plunged her ram into her side, heeling her heavily to starboard. While the *Maximilian* backed slowly away, the *Re d'Italia* righted herself and then heeled on over to port from the force of her own momentum and the weight of tons of water rushing into a great hole in her side. As she capsized and sank, her ill-trained but spirited crew shouted a cheer for their king.

The loss of the *Re d'Italia* effectively ended the battle. The Italian fleet retired to the west. Since the Austrian fleet had several vessels damaged and was still inferior to the enemy, Tegetthoff did not pursue. In any event, he had accomplished his mission by saving Lissa. He returned to Austria a national hero. Admiral Persano was dismissed from the service.

Naval strategists rightly condemned Persano's assault on Lissa in the face of an undefeated enemy fleet. Tacticians noted that a fleet fighting bows-on in divisions had defeated a fleet in column that had at least attempted to fight as a unit. The puzzler was what to make of the spectacular sinking of the *Re d'Italia*. Did that example and that of the *Merrimack* sinking the *Cumberland* mean that the ram had achieved ascendancy over the gun? Ship designers were uncertain, but to be on the safe side they provided all capital ships with underwater rams until well into the twentieth century.

Guns versus Armor

During the Civil War, inventors such as Ericsson, Isherwood, and Dahlgren placed the U. S. Navy in the forefront of technological innovation. But postwar austerity forced the phasing out of their programs. Technological leadership thus passed to the British, French, and Germans.

In 1879 the explosion of a muzzle-loader in HMS *Thunderer* convinced the British Admiralty that such guns were not safe and led to the gradual adoption of breech-loading guns in the Royal Navy. A tendency of breech-loaders to burst was overcome through the development by the French navy of the interrupted screw for breech-closing mechanisms. Wrought iron replaced cast iron in gun barrels, and steel replaced wrought iron for sleeves that were shrunk on the liners of built-up guns. By 1881 naval rifles were being made entirely of steel.

At the same time slow-burning "brown" powder, in which slightly charred straw was used as charcoal and the sulfur content was reduced, permitted the lengthening of gun barrels to secure higher muzzle velocity and greater range. In 1887 the French adopted smokeless powder, or guncotton, made by nitrating cellulose—an improvement quickly copied by the rest of the world.

The penetrating power of armor-piercing shells was increased by improvements in design of the point. But the great guns would have wrought destruction only upon their own crews had it not been for the concurrent development of hydraulic mechanisms that could absorb the force of their recoil—amounting to as much as a hundred million foot-pounds—and return them to battery without a jar. As a result of all these technological improvements, toward the end of the century naval guns could shoot many times the range at which they could be accurately aimed, and it was a rough rule of thumb that at battle ranges a naval gun could penetrate as many inches of the finest armor as its own caliber.

Even this degree of resistance in armor was achieved only by a long and complicated process of improvement in metallurgy. The tern "ironclad" correctly indicated the material with which early armored ships were protected. It began to be a misnomer when compound armor, made of iron plates covered with a steel face, was used on the turrets of the British *Inflexible*, designed in 1874. Her waterline belt of 24-inch wrought iron, the ultimate in thickness, could just be penetrated at close range by 16-inch muzzle-loading guns like her own. The complete use of compound armor in HMS *Colossus*, designed in 1879, permitted the reduction of the waterline belt to 18 inches. Thereafter, the introduction of nickle-steel armor made possible further gradual reductions of armor thickness, until the Harvey process for face-hardening steel by heat and water treatment, and the even better Krupp process of 1895, reduced capital-ship belt armor to its minimum thickness of six inches in the Royal Navy's *Canopus*, authorized in 1897.

Hull Design

Improvement in ship armor was paralleled by evolution in hulls built to carry it. With the launching of the *Warrior* in 1860, the British established a policy of using only iron hulls in new construction. The French, whose timber reserves were greater but whose iron industry was weaker than England's, continued to build wooden-hulled ironclads until 1872, when they took a long step ahead of the British by using steel combined with iron in the hull structure of the *Redoutable*. The British regained their technological lead in 1886 as they began launching all-steel-hulled warships.

From the earliest days of the ironclad, designers had been obliged to compromise between inadequate protection everywhere and absolute protection in the most vital areas. Because the earliest ironclads, like their all-wood predecessors, carried guns along nearly their entire broadside, the armor also had to extend along the whole broadside. As guns grew in size and power, designers began to concentrate them in the central portion of the ship, around which the armor could be concentrated. With less area to be armored, heavier armor could be used. Further concentration was possible with the introduction of the barbette, a stationary, circular wall, inside of which the gun rotated, firing over the uncovered top, and the turret, which partly covered, and rotated with, the gun.

Toward the end of the century, designers could no longer provide absolute protection for any part of the ship. The best that could be achieved was a reasonable degree of protection at battle ranges for guns, magazines, waterline, and machinery, and some protection for personnel elsewhere against quick-firing guns.

An additional safeguard was compartmentation, which could at least keep the ship from sinking after she was hit. In warship design, bunkers were located in outboard compartments, where the coal would absorb the force of shells that might penetrate them.

A feature closely related to compartmentation was the protective deck—to guard the vitals of the ship against plunging fire. Located at the waterline, a full deck of armor strong enough to stop plunging shells enclosed a space below of sufficient displacement to float the ships, no matter how many holes were shot through the sides above. Such decks were the only protection of the so-called protected cruisers in the last quarter of the century.

The Torpedo and its Carriers

As we have seen, the stationary marine explosive of Civil War days was called a torpedo. When the term came to be applied to movable marine weapons that carried explosive charges to their targets by means of internal engines, the stationary charges became known as mines.

The first successful automotive torpedo, propelled by a compressed-air engine driving a single propeller, was completed in 1866 by Robert Whitehead, British manager of a machine-building firm at Fiume on the Adriatic Sea. During the next 30 years, the addition of a hydrostatic depth regulator and gyroscope rudder controls greatly increased its accuracy. Almost from the beginning, navy men everwhere regarded the torpedo as a formidable weapon because it, and its means of delivery, cost so little in comparison with the damage it could inflict on large vessels. It appeared that nations with insignificant navies would, by using torpedoes, be able at little expense to challenge even the largest naval powers. The mere existence of the torpedo early led to increased compartmentation in warships.

Great Britain, whose navy had the most capital ships and was thus most challenged by the torpedo, took the lead in developing vessels both to launch torpedoes and to defend against them. Early torpedo-launching craft, called torpedo boats, were light and carried no armor, relying on speed to evade fire from their victims.

To counter attacks by such craft, the British armed their ships with light, quick-firing guns, but it soon became clear that the gunners could not react rapidly enough to the swift torpedo boats. Hence, a new type of speedy ship, the torpedo-boat destroyer (later called simply destroyer), was developed to shield larger ships from torpedo attacks. The first of the type, the *Havock*, armed with quick-firers and torpedoes and slightly larger and faster than a torpedo boat, was launched by Britain in 1893. The first U. S. destroyers, the 16-ship *Bainbridge*-class, authorized in 1898, were 420-ton coal burners. All saw service in World War I.

Quick-firers gave rise to two new classes of ship, both anti-destroyer cruisers. Heretofore, cruisers, like their predecessor frigates, had been used during peacetime for protecting commerce and for showing the flag on foreign stations, and during wartime for protecting one's own commerce and raiding the enemy's, in scouting for the battle fleet, and for fighting ships of their own class. The new cruisers of the late nineteenth century were of two classes: swift, lightly armored light cruisers armed with 4.7- to 6-inch guns; and slower protected or armored cruisers, which had armored decks and carried two or more heavier guns in addition to their quick-firers. Both classes were used to protect capital ships from destroyers.

Another new type, the submarine, was developed to launch the torpedo. The first practical submarine was completed in France in 1864, but truly modern submarines could not be built until a number of problems were solved. For example, during the 1880s, electric engines powered by storage batteries were introduced to drive the craft when it was submerged, and hydroplanes were developed to provide stability. During the next decade, gyroscopic mechanisms similar to those used in torpedoes solved the problem of steering. The United States and France led in the development of submarines, but such boats were not perfected for combat until the first decade of the twentieth century.

Propulsion

The high speed of the first destroyers was made possible by developments in boilers and engines following the American Civil War. Early boilers were simply iron boxes reinforced internally by iron stay rods. Metallurgical advances made possible stronger box boilers that could contain twice the steam of midcentury boilers. During the same period a water-tube boiler was developed that increased efficiency by passing water in steel tubes through gases heated by combustion. Such boilers

by the end of the century employed pressures of up to 250 pounds to drive triple-expansion engines capable of producing 14,000 horsepower, resulting in speeds of 18 knots for battleships and 24 for cruisers. In destroyers steam turbine engines replaced reciprocating engines to propel the ships at 36 knots.

By the late 1890s, all the basic warship types of the next quarter-century, except the submarine, had evolved, and their capabilities were nearly equal to those of similar types in World War I. Battleships, displacing up to 15,000 tons, carried armor of face-hardened nickle-steel up to 14 inches in thickness and mounted breech-loading rifles up to 16.25 inches in heavily armored turrets. Armored cruisers, often nearly as large as battleships, carried armor up to 6 inches and mounted guns up to 9.2 inches. Protected cruisers, displacing up to 5,600 tons, had armored decks as much as 2.5 inches thick and mounted quick-firing guns as large as 6 inches. Destroyers were small, the largest not much over 400 tons, but as noted they made trial speeds up to 36 knots.

The New U. S. Navy: Ships

In the 1880s the United States began rebuilding its neglected navy. The timing was favorable. The evolution of ships and weapons had reached a plateau; a fleet built in accordance with the latest designs was not likely to become quickly obsolete. The country had the means and the will. Postwar depression had been succeeded by a wave of prosperity. Reconstruction and other domestic political issues were moving into the background, and Americans were taking increasing interest in foreign affairs. The country was industrializing at such a rate that American manufacturers foresaw saturation of their domestic markets. The obvious outlet for surplus goods was foreign trade, but European nations, particularly Britain, France, and Germany, in a new surge of imperialism, were seizing economic control of world markets. To compete with these growing monopolies, American business leaders contended that the United States should revive its merchant marine and build a navy capable of supporting it.

In 1880 the Republican Party, sensitive to business pressures, confirmed its grip on the national government by taking control of both houses of Congress as well as the presidency. The new president, James A. Garfield, named big-navy-advocate William H. Hunt secretary of the navy. Hunt appointed a board of line and staff naval officers to advise what types and numbers of ships he should recommend. The board's report, which Hunt forwarded to Congress, called for the construction of no fewer than 68 new vessels. The administration, shocked by the huge number, which implied governmental neglect, kicked Secretary Hunt upstairs into an ambassadorial post and appointed a second, tamer, board, which came forward with a less ambitious recommendation.

Congress, after whittling down the second board's modest recommendation, in 1883 authorized construction of the protected cruisers *Atlanta, Boston,* and *Chicago* and the dispatch vessel *Dolphin*—a squadron the public promptly tagged "the Navy's ABCDs." These ships, tiny by post–World War II standards, mark the transition from the old U. S. Navy to the new. They were built of steel, were steam-propelled, had double hulls and watertight compartments, and were fully electrified, but they proclaimed their pedigree by carrying partial sail rig. Congress encouraged retirement of the outmoded wooden ships by limiting the amount that could be spent on their repair to 20 percent of the cost of a similar new vessel.

Beginning in 1885, Congress each year authorized funds for naval construction. As the shore establishment readied itself to support a new fleet, the forces grew slowly in numbers and modernity. The work was handicapped at first by American inexperience in modern ship design and lack of steel shipbuilding capacity. Construction plans for some of the earlier American steel warships had to be purchased from England, and armor, shafting, and heavy gun mounts had to be supplied from abroad.

To overcome the latter deficiency, Secretary of the Navy William C. Whitney combined steel orders for several ships into one $4.4 million contract, thereby providing the impetus to get the fledgling domestic steel industry moving. He thus assured the Navy of a continuous supply of steel armor plating—and, incidentally, of a new ally in its battles for congressional funding.

Early products of the new policy were America's first battleships, the *Texas* and the *Maine*, authorized in 1886. These, however, were soon recognized as second-class warships, fit for little except coast defense. Though the *Maine* was fated to blow up in Havana harbor while still rated a battleship, other vessels of her type were more properly designated armored cruisers. But American marine designers and shipbuilders were learning their craft, and by the end of the 1880s they were producing such fine ships as the *New York* and the *Olympia,* which could stand comparison with any cruisers in the world.

Many congressmen and thoughtful public spokesmen were beginning to express doubts about the effectiveness of the time-honored American commerce-raiding naval war plan. After all, neither the American privateers of the War of 1812 nor the Confederate cruisers had been able to get their prizes into port through the enemy blockade. Senator Matthew C. Butler of South Carolina scoffed at commerce raiding as an "insignificant kind of guerrilla, bushwhacking warfare." What he, but by no means all congressmen, demanded was a battleship fleet that could break up a blockade and defeat any enemy fleet that attempted to support a coastal invasion of the United States.

In his annual report of 1889, Secretary of the Navy Benjamin F. Tracy, reflecting the Butler view, called for the building of two battle fleets, one of 8 battleships for the Pacific Ocean and one of 12 for the Atlantic—the fleets to be backed by at least 60 cruisers. "This country," Tracy concluded, "needs a navy that will exempt it from war but the only navy that will accomplish this is a navy that can wage war."

Congress was not ready to build a fleet according to the Tracy specifications, but in 1890 it authorized the building of 3 seagoing battleships, the *Indiana,* the *Massachusetts,* and the *Oregon,* each displacing 10,288 tons, capable of 16 knots, and armed with four 13-inch, eight 8-inch, and four 6-inch guns—formidable vessels for their day. In 1892 it authorized the building of the battleship *Iowa,* somewhat heavier and faster than the *Indianas.*

By the eve of the Spanish–American War, the United States had acquired a fleet that, though far from being the world's most powerful, was eminently respectable: 4 first-class battleships, 2 second-class battleships, 2 armored cruisers, 10 protected cruisers, and a considerable number of gunboats, monitors, and torpedo boats.

The New U. S. Navy: Officers and Men

During the American Civil War, the students and faculty of the United States Naval Academy who did not go south to fight for the Confederacy retired to Newport, Rhode Island for the duration. Here under inadequate leadership the school deteriorated. At the end of the war, Secretary of the Navy Welles returned the Academy to Annapolis and gave the job of rehabilitating it to two of his ablest officers, Rear Admiral David D. Porter and Lieutenant Commander Stephen B. Luce, serving respectively as superintendent and commandant of midshipmen. Porter and Luce weeded out undesirables from faculty and student body, raised academic standards, and introduced an honor system. By 1869 the Academy had gained sufficient renown to attract the gifted Albert Michelson, first as a midshipman and later as an officer instructor. In the latter capacity he measured the speed of light more accurately than it had been measured before, a major step in a career of scientific experimentation, in which he became the first American recipient of the Nobel Prize for physics.

In 1873 a group of the Naval Academy's officer and civilian faculty members formed the United States Naval Institute in order to hold discussions and present papers regarding professional naval matters. The Institute from time to time published its papers and other pertinent matter as the *United States Naval Institute Proceedings*, at first as a series of pamphlets, ultimately as a monthly magazine—the principal forum for articles and discussions concerning the U. S. Navy. Eventually the Institute became also an important publisher of books on naval matters.

Luce, on returning to sea duty in 1868, was shocked at the sort of seamen he found manning the U. S. warships. During the Civil War eager young Americans of all classes had manned the decks. Now, as in prewar days, the sailors in a U. S. man-of-war were likely to be mercenaries, recruited from among waterfront drifters around the world. Matthew Perry's cherished plan for apprentice-school ships to train young Americans to be sailors had been scotched by the 1842 hangings on board the brig *Somers*. The plan had been revived before the end of the war but was only beginning to show results. Luce, volunteering to participate, was given command of one of the training ships and later of the entire practice squadron. With his characteristic energy and enthusiasm, he instilled new life into the program, which he made into a sort of game involving competitive drills and mass singing of sea songs. The program as developed by Luce remained in effect until the increasing complexity of naval instruments and weapons required seamen to receive their basic training ashore in fully equipped schools.

Long before that day, Luce had focused his attention on the need to educate future naval leaders beyond the basic professional education of the Naval Academy. He proposed establishing a naval war college, where selected officers would study the art of war. He met instant opposition from senior naval officers, who saw no advantage to be derived from such an ivory-tower proceeding. But Luce obtained the consent of Secretary of the Navy William E. Chandler, who issued the necessary authorization. In September 1885, Luce, now a rear admiral, established the Naval War College in a former almshouse on Coasters Harbor Island off Newport, Rhode Island, with three instructors, including himself, who also served as president of the college. After many ups and downs, the Naval War College so proved its worth that the major navies of the world established similar colleges.

Of major importance was the founding in 1882 of the Office of Naval Intelligence. The new organization, through its naval attachés stationed abroad at American ministries, collected information on foreign navies as an aid to formulating U. S. war plans. Shortly after its founding, ONI began publishing a series of analytical reports on naval subjects. These served as official counterparts to the unclassified articles published in the Naval Institute's *Proceedings*.

Following the formation of the Navy Corps of Engineers in 1842, its officers had demanded equality with the Navy's line officers—in rank, berthing, wardroom privileges, and pay. The line officers long balked at these demands, insisting that the engineers should remain staff officers, subservient to the line. By the 1890s, however, machinery on board ships had become so complex that not even the proudest line officers could any longer look down on the engineers who operated them as mere mechanics. A Naval Personnel Board of line and staff officers presided over by Assistant Secretary of the Navy Theodore Roosevelt, after extended deliberations, recommended amalgamation of the line and engineering officers. Congress in 1899 enacted legislation based on the board's recommendation. Though the engineers had won the dignity of the line, it proved impractical for the specialists among them to advance to the command of ships and naval forces. The solution was the establishment of a corps of engineering specialists within the line, set apart by the letters EDO (engineering duty only).

Alfred Thayer Mahan

In 1886 Admiral Luce left Newport to assume the senior professional post in the U. S. Navy, command of the North Atlantic Squadron. Relieving him as president and chief instructor of the Naval War College was Captain A. T. Mahan, whom Luce had selected partly on the basis of Mahan's recently published *The Gulf and Inland Waters*, a naval history of the American Civil War.

Mahan initially believed that the United States should avoid acquiring territorial possessions overseas, not only to save the expense of the large navy that would be needed to protect them, but also to avoid the dominance of a powerful military caste over the democratic processes of government. In line with these opinions, he accepted the naval doctrine of his time and country that coast defense and commerce raiding were the only tasks the U. S. Navy needed to perform in time of war.

But as Mahan began to study history in preparation for assuming his duties at the War College in the fall of 1886, he discovered that "control of the sea was an historic factor which had never been appreciated and expounded." From this time on he had his vocation. Examining the situation and characteristics of nations that had become great sea powers, especially England, he perceived certain factors of geography, demography, politics, and national character that favored the development of sea power.[1]

The concrete result of Mahan's studies he published in two books based on his War College lectures: *The Influence of Sea Power upon History, 1660–1783*, in 1890, and *The Influence of Sea Power upon the French Revolution and Empire*, two years later. These volumes trace Britain's use of sea power to attain her worldwide trade and colonial empires. An island nation, she was exempt from the expense of maintaining a large, defensive army and could devote the bulk of her military expenditures to acquiring a powerful, capital-ship navy. Her navy, taking advantage of England's position on the approaches to western Europe, dominated the North Atlantic and, ultimately, the seas of the world.

In *The Interest of America in Sea Power, Present and Future*, published in 1897, and in various articles, Mahan pointed out that most of the sea-power factors that had made Great Britain mistress of the seas were potentially present in the situation of the United States. What the country needed was a fleet of capital ships that could break up a blockade and meet the fleets of any possible enemies on favorable terms. As we have seen, this concept was already widely accepted and being acted upon when Mahan published his sea-power books, but Mahan gave it the sanction of history and the support of close reasoning, and at the same time vindicated the new imperialism of the major industrial nations.

It was not sufficient merely to convince the people and their government of the advantages of sea power and show them how it could be developed. It was equally important to show them

how it could be used. According to Mahan the principal mission of a navy in warfare was to control the areas of sea communication in order to secure their use to one's own cargo vessels and transports while denying their use to the enemy. In a conflict with another sea power that possessed a strong fleet of capital ships, such control could be achieved only by destroying or neutralizing the enemy's fleet with a more powerful fleet of one's own. Commerce warfare by fast cruisers might in part deny the use of the sea to the enemy's merchant marine, but it could not secure its use to one's own; it was merely an adjunct to the main objective of destroying the enemy's most powerful fighting force wherever it might be.

But modern warships could not carry sufficient coal to cross an ocean and fight an enemy fleet on equal terms. Hence the need for overseas bases to extend the range of the fleet in any area where one's sea communications might be threatened. Because a base exists to support the fleet, and not the fleet to support the base, ideally a base should be self-sufficient. Thus overseas bases are most favorably located in colonies, which can provide resources and are under one's own control. Colonies in turn make trade more profitable and thus nourish the merchant marine, which is the *raison d'être* of sea power in the first place. Thus Mahan's line of reasoning led him from his original isolationist politics and defensive naval strategy to a position that was politically imperialistic and strategically offensive.

In any tactical or strategic military situation, the commander endeavors to defeat the enemy in fractions. He does not, if he can avoid it, send his force spread thin against the whole of the enemy force at one time. Instead he endeavors (1) to bring his chief attack against part of the enemy force while (2) the rest of the enemy force is being held out of the main action. Mahan described this technique as "so distributing your own force as to be superior to the enemy in one quarter, while in the other you hold him in check long enough to permit your main attack to reach its full result." This dual operation, involving hitting one fraction of the enemy force while holding the other, is part of what Mahan meant by the word *concentration*. To be perfectly concentrated, however, a force must be under unified command, its elements must be mutually supporting, it must be in pursuit of a single main objective, and it must be disposed with regard to the strategic center.

Although Mahan's lectures at the Naval War College had interested a number of American naval officers, his *Influence of Sea Power upon History*

---

[1]Chapters 2–8 of this book generally develop Mahan's sea power thesis. All other chapters reflect it.

did not immediately receive the acclaim in the United States that it was accorded abroad—especially in Britain, Germany, and Japan, just then embarking on an unprecedented capital-ship race.[2] British commentators saw the book as a reasoned exposition of the principles that many of their officers and statesmen had followed instinctively. The German Kaiser ordered translations placed in the wardroom of every ship in his new navy, and his admiralty distributed it to all schools, public libraries, and government departments. The Japanese government provided translated copies to its army and naval officers, political leaders, and schools. In the United States, where Mahan's books were not at first widely read, his influence was wielded chiefly through his early interpreters, notably Secretary of the Navy Tracy; Henry Cabot Lodge, chairman of the Senate Naval Affairs Committee; and Theodore Roosevelt, as assistant secretary of the navy, vice president, and president.

Summary

Following the American Civil War, the United States, absorbed by internal affairs and anticipating no national danger from without, permitted its navy to decline in both strength and technological leadership. The British, French, and German navies made the expensive trial-and-error experiments that produced the steel fleets of the late nineteenth century.

Naval guns, hulls, and armor shifted from cast

---

[2]Britain's Naval Defense Act of 1889 committed the Royal Navy to a two-power standard, that is, to maintaining a battleship fleet equal in size to the combined fleets of Britain's two closest competitors. Most other maritime powers followed Britain's lead and devoted the bulk of their naval resources to building battleships.

iron to steel. As the strength of armor increased, so did the power of guns to penetrate it. As the guns grew in size and power, designers massed them in the centers of ships, around which armor could be concentrated—culminating in the general adoption of the turret, which partly covered the guns and rotated with them. Since armor could not prevent gunfire from penetrating hulls, the hulls were divided into watertight compartments, which could at least prevent ships from sinking after they had been hit.

In the new navies, the choice of weapons lay at first between the gun and the ram. Study of the Battle of Hampton Roads (1862) and the Battle of Lissa (1866) led some theorists to advocate the latter. The automotive torpedo emerged as a challenger for both and posed new problems for solution. It led to the torpedo boat and the submarine to carry it. The destroyer, developed to attack the torpedo carriers, became itself also a torpedo carrier.

A revival of the U. S. Navy, begun in the 1880s, profited by the technological and intellectual developments in other navies. By 1898, the United States had a navy of steel, well prepared to meet its first challenge, in the Spanish–American War. Chief spokesman for the capital ship was the American A. T. Mahan, who pointed out in his influence-of-sea-power books that England, taking advantage of geographical and other factors, had built a world empire and risen to dominate the seas through wise use of capital-ship fleets.

Mahan had come into prominence on the crest of a new intellectual wave in the U. S. Navy, a wave that had seen improvements in the U. S. Naval Academy; the establishment of the U. S. Naval Institute, the Office of Naval Intelligence, and the Naval War College; and the integration of engineering officers into the line.

Chapter 16
The Rise of Japanese Naval Power

Insular Japan, like insular England, was early the target of expanding continental powers. In 1274 and again in 1281 Kublai Khan, heading massive expeditionary forces, attempted to invade Japan. Under the Mongol threat, the Japanese temporarily abandoned their internal strife and united to contain the enemy beachheads. They were successful, thanks in part to providential typhoons that on both occasions scattered and sank much of the invasion fleet. Thus the *kamikaze* ("divine wind") became a part of the Japanese patriotic tradition.

Once more united, this time under the strong rule of the Shogun Hideyoshi, the Japanese in 1592 and again in 1597 undertook to invade the continent via Korea. In both attacks, the Japanese invaders overran part of the Korean peninsula but were eventually thrown back by a combination of Chinese armies and the Korean navy.

The Far Eastern fleets, like the Christian–Muslim fleets in the contemporary Battle of Lepanto, were made up mostly of galleys armed with light cannon. Naval victory in the Far East, as in the Mediterranean, was achieved in most instances by grappling and boarding. But in 1592 the Koreans, led by Yi Sun Sin, "the Eastern Nelson," rammed their way through the Japanese line with the aid of a special galley fitted with an iron-plated turtleback having gunports forward. The confusion caused by this novel weapon enabled the conventional Korean galleys to keep clear of Japanese boarding parties while pouring in cannon and musket fire and flaming arrows.

Even more inglorious for the Japanese was the end of their 1597 invasion. Yi Sun Sin, in an Asian Trafalgar that cost him his life, gallantly attacked the numerically superior invaders at sea and destroyed their navy as an effective fighting organization. Three centuries were to elapse before a Japanese fleet again ventured into Korean waters.

After the death of Hideyoshi, the intense nationalism of the unified Japanese archipelago turned inward upon itself. Japan, as a great trading nation with geographical advantages similar to those of England, might have become the Great Britain of the East. Instead, the shogunate chose to discourage trade and exclude foreign influence of all sorts. Japan deliberately cut herself off from the rest of the world for 250 years.

The Reopening of Japan

After 1830 the U. S. whaling fleet gradually shifted its center of operations from below the equator to the North Pacific waters off Hokkaido. Hence the attitude of the Japanese became increasingly a matter of concern to the U. S. government. The acquisition of California and the development of the Oregon territory made the United States a Pacific power. Projected transpacific steamship service forecast a need for port privileges in Japan, which lay directly athwart the great circle route to Shanghai. Unsuccessful American attempts to establish diplomatic relations with the Japanese at length persuaded President Fillmore that a show of force was required.

To Commodore Matthew Calbraith Perry, commanding the U. S. East India Squadron, the president gave a personal letter from himself to be delivered to the emperor of Japan. Perry was instructed to negotiate a treaty guaranteeing protection for American persons and property in Japan and a free access to one or more ports for supplies and trade. He was to use force if necessary, but only as a last resort.

After carefully studying all available information about Japan, the commodore concluded that his best approach would be to demand all courtesies due from one nation to another and to deal with only the highest officials. He was aware, he reported to the secretary of the navy, that a haughty, exclusive demeanor would secure most respect from "these people of forms and ceremonies." For such a mission, so conducted, Perry was eminently fitted. Impressive, able, somewhat pompous, he was just the man to match dignified behavior with the Oriental specialists in dignity.

After a protracted fitting-out period during which the commodore accumulated a large assortment of gifts—typical American machinery and other industrial products—the expedition got

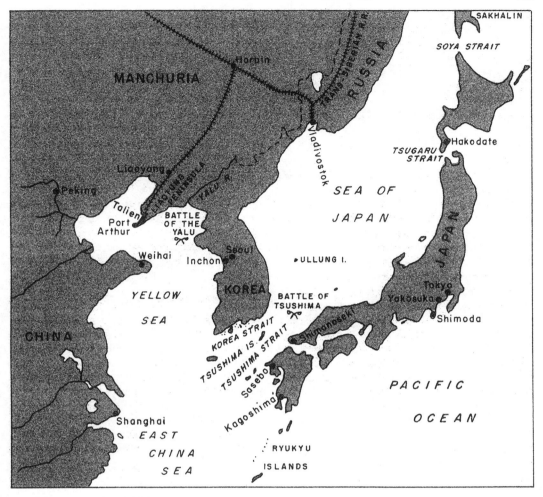

Northeast Asia, 1894–1905

under way in early 1853. The squadron that Perry took to Japan consisted of the paddle frigates *Susquehanna* and *Mississippi* and the sailing sloops-of-war *Plymouth* and *Saratoga*. Anchoring in Tokyo Bay in July, Perry went ashore in a stately procession and ceremoniously delivered the president's letter, inscribed on vellum and enclosed in a gold-mounted rosewood box, to two imperial princes, representatives of the emperor.

He announced that he would come back for the imperial reply the following spring. Returning to his flagship he disregarded the protests of the authorities and took his squadron to within six miles of Tokyo. After the city's two million inhabitants had obtained a good view of the ships, the commodore left for China. Perry's gifts as a negotiator nowhere showed to better advantage than in the timing of his departure. He knew better than to press the Japanese for a decision when they had a valid reason to reject his demands for lack of discussion.

While the squadron wintered in China, its strength now increased by a paddle frigate and two sailing sloops, the appearance of a Russian squadron at Shanghai prodded Perry into expediting his second visit to Japan. To prevent the Russians from reaping where he had sowed, he hastened back to Tokyo in midwinter.

In the ensuing negotiations, Perry matched the Japanese in obstinacy. The Council of State, aware of Japan's military weakness, finally bowed to the inevitable. The Treaty of Kanagawa, completed at the end of March 1854, guaranteed protection to Americans and provided for the opening of the ports of Shimoda and Hakodate to American shipping, but there were no concessions on trade.

Perry's firm but judicious pressure had yielded the most that could be obtained under the circumstances. Townsend Harris obtained more generous terms two years later, but that was after the shogun had come to recognize foreign trade as a means of promoting the technical and industrial revolution that Japan had to undergo to ensure her security and independence.

The treaties and the arrival of foreigners to implement them enraged some Japanese clan leaders, who took matters into their own hands. When the Satsuma clan committed atrocities against some Englishmen, however, six British men-of-war bombarded and burned their stronghold of Kagoshima. Mori, lord of the clan of Chosu, began firing on foreign vessels using Shimonoseki Strait. Opening this passage required the naval efforts of three nations in four expeditions of increasing power during 1863 and 1864 before the stubborn chieftain could be brought to terms.

These punitive measures opened the eyes of the clan chiefs, who developed great respect for naval power. They abandoned their xenophobia and welcomed intercourse with other nations, at least to the extent of acquiring Western military techniques. They now turned their warlike energies against the shogun, whom they overthrew in the course of a two-year civil war, and "restored" the emperor. Under the "Meiji Restoration," Japan became Westernized with a rapidity that amazed foreigners; and in the forefront of institutions that underwent reform were the army and the navy.

The modernization of the navy had been taken in hand even before the downfall of the shogunate, the first dockyards and slipways of the Yokosuka navy yard having been laid out in 1865. Officers and officer-candidates were sent abroad, principally to Great Britain and the United States, to attend naval schools of all levels.[1]

Beginning in 1874, the Japanese commissioned foreign yards to construct warships, at the same time making every effort to construct improved imitations at home. By the last decade of the nineteenth century, they were launching cruisers as good as any built in Europe.

The strategic problem confronting Japan after 1870 was in many respects analogous to that faced by Great Britain. Both nations occupied insular positions off continents that were liable to domination by one or a combination of dynamic land powers. What Japan had to fear most was the emergence of China as a naval power and the march of Russia toward ice-free ports. Strategically, Japan was in a stronger position than either of her rivals, for her strength was concentrated by her geographic situation. While she was weaker numeri-

cally than either of her presumptive antagonists, neither of them could employ full strength against her as long as she remained undefeated at sea.

To strengthen her position, however, Japan pursued a policy that aimed first to establish a defensive barrier off the east coast of Asia and then to exercise political control of the enclave formed by it. She began by annexing the Bonin Islands in 1876 and the Ryukyus three years later. Formosa and the Pescadores belonged to China, and Korea, the central corridor, was nominally China's vassal. Sakhalin, the northern flank, was Russian. To complete her proposed barrier, Japan would have to seize all these territories, and acquiring them meant warfare with both China and Russia. The Japanese leaders accepted the necessity. In 1894 they attacked China, the weaker of the two.

The Sino–Japanese War, 1894–95

The pretext for war was provided by a Japanese-fomented rebellion in Seoul, the Korean capital. China moved in forces to restore order, whereupon Japan seized upon a treaty technicality to land troops at Inchon. Advancing to Seoul, the Japanese replaced the Korean king with a puppet "regent" and demanded that the Chinese withdraw from the peninsula. When China, instead of submitting to this demand, began rushing troops to Korea by sea, four cruisers sortied from the Japanese naval base at Sasebo and without formal declaration of war attacked the Chinese troop convoy, battering a cruiser, destroying one gunboat and capturing another, and sinking a loaded transport. Japan had inaugurated the practice she was to employ in subsequent wars—strike first, declare war afterward. Both sides declared war on 1 August 1894.

While the Japanese rushed troops and supplies to Korea by sea, China for some time used the slow, roundabout land route. But rapid Japanese advances obliged the Chinese in mid-September to resort again to sea transport. Escorting their first convoy was a squadron of ten warships commanded by Admiral Ju-ch'ang Ting. The squadron's main strength was concentrated in two slow German-built, 7,400-ton armored battleships, the *Ting Yuen* and the *Chen Yuen*.[2] Each carried four 12-inch guns in two barbettes disposed on the beam in echelon. In addition to these big guns, the Chinese force mounted a bewildering variety of smaller calibers, including only three quick-firers, all 4.7-inch. Having detached the troop transports at the mouth of the Yalu River, Ting's battle line stood guard at anchor.

At ten o'clock the next morning, 17 September,

[1]The U. S. Naval Academy admitted its first Japanese student in 1869; its last, in 1906. A total of 16 Japanese attended the Academy, and 7 graduated.

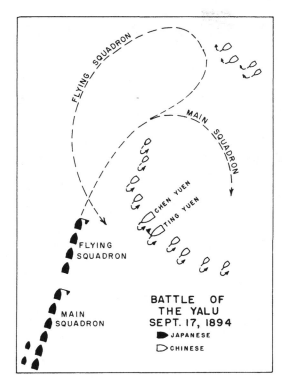

FLYING SQUADRON

MAIN SQUADRON

CHEN YUEN

TING YUEN

FLYING
SQUADRON

MAIN
SQUADRON

BATTLE OF
THE YALU
SEPT. 17, 1894
◣ JAPANESE
◻ CHINESE

the Chinese crews were exercising at general quarters when lookouts reported heavy smoke at sea to the southwest. Evidently the Japanese fleet was approaching. Ting, in order to have sea room to maneuver, at once ordered his ships to get up steam and prepare to advance on the enemy. The battle line was under way by 11 a.m., deploying from column to line abreast, the standard approach formation.

The Japanese fleet, commanded by Vice Admiral Ito, had as its principal armament sixty-seven 4.7- and 6-inch quick-firers, the most effective type of naval gun in the period before improved techniques of aiming gave the advantage to long-range fire by heavier guns. The fleet was divided into two semi-independent squadrons. The Flying Squadron, commanded by Rear Admiral Tsuboi, comprised four cruisers capable of 17 knots. The Main Squadron, under Ito's direct command, was composed of four more fast cruisers, followed by a pair of obsolescent ironclads that managed to keep up only by cutting corners during evolutions. None of Ito's ships was heavily armored.

The opposing battle lines, ten ships in each, made visual contact at 11:40. At the Chinese center

[2]The acting executive officer of the *Chen Yuen* was an American, Philo McGiffen, a graduate of the U. S. Naval Academy.

were the two battleships *Ting Yuen* and *Chen Yuen*, flanked by five cruisers and three sloops.[3] Ting thus had left his flanks fatally weak, with two sloops on his extreme right and a sloop and a light cruiser on his extreme left. Ito, approaching in column from the left at double Ting's speed, headed diagonally across the Chinese front. His intention was to strike first at Ting's weak right flank—even at the risk of leaving stragglers in the path of their oncoming opponents. Tsuboi, disregarding futile Chinese fire, which opened at 6,000 yards, held his own fire until he was close enough to make effective use of his quick-firers. These at length he turned with deadly effect on the two sloops on Ting's right as he steamed across their bows and doubled around the Chinese flank.

It had been Ito's intention after rounding the flank, to steam across the Chinese rear. This his Main Squadron did, coming up on the Chinese left. But Tsuboi's Flying Squadron turned first to the north to chase away four Chinese reinforcements coming from the Yalu. Tsuboi then turned south to support the weak Japanese rear, which had come under heavy Chinese fire. As a result, Ting's formation was caught between two fires and quickly disintegrated. Already ablaze, one of the sloops of the Chinese right went down; the other grounded on a nearby island. The two ships on the Chinese left, heavily damaged, ran for Port Arthur. Two Chinese cruisers became separated from the battleships and were sunk by Tsuboi's squadron, which steamed widely through the battle area seeking out stragglers and disabled.

Ito concentrated upon the *Ting Yuen*, the *Chen Yuen*, and two cruisers—all of Ting's fleet that had not fled or been sunk. Circling at 2,500 yards, he kept up a rapid and steady fire, taking the two battleships as his special targets. His heavy shells riddled their superstructures. His quick-firers repeatedly swept their decks, killing gun crews in exposed stations. Yet the vitals of the big ships, protected by 14 inches of armor, remained unimpaired. Keeping their bows turned toward their attackers, they continued to fire slowly. Though a corrupt government had provided them with faulty ammunition—including shells filled with sawdust or sand—they gave a good account of themselves. Toward 3:30 one of their 12-inch projectiles detonated ready ammunition in Ito's flagship, causing a

[3]Unarmored vessels under 2,000 tons displacement that were not primarily torpedo craft were called sloops. The sloop of the late nineteenth century was the predecessor of the twentieth-century destroyer, that is, the type next after the cruiser in size and armament.

hundred casualties and putting the ship out of action.

Ito at length concluded that the battleships were indestructible with the armament he carried. At 5:30, fearful of a night attack by torpedo boats out of Port Arthur, he broke off action. At that time the *Chen Yuen* had only three 12-inch shells left; these were loaded in the guns for a final salvo. The *Ting Yuen* was in almost as bad a situation. The antagonists kept each other in sight until dark and then lost contact. Early the next morning the four surviving ships of the Chinese battle line reached Port Arthur.

Because the Japanese had clearly outfought the Chinese and won a victory of sorts, naval theorists examined their tactics for useful lessons. This analysis proved something of a puzzle. The Battle of the Yalu provided a situation similar to that at the Battle of Lissa—a broadside attack in column opposed to a bows-on attack. Thus the tactical lessons of the two battles seemed to cancel each other out, except for one fact—at Lissa and again at Yalu, as at Trafalgar long before, the victorious fleet had fought in separated divisions. The tactical flexibility and the possibilities for achieving winning combinations through dividing one's force were keenly studied by naval officers everywhere.

The controversy then raging over the rival claims of the big gun and armor were left unsettled, inasmuch as the heavier Japanese guns did not actually hit Chinese armor. The Japanese had won their victory mainly through possession of an overwhelming superiority in quick-firers.

As the Japanese army, victorious in Korea, crossed the Yalu and invaded Manchuria, Ito's fleet escorted a large infantry force from Japan to the Liaotung Peninsula with the aim of isolating and laying siege to Port Arthur. While Ito was so employed, Ting's force slipped out of Port Arthur and escaped to Weihaiwei.

In mid-November, Ito covered the landing of siege guns at Talien Bay, to which the newly landed Japanese army had advanced. Three days later the army assaulted the Port Arthur defenses. To the astonishment of the world, the forts were overrun in six hours.

The Chinese squadron at Weihaiwei had to be destroyed, because it threatened the flank of a scheduled Japanese advance on Peking. Cutting out the ships required more joint operations, this time in the depths of a particularly severe winter. A 32,000-man invasion force, landed by Ting west of Weihaiwei, advanced to the base and quickly captured the forts and harbor shore. Ito's naval force, blockading outside, launched a series of night torpedo-boat attacks that sank the *Ting Yuen* and a cruiser. Admiral Ting ordered the surviving ships to make a dash for freedom. Only 3 managed to reach safety; the other 13 were captured or driven on the rocks.

His situation hopeless, Ting on 12 February arranged for surrender and then drank a lethal dose of opium. Two weeks later, the Chinese Manchurian army was decisively defeated at Liaoyang, whereupon the Chinese viceroy opened negotiations for peace.

The Treaty of Shimonoseki (17 April 1895), ending the Sino–Japanese War, was dictated by the victors. In addition to paying the full costs of the war, the Chinese withdrew from Korea and ceded Formosa, the Pescadores, and Port Arthur.

Events Leading to the Russo–Japanese War

Russia, with eyes on Port Arthur as a potential warm-water port, reacted promptly. St. Petersburg secured the cooperation of the French and German governments in warning that acquisition by Japan of any part of the Chinese mainland would create a "permanent obstacle to peace in the Far East." The Japanese yielded to "the dictates of humanity" and forthwith proceeded to double their army and triple their navy.

While Japan was obliged to withdraw her army from Korea and abandon possession of Port Arthur, Russia was pushing her Trans-Siberian Railway across north Asia. In 1896, in return for a treaty of alliance and loans to pay her war indemnity to Japan, China granted Russia the right to extend her railroad line to Vladivostok by the most direct route, through Manchuria. The next year the Russians secured a lease on Port Arthur and the right to connect it with the Manchurian segment of their railroad. Two years later Russia coolly appropriated Port Arthur outright and extended her control over all Manchuria. She then began intrigues to acquire a dominant position in Korea.

Japan, forced to stand by while Russia took over the fruits of her conquests, grimly prepared for war. While six battleships and six heavy cruisers were building for her in Europe, her diplomats worked to ensure that when war came the ring should be clear in the Far East. In 1902 they negotiated the Anglo–Japanese Alliance guaranteeing mutual support should either nation become involved with more than one enemy over China or Korea. The Japanese then demanded the withdrawal of Russian troops from Manchuria. Evacuation was postponed and negotiations dragged on until February 1904. On 6 February, Japan broke off diplomatic relations with Russia.

The Japanese went to war in the face of apparent disadvantages. They had to capture enemy-occupied territory by amphibious assault. They had less than half as many troops as Russia had. Their fleet was numerically weaker—6 modern battleships to Russia's 15, 21 destroyers to Russia's 38, though the Japanese also had 39 seagoing torpedo boats, and 25 cruisers to Russia's 19. Russia was economically the more self-sufficient and was allied with France, the leading creditor nation of continental Europe.

But Russia's advantages in numbers and finance were more than offset by Japan's military concentration at the strategic center. Most of Russia's troops were at the far end of the Trans-Siberian Railroad. Her naval forces were divided into three fleets of nearly equal strength—in the Baltic, in the Black Sea, and in East Asia. The uncertain attitude of Great Britain contained the first of these in Europe until after the outbreak of the war. The second was confined to the Black Sea by the London Treaty of 1870, which closed the Dardanelles to foreign warships. Most of Russia's Far Eastern squadron was at Port Arthur, but four heavy cruisers were at Vladivostok, and a cruiser and a gunboat were at Inchon, Korea.

The Russians had no first-class naval base in the Far East, and the best of what repair facilities they had were at the undefended commercial port of Dalny, 20 miles from Port Arthur. The Japanese, on the other hand, had four major naval bases and eleven large commercial docking and repair establishments in their home islands.

In the circumstances, Japan's obvious strategy was to hit first and hit hard; Russia's was to delay—to avert a decision on land and sea and gain time to reinforce her military strength in the Far East.

Operations in the Port Arthur Area

As in her war with China, Japan opened hostilities with an attack on the enemy fleet before war was formally declared. In the evening of 8 February 1904, Vice Admiral Heihichiro Togo arrived off Port Arthur with the main body of the Japanese Combined Fleet and sent in ten destroyers for a night torpedo attack on the unsuspecting, brilliantly lighted battleship–cruiser force anchored in the outer roadstead. Two battleships and a cruiser were hit. The next day a Japanese cruiser–destroyer force attacked and crippled the Russian cruiser at Inchon, obliging both it and the accompanying gunboat to scuttle themselves to avoid capture.

A week later, after war had been declared, the Japanese First Army went ashore at Inchon under cover of Togo's battleships. The Russian Port Arthur squadron did nothing to interfere.

Early in March all such passivism was temporarily swept away with the arrival at Port Arthur of dynamic Vice Admiral Stepan Osipovich Makarov, newly appointed commander of Russia's East Asia naval forces. Makarov set about at once to restore morale, develop an aggressive spirit, and establish high standards of material and performance. The day after his arrival, his destroyers engaged the Japanese patrols and inflicted considerable damage. Admiral Togo quickly realized that his opponents had at last discarded their no-risks policy.

Unhappily for the Russians, the new broom did not last long enough to sweep away all the defeatism and inefficiency that lay like a pall upon Port Arthur. A month after his arrival, while chasing a Japanese mining force, Makarov's flagship, the battleship *Petropavlovsk*, struck a mine and went down, carrying the new commander and 600 of the crew. Makarov's death was an irreparable loss for Russia. "With him," wrote a destroyer commander, "all hope of rendering the squadron efficient was buried."

Rear Admiral Vilgelm Karlovitch Vitgeft, Makarov's successor, promptly resumed the defensive. Soon afterward came an announcement from St. Petersburg that the Baltic squadron would leave the Baltic at the end of July and arrive in the Yellow Sea four to five months later. This information merely confirmed Vitgeft in his decision to wait, conserving his force until the squadron from the Baltic could arrive with reinforcements.

The Japanese, on the other hand, began to move with quickened determination. By early May their First Army was across the Yalu and extending its left toward Port Arthur. Their Second Army, covered by Togo's fleet, landed on the Liaotung Peninsula and stormed the narrow neck leading down to the Russian base. Vitgeft meanwhile lay at anchor, disregarding his opportunity to make a surprise appearance and sweep the flanks of the assaulting columns with naval gunfire.

In mid-May fate presented Vitgeft with yet another opportunity. Within a few hours Russian mines sank two of Togo's battleships. Though Vitgeft now had six battleships to Togo's four, he still did not move.

So long as Port Arthur held out, Vitgeft's inactivity was not entirely illogical. Now that the Baltic squadron was on the way, the Japanese faced a convergence of naval power that would outnumber them two to one. But in early August 1904, when Port Arthur came under fire by Japanese artillery and the fall of the base was imminent, Russian fleet action of some sort was clearly called for. Vitgeft should doubtless have launched his squadron at Togo to do as much damage as possible. Even if he were beaten, he had a chance of so weakening the Japanese fleet that it could easily be defeated by the approaching Baltic fleet. Instead, orders from above forced him into flight. From the czar came a peremptory message: "Put out with full strength for Vladivostok."

Seventy-two hours later, at dawn on 10 August, the Port Arthur squadron—six battleships, four cruisers, and eight destroyers—made its dash for freedom. Japanese scouts soon picked up the fugitives and radioed Togo. When the latter sighted the Russians at noon, he had with him six armored vessels and nine cruisers. Vitgeft managed to slip past the Japanese fleet and head at top speed for the Straits of Korea. There ensued an afternoon-long battle of the boilers that was also a race with the sun. Toward sunset the Japanese at length pulled abeam of Vitgeft's fleeing column and opened fire.

Togo, fearful of torpedo attack and mindful that he had to preserve his ships to meet the approaching Baltic squadron, held off at long range. A pair of lucky 12-inch shots, however, hit the Russian flagship *Czarevitch*, killing Vitgeft and so jamming the helm that the ship swung left, away from the enemy, and continued on around as if to ram her own column. The Russian fleet, now leaderless, baffled by the strange antics of the *Czarevitch*, fell into confusion.

Togo closed to 4,000 yards for the kill but, sighting Russian destroyers approaching in the darkness, as if for a torpedo attack, he broke off action. During the night the Russians scattered. Five battleships, a cruiser, and three destroyers fled back to Port Arthur. The rest of the Russian vessels took shelter in neutral ports and were out of the war.

Three Russian cruisers at Vladivostok set out to facilitate the escape of the Port Arthur squadron. Ignorant of Vitgeft's defeat, they arrived off the island of Tsushima in the Straits of Korea on 14 August. Here they ran into a force of four Japanese cruisers under Vice Admiral Kamimura, who instantly gave chase. Superior Japanese gunnery soon forced the slowest of the Russian cruisers out of line, so wrecked and helpless that she was scuttled by her crew. The other two, badly battered, made it back to Vladivostok. Here, with a cruiser that did not sortie, they constituted a still formidable squadron. But news of the fate of the Port Arthur squadron so shattered morale at Vladivostok that they were of little further use in the war.

Knowledge of the approaching Russian naval reinforcements from the Baltic spurred Japan into a supreme effort against Port Arthur. Abandoning orthodox siege tactics, the Japanese troops made a general assault, introducing the "banzai charge" and the use of human torpedoes to blast paths through barbed wire entanglements. But the Russian resistance also was desperate. The advance of the Japanese in December to the high ground overlooking the base cost them 60,000 men.

By this time the Port Arthur squadron had long since ceased to be even a fleet in being. Its secondary batteries and a large proportion of its crews had been incorporated in the land defenses. Now the squadron suffered the ultimate humiliation for a naval force: artillery ashore began to batter it to pieces. Port Arthur surrendered on 2 January 1905, though not before the last of the Russian ships had been sunk or scuttled. Russia now had to attempt with her squadron from the Baltic what she should have undertaken earlier in the war with her whole fleet.

The Voyage of the Baltic Squadron

On 14 October 1904, after numerous frustrating delays, the Baltic squadron of 7 battleships, 5 cruisers, 7 destroyers, and a fleet train of 9 auxiliaries departed the Baltic port of Libau for its 18,000-mile cruise to Vladivostok. In command was Vice Admiral Zinovi Petrovich Rozhestvenski, whose indefatigable zeal and fiery temper had not been enough to hurry the fleet into readiness on schedule.

The voyage had barely begun when the Russians, apprehensively aware of the Anglo–Japanese alliance, became involved in an international incident that almost brought Britain into the war against them. On the night of 21 October, while steaming through the North Sea, the squadron opened fire on British trawlers under the impression that they were destroyers coming in for an attack. In a brief but heavy fusillade, with some Russian ships firing at each other, one of the fishing vessels was sunk.

The squadron continued on its way without attempting to rescue survivors, but cruiser divisions of Britain's Royal Navy closed the Russians and kept them under observation all the way to Gibraltar, being called off only when the czar's government agreed to submit the case to arbitration.

On arriving at Tangier, Rozhestvenski detached his lighter craft under Rear Admiral Folkersam to proceed via the Suez Canal. With his deeper-draft ships, which might run aground in the canal, he pushed south around Africa. En route his force refueled from German colliers in several French and German ports. The divisions rejoined on 9 January 1905, at the island of Nosy Bé off Madagascar. Here they were soon reinforced by 5 cruisers and 2 destroyers from Russia. Here too the squadron learned that Port Arthur had just surrendered.

The government might properly have called Rozhestvenski home to await the completion of a really formidable fleet, already approved. But it was now more urgent than ever that he take his squadron promptly to Vladivostok, at whatever cost, because the Trans-Siberian Railway had proved utterly unable to maintain an adequate flow of men and material into Manchuria. Unless Russian naval forces arrived to intercept reinforcements and supplies moving freely from Japan to the continent, the Russian army faced disaster. So the Admiralty ordered Rozhestvenski to press on, informing him that he would be joined by Rear Admiral Nebogatov with an old slow battleship, a cruiser, and three antique coast defense ironclads, "superfluous encumbrances" that Rozhestvenski would willingly have done without.

Commander Baltic Squadron would have preferred to depart the vicinity of Madagascar at once, but two months of negotiation in Europe were necessary to obtain from the Germans a renewal of their coal contract. Meanwhile, the ships and men of the Baltic squadron deteriorated in the steaming heat of the tropics. At last the squadron pushed on to French Indochina where, after another month of waiting, Nebogatov arrived with his old ships, which the disgusted sailors named the "auto-sinker class."

On 14 May, the combined Russian forces, 53 ships in all, left Indochina for the final run to Vladivostok. To arrive there, Rozhestvenski had to transit the Sea of Japan. He had a choice of three routes: through the Korean, the Tsugaru, or the Soya straits. Strategically it made little difference which he chose, because Admiral Togo, having the interior position, could arrive first at any of the three. So Rozhestvenski decided to take the shortest route, the Strait of Tsushima on the eastern side of the Korean Straits, though he suspected that this was where Togo was waiting to waylay him.

On 23 May, near the Ryukyus, colliers came alongside the Russian squadron for the last time, and each ship was ordered to take on board only enough coal to ensure good battle trim on the 27th,

the day they expected to meet the Japanese fleet. Soon afterward Rozhestvenski turned northeastward and shaped course for the Tsushima Strait. During the approach, Admiral Folkersam died of a heart attack, but his death was not disclosed to the fleet—or to Nebogatov, who thereby automatically became second-in-command. Folkersam's flag was kept flying on the *Osliabya*, and her captain was directed to exercise command of the division.

Here it should be pointed out that Rozhestvenski was faced with an almost insoluble problem. One of the oldest principles of warfare required that a commander undertake to attain only one major objective at a time. Rozhestvenski was confronted with three: (1) meeting the opposition of the Japanese fleet; (2) taking his own fleet to Vladivostok; and, (3) because the breakdown of the Trans-Siberian Railway had created shortages at Vladivostok, taking his service force with him. He was obliged thus simultaneously to solve the problems of combat, flight, and convoy protection. His opponent, on the contrary, would have to concern himself exclusively with defeating the Russian fleet.

Fearing a nocturnal torpedo attack, Rozhestvenski timed his approach so as to pass through Tsushima Strait in daylight. His battle line, three divisions of four ships each, now included eight battleships of varying speeds and armament. It was held to ten knots by the auxiliaries and by Nebogatov's obsolescent warships in the rear division. The battle line was to fight in column. The cruisers would support the battle line or cover the convoy as directed. A purely defensive role was assigned to the destroyers in daytime action and to the heavier ships at night. At noon on 27 May, as the squadron entered the strait, a signal fluttered up the halyards of Rozhestvenski's flagship *Suvorov*: "Steer north 23 degrees east"—the course for Vladivostok. It was kept flying as long as the *Suvorov* remained afloat.

The Battle of Tsushima, 27–28 May 1905

As Rozhestvenski had anticipated, Togo with his battle line of four battleships and eight heavy cruisers was waiting for him—on the western side of the straits, off Korea. A little before dawn on the 27th, one of Togo's scouts flashed the word by radio: the Russians were coming, headed for the Strait of Tsushima. At sunrise Togo headed east to intercept—leading the First Division in the *Mikasa*, closely followed by Kamimura, leading the Second Division. Togo planned to move his battle line like an articulated barrier back and forth across the Russians' line of advance in order to turn them back. His light cruisers were to engage the Russian cruisers and auxiliaries. At nightfall all gunnery ships would hand over the enemy to the destroyer flotillas and withdraw to the north to give them a clear field. At dawn the next day, the Japanese battle line would sweep south to reengage. The pattern would be repeated until the Russian fleet was annihilated.

Togo sped to the waters north of Tsushima Strait and around 1 p.m. crossed the Russians' estimated

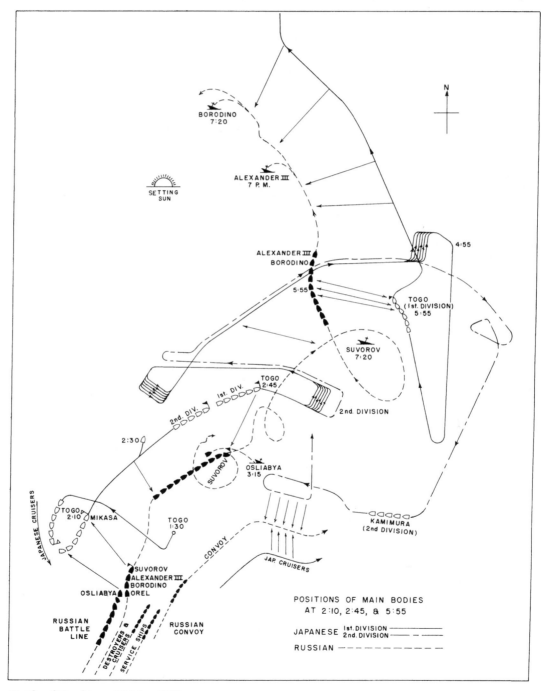

Battle of Tsushima, 27 May 1905

line of advance from west to east, then turned south in order to attack them from the east. On this heading he at length made out the enemy fleet eight miles away. On course 023 for Vladivostok, it was on a more northerly heading than that last reported to Togo. This new line of advance called for an attack on the Russians' left flank in order to turn them away. Thus Togo a little after 1:30 p.m. changed to course northwest and led his divisions back across the head of the oncoming enemy, still out of range at 15,000 yards. He turned his line left in succession and came down on the port side of the Russians on an opposite course. At this moment signal flags started up from the *Mikasa*'s bridge, reading: "The fate of the Empire depends on this day's battle. Let every man do his utmost."

Rather than let the Russians slip past him, Togo signaled, "Follow me," and led his division around to left in a reversal of course. Kamimura followed his example. Togo turned his ships in succession in order to retain his position in the van. It was a dangerous maneuver because the leading ships masked the fire of those following, and all ships turning in the same water provided the enemy with a stationary target at the knuckle. However, as Togo had noted, the Russian ships were in a state of too much confusion to take full advantage of the opportunity thus presented. Belatedly and awkwardly trying to form single column, they had fallen into disarray, masking some of their own fire and forcing the battleship *Osliabya* out of line. The Japanese divisions completed their vulnerable 16-minute countermarch with only minor damage. Rozhestvenski's chance for escape or victory had now passed.

The Japanese pressed toward the Russian van and fired a hail of projectiles that quickly found the range. Steaming at 14 knots, Togo and Kamimura drew ahead and gradually came right in an effort to cross the Russian T.[4] Rozhestvenski countered by giving way to the right, but the speed advantage of the Japanese enabled them to draw ahead and mass fire on the Russian van, including the *Osliabya*, still out of line to port. Meanwhile, the Russians concentrated fire on Togo's rear ships and forced one out of line, unable to steer.

Toward 3 p.m. the *Suvorov*, under intense fire at the head of the Russian line, sheered to the right out of control, one funnel and a mast shot away and

[4]To cap, or cross, the T of an enemy, the attacking column crosses ahead, at 90 degrees more or less, to the enemy's line of advance. The attacker is thus able to bring full broadsides to bear, massing his fire on the head of the enemy column, while his opponent finds his after guns able to bear, if at all, only on the extremities of the attacker's column at relatively long range.

her upper works a shambles. She circled once and staggered off to the northeast, carrying Rozhestvenski wounded and unconscious out of the battle. Exploding shells meanwhile had torn huge holes in the *Osliabya* just above the waterline forward. Inrushing seas brought her down by the bow until her gun ports were submerged. Rapidly flooding through the gun ports, she rolled over, hung on her beam ends for a few minutes, and at last capsized and plunged with the loss of 600 of her 800 men.

Because Nebogatov was yet unaware that the command had devolved upon himself, the Russian fleet was now leaderless. It could only try to obey Rozhestvenski's last signal, which was to steer course 023, for Vladivostok. This it endeavored repeatedly to do, but each time it was foiled by the Japanese divisions, which used their superior speed to sweep back and forth across its line of advance. The Russians, to avoid being capped and to return to a northerly course, steamed clockwise through two complete circles.

At 4:35, after a half-hour exchange of fire at 7,000 yards, Togo disengaged and ordered his destroyers to make a torpedo attack. Twenty minutes later, learning that the destroyers were unable to carry out this assignment, Togo and Kamimura hurried south toward gunflashes on the horizon. The Japanese battle line missed the Russian main body in the smoke to westward but soon found itself heading into the battle of the light cruisers, which had been going on indecisively since noon. Kamimura stayed to lend support in this area, while Togo headed northwest after bigger game.

The third phase of the battle began at 5:55 as the north-steaming Japanese First Division again sighted Russian battleships bearing northwest on their port bows. Togo turned in four points to close the range quickly before dark. But the Russians were still full of fight, and he found himself running into heavy fire with all the advantages on the other side, since the sun was setting directly in the eyes of his pointers, and his six ships were engaging ten. A quick turn to the right opened the range another 2,000 yards, and Togo came to a parallel course. As the light gradually shifted in the Japanese favor, silhouetting the Russians against the afterglow, Togo's vessels massed a deadly, accurate fire on the *Alexander III*, at the head of the line. Fifteen minutes later, burning fiercely, her bows nearly blown off, she turned out of line, capsized, and went down. The Japanese had already shifted fire to the new van ship, the *Borodino*. As darkness came on, she caught fire, thus presenting an easy target to the Japanese range finders. At 7:20 two of her magazines exploded, whereupon she capsized, floated bottom upward a few minutes, and then sank.

The loss of the *Borodino* broke up the Russian column. Nebogatov, in the *Nicholas I*, at last informed that he was in command, signaled "Follow me" and led a disorganized mass of ships to the southwest. The Japanese battleships and cruisers now left the area according to plan and steamed north toward the morning rendezvous near Ullung Island. With their departure, the battle entered a fourth phase; a series of scattered and fiercely contested night torpedo actions.

The Japanese destroyers had already sunk the battered *Suvorov*, but not before a Russian destroyer had come alongside and removed Rozhestvenski, still insensible from head wounds. In the darkness the Japanese torpedo craft, 21 destroyers and 37 torpedo boats, now closed in on the bewildered Russian fleet from all directions, sinking two battleships and so damaging two cruisers that they were scuttled to avoid capture.

At dawn on 28 May, 140 miles north of the previous day's battle area, Togo's staff were sweeping their glasses over an empty horizon when a light cruiser division 60 miles to the south reported Russian ships. The Japanese battle divisions steered toward the contact and at 9:30 sighted the battleships *Orel* and *Nicholas I*, two coast defense ironclads, and a cruiser. Shots fired from beyond the Russian range brought no response save the appearance of a table cloth on the *Nicholas*, hoisted in lieu of a white flag by order of Admiral Nebogatov. The Russian cruiser made off at high speed.

Of the separated Russian units, a coast defense ironclad of the battle line was heavily hit and scuttled; 2 cruisers were driven ashore; 4 destroyers and 4 auxiliaries were sunk; 2 destroyers, including the one with Rozhestvenski on board, were captured; and 3 cruisers, 3 auxiliaries, and a destroyer made neutral ports, where they were interned. In the course of the battle, 8 of the 12 Russian armored vessels, including 5 battleships, had been sunk. Of the 53 ships that had left the Baltic, a cruiser and 2 destroyers reached Vladivostok.

The Battle of Tsushima was decisive in every sense. Russia could no longer hope for victory on land because internal revolt prevented her from further reinforcing her Far Eastern armies. When the defeat at sea dashed her final hopes, she welcomed the mediation of U. S. President Theodore Roosevelt. At the Portsmouth, New Hampshire peace conference, her delegates did not do badly. They obtained for Russia a much-needed treaty of peace at the cost of Port Arthor and southern Sakhalin, both ceded to Japan. The mediators rejected a Japanese demand for cash indemnity on the ground that the Russian army, though defeated, withdrew intact and was still in the field.

Had Togo lost the battle, the Japanese army would have been isolated in Manchuria with its supply lines severed. Russia would undoubtedly have imposed heavy terms that would have made her the paramount power in the Far East.

Russia's defeat further undermined the confidence, already deeply eroded, of the Russian people in their leaders. What particularly rankled in all classes, however, was the tame surrender of Nebogatov and several of his captains. After the war they were court-martialed and sentenced to death, a punishment that was never carried out. What in fact was killed was the ancient tradition that a ship captain or squadron commander, after a valiant but hopeless fight, might honorably strike his colors. The precedent of Tsushima and its aftermath established a new and more implacable tradition: that warships and naval squadrons do not surrender under any circumstances.

The Battle of Tsushima demonstrated the value of heavy armor and the need for heavy guns. The Japanese enjoyed a great advantage through having in their battle line only swift homogeneous ships with uniform tactical characteristics. Togo's tactics, generally skillful, appeared brilliant because the Russians fought for the most part without leadership. Kamimura, like Collingwood at Trafalgar, was given a large measure of initiative, which he used effectively. His contributions to the victory further confirmed many officers, particularly in the Japanese navy, in their opinion that much was to be gained by operating in semi-independent divisions.

As for strategy, the lessons of the war have nowhere been more trenchantly summarized than in a letter of 3 March 1909, that President Roosevelt wrote to his successor, William Howard Taft, at the urgent request of Mahan:

> Dear Will: One closing legacy. Under no circumstances divide the battleship fleet between the Atlantic and Pacific Oceans prior to the finishing of the Panama Canal. . . . It is nearly four years since the Russian-Japanese War. There were various factors that brought about Russia's defeat; but the most important by all odds was her having divided her fleet into three utterly unequal divisions. The entire Japanese force was always used to smash some fraction of the Russian force.

Summary

Among the established and rising sea powers in the early twentieth century, Japan was unique in that she had completely skipped the Age of Sail. The defeated fleets of Hideyoshi in the late sixteenth century were composed mostly of galleys. The victorious fleets of Ito in the Battle of the Yalu in 1894 and of Togo in the Battle of Tsushima in 1905 were composed of steamships of the most advanced design.

Japan had been induced to open her ports and rejoin the industrialized world by Commodore Perry of the U. S. Navy, who in 1853 demonstrated Japan's military weakness by taking two steam frigates and two sailing sloops-of-war into Tokyo Bay and defying the Japanese to oust them.

Perry's demonstration, followed by naval bombardments against Kagoshima and the Strait of Shimonoseki, convinced Japanese leaders that to survive they would have to deal with other nations, at least to the extent of acquiring Western military techniques. With remarkable astuteness, they not only assimilated the lessons of three centuries of sea warfare in the West, but actually outstripped many Western innovators in developing naval weapons and strategic and tactical concepts.

The Japanese leaders concluded that to protect their country from her continental neighbors, Japan would have to take possession of Formosa, Korea, and Sakhalin. That meant going to war successively with China and Russia.

To begin hostilities with China, the Japanese attacked a Chinese troop convoy before war had been declared. In the ensuing Sino–Japanese War (1894–95), the Japanese were victorious on land and sea. Ito's Japanese fleet defeated Ting's Chinese fleet in the Battle of the Yalu, and afterward cooperated with the Japanese army in the capture of Port Arthur and the destruction of the remains of Ting's fleet at Weihaiwei. The peace treaty required the Chinese to withdraw from Korea and transferred Formosa, the Pescadores, and Port Arthur from China to Japan.

To open hostilities with Russia, the Japanese attacked the Russian fleet at Port Arthur prior to a declaration of war. In the ensuing Russo–Japanese War (1904–5), the Japanese army captured Port Arthur and the Japanese navy used its interior position to neutralize successively the three segments of Russia's Far East fleet—at Port Arthur, at Inchon, and at Vladivostok. Then, conserving their ships and practicing continually at gunfire and maneuver, they were prepared with the same naval forces to defeat the Russian Baltic squadron when it arrived.

In tactics, the Japanese early perceived the paramount value of the column and of broadside fire. Using speed and maneuver, they generally succeeded in breaking up enemy formations and bringing a preponderance of fire against successive fractions of the enemy fleet. In accordance with the principle triumphantly demonstrated by Nelson at Trafalgar, they operated in semi-independent divisions in order to attain great flexibility in battle and to permit part of the fleet to proceed at any time by the shortest line to the point where it was most needed.

As a result of her victories over China and Russia, Japan in the early twentieth century emerged as a first-class naval power—a power with which the acknowledged Mistress of the Seas did not hesitate to conclude an alliance. But Japan, regarding herself as robbed by the West of the fruits of her victories, continued to strengthen her fleet against the day when opportunity would enable her to assert her supremacy in the Far East.

Chapter 17
The Spanish–American War

If any single event marks the emergence of the United States as a major power, it is the Spanish–American War of 1898. Lasting a little over a hundred days and costing some 3,000 American lives, this brief, one-sided conflict involved the United States in the complex problems of the Far East and served notice on the European powers that henceforth American military strength would have to be reckoned with. For the Americans themselves it marked a turning point toward greater participation in world affairs.

Although the first major sea battle of the Spanish–American War was fought half a world away in the Philippines, the conflict arose out of the anarchy in Cuba. Here a chronic state of revolution against Spanish misrule finally erupted into fiery rebellion in 1895. The *insurrectos*, vying in cruelty with their Spanish masters, set about a policy of deliberate devastation in which the property of American citizens was not spared unless protection money was paid, and this in turn was expended to finance the revolt or to spread propaganda. Indeed, a major reason for U. S. intervention was to protect the large American-owned cane plantations and sugar mills. These interests were not inconsiderable, amounting to $50,000,000 in investments and $100,000,000 in annual volume of trade. Determined to put an end to the intolerable conditions in Cuba, the Spanish government early in 1896 sent General Valeriano Weyler to Havana, with orders to apply stern measures. Weyler's solution was to herd civilians into reconcentration areas, where they could not support the rebels. Here unhygienic conditions brought death to thousands, mainly women and children. The American public, already stirred by the skillful efforts of the Cuban junta in New York, reacted violently against the inhuman methods of "Butcher Weyler," and many urged that the rebel "government" be accorded recognition forthwith. Responding to the clamor, Congress passed a resolution demanding recognition of Cuban belligerency. Anti-imperialist President Cleveland ignored the resolution as an intrusion upon his executive powers, declaring that he would refuse to call out the Army rather than go to war with Spain, but to the Spanish government he

intimated that American respect for Spanish rule in Cuba might be "superseded by higher obligations, which we can hardly hesitate to recognize and discharge."

When a new, liberal Spanish ministry in 1897 recalled Weyler, modified the reconcentration system, and granted the Cubans a certain degree of autonomy, Americans began to lose interest in the Cuban cause. Then in February 1898 there occurred two events which aroused a storm of public indignation in the United States. One was the publication in the New York *Journal* of an indiscreet private letter written by Dupuy de Lôme, Spanish minister in Washington, and somehow obtained by the Cuban junta. In his letter the minister hinted at Spanish duplicity in discussions on pending trade agreements and referred to President McKinley as a "small-time politician." A week later, the battleship *Maine*, which had been ordered to Cuba to protect American lives and property, was torn apart by an explosion that killed 260 of her crew. The American public believed that the explosion was external, caused by a mine planted and set off by the Spaniards. The New York *Journal* offered a $50,000 reward, never claimed, for the apprehension and conviction of the perpetrators. Though subsequent studies have shown that the explosion might well have been internal and accidental, the United States was brought to the brink of war.[1]

---

[1]Admiral Hyman G. Rickover, USN, gathered all available data, including the numerous photographs taken of the wreckage when the *Maine* was raised in 1911, and in 1975 submitted it to Ib S. Hansen, assistant for design applications in the Structures Department at the David W. Taylor Ship Research and Development Center, and Robert S. Price, research physicist for the Naval Surface Weapons Center. These experts, operating in the light of modern technical knowledge and recent wartime experience and testing programs, concluded that "the characteristics of the damage are consistent with a large internal explosion." They theorized that spontaneous combustion in inadequately ventilated bituminous coal ignited gunpowder in an adjacent magazine, and this in turn set off explosions in adjoining magazines. (H. G. Rickover, *How the Battleship* Maine *Was Destroyed*, Washington, D.C., 1976)

Because, in event of armed conflict with Spain, Cuba would be the primary military objective and Puerto Rico a secondary one, the bulk of the U. S. fleet was concentrated in the Atlantic. To strengthen forces already there, the battleship *Oregon* made her celebrated voyage from Puget Sound around South America to the Caribbean, a 15,000-mile passage completed in 66 days at an average speed at sea of nearly 12 knots. Her arrival raised the strength of the North Atlantic Squadron to five battleships, the *Iowa, Indiana, Massachusetts, Texas,* and *Oregon,* and two armored cruisers, the *New York* and the *Brooklyn,* plus smaller types. Meanwhile, the Navy Department maintained only a small Asiatic Squadron of light cruiser types in the Pacific, which was generally regarded as an area of lesser naval significance.

The effect of the *Maine* disaster was not lost upon the Spaniards, who tried to appease American wrath, but at the same time prepared for war. Upon learning of the explosion, the Spanish Minister of Marine alerted the fleet and advised Admiral Pascual Cervera, commanding the main home force, to be ready to destroy the American base at Key West and then to blockade the American coast.

To Cervera, constitutionally pessimistic, such an assignment appeared fantastic in the extreme, for his operational strength consisted only of four cruisers and two destroyers, all in poor shape. He pointed out his naval inferiority in comparison to the Americans, the absence of powerful Spanish bases beyond the Atlantic, and the probable lack of adequate logistic support for his fleet in Cuba and Puerto Rico. He expressed the opinion that the most practical naval strategy for his country in event of war would be to retain forces for defense of the homeland, and asserted that his fleet could make the American coast a profitable military objective only if Spain could enlist a powerful naval ally capable of furnishing assistance. The Ministry thereupon modified its directive but insisted that the naval forces should at least defend Puerto Rico. On 8 April 1898, Cervera, still regarding his mission as hopeless, steamed from Cadiz and advanced to the Cape Verde Islands to await further political developments.

Word of the sortie of the Spanish home fleet caused a tremendous war scare along the American East Coast. Badly informed citizenry everywhere had visions of coastal bombardment and invasion by the enemy. Both Army and Navy received frantic calls for coast defense. Secretary of War Russell Alger afterwards remembered that "calls made upon the department for immediate rescue from the advancing Spanish fleet were pathetic in their urgency. Telegrams, letters, and statesmen representing the imperiled localities poured into the War Department. They wanted guns everywhere; mines in all rivers and harbors on the map."[2] Theodore Roosevelt later recalled that nervous Boston financiers, fearful for the safety of their investment securities, removed them 50 miles inland to Worcester for safer keeping.

No harm was done, and some nerves were calmed, by a general trundling out of obsolete Civil War guns to points along the coast, whence they were aimed futilely at the empty Atlantic. But demands for fleet protection simultaneously of all parts of the East Coast were something else again, for a fleet is by reason of its mobility a weapon of attack. Even when its mission is defensive in purpose, its units should never degenerate into static platforms for guns.

The Navy Department was well aware that the North Atlantic Squadron ought in the circumstances to operate as a unit. Even if Cervera should strike elsewhere than in the Caribbean, where he was expected, a fleet with its integrity preserved could still strike a retaliatory blow. Spreading the fleet thin along the coast could prove military suicide; yet the clamor of the coastal cities for naval protection had to be satisfied in some manner. The solution was a compromise—the North Atlantic squadron was divided into two main parts. One, under Acting Rear Admiral William T. Sampson, was based at Key West, poised and ready for offensive operations against Cuba and Puerto Rico. The other, the so-called Flying Squadron, was organized at Norfolk under the command of Commodore Winfield Scott Schley, as a mobile fortress fleet for the roving protection of the Atlantic seaboard. A smaller Northern Patrol Squadron of obsolete and generally useless vessels guarded the coast from the Delaware Capes northward.

Meanwhile, the Spanish Ministry was vacillating over American demands that Spain grant an armistice to the *insurrectos* and put an end to reconcentration—fearful of revolution at home if they capitulated and of war with the United States if they did not. By 9 April, the Ministry had given in on both points. It was already too late, however, for President McKinley had now come to realize that the Democrats with their cry of "Free Cuba!" would defeat him in the next elections unless he put a definitive end to the wretched conditions in the Spanish colony. So he sent a war message to Congress on the 11th, requesting authority to use

[2]Russell A. Alger, *The Spanish-American War* (New York, 1901), 38.

the Army and the Navy. A week later Congress passed a joint resolution declaring Cuba free and independent, demanding the withdrawal of Spanish forces, and directing the president to use armed force to put the resolution into effect. A final clause, the so-called Teller Amendment, pledged that whatever the outcome the United States would not annex Cuba.

On 22 April 1898 the Navy Department directed Sampson to establish a blockade of Cuban waters from Havana around the western tip of the island to Cienfuegos on the south coast. On 25 April Congress declared a state of war to have existed since 21 April. On the 29th Cervera's fleet left the Cape Verdes and steamed to the defense of Puerto Rico. Cervera was given "entire freedom of action as to route, port, and cases and circumstances in which battle should be sought or eluded."

The Philippine Campaign

No cries for coastal protection split the small American naval force in the Pacific. Indeed, many Americans were scarcely aware that Spain had possessions in that area. One man in Washington, however, knew very well that the Spaniards owned the Philippines and had a fleet of sorts there. That man was Theodore Roosevelt, assistant secretary of the navy. When trouble with Spain loomed, Roosevelt decided that the United States must be prepared to strike in the Pacific as well as in the Atlantic. Casting about for a man capable of striking a quick and effective blow against naval forces in the Philippines, he selected Commodore George Dewey and had him appointed commander in chief of the U. S. Asiatic Squadron.

Dewey at the time of his appointment was holding the routine administrative post of president of the Board of Inspection and Survey, but he had experienced extensive combat duty in the Civil War and had a reputation for aggressiveness. Dewey was much more than merely aggressive. Like his old commanding officer, David Glasgow Farragut, he combined a keen eye for tactical situations with a capacity for meticulous attention to detail. Before leaving Washington he read everything he could find on the Philippines and studied all available charts of the surrounding waters. Urgently requesting the Navy Department to forward ammunition as soon as possible, he left for Japan in early December 1897. A month later he boarded the flagship Olympia at Nagasaki and assumed his new command.

Dewey soon moved his squadron to Hong Kong in order to be nearer Manila. Here he received a cablegram from Roosevelt, then Acting Secretary: "Keep full of coal. In the event . . . of war your duty will be to see that the Spanish squadron does not leave the Asiatic coast, and then offensive operations in Philippine Islands." Dewey needed no such prompting, for he was already furiously at work in preparation for his coming task. He purchased a collier and a supply steamer to serve as fleet train. He had his warships docked, the machinery overhauled, the underwater hulls scraped, and the white sides painted battleship gray. The commodore personally inspected all details, seeing to it that crews underwent daily drill and that all machinery was ready for sustained operation at a moment's notice. Lacking information on the Spanish fleet and fortifications in the Philippines, he sent a spy to Manila and disguised his own aide as a tourist to pick up data from travelers arriving in Hong Kong. To evade British neutrality rules once war was declared, he arranged for a temporary anchorage at Mirs Bay in Chinese waters some distance up the coast.

On 25 April came a cable from the secretary of the navy: "War has commenced between the United States and Spain. Proceed at once to Philippine Islands. Commence operations at once, particularly against the Spanish fleet. You must capture vessels or destroy. Use utmost endeavors." Dewey waited 36 hours until the American consul arrived from Manila with the latest word concerning Spanish preparations. On the 27th Dewey sailed for the conquest of the Philippines.

The American squadron comprised four cruisers, including the flagship Olympia (5,870 tons), the Baltimore, the Raleigh, and the Boston; two gunboats, the Petrel and the Concord; and the revenue cutter McCulloch. These vessels totaled about 20,000 tons and carried some 100 guns, only half of them larger than 4-inch. Six hundred miles away in the Philippines waited the fleet of Rear Admiral Don Patricio Montojo. Montojo's only modern vessel of any real consequence was the Reina Cristina, of about 3,500 tons, mounting 6.2-inch guns. Another of his cruisers, the old wooden Castilla, was unable to move under her own power. In addition, he had five ships of 500 to 1,100 tons. Estimating that he would have no chance of defeating the American squadron in a battle of maneuver, Montojo planned to fight at anchor, using his ships as a fortress fleet to supplement shore batteries.

En route to the Philippines, the American squadron made final preparations for action, including battle drills in daylight and darkness, practice in fire fighting and damage control, and removal of practically all woodwork to lessen fire hazards. In the afternoon of 30 April, after reconnoitering Subic Bay and finding the Spanish fleet not there, Dewey remarked, "Now we have them," and headed for the passage south of Corregidor leading into landlocked Manila Bay.

Despite his outward assurance, the commodore had inward qualms. Manila was regarded throughout the Far East as impregnable. The passages into the bay had been mined. Thirty years before, his old commander Farragut had damned the torpedoes, in deed if not in word, and steamed into Mobile Bay. Since then, of course, mines had greatly improved, but Dewey, judging that there were no engineers in Manila skillful enough to place mines properly in the deep waters off Corregidor, determined to take his fleet in under cover of darkness. "Whenever I have been in a difficult situation, or in the midst of such a confusion of details that the simple and right thing to do seemed hazy," he wrote afterward, "I have often asked myself, 'What would Farragut do?' In the course of preparations for Manila Bay I often asked myself this question, and I confess I was thinking of him that night when we entered the bay, and with the conviction that I was doing precisely what he would have done."[3]

On 1 May 1898, a little after midnight, when the American squadron had almost completed its passage into the bay without encountering any live mines, a few of the batteries on shore opened fire. But shells from the American ships quickly silenced the guns and the entire line passed through the strait unscathed. At dawn, Dewey's squadron was off Manila looking for the Spanish fleet. The city batteries opened fire but made no hits.

To spare the city bombardment by American guns, Montojo had placed his squadron off Cavite. Here Dewey found him and closed to 5,000 yards to conserve ammunition, since there was no nearby source of replenishment. At 5:40 a.m. the commodore said to the captain of the *Olympia*, "You may fire when you are ready, Gridley." Firing steadily, the Americans passed and repassed the Spanish ships in a series of countermarches reminiscent of Du Pont's tactics in Port Royal Sound. Several Spanish ships, including the *Reina Cristina*, made futile attempts to advance but were sunk or driven back. When Dewey temporarily withdrew at 7:35 because of an erroneous report of ammunition shortage, the *Cristina* and the *Castilla* had already been abandoned. At 11 o'clock Dewey resumed battle and in another hour of firing completed the annihilation of the Spanish squadron.

[3]*Autobiography* (New York, 1916), 50.

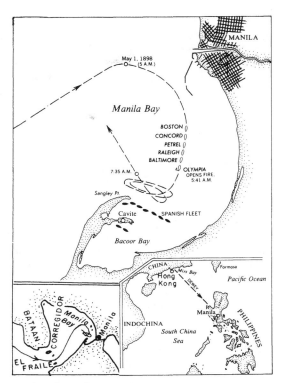

Battle of Manila Bay, 1 May 1898

When he ceased fire, all of Montojo's warships were burned, sunk, or abandoned.

Spanish casualties, in the fleet and ashore on Cavite, were 381 killed or wounded. Dewey's squadron had suffered no fatalities and only seven wounded. The Americans, who had drilled regularly at gunnery, had made at least 170 hits; the Spaniards, who had had no practice at all, made only 15. The American victory was as much a result of superior preparation as of superior power. "The battle of Manila," said Dewey, "was won in Hong Kong harbor." He might have added that it was a timely victory, for had he not promptly located and defeated Montojo's force, his supply situation would have become precarious.

With no Spanish naval power left in the area, Dewey anchored off Manila to hold the Philippines against outside interference. His problem was complicated by the arrival of five German warships on the lookout for a chance to pick up the Philippines for colony-hungry Germany, should the United States not be interested. The United States, however, was very much interested. Some 11,000 army troops were soon on the way from San Francisco to seize Manila and occupy the islands. En route to the Philippines the cruiser *Charleston*, escorting the troop convoy, made a bloodless capture of Spanish Guam, where the governor had not even heard of the war. Less than a month later, the United States, with visions of growing empire, at long last annexed the independent Hawaiian Islands.

On 13 August 1898, under combined army and naval bombardment, Manila capitulated after a token resistance. Thereafter the Army and the Navy faced the three-year task of putting down an insurrection among the Filipinos, who had hoped for independence and not merely an exchange of imperial masters. Nearly half a century would pass before the United States would deem the Filipinos ready to govern themselves. Meanwhile, with the cession of the Philippines by the treaty of peace, the United States became permanently involved in the affairs of the Far East.

The Caribbean Campaign

Admiral Sampson, intellectual, somewhat remote, but by no means lacking in aggressiveness, proposed opening hostilities against Spain with an amphibious assault upon Havana. By capturing the capital and military stronghold, he hoped to bring the conflict to an early end. Secretary of the Navy John D. Long disapproved Sampson's proposal be-cause the Army was far from ready and also because he considered it unwise to risk the American fleet against the guns of Havana while an enemy fleet was still at large. The accumulated experience of warfare suggested that before exposing one's ships to the perils of attack against a fortified coast one must either have gained command of the sea by destroying any enemy forces that might interfere, or else one must have the equivalent of two fleets, a Support Force to attack the coast and protect the invasion troops and a Covering Force to act as a shield to the beachhead and Support Force, fending off any approaching enemy fleet.

With the North Atlantic Squadron divided between Norfolk and the Caribbean, Long simply did not feel that Sampson had sufficient strength for amphibious operations while Cervera's fleet remained intact. In this opinion he was seconded by the new Naval War Board. This board, composed of Rear Admiral Montgomery Sicard, retired commander of the North Atlantic Squadron, Captain Arent S. Crowninshield, chief of the Bureau of Navigation, and Captain Mahan, the naval historian and philosopher, was intended originally as a mere intelligence agency but came in time to act as a central strategy board. As such, it served to unify the efforts of the Navy, though it sometimes embarrassed local commands when it ventured into tac-

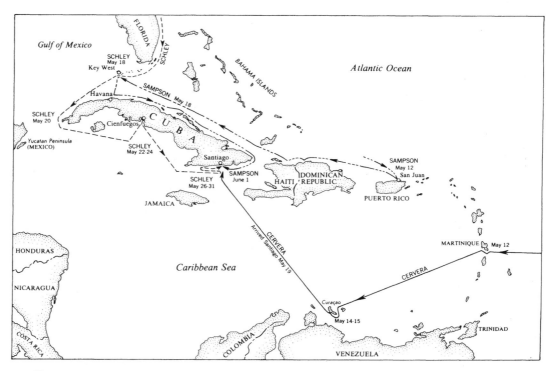

Caribbean Campaign, 1898

tical directives. The Board was a great step forward from the somewhat hit-or-miss central direction in earlier wars, but no machinery had yet been developed that, like the Joint Chiefs of Staff in World War II, could coordinate army and naval operations.

When Cervera, on orders from Madrid, cleared the Cape Verde Islands on 29 April, he was as gloomy as ever. He knew he was hopelessly outmatched. Moreover, his best cruiser, the *Cristóbal Colón*, lacked her two 10-inch guns, and another, the *Vizcaya*, was slowed by a badly fouled underwater hull.

Sampson soon learned of Cervera's sortie and at once conceived the plan of going out to meet him at San Juan, Puerto Rico, where he believed the Spanish fleet would have to put in for coal. Mahan also had estimated that the Spaniards would touch first at San Juan and had suggested placing scout cruisers in that area to detect Cervera and notify Sampson. The American fleet could then advance to San Juan and seek a decisive naval action. However, Sampson partially lifted his blockade of Cuba on 3 May and headed for Puerto Rico with the battleships *Iowa* and *Indiana*, the armored cruiser *New York*, two monitors, and a torpedo boat. Slowed down by the monitors, which had to be towed, he did not reach San Juan until the 12th. Finding no signs of Cervera, he bombarded the port for an hour, taking eight personnel casualties from shore guns and doing only minor damage.

Mahan condemned Sampson's advance to Puerto Rico. The main objective of American operations in the Caribbean was capture of Cuba by invasion, following defeat or blockade of the Spanish fleet. Until Cervera was located, therefore, Cuba was the strategic center of the campaign. In the circumstances Sampson in abandoning Cuba was, in Mahan's terms, sacrificing his position at the strategic center for an eccentric operation of dubious advantage.

As a matter of fact, Cervera had outguessed Sampson by estimating that Sampson would do exactly what he did. While the North Atlantic Squadron was widely scattered, with Schley at Norfolk, Sampson at San Juan, some vessels at Key West, others on blockade duty off Cuba, and the *Oregon* en route from the Pacific, the Spaniards successfully eluded them all and slipped into Cuba's back door. After crossing the Atlantic at less than seven knots, Cervera had applied for coal at Martinique. Refused assistance there by the French, he had proceeded to Curaçao, where the Dutch authorities proved more hospitable. Thence he proceeded straight for Cuba.

Sampson was already returning from his fruitless advance to San Juan when he learned of Cervera's arrival in the Caribbean. He thereupon dropped his monitors and made full speed for Key West, arriving on 18 May, a few hours after Schley's Flying Squadron had arrived from Norfolk. Believing that the Spanish fleet was bringing ammunition for defense of the capital, Sampson strengthened his blockade of Havana and sent the Flying Squadron, reinforced by the *Iowa*, around to the south coast of Cuba to blockade Cienfuegos, which was connected to Havana by rail. In the meantime, once more outguessing Sampson, Cervera had made directly for the isolated port of Santiago, far to the southeast. Here on the morning of the 19th he was received with congratulations when he steamed through the narrow channel into the harbor. Merely reaching Santiago safely was a real achievement. But now he could think of nothing better to do than remain anchored in the harbor until the American blockade closed on him nine days later.

Meanwhile Schley was taking his time getting to Cienfuegos. Once there he found he could not see inside the harbor, but he did see smoke and from that assumed that the Spaniards might be present. With evidence piling up that Cervera was elsewhere, Sampson sent Schley word by fast dispatch boat: "Spanish squadron probably at Santiago. . . . *If you are satisfied they are not at Cienfuegos*, proceed with all despatch, but cautiously, to Santiago de Cuba, and if enemy is there blockade him in port." On the 24th Schley made contact with Cuban insurgents ashore and, determining at last that Cervera was not at Cienfuegos, headed for Santiago. Keeping down for a while to the six-knot speed of one of his gunboats, which was having trouble in the mounting seas, he did not complete the 315-mile run until 26 May. While still 20 miles from Santiago he made contact with three American scout cruisers, none of which had sighted Cervera.

Schley now began to worry about the state of his coal supply, and though he had a collier with him, the rough seas made coaling at sea impossible. So that night he ordered his squadron to head back toward Key West for recoaling. Delayed by engine trouble in his collier, he was overtaken by a scout cruiser next morning with a terse message from Washington: "All Department's information indicates Spanish division is still at Santiago. The Department looks to you to ascertain facts, and that the enemy, if therein, does not leave without decisive action." To which Schley replied: "Much to be regretted, cannot obey orders of the Department;

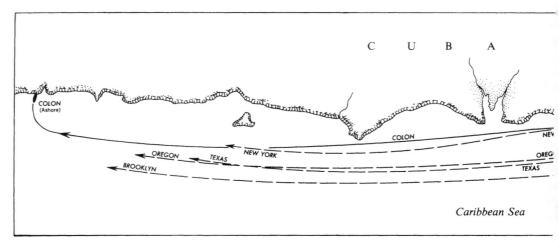

Battle of Santiago, 3 July 1898

forced to proceed for coal to Key West, by way of Yucatan passage; cannot ascertain anything respecting enemy."[4] Luckily, the seas soon calmed so that the Flying Squadron was able after all to take on coal. Schley therefore returned to Santiago and took station off the harbor in the evening of 28 May. The following morning the *Cristóbal Colón* was clearly visible anchored at the entrance, where she had been for the past four days. On 1 June Sampson arrived off Santiago, his squadron strengthened by the newly arrived *Oregon*, and assumed overall command. At last the various parts of the North Atlantic Squadron had been brought together.

The American vessels now took blockading stations, with the five battleships in a semicircle four to six miles off the entrance and smaller craft patrolling closer inshore. At night the ships closed in somewhat, and a searchlight from one of the battleships played upon the harbor mouth. During the month-long blockade the fleet frequently bombarded the Morro and other shore batteries guarding Santiago harbor, and at night the experimental cruiser *Vesuvius* participated spectacularly but not very effectively, firing 1,500-pound dynamite shells by compressed air from three fixed 15-inch tubes. In order to secure an advanced base near Santiago for coaling, supply, and general maintenance of the blockading vessels, some 650 marines seized Guantanamo, Cuba on 10 June and in a week of fighting made good their position. These were the first Americans to fight on Spanish soil.

Cervera in the landlocked harbor of Santiago was harmless enough, yet his squadron still consti-

tuted a fleet in being that exerted a restraining influence upon American operations elsewhere, because there always existed the possibility that he might escape. The United States could not exercise unchallenged command of the seas around Cuba so long as there was any likelihood that Spanish warships might interfere with landing or other operations. Sampson's fleet could not, however, penetrate the narrow, winding channel into the harbor because of minefields planted there, and the minefields could not be cleared because of the nearby shore batteries. Any attempt to run through the mines might result in a vessel in the middle of the attacking column being sunk and so splitting the fleet by blocking the ships already inside from those still outside. The alternative to going in and destroying Cervera's squadron was to close the harbor entrance with a sunken hull that could not be bypassed at night or blown away by storms. For such a stopper Sampson chose a small collier and sent her in with a picked crew of seven under Naval Constructor Richmond P. Hobson to blow her up and sink her across the narrowest part of the channel. But the collier was detected by the Spaniards, whereupon shore batteries opened fire and so smashed her steering gear that she drifted past the narrows and sank in a position where she was only a minor obstacle.

With the failure of the harbor-blocking experiment, it became clear that if the danger was to be removed, the Spanish squadron would have to be induced to come out and fight or Sampson's fleet would have to go into the harbor after it. Sampson therefore called on Washington for sufficient troops to capture the shore batteries so that he could send in boats to clear the mines.

[4]Schley communicated with the Department via dispatch cruiser to nearby Haiti, which had cable-telegraph connections with Washington.

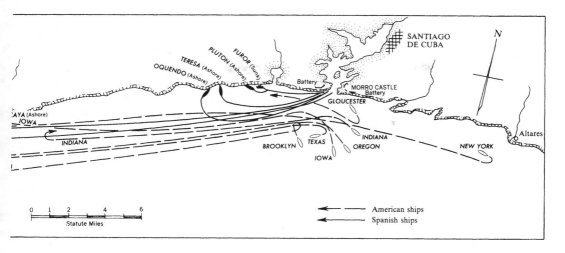

Meanwhile the Army, eager to take part in the war which up to then had involved only the Navy and a few marines, quickly assembled 16,000 soldiers at Tampa under command of Major General William R. Shafter. On 31 May the War Department sent Shafter his orders, which read in part:

Proceed under convoy of the Navy to the vicinity of Santiago de Cuba, land your force at such place east or west of that point as your judgment may dictate, under the protection of the Navy, and move it onto the high ground and bluffs overlooking the harbor or into the interior, as shall best enable you to capture or destroy the garrison there, and cover the Navy as it sends its men in small boats to remove torpedoes, or, with the aid of the Navy, capture or destroy the Spanish fleet now reported to be in Santiago harbor.

Shafter thus had been given considerable latitude, including the right to exercise his own judgment and, if he saw fit to do so, initiate a campaign against the city of Santiago and the main Spanish army. The fact that he was given a choice of operations, when the Navy had asked for one specific task to be done, reveals serious lack of liaison between the War and Navy departments. Moreover, Shafter and Sampson, who would have to work together closely in mutual support, had no common superior below the level of the president of the United States.

Sailing from Tampa in mid-June in commercial transports escorted by naval vessels, the expeditionary force reached Santiago on the 20th. Present were General Leonard Wood's Rough Riders, including Theodore Roosevelt, who could not bear to

remain behind his desk at the Navy Department when fighting was in prospect. Four days were consumed in leisurely, laborious landing operations at Daiquiri, 18 miles east of Santiago, with the Navy standing by to lend support and providing boats to ferry the troops to the beach.

On 20 June Admiral Sampson, together with General García and other Cuban officers, held his only conference with General Shafter. There appears to have been no firm decision reached, but Sampson left the conference satisfied that Shafter had accepted the harbor batteries as his objective. Shafter left equally convinced that the admiral had agreed to the city of Santiago as the Army's proper objective. The general afterward asserted that his decision to attack Santiago was included in a memorandum he dictated to a member of Sampson's staff. In any event, when Shafter directly afterward plunged into the interior with his troops, Sampson seems to have regarded the move as a feint, to be followed by an early attack on the batteries. He was astounded a few days later when the general informed him by message that the city was the true objective of his march.

Meanwhile, hampered by rough bridle paths and barbed wire, the soldiers had advanced slowly under the blazing tropical sun, many dropping out with heatstroke or typhoid fever. At San Juan Hill and El Caney the Spaniards took a stand and inflicted on the invaders casualties amounting to nearly 10 percent. Alarmed, on the verge of retreating, Shafter, who was 63, weighed more than 300 pounds, and was confined to his tent with fever, sent Sampson an urgent message: "Terrible fight yesterday, but my line is strongly entrenched three-quarters of a mile from town. I urge that you make effort immediately to force the entrance to avoid future losses among my men." Thus the Army, halted by a variety of causes at the city's outskirts, was now requesting the Navy to enter live minefields in order to assist the land forces in a campaign the admiral regarded as a misconception of the Army's proper mission. Exasperated by his inability to reach an agreement with Shafter by messenger regarding the respective roles the Army and the Navy should play, Sampson on 3 July steamed eastward along the coast in his flagship *New York* for a personal interview with the general. Sampson's departure from the Santiago blockade set the stage for a subsequent dispute involving Schley.

Before Sampson could set foot ashore, his differences with Shafter were resolved by Cervera himself. Though the situation looked grave enough to the Americans, it looked graver still to the Spaniards, who were convinced that Santiago was about to be captured and the fleet with it. Rather than see that happen, Governor General Blanco, at Havana, telegraphed Cervera to get out of port at any cost, and Cervera seized the opportunity of making his sortie while Sampson was off station in the *New York*, and the *Massachusetts* was coaling at Guantanamo. The Spanish flagship *Maria Teresa* led the way at 9:35 a.m., followed by the cruisers *Vizcaya*, *Cristóbal Colón*, and *Oquendo* and two destroyers. Sighting the smoke of the *Teresa* as she approached the entrance, the *New York* promptly came about, hoisted the signal for action, and sped westward trying to catch up with the running battle being fought by Schley, whom Sampson had left in tactical command during his absence.

Off Santiago harbor, the blockaders closed in, firing at the *Teresa* as she emerged. The *Brooklyn*, Schley's flagship, with the *Teresa* approaching as if to ram, swung to starboard across the bow of the nearby *Texas*, which had to back all engines to prevent a collision. Making almost a complete circle the *Brooklyn* finally headed west with the rest of the ships. These were already pursuing the Spaniards, who had broken through the blockade. Why the *Brooklyn* at first turned east instead of west, whether to avoid being rammed, to unmask the batteries of other American ships, or to open the range, was never satisfactorily explained, even by Schley, who stated merely that "it was the proper military maneuver under the circumstances" and that "it saved the day beyond any doubt."[5]

⁵Winfield Scott Schley, *Forty-five Years under the Flag* (New York, 1904), 302.

Soon the swift *Brooklyn* made good her loss in range and took the lead among the pursuers, with the *Oregon, Iowa, Texas,* and *Indiana* following. At the same time the little converted yacht *Gloucester* closed on the two Spanish destroyers. Coming under concentrated fire from the American battle line, the *Teresa*, hit about 30 times, her steam lines severed, her wooden decks on fire, turned toward shore and beached herself six miles west of the harbor mouth.

The *Oquendo* and the *Vizcaya* next came under heavy fire, began to blaze, and likewise grounded. Only the *Colón*, last and swiftest of Cervera's cruisers, outran the range of American shells and made a gallant bid to escape. Her stokers spurred to extraordinary exertion by libations of cognac, she steamed westward at 14 knots. After a 55-mile chase, when the alcoholic stimulation of her black gang had turned to drowsiness, the *Brooklyn* and the *Oregon* finally caught up with her and began making hits. At that, the *Colón*, only slightly damaged, struck her colors, steered for the beach, and surrendered. Meanwhile, the two Spanish destroyers, hotly engaged by the little *Gloucester*, had come under fire of the *Indiana* as she sped by. One destroyer was almost cut in two by a 13-inch shell; the other, heavily damaged by a smaller shell, sank after lowering her colors to the *Gloucester*.

As in the Battle of Manila Bay, an inferior fleet had been annihilated by a superior, better-managed fleet. Spanish losses in the Battle of Santiago were 160 men killed and 1,800 captured, including Cervera himself. American losses were one man killed and one wounded.

The defeat of Cervera had far-reaching effects. Within a fortnight, Santiago, under naval bombardment and running short of food, became untenable, whereupon General Toral formally surrendered the city and his 22,000 troops to General Shafter. Spain's few remaining warships, en route to attack Dewey in Manila Bay, turned around in the Red Sea and headed back home to defend Spanish shores from a possible attack by the victorious North Atlantic Squadron. Now that the United States was in undisputed command of Caribbean waters, American expeditionary forces, with naval support, landed in Puerto Rico and headed for the capital. By the end of July, with U. S. forces victorious everywhere, the Navy laid plans for a cruise against the Spanish mainland, whereupon the Spaniards promptly sued for peace. In the final treaty, signed on 10 December 1898 in Paris, Spain relinquished all claim to Cuba and ceded Puerto Rico, Guam, and the Philippines to the United States.

The Sampson–Schley Controversy

For their services in the Spanish–American War, Dewey, Sampson, and Schley were made permanent rear admirals. It would appear that there was glory enough for each, but bitter recriminations arising between the adherents of Sampson and Schley served in some measure to dim the renown of both.

In the first newspaper stories of the Battle of Santiago, genial, obliging Schley, a favorite of the press, received almost unanimous credit for the victory, though the preliminary planning had been done by Sampson, who, unluckily, was off station when the enemy fleet emerged. As newspapers began to reach the fleet off Santiago a week after the battle, Schley went to Sampson with a message which he asked him to transmit to the secretary of the navy: "Feel some mortification that the newspaper accounts of July 6th have attributed victory on July 3rd almost entirely to me. Victory was secured by the force under command Commander-in-Chief, North Atlantic Station [Sampson], and to him the honor is due." After reading the message, Sampson said, "Schley, this is kind and generous; I will transmit it at once." He did, but that same day he wrote a secret message of his own to the secretary in which for the first time he complained about Schley's procrastination in locating and blockading Cervera more than a month earlier. "This reprehensible conduct," wrote Sampson, "I cannot separate from his subsequent conduct, and for this reason I ask you to do him ample justice on this occasion."

Sampson's secret letter came out several months later when the promotions to rear admiral were being considered for confirmation by the Senate, and Secretary Long advocated that Sampson be advanced several numbers over Schley. Schley defended his conduct so well in a letter to the Senate Naval Affairs Committee that the inequity was canceled. Two years later, however, Schley's indignation was again aroused by the appearance of a third volume of Edgar Maclay's *History of the United States Navy*, the first two volumes of which were in use as textbooks at the U. S. Naval Academy. Maclay not only put the severest interpretation upon Schley's action preceding the blockade but implied that Schley's turnaway to starboard in the *Brooklyn* was an act of cowardice. At this Schley requested a Court of Inquiry to determine what his war record had been.

For 40 days the court held session under the chairmanship of Admiral Dewey. After 2,000 pages of testimony and findings had been assembled, the court issued a majority and a minority report. The majority found that Schley's conduct prior to 1 June 1898 "was characterized by vacillation, dilatoriness, and lack of enterprise" and concluded that "the turn of the *Brooklyn* to the eastward was made to avoid getting her into dangerous proximity to the Spanish vessels." The brief minority report just as vigorously praised and defended Schley's conduct.

Schley protested the majority findings to Theodore Roosevelt, then president of the United States. Roosevelt concluded that there was "no excuse whatever from either side for any further agitation on this unhappy controversy." So the matter rested.

Lessons and Consequences of the War

The war dramatized for the American public and for the world the emergence of the United States as a major naval power. The overwhelming and apparently easy victories of Dewey and Sampson and the epic 15,000-mile voyage of the *Oregon* provided a popular emotional point of departure for acceptance of a "big navy" policy.

At the same time, the thoughtful student of the Spanish–American War was forced to the conclusion that the U. S. Navy, though performing creditably, still showed much room for improvement. It was not likely to repeat the sweeping victories of Manila and Santiago without better material, better techniques, and better understanding of principles. "We cannot," warned Mahan, expect ever again to have an enemy so entirely inapt as Spain showed herself to be."[6]

The most important long-term consequence of the war was that the United States had acquired an overseas empire. The occupation of Puerto Rico and Guantanamo would aid the Navy in its mission of defending the continental United States. But the new Pacific possessions posed far more problems than they solved.

Attempts to find solutions to these problems dominated much of the Navy's thinking for the next 40 years. Most perplexing was the question of how to defend the Philippine archipelago—7,000 miles from the United States but only 1,000 from Japan and less than 300 miles from Japanese-held Formosa. Against a militaristic, expansionist Japan, the Philippines could be defended only by maintaining

[6]*Lessons of the War with Spain* (Boston, 1899), 157.

effective fleet superiority in Far Eastern waters. Once lost to Japan, or any other strong Oriental power, they could be recovered only by securing control over most of the Pacific. Either alternative would require fortified base facilities far beyond anything the United States possessed.

Dewey's overwhelming victory over the Spaniards in Manila Bay so strengthened the expansionists in Congress that by mid-1898 they were able to ride down opposition and by joint resolution annex the island chain of Hawaii. Early the following year the United States laid claim to the tiny atoll of Wake, and late in 1899 annexed part of the Samoa Islands, including the fine harbor of Pago Pago. In the face of anti-imperialist sentiment, that was as far as Congress could go.

Spain, having lost her principal colonies, decided to divest herself of the cares of empire and concentrate on domestic development. In 1899 she put up for sale, at a bargain price, all her remaining Pacific possessions—the Marshalls, the Carolines, and all the Marianas except Guam, nearly a thousand islands, most small but, as it turned out, adequate for the construction of numerous airfields and the provision of not a few good anchorages. The United States was not interested. Germany, tardy participant in the new imperialist race, snapped them all up.

Summary

The American people, angered by persistent Spanish misrule in Cuba, were infuriated by the blowing up of the battleship *Maine* in Havana harbor and blamed it on the Spaniards. Shortly afterward, in April 1898, Congress declared Cuba free and independent, and Spain and the United States each declared war on the other.

Commodore Dewey, forewarned by Assistant Secretary of the Navy Roosevelt, had his Asiatic Squadron ready. With four cruisers, two gunboats, and a revenue cutter, he proceeded from the China coast to the Philippines. On 1 May, after midnight, he entered Manila Bay where the next morning his squadron, in the Battle of Manila Bay, destroyed the much inferior Spanish fleet.

Rear Admiral Sampson, Commander North Atlantic Squadron, was blockading Havana. He had four battleships and a fifth, the *Oregon*, en route to the Caribbean from the West Coast, be-

sides three armored cruisers and several smaller vessels. His Spanish opponent, Admiral Cervera, was en route toward Cuba with four armored cruisers and three destroyers, all in a state of extreme neglect.

Sampson's victory in the Battle of Santiago, 3 July, was no less complete than Dewey's, but it was achieved under more complex circumstances. Assuming that Cervera would coal at Puerto Rico, Sampson went there, while Cervera coaled at Curaçao and slipped into Santiago. Schley, sent by Sampson to look for Cervera, lost time before the port of Cienfuegos, where he supposed the Spanish fleet to be. On reaching Santiago, Schley headed back toward Key West for coal. The weather abating, he coaled at sea and returned to Santiago, where he was joined by Sampson with the rest of the North Atlantic Squadron.

Sampson, unable to enter Santiago harbor because of mines, and unable to sweep the mines because of shore batteries, called for U. S. troops to capture the batteries. General Shafter arrived with 16,000 soldiers but headed for the city of Santiago instead of the batteries. Meeting heavy resistance, he called on Sampson to force the harbor entrance with his fleet and come to the aid of the army. When Sampson, exasperated, headed east in the *New York* to consult with Shafter, Cervera debouched from the harbor with his whole fleet and raced westward along the coast.

The U. S. squadron was soon in hot pursuit, though Schley's flagship *Brooklyn* first turned east and had to circle to join the chase. The *New York* also came about and tried to catch up. In the ensuing battle, fought on the run, the entire Spanish fleet was destroyed.

Santiago fell, and U. S. troops, with naval support, landed on Puerto Rico. Spain sued for peace and in the final treaty relinquished all claim to Cuba and ceded to the United States Puerto Rico, Guam, and the Philippines.

The defeat of the Spanish forces marked the emergence of the United States as a major power, but the subsequent controversy over Schley's dilatoriness in blockading Santiago, over his wrong-way turn at Cervera's emergence, and over who in fact, Sampson or Schley, was the victor in the Battle of Santiago, somewhat dimmed the luster of both the naval commanders.

Chapter 18
The Rise of
American Naval Power

The first decade of the twentieth century witnessed major shifts in the world balance of naval power. Japan astonished the Western nations by her defeat of Russia in 1904–5, largely by means of a more effective fleet. Germany launched a major ship-building program designed to challenge Britain for command of the North Sea. The United States, whose naval forces had recently destroyed two Spanish fleets, embarked on a new era of assertiveness in which her modern steel navy played a prominent part. Though America's emergence as a naval power was not as surprising or dramatic as that of Japan or Germany, it was destined to be of more lasting consequence.

The central figure in America's rise to world power was her dynamic young president, Theodore Roosevelt. In an age when erudition was an uncommon attribute for a political figure, Roosevelt was a phenomenon. He was an omnivorous reader, with a keen appetite for history. In 1882, at the age of 24, he published *The Naval War of 1812*, a precocious monument to its author's interests and to his firm grasp of naval first principles. In 1888 he addressed the Naval War College on the subject of the same war. There he met Alfred Thayer Mahan, who was to become his mentor on the subject of naval warfare. In 1890, while a civil service commissioner, he reviewed for the *Atlantic Monthly* Mahan's recently published *The Influence of Sea Power upon History, 1660–1783*, publicly congratulating the author and stating his own conviction that the United States needed "a large navy, composed not merely of cruisers, but containing also a full proportion of powerful battleships able to meet those of any other nation."

In the fall of 1901, an assassin's bullet made Roosevelt, recently elected vice-president, the youngest president in American history. The brash young assistant secretary of the navy of four years before was now chief executive of the United States. Through his own terms of office and that of his handpicked successor, William Howard Taft, such were Roosevelt's prestige and personal force that his concept of correct foreign and naval policy was to a large degree the country's.

Various private industrial interests in the United States had a stake in continued expansion. Shippers and exporters and especially shipbuilders and steel companies not unnaturally favored a large navy. In 1903, these groups joined retired officers and disinterested citizens in founding the Navy League of the United States. As a prosperous organization with a limited and definite aim, it was immediately effective.

Beginning in 1903, the U. S. Navy Department began laying down two capital ships a year. Though there were exceptions in the ensuing decade, this came to be the norm of naval construction. Generally speaking, the building policy of Taft's administration (1909–13) continued the aims of Roosevelt's.

Some idea of the increased emphasis on the Navy can be gained from the following table.

Fiscal year	Total federal expenditures	Naval expenditures	Percent of total
1890	$318,040,711	$22,006,206	6.9
1900	520,860,847	55,953,078	10.7
1901	524,616,925	60,506,978	11.5
1905	567,278,914	117,550,308	20.7
1909	693,743,885	115,546,011	16.7
1914	735,081,431	139,682,186	19.0

Most of the increase in the costs of the naval establishment was due to the increase in the size and complexity of war vessels. In 1903, a first-line battleship cost $5,382,000. The *Delaware* and the *North Dakota* of the 1907 program, with standard displacement of 20,000 tons, cost $8,225,000 each. By the time of World War I, costs had soared (in the United States) to $15–20,000,000. The typical first-line battleship at the turn of the century was less than 400 feet long and displaced 15,000 tons. By 1914 U. S. battleships of 32,000 tons were being built.

An obvious weakness of the U. S. building program was its dominant emphasis on capital ships. The Roosevelt and Taft administrations and their professional advisers were aware of this. Their reasoning was that battleships took up to four years to build, and that smaller craft could be constructed in case of need in a much shorter time. As it turned out, in the sort of war the U. S. Navy was called on to fight in 1917–18, this emphasis in building policy proved to have been especially unfortunate.

The General Board and the Joint Board

During the Spanish–American War, the Naval War Board proved its worth in keeping the North Atlantic Squadron informed and in directing its elements toward unified objectives. When at the end of the war the Board was dissolved, movements got under way to establish something of the sort on a permanent basis in both armed services, and also to set up a coordinating authority to achieve better Army–Navy cooperation. What the proponents had in mind was committees of senior officers, with some overlapping memberships.

In both services the question arose as to whether what was needed was general staffs, with command authority of their own, or general boards, whose duties would be limited to providing expert advice to the civilian authorities. Senior officers in both Army and Navy almost to a man favored the general staff concept. Secretary of War Elihu Root agreed. He sponsored and established an Army General Staff, headed by the army chief of staff, with authority to supervise and coordinate the entire army establishment. Secretary of the Navy Long, distrustful of placing overall executive power in the hands of officers, adamantly opposed the general-staff concept for the Navy. In March 1900 he established the General Board of the Navy, with advisory duty only.

In 1903 the two secretaries set up the Joint Army–Navy Board, with the function of ensuring Army–Navy cooperation. Composed of four officers from the Army's General Staff and four men from the Navy's General Board, it was charged with "conferring upon, discussing and reaching common conclusions regarding all matters calling for cooperation of the two services." Because the army and navy members distrusted each others' motives, the Joint Board did a good deal of wrangling, over such matters as location of bases and who would control what, but it performed a valuable service in preparing and constantly updating war plans. These were known as the "color plans," because each of the nations involved was given a color code name: United States, blue; Japan, orange; Great Britain, red; Germany, black; Mexico, green; and so on.

The members of the Navy's General Board were virtually all disciples of Mahan in that they advocated (1) a large battleship force, which should be kept concentrated in order to constitute a "fleet in being," (2) the possession of overseas bases, especially in the Pacific, as repair facilities and coaling stations, and (3) the construction of a canal across the Central American isthmus in order to facilitate moving the fleet from ocean to ocean. One of the few complaints concerning the General Board, heard most often in Congress, was that in its propaganda efforts to expand the Navy, it tended to mark off powerful American warships as obsolete while listing inferior foreign vessels as serviceable.

Big Stick Diplomacy and the Panama Canal

None of Theodore Roosevelt's public remarks captured the public imagination more than his admonition to "speak softly and carry a big stick." Political cartoonists pictured him striding into action with an enormous club over his shoulder. More often than not, the "stick" was the Navy. The Navy's value in enforcing America's policies abroad is nowhere more clearly illustrated than in the maneuvers leading to the digging of the U. S.–controlled Panama Canal.

The obvious value of a canal across the Central American isthmus had been recognized for at least two hundred years. In the last quarter of the nineteenth century a French corporation headed by Ferdinand de Lesseps, who had directed the digging of the Suez Canal, attempted to construct a sea-level waterway across Panama. Sea-level construction had proved eminently practical in the Suez desert, but in Panama it meant digging through the continental divide. A poor plan and disease caused the project to end in failure and financial collapse.

The United States refused to let the project be shelved. The long voyage of the *Oregon* around South America during the Spanish–American War and the subsequent U. S. acquisition of possessions in the Pacific emphasized to Americans the need for a U. S.–controlled isthmian canal to permit quick transfer of naval forces from one ocean to the other. Secretary of State John Hay paved the way by negotiating with the British a treaty invalidating an 1850 agreement that any such canal must be jointly built and owned and should remain unfortified. Congress rejected the first Hay-Pauncefote Treaty but accepted the second (1901), which gave the United States not only exclusive control of the canal but the right to fortify and defend it.

The U. S. government, assuming from the French failure that the Panama route was not feasible, inclined toward an alternate route, across Nicaragua. This was bad news for the French holding company that had taken over the assets of the bankrupt de Lesseps organization and hoped to sell them to the United States. The holding company's spokesman, a heavy stockholder, was the highly persuasive Monsieur Philippe Bunau-Varilla. He embarked upon a campaign to convince the American public, and their elected representatives, that the Panama route was superior after all. Bunau-Varilla won his point, and Secretary Hay proceeded to negotiate with representatives of Colombia, of which Panama was then a province. The result was a preliminary agreement (the Hay-Herran Treaty) whereby the United States was to secure a six-mile-wide transitway for $10,000,000 and a $250,000 annuity.

The Colombian senate refused to approve the treaty. The French company was to receive $40,000,000 from the United States for its work and equipment. Its concession, however, ran out in October 1904, at which time all its physical assets reverted to Colombia. From the Colombian point of view, the simple exercise of a year's patience promised to be very profitable.

This view was ill grounded, for it neglected the entrepreneurial talents of Bunau-Varilla, who, from his headquarters in the old Waldorf-Astoria Hotel in New York, engineered a revolution in Panama. It also failed to take into account the impatience of President Roosevelt, who was eager to "make the dirt fly."

Revolution in Panama was no novelty. According to Roosevelt's count, there had been 53 in 53 years. But the revolution of 1903 had a synthetic look, for the patriot army of 500 men had cost $200 a head and was supplemented only by a reserve of 441 members of the Panama fire departments. But Bunau-Varilla was fairly confident that American support would sustain his patriotic efforts.

Under the terms of the Treaty of 1846 with New Granada (Colombia), the United States was pledged to maintain "perfect neutrality" and "free transit" on the Isthmus. Ostensibly in support of this pledge, on 2 November 1903, the USS *Nashville* arrived at Colón. On 3 November the standard of revolution was raised ashore, and on 4 November the Republic of Panama was born officially. There was no overland route from Bogotá, and Colombian troops sent by water were politely told they could not land, since America had treaty obligations to uphold, and for them to proceed would obviously create an unneutral disturbance. The guns of the *Nashville* were an eloquent unspoken argument. Presently the *Dixie* arrived with

a force of marines for any necessary policing ashore. On 6 November, the United States recognized the revolutionary government of Panama.

Bunau-Varilla, who never relinquished his French citizenship, now appeared in Washington as agent plenipotentiary for the new Republic of Panama. On 18 November, some 15 days after the revolution, the Hay-Bunau-Varilla Treaty conveyed to the United States a zone ten miles wide in perpetuity for $10,000,000 and a $250,000 annuity. On 23 November the treaty was ratified by the U. S. Senate. Though the revolutionary government of Panama owed its existence to the timely arrival of the *Nashville*, members of that government found fault with the terms of the treaty. For a time it seemed likely that the Panamanians, like the Colombians, would reject the American terms. But hints from Bunau-Varilla (still in Washington) that the United States might withdraw her support in such an event led to a speedy, if reluctant, ratification.

The organizing ability and technical skill of the U. S. Army Corps of Engineers and a decade of labor by an army of workers produced the desired result. The canal was opened in August 1914 as the world was going to war. The U. S. Navy had its priceless transitway between the country's widely separated coasts.

Whether U. S. acquisition of the Canal Zone constituted "international piracy," as some liberal journals claimed, or simply an indirect exercise of a kind of "right of eminent domain," it was not calculated to increase the popularity of the United States in Latin America, particularly in Colombia. In 1921, the United States paid $25,000,000 "conscience money" to Colombia as a belated apology; and in 1978, a new agreement between the United States and Panama established procedures for an ultimate return of sovereignty over the Canal Zone to Panama.

Intervention in Latin America

In 1901 President Roosevelt made a statement that he afterward regretted. "If any South American country misbehaves toward any European country," he said, "let the European country spank it." Taking him at his word, Britain the following year persuaded Germany and Italy to join her in blockading the coast of Venezuela, which had repudiated her international debts. The blockading warships seized several gunboats and sank two, and the Germans bombarded a fort and incidentally destroyed an adjoining village. Thus pressured, Venezuela hastened to accept arbitration of the claims.

The episode caused Roosevelt intense concern. He even considered intervening. The prospect of a Panama canal had given a new importance to the Caribbean. Decay of the eighteenth-century sugar trade had made the sea a cul-de-sac, far removed from the major trade routes, but with the completion of the canal it would become a vital maritime artery in peace and war. Blockade and bombardment of a coast on the canal's approaches must not again be tolerated. The operations might lead to a landing, with a temptation to stay. Such a lodgment would not only violate the Monroe Doctrine; it would also imperil America's new lifeline via the canal.

In 1904 the Dominican Republic after a series of bloody revolutions was heavily in debt and bankrupt. Certain European states, notably Germany, were considering collecting their debts by force. To forestall any such encroachment, Roosevelt proclaimed what has come to be called the "Roosevelt Corollary" to the Monroe Doctrine. It affirmed that the United States might feel obligated ". . . in flagrant cases of . . . wrongdoing or impotence [in Latin America] to the exercise of an international police power." In other words, if any situation appeared to demand intervention to protect lives or enforce treaty rights, the United States and a force of marines would do the intervening.

The United States first applied the Roosevelt Corollary to the situation in the Dominican Republic, taking over the country's customs collection and allocating 55 percent of the receipts to the settlement of her foreign debts. In subsequent years, small-scale U. S. intervention in various revolution-torn countries of the Caribbean area was common. Naval and marine forces were involved in both campaigning and governmental administration in Nicaragua, Haiti, and the Dominican Republic. Usually U. S. military occupation promptly brought law and order. Where the occupation was of long duration, there were normally also spectacular improvements in public-health measures and road building. Administration of civilian government functions by professional military men tended to be fair but paternalistic—often resented more by neighboring countries than by the ones occupied. To the stronger, stable countries of Latin America, this casual exercise of military and naval power by the United States was simply another example of "Yankee imperialism."

Outbreaks of anarchy brought U. S. marines into Cuba in 1906, 1912, and 1917. The authority for these interventions was not the unilateral Roosevelt Corollary but the Platt Amendment, which permitted American armed forces to intervene if needed to preserve order or to maintain Cuban independence. The amendment had the force of a treaty between Cuba and the United States, and through U. S. insistence it had been incorporated into the Cuban constitution. By a provision of the amendment, the United States leased Guantanamo, Cuba for use as a naval base. Failure of Congress to provide funds for additional bases in the area made Guantanamo the hub of America's Caribbean defense. The Platt Amendment was abrogated by treaty in 1934, but the U. S. Navy continued to use the Guantanamo base then, and even after 1961, when diplomatic relations were severed between Cuba and the United States.

In 1914 President Woodrow Wilson's efforts to foster democratic government for the Mexican people and the arrogance of Rear Admiral Henry T. Mayo brought the United States to the verge of war with Mexico. Over the protests of American interests, which had a billion dollars invested in Mexican railways, oil wells, and mines, Wilson refused to recognize the government of Victoriano Huerta, who had established himself as president of Mexico by murdering his predecessor. When rising anarchy under Huerta cut off their dividends, the same interests demanded that Wilson intervene, but the most the American president would do was to station U. S. naval forces off the Mexican coasts, permit the sale of munitions to Huerta's rivals, and call on Huerta to resign.

In this tense situation, Mexican authorities on 9 April 1914 arrested a U. S. naval boat-party loading gasoline at a pier at the port of Tampico. The Americans were quickly released, with an apology, but Rear Admiral Mayo, commanding the U. S. squadron, was not appeased. He sent an ultimatum to the Mexican general at Tampico, directing him within 24 hours to "publicly hoist the American flag in a prominent position ashore and salute it with 21 guns." The general, on orders from Huerta, refused thus to grovel. Wilson, feeling obliged to support his admiral, ordered the commander of the U. S. squadron off Veracruz to seize the customhouse there. He thereby nearly touched off a second Mexican War.

Supported by naval gunfire from the *Prairie*, the *Chester*, and the *San Francisco*, a mixed force of marines and bluejackets on 22 April fought their way into the city, occupying the customhouse, the cable office, and other waterfront buildings. By this time Rear Admiral Charles J. Badger, Commander in Chief of the United States Fleet, had arrived with five battleships. The force ashore was powerfully reinforced, and the occupation of the entire city was accomplished by noon of the 22nd. Presently a U. S. army detachment came to take over the occupation.

Before hostilities could spread, a joint arbitration proposed by Argentina, Brazil, and Chile was accepted, and all-out war was averted. In July Huerta went into voluntary exile, and in November the American warships withdrew from the Mexican coasts.

Problems In the Far East

The U. S. Navy's need for a base in the western Pacific had been sharply demonstrated in the war with Spain. Dewey, forced by British neutrality to leave Hong Kong, was cut off from all prompt logistic support. Had he lost the Battle of Manila Bay, he would have found himself in a predicament, lacking a friendly port where he could refit. The Navy's requirement for a base in the Philippines became an important consideration in the peace negotiations. In the event, the United States took the entire archipelago. As we have seen, the need to protect this new and distant acquisition led to the American annexation of Guam, Hawaii, American Samoa, and Wake, and provided a powerful argument for the building of a U. S.–controlled isthmian canal.

If the annexation of the Philippines posed new problems for the United States, it seemed also to open opportunities for an expanding trade in the Far East, particularly in China, where U. S. merchants fancied they saw an enormous potential market for American goods. But European powers had already secured for themselves a near-monopoly of the China trade. When the Sino–Japanese War demonstrated the impotence of the Chinese government, the powers began to move in—establishing footholds and staking out "spheres of influence" guarded by naval squadrons. Though the technicality of Chinese sovereignty was maintained, it appeared that China was about to be partitioned, in which case the Americans would lose all access to the China market.

To forestall such exclusion, the United States would have either to join the scramble for a sphere of influence of her own, or somehow deter the other powers from dividing China up among themselves. Many naval officers favored the former alternative, arguing for the establishment of an American naval base in the Chusan Islands, or at Samsa Inlet, across the strait from Formosa. But the U. S. government, reluctant to embark on a policy of such obvious imperialism, sought a means to prevent the other powers from consolidating their footholds in China. A solution of sorts was found by Secretary of State Hay, who in 1899 drafted a paper requesting assurances from each power that every part of China would be open to the trade of all friendly nations regardless of spheres of influence, a policy that came to be known as the "Open Door."

Acceptance of the Open Door Policy had the effect, as intended by Hay, of alleviating the threat to China's sovereignty and of lessening distrust among the European powers, each of which had suspected the others of planning to carve out an exclusive protectorate. But Hay's note was not a final solution to the rivalry in China. To protect their interests, the powers routinely kept warships in Chinese waters, and increasingly the Chinese grew to resent their presence.

In 1900, a group of young Chinese patriots called the I Ho T'uan (Righteous and Harmonious Fists), or Boxers, began a campaign to rid their nation of foreigners. The Chinese government at first tried to stop the Boxers for fear that their activities would incite the foreigners to exert more dominance. But as the Boxers waxed in strength, the government began to support them. In the late spring of 1900, the foreign legations in Peking began requesting military and naval support from their home governments. The United States sent the cruiser *Newark* to the Hai ho River, and her commanding officer, Captain B. H. McCalla, led about a hundred bluejackets to join an improvised international army of some 2,000 men under British naval command that tried unsuccessfully to fight its way inland to Peking. The United States, anxious not to become tainted by association with imperialist powers, announced that her troops were acting independently.

A second international army of 18,600 men, including 2,500 American soldiers and marines, on 4 August 1900, succeeded after hard fighting in occupying Peking and raising the siege of the legations. In September 1901 the Chinese government acceded to a joint allied protocol that engaged her to pay an indemnity of $333,000,000 in 39 annuities. The United States later returned most of her share to China to provide scholarships to enable Chinese young men to study in the United States.

The Boxer Rebellion might well have provided the excuse for a final partitioning of China into European dependencies and spheres of influence. American participation in the fighting, however, gave the United States a voice in the councils of the nations concerned. Secretary Hay made this the occasion of a new affirmation of his Open Door Policy, calling on the powers to "safeguard for the world the principle of equal and impartial trade with all ports of the Chinese empire," and this time stating specifically that the United States stood for the territorial integrity of all China.

Russia seized upon the opportunity presented by the Boxer uprising and the occupation of Peking to tighten her grip on Port Arthur, occupy Manchuria, and dominate Korea. The Japanese, who had been ousted from Port Arthur and had their own designs on Korea, prepared for war.

President Roosevelt was initially a great admirer of Japan and her people. He saw the Japanese as efficient and energetic—very much like himself. He rather welcomed the Anglo–Japanese Alliance of 1902 as a makeweight against Russia. When Japan and Russia went to war in 1904, he ardently hoped for a Japanese victory. Since Russia was generally thought to be the stronger of the two, Roosevelt believed that a Japanese victory would help assure a continuation of the balance of power in the Far East that favored the Open Door. Far from deploring the Japanese sneak attack on Port Arthur, Roosevelt applauded it. Secretary of War Root called it "bully."

Japan's dramatic, one-sided victories at Port Arthur and Tsushima electrified the world, but they had drawn so heavily on Japanese manpower and financial resources that they left the victor exhausted. The victories also startled Roosevelt, who began to see Japan as a threat. Directly following the Battle of Tsushima, the Japanese government secretly requested the good offices of Roosevelt to serve as mediator to end the bloody conflict. With some reluctance Roosevelt accepted, seeing an early ending of the hostilities as the best way to retain the balance of power.

The 1905 Treaty of Portsmouth, ending the war, was far from popular in Japan, because the people had expected that Russia, in addition to ceding territory, would be forced to pay an indemnity that would restore Japan's ravaged treasury. Crowds in the streets of Tokyo demonstrated angrily, blaming Roosevelt, and Japanese–American relations began to sour.

In 1906 the Japanese were further irritated by the action of the San Francisco school board in segregating Oriental school children. The arrival of many Japanese laborers in the San Francisco area following the Russo–Japanese War had aroused resentment there, because the willingness of the immigrants to work for low wages presumably jeopardized the living standards of white labor. The

situation was aggravated by the flow into the public school system of Japanese children with little knowledge of English. Attempts to cope with the language problem by putting teen-aged Japanese in easy elementary classes proved disruptive. The board of education thought it had solved the problem by setting aside a public school specifically for the young Orientals.

When news of this school action reached Japan, it triggered an outburst of public indignation. The proud recent victors over the world's most populous white country were outraged at the apparent imputation of racial inferiority. Magnified by yellow journalism in both Japan and the United States, the situation produced a full-blown diplomatic crisis. Roosevelt, with no authority over the internal operations of the state of California, somewhat mollified the Japanese by assailing the San Franciscans in his next annual message. He finally achieved a compromise, in the so-called Gentlemen's Agreement, whereby Japan engaged to restrict emigration to the United States, in return for which the city of San Francisco was persuaded to rescind its objectionable school policy.

Having induced the San Franciscans to back down, Roosevelt wanted by a dramatic gesture to show Japan the power (the "big stick") that lay behind the soft words of American diplomacy. This gesture he made with his order for a round-the-world cruise to be taken by the 16 first-line battleships of the U. S. fleet. On invitation, Yokohama was included as a port of call.

In December 1907 the battle line under the command of Rear Admiral Robley D. Evans steamed south from Hampton Roads, heading for South America and the Straits of Magellan, the first leg of its 46,000-mile, 14-month voyage. In addition to demonstrating to the Japanese and to the rest of the world that the United States had become a formidable sea power, the cruise was counted on to stimulate domestic support for Roosevelt's naval building program, and to test the ability of the battle fleet to steam around a continent, cross an ocean, and arrive in Oriental waters still in fighting trim—a test that Rozhestvenski's Baltic Squadron had signally failed to pass in 1905.

The cruise succeeded in achieving all three goals. The Japanese public, as if to atone for its former bitterness, welcomed the American ships with enthusiasm. In the Antipodes and in Middle Eastern and European ports of call, the fleet was hailed as exciting and tangible evidence not only of the might but of the good will of the United States. Materiel performed well. Coaling at sea was accomplished with a minimum of accidents. The performance of the fleet was a proud dramatization to the American people of their collective might.

There were just two flaws. In Japan, the militarist clique argued that this display of American naval strength only proved that Japan would have to make even greater sacrifices to surpass it. In Britain, just as the U. S. fleet was about to set out on its world cruise, the Royal Navy unveiled its secretly built *Dreadnought*, a battleship with features that made every other battleship in the world obsolete. To knowledgeable navy men everywhere, Roosevelt's vaunted Great White Fleet had become a parade of handsome floating antiques.

The Japanese victory over Russia, demonstrating that Japan was capable of threatening American interests in the Pacific, gave the U. S. Joint Board something to think about besides interservice bickering. At the time of the war scare resulting from Japan's reaction to the San Francisco school segregation order, the Board hastily drew up plans to defend the Philippines from a possible Japanese attack. Thereafter, in U. S. war planning Japan was cast in the role of a potential enemy. Beginning in 1911, the Navy's General Board, the Army's General Staff, and the U. S. Joint Board cooperated in drawing up a series of full-scale "color" war plans, called Orange Plans, for rescuing the Philippines—on the assumption that in any war with Japan, the Philippines would be the enemy's first objective.

U. S. Relations with Britain and Germany

Toward the end of the nineteenth century, England, traditional "enemy" in American Fourth of July orations, had begun to display a new friendliness toward the United States. During the Spanish–American War, Britain alone of the major powers expressed approval of U. S. goals. During the hostilities, she undertook to guard American interests in Spain. She put no bar in the way of American acquisition of two cruisers building in English yards, originally on Brazilian order. She encouraged Canada to permit transfer of U. S. revenue cutters from the Great Lakes to the Atlantic via the St. Lawrence River.

The British concession of exclusive U. S. control of the projected canal in Panama was widely and correctly judged to be evidence that Britain meant to meet the United States more than halfway in any clash of interests. The permanent withdrawal of the British West Indies Squadron from Jamaica (1904–5), though part of a long-term policy of fleet concentration in home waters to overbalance the growing German strength in the North Sea, amounted to an unspoken acknowledgment of American supremacy in the Caribbean. Responsible Britons and Americans were beginning to refer to the chance of any further war between their two countries as an "impossibility." The U. S. Joint Board, as its duties required, drew up a Red Plan for possible war with Britain, but no one took it very seriously.

On the contrary, Germany, last of the major European powers to adopt an avowed imperialist policy, repeatedly aroused American suspicions and hostility. To such an expanding power as Germany, the poorly defended, generally ill-governed countries of South America were a standing invitation, their only safeguard the Monroe Doctrine. German Chancellor Otto von Bismarck slightingly called the Doctrine "a species of arrogance peculiarly American," but he kept hands off. Kaiser William II, less circumspect, in 1902 permitted his fleet to bombard the coast of Venezuela, a major provocation leading to President Roosevelt's proclamation of his Corollary.

In the last quarter of the nineteenth century, Germany's quest for colonies followed her trade into the Pacific, where the United States was beginning to look for potential naval bases. In 1878, the United States signed with the kingdom of the Samoa Islands a treaty offering protection in exchange for the right to establish a naval station in the harbor of Pago Pago. The next year Germany and Great Britain negotiated treaties with Samoa. There followed 20 years of off-and-on wrangling. At last in 1899 Britain withdrew, and Germany and the United States divided the islands between them. Meanwhile Germany in 1884 had caused some alarm in Britain and Australia by annexing the Bismarck Archipelago and northeastern New Guinea. The following year Germany declared a protectorate over the upper Solomon Islands, but in 1899 she ceded all of these territories except Buka and Bougainville to Britain in exchange for recognition of German rights to western Samoa.

Following the 1898 Battle of Manila Bay, Dewey blockaded Manila while awaiting occupation troops from the United States. Several nations sent vessels to the bay to observe and to be on hand if needed to provide services for their nationals ashore. Most of the visiting commanders properly reported to Dewey, who assigned them anchorages. Not so German Vice Admiral von Diederichs, who pointedly ignored Dewey's blockade regulations and even established contacts ashore. He had arrived with a force stronger than Dewey's, with the object of acquiring for Germany some of the Philippine archipelago, by purchase or otherwise, if opportunity offered. Dewey, overtaxed by his daily routine, after enduring several days of Diederichs's contemptuous treatment, lost his temper. "Listen to me," he said to a German officer who had arrived with complaints from Diederichs. "Tell your admiral that the slightest infraction of these orders by himself or his officers will mean but one thing. Make no mistake when I say it will mean war. If you people are ready for a war with the United States, you can have it in five minutes."

Captain Sir Edward Chichester, RN, present with cruisers, had conscientiously observed Dewey's regulations and had maintained cordial relations with the Americans. On the day that Manila fell to U. S. troops ashore, all ships moved shoreward for closer observation. Captain Chichester happened to place his cruisers between Dewey's ships and those of Diederichs. From this chance movement arose the legend that the German fleet was about to attack the American fleet, and that the British had served notice that in event of a showdown the Anglo-Saxons would stand together.

Thus in an atmosphere of some hostility, the Americans set out to surpass the German naval program, determined that the United States, and not Germany, should be the possessor of the "navy second only to Britain's." Germany continued to arouse American suspicions by the arrogant public utterances of her Kaiser, by the brutal efficiency with which she developed her new colonies in Africa and her leasehold at Tsingtao, and by her purchase from Spain of the Carolines, the Marshalls, and the Marianas—all islands lying between the United States and the Philippines.

The Joint Board, in preparing its Black Plan for possible war with Germany, unrealistically assumed that any war between the United States and Germany would be solely a naval war, that it would be fought singlehandedly by the U. S. capital ship fleet against the German capital ship fleet, and that the German navy would be free to maneuver in the Atlantic and the Caribbean. This miscalculation influenced the U. S. building program toward heavy emphasis on battleships, which proved virtually useless in World War I, and neglect of destroyers and other small vessels, which were sorely needed for convoy escort and antisubmarine warfare.

Technological Developments

One reason for the early close-range fighting at sea was that clouds of gun smoke obscured sight and made aiming of guns difficult. With the general adoption of the new smokeless powder at the end of the nineteenth century, fighting at maximum range became practical. The Royal Navy made a serious attempt to bring fire control up to the challenge of the new ranges, but the U. S. Navy was slow to follow the example. In the Battle of Santiago only a little over 3 percent of U. S. shells fired hit the Spanish ships. Lieutenant William S. Sims, USN, while serving in the Far East, observed the superior gunnery of the Royal Navy and became acquainted with Captain Percy Scott, the British gunnery expert, inventor of the "master sight" or director. Scott had devised an elaborate training routine based on a sort of time-and-motion study of a typical gun crew. He showed it was possible, with the improved elevating gear then used, to keep the gun on target throughout the roll of the firing ship.

After studying Scott's methods, Sims returned to the United States afire with enthusiasm for improving the U. S. Navy's gunnery. When his preachments fell on deaf ears, he defied regulations by ignoring the chain of command and writing directly to the president. Roosevelt, far from taking umbrage, gave Sims's report a favorable endorsement, and Rear Admiral Henry C. Taylor, the progressive new chief of the Bureau of Navigation, appointed Sims Inspector of Target Practice, a billet he held from 1902 to 1909. In this post he imposed the new methods on the U. S. Navy. The fact that they worked converted even those officers who were personally resentful of Sims's often imperious manner.

The typical U. S. battleship authorized at the turn of the century (e.g., the New Jersey, the Rhode Island) displaced about 15,000 tons, had a speed of 19 knots, and was armed with four 12-inch, eight 8-inch, and twelve 6-inch guns. American officers were beginning to ask, "Why the mixed calibers?" With smokeless powder and improved gunnery, the optimum range would seem to be the maximum range of the biggest guns, and at that distance the smaller guns would be unable to reach the enemy. Why not eliminate the secondary battery and add more big guns? In 1901 Lieutenant Homer Poundstone, USN, designed such an all-big-gun battleship, but he was ahead of his time—at least in the opinion of the Navy Department, which rejected his design.

At last in 1905 the Department recommended and Congress authorized the laying down of the battleships Michigan and South Carolina, which had an armament of eight 12-inch guns and no secondary battery. The guns were in four two-gun turrets, with the turrets arranged in pairs on the centerline fore and aft, the inner ones elevated so as to fire over the outer. Thus the ships could fire eight guns in broadside, or four guns forward or to the rear. In the next two years the *Delaware* and the *North Dakota* were authorized, armed with ten 12-inch guns, but also provided with anti–torpedo-boat batteries of 5-inch guns.

But it was the Royal Navy that had the first all-big-gun battleship in actual operation. This was the famous *Dreadnought*, sponsored by Britain's First Sea Lord, the brilliant, dynamic Sir John Fisher. Laid down in October 1905 and rushed to completion in utmost secrecy, she was launched in February 1906, an all-time record in battleship construction. She was completed, commissioned, and revealed to the world in late 1907, while the American all-big-gun ships were still on the ways. Hence *dreadnought* became the type-name for all the big-gun battleships that came after her, and the mixed-caliber capital ships, now outmoded, were called predreadnoughts.

At the time of her commissioning, the *Dreadnought*, with ten 12-inch guns mounted in five deck-level turrets, had 2½ times the firepower of any other battleship afloat. The Germans lost no time in building dreadnoughts of their own.

In another respect, too, the *Dreadnought* led the world and was much imitated. The first large warship to be propelled by turbine engines, she outsped all other battleships at 21 knots.

For some time petroleum products had been used to propel smaller craft, either in internal combustion engines, as in submarines, or as a source of heat to produce steam. Winston Churchill, First Lord of the British Admiralty, sponsored the adoption of oil for the Royal Navy's big ships. The initial oil-fueled battleships were Britain's 27,500-ton *Queen Elizabeth* class, the first of which was laid down in 1912. They participated importantly in both world wars.

As compared to coal, oil afforded greater speed (the *Queen Elizabeth*s made 25 knots), greater radius of action, and far greater ease of stowage and handling, including the capability of refueling under way in all but the most tempestuous seas. Other major navies, as usual, followed the British lead. For the United States, with ample domestic petroleum, the shift was an unqualified improvement, but for Britain the change was not without risk, because she had to depend on foreign sources. Understandably the Admiralty lost no time in signing a long-term contract with the Anglo–Persian Oil Company, an enterprise in which the British government subsequently purchased a controlling interest.

Also fostered by the innovative Admiral Fisher were the first battle cruisers—the *Indomitable*, the

Inflexible, and the *Invincible*. They were armed like the *Dreadnought* but carried less armor and hence could make speeds up to 26 knots. Designed as "cruiser-killers," they could outrun battleships and outgun everything else. Germany also began building battle cruisers, but the United States and other principal naval powers preferred to put their appropriations for major naval vessels into the slower but more heavily armored battleship.

The destroyer, designed originally to attack torpedo boats, evolved into the main surface torpedo carrier for operations against large enemy vessels. Five American destroyers of 1907, displacing 800 tons each, were the first turbine ships of the U. S. Navy. Destroyers of the 1911 building program displaced more than 1,000 tons. By this time the tactical use of destroyers as a screen for capital ships had become doctrine in all navies, and the destroyer flotilla was becoming a necessary adjunct to the scouting line. World War I was to demonstrate the destroyer's value in antisubmarine warfare.

The first submarine purchased for the U. S. Navy was the *Holland* (1900), named for her designer and builder, John P. Holland. She was 54 feet long and displaced 74 tons submerged. Her single screw was driven on the surface by a gasoline engine, and she had batteries and an electric motor for underwater propulsion. United States naval authorities were sufficiently impressed at her trials to order five similar, slightly larger vessels from the builder. The English Vickers Company purchased rights to the *Holland* design, and from Vickers the British Admiralty in late 1900 ordered five boats of that type.

In the ensuing decade all navies adopted the submarine. Bigger and bigger submarines were built, so that by 1914 the newer types were of 500 to 800 tons, capable of long voyages at sea. The problem of accurate underwater navigation with a magnetic compass proved insoluble because of the unpredictable and erratic deviation caused by changes in the magnetic field of the electric cables. The perfection of the gyrocompass (1908) at last made relatively sustained submerged cruising possible. The German diesel engine (1909) was promptly and universally adopted for submarine surface propulsion, adding enormously to safety and cruising range.

The submarine had been conceived as a device primarily for attacking armored vessels. Oceangoing types were expected to accompany the fleet. Smaller submarines were for harbor and coast defense—inhibitors of close blockade. The potentiality of the submarine against merchant shipping was largely unrecognized. Certainly it was not appreciated by the Germans, who were slow to adopt the new weapon (1906), and who built relatively few of them before 1914. When World War I began, there was no weapon that could reach a submarine submerged below ramming depth, and no admiralty had been much concerned with finding one.

Of all weapons of war, none is so characteristically American as the airplane. The first successful heavier-than-air flight was made by Wilbur and Orville Wright at Kitty Hawk on Nag's Head, North Carolina in 1903. Military potentialities of aircraft were at once recognized by certain officials of the U. S. Army and Navy. The destructive employment of planes was too remote to be anticipated at this time, but as a means of scouting and fire control at long ranges the invention was considered very promising. In 1910 and early 1911, Eugene Ely made successful takeoffs from a ship and landings on an improvised flight deck, thus demonstrating the feasibility of the aircraft carrier. Glenn H. Curtiss developed and built the first seaplane in 1911. The same year the U. S. Navy purchased two planes from Curtiss and one from the Wright brothers. In 1912, Lieutenant T. G. Ellyson (Naval Aviator Number One) flew a plane from a compressed air catapult mounted on a barge in the Potomac River. Rear Admiral Bradley Fiske, one of the most inventive and progressive officers in the service, proclaimed the practicability of the torpedo plane and designed a workable torpedo release gear.

In 1912 the first naval aviation unit was established in a camp at Annapolis, Maryland. The following year it was transferred to Pensacola, Florida. Here it developed into the Pensacola Naval Air Station, the Navy's academy of the air. That year Lieutenant John H. Towers, future chief of the Bureau of Aeronautics and post–World War II commander in chief Pacific Fleet and Pacific Ocean Areas, made the first scouting flight in fleet exercises. Scouting and spotting flights were made in 1914 during the Veracruz operation.

The adoption by navies of the greatest immediate consequence was radio, because its possibilities, unlike those of the submarine and airplane, were largely foreseen and applied. In providing a permanent link between ships and fleets and shore stations near and far, radio changed the application of naval strategy by promoting greater coordination of scattered elements.

By 1914, the newest ships in the world's navies were beginning to acquire a "modern" look. And indeed some of them were still to have real combat value as much as 30 years later.

Summary

Around the beginning of the twentieth century, Great Britain, which had been unquestioned Mistress of the Seas since Trafalgar, found her seapower eminence challenged by three rising naval powers: Japan, which defeated the fleets of China and Russia; Germany, which launched a shipbuilding program to contest Britain's command of the North Sea; and the United States, which defeated the fleets of Spain. The United States, under the dynamic leadership of President Theodore Roosevelt, embarked on a shipbuilding program to attain a "navy second only to Britain's." To guide the burgeoning U. S. Navy, the secretary of the navy established a General Board of senior naval officers, and with the secretary of war set up a Joint Board of senior officers of both services to ensure Army–Navy cooperation and to draw up war plans.

With the admonition "Speak softly and carry a big stick," Roosevelt announced a tough foreign policy, in which naval power was his usual "big stick"—employed chiefly against or on behalf of the Latin-American countries bordering the Caribbean. It was first applied to separate Panama from Colombia, in order to expedite treaty rights for digging a U. S.–controlled canal through Panama.

To prevent foreign nations from intervening in Latin America (usually to collect defaulted debts), Roosevelt announced that if intervention became necessary, the United States would do the intervening—a policy called the Roosevelt Corollary to the Monroe Doctrine. Applying the Corollary, U. S. naval and marine forces intervened in Nicaragua, Haiti, and the Dominican Republic—to collect debts or to restore order. By authority of the Platt Amendment, incorporated in the Cuban constitution through American insistence, U. S. marines thrice occupied Cuba. The United States came to the verge of war with Mexico when U. S. forces occupied the port of Veracruz in retaliation for Mexican refusal to salute the American flag in apology for the false arrest of a boat party.

United States acquisition of the Philippines was followed by American involvement in Far Eastern affairs. The United States announced the Open Door Policy to prevent partitioning of China by foreign nations, joined the foreign nations in defeating the Boxer Rebellion, and mediated the war between Japan and Russia. The 1905 Portsmouth Treaty, result of the mediation, disappointed the Japanese, who were subsequently outraged by segregation of Oriental children in San Francisco schools. In the diplomatic crisis that resulted, the U. S. Joint Board made preparations—subsequently embodied in the Orange Plans—for defending the Philippines from Japanese attack, and Roosevelt sent the U. S. battleship fleet around the world, partly to impress the Japanese with American military power.

While Great Britain was winning American friendship by supporting the United States in the Spanish–American War, conceding to the United States exclusive control of the Panama Canal, and withdrawing her naval squadron from the Caribbean, Germans were arousing American suspicion and hostility by bombarding the coast of Venezuela, wrangling with the United States over Samoa, ignoring Dewey's blockade regulations in Manila Bay, developing colonies with brutal efficiency, and acquiring most of the Pacific islands between the United States and the Philippines.

The adoption by navies of smokeless powder and improvement in naval gunnery (promoted in the Royal Navy by Percy Scott and in the U. S. Navy by William S. Sims) led logically to all-big-gun battleships, the first afloat being the British *Dreadnought*. The British and the Germans, but not the United States, built battle cruisers, all-big-gun ships that sacrificed armor for speed.

The U. S. Navy was the first to commission a submarine, the *Holland*, and other navies followed suit. All saw the submarine as useful for harbor and coast defense and for attacking armored warships. None foresaw it as the preeminent commerce raider. The airplane, invented by Americans, was assessed as useful in war for scouting and distant fire control. No one anticipated its great destructive power. The possibilities of radio, however, were early perceived and applied.

Chapter 19
World War I: Surface Actions

In the late summer of 1914, Europe was plunged into a war that impoverished Great Britain and France, destroyed Imperial Germany and the Austro-Hungarian Empire, and brought revolution and civil war to Russia. World War I undermined the social, political, and moral order of continental Europe, making possible the rise of Fascism in Italy and Nazism in Germany. Thus World War I set the stage for World War II.

Of crucial importance among the causes of World War I were the elaborate alliance systems that had grown up, each secured by a network of secret treaties, financial arrangements, and military "understandings." In 1914 power appeared to be about equally balanced between the major groupings—the Triple Alliance (Germany, Austria-Hungary, and Italy) and the Triple Entente (France, Russia, and Britain).

The immediate cause for the outbreak of war was the assassination at Sarajevo of the heir apparent to the Austrian throne by a Serbian patriot. The Austrian foreign minister, emboldened by Germany's unqualified support (the so-called blank check), fired off an ultimatum to Serbia demanding compensation and punishment of the guilty. These Serbia could promise. But Austria also demanded the right to police Serbian territory, a demand the Serbs rejected.

Russia, whose foreign office for a generation had been preaching "pan-Slavism" in the Balkans, had a mutual defense pact with Serbia. When Austria and Serbia mobilized, so did Russia. The Germans, whose strategy for a two-front war was to overwhelm the French first in a lightning thrust through neutral Belgium before Russia could fully mobilize (the Schlieffen Plan), felt compelled to move at once. Austria declared war against Serbia on 28 July 1914. Germany declared war against Russia on 1 August, against France on 3 August, and against Belgium on 4 August. The British government, bound by honor and interest to support France and defend Belgium, at midnight on 4 August declared war against Germany.

Opposing Naval Strategies

As we have seen, Germany, in the years preceding the outbreak of World War I, had embarked on an ambitious naval building program. Chancellor Bismarck had declined to build a substantial seagoing navy, lest such an action stimulate a naval race with Britain. After Bismarck's departure from office, William II, the new Kaiser, allowed himself to be persuaded by the dubious logic of Alfred von Tirpitz, secretary of state for the Imperial Navy Department, that a German High Seas Fleet would be more likely to bring about an alliance with Great Britain than to stimulate competition between the two powers. According to Tirpitz, Britain would seek friendship with Germany rather than challenge the powerful fleet Germany would build.

German naval planners, including Tirpitz and Kaiser William, believed in the primacy of the battleship, with other types subordinated to scouting and protecting roles. Concurring with Mahan that *guerre de course* was ineffective against a naval power, they made few preparations for that type of warfare and regarded the submarine as a fleet auxiliary. Hence, at the outset of the war the Germans had fewer than 50 U-boats.

As Bismarck had foreseen, Germany's decision to construct a battle fleet aroused British suspicions. Noting that the new German ships were "short-legged," suitable only for operations in the North Sea, the British rightly concluded that the German naval program was directed at them. Hence, when in 1908 the Germans announced another expansion of their building program, the British responded by doubling their own construction plans for 1909. Still Tirpitz did not give up. In 1911, faced with evidence of increasing Anglo–French rapprochement, he asked for a supplement to the 1908 program. By then the cost of naval arms was creating political problems in London. In 1912, the British sent Viscount Haldane, their war minister, to Berlin to see if some accommodation could be made, but the German price for a naval agreement was too high: a promise of British neutrality in event of a Franco–German war. The consequence was that both sides entered the war with powerful navies. Neither, however, had acquired the established policies, the developed doctrines, or the top-level organizations needed to handle their navies properly.

During the prewar years, the Royal Navy was dominated as never before by one man, Sir John Fisher, the hard-driving First Sea Lord. In 1904 the British elevated the office he held to supremacy over the other sea lords, and Fisher characteristically took full advantage of the change. Although at that time the First Sea Lord had little control over operations, he exercised great authority over administration, planning, and policy. Anxious to modernize the Royal Navy, Fisher instituted reforms that brought controversy as well as improvement. He supported officer education, the scrapping of obsolete warships, and a nucleus-crew system designed to bring reserve ships quickly up to battle efficiency. The two most controversial of his reforms were the redistribution of the fleets and the rebuilding of the Navy around the all-big-gun ships exemplified by the *Dreadnought*.

In the nineteenth century, Britain's worldwide interests had so directed the deployment of her navy that in 1904 she had nine fleets stationed in various locations around the world. The growing threat of German naval power in the North Sea made this dispersion of force dangerous for Britain. Fisher, believing that Dover, Gibraltar, Suez, the Cape of Good Hope, and Singapore were strategic keys locking up the seas of the world, merged the nine fleets into five and based one at each of these key points. The Home Fleet he made by far the most powerful. Two-thirds of Britain's naval strength was in fact concentrated in home waters, a concentration made acceptable in part by the Anglo–Japanese Alliance of 1902, the Anglo–French Entente of 1904, and a growing rapprochement with the United States.

Along with the rest of the world's battleships, those of Britain were rendered obsolete by Fisher's introduction of the *Dreadnought*. Thus, said Fisher's critics, Britain had sacrificed her leading position in the shipbuilding race and encouraged Germany to resume the contest on a more nearly equal basis. Fisher's rebuttal was that the innovation would have come sooner or later; so much the better if Britain led the way.

Sir John was far from popular among many of the tradition-bound admirals of the Royal Navy. In early 1910 their criticism forced him out of office, a retirement made more palatable by the granting of

a barony. His influence continued to pervade the Navy, however, and his successor at the Admiralty, Sir Arthur Wilson, adhered to his policies.

Since 1904, British national strategy had been the responsibility of the Committee of Imperial Defence. From the time that the outbreak of war was foreseen and increasingly regarded as inevitable, the committee debated how Britain could best employ her armed forces against the enemy. All members accepted the blockade of Germany and the protection of shipping as appropriate tasks for the Royal Navy. But Britain had more naval power in certain categories of ships than she needed to carry out these functions. The debate concerned how best to use this excess and how best to employ Britain's efficient and growing army.

One view, which Admirals Fisher and Wilson espoused, looked for its inspiration to Britain's strategy in the Seven Years' War and in the first three Coalitions of the Wars of the French Revolution and Empire. Holders of this view preferred a peripheral strategy and opposed, for British arms at least, the continental strategy of driving straight at the enemy. They argued that Britain should use the mobility conferred by her geographical position and her sea supremacy to strike around the periphery of the enemy's position, probing for weak spots where amphibious attacks could weaken his military strength, draw his forces from the main theaters, and break up his potential alliances. The war in the main continental theaters, they said, should be left to the armies of Belgium, France, and Russia, and any other powers that could be attracted to the Allied cause. These forces Britain would support by subsidy, partly financed by capture of German trade, and by any other means short of actually providing large numbers of troops at the main fronts. The peripheral strategists, in short, called for a return to the main features of Pitt's Plan, the strategy on which the British Empire was founded.

The opposing view, espoused by General Sir Henry Wilson, British Director of Military Operations, saw no alternative to putting a major British army in the main western theater of the continental war. It drew its inspiration from the War of the Fourth Coalition, which had finally defeated Napoleon. A British army, supported by the armies of Spain and Portugal, had driven up from the south, while the army of Russia, combined with those of Austria and Prussia, advanced from the east. Between them, these forces had crushed the Napoleonic empire. The diplomatic and geographical situation in 1914 provided, it was argued, a close counterpart to this decisive combination.

The Kaiser, like Napoleon, was surrounded. He had no choice but to fight a two-front war. Britain's best contribution, said the continental strategists, was to place her main army at once on the Continent.

Prime Minister Herbert Asquith, desiring to have a settled strategic plan, on 23 August 1911 called a special meeting of the Committee of Imperial Defence, to which selected cabinet members and senior officers of the Army and Navy were invited. In the morning General Wilson presented the continental plan, which the Army favored. In the afternoon Admiral Wilson explained peripheral strategy, which the Navy preferred. The sense of the meeting was that the general had advocated the wiser course.

Admiral Wilson was now expected to provide plans for naval support of the Army, specifically for the prompt transportation of a British Expeditionary Force to France. If the admiral developed any such plans, he kept them strictly to himself. Haldane, at the War Office, complained to Asquith, who wrote to an intimate, "The present position, in which everything is locked up in the brain of a single taciturn Admiral is both ridiculous and dangerous."

Evidently Reginald McKenna, the First Lord, was unable or unwilling to prod Admiral Wilson into action. A more resolute First Lord was needed, and Asquith believed he had found him in Winston Churchill, outspoken head of the Home Office. The prime minister simply had McKenna and Churchill exchange jobs.

Churchill came to the Admiralty with the understanding that his immediate tasks were to get rid of Admiral Wilson, organize for the Royal Navy a war staff comparable to the Army's General Staff, and initiate plans for transporting the British Expeditionary Force to France.

For Churchill, ousting Admiral Wilson proved no great problem, but assembling a functional Naval General Staff presented difficulties. British naval officers were not trained for general staff work. They lacked the military education and the breadth of understanding needed to think in grand strategic terms. "There was no moment in the career and training of a naval officer," said Churchill, "when he was obliged to read a single book about naval war, or pass even the most rudimentary examination in naval history." He continued:

"The Silent Service" was not mute because it was absorbed in thought and study, but because it was weighted down by its daily routine and by its ever complicating and diversifying technique. We had competent administrators, brilliant experts of every description, unequalled navigators, good disciplinarians, fine sea-officers, brave and devoted hearts: but at the outset of the conflict we had more captains of ships than captains of war.[1]

The continuing threat of the German naval building program drove Britain ever closer to France. In 1912 the Committee of Imperial Defence concluded that Britain must further concentrate her fleet in home waters. Accordingly, by agreement, the Royal Navy recalled its entire battle fleet to the North Sea, while France transferred all her battleships to the Mediterranean. The British and French governments further agreed that in event of war in which both nations participated, the Royal Navy would protect the northern and western coasts of France. This understanding, however, did not constitute an alliance. Neither did the Anglo–French Entente of 1904, or General Wilson's pledge to provide an expeditionary force to fight on the Allied left flank in western Europe under French strategic direction. There was in fact no political obligation on the part of the British government to come to the aid of France should she be attacked, but many British leaders were of the opinion that Britain was morally bound to help defend France.

Thus when the assassination of Austria's Archduke Ferdinand touched off a chain of events that led to Austrian, Russian, German, and French mobilization, the role Britain would play in the coming war was still uncertain. The French, however, relying on General Wilson's pledge, were shocked and dismayed to learn that the British Expeditionary Force was not on its way. Not until Germany refused to give assurance that it would respect Belgian neutrality did the British cabinet vote for war. At midnight, 4 August 1914, a signal was flashed to all Royal Navy commands: "Commence hostilities against Germany."

Opening Operations

Germany had been shrewdly cultivating her influence with Constantinople for a dozen years, and had high hopes of a successful economic thrust into the underdeveloped but potentially valuable Middle East. The convention of 1907 between Britain and Turkey's ancient enemy Russia made the Turks more willing to strengthen their rapprochement with the Germans, and in due course, they invited Germany to furnish a military mission to train the Turkish army. In response, General Otto Liman von Sanders in December 1914 arrived at Constan-

[1] *The World Crisis* (New York, 1931), 62–3.

tinople to assume the post of inspector general of Turkey's land forces. The following July, Turkey, expecting Britain to remain out of the war, offered Germany a secret alliance, which the Germans eagerly accepted.

As war approached, the British planned to requisition for their own use all ships being built in British shipyards for foreign powers. By far the most valuable, and potentially dangerous, of these were two Turkish battleships, one of which was already completed. The Turkish government reacted with rage and dismay at the news that they were to be denied their new ships. The Germans, shrewdly capitalizing on this situation, offered Turkey as substitutes the battle cruiser *Goeben* and the light cruiser *Breslau*, which had been caught in the Mediterranean and had no hope of reaching Germany. Because of a series of intelligence lapses and command mistakes, the British and French failed to intercept the two German ships as they were making for Constantinople under the command of Rear Admiral William Souchon. On 13 August, three days after their arrival, the Turks announced the "purchase" of the *Goeben* and *Breslau*, but the original crews remained on board, and Souchon remained their commander. In late October Souchon led a Turco–German squadron against the Russian Black Sea ports of Odessa and Novorossysk, laid mines off Sevastopol, and sank a Russian gunboat. These provocative acts resulted in war between Turkey and Russia.

When hostilities in western Europe appeared imminent, the British Home Fleets and the German High Seas Fleet had gone to war stations. The principal combat strength of the British Home Fleets was concentrated in the Grand Fleet, commanded by Admiral Sir John Jellicoe, with a main base at Scapa Flow in the Orkneys and subsidiary bases in the Scottish firths. The Grand Fleet included 20 first-line battleships and 4 battle cruisers. Its principal functions were to prevent the escape of German ships into the Atlantic, to guard the North Sea, and to watch the High Seas Fleet, bringing it to battle and destroying it if a favorable opportunity arose. Cruiser–destroyer patrols operated out of Dover, Harwich, and the Humber to guard the British coast. After the outbreak of war, a Channel fleet, including 17 predreadnought battleships, was organized to assure the safe passage of British troops and supplies to France.

The German High Seas Fleet, commanded by Admiral Friedrich von Ingenohl, included 13 first-line battleships, 3 battle cruisers, and 8 predreadnoughts. It was based in the estuaries of the Weser and Elbe rivers and in Jade Bay. Its assigned functions were to guard the German coast from British attack and to seek opportunities to weaken the British fleet.

The British Home Fleets were first put to the test as the movement of British troops began, chiefly from Southampton to Le Havre. It was a risky business, one that the Germans might well have made an all-out effort to interrupt. But in contrast to the failure in the Mediterranean, this carefully planned operation was executed with flawless precision. The Grand Fleet moved out into the North Sea, ready to pounce upon the High Seas Fleet should it venture from its base. The Channel fleet with the assistance of British and French coastal patrols closed both ends of the English Channel, maintaining ceaseless watch against raids by enemy ships and submarines. The troops meanwhile crossed in independently sailing transports, which shuttled back and forth as fast as loading, unloading, and fuel endurance would permit. Between 9 and 22 August 1914, a British Expeditionary Force of five divisions crossed to France in complete safety and, what is more remarkable, in almost complete secrecy.

The Germans were already initiating the western phase of their modified Schlieffen Plan: to sweep through Belgium, capture Paris in a great wheeling movement, and thus put France out of the war. But in the First Battle of the Marne, fought in early September on Paris's doorstep, a hundred thousand British regulars held the Allied left flank and helped drive a wedge between two separated German armies. The invaders were pressed back to the line of the Aisne River, and Paris was saved.

Allied sea power, which had made possible the presence of the British troops, indirectly provided the thin margin of successful resistance to the German surge. By the end of September a quarter of a million soldiers, virtually all of Britain's professional army, had landed in France. Through the entire war, the "sea bridge" across the Channel was never to be successfully attacked by the German navy.

The location of the British Isles astride the exits from the North Sea made the High Seas Fleet virtually a prisoner of the Grand Fleet, which by simply remaining at anchor as a fleet in being had the effect of blockading the Germans. Obviously the inferior High Seas Fleet was not going to come out and challenge the assembled Grand Fleet. On the other hand, the threat of minefields and submarine and dirigible attack deterred the Grand Fleet from going into Jade Bay to attack the German fleet—as Dewey had gone into Manila Bay 16

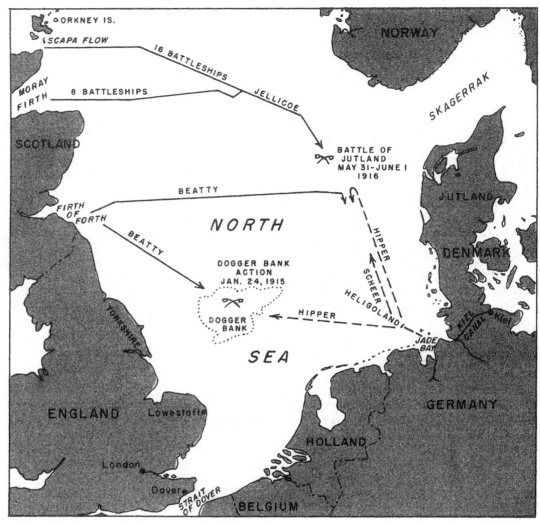

Fleet Operations in the North Sea, 1915–16

years before. The British aim was to lure out the High Seas Fleet, or some part of it, for destruction. The Germans hoped to entrap and destroy successive portions of the Grand Fleet and thus whittle it down to a size they could handle.

The Heligoland Bight Action, 28 August 1914

The first surface action in the North Sea set the pattern of ambush and counter-ambush that characterized later operations in this area. British submarines of Commodore Roger Keyes's command reported German scouting missions in the Heligoland Bight, the triangular body of water off the mouths of the Elbe and Weser rivers. Late each afternoon, German light cruisers escorted destroyers to sea for a night patrol. At dawn the

cruisers met the destroyers 20 miles northwest of Heligoland Island and shepherded them back home. Keyes, seeing in this regularity an opportunity for the British fleet, worked out a plan for taking the enemy by surprise. Using his submarines as bait, and holding strong surface support just over the horizon, he would lure the Germans into the waters west of Heligoland, whereupon the British surface vessels would sweep down from the north and then turn west, cutting out any enemy vessels they encountered. Keyes believed that the British could thus smash the night destroyer patrol and with a little luck get the cruisers as well.

Going in person to London, Keyes submitted his plan to the lords of the Admiralty. The Admiralty accepted the plan and the proposed date of 28 August 1914, but at first limited the surface support to 2 light cruisers and 33 destroyers under Commodore Richard Tyrwhitt. After Keyes had departed, however, the Admiralty decided to send also 6 light cruisers under Commodore William R. Goodenough and 5 battle cruisers under Vice Admiral Sir David Beatty. As a result of incredible bungling at the Admiralty, neither Keyes nor Tyrwhitt, as they headed for Heligoland, was informed of this powerful reinforcement.

The situation was further complicated by the fact that the Germans had got wind of Keyes's scheme and were planning to spring a counter-ambush. Like Keyes and Tyrwhitt, however, they had no information that Goodenough's and Beatty's squadrons were on their way. Near Heligoland the Germans had 19 destroyers and 2 light cruisers. To the east and south they had 4 more light cruisers, and inside Jade Bay, 50 miles away, was the German Battle Cruiser Squadron. Each side was trying to trap the other, and if Tyrwhitt's force had not had the backing whose presence he did not suspect, matters might have turned out ill for him.

Keyes's plan seemed to work to perfection. Three of his submarines, acting as bait, took surface stations west of Heligoland. When the German destroyers came out to investigate, Tyrwhitt's ships swept down and pursued them, whereupon two German light cruisers darted out from behind Heligoland. The British sent one of the cruisers reeling back toward Wilhelmshaven with 50 casualties; then, turning back westward, they encountered a lone German destroyer and quickly reduced her to flaming wreckage. Keyes, now also on a westerly course, was startled to see Goodenough's cruisers approaching through the morning mist and, supposing them to be enemy, radioed for help. Tyrwhitt came dashing up, and a hot battle between friendly forces was averted only by timely mutual recognition.

Admiral Ingenohl had ordered the German battle cruisers to proceed to Heligoland when needed, but he apparently forgot about the tide. Not until early afternoon would the tide be high enough for them to get over the Jade bar. Meanwhile, the five German light cruisers in the area advanced to the attack. Goodenough's force sank one, and before the others could escape, Beatty's battle cruisers came charging down from the northwest and with their 13.5-inch guns shattered two more. The two surviving German light cruisers, badly battered, managed to slip away and fall back on the battle cruisers from Jade Bay, now belatedly hastening to the scene of action. When these at last arrived, all the British ships had departed.

The British had drawn first blood in a surface action, sinking three enemy light cruisers and a destroyer, with more than 700 Germans killed and 400 taken prisoner. The British experienced only slight damage and lost 35 men. Coming at a time when the German armies were rolling across Belgium and northern France, the news of the British victory was a welcome tonic to the Allied peoples. But officers of the British Admiralty were aware that they had served the fleet ill. The last-minute change of plans and the failure to warn the sea commanders almost resulted in British ships sinking other British ships.

The German Admiralty was no less aware that it had mishandled operations. Despite advance warning of the British ambush, German forces powerful enough to destroy the attackers on Germany's doorstep were caught unready, or unable, to put to sea. The Kaiser, shocked at the loss of his ships and men, determined henceforth to take control of fleet movements into his own hands. He advised Ingenohl that no sortie should be made without his personal approval. The Heligoland area was mined. A battleship division was held in readiness, and battle cruisers with steam up were stationed outside of Jade bar, prepared for counter-attack should the British make a second venture.

The confidence the Heligoland victory brought the Royal Navy was soon offset by losses to German submarines. In September 1914, the U-boats sank four British cruisers in the North Sea. The cruisers' 1901 and 1902 hulls and compartmentation were defenseless against the improved and efficient German torpedo. The ships sank quickly with great loss of life. Through the rest of the war, British fleet operations in the North Sea were hampered by somewhat excessive caution—particularly in chase situations, in which the enemy might lead Royal Navy units over minefields or into submarine ambush.

The German Pacific Squadron

In 1898 Germany had acquired a naval base at Tsingtao, China. The following year, as we have seen, she purchased from Spain the Caroline, the Marshall, and most of the Mariana islands. Subsequently she developed a number of her new island colonies as coaling stations. In the summer of 1914, a half dozen German cruisers were operating in the Pacific under the command of Vice Admiral Graf von Spee.

Since Germany, at the end of the Sino–Japanese War, had been instrumental in forcing Japan out of Port Arthur, the Japanese had been resentful of the Germans. To resentment was added alarm when

Germany secured her new Chinese and Pacific bases. Nothing in the Anglo–Japanese Alliance of 1902 required Japan to participate in a European war, but shortly after the outbreak of World War I among the European powers, she invoked the alliance to send an ultimatum to Germany demanding the withdrawal of her warships from China and Japan and the surrender of Tsingtao. Japan's long-range plan in declaring war was to oust the Germans from their possessions in the Pacific area and take them over for herself.

Spee was then at Ponape in the Carolines with his 11,600-ton armored cruisers *Scharnhorst* and *Gneisenau* and his light cruisers *Emden* and *Nürnberg*. At Ponape, 2,700 miles from both the British China Squadron at Hong Kong and the considerable Australian force at Sydney, and almost as far from the Japanese fleet in Japan's Inland Sea, the Germans were for the time being relatively safe. But Spee knew that if he ventured into the western Pacific or remained in the central Pacific, he would eventually be hunted down. So he decided to cruise to the South American west coast. Here friendly Chile would supply him with coal to continue operations. He dismissed commerce warfare as a primary objective for his squadron as a whole, but detached the *Emden* with a collier to proceed westward across the Pacific in order to raid British shipping in the Indian Ocean.

En route to South America by easy stages, Spee picked up the protected cruiser *Leipzig* and the light cruiser *Dresden* at Easter Island. Then, receiving intelligence that British cruisers were already operating off the west coast of South America, he proceeded thither at once. By the end of October, the German squadron was cruising off Chile, with the *Leipzig* breaking radio silence in an effort to deceive the British into supposing that only one German ship was in the area.

In early September, Rear Admiral Sir Christopher Cradock had been appointed commander of a force of British cruisers operating off the coast of Brazil, in an area where two German ships had been raiding merchantmen. On 21 October Cradock left Port Stanley in the Falklands with the 12-knot predreadnought *Canopus*, the armored cruisers *Good Hope* and *Monmouth*, the light cruiser *Glasgow*, and the auxiliary cruiser *Otranto*. Passing into the Pacific via the Straits, he took a northerly course, ordering the slow *Canopus* to join him west of Valparaiso. The fast *Glasgow*, forging on ahead, arrived off Coronel and heard German naval radio signals, which she correctly identified as coming from the *Leipzig*. Spee's ruse was working.

The Battle of Coronel, 1 November 1914

Early on 1 November, a German merchant steamer signaled Spee that the *Glasgow* had anchored off Coronel, to the south. The German commander quickly headed for that area. At the same time, Cradock's main body, hearing strong radio signals, was sweeping north seeking the *Leipzig*. Picking up the *Glasgow*, Cradock did not consider it necessary to wait for the plodding *Canopus* to join.

Shortly after 4 p.m., the two forces came within visual range, and each commander was surprised to find that he was encountering more than one opposing cruiser. The *Scharnhorst* and the *Gneisenau* cleared for action with significant advantages over their main antagonists, the *Good Hope* and the *Monmouth*. Only the two 9.2-inch guns of the *Good Hope* were in a class with the sixteen 8.2-inch guns of the two German armored cruisers. The German crews, who had served together for three years, were famous for their excellent gunnery, the *Scharnhorst* having won the Battle Practice Cup in 1913 and placed second in 1914 to the victorious *Gneisenau*. Of great importance also was the German possession of a director system, not yet introduced into British cruisers.

A little after 6 p.m., Cradock attempted to cross the German T. Failing, he shifted to a southerly course, parallel to and westward of the Germans. Spee, with the setting sun in his eyes, held his fire and kept the range open. But as soon as the sun had gone down, silhouetting the British cruisers in the afterglow, he moved in and opened fire at 11,370

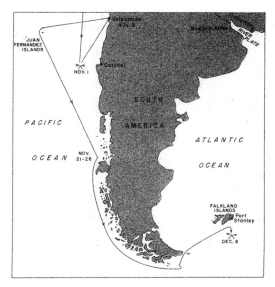

Spee's Operations in South American Waters, 1914

yards. Within five minutes superior German gunnery had obtained decisive hits, destroying the forward turret and conning tower of the *Good Hope*. The strong southeasterly winds drove heavy seas against the port bows of all the warships, thereby interfering more with British than with German gunnery. By 6:50 the *Monmouth* was limping south out of the battle lines, fires raging within her hull; shortly afterward her guns went silent. At 7:26 the two German van cruisers ceased fire. A series of gusty rain squalls so limited their vision that they did not learn the fate of Cradock's flagship *Good Hope*, which, after taking some 30 hits from the *Scharnhorst*, was destroyed by an exploding magazine.

Spee, eager for the kill, directed his force to locate and finish off the British vessels. In the gathering darkness, the *Leipzig* actually charged at high speed right through the *Good Hope* wreckage without realizing it. Toward 9 p.m. the *Nürnberg* chased and destroyed the crippled *Monmouth*. Meanwhile, the *Otranto* and the speedy *Glasgow* had escaped to westward.

Strategically the Germans had gained little. For a short time the nitrate, copper, and tin shipments from Peru and Chile were held up, but the River Plate trade continued in undiminished volume. On the other hand, the Germans had clearly won a tactical victory. Two British cruisers and their crews had been wiped out, whereas Spee's force had received only six inconsequential hits and had two men wounded. The German admiral had used shrewd tactics with superior force, and had taken skillful advantage of position, light, wind, and sea. Yet even in defeat, Cradock had lessened the chances of continued German success, for Spee's squadron had expended 42 percent of its 8.2-inch ammunition in an area where there was no replenishment to be had.

As soon as the British Admiralty heard the grim news of Coronel, battle-cruiser support suddenly was no longer reserved for waters nearer home. Lord Fisher, whom Churchill had brought back as First Sea Lord just two days before the Coronel action, ordered Vice Admiral Sir Doveton Sturdee to proceed with the fast battle cruisers *Invincible* and *Inflexible* at best possible speed to the Falkland Islands, where British intelligence estimated Spee might next appear. Meanwhile, to bolster defenses in the Falklands, the old *Canopus* was lightly grounded in Port Stanley harbor for protection of the anchorage. Sturdee's force arrived on 7 December, joining six British cruisers already there.

Spee had inched his way around the tip of South America, spending three days coaling from a captured Canadian sailing ship. This lost time he could never recover. On the morning of 6 December, he held a conference with his captains, who recommended attacking Port Stanley in order to destroy the radio station, capture the British governor, and seize the coal stored there. The admiral accepted this objective.

The Battle of the Falkland Islands, 8 December 1914

Off the Falklands on the morning of 8 December, Spee ordered the *Gneisenau* and the *Nürnberg* to advance on Port Stanley harbor to reconnoiter and take the radio station under fire. At this time the British were coaling inside the harbor for a sweep south. When the two German cruisers were sighted from the signal tower at 7:50 a.m., Sturdee's force was taken completely by surprise and could not immediately sortie. At 9:20, however, the *Canopus* opened indirect fire, which fell short. Soon afterward the *Gneisenau*, moving toward the harbor entrance, caught sight of the tripod masts of the British battle cruisers and flashed the alarm. As the British piped "action stations," and their engineers hastened to get up full steam, the Germans beat a hasty retreat and gained a head start of 15 miles. The sea was calm, the sky clear, and visibility good—all factors favorable to British engineering and gunnery.

By 12:50 p.m. the British were within range of the rearmost German ship, the *Leipzig*. Spee, realizing that the battle cruisers would quickly exploit their superior 12-inch guns, decided that his situation would be hopeless if he kept his force concentrated. So he elected to sacrifice his main units in order to facilitate the escape of his three smaller cruisers. These dispersed to the south, pursued by the cruisers *Glasgow*, *Cornwall*, and *Kent*.

In a running battle the British battle cruisers held off a thousand yards beyond the extreme range of the enemy guns and methodically battered the two German armored cruisers into helplessness. At 4:17 the *Scharnhorst* listed heavily to starboard, burning furiously, and then plunged to the bottom with her entire crew. By 5:30 the *Gneisenau's* speed had been reduced to five knots. Her captain ordered her sea cocks opened, and she quickly heeled over and sank. Their sacrifice was in vain, for two of the three smaller German cruisers were soon overhauled and destroyed. The British returned to Port Stanley triumphant, having sustained slight battle damage and few casualties. The battle had eliminated the last major German naval surface forces outside the North Sea.

The Dogger Bank Action, 24 January 1915

Meanwhile the game of ambush and counter-ambush continued in the North Sea. In December 1914, German battle cruisers bombarded the Yorkshire coast. The following January, Beatty's battle cruisers, seeking to retaliate, made a fruitless sweep west of Heligoland Bight. As a result of Beatty's sortie and British operations in a shallow area of the North Sea known as Dogger Bank, Admiral Ingenohl on 23 January ordered Vice Admiral Franz von Hipper to sea.

Hipper's force comprised three battle cruisers and an armored cruiser, supported by a half dozen light cruisers and more than a score of destroyers. His orders were to reconnoiter Dogger Bank in the early hours of the 24th in order to intercept and destroy any British scouts in the area. The German plan was thus a simplified version of the British plan that led to the Heligoland Bight action: to bring a superior concentration by surprise against enemy light units.

Unknown to the Germans, however, the British had gained a secret advantage that almost precluded the possibility of their being surprised. The Russians had captured the hulk of a German light cruiser that grounded in the Baltic; and in the shallows alongside, one of their divers recovered a jettisoned code book, waterlogged but still legible, including the German military grid of the North Sea. This priceless find the Russians turned over to the British Admiralty. Because the Germans never radically changed their code, the British navy thereafter usually had advance information of High Seas Fleet operations. Radio direction-finder stations, spaced along the British east coast from Scotland to the Strait of Dover, picked up most German surface and submarine dispatches, pinpointed their origin, and forwarded them to the Admiralty for decoding and possible action. Thus British radio intelligence intercepted and decoded the message to Hipper ordering a sortie.

Fifteen minutes after Hipper cleared Jade Bay in the late afternoon of 23 January, Beatty was leaving the Firth of Forth with five battle cruisers and the usual accompanying light cruisers and destroyers for scouting. Beatty reached the intercepting position slightly ahead of time on the morning of the 14th, on a calm sea with a light breeze from the northeast and good visibility.

A few minutes later, Hipper's force, promptly on schedule, came steaming up from the southeast. The Germans, recognizing the tripod masts of the British battle cruisers, quickly reversed course and sped back toward base, with Hipper's flagship *Seydlitz* leading and the slower armored cruiser *Blücher* in the rear. The British promptly gave chase.

A little before 9 a.m., the *Lion*, Beatty's flagship, leading the British force, opened with a slow and deliberate ranging fire and soon made her first hit, on the *Blücher*. As the swift British battle cruisers closed the range, Beatty signaled: "Engage your opposite number." Since there were five British vessels to four German, the command produced some confusion, and one German ship, the *Moltke*, did not come under fire from any of the British vessels. The *Blücher*, however, slow and exposed at the end of the German line, got more than her share and was soon afire, listing, and dropping out of formation.

The retiring German battle cruisers, meanwhile, all massed fire on the *Lion*, endeavoring to put her out of action. The British flagship, struck by several shells in succession, slowed and listing, was obliged to fall out of line. As she did so, Beatty signaled, "Attack the enemy rear," meaning the rear battle cruiser of the still-operational German force. But Rear Admiral Archibald Moore, in the *New Zealand*, who now took command of the British force, assumed that Beatty meant the *Blücher*, formerly at the German rear but now a flaming hulk off to the northeast. Obeying what he believed to be an unequivocal order, Moore led the entire force to join the British light cruisers in overwhelming the *Blücher* in a tornado of shells. The chance for a major British victory was thereby lost. The old armored cruiser went down after a gallant, hopeless fight, but the rest of Hipper's force made good its escape.

The Dogger Bank action was hailed in the British press as a victory for the Royal Navy, but when the details became known, among senior British naval officers there was general indignation. Commodore Keyes snorted, "The spectacle of Moore and company yapping around the poor, tortured *Blücher*, with beaten ships in sight still to be sunk is one of the most distressing episodes of the war."

Officers expressed the opinion that in this situation Moore should have followed the dictates of common sense, rather than blind, uncritical obedience. Old Lord Fisher thundered, "He ought to have gone on, had he the slightest Nelsonion temperament in him, regardless of signals! Like Nelson at Copenhagen and Cape St. Vincent! In war the first principle is to disobey orders. *Any fool can obey orders!*"

Beatty was distraught. "The disappointment of that day is more than I can bear to think of," he said

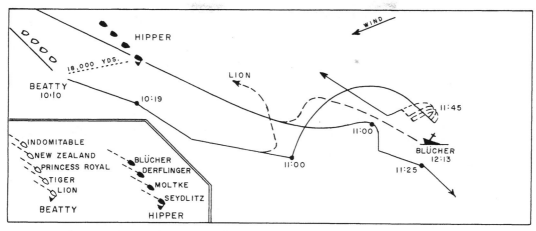

Dogger Bank Action, 24 January 1915

later. "Everybody thinks it was a great success, when in reality it was a terrible failure. I had made up my mind that we were going to get four, the lot, and four we ought to have got."

The Kaiser was no less indignant than Lord Fisher. Admiral Ingenohl had failed to have battle cruisers ready, available for action, at Heligoland Bight. Now he had failed to have battleships ready to support Hipper in the Dogger Bank action. The Kaiser summarily relieved Ingenohl of his command of the High Seas Fleet, replacing him with Admiral Hugo von Pohl, whom he advised to be more cautious than his predecessor. Pohl adhered to the imperial advice with complete fidelity, adopting a policy of absolute fleet inaction.

The Battle of Jutland, 31 May–1 June 1916

Admiral Beatty ached to get another crack at Hipper and his battle cruisers, and Admiral Jellicoe was almost equally anxious to bring the High Seas Fleet into action. But Admiral Pohl's policy of inaction left the British fleet commanders little to do but twiddle their thumbs. The real battle at sea in 1915 was against the German U-boats.

In January 1916, Admiral Pohl retired in poor health and was succeeded as commander in chief of the High Seas Fleet by Vice Admiral Reinhard Scheer, a more aggressive officer. Scheer laid plans to bring down the strength of the Grand Fleet to parity with his own. He would have U-boats mine the vicinity of British bases and patrol off the entrance channels. German surface forces would skillfully bait traps to entice Admiral Jellicoe to divide his fleet and thus provide an opportunity for the Germans to cut off and destroy a portion. Scheer could afford to gamble. With boldness he might gain much from his opponents' mistakes—

perhaps control of the North Sea. On the other hand, defeat could not greatly worsen the strategic situation of the High Seas Fleet.

Britain, on the contrary, had everything to lose from defeat or severe attrition at sea. She was not only the chief transshipment base for Allied war supplies; she was obliged also to import her own foodstuffs and basic war materials. Hence, despite the superiority of the Grand Fleet, Jellicoe felt obliged to avoid risks. Churchill called him "the only man on either side who could lose the war in an afternoon." To dig the High Seas Fleet out of its fortified and mined bases was out of the question. Like Scheer, therefore, Jellicoe resorted to ambush, but with a difference: his objective was to bring on a decisive fleet engagement. To that end he made periodic sweeps of the North Sea.

Jellicoe, believing that with his numerical superiority he could annihilate the enemy in a day gunnery duel, was determined to fight under conditions of his own choosing. At whatever cost to his reputation, the Grand Fleet must come out of an engagement preponderantly superior to the High Seas Fleet. In summarizing his tactical views for the Admiralty, Jellicoe stated:

> The Germans have shown that they rely to a very great extent on submarines, mines, and torpedoes, and there can be no doubt whatever that they will endeavour to make fullest use of these weapons in a fleet action, especially since they possess an actual superiority over us in these particular directions. It therefore becomes necessary to consider our own tactical methods in relation to these forms of attack. . . .
>
> If, for instance, the enemy battle fleet were to turn away from an advancing fleet, I should assume that the intention was to lead us over mines and submarines, and should decline to be so drawn.

Battle of Jutland, 31 May–1 June 1916*

I desire particularly to draw the attention of their Lordships to this point, since it may be deemed a refusal of battle, and, indeed, might possibly result in failure to bring the enemy to action as soon as expected and hoped.

The new offensive strategy of the High Seas Fleet got under way in late April 1916 with a bombardment of Lowestoft by a force of battle cruisers and light cruisers. Jellicoe countered with an attempt to lure the Germans into battle, but to no avail. A month later Scheer prepared to launch a raid on Allied shipping off southern Norway, hoping thereby to attract British fleet units. Here the Skagerrak provided a ready avenue of escape to Kiel should he be cut off from his North Sea bases.

In the early hours of 31 May 1916, the High Seas Fleet began to sortie from Jade Bay to carry out the Norway raid. Leading the way out of the Bay was Hipper's Battle Cruiser Force, five battle cruisers in column, with destroyers screening, and light cruisers and destroyers scouting in an arc out ahead. When Hipper was well out at sea on a northerly course, the German Battle Fleet, under Scheer's direct command, followed in single column—16 dreadnoughts, trailed by 6 predreadnoughts, with light cruisers and destroyers in screening and scouting positions.

Unknown to Hipper and Scheer, the Grand Fleet was already at sea, having sailed the evening before from its bases at Scapa Flow and the Scottish firths. The Royal Navy, informed by radio intelligence and code breaking that a German force was preparing to sortie, had come out to do a little

*I: The Battle Cruiser Action—the Run to the South
II: The Run to the North
III: The Main Fleet Action
  1. Jellicoe's battle line deploys into column.
  2. Jellicoe caps Scheer's "T."
  3. The Crisis. Jellicoe again caps Scheer's "T."
  4. Jellicoe turns away.
IV: The Night Action

trapping of its own. Jellicoe had no inkling, however, that the whole High Seas Fleet had emerged.

In the early afternoon of the 31st, the British Battle Fleet, under Jellicoe's direct command, was some 90 miles off the coast of Norway. Included were 24 dreadnoughts in six columns abreast, with destroyers screening and cruisers and destroyers scouting out ahead. Seventy miles southeast of the Battle Fleet, and much nearer the oncoming Germans, was Beatty's Battle Cruiser Force, with the usual light cruisers and destroyers attending. Attached to Beatty's force was a squadron of four fast dreadnoughts under Rear Admiral Evan-Thomas.

Thus at one time on the North Sea, in four groups, were 151 British and 99 German ships. The Grand Fleet and the High Seas Fleet, unaware of each other's presence, were almost on a collision course.

At 2:20 p.m. one of Beatty's light cruiser scouts signaled "Enemy in sight," whereupon Beatty brought his battle cruisers to course south–southeast and increased speed in an attempt to get between the enemy and his base. Evan-Thomas's four battleships delayed several minutes in changing course, because heavy funnel smoke obscured Beatty's turning signal. At 3:25 Beatty came within sight of the enemy force and with great satisfaction recognized it as Hipper's battle cruisers. He had been waiting nearly a year and a half for this opportunity and was determined that Hipper should not elude him again. Beatty now apparently had everything in his favor: six battle cruisers to Hipper's five, and Evan-Thomas's four dreadnoughts, ten miles to the rear and racing to catch up—not to mention Jellicoe's 24 dreadnoughts, out of sight over the horizon.

Hipper promptly countermarched. Beatty assumed that, as in their previous encounter, he was fleeing back toward Jade Bay. This time, however, Hipper was intent on luring the British battle cruiser force under the guns of Scheer's battleships. Both sides opened fire, and at 3:55, when the converging squadrons had closed to 13,000 yards on parallel courses, shells began to find their targets, thus initiating combat in the opening phase of the Battle of Jutland, a phase called the Battle Cruiser Action, or the Run to the South.[2]

Within a few minutes the opposing flagships, the *Lion* and the *Seydlitz*, each had a turret knocked out by enemy fire. Shortly afterward the *Indefatigable*'s magazines exploded, and she rolled over and sank. Twenty minutes later an explosion shattered the *Queen Mary*, and she disappeared in a pall of smoke. On seeing his second battle cruiser go down, Beatty remarked, "There seems to be something wrong with our bloody ships today." Indeed there was. They were inferior to the German ships in armor, gunnery, and the explosive power of their shells.

By 4:30 Evan-Thomas's battle squadron had nearly caught up and was making hits on the enemy battle cruisers. At the same time British destroyers, forging ahead, were approaching the German line of advance for a torpedo attack. Thus menaced, Hipper turned away to disengage. Almost immediately afterward, the commander of one of Beatty's light cruiser squadrons, scouting ahead, flashed back the electrifying report: "Battleships southeast."

Beatty held his course until he saw a long line of masts and funnels on the southern horizon coming directly toward him; he then signaled his ships to reverse course in succession. Now he had an opportunity to turn the tables and lead the whole High Seas Fleet within range of Jellicoe's guns. Evan-Thomas delayed executing the order until Beatty had passed on the opposite course, then fell in behind him. In this position his ships came under fire both from Hipper's battle cruisers, which had countermarched and taken station in the van of Scheer's battle fleet, and from the battle fleet itself—a bombardment that Evan-Thomas's dreadnoughts returned with interest.

The second phase of the battle had now begun, the Run to the North, with Beatty and Evan-Thomas pursued by the combined forces of Hipper and Scheer. Jellicoe, informed of the situation by radio, raced to meet Beatty. He planned to deploy his 24 battleships in a single column like a wall

across Scheer's line of advance—to prevent the High Seas Fleet from escaping through the Skagerrak and back through the Kiel Canal to base.

For his blocking plan to succeed, Jellicoe had to know how to deploy—which of his six divisions should lead the way into a single column and what course it should take. To make the right decision he needed to be informed of the position and course of the High Seas Fleet. This Beatty was not able to provide with any degree of exactitude. He reported Scheer's bearing from his flagship *Lion*, but he could not state with any certainty what his own position was. Low-lying smoke and mist concealed the horizon, making astronomical fixes impossible, and after 17 hours at sea dead reckoning was not to be depended upon.

At 5:42 one of Jellicoe's scouting cruisers reported the British Battle Cruiser Force dead ahead. Beatty was then heavily engaged with Hipper, trying to force the Germans eastward, away from the path of Jellicoe's oncoming battleships. At 6 p.m. Jellicoe, from his flagship, the *Iron Duke*, could make out Beatty's ships through the mists but could not see Scheer's or Hipper's. Deciding he could wait no longer, he ordered a deployment on the left, on an easterly course. Beatty with his battle cruisers sped ahead to lead the British battleships, and Evan-Thomas fell in behind them. The scout cruisers meanwhile scrambled to get to the disengaged side. Here at "Windy Corner," as this general meeting point came to be called, "there was handling of ships . . . such as had never been dreamt of by seamen before."[3]

Phase three, the Main Fleet Action, was about to begin. As it turned out, Jellicoe could not have achieved a more effective deployment even if he had controlled the movements of both opposing fleets. His long column of battleships, on its easterly course, capped the T on Scheer's column coming up from the southwest. Under the misty conditions of the North Sea, however, Jellicoe was not fully aware of his opportunity and failed to open decisive fire. Scheer, seeing nothing in the mists ahead but gun flashes, at 6:35 began executing a carefully rehearsed "battle turn" to disengage.

In other circumstances, the British battle line might have turned at once in pursuit and brought the battle to a quick end with overwhelming fire.

---

[2]Courses and bearings in the official reports of this battle are all magnetic. Local variation was 13° 15′ W, which would have to be subtracted to obtain true directions. In the heat of battle the recorders simply noted the bearings indicated on magnetic compasses, a safe-enough procedure when the action is some distance from land.

[3]Quoted by Holloway H. Frost, *The Battle of Jutland* (Annapolis, 1936), 305. In 1922, student officers at the U. S. Naval War College, studying Jellicoe's complicated deployment and looking for something simpler, hit upon the easily maneuverable circular formation for daylight operations. The following summer student-officer Commander Chester W. Nimitz introduced the circular formation to the U. S. Fleet.

But Jellicoe, as we have seen, had no intention of letting himself be drawn into a stern chase, the contingency he so greatly feared. He continued on his easterly course for some time and then turned south by divisions in order to block Scheer from his base at Jade Bay.

Scheer, for his part, at 6:55 turned east, probably hoping to escape across the British rear and so get back to base. But Jellicoe had not got as far south as Scheer calculated he would be. The latter's eastward turn carried the German column head-on through smoke and mists once more into the center of the British Battle Fleet, which thus again capped his T. Scheer, concluding that he could neither elude nor penetrate the British fleet, at least by daylight, repeated his turnaway, covering his countermarch with a destroyer attack and with a battle-cruiser sortie to draw the British fire.

At this moment, the crisis of the battle, Jellicoe again declined to follow the enemy. Instead, he turned away by subdivisions to avoid torpedoes fired by Scheer's destroyers. This move again broke off the engagement. An hour later, almost by

chance, the fleets drew together once more. There was an exchange of fire by the vans, but Jellicoe refused to develop the contact because of the approach of nightfall. When darkness came, the fleets were steaming on parallel southerly courses. Jellicoe, planning to renew the action at daybreak, was between Scheer and his base.

The fourth phase, the Night Action, occurred between darkness, 31 May, and dawn, 1 June. Scheer fully grasped the desperation of his position. If he remained blocked from his base through the night, the British would have a whole day to find means of bringing their great preponderance of strength against him. Rather than risk that contingency, he chose the scarcely less hazardous alternative. Even though he was fairly sure that the Grand Fleet lay in his path, he decided to head for home by the shortest route. Shifting his crippled battle cruisers to the rear, he ordered the fleet to turn southeast in succession and hold the course regardless of cost—"*durchhalten.*" Between 10:15 p.m. and 2 a.m., a series of short and deadly encounters at point-blank range flared up as the Ger-

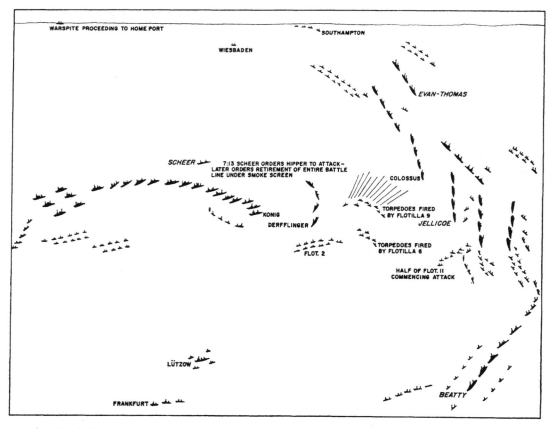

Battle of Jutland: The Crisis, 7:15–7:20

man battleships and cruisers bulldozed their way through British light forces, passing a scant half dozen miles astern of the British Battle Fleet. Scheer succeeded in breaking through the British rear, with the loss only of an old predreadnought and two light cruisers, while sinking an armored cruiser and five destroyers. He had completed his breakthrough before Jellicoe could get a clear picture of the situation in his rear.

At 2:30 Jellicoe, at last realizing that his quarry had escaped, and not daring to venture closer to the German minefields, turned his fleet north. The Battle of Jutland was over. Scheer reached Jade Bay that afternoon.

While the retreat of the High Seas Fleet could not be called a victory, the Germans were elated that they had more than held their own against a superior force. The ratio of fleet strength in the battle had been 8 to 5 in favor of the British. The ratio of losses was about the same, but in favor of the Germans. The British lost 3 battle cruisers, 3 armored cruisers, and 8 destroyers, displacing a total of 111,980 tons. The Germans lost 1 old predreadnought, 1 battle cruiser, 4 light cruisers, and 5 destroyers, amounting to 62,233 tons.

The blunt communiqué released by the British Admiralty after the battle made no attempt to conceal the losses. It was received by the British public and the Royal Navy with bitter disappointment, the more so because both had been schooled in the Nelsonian tradition of annihilation. Jellicoe was widely denounced. To armchair tacticians it appeared that he had repeatedly backed off from opportunities to come to grips with the enemy. When he was elevated to the post of First Sea Lord, the promotion was generally but erroneously interpreted as a classic example of kicking upstairs.

For the moment, the German navy was left with a sense of achievement, but the moral effects of its excellent showing against the world's most powerful fleet were gradually dissipated by continued inactivity in port. For after Jutland, as before, the High Seas Fleet dared not risk battle with the British main body. Save for an occasional timid training sweep and two abortive hit–run attempts on convoys to Norway, it was bottled up in port for the rest of the war. Continued idleness, followed by moves of the German Admiralty to transfer men from the inactive fleet to the very active submarine service, set off mutinies that spread to the German public and to the German soldiers in the field, so that Germany's defenses collapsed almost as much from internal revolt as from outside pressure.

The Battle of Jutland was the culminating surface action of the Age of Steam—as Lepanto was the culmination of the Age of the Galley; and Trafalgar, of the Age of Sail. For the next quarter century naval establishments the world around gave it the most intensive study. Yet, for all its sound and fury, Jutland had few lessons of abiding value to teach. The next great battles at sea would be fought between carrier forces, able to strike an enemy 200 or more miles away, far beyond the reach of a dreadnought's guns.

Chapter 20
The Campaign for Constantinople

When the Anglo–French armies succeeded in stopping the initial German drive short of Paris, members of the British cabinet predicted that the war would be over in 90 days. Field Marshal Lord Horatio Kitchener, Secretary of State for War, scoffed at such rosy forecasts. He declared flatly that the war would continue at least three years and that it would be won by the last power that could put a million trained men on the field of battle. Before the end of 1914, the rest of the cabinet were ready to agree, at least with the proposition that this was not going to be a short war. On the Eastern Front the Germans were employing no more than 20 percent of their available force to thrust back hordes of Russians. The latter were by no means lacking in valor, but they were miserably armed. Their army lacked adequate artillery, and many of their soldiers had no rifles. The United States, extending credit, was beginning to make up the Allied shortfall in munitions, but Russia could not participate in this or any other international trade, because her only two practical routes to the outside world were via the Baltic Sea, which the Germans controlled, and via the Black Sea, which the Turks had blocked by closing the Dardanelles.

The Western Front had reached a deadlock, with the antagonists facing each other in 350 miles of trenches meandering across northern France from the North Sea to Switzerland. Every attempt by either side to break through the opponent's barbed wire and machine-gun defenses resulted in fearful losses; by the end of the year each side had suffered more than a half-million casualties. Outflanking the enemy line by land was out of the question, since one end was anchored on the coast and the other ended at the frontier of a neutral power. Outflanking the Western Front by water, however, was possible, and Britain and Germany, both naval powers, studied means of doing so.

Germany's solution was to raid Britain's oceanic lifelines. At first with surface raiders and then with submarines, Germany attacked the shipping bringing in the supplies and foodstuffs on which Britain's very existence depended. Germany's unrestricted submarine warfare brought Britain to the verge of

defeat, but it eventually drew into the war the United States, which provided those last million trained men that Kitchener predicted would be needed to achieve victory.

Most British plans to outflank the Western Front involved joining hands with Russia in order to arm and make use of Russia's immense reserve of manpower, free shipping blockaded in Russian ports, and release Russia's surplus wheat, much needed in Britain and France. Lord Fisher proposed sending an amphibious fleet into the Baltic to embark Russian infantrymen at Riga and land them on the Baltic beaches of Germany for a 90-mile drive on Berlin. It looked like a quick way of ending the war. But first the British would have to remove the High Seas Fleet from the board—either by blockading it in port with mines and submarines or by luring it out for destruction. Should the High Seas Fleet be lured into battle with the Grand Fleet, few Englishmen doubted in 1914 that the former would be reduced to impotence.

Within the British War Council, sentiment was growing for an attack on Turkey. Already in the Aegean Sea the Allies had a blockading squadron of old predreadnoughts watching the Dardanelles lest the *Goeben* and *Breslau* emerge to raid Britain's Mediterranean lifeline. Supported by this squadron, an invasion of Asian Turkey by Allied forces might bring neutral Italy in on the Allied side and also encourage the wavering Balkan states to attack European Turkey and the ramshackle Austro-Hungarian Empire.

Events in the Middle East brought the issue to a head. At the end of 1914, Turkey, in line with her expansion plans, prepared to invade the Russian Caucasus. The Grand Duke Nicholas, Supreme Commander of the Russian Armies, asked if Britain could manage a diversion against the Turks that would draw Turkish infantry from the Russian border. On receipt of this query, Kitchener gave prompt assurance that Britain would act. Convincing himself that there were no troops to spare, he put the matter to Churchill. Could the Admiralty arrange some sort of naval demonstration at the Dardanelles?

Churchill discussed the problem with Fisher. In the years they had known each other, there had grown between them a warm friendship, a sort of father–son relationship. Churchill valued the older man's encyclopedic knowledge of the Navy and his keen understanding of naval problems. Fisher was fascinated by Churchill's brilliance of mind and power of expression. Thus far, since Fisher reentered the Admiralty, they had made an effective team.

On pondering the Turkish problem, Fisher saw vistas opening up. In a burst of enthusiasm, he dashed off for Churchill one of his flamboyant, handwritten "Dear Winston" letters, filled with underlinings, capital letters, and exclamation points. "I CONSIDER THE ATTACK ON TURKEY HOLDS THE FIELD!" he wrote in capitals, "but ONLY if it's IMMEDIATE!" He proposed that all available Indian troops and 75,000 seasoned British soldiers be drawn from the Western Front and landed on the Asian side of the Dardanelles, while the Greeks attacked the Gallipoli Peninsula, the Bulgarians moved on Constantinople, and the Russians, the Serbians, and the Romanians attacked Austria-Hungary. At the same time the predreadnoughts of the blockading squadron would force the Dardanelles.

It was a breathtaking proposal, but utterly unrealistic. Kitchener had stated categorically that no soldiers could be spared. The participation of Greece, Bulgaria, Serbia, and Romania was exactly what the Allied leaders desired, but these states were unlikely to be drawn in unless the Allies first demonstrated their dependability by winning a victory in the Middle East. All that was left of Fisher's plan was the suggestion of forcing the Dardanelles with the old battleships. On this proposition Churchill now focused his attention.

On 3 January 1915, Churchill sent a telegram to Vice Admiral Sackville H. Carden, commanding the Dardanelles blockading squadron. Did he consider forcing the Dardanelles by ships alone a practicable operation? "Importance of results," said Churchill, "would justify severe loss."

The 58-year-old Carden, who had been ordered to his current command from four peaceful years as superintendent of the Malta dockyard, must have been surprised to receive the query directly from the First Lord and possibly felt it required an affirmative answer. His reply reached the Admiralty on the 5th: "I do not consider Dardanelles can be rushed. They might be forced by extended operations with large number of ships."

Both the War Council and the Admiralty officers were favorably impressed by this opinion

from the officer on the spot. Churchill cabled back to Carden: "Your view is agreed with by high authorities here. Please telegraph in detail what you think could be done by extended operations, what force would be needed, and how you consider it should be used."

Carden's plan, prepared by his staff, arrived in London 11 January. It divided the proposed attack into four steps:

1. Destroy all forts at the Dardanelles entrance.
2. Sweep minefields as far as the Narrows, and reduce forts supporting them.
3. Reduce forts at the Narrows.
4. Sweep mines from the Narrows, eliminate forts and mines above the Narrows, and enter the Sea of Marmara.

To carry out this schedule, Carden professed to need 12 battleships, 3 battle cruisers, 3 light cruisers, 1 flotilla leader, 16 destroyers, 6 submarines, 4 seaplanes, 12 minesweepers, and miscellaneous auxiliaries.

The Naval War Staff discussed the Carden plan with approval. Churchill was gratified when Lord Fisher suggested that, in addition to the dozen old predreadnoughts Carden had requested, they should send out the new dreadnought *Queen Elizabeth*. She was due to go to Gibraltar to have her powerful 15-inch guns tested. Why not send her to the Dardanelles to test them on the Turkish fortifications while standing well out beyond range of the Turkish guns? The suggestion was promptly accepted. The French navy, on being queried, agreed to provide four old battleships for the enterprise.

At a meeting of the War Council on 13 January, with Fisher present, Churchill set forth the Carden plan with all the forcefulness and persuasiveness at his command. The Council was interested. Kitchener thought the plan worth trying, pointing out that the bombardment could be discontinued if it proved ineffective. Without a dissenting vote, the Council directed the Admiralty to draw up plans "for a naval expedition in February to bombard and take the Gallipoli Peninsula with Constantinople as its objective."

The "taking" of the Gallipoli Peninsula would be done by two battalions of marines and by some rifle-bearing bluejackets of the Royal Naval Division—after the ships had wrecked the forts and forced their abandonment—as Du Pont's fleet had done at Port Royal in 1861; or, by getting upstream, had forced their submission by blocking their essential waterborne supply, as Farragut's fleet had done at New Orleans in 1862 and at Mobile Bay in 1864.

Toward the end of January, the planning for the Dardanelles operation was well under way. The necessary ammunition had been assembled, and the additional ships were en route to the Aegean Sea. The Naval Staff's chief concern now was about the qualifications of Admiral Carden, who had never before commanded so much as a cruiser squadron. "I am not aware," said the First Lord, "of anything he has done which is in any way remarkable." To advise Carden, and to stiffen his resolve should it falter, Churchill appointed to his staff two able and experienced officers: Rear Admiral John de Robeck, as second-in-command, and Commodore Roger Keyes, as chief of staff.

At this point Lord Fisher confounded everybody by suddenly announcing his unqualified disapproval of the whole enterprise. His opposition was aroused apparently by a letter from Sir John Jellicoe, complaining that the superiority of the Grand Fleet was insufficient to assure a victory over the High Seas Fleet should it emerge. Fisher agreed and fired off a protest to the First Lord. He opposed the transfer of destroyers and battle cruisers to the Aegean. He was concerned, not about probable loss of predreadnoughts, which were due for early scrapping, but about their crews—trained men needed to man the new British warships coming off the ways. He returned to his early insistence that success at the Dardanelles was contingent upon the cooperation of a formidable army force.

On 27 January, Lord Fisher sent Prime Minister Asquith a note stating that, being in disagreement with the First Lord, he would not attend the War Council meeting scheduled for the next day, and in effect resigning his post. "I am very reluctant to leave the First Lord," he concluded. "I have great personal affection and admiration for him, but I see no possibility of a union of ideas, and unity is essential in war, so I refrain from any desire of remaining as a stumbling block."

The next morning, before the meeting, Churchill persuaded Fisher to join him in putting their differences privately before Asquith. The prime minister heard them out. He then made his decision: "The Dardanelles will go on." The three men proceeded together to the meeting. Here, when Churchill began his report on the preparations for the Dardanelles operation, Fisher protested that he understood the matter would not be raised that day. On being overruled by the prime minister, Fisher rose abruptly from the table and headed for the door, intending to write out his resignation then and there. Kitchener rose also, intercepted the admiral, and drew him into a window alcove,

where he pointed out that, the prime minister having made his decision, it was Fisher's duty to do his utmost to see it carried out. Fisher relented and sat down again.

After the meeting, Churchill invited Fisher to his office and there in a long and friendly discussion won the old man over. Fisher could not bring himself to approve of the forthcoming operation, but Churchill convinced him that it was more likely to fail in his absence than if he remained at his post. Moreover, only by remaining at the Admiralty could Fisher push forward his cherished building program. "When I finally decided to go in," he said later, "I went the whole hog, *totus porcus.*"

The Dardanelles Campaign

The Turks had concentrated their Dardanelles defenses in the 12 miles nearest the Aegean Sea. There were 27 guns in 4 forts at the entrance headlands and 88 guns in 11 forts a dozen miles upstream at the Narrows. Between these two strongpoints, spaced along the steep shores, were smaller-caliber guns.

In November 1914 Admiral Carden's Aegean squadron, on orders from Churchill, had bombarded the entrance forts. This hostile act, the purpose of which was never satisfactorily explained, spurred the Turks into strengthening their defenses. With help and advice from a German naval mission, they extended a minefield at the Narrows and laid a new field off Kephez Point, three miles downstream. They installed additional batteries to protect the mines and arranged searchlights to illuminate nighttime minesweepers. On the high banks between the entrance and Kephez Point, they placed mobile howitzers that could be shifted from spot to spot. The weakness of the Dardanelles defenses, otherwise formidable, was shortage of large-caliber shells for the big guns in the forts. None could be sent from Germany except by clandestine means, because Russia and neutral states lay between Turkey and the Central Powers.

Churchill sent Carden additional firepower, but he failed to provide him with an advanced base in the Aegean. At Tenedos, an island 15 miles south of the Dardanelles mouth, Carden's squadron used an anchorage lacking facilities for even emergency repairs. By arrangement with the Greek government, Churchill planned in due course to set up an amphibious base on Mudros Harbor at the island of Lemnos, 50 miles southwest of the Dardanelles mouth, but in early 1915 there was at Mudros only a fishing village with a small pier to serve a large and windy anchorage. The nearest place suitable for combat loading of ships was Alexandria, 700

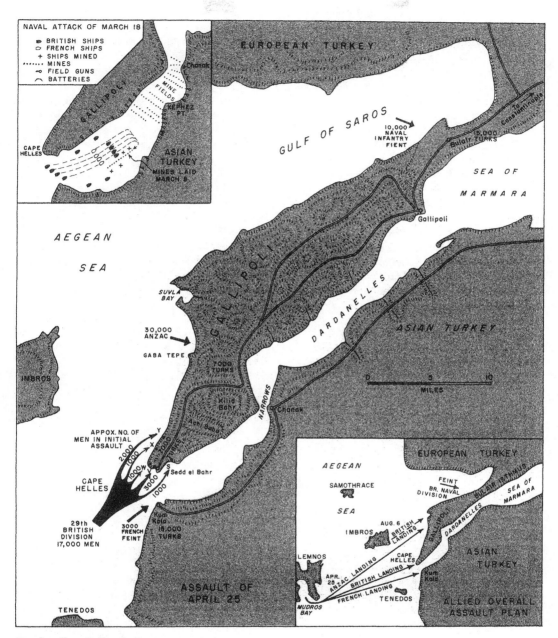

Dardanelles–Gallipoli Campaign, 1915

miles by sea from the Dardanelles. The nearest fleet base was at Malta, even farther away.

The Anglo–French naval attack on the Dardanelles began in the morning of 19 February 1915. From the Tenedos anchorage, Admiral Carden in the battle cruiser *Inflexible* led out five predreadnoughts. On the distant shore to their left as they approached the Dardanelles mouth were two forts flanked by Cape Helles and the nearby village of Sedd el Bahr. Behind these fortifications were the heights of Gallipoli Peninsula, many steep-rising hills sparsely covered with brown scrub and an occasional dwarf pine. To their right, on the Asian shore near the village of Kum Kale, were two additional forts, behind which were more steep hills.

After the winter sun had dispersed morning shadows, Carden's ships, standing off at maximum range, began a slow, deliberate fire against all four forts. The Turks wasted no ammunition on vessels they knew their guns could not reach, but when, toward the end of the day, some of the ships moved in to inspect the damage, two of the forts opened fire and chased them away. Stormy weather and low visibility, usual at this time of the year in the Aegean, postponed resumption of the attack until 25 February. On that day the ships moved in close, taking some damage, and in a daylong bombardment battered the headland forts into abandoned ruins.

During the following week, each day that weather permitted, demolition parties of English bluejackets and marines went ashore on both headlands and blew up Turkish artillery the fleet had not shattered. Covered by ships' guns, the shore parties were at first harassed only by desultory rifle fire from a distance. But the Turks began digging their way forward, in deep trenches that protected them from the naval gunfire. Thus sheltered, they shot and killed 20 men in one landing party. On 4 March the demolitions were completed, and Admiral Carden announced that the objectives of Step 1 had been attained.

The news elated the British War Council and caused panic in Constantinople. In Chicago the price of wheat fell abruptly, on the assumption that Russia would soon be exporting her surplus grain. The Greek government offered three divisions to land on Gallipoli, but Russia, averse to seeing Greeks in Constantinople, which she wanted for herself, opposed accepting the offer and planned to send an army corps of Russians to occupy the city once it surrendered.

Meanwhile, Step 2 was under way: operations to sweep the mines within the strait and to suppress their supporting artillery along the banks. Each clear day warships entered the straits and fired at the shores, but with little effect. The mobile howitzers, concealed in the scrub, provided no point of aim, and they were frequently shifted.

Seaplanes equipped with radio were counted on to spot Turkish guns, but most days the water was too rough or two smooth for the planes to take off. When they did become airborne, they rarely succeeded in climbing beyond the reach of enemy rifle fire. Their chief contribution, as it turned out, was locating the Kephez Point minefield, laid in a series of cross-channel lines beginning seven miles inside the Dardanelles entrance.

The most ineffectual operation of the whole attack, nullifying all the rest, was the minesweeping. It was carried out by unarmed wooden fishing trawlers, jury-rigged for sweeping and manned by civilian fishermen from North Sea ports. The wooden sweepers, standard at that time, had performed well enough in quiet, uncontested waters, but in the four-knot current of the straits they could make little headway, particularly with their sweeps out. More serious, the operators, lacking experience under fire, tended to bolt when exploding shells raised geysers around them.

After an abortive daylight sweep on 26 February, the sweepers were sent out only after dark. However, the defenders turned night into day with their searchlights, which the accompanying warships could not succeed in shooting out. Each night, as soon as the shore guns began firing, the trawlers turned and fled—usually far short of the minefield. Churchill, increasingly impatient at the reports he was getting, telegraphed: "I do not understand why minesweepers should be interfered with by firing which causes no casualties. Two or three hundred casualties would be a moderate price to pay for sweeping up as far as the Narrows."

Carden, growing desperate, put a commissioned officer from the fleet in command of each trawler and stiffened the crews with midshipmen and warrant and petty officers. The effect was dramatic. The trawlers cut deep into the Kephez field. Under heavy fire, they took numerous hits and had much of their gear shot away, but they suffered only nine casualties—five killed and four wounded.

The warships, under orders from Churchill under no circumstances to enter an unswept minefield, did what they could from a distance— firing at the Narrows forts from the edge of the Kephez field or over the Gallipoli hills from the Aegean Sea. The range was too great to achieve decisive results.

A Turkish mine expert, observing that the Allied battleships entering the straits tended to retire along the Asian side, went out in a small steamer after midnight on 8 March and laid 20 mines in a line parallel to the Asian coast. These mines were never sighted, and only three of them were swept, rather by accident than by design.

To Churchill the light casualties implied that there was lack of daring at the scene, a reluctance to take the risks needed to achieve a breakthrough. On 11 March, he telegraphed Carden: "We do not wish to hurry you or urge you beyond your judgment, but we recognize clearly that at a certain period in your operations you will have to press hard for a decision, and we wish to know whether you consider that point has now been reached."

Depressed by Churchill's goading and increasingly conscious that he had assumed a task beyond his capacity, Carden was eating little and sleeping scarcely at all. On the 16th he sent word to Churchill that the climactic effort would begin as soon as weather permitted. Then, at the urging of physicians who feared his nervous collapse, he resigned his command. With Churchill's approval, Admiral de Robeck took over the command and scheduled the all-out effort for 18 March.

De Robeck decided to try what sheer volume could do, using all his battleships. Since the strait was not wide enough for all of them to operate effectively at the same time, he planned to bring them forward by fours to hammer at the Narrows forts, while the older battleships on the flanks engaged the shoreline mobile howitzers and minefield batteries. He gambled that a day of this treatment would sufficiently subdue the forts for the trawlers to sweep a channel through the minefields. The fleet would then advance, destroy the forts with point-blank fire, and proceed to the Sea of Marmara.

De Robeck led off the 18 March attack with his four hardest hitters, the *Queen Elizabeth*, *Agamemnon*, *Lord Nelson*, and *Inflexible*, in line abreast at 14,000 yards from Chanak. Beyond reach of the Narrows guns, they were hit repeatedly by the shoreline artillery but suffered only moderate damage. After the four British ships had pounded the forts for half an hour and visibly made a number of destructive hits, de Robeck signaled the second line, comprising the four French battleships, to move forward. While the British vessels continued to fire, the French ships passed between them and advanced to a line 10,000 yards from the main targets. Here they opened fire, while the British ships behind them continued their own bombardment. For two hours the French vessels, backed by the British support line, fired steadily at the Narrows forts. Turkish shells, from ahead and from the adjacent shores, battered their topsides and holed one French hull below the waterline.

When the fire from the Turkish forts had considerably abated, de Robeck, according to plan, recalled the French ships and moved up four British replacements that had been waiting in the rear. As the French vessels wheeled right into column on a prearranged retirement course along the Asian shore, they ran down the line of unswept mines laid on 8 March. One battleship, the *Bouvet*, struck a mine and sank like a stone, taking down more than 600 of her ship's company.

Most of the officers and ratings who had lately stiffened the resolution of the sweepers' crews had now returned to their places in the fleet. That proved unfortunate. As the wooden craft advanced, Turkish guns on either shore took them under fire. It was no more than the naval personnel had been enduring all day, but it was too much for the civilian fishermen. Despite the efforts of accompanying picket boats to force them forward, the trawlers turned and fled at their best speed out of the strait.

De Robeck, seeing the trawlers depart, knew the attack was over. There would be no prompt breakthrough. He ordered the forward line to retire. Almost immediately afterward the *Inflexible*, nearest the Asian shore in the support line, struck a mine close to the position where the *Bouvet* had gone down. Listing to starboard and down by the bow, she headed out of the strait. The retiring forward line now reached the row of unswept mines. The old battleship *Irresistible* struck one and began to drift toward the Asian shore under heavy fire from the mobile guns. A destroyer approached the stricken vessel and managed to take off most of her crew. While the rest of the fleet retired, the battleship *Ocean*, ordered to take the stricken *Irresistible* in tow, struck another of the 8th of March mines. Both battleships sank during the night.

Surprised and relieved, the Turks and Germans defending the Narrows watched the Allies retire. With many of the Turkish guns dismounted or destroyed and most of their ammunition expended, the defenders knew that if the battleships had penetrated the minefields, they could easily have fought their way through the Narrows. It had been a near thing, and in their opinion the Allies were certain to repeat the attack without delay. They passed the word to Constantinople, and the government made final preparations to abandon the capital and also remove gold, art treasures, and other valuables.

In the Aegean and at London likewise there was every expectation that the attack would soon be renewed. The *Inflexible* and two damaged French battleships departed for repairs at Malta. Churchill assured de Robeck that the lost warships would be promptly replaced. The admiral sent the fishermen home and ordered destroyers rigged for minesweeping. He notified the Admiralty that he "hoped to be in a position to commence operations in three or four days."

But a new element had entered the operational plan. Even before the attack on the outer Dardanelles forts, Lord Kitchener decided that it would be useful to have army forces at the scene. Because the Turks were unlikely to launch an attack on the Suez Canal while Constantinople was threatened. he ordered the Australian and New Zealand Army Corps (Anzac) in Egypt transferred to Lemnos. He planned also to transfer the crack 29th Division, then in England, but temporary concern about the situation on the two main fronts caused him to delay sending the 29th Division until 16 March. He also arranged for the Admiralty to provide the Royal Naval Division of infantry and for the French to contribute a division from Africa.

Thus by the third week in March, 81,000 infantry-men and artillerists were at Lemnos or on the way thither.

On 22 March, Admiral de Robeck, expecting to make a second all-naval attack on the Narrows with-in a few days, went in the *Queen Elizabeth* to Lemnos to confer with, among others, Major General Sir William Birdwood, who commanded the Anzacs, and General Sir Ian Hamilton, who had arrived on the 17th to assume overall command of Allied army forces in the Aegean. Accounts differ as to who said what at that meeting, but the important result was that Admiral de Robeck came away with a complete change of mind. He had become con-vinced that the Navy should not resume the cam-paign against the Dardanelles except in conjunc-tion with army operations ashore. He so notified a dumfounded Churchill. Lord Fisher and officers of the Naval General Staff accepted de Robeck's view, and Churchill sorrowfully announced it to the War Council. Lord Kitchener thereupon assumed re-sponsibility for the campaign.

The Gallipoli Campaign

From the day Kitchener appointed him to the Ae-gean command, General Hamilton had been study-ing Gallipoli—at first by means of maps; then, after his arrival at Lemnos, through discussion and per-sonal observation. Because forts on the plateau of Kilid Bahr dominated the approach to the Narrows via the Dardanelles, he recognized that Kilid Bahr had to be the principal objective of his invading army.

Studying the Gallipoli coast from the bridge of a cruiser, he mentally assigned the capture of Kilid Bahr to his only experienced troops, the 29th Divi-sion. They would land at Cape Helles, he decided, for here on relatively flat ground the landing parties could be closely supported by naval gunfire. Moreover, the area was familiar, having been re-cently reconnoitered by Carden's demolition par-ties. The beaches were so narrow, however, that the invasion would have to be carried out over several of them at the same time in order to get an adequate force ashore fast enough to meet any gathering opposition. Clearly visible five miles be-hind Cape Helles was the ridge of Achi Baba. Ships' guns could support the invaders thus far. Allied artillery placed on Achi Baba could support a fur-ther drive on Kilid Bahr. Hamilton counted on having his troops on Kilid Bahr within 48 hours of their landing.

The general's next problem was that of how to isolate the Turkish defenders of Cape Helles from supply and reinforcement. To that end, he was tempted to schedule a landing at the opposite end of Gallipoli on the Bulair Isthmus, the obvious route for overland supplies from Constantinople. But the approaches here were so shallow that trans-ports would have to anchor far out, necessitating a long and vulnerable ship-to-shore movement. Moreover, studying the Bulair coast with powerful field glasses, he found it heavily defended, with an elaborate system of trenches and gun positions.

Moving in his cruiser down the coast, Hamilton looked for a good landing beach near the narrow waist of Gallipoli proper. He spotted one a little north of the promontory of Gaba Tepe. Here a clear, sloping shore provided a gateway to the high backbone of the peninsula. Artillery placed on these heights, backed by naval gunfire, could inter-cept supplies or reinforcements passing through the Dardanelles or along the north–south road, which at this point ran along the Dardanelles shore. A landing at the waist, together with feints at Bulair and Kum Kale, could immobilize all Turks outside southern Gallipoli long enough for the 29th Divi-sion to capture Kilid Bahr. Hamilton's overall plan thus was settled, with only the details to be worked out.

General Hamilton was shocked to learn that the transports bringing the 29th Division from En-gland had not been combat-loaded. Guns and their ammunition, for example, were in separate ships, and machine guns were stowed inaccessibly under everything else. Because reloading would be im-possible at Mudros, with its few boats, single pier, and feeble shore establishment, Hamilton had the entire convoy diverted to Alexandria and pro-ceeded there himself.

In Egypt the soldiers encamped, while supply officers directed stevedores and sailors in the labo-rious task of unloading, rearranging, and reloading, so that items used together would be stowed together, and so located as to permit debarkation in predetermined order as needed. General Hamil-ton, between inspections, conferred with Lieu-tenant General Sir Aylmer Hunter-Weston, com-manding officer of the 29th Division, or joined his own staff in completing plans for the forthcoming campaign. On 10 April, Hamilton was back in Mud-ros Harbor, on board the *Queen Elizabeth*, pre-senting his plan to Admiral de Robeck and his staff. Two days later de Robeck issued his *Orders for the Combined Operation*.

As the reloaded transports came straggling into Mudros Harbor from Egypt, the naval officers made contact with the army units they were to work with and carried out landing rehearsals, put-ting the troops through a strenuous course in rapid and silent debarkation and handling of boats in ship-to-shore movement. All invasions were scheduled for the morning of 25 April.

Following the aborted Allied naval attack of 18 March, a desperate Turkish government had offered the Gallipoli command to General Otto Liman von Sanders, head of the German military mission in Turkey. Liman accepted the command with the proviso that every available gun be transferred to the peninsula and that a division of infantry be added to the five already there.

Liman von Sanders made good use of the month of grace bestowed by Kitchener's delay in sending the 29th Division and by the War Office's failure to make sure it was shipped out in combat-ready units. He put his soldiers through a stiff training regimen, including forced marches. Behind all likely landing beaches he had his Turks dig interconnected trench systems, which they protected with machine-gun posts and miles of barbed wire.

In deploying his troops, however, Liman misestimated where the Allies intended to land. On the assumption that the invaders would try to cut his land communications with Constantinople, he placed two divisions (15,000 men) in the Bulair area and established his own headquarters at the nearby town of Gallipoli. He placed two more divisions near Kum Kale on the Asian headland, and only one division in southern Gallipoli, where Hamilton intended to make his main landing. His sixth division Liman held in reserve, to be shifted rapidly to any danger spot on either side of the Dardanelles. By a fateful coincidence, this reserve division was encamped in the narrow waist of the peninsula, less than four miles from the beach where the Anzacs were scheduled to invade. Its commanding officer was the redoubtable Mustafa Kemal, who eight years later would found the Turkish Republic and become its first president.

In the evening of 24 April, more than 200 Allied ships were moving through the Aegean toward their targets, these vessels carrying 10,000 naval infantry for the feint at Bulair, 3,000 French soldiers for a diversionary landing at Kum Kale, 30,000 Anzacs for the invasion near Gaba Tepe, and 17,000 Englishmen, mostly of the 29th Division, for the landings at Cape Helles. As in past British amphibious operations, there was no unified army–navy command, but to assure close cooperation between the services General Hamilton and his staff were embarked in Admiral de Robeck's flagship, the *Queen Elizabeth*.

General Birdwood, hoping to achieve surprise, landed the spearhead of his Anzac force before dawn. Confused in the darkness, the men rowed ashore a mile north of the assigned area. Here they found not the easy slope Hamilton had seen from

his cruiser, but a steep hill, which they had to climb in the face of intermittent rifle and machine-gun fire. Fortunately for the Anzacs, the nearby coast defenders, few in number, soon ceased fire and melted into the interior. Dawn revealed to the invaders nightmarish terrain, far too broken for organizing battalions as they came ashore. Detachments climbed the coastal ridge, only to find beyond it a ravine and more sharp ridges.

General Hamilton and Admiral de Robeck, on board the *Queen Elizabeth*, remained off the Anzac beachhead until they were satisfied that the landing there was a success. They then went steaming southward to inspect the Helles beaches. In the Helles area it had been deemed unwise to attempt night landings because of the strong currents. At dawn Hamilton and de Robeck had heard the distant thunder of the naval bombardment, followed by silence as the landing forces headed for the beaches.

General Hamilton had delegated the tactical control of the Cape Helles assault to General Hunter-Weston, who was to land his principal assault force of some 3,000 troops on a 300-yard-wide stretch of beach designated Beach V, just east of Sedd el Bahr. At the same time a total of five battalions (5,000 troops) would go ashore on Beaches S, W, X, and Y, which flanked Beach V. To forestall independent action, Hunter-Weston had ordered each flank battalion to wait at its own beach until the main body from Beach V moved up Gallipoli. They were then to join the advancing 3,000. He had expected to capture the ridge of Achi Baba the first day and the plateau of Kilid Bahr the second.

Toward 6 a.m. the southbound *Queen Elizabeth* approached Beach Y, actually a mere landing area at the foot of a path leading up a cliff. Hamilton was surprised to see British troops idling on the cliff with no sign of any enemy. Clearly the main body had not arrived so far, and thus the Helles invasion was behind schedule. The general's chief of staff urged him to order the Naval Division down from its diversionary operation off Bulair and land them here at this peaceful beach for a dash to the heights of Achi Baba, less than three miles away. Hamilton refused. It was far too early, he said, to commit his strategic reserve.

From the *Queen Elizabeth*, the general observed the operations on Beaches X and W with satisfaction. The landing at W had been costly, to judge from the many bullet-riddled landing boats and the bodies along the shorelines, but troops from both beaches were now well inland, engaging the enemy. When, however, the *Elizabeth* rounded Cape Helles, and Hamilton turned his binoculars on Beach V, the site of the main landing, he was appalled.

Beach V was a cove rimmed with a narrow strip of sand, from which the ground sloped upward, forming a sort of amphitheater with Turkish trenches at the top and the battered fort of Sedd el Bahr on its eastward flank. Just off the beach, toward shore, was the collier *River Clyde*, which had hastily been converted into an infantry landing ship. Turks were firing rifles and machine guns from the trenches and the rubble of the fort. Englishmen were firing back at them from sandbag-protected machine guns on the bow of the collier. The only living British troops on the beach were huddled where they had taken shelter, behind a low bank near the water's edge.

The rest was a scene of horror. The piled-up British dead lay along the beach and on several lighters, now adrift, which had earlier served as parts of a floating gangway from the collier. A few brave invaders had made it part way up the slope in the face of massed enemy fire. Their bodies lay where they fell, testimony to their courage and hardihood. The water near the shore was reddened.

Concealed on board the *Clyde* were follow-up troops, possibly as many as a thousand. More hundreds were in boats some distance from the shore. Apparently nobody was willing to transmit a new landing signal that would send these men to certain destruction.

Commodore Keyes suggested having them towed around to Beach Y. From there they could open up Beach V by attacking the defenders from the rear. Hamilton concurred, but he was reluctant to interfere with the tactical commander's conduct of operations. Finally he passed the suggestion by radio to Hunter-Weston, who was off Beach W, but put it rather oversubtly in the form of a question: "Would you like to get some men ashore on Y Beach? If so, there are trawlers available." To which, after some delay, Hunter-Weston radioed back his opinion that any change in the present arrangements would retard the landing. Hamilton said no more. By this time he had the bad news that Mustafa Kemal's reserves, though heavily outnumbered, had blocked the Anzacs advance from Gaba Tepe.

At Helles, when dusk concealed them from the Turkish snipers, the boated infantrymen at last broke through to Beach V. The *Clyde* survivors landed under cover of darkness and joined them in a thin perimeter. Here weary men stood to arms all night, firing sporadically at Turks who clung to rubble in the ruined fort.

Farther north, the Turks at last discovered the two British battalions at Beach Y and harassed them through the night. The next morning the British at this beach withdrew by boat without orders, but the battalions at the other beaches held fast. Before noon on the 26th, the beachhead at V was handling supplies. By nightfall the British had a secure line from Beach X across to Beach S.

On the 27th the French division, including the regiment that had made a diversionary landing at Kum Kale, took over the right wing of the British line. But the 29th Division, virtually without sleep for three nights and burdened by the necessity of manhandling supplies up from the waterfront, could not move. When at last Hunter-Weston's command pressed forward on 28 April, it was too late. Fresh Turkish units, rushed in from Bulair and Kum Kale, quickly halted the Allied advance.

Stalemate and Evacuation

The Allies never got to Kilid Bahr. They never got to Achi Baba. In Gallipoli a deadlock quickly developed as immobile as that on the Western Front.

Turkish guns, moved away from the strait into strong redoubts at Helles, held their own against naval ordnance and stopped each British charge by firing into the flanks of the advancing infantry. At the Anzac beachhead, continual harassing fire kept the Australians and the New Zealanders from assembling an assault force. Allied naval gunners improved with practice, but they never learned to deliver on call the pinpoint fire required to support an infantry breakthrough. When some ship registered her guns on an enemy trench, the Turks, under cover of darkness, simply dug forward so close to British lines that the naval shells struck friend as well as foe. Whenever the Turks left their trenches, a combination of fire from small arms and naval guns always stopped them. Throughout the long stalemate, trench systems expanded, logistic demands increased in geometric progression, and casualties mounted.

On 6 August General Hamilton, by then commanding 120,000 men, set ashore two green divisions at Suvla Bay on the Anzac left. The new invaders were to coordinate with the Anzacs in a move to cut across Gallipoli. The effort was neutralized by knife-sharp ridges, dead-end ravines, disjointed effort, and most of all by poor leadership. A mixed battalion of English and Gurkhas after heroic effort reached the heights and at last looked down upon the Dardanelles, only to be struck by a salvo of high-explosive shells, possibly from the fleet. Nevertheless they held on until Liman von Sanders sent in Mustafa Kemal to command their opponents. The Turkish general, three days and nights without sleep, drove his exhausted men harder than the British were driven. Under Mustafa's leadership the Turks thrust the invaders off the key ridges and back into an entrenched beachhead line that neither antagonist was able to break.

The only independent naval contribution to the campaign during the stalemate was made by Allied submarines. From late April through December a heroic handful of British and French submariners proved that determined men can make the "impossible" look easy. In small submarines they repeatedly penetrated the Dardanelles to patrol the Sea of Marmara. When the Turks submerged a steel net across the Narrows, the submariners broke through by ramming into the barrier and surging ahead or astern until something gave way. In the Marmara one- or two-boat patrols harassed Turkish shipping for seven months. They destroyed supply vessels, sank two ships moored at Constantinople, shot up trains, and briefly raided ashore. Liman was obliged to bring in most supplies and all reinforcements via Bulair Isthmus—the troops coming on foot and the supplies by camel and ox cart.

By November it had become obvious that Allied forces would not move from Gallipoli to Constantinople. Nearly half a million soldiers, British and French, had been employed in the attempt. Nearly a quarter of a million were casualties, but the Allies were no nearer Constantinople than they had been in April. The Turks had used about the same number of men and suffered similar casualties, but they still held Kilid Bahr, the key to the Dardanelles and to Constantinople. Reluctantly Kitchener ordered Gallipoli evacuated.

The Anzac troops were particularly ingenious in devising tricks to simulate the usual pattern of rifle and artillery fire, even after their trenches were empty. In the course of five nights, units withdrew on a carefully worked-out timetable, and during four days men still ashore skillfully counterfeited the normal appearance of a crowded beachhead. British sharpshooting had set the stage for this piece of illusion. So wary had the Turks become of snipers that they dared not risk the daylight reconnaissance and observation that would have unmasked the British deception.

When the Turks at Anzac found the British beachhead empty, they marched down to reinforce their troops at Helles. Nevertheless, the Allies in this area also successfully withdrew, pulling out all infantry and artillery in little over a week, despite one heavy Turkish attack. The success of this evacuation, like that at Anzac, was due partly to Turkish respect for Allied small-arms fire. It was facilitated also by the fact that the Turks had no real desire to hinder the Allied departure. But mainly it was the result of meticulous planning, rigid discipline, and strict adherence to a realistic timetable. The Allied withdrawal from Gallipoli is rightly considered one of the most remarkable amphibious evacuations in the history of warfare.

The Aftermath

The Gallipoli fiasco was a great spoiler of reputations. Few of the highly placed officials who made the decisions for the campaign entirely escaped its stigma. Lord Fisher ended his career in May 1915 by resigning in protest against sending more ships to the Aegean. Soon thereafter Churchill was forced out of the Admiralty with a tarnished reputation that he did not fully retrieve until World War II. Hamilton was never again entrusted with a field command. Kitchener, his prestige undermined, ceased to dominate the War Council. The further decline of his prestige, and doubtless his expulsion from office, were averted only by his untimely death when the cruiser conveying him to an official visit to Russia, struck a mine and went down off the Orkneys. Asquith outlasted the others in office, but he never expunged the blot on his name left by his participation in the Dardanelles decision. At the end of 1916, he was succeeded as prime minister by David Lloyd George, who had previously succeeded Kitchener as secretary of state for war.

Yet the campaign for Constantinople, viewed in retrospect, was one of the soundest strategic concepts of World War I. Had it succeeded, as it nearly did, Russia with her massive manpower might have been provided with the munitions to drive into Germany from the East as her allies struck from the West. The two drives, between them, could have crushed the Central Powers—just as a similar dual drive crushed Hitler's empire in 1945.

Had the Allies in February 1915 applied, under decisive leadership, all the force they had committed by mid-August, they could hardly have failed to conquer Constantinople and open the Black Sea route to Russia. The enterprise ended in failure as a result of mismanagement, hesitation, delay, use of inadequate minesweepers, inability of ships to suppress shore artillery and knock out shore defenses, failure to commit reserves when opportunity offered, underestimation of the Turks' fighting skill and prowess, and sheer hard luck.

Though the Allied Gallipoli campaign, the greatest amphibious assault in history up to its time, had proved a fiasco, it provided a textbook full of lessons on which the successful amphibious assaults of World War II were largely based.

Chapter 21
The War Against Shipping

Throughout World War I, the conflict at sea was waged primarily for the protection, interdiction, or destruction of shipping—military and mercantile. Britain, following her traditional maritime strategy, promptly imposed a distant blockade on Germany, expecting that a nation so highly industrialized would be devastated by a sudden denial of foodstuffs and vital materials. But Germany, through judicious stockpiling, development of substitute materials, and imports through neutrals, endured four years of relative isolation from world markets. Moreover, she struck back at sea, ineffectually at first, by means of surface commerce raiders, but with increasing effectiveness as she resorted to her navy's growing submarine arm.

Establishment of a blockade against Germany was not as simple as it had been against France in the Napoleonic era. Germany controlled the Baltic and could import freely from northern neutrals. Under international law, a blockade to be legal had to be effective if not absolute. But the advent of the high-seas mine and the submarine and the threat of land-based aircraft made close blockade virtually impossible, yet a distant blockade could clearly not be fully effective. To resolve this dilemma, an international commission met in London in 1908–9. The resulting Declaration of London ruled that all goods except munitions and other obvious war materials were immune to seizure if shipped to a neutral country, even if intended for transshipment to a belligerent.

Britain had refused to ratify the declaration, which would have vitiated her sea strategy. When the war broke out, she adhered to its provisions only briefly, and then only as she chose to interpret them. To control neutral shipping, she proclaimed a mined area from the Thames Estuary to the Belgian coast. Neutrals had to call at British ports for contraband control before receiving sailing directions through the minefield. A month later the Admiralty proclaimed the entire North Sea and the waters between Iceland and the Norwegian coast a war zone, while prescribing one swept route through the Channel and into the Skagerrak. Britain enforced contraband control primarily by means of the Tenth Cruiser Squadron based on

Liverpool and the Shetland Islands, but the characteristic low visibility in the North Sea made total interdiction impossible.

Germany branded the blockade as uncivilized warfare against women and children and strove by all possible means to break it. Her first U-boat operations, directed at the blockading warships, were marked by the startling success of *U-9* in sinking the cruisers *Aboukir*, *Hogue*, and *Cressy* in succession off the Netherlands coast. Such operations, however, failed to improve Germany's situation. As her merchant marine was swept from the sea, she turned to using neutral bottoms to import the necessities of life. British inspections of neutral vessels resulted in the confiscation of any contraband consigned to Germany. Britain also rationed neutral imports to prewar levels so as to reduce transshipments of goods to Germany. These measures aroused resentment among the neutrals, but the British ignored such reactions in order to keep the blockade effective.

German Surface Raiders

The British had a brief scare in the early months of the war when Germany sent out surface raiders to attack their merchantmen. The most successful of the raiders was the light cruiser *Emden*, detached from Spee's Pacific Squadron. In September 1914, disguised with a dummy extra stack to make her look like a British county-class cruiser, she entered the Bay of Bengal. Here she sank three British freighters and captured a fourth, and set oil storage tanks at Madras ablaze with shellfire. Proceeding to the conflux of trade routes west of Ceylon, she sank five ships in 48 hours. After overhaul and coaling at the lonely island of Diego Garcia, where the British inhabitants were unaware that a war was in progress, the *Emden* returned to the hunting grounds near Ceylon and within a few hours on 20 October sank five British ships and captured two more. She then headed east to the Malay Peninsula, where in a daring early morning raid in the harbor of George Town she sank a Russian light cruiser and a French destroyer. By this time scores of Allied ships were on her trail.

She was finally run down near the Cocos Islands south of Sumatra by the Australian light cruiser *Sydney*, which with superior speed and gunpower left the *Emden* a helpless wreck on a reef.

The fast light cruiser *Karlsruhe* did almost as much damage as the *Emden*. Between 31 August and 24 October 1914, operating off the Brazilian coast, she sank or captured 14 British merchantmen. But in early November, while descending on the Bahamas for a surprise attack, she was blown apart by an accidental explosion. Germany continued to send out surface raiders from time to time, but their effect on the conduct of the war was not significant. Radio made such extended cruises as that of the *Alabama* impossible. It was simply a question of time, rarely more than a few weeks, before a raider was run down and eliminated. Some were destroyed at sea. One was chased up an African river and blockaded. Two sought sanctuary in the neutral port of Norfolk, Virginia and were interned. By early 1915 the German surface-raider threat was virtually ended. It appeared that Allied overseas communications were safe.

The First U-boat Campaign, 1915

Communications, in fact, were far from safe. In response to the British declaration that the entire North Sea was henceforth a war zone, the German Naval Staff considered the use of U-boats against Britain's trade. The political implications, including possible U. S. entry into the war, could not be taken lightly. Finally, on 4 February 1915, Admiral von Pohl published the following warning in the *Imperial Gazette*:

(1) The waters around Great Britain and Ireland, including the whole of the English Channel, are hereby declared to be a War Zone. From February 18 onwards every enemy merchant vessel encountered in this zone will be destroyed, nor will it always be possible to avert the danger thereby threatened to the crew and passengers.

(2) Neutral vessels also will run a risk in the War Zone, because in view of the hazards of sea warfare and the British authorization of January 31 of the misuse of neutral flags, it may not always be possible to prevent attacks on enemy ships from harming neutral ships.

The initial attack took place in February in waters off the east coast of Britain and in the Western Approaches north and south of Ireland. Striking without warning, German submarines sank an average of 1.9 ships daily, nearly 100,000 gross

register tons per month.[1] British minelayers soon undertook to check the threat, but not until the summer of 1918 was the Dover Strait effectively closed to U-boats.

In May *U-20* sank the British liner *Lusitania* off the south coast of Ireland. Among the dead were 128 Americans. The United States dispatched a sharp protest to Germany, demanding guarantees for the safety of Americans on the seas and immunity of passenger liners from attack. Germany dismissed the note, claiming that the *Lusitania* carried war materials and was therefore a legitimate target. Great was American indignation, but, as Germany had foreseen, the United States was not prepared to go to war.

In August 1915, the British passenger steamer *Arabic*, off Kinsale, Ireland, crossed the path of *U-24*, which promptly sent her to the bottom. The loss of three Americans in the sinking brought U. S. protests to the point of threatening war. Germany wavered, and on 20 September the first phase of the U-boat campaign ended with orders approved by the Kaiser that passenger liners would henceforth be immune from attack. The Germans shifted the focus of U-boat attack to the Mediterranean, where during the rest of the year more than a hundred Allied merchantmen were sunk.

The Second U-boat Campaign, 1916

Early in 1916, Admiral Tirpitz and General Ludendorff concluded, on grounds no one has been able to discover, that the United States had become somewhat more sympathetic toward submarine warfare. The Kaiser, however, refused to consider sinkings outside the prize rules and ordered that attacks without warning be made only in the war zone and only on armed merchant ships. Within two weeks, however, a new German–American crisis arose. On 24 March the unarmed, unescorted French steamer *Sussex* was sunk in the Channel by *UB-29*, which mistook her for a warship. Casualties in the sinking included injury to three Americans, leading President Wilson on 18 April to threaten to break diplomatic relations with Germany. The German government replied on 4 May with its "*Sussex* pledge," promising that U-boat attacks on commerce would in the future be conducted in strict conformity with Prize Law, which required

[1]Gross Register Ton (G.R.T.) is an international measure of the carrying capacity of a cargo ship, computed on the basis of 100 cubic feet of cargo space per ton. Warship tonnage is measured in displacement tons. A freighter of 3,000 G.R.T. would have about 5,000 tons displacement.

visit and search and provisions for the safety of passengers and crew before a ship could be sunk. Admiral Scheer, convinced that warfare conducted by U-boats under Prize Law could not possibly succeed, deliberately recalled his North Sea U-boat flotillas from western waters and announced that the submarine campaign against British commercial shipping had ceased. The Kaiser approved and ordered a vigorous U-boat campaign, to be directed against Allied warships only.

Hence, from May to September 1916, the Germans attempted U-boat ambushes of naval forces. Scheer planned to use cruisers to lure out elements of the Grand Fleet and lead them to where waiting U-boats could torpedo them. A dozen U-boats were thus deployed when the Grand Fleet sortied for the sweep that led to the Battle of Jutland.

Meanwhile, German submarines continued the attrition of weakly protected ships in the Mediterranean, observing Prize Law. These losses obliged the British in mid-March to divert Far Eastern shipping to the longer but safer passage around the Cape of Good Hope.

Germany's Decision to Adopt Unrestricted U-boat Warfare

As 1916 closed, Field Marshal Paul von Hindenburg, now chief of the German General Staff, realized that the Central Powers were losing the war simply because they were not winning. The failure of the great Verdun offensive had severely drained German manpower, while the British blockade caused ever greater suffering in the Fatherland. All weapons had been exploited to the full except one—the U-boat. German analysts concluded that the weakened British merchant marine was ripe for a coup de grâce, and that the U-boat arm could deliver it.

In an appreciation of 22 December 1916, Admiral Henning von Holtzendorff flatly stated that the U-Waffe, if unleashed in February 1917, could force Britain to surrender by June, before the summer harvests could be reaped. German economists estimated that if the U-boats could sink 600,000 tons monthly for five months, neutral shipping would be driven away from Britain, and that the British merchant marine would be insufficient to prevent famine in the United Kingdom. Von Holtzendorff considered that American aid, if given at all, would be too little and too late. He was of the opinion that if the British had intended to institute convoys, they would have done so, and that therefore convoys must be impractical. Finally, he believed that the efficiency of the U-boats

would overcome any Allied improvements in antisubmarine warfare. He was wrong in every particular except for his estimate of tonnage to be sunk.

Impressed by these estimates, Chancellor Bethmann-Hollweg finally withdrew his objections to unrestricted submarine warfare. Now the Supreme Command was prepared to take the climactic gamble and disregard the near certainty of U. S. entry into the war. "The U-boat is the last card," commented the chancellor ominously.

In launching the 1917 campaign, the first wave of U-boats risked the mine-strewn Channel route to the Western Approaches, thus adding substantially to their patrol time. Defective British mines redeemed the gamble. Other U-boats operated in the Channel and in the North Sea. Despite the lack of a central U-boat command control, the curve of sinkings shot up sharply. Although the Germans overestimated Allied losses by about a third, the actual sinkings exceeded Holtzendorff's estimate.[2] British economy and war potential reeled under the relentless onslaught. It soon became obvious that if sinkings continued at the current rate, Britain would have to yield.

British Antisubmarine Warfare

The Admiralty and War Council had concluded at the war's outset that the convoy system, which had safeguarded British shipping during the wars with France, should not be reinstituted against the seemingly landlocked Central Powers. A consensus in the Royal Navy held that the best way to deal with U-boats was blockade, patrol of the sea lanes, and attacks on submarine bases. Convoys, it was pointed out, served to bunch targets, added to the dangers of collision, delayed sailings, and cut military efficiency of shipping unacceptably. If ships were well spread out in their customary routes, the enemy could not hope to destroy more than single units, while he might wipe out an entire

[2]Allied and neutral losses for the first six months of unrestricted U-boat warfare as estimated by the Germans, and the actual figures:

Month of 1917	German estimate (G.R.T.)	Admiralty record (G.R.T.)
February	781,500	536,334
March	885,000	603,440
April	1,091,000	875,023
May	869,000	594,654
June	1,016,000	684,667
July	811,000	549,047
Monthly average	908,917	640,528

convoy. The Admiralty believed it could make the sea routes safe by means of traditional cruiser patrols.

Behind the term "sea routes" lay a curious misconception traceable to the writings of Mahan, who had borrowed from land warfare such phrases as "lines of communication," "communication routes," and the like. His terms "sea routes" and "sea lanes" became facile phrases for naval strategists, who tended to use them without thinking. Peacetime great-circle lines connecting sea ports on charts, became "sea lines of communication," and by 1914 naval strategists conceived it their duty to protect those "lines." Actually their business was and is to protect *ships*. Sea lines of communication carry nothing; ships carry the trade of the world. No major naval power has ever failed to protect a reasonable number of its ships when it did not divert its efforts to protecting sea routes.

When German submariners initiated commerce raiding in 1915, the Admiralty continued its established practice of patrol and minesweeping. The U-boat commanders merely kept out of the way until the patrols had passed on and then waited, confident that a freighter would blunder along shortly. Opposed only by this misguided system of "offensive patrolling," U-boats had by the end of 1916 sunk 1,660 ships.

The British, meanwhile, sought stratagems to carry the war to the U-boats. Large merchant ships were armed so that they might engage submarines that had surfaced to sink their victims by gunfire. Other vessels—freighters, trawlers, sailing ships—carried concealed guns. Known as Q-ships, they were used specifically to decoy submarines within gun range. Few U-boats were destroyed by such means. The submariners became wary and tended to attack with torpedoes any vessels they suspected of being armed. Even those U-boats that rose to the bait usually escaped unscathed, because their low silhouettes presented only a small target for the gunners.

Means of locating and attacking submerged U-boats were primitive and generally unsatisfactory. The hydrophone, developed in 1915, could give only the bearing of a submerged submarine, and early depth charges were small and scarce. In narrow waters, as in the Dover Strait, good results were achieved by a combination of nets and mines, with patrolling aircraft and surface vessels to force the U-boats to remain submerged.

By the end of 1916 the best efforts of the Royal Navy had proved largely ineffective. Despite the employment of thousands of surface craft and hundreds of aircraft and the laying of 22,000 mines, merchant-ship sinkings continued to mount. The Germans were sinking an average of 150 ships a month, and prominent naval leaders, including Admiral Jellicoe, were predicting Britain's collapse unless means could be devised to counter the U-boat.

On taking office as Prime Minister in December 1916, David Lloyd George brought Jellicoe to London as First Sea Lord, giving him the specific task of coping with the U-boat peril. Jellicoe realized that he was facing nothing less than a revolution in naval warfare, in which a minor naval power was exploiting a new weapon to defeat a major maritime nation dependent on its shipping for its very survival. To give himself the power to deal with the situation, Jellicoe succeeded in reorganizing the Admiralty so that the First Sea Lord became also Chief of Naval Staff and thus directly controlled operations. He thus had a role equivalent in function to that of the U. S. Chief of Naval Operations, an office established two years earlier.

The U. S. Navy

The U. S. Navy, with a formidable battle line of dreadnoughts, constructed through the efforts of President Theodore Roosevelt, was ill suited for the demands of the war in the Atlantic. Thinking in terms of a navy "second only to Britain's," the planners had built a fleet without giving enough thought about how it was to be used. Especially lacking were small ships that would be useful in antisubmarine work, and many of those that were authorized were canceled during the Wilson administration as a result of the parsimony of Secretary of the Navy Josephus Daniels.

Strategic thinking among American naval officers was significantly conditioned by the war games of 1915, based on War Plan Black, which envisaged engagement with an enemy fleet in the Caribbean. The Navy Department, keenly conscious of its role in defense of the recently completed Panama Canal, found it difficult to shift its strategic vision to North Atlantic and European waters.

In 1915 the U. S. Navy achieved one of its desired reforms with approval of the establishment of the Office of Naval Operations. Its authority provided a chief "who shall, under the direction of the Secretary of the Navy, be charged with the operations of the fleet, and with preparations and readiness of plans for its use in war." Rear Admiral William S. Benson became the first Chief of Naval Operations. He tightened up administration by requiring the bureaus to report the state of their war preparedness. He gave full support to improvements in communications and in procurement of ordnance and ammunition. He encouraged contact with prominent scientists of the day and established a Naval Consulting Board, including such outstanding men as Thomas A. Edison, Elmer Sperry, and William Coolidge. Thus began the Navy's close alliance with science and industry, which made possible some of the major technological advances of the twentieth century.

America's Road to War

When war broke out in August 1914, the United States was disturbed more by the British blockade measures than by the activities of the Germans. Insisting on freedom of the seas, the U. S. ships inevitably ran afoul of the British patrols, and the ship owners were infuriated at the long delays encountered in inspections. In the course of time, however, American shippers found it profitable to send more and more ships to Britain and France with war cargoes. This commerce brought about sinkings by U-boats and, partly as a result of skillful British propaganda, a shift in American opinion in favor of the Allies. The *Lusitania* case discredited the remaining German sympathizers in the United States and at the same time stiffened Woodrow Wilson's determination to insist on American rights on the high seas. So strong was Wilson's second note on the *Lusitania* sinking that his pacifist secretary of state, William Jennings Bryan, resigned in protest, asserting that it would bring war.

Wilson joined the advocates of preparedness and swung his influence behind the naval building program then before Congress. The president took his case directly to the nation, advocating America's need for "the greatest navy in the world." After much maneuvering, the Naval Act of 1916 became law on 29 August. Behind it lay America's new desire to possess "a navy second to none." During the debates, the Battle of Jutland had strengthened the hand of those favoring big ships. If Germany could defy the Grand Fleet, America must look to her own navy, for the British might not be there the next time to block the Germans. The act proposed to add to the U. S. Navy in the short space of three years 10 battleships, 6 battle cruisers, 10 scout cruisers, 50 destroyers, and 67 submarines. The act further authorized a Naval Flying Corps and a Naval Reserve Force.

The passage of the Naval Act did not mean that the U. S. Navy was getting ready to participate in the war. The act was long-range in its aims, being interpreted by the administration as a plan to en-

sure "normal growth," envisioning a postwar situation when the United States would take its rightful place as a world leader. Meanwhile, despite protests from administrative offices and from the Chief of Naval Operations, Secretary Daniels resisted all pressure to prepare for war, in which the country might become involved despite its peaceful intentions. Daniels refused to equip and man the ships the Navy already had in commission, or to put the ships themselves in top condition. President Wilson was running for reelection on the slogan "He kept us out of war." The secretary regarded effective war preparation as politically inexpedient.

Even before Wilson had taken the oath of office for his second term, Germany announced her fateful policy of unrestricted submarine warfare. The message to the United States specified that one American vessel a week would be allowed to proceed to and from Britain, provided it carried no contraband and conformed strictly to German instructions. In the face of this effrontery, Wilson, as bound by his stand on the *Sussex* pledge, on 3 February 1917 severed diplomatic relations with Germany. American indignation was heightened by publication of the notorious Zimmermann Telegram of 19 February, a fantastic attempt to bribe Mexico to join Germany in event of war with the United States, in return for the prospect of regaining Texas, Arizona, and New Mexico. Intercepted by the British, this sensational proposal was published on 1 March, rousing even those Americans still counseling neutrality.

Wilson issued orders for American vessels bound for the war zone to be armed, and in March the first American merchantmen so armed put to sea. Wilson still hoped that Germany would not go to the length of sinking American ships. Lacking overt acts, he was prepared to go no further. On 12 March, the American steamer *Algonquin* was sunk without warning near the British Isles. A week later three more American ships went down before U-boat attack with the loss of 15 lives. On 2 April, Wilson grimly told Congress, "The world must be made safe for democracy. . . . The right is more precious than peace, and we shall fight for the things which we have always carried nearest our hearts." Four days later the United States declared war.

Adoption of Convoy

The Admiralty was still clinging adamantly to the defense-of-routes theory when, in early April 1917, Rear Admiral William S. Sims, USN, was sent to England to study the shipping situation and make recommendations for the employment of the U. S. Navy in event of war with Germany. By the time he arrived, the United States had entered the war. On learning of the desperate condition of British shipping—over a million tons sunk in February and March—Sims was appalled. April promised to be even worse. Royal Navy planners frankly predicted defeat by November unless the U-boat could be conquered. Jellicoe could see no solution except additional patrolling, mining, and evasive routing—intensification of methods already proved unsuccessful.

A group of younger officers at the Admiralty, headed by Commander Reginald Henderson, RN, had been quietly studying shipping operations and losses. They found that cross-Channel coal convoys, which the French had insisted on, were getting across almost unscathed. Out of 2,600 sailings in that service, the U-boats had sunk five ships, a loss rate of 0.19 percent, as opposed to a loss rate of nearly 25 percent of ships sailing independently in *the same waters*. The result was similar when convoys were instituted between England and Norway: losses decreased 120-fold.

Armed with such figures, Henderson's group recommended that the Admiralty adopt convoy generally, especially ocean convoy. The Sea Lords flatly refused. Escort of convoy, they said, was only defensive. Offensive measures were required to defeat the U-boat. And they trotted out the rest of the old arguments against convoy.

Admiral Sims, learning of the findings and recommendations of Henderson's group, became an enthusiastic convert. Having an opportunity for discussions with Prime Minister Lloyd George, Sims forcefully argued for the convoy system. Lloyd George, once convinced, became one of the strongest supporters of convoy. He put pressure on the Admiralty, which Jellicoe countered by directing Henderson to prepare an even more systematic study. As a result, the Admiralty finally concluded that convoys were "entirely practicable." On 30 April the Sea Lords assented to an experimental ocean convoy.

Sims, in his new capacity as Commander United States Naval Forces Operating in European Waters, threw himself and his gradually growing forces into the battle against Germany's U-boat offensive. The first six American destroyers, Division Eight, arrived at Queenstown in early May 1917. In the ensuing three months, 31 additional destroyers and two tenders arrived.

Meanwhile the convoy system was getting under way. Convoy of ships bound for the British Isles began in mid-July, for outward-bound ships a month later. As the number of ships convoyed increased, the sinkings steadily decreased, despite increasing numbers of U-boats at sea in the proclaimed war zone.

In November the convoy system was extended to the Mediterranean. There, despite shortage of convoy escorts because the commander in chief preferred patrol, the convoy loss rate was only 1 percent, and convoy escorts accounted for two-thirds of all U-boats sunk in that area.

All the old arguments against convoy proved unfounded. Forming a convoy took no longer than it had taken to "sanitize" a lane by minesweeping and patrol. Scheduled arrival of convoys made it possible to plan port usage efficiently. Merchant officers proved as capable of keeping station and avoiding collision as their naval counterparts. Providing convoy escorts never required more than 15 percent of the naval ships in commission, and the escorts came from the useless patrols and were not suited for fleet operations.

As the convoy system expanded, the sinkings by U-boats fell almost in proportion. The U-boats now found their victims among vessels sailing independently. The loss rate of independent ships compared to those sailing in convoy averaged 12 to 1.

The Germans committed all available boats to implement the political decision to wage unrestricted U-boat warfare. Based on the estimate that Britain could be brought to her knees in five months, the U-boat command went all out, neglecting maintenance and repair. They were thus enabled to keep a daily average of 45 boats at sea, rising to a peak of 52 in July 1917. The results of the injudicious policy on maintenance soon made themselves felt. With increasing losses of U-boats and a cutback in U-boat building, another result of the wishful estimate of early Allied collapse, the number of U-boats at sea at length began a steady decline.

Belatedly the Germans undertook large U-boat construction programs. By September 1918 the delivery rate of new boats approached 30 a month, and Scheer obtained the Kaiser's approval to increase it to 40 a month. By this time, however, the increased production was too late to have any effect on the war.

Other Antisubmarine Measures

In an attempt to prevent U-boats from getting into the operating areas, the Allies decided on three mine barrages. The most famous, the vast North Sea Mine Barrage extending from the Orkneys to Norway, received Allied approval at the end of

November 1917, despite Sims's active opposition. Events proved Sims right, for in spite of 70,000 mines laid in a field 230 miles long and 15 to 20 miles wide, the results were minimal. Possibly one U-boat was lost as a result of the huge undertaking. The conditions of visibility and the great distances involved in the North Sea made effective anti-sweeper patrol impossible. U-boats continued to use the waters at will, occasionally escorted by German minesweepers.

The second barrage had no better success. The British attempted to close the Strait of Otranto and bottle the Mediterranean U-boats up in the Adriatic. The barrage sank one U-boat, but the Germans used the route freely until the end of the war.

The only successful minefield was the Dover Strait Barrage, laid during the winter months of 1917–18. Because this was a relatively small area, easy to patrol against German minesweeping operations, and offering easy opportunities for replacing lost mines, the Dover Barrage proved highly effective, destroying some 12 U-boats by August 1918, completely closing the Strait, and forcing abandonment of the Flanders U-boat base.

Before the Dover barrage forced closing of the Flanders base, the British hoped to strike at "the hornet's nest," as Woodrow Wilson put it, instead of "hunting hornets all over the farm." They proposed a raid on the harbors of Zeebrugge and Ostend, which were interconnected by ship canals through Bruges. Under the command of Vice Admiral Roger Keyes, the raid attempted to sink blockships in the channel entrances. As it turned out, the operation, on 22 April 1918, was completely unsuccessful, even though it was proclaimed a triumph in the Allied press. None of the blockships was able to reach its assigned position. The operation cost the British more than 1,200 casualties, and in a few weeks the ports were operating as before. The raid, however, gave rise to the idea of specially trained raiding troops, which resulted in the formation of the famous Commando and Ranger units of World War II.

One of the most effective killers of the U-boat turned out to be another submarine. The Allied boats sank 19 Germans, and the psychological effect on the Germans was even greater than the actual losses, for the threat of an unexpected torpedo in a U-boat forced to surface to recharge batteries sharply reduced morale in the U-boat service. As a captured German submarine officer put it: "We got used to your depth charges and did not fear them, but we lived in constant fear of your submarines."

U. S. Contributions

The participation of the Americans in the war at sea was undramatic. In addition to taking part in convoy operations, to which they contributed, among other craft, a wood-hulled 110-foot submarine chaser, they reversed an earlier policy on piecemeal commitment of the U. S. fleet. They sent five battleships to Scapa Flow to reinforce the Grand Fleet. Battleship Division Nine, commanded by Rear Admiral Hugh Rodman, operated as Battle Squadron Six.

The U. S. Navy bore primary responsibility for the safe transport of American troops and supplies to France. Here again convoy proved its worth. Strongly escorted troop convoys regularly made the transatlantic passage with no losses on the eastbound run. The more lightly escorted westbound troop convoys lost only three ships. By midsummer 1917, 50,000 troops a month made the crossing to France in convoys of 4 to 12 heavily escorted transports. A year later the monthly average reached 200,000. In all, over two million American troops crossed the Atlantic, some in American and some in British ships. Americans provided almost all the escort forces.

Because the United States had only about a million tons of shipping available at the outset of the war, the U. S. Shipping Board organized an immense program for building up the American merchant marine. The Board's first move was to seize and recondition all interned enemy ships, including the huge German passenger liner *Vaterland*, renamed the *Leviathan*. Newly designed, mass-produced Liberty ships appeared in large numbers, while experimental ships of wood and even of concrete carried vital supplies.

The 1918 Crisis and Allied Victory

The transfer of German troops from the Eastern Front as a result of the Russian collapse gave Germany a numerical superiority on the Western Front for the first time since 1914. Germany hoped to exploit this advantage to force a decision before the United States could make her weight felt. On 21 March 1918, Ludendorff hurled a massive offensive against the British. In this military crisis, the Allies agreed to the appointment of a supreme commander in France and designated Field Marshal Ferdinand Foch for the post. There followed a race against time as the Americans and British attempted to transport enough troops to Europe to alter the balance before Germany could win the war.

On the Western Front the crisis came on 18 July 1918, when Paris was threatened in the Second Battle of the Marne. American troops aided the Allies in repulsing the attack and then driving the Germans back toward Germany.

Part of the U. S. Navy went ashore during the campaign. Some of the heaviest fighting fell to the 25,000 U. S. marines at Château-Thierry, Aisne-Marne, St. Mihiel, and Meuse-Argonne, where they suffered some 2,500 casualties. Meanwhile, large-caliber naval guns mounted on railway flat cars struck at German railroads, bridges, and ammunition dumps.

Germany's 1918 offensive had been a last, desperate gamble. She could not make another. The strangling blockade had done its work, and at sea the convoy system had defeated the U-boats. Her armies reeling back to German soil, her High Seas Fleet in mutiny, her population reduced to near-starvation, and with revolution imminent, Germany could see no solution but surrender. On 9 November, the Kaiser abdicated, and two days later German representatives affixed their signatures to the Armistice documents.

Summary

In World War I the Central Powers occupied the interior position relative to the Allied Powers. Anticipating the alignment of the belligerents, the German General Staff planned to overwhelm France first, driving in through Belgium, and then use the same force to defeat the Russian army, which presumably would be slow to mobilize. But British and French leaders also foresaw the alignment of powers and anticipated the German strategy. After the outbreak of war in the summer of 1914, Britain promptly placed an army in France, which together with the French army blunted the German drive and gave Russia time to mobilize, so that the Central Powers were obliged to fight a two-front war.

The only German warships at sea at the outbreak of war were the battle cruiser *Goeben* and the light cruiser *Breslau* in the Mediterranean and several cruisers in the Pacific. The *Goeben* and the *Breslau* escaped to Turkey, with which Germany had a secret alliance. The Pacific cruisers, forming a squadron under Admiral Graf Spee, defeated a British cruiser squadron off Chile in the Battle of Coronel (November 1914). Then, in the Battle of the Falkland Islands (December 1914), the German squadron was itself devastated by British warships, including two battle cruisers rushed from Britain.

In a prewar building race, the British Grand Fleet, thanks largely to Admiral Fisher, remained considerably more powerful than the competing German High Seas Fleet. However, the Grand Fleet, for fear of submarines and mines, dared not venture into German waters to strike the enemy. The High Seas Fleet refused to come out and challenge the Grand Fleet until the latter had been brought down to parity by destruction of detached elements. Hence both sides resorted to ambush and entrapment, resulting in three engagements: the Heligoland Bight Action (August 1914) and the Dogger Bank Action (January 1915), battles between elements of the opposing navies, and the Battle of Jutland (May–June 1916), involving the entire Grand and High Seas fleets. In all three battles the British won, but they achieved only limited victories because of the Royal Navy's faulty communications, defective materiel, inept gunnery, and the dubious judgment of some of its officers.

The Battle of Jutland, the last of the great battleship battles, came about as a result of a double entrapment. The opposing battle-cruiser squadrons made contact, opened fire, and drew in the opposing battleship fleets, neither of which realized that the other was at sea. Jellicoe, the British admiral, used his column of battleships to block the High Seas Fleet, first, from escape via the Skagerrak and then from returning to base in Jade Bay. Scheer, the German admiral, succeeded in getting his inferior fleet back to the bay by breaking through the British rear at night. Jellicoe failed to win a victory commensurate with his superiority in numbers, because (1) he would not be drawn into a stern chase lest he be led over mines and submarines, (2) he turned away from German torpedoes and broke off action, and (3) he would not risk fighting at night.

Meanwhile, the land warfare in France had long since reached stalemate. Britain early sought means of outflanking the Western Front to join hands militarily with Russia in order to strengthen the Eastern Front. This meant a return to Britain's traditional peripheral strategy, using the mobility conferred by her sea supremacy to strike at weak points around the enemy's position. The plan finally adopted, largely through Churchill's strong support, was to advance up the Dardanelles and capture Constantinople, thereby establishing communications between the Allied fronts via the Black Sea. The operation (March–December 1915), though strategically sound, failed through inadequate intelligence, poor planning, poor generalship, and a series of tactical errors. The Allies were repulsed both in their attempt to drive up the Dardanelles with naval forces and in their subsequent campaign to seize the Gallipoli Peninsula.

Germany's early attempts at commerce raiding by use of cruisers produced only limited results. Some of her cruisers, notably the *Emden*, wreaked havoc for a while on Allied shipping, but in due course the Royal Navy ran all the cruisers down. The submarine, however, proved the perfect commerce raider, catching the Allies by surprise with no immediate countermeasures. The German U-boat, in fact, very nearly won the war for the Central Powers. While losing 187 of their number, the U-boats sent to the bottom, through direct attack or minelaying, 5,234 merchant ships amounting to 12,185,832 G.R.T. In addition, they sank 10 battleships, 18 cruisers, 20 destroyers, and 9 submarines.

Until mid-1917 no Allied commander in a position of high responsibility could see a means of averting defeat through submarine attacks on Allied commerce. Then with the institution of convoy, losses to U-boats fell steadily, while sinkings of U-boats mounted rapidly. More than two-thirds of all U-boats lost were sunk during the period of extensive convoy operations. By mid-1918 the U-boat had ceased to be a serious menace except to the vessels that continued to sail independently.

Germany's unrestricted submarine warfare, while threatening the Allies with defeat, brought the United States into the war on their side. The defeat of the U-boat by the convoy system helped make possible the transportation of two million American soldiers to France, more than enough to offset the collapse of the Russian army, enough in fact to ensure Allied victory.

Chapter 22
Disarmament and Rearmament

Immediately after the Armistice of 1918, the U. S. Navy turned to the formidable tasks of bringing home the American Expeditionary Force and of lifting the North Sea Mine Barrage. Somewhat later the Navy sent cruisers and destroyers to Russian Black Sea ports to help evacuate White refugees from the Red victories, and cooperated in the evacuation of 262,000 Greeks from Asia Minor after Turkish victory in the Greco–Turkish War.

Combined Allied expeditionary forces with strong naval support proceeded to Archangel and Vladivostok to guard or destroy war materials that had been shipped there before the collapse of the czar's armies. In Siberia the well-founded fear that a large Japanese force there intended to use the expedition as a step leading to permanent occupation kept the American army contingent and most of the U. S. Asiatic Fleet at Vladivostok until April 1920. A Yangtze patrol of light units was established to serve as a symbol of America's Far Eastern interests.

The End of the German Fleet

The Armistice had specified that Germany must immediately submit to internment 10 battleships, 6 battle cruisers, 8 light cruisers, and 50 destroyers, and surrender all of her submarines. The larger warships demanded were specified by name and included the newest and finest vessels in the High Seas Fleet.

On 21 November 1918, with the Grand Fleet, and attached American dreadnoughts, lined up in parade-ground regularity off the headlands of the Firth of Forth; the best ships of the German fleet steamed slowly inside, anchored, and hauled down their flags in token of surrender—a navy undefeated, but the navy of a defeated nation. These were the ships that had fought at Jutland—the *Friedrich der Grosse*, the *Koenig Albert*, the *Kaiser*, and the rest. There too were the battle cruisers—the *Seydlitz*, the *Moltke*, the *Derfflinger*, the *Von der Tann*. Tears streamed down the cheeks of the German officers and veteran ratings alike at this hour of humiliation. For them it signaled not only

the end of a career; it seemed the end also of a tradition they had devoted their lives to building. The German submarines were ordered to Harwich. They came in batches of 20 or so and surrendered to Rear Admiral Sir Reginald Tyrwhitt's force.

The Germans had understood that their disarmed vessels were to be interned in a neutral port, hostages for their good behavior until the peace treaty could be arranged. Instead, they were ordered to Scapa Flow. The British and French, who disagreed about so much in writing the treaty, had no trouble in agreeing that Germany should never have the ships back. By the terms of the Treaty of Versailles, the German navy was to be stripped down to 6 predreadnoughts, 6 light cruisers, 12 destroyers, and 12 torpedo boats. All other German warships were to become the property of the Allies for such disposition as they might agree on. All German naval construction under way was to be broken up. The Germans were to have no submarines, then or later.

The Germans at Scapa Flow, cut off from dependable, up-to-date news sources, learned that their countrymen strongly objected to the treaty, and they received the impression that the Allies were about to reopen the war unless the treaty was promptly signed. Determined that their ships should never be used against the Fatherland, they secretly loosened seacocks and removed watertight doors. On the final day of the Allied ultimatum, 21 June 1919, the British guard squadron left Scapa Flow. It had put to sea merely for target practice, but the Germans took its departure as evidence that the war had been renewed. At an agreed-upon signal from the flagship *Emden*, every captain in the German fleet ordered seacocks opened. Almost before the remaining British realized what was happening, the scuttled German vessels had sunk at their moorings.

This gesture, which in retrospect has a certain magnificence, had a peculiarly infuriating effect on British and French public opinion. It was as though a hated criminal had forestalled the executioner by a secret dose of cyanide. As condign punishment,

231

Germany was compelled to deliver five of her remaining light cruisers, 300,000 tons of floating docks, and 42,000 tons of dredges, tugs, and floating cranes—practically everything still afloat in her silent harbors.

Postwar Building Programs

The destruction of the German fleet had important implications for U. S. naval building policy. Prior to World War I, building a fleet to parity with, or superiority over, the German or the Japanese fleet (whichever was deemed stronger) had been a consistently maintained long-run U. S. policy. A navy "second only to Britain's" had been the prewar goal. Through the postwar decades, it was the Japanese fleet that was dominant in the Navy's assessment of its own needs. Furthermore, since the United States required some naval protection of her Atlantic seaboard as well as a major fleet in the Pacific, it was accepted doctrine that the U. S. Navy must be considerably larger than that of her potential Pacific enemy.

Like the United States, Japan had emerged from World War I stronger than before. And whereas the United States, during her involvement, had devoted most of her shipbuilding capacity to destroyers and other escort vessels the antisubmarine campaign required, the Japanese were pushing to completion several battleships on the ways. France and Italy had largely suspended ship construction, and their exhausted national treasuries gave little immediate prospect of competitive building. England remained, statistically at least, the dominant naval power. She had more than replaced her naval vessels lost during the war, and for what it was worth received the bulk of the surviving German submarine force.

Like her continental allies, England too was exhausted by the war. With her Far Eastern interests presumably protected by the Anglo–Japanese Alliance, she was content with the naval status quo, and indeed prepared to reduce by half her swollen wartime fleet. But British complacency was shattered by a threat from a surprising source, President Wilson, who proposed to build an overwhelmingly superior U. S. fleet.

Technically, at least, the United States had declared war on Germany to preserve neutral rights on the high seas. The second of Wilson's celebrated Fourteen Points provided for:

> Absolute freedom of navigation upon the seas, outside territorial waters, alike in peace and war, except as the seas may be closed in whole or in part by international action for the enforcement of international covenants.

Literally interpreted, this proposal denied the right of unilateral blockade, not to speak of the long-sanctioned right of search and seizure of contraband. To accept such a proposition would be to throw away much of the advantage of superior sea power; hence the British succeeded in getting it struck from the peace conference agenda. Wilson's reaction was to request Congress not merely to revive the suspended capital-ship building program of 1916 but to ask for a doubling of this heavy schedule.

At the end of the war, the U. S. Navy already had 16 formidable dreadnought battleships, none over eight years old. The British total was 42 ships, but as the British naval leaders well knew, this was a deceptive comparison. Thirteen of the British total were overage, obsolescent vessels due for scrapping. The Battle of Jutland had demonstrated that the nine battle cruisers were not fit for the battle line.. So, in effect, the Grand Fleet possessed a statistical superiority of 20 first-line battleships as compared to the 16 of the United States. For the latter merely to complete the 1916 program, incorporating the lessons of the war in the design of the new ships, would provide a fleet of 35 modern units, all superior to Britain's. The newly proposed U. S. 1919 program would mean a fleet of more than 50 first-line vessels, utterly eclipsing the British navy unless Britain strained every resource in an untimely naval arms race.

British reaction, both popular and official, was predictably one of outrage. The tenet that naval supremacy was the cornerstone of British power and empire was so universally accepted that it seemed almost a betrayal of trust for an ally to fail to accept it also. The British government and the Admiralty grimly set to planning their own inflated building program.

There is no clear record of either Wilson's precise motivation or his expectations. Certainly from the point of view of defense needs the 1919 program would have been excessive. Even for the rich United States it would inflate the budget for many years to a burdensome level. It seems probable that, exasperated over the British attitude on the freedom-of-the-seas issue, and concerned over Japanese saber-rattling in the Far East, the president really did want and expect a much-enlarged navy. He could realistically assume that the Congress would whittle down any administration request and may therefore have been asking for much more than he really deemed essential. It is also most likely, however, that he intended the threat of the 1919 program as a club over the heads of the British, who did not then appear enthusiastic about Wilson's cherished dream—the League of Nations.

Since he had emphasized that any arms limitation should take place through the mechanisms of such a permanent organization, presumably an astronomical competitive-building program would appear to England as an unattractive alternative to supporting the League.

The Washington Conference

England never had to make the choice. Congress rejected the 1919 program. The Senate rejected the League of Nations. The country in the 1920 election rejected the Democratic Party. Embittered and terminally ill, Wilson left the White House excoriating America's "sullen and selfish isolation."

Newly elected President Harding urged a return to "normalcy"—an important component of which public opinion the world over took to be a reduction in armaments. Congress in early 1921 overwhelmingly passed a joint resolution favoring a disarmament conference. Secretary of State Charles Evans Hughes accordingly invited to Washington appropriate delegations from Britain, France, Italy, and Japan. Only the Japanese hesitated, rightly suspecting that American aims included not only a permanent inferiority for them in fleet units but also an abrogation of their valued alliance with Britain. On the other hand, they were in no position to afford an all-out armaments race with the United States. After a two-and-a-half-week delay, they agreed to participate.

The conference met in Washington on 12 November 1921, with all the fanfare appropriate to the first international congress of this kind ever to be held in the Western Hemisphere. At the first plenary session, Secretary Hughes astonished his listeners and delighted the newspaper-reading public of the world by dismissing polite generalities and laying specific American proposals on the table at once.

These proposals included: an agenda based on the existing strength of navies;[1] a ten-year "holiday" in construction of capital ships (battleships and battle cruisers); a scrapping program (with specific ships named) that would result in a 5:5:3 ratio for the United States, Great Britain, and Japan. The scrapping schedule Hughes proposed went far beyond anything the foreign delegates had contemplated. Of America's postwar fleet, including vessels on the ways, the secretary calmly proposed to scrap 30 ships, aggregating 847,750 tons.[2]

The British and the Japanese applauded Hughes with some enthusiasm at this point in his address. He had disposed of their countries' fears of a naval armaments race. But they were a bit premature. They listened in glum silence as the American secretary went on to tell them what the United States would regard as a commensurate sacrifice on their part. He enumerated 36 British and Japanese vessels with a total tonnage of 1,032,303, which also must be junked. One Briton observed dourly, "Secretary Hughes sunk in 35 minutes more ships than all the admirals of the world have sunk in a cycle of centuries."

Hughes has been criticized for putting his cards face up on the table before the game began. But it was a calculated move, tremendously effective because totally unexpected. Whatever may be said for the American objectives in the conference, there can be little doubt that this dramatic opener vastly shortened negotiations and helped assure acceptance of most of the American proposals. Press and public all over the world were enthusiastic. If Hughes's address was a bid for popular support, it was an outstanding success.

Technical committees, in which France and Italy were represented, next hammered out the text of the Five-Power Naval Limitation Treaty. The treaty adopted the ten-year holiday in capital-ship construction. It limited overall tonnages in capital ships and aircraft carriers. In capital ships the United States and Britain were allowed 525,000 tons; Japan, 315,000 tons; France and Italy, 175,000 tons. In carriers the United States and Britain were limited to 135,000 tons; Japan, 81,000 tons; France and Italy, 60,000 tons. No capital ship could exceed 35,000 tons; no carrier, 27,000 tons. Capital-ship guns were limited to 16 inches, carrier guns to 8. Exceptions permitted the Japanese to retain the new 39,000-ton battleship *Mutsu*; the British, to complete the 41,000-ton battle cruiser *Hood*; and the United States, to complete the 33,000-ton carriers *Lexington* and *Saratoga*—all to be accommodated within the overall tonnages allowed.

Japan's delegates sturdily resisted accepting the 5:5:3 ratio with its imputation of Japanese inferiority. But the American delegates were rather precisely informed of the limits to the bargaining powers of the Japanese (and other) delegations, since

---

[1]Defined to mean "ships built and ships building." To have admitted only ships built would have rendered permanent a British superiority that was no part of the American aim.

[2]This figure invites comparison with the 525,000 tons that became the legal limit to U. S. and British capital-ship tonnage under the terms of the treaty.

the U. S. State Department's celebrated Black Chamber was regularly decrypting their home governments' encoded radio instructions as quickly as their own embassies could decode them.

As a concession to Japanese fears and sensibilities, the United States and Great Britain agreed to insertion in the treaty of the controversial nonfortification clause. By its terms no further fortification in the Pacific Ocean area would be carried out by Japan outside her home islands; by the Americans, in any of their possessions west of Hawaii; by the British, anywhere east of Singapore and north of Australia.

An American effort to extend the ratios to cruisers and lesser naval types came to nothing because of the reluctance of both Britain and Japan. The American delegation could not afford to be insistent because in existing strength of cruisers the United States was not only far behind Great Britain but also considerably weaker than Japan.

The Naval Limitation Treaty was related to the simultaneously negotiated Four-Power Pact and Nine-Power Treaty. The former was designed to save face for Japan in the abrogation of the 1902 Anglo–Japanese Alliance. It provided that the signatory powers—Britain, the United States, Japan, and France—would "respect" each other's Far Eastern possessions. The same signatories joined Italy, the Netherlands, Belgium, Portugal, and China in signing the Nine-Power Treaty reaffirming the territorial integrity of China, essentially a multilateral endorsement of the Open Door Policy.

The Washington Conference was an American success insofar as most of the objectives of the State Department were incorporated in the treaties. However, in failing to limit cruiser tonnage, the Naval Limitation Treaty allowed Britain and Japan to divert appropriations into these and lesser types, in which the United States was becoming more and more inferior. The issue of reduction of armies and of land disarmament, which Secretary Hughes would also have liked to sponsor, was never addressed. The French, ever fearful of Germany, made this omission a condition of their attending the conference.

Senior American officers, army as well as naval, deplored the nonfortification agreement as practically underwriting Japan's naval supremacy in the Far East. But the American negotiators rightly surmised that what they bargained away was an empty right, one that Congress would never exercise anyway. The Philippines and Guam had already been American possessions for 23 years without their being fortified. And indeed after the expiration of the treaty in 1936, Congress failed to act. On the other hand, there was at least some chance that Japan might refrain from fortifying her outlying island possessions if bound by the treaty.

In the hindsight of half a century, the most serious mistake of the conference was the tacit acceptance of an adversary relationship by the United States and Britain. The possibility of a war between them was too remote to be considered in planning. And they had an obvious identity of interest in the Far East. It made no sense to bargain themselves into a position that would allow Japan a free hand in that area even in the face of their joint forces.

Later Naval Disarmament Conferences

The Geneva Naval Conference, called by President Coolidge in 1927 specifically to impose the 5:5:3 ratio on cruiser tonnage, was a total failure. France and Italy refused to participate. The British delegation, agreeing in principle to the proposal of parity with the United States, insisted on a tonnage figure much higher than the American delegation deemed necessary. For the Americans to have reverted to Hughes's 1921 Washington formula of basing ship ratios on "existing strength" would have obliged them to accept permanent inferiority—not only to Britain, whose worldwide empire at least gave an excuse for a very large cruiser force, but to Japan as well. At that time Japan had in commission or under construction 214,000 tons of modern cruisers; the United States, only 155,000.

The British and American delegates wrangled without reaching agreement over the size and gun calibers allowable to a cruiser, the British preferring more but smaller ships armed with 6-inch guns, the Americans demanding a 10,000-ton allowance and 8-inch caliber guns. Sometimes credited with an assist in wrecking the conference is the clandestine lobbying in Geneva of one William B. Shearer, hired by certain American shipbuilding interests to try to disrupt the negotiations. In any event, the Geneva Conference broke up without even a face-saving pretense of any agreement whatever.

The growing common interests of the United States and Britain made cooperation increasingly important. Careful advance preparation enabled the two countries to settle the troublesome cruiser issue in the London Conference of 1930, each to be allowed to have more of the cruiser type it preferred. The types were designated heavy cruisers or light cruisers, depending on whether their main battery guns were more or less than 6.1 inches.

Heavy cruisers normally carried 8-inch guns; light cruisers, 6-inch. France and Italy, unable to settle their differences, did not participate in the new treaty. Japan acceded to the London agreement conditional to an altered 10:10:7 ratio in cruisers and destroyers and parity in submarines. The limitations finally agreed upon, stated in displacement tons, were:

Types	United States	Britain	Japan
Heavy cruisers	180,000	146,800	108,400
Light cruisers	143,000	192,200	100,450
Destroyers	150,000	150,000	105,000
Submarines	52,700	52,700	52,700

The ban on capital-ship construction was extended to the end of 1936.

Throughout the decade of the 1930s, the post-Versailles international political system was on greased skids inclining toward war. A General Disarmament Conference in 1932–33 at Geneva failed abjectly. The Second London Naval Disarmament Conference (1935–36) was a final effort at perpetuating the principle of treaty limitations of navies. The aggressions of Japan, Italy, and Germany, and their manifest contempt for existing treaties, foredoomed the Second London Conference. Britain had already surrendered a principle to Germany in a bilateral naval treaty in 1935, by the terms of which Germany was "allowed" 35 percent of Britain's naval tonnage and parity in submarines. The Japanese demanded full parity in all categories. When the United States and Britain refused to assent to such an arrangement, the Japanese withdrew from the conference.

The United States, Great Britain, and France finally signed a treaty so watered down with "escalator clauses" as to be virtually meaningless. For all practical purposes, treaty limitations of navies expired 31 December 1936.

American Building Policy in the 1930s

Congress in 1924 had authorized construction of eight cruisers, but President Coolidge, no naval enthusiast, suspended funds for all but two. Then, stung by the failure of the Geneva Conference, Coolidge sponsored legislation that would bring the U. S. Navy to full parity with Britain's. Congress, however, influenced by pacifist protests, sharply cut back the program. Under President Hoover, himself a pacifist, not a single combatant ship was laid down.

American building policy entered a new phase following the inauguration of Franklin D. Roosevelt in 1933. Like Theodore Roosevelt, his distant cousin, Franklin Roosevelt showed a perception of the intimate relation between diplomatic and military strength. He recognized the true seriousness of the deteriorating world situation, and knew that navies cannot be improvised in the face of an emergency. Furthermore, again like the earlier Roosevelt, he had gained professional knowledge of the service as assistant secretary of the navy and had a hobbyist's enthusiasm for the sea service.

The first substantial naval authorization of Roosevelt's first term was a relief measure to assist the depressed steel and shipbuilding industries; the National Recovery Act of June 1933 authorized new construction in cruisers and lesser types to full treaty strength. In March 1934 the Vinson-Trammel Bill passed, providing for an eight-year replacement building program amounting to 102 ships. From 1934 to 1940, the American naval appropriations implementing the Vinson-Trammel program grew year by year, finally approaching a billion dollars annually. The Second Vinson Act of 1938 authorized a 20 percent overall tonnage increase above the former treaty limits. In addition to new construction, modernization of older vessels was undertaken. New emphasis was put on naval aircraft and carriers. New naval bases and air stations were established.

After the fall of France, in June 1940, the limiting factor in American defense expenditures ceased to be congressional reluctance to underwrite the service's maximum programs; it was from then on simply the physical limitations of America's industrial capacity. By the time of the Pearl Harbor attack (7 December 1941), the U. S. Navy had the following combatant vessels in commission or on the ways:

	In commission	Building
Battleships	17	15
Carriers	7	11
Cruisers	37	54
Destroyers	171	191
Submarines	111	73

The U. S. Merchant Marine

Virtually since the U.S. Civil War, the U. S. merchant marine has been at a competitive disadvantage in comparison with the shipping of other countries. In the twentieth century this situation has

stemmed from both high construction costs and
high costs of operation. In spite of abundant tariff
protection, American shipbuilding and operation
could never compete effectively with those of other
countries except with the additional crutch of
federal subsidy. Up to 1936, this subsidy took the
disguised form of a liberal government loan policy
and of excessive payments for carrying the mail. In
addition, American shippers after World War I had
been able to purchase surplus vessels from the
government at bargain prices.

In 1936 Congress passed an important Shipping
Act, which established a five-man Maritime Commission under Rear Admiral Emory S. Land, USN
(Ret.), and initiated a new program of direct subsidy for both construction and operation. Designs
for subsidized construction had to meet the approval of the commission, which examined them
with an eye to wartime auxiliary use. To qualify for
subsidy, an operator had to carry crews two-thirds
of whom were U. S. citizens and submit to certain
investigatory and regulatory powers exercised by
the commission.

Beginning in 1938, the Maritime Commission
fostered in the merchant marine a replacement
program that aimed to retire slow, obsolete craft at
the rate of 50 ships a year. The following year this
rate was stepped up. Under the forced draft of
wartime, new construction was enormously increased. Yard capacity and the availability of ship-
yard workers were the only effective limiting factors after the Pearl Harbor attack. By September
1942, 300 tankers and 2,000 standard-design Liberty and Victory ships had been contracted for.
Even after allowing for large losses to submarines,
the American merchant marine had a net growth by
the time of the German surrender to more than
30,000,000 tons.

Technology and Doctrine
in the Interwar Period

In the two decades following World War I, the
policies of the U. S. Navy were to a large extent
based on the possibility of a war with Japan. Despite clashes at the disarmament conferences, the
United States tacitly recognized Britain as a permanent ally, whose fleet would serve as a barrier to
threats against the U. S. east coast. But the militant
and nationalistic Japanese posed a real and continuing threat to the Philippines and to the U. S.
Open Door Policy in China. Strategic thinking in
the U. S. Navy Department and war-gaming at the
Naval War College were dominated by the fre-

quently revised Orange Plan, which was at once a
scenario and a solution. The Orange Plan hypothe-
sized a Japanese amphibious attack on the Philippines (and perhaps other objectives in the Far
East). United States army and naval forces on the
scene would back Filipino resistance, but only to
buy time. It was assumed that the Japanese could
conquer the islands. In due course, however, the
main U. S. fleet, when concentrated and ready,
would advance across the Central Pacific, threatening the Japanese home islands and forcing a decisive naval battle. This was generally imagined to be
a line-of-battle action along the pattern of Tsushima
or Jutland. With the back of the Japanese navy
broken, Japan could be brought to heel, by blockade if necessary.

Acceptance of the Orange Plan by U. S. naval
leaders strongly influenced the Navy's building
plans and budgets. It also promoted some fruitful
thinking and doctrinal planning. The 15-year building holiday frustrated the "battleship admirals"
somewhat, but their insistence on the 8-inch-gun
cruiser demonstrated their honoring of the traditional American insistence on qualitative superiority. After 1936 they pushed the procurement of a
new battle line.

First of the new U. S. battleships was the *North
Carolina*, laid down in 1937, commissioned in
1941. Her improvements over the *West Virginia*
(commissioned in 1923, last of the Treaty ships)
were refinements rather than innovations. Even
so, the *North Carolina* was seven knots faster and
more heavily armored, and she had a much heavier
antiaircraft battery and much more sophisticated
fire control.

The submarine force of the postwar period was
expanded, and the new boats, much larger than
those of World War I vintage, had the enormously
greater range needed for effectiveness in the vast
Pacific. Improved submarine rescue devices and
techniques were perfected. Antisubmarine detection and attack equipment and antisubmarine tactics were also the subject of a continuing research
and development program.

But it was the development of the aircraft carrier that best gave scope to the Navy's innovative
energies. Even a battleship man could see that in
clear weather a fast, high-flying airplane would be a
far better observation platform for scouting purposes than the crow's nest of a 30-knot cruiser. In
1919–21 the collier *Jupiter* was converted into
CV 1, the *Langley* (19,360 tons), the U. S. Navy's
first carrier. Two battle-cruiser hulls, which otherwise would have been scrapped under the Naval

Limitation Treaty, were converted to the 33,000-ton *Lexington* and *Saratoga*, both commissioned in 1928. It was on the flight decks of these three vessels that the operational techniques were developed that made the U. S. Navy's air arm the world's finest.

When the USS *Ranger*, the first American vessel conceived as a carrier from the keel up, joined the fleet in 1934, carrier concepts had developed beyond her. Designed to carry fleet reconnaissance aircraft, she was never modified for assault missions. The *Langley*, long obsolete as a carrier, was converted in 1936 into a tender. Not until the *Yorktown* was commissioned in 1937 did the fleet acquire a third assault carrier. By then flight techniques and aircraft design had progressed far enough to justify steady building. The carriers *Enterprise*, *Wasp*, and *Hornet* were all commissioned before the outbreak of the Pacific war in 1941. Nineteen more were then on order, but on Pearl Harbor day the U. S. Navy had only six assault carriers. These were to constitute the nucleus of a truly radical "battle line."

Until the Pearl Harbor attack, however, the carrier as the main weapon system for attack was not generally recognized. Almost from the time of the Armistice in 1918, the role of aircraft in future wars was loudly and publicly debated. The most zealous and articulate proponent of the bomber plan was Brigadier General William ("Billy") Mitchell of the Army Air Corps. In 1921 he was permitted to have planes drop 2,000-pound bombs on an obsolete German battleship and cruiser anchored off the Virginia capes. That the air attack finally sank the vessels was proclaimed by Mitchell as proof that all navies were obsolete.

Naval observers regarded the demonstration as unrealistic. The vessels were not maneuvering under way. They were not shooting back. They had no damage-control parties on board. However, the naval flyers saw it as a powerful argument for carriers. This well-publicized experiment undoubtedly made it easier for them to persuade their conservative seniors to divert a portion of the Navy's budget to fostering naval air. It began to be generally accepted that in addition to being the "eyes of the fleet," carrier aircraft conceivably could slow an enemy fleet by damaging one or more of its major units.

As early as the 1929 fleet exercises, the *Saratoga* sent in over the Panama Canal planes that theoretically "destroyed" two of the vital locks. In later maneuvers, simulated air attacks on Pearl Harbor and the Mare Island Navy Yard in California were ruled by the referees as successful. But the implications of these exercises were not generally appreciated; the carriers had no cruiser–destroyer screens permanently assigned.

Carrier aircraft were early specialized in function, an attack carrier operating squadrons of fighters, bombers, and torpedo planes. The planes themselves had to have special characteristics adapting them to making arrested landings on heaving flight decks. The U. S. Navy was in no hurry to adopt standardized designs for mass production. Hence, some of its flyers began World War II in obsolescent aircraft. But the new generation of planes, the workhorses of the war, were of excellent quality. The Grumman Wildcat (F4F) fighter and the Douglas Dauntless (SBD) dive bomber joined the fleet in 1941. The Douglas Devastator (TBD) torpedo plane was available as early as 1938, but the improved Grumman Avenger (TBF) did not reach the fleet until after the Battle of Midway in June 1942. Before the end of the war the Grumman Hellcat (F6F) displaced the Wildcat as the first-line carrier interceptor.

The naval dive-bomber was to prove the hammerhead of the naval war. In attacking a maneuvering target such as a ship, a bomber in level flight is much more prone to err in range than in deflection. Obviously the steeper the glide or dive made in the attack, and the closer the point of bomb release to the target, the less is the hazard of missing. Naval and marine flyers generally adopted an 85-degree dive. Such an operation required a specially designed plane, with wing flaps rugged enough to serve as "brakes" in a steep dive, and an airframe and wings stout enough to take the stresses of multi-G pullouts after drop.[3] The SBD was such an airplane.

The Orange Plan contemplated an advance by the Navy through 6,000 miles of the island-studded Central Pacific Ocean. Until the late 1930s, it was accepted that a steam-driven fleet could operate only within a radius of 2,500 miles or so from a major base. Since the League of Nations had mandated the former German island possessions north of the equator to Japan—including the Marianas (less U. S.–owned Guam), the Marshalls, and the far-flung Carolines—and since it was suspected that the Japanese were fortifying some of these

---

[3]During World War II, U. S. naval and marine corps flyers were unique in their ability to make real dive-bombing attacks. Other so-called dive-bombers (e.g., the German Stuka) attacked in a steep glide. Their structures were too frail for the pullout stress of near-vertical attacks.

islands, contrary to the terms of the mandate, it was necessary to assume that Japanese bases would have to be taken by amphibious assault. Planning officers of the U. S. Navy and Marine Corps, studying with painstaking care the British mistakes in the essentially amphibious Gallipoli campaign of World War I, developed a detailed amphibious doctrine, which they incorporated in the *Landing Operations Manual*, first published for service use in 1934. Training exercises in subsequent years refined details, but most of the theoretical "textbook solutions" of the original stood up well under trial.

Among the more obvious provisions of the U. S. amphibious doctrine were the absolute necessity of detailed and exact planning of all aspects of the operation, the need for careful briefing of all participants, the value of surprise, and the desirability of speed in exploiting any advantage won. Ship bombardment must be supplemented by close support of ground units by aircraft used as flying artillery. Supply vessels must be combat-loaded (i.e., equipment must be readily off-loaded in the sequence desired during the landing), and vital stores must be distributed among supply ships so that the loss of one or more vessels would not create an insuperable bottleneck. In view of all that could go wrong in this most complicated and vulnerable of operations, realistic rehearsal by all units involved was strongly recommended.

Wartime experience led to only two significant changes in American amphibious doctrine. The *Landing Operations Manual* (and its 1938 revision, *Fleet Training Publication 167*) had assured "unity of command" by leaving the admiral commanding the approach in charge throughout the operation. In the war it was found expedient for him to turn over command to the marine or army general once that officer had his headquarters functioning on the beach. Also the manual had presupposed that support fire would be delivered by the gunnery vessels while they were maneuvering at long range. In practice, even the larger vessels had to brave the hazards of air and submarine attack while they laid down deliberate, aimed fire from close ranges. In fact it came to be standard practice for ships' officers to accompany the troops ashore as gunnery spotters, to radio for call fire on specific enemy targets.

To get artillery and armor ashore with the first wave, specially designed landing craft were needed. The Navy and Marine Corps, using as prototypes powered craft developed for oil prospecting in Louisiana's swampy bayou country, developed the LCVP (Landing Craft, Vehicle and Personnel), which could discharge tracked vehicles directly onto the beach from a ramped bow, and the LVT (Landing Vehicle, Tracked), which could claw over coral reefs and then come ashore like a true amphibian. The larger LSTs (Landing Ships, Tank), attack transports, command vessels, and many supporting systems were at least in the blueprint stage when the United States entered the war.

Logistic doctrine, comprising all the services of support and supply, is inherently less dramatic than the development of the fast carrier task force or the techniques of beach assault, but in any protracted war, carried out over immense distances, it is equally vital. The step-by-step advance on Japan from Pearl Harbor through the island-studded Central Pacific that was contemplated in updated versions of the Orange Plan would require not merely conquest of islands but the facility to convert them speedily into operational bases. The solution to this problem was the Navy's Construction Battalions ("Seabees"), recruits already experienced in heavy construction work, uniformed, and placed under naval discipline. Coming ashore at an early stage in an amphibious assault, the Seabees often operated their bulldozers and other heavy equipment under enemy fire. Even the marines soon came to sing their praises. Later, as the naval front moved west, carefully planned special service commands were spun off from the Construction Battalions—Patrol Aircraft Service Units (PATSUs), Carrier Aircraft Service Units (CASUs), and others. These units could be moved about on short notice, and each could typically service a three-squadron wing.

In the course of the war, the Bureau of Supplies and Accounts developed standardized base components, each of which included the personnel and equipment needed to set up a base of a certain type. LIONs were for major naval bases; CUBs were for smaller bases; ACORNs were for naval air bases. This packaged-base system could at times result in wasteful assignment of unneeded spare parts and redundant equipment, but some flexibility could be effected through skillful use of the multivolume *Catalogue for Advanced Base Functional Components*.

Apart from bases, the fleet would need extensive support by seaborne supply—oilers, tenders, repair ships, floating drydocks, ammunition carriers, and more. The somewhat inexact concept of the Fleet Train was refined to become the Service Force Pacific, whose mobile service squadrons kept up with the advancing fleet, anchoring prepared for immediate business in any handy harbor or lagoon. More than any other single factor, the Service Force gave the fleet the 6,000-mile operating range that the campaign required.

American Public Opinion in the 1930s

The isolationism deplored by Wilson after the Senate rejected the League of Nations persisted through the twenties and became a political force in the thirties. Many Americans accepted the revisionist thesis that U. S. entrance into World War I had been a mistake, and strongly opposed American commitments that might again involve the country in a foreign war. In 1934 headlines were made by hearings of the Senate's Nye Committee, which rehearsed in detail the fact that American steel companies and munitions makers profited handsomely from the war. World Peaceways and similar pacifist pressure groups promoted the erroneous belief that somehow these corporations were responsible for America's involvement. This "merchants of death" propaganda helped to engender the neutrality legislation of the late 1930s, which unilaterally surrendered those neutral rights the United States had four times gone to war to preserve. The 1935 Neutrality Act forbade the sale or transport of munitions to a belligerent. The 1936 amendment prohibited loans to belligerents. The 1937 Act permitted the sale to belligerents of goods, other than munitions, but only on a cash-and-carry basis. The United States would sell to belligerents only if they paid cash for U. S. products and carried them away in their own ships. If these ships were sunk, it was not the business of the United States. The 1939 Act lifted the arms embargo but empowered the president to forbid U. S. ships from entering the war zone. To avoid being challenged on the seas, Americans planned to retreat from the seas.

As in England and France, there was in the United States a widespread feeling that no war was worth fighting. Contemporary literature reflected a deep cynicism about the motives and competence of World War I leaders.[4] A great many American students gave vociferous approval to the Oxford Pledge, by which British undergraduates were swearing "under no circumstances" to fight for king and country.

Thinking on Grand Strategy

Along with an isolationist and somewhat pacifistic public opinion went a popular misconception of grand strategy that made many persons feel that in any conceivable European war American involvement would never be necessary. Most of the writers on military subjects in popular journals condemned Allied generalship in World War I for useless sacrifice of men in trying to penetrate the German trench line. With this lesson learned and digested, it was assumed that in event of war the Allies in their impregnable Maginot Line would simply allow the Germans—finally driven to desperate action by the relentless pressure of naval blockade—to throw away their armies in futile attack.[5]

The Maginot Line was of course to prove anything but impregnable. Moreover, the role assigned sea power in this strategy was not realistic. An island nation, such as England or Japan, can be defeated wholly or mainly by blockade. A continental power cannot. Though German industry might be weakened by shortages of, say, alloy metals, the development of synthetic gasoline and synthetic rubber supplied at home the two vital bulky materials Germany needed for protracted war.

As the prewar German building program showed, Hitler and his generals tended to discount the relevance of sea power to Germany's situation and to place naval construction in a third priority behind that for the army and the Luftwaffe. Not until 1938 did Hitler begin a substantial buildup of his fleet.

Rather than stemming from Mahan, the theoretical underpinnings of Nazi world strategy derived from Karl Haushofer's geopolitical writings, which in turn were based on the writings of a British geographer, Halford J. Mackinder.[6] Written in 1919, Mackinder's *Democratic Ideals and Reality* was meant as a warning to his countrymen. In essence, its message was that Mahan's seapower thesis was being rendered outmoded by the development of roads and railroads in the great continents. Steam and gasoline engines were de-

---

[4]Dozens of titles might be cited. Ernest Hemingway's *A Farewell to Arms*, C. S. Forester's *The General*, and Erich Maria Remarque's *All Quiet on the Western Front* are examples from the novels. Plays and movies with a strong pacifist overtone reached nearly all of the population in the Western democracies.

[5]Maginot Line: a heavily armed line of concrete fortifications built by the French along the Franco–German border to frustrate any German attempt to invade France. In World War II the Germans outflanked the Maginot Line, invading France through Belgium as they had done in World War I.

[6]Professor General Karl Haushofer was the founder and head of the Institut für Geopolitik in Munich. In addition to his extensive writings, his personal prestige with the Nazi hierarchy was important in influencing German grand strategy.

priving the sea of its monopoly of bulk transportation. In the long run the power or powers controlling the center of the greatest landmass, Eurasia, would be able to conquer and control the world. This "Heartland" the Germans might have captured in World War I if they had not made the error of waging war on two fronts. In the future, a German–Russian alliance or conquest by one nation of the other could set the stage for Mackinder's gloomy scenario.

Accepting the validity of Mackinder's views, Haushofer attempted to orient German territorial aspirations to the East. In the opinion of the Nazi geopoliticians, with a conquered Russia as a German base, Hitler could afford at last to defy the superior British fleet.

Herein lies the ultimate rationale of Germany's attack on Russia in 1941, and perhaps also the adventures of Rommel's Afrika Korps in Germany's North African campaign. Haushofer himself, through whom Mackinder's ideas reached Hitler, cannot be deemed responsible for the poor timing of the Russian campaign, since his program insisted that Germany should at all costs avoid another two-front war. But the idea of conquering Russia sooner or later, of making a large part of her a German colony, was consistent with his program.

The Breakdown of Collective Security

Throughout the between-wars period, the diplomacy of the Western democracies aimed at providing a collective security system. The original cornerstone was conceived to be the enforcement of the Versailles Treaty, which undertook to insure the permanent disarmament of Germany, and the strengthening of the League of Nations. The Bolshevik threat was "solved" by the *Cordon Sanitaire*, a row of small buffer states along Soviet Russia's western border. France by loans and diplomacy promoted in middle Europe a Little Entente (1924) of friendly states—Yugoslavia, Czechoslovakia, and Romania, all of which had received territory from the dismembered Austrian Empire.

Joint international action was the order of the day. Besides the disarmament conferences, there were war debts and reparations settlements (Dawes and Young plans) and treaties of conciliation—the Treaty of Rapallo between Germany and Russia (1922) and the multinational Pact of Locarno (1925). In 1926 Germany entered the League of Nations. Even Communist Russia, outcast among nations, was, at the behest of France, admitted to the league in 1933. Through the decade of the 1920s, there seemed no good reason to think a new war inevitable. Probably most statesman, and certainly most ordinary people, felt that diplomacy had displaced large-scale war, for their lifetime at least. Indeed the Kellogg-Briand Pact, signed by representatives of all major powers, pledged to outlaw all but defensive wars. It was a meaningless incantation, however, since very few wars, even those initiated by a preemptive strike, are acknowledged by the initiator as aggressive.

In any event, the apparent stability was short-lived. Britain, France, and the United States, with pacifistic populations and inadequate armaments, failed to take effective joint action when it might have saved the peace. Soviet Russia, received grudgingly and suspiciously in the councils of the democracies, was preoccupied by a gigantic effort to industrialize and build a modern economy.

Japan, Germany, and Italy, the self-styled "have-not" nations, nationalistic, imperialistic, and opportunistic, came to assume the dynamic roles in the history of the 1930s. They were not satisfied with the status quo, and were prepared to risk war to remold their corners of the world.

The proximate causes of the aggressions of the Fascist countries in the 1930s may well have been the alleged injustices of the Versailles Treaty (in the case of Germany), and the Great Depression, which by destroying the means of livelihood of millions of men made them ready to follow any demagogue. But the deep-rooted underlying causes were the grandiose national objectives of Germany, Italy, and Japan—unchallengeable dominance in middle Europe, in the Mediterranean, and in the Far East.

For Adolf Hitler's Germany the immediate objective was the absorption of all German-speaking areas—Austria, Sudetenland, Polish Silesia, and Danzig; the ultimate objective was to subjugate the Balkans and the Ukraine. For Mussolini's Italy the short-term goal was an African empire comparable to France's—Ethiopia supplementing Libya, Eritrea, and Italian Somaliland; and a foothold on the east shore of the Adriatic— Albania, perhaps later a part of Greece. For Japan the irreducible minimum was Manchuria; the more distant objective, hegemony over China, Malaya, and the East Indies.

In a sense World War II may be said to have begun on 18 September 1931, when a bomb explosion on the track of the South Manchurian Railway near Mukden signaled the beginning of the first "Chinese Incident," the invasion of Manchuria by the Japanese. The failure of the democracies to cope with this treaty-breaking threat to the general peace was a lesson not lost on Mussolini and Hitler.

Italy next broke the peace by her 1935 invasion and conquest of Ethiopia. It was not so much the intrinsic importance of Manchuria and Ethiopia to the democratic world that mattered. Rather it was that these naked aggressions proved at once the impotence of the League of Nations at its designed function and the bankruptcy of the collective security system. With the advance connivance of the conservative governments of France and Britain, Mussolini manufactured a border incident and made it an excuse for an aggressive war. After a brave but futile fight, the tribesmen of Ethiopian Emperor Haile Selassie were defeated.

Meanwhile, popular support for the League proved surprisingly strong in Britain and France. The League did act to the extent of applying economic sanctions—that is, forbidding loans or financial assistance to Italy. It also embargoed munitions for the Italians. As could have been predicted, such measures were entirely ineffective in arresting a small-scale colonial war. Oil sanctions, which might have been effective, were not applied. Britain ostentatiously moved a fleet into the Mediterranean, apparently for the purpose of allowing its personnel to watch Italian transports carry an army through the Suez Canal to Eritrea. About the only solace friends of the League could distill from the sorry story was that the double-dealing foreign ministers of Britain and France, Sir Samuel Hoare and Pierre Laval, were forced by popular indignation to resign.

The mere threat of oil sanctions, and the disturbing reports he received of public hostility to Italy in the democracies, caused Mussolini to reassess his relations with Nazi Germany—with which Italy had recently been distinctly unfriendly. Up to 1935 Germany had been largely unarmed. But in that year, after some domestic massacres to consolidate his power at home, Hitler felt secure enough to denounce the Versailles Treaty and to announce to the world the rearmament of Germany. A rearmed Germany would be worth Italy's sympathetic attention, reasoned Mussolini. The Rome–Berlin Axis dates from 1936.[7]

Adolf Hitler, an ill-educated demagogue, brilliant but with paranoic tendencies, had come to power in Germany in 1933, pledged to cure unemployment and to destroy the Versailles settlement. By rearming Germany, he did both. In 1936, in the face of French threats, he marched his new armies into the "permanently demilitarized" Rhineland, a necessary preliminary to defense of the industrial Ruhr should major war develop later.

In the Spanish Civil War (1936–39) both Hitler and Mussolini intervened on the side of the rebels with men and material—perhaps decisively. Though in the beginning popular sympathy in the democracies was 2 to 1 in favor of the Loyalist government, it was not the democracies but Russia that provided material assistance to the Loyalists, and that was too little and came too late. As the Spanish War dragged to its miserable conclusion, the small Spanish Communist Party, by virtue of its determined and ruthless leadership, became the dominant group in the Loyalist government. This situation of course made effective intervention by the democracies even less a political possibility.

In early 1938 German rearmament had made Hitler bold enough to undertake his first really big gamble. With the cooperation of the Nazi party in Austria, he simply marched to Vienna and announced an *Anschluss*—a union of Austria with Germany. Not being challenged, later in the year he demanded of Czechoslovakia that she cede to Germany the German-speaking Sudetenland, a fringe of parishes along Czechoslovakia's borders.

Unlike the Austrians, the Czechs are primarily a Slavic, not a Germanic, people. They had military alliances with France and Russia. With mountainous frontiers, a good army, and a substantial armaments industry, they were prepared to fight. Nearly everyone in Europe expected war. Instead, the prime ministers of France and Britain flew to Munich for a personal conference with Hitler. In return for Hitler's empty promise, "This is the last territorial demand I have to make in Europe," the ministers signed the notorious Munich Agreement, which let him have his way. Six months later Hitler seized most of the rest of Czechoslovakia. Russia, seeing this sellout as a Franco–British move to turn Hitler's aggressions eastward, toward the Soviet Union, on 23 August 1939, signed a nonaggression pact with Germany. Hitler, meanwhile, was threatening the Poles. Britain and France, at last recognizing the futility of appeasement, pledged support to Poland if her independence were threatened, and, on 25 August 1939, signed a treaty of alliance with Poland.

---

[7]The German–Japanese Anti-Comintern Pact later in the year made Germany the kingpin in a later Rome–Berlin–Tokyo Axis. The term Axis was in common use from 1937 on.

Summary

Prior to World War I, the United States competed with Germany and Japan to build a navy second only to Britain's. At the end of the war, France and Britain deprived Germany of her fleet, part of which deliberately sank itself while interned at Scapa Flow. Thereafter the U. S. Navy was in competition mainly with the Japanese. President Wilson's plan to equal or outstrip rivals by means of a heavy shipbuilding program was vetoed by Congress. Wilson's successor, President Harding, proposed to attain the same aim by scrapping ships. At an international conference called at Washington in late 1921, the United States recommended that the United States, Britain, and Japan scrap 66 ships, built and building, for a total of nearly 2,000,000 tons displacement. The Washington conference produced three treaties:

Five-Power Naval Limitation Treaty. This treaty established a 5:5:3 tonnage ratio for capital ships and aircraft carriers among the United States, Britain, and Japan respectively, with France and Italy allotted lesser tonnages, thus;

	Capital ships	Aircraft carriers
United States and		
Britain	525,000	135,000
Japan	315,000	81,000
France and Italy	175,000	60,000

Capital ships were limited to 35,000 tons displacement and 16-inch guns; carriers, to 27,000 tons and 8-inch guns. There was to be no construction of capital ships for ten years. There was to be no arming or fortifying of Pacific islands north of Australia—a provision not applicable to the Japanese home islands or the American Hawaiian Islands.

Nine-Power Treaty. This treaty guaranteed the territorial integrity of China.

Four-Power Pact. Abrogating the 1902 Anglo–Japanese Alliance, Britain, France, Japan, and the United States guaranteed to respect each other's rights and possessions in the Pacific area.

In the London Conference of 1930 the United States, Britain, and Japan agreed on a 10:10:7 ratio in the cruisers and destroyers and parity in submarines. The ban on capital-ship construction was extended to 1936.

American ship construction lagged behind treaty limitations until 1933, when President Roosevelt, as a relief measure to help the depressed steel and shipbuilding industries, sponsored legislation to build cruisers and lesser types to full treaty strength. The first Vinson-Trammel Bill (1934) authorized an eight-year replacement building program amounting to 102 ships. The Second Vinson Act (1938) authorized a 20 percent tonnage increase above the former treaty limits. After the fall of France (1940) U. S. naval building was limited only by America's industrial capacity. At the same time the Maritime Commission, established by Congress in 1936, was fostering a rapid buildup of the U. S. merchant marine.

In the two decades following World War I, the policies of the U. S. Navy were focused mainly on the possibility of a war in the Pacific with Japan. United States strategic thinking was dominated by the Orange Plan for projecting American military power across the Pacific, through the many Japanese-held islands, to the rescue of the Philippines. Solutions would be required for the following problems: (1) how to bring superior air power against the land-based air of the islands, (2) how to assault the strongly defended island bases, (3) how to free the fleet from dependence on rearward bases, and (4) how to defeat the Japanese fleet. Solving these problems required (1) a fleet buildup with emphasis on aircraft carriers and improved carrier planes, particularly dive-bombers, (2) developing an amphibious doctrine and suitable landing and beaching craft, and (3) developing a logistic doctrine whereby the fleet and other forces in effect carried their bases forward with their advance.

The American public remained largely pacifistic, and the belief was widely held that France was safe from German attack behind her Maginot Line. As a means of keeping out of any war that might erupt, the United States passed neutrality acts forbidding the sale of munitions to belligerents and specifying that she would sell other products to belligerents only if they paid cash and carried away the goods in their own ships.

The German government, meanwhile, inspired by Mackinder's *Democratic Ideals and Reality*, as interpreted by Karl Haushofer, dreamed of seizing the heartland of Eurasia as an impregnable base from which to launch world conquest. Under Hitler, the Germans, in defiance of the Versailles Treaty, rearmed the Rhineland. They then marched into Austria and added that country to Germany. Also aspiring to imperialistic adventure, Italy invaded Ethiopia, and Japan invaded China. The failure of the League of Nations to take adequate measures against these aggressions cost it its last shreds of authority and presaged its early demise.

When Hitler declared his intention of adding

the Sudetenland of Czechoslovakia to his growing German empire, the prime ministers of Britain and France flew to Munich to dissuade him. In return for Hitler's empty promise, "This is the last territorial demand I have to make in Europe," the ministers signed the notorious Munich Agreement, which let him have his way. Six months later Hitler seized most of the rest of Czechoslovakia. Russia, seeing this sellout as a Franco–British move to turn Hitler's aggressions eastward, toward the Soviet Union, signed a nonaggression pact with Germany. Hitler, meanwhile, was threatening the Poles. Britain and France, at last recognizing the futility of appeasement, pledged support to Poland if her independence were threatened, and, on 25 August 1939, signed a treaty of alliance with Poland.

Chapter 23

World War II: The German–Italian Offensive

"It is peace in our time," said Britain's prime minister, Neville Chamberlain, when he returned from the Munich Conference with Hitler. Less than a year later, at 0445[1] on 1 September 1939, Nazi armies hurled themselves against Poland, and the holocaust of World War II began. England and France had mutual aid treaties with Poland, but Hitler had no reason to believe that they would honor them any more than they had fulfilled their Munich-repudiated moral obligations to Czechoslovakia. The German Führer planned a swift campaign that would smash Poland while Britain and France vacillated. He thus would present them with a fait accompli. But he failed to realize the change in temper of both leaders and people in the two western countries. In the evening of 1 September, the British presented the Germans an ultimatum. At 0900 on the 3rd, they issued them a final warning. Two hours later, Prime Minister Chamberlain, in a broadcast to the nation, announced that His Majesty's Government was at war with Germany. France followed suit that afternoon. The same day in London a round-faced, chubby man of dynamic fighting spirit returned as First Lord of the Admiralty, an office he had relinquished 24 years earlier. A signal was flashed to the fleet: "Winston is back."

In a few weeks all was over on the Polish front. Here blitzkrieg tactics had done their work. But all was not over in the West. Though British and French mobilization had come too late to help Poland, Britain and France executed plans to meet any westward thrusts of the German Wehrmacht—France by means of her armies sheltered behind the Maginot Line; Britain primarily through use of her sea power. The Royal Navy promptly blockaded Germany by covering all exits from the North and Baltic seas with cruiser patrols, while the Home Fleet was poised at Scapa Flow to deal with any breakout.

Hitler had no wish to face a real war with Britain and France—at that time. Hence, after the Polish

operation had been completed, he refrained from any offensive action on the Western Front, a measure of restraint that brought about what has been called the Phony War. Through the winter of 1939–40, German troops in the Siegfried Line faced French troops in the Maginot Line with only small skirmishes relieving the monotony.

The War Begins at Sea

The Germans at sea, on the contrary, struck hard from the first. The day England entered the war, the British passenger liner *Athenia* was sunk by Lieutenant Fritz-Julius Lemp, of *U-30*. Commodore Karl Dönitz, officer commanding U-boats; Grand Admiral Erich Raeder, commander in chief of the German fleet; and Hitler himself issued denials of German responsibility—in good faith because they could not believe a U-boat commander had disobeyed their orders to spare passenger ships. In less good faith was Propaganda Minister Josef Goebbels's charge that Churchill had engineered the whole thing himself in the hope of involving the United States in the war.

As a result of the *Athenia* sinking, the Admiralty lost no time in adopting convoy. The first sailed for Halifax on 8 September. Its escort accompanied it out for 300 miles, then picked up an inbound convoy and brought it safely to United Kingdom ports—an early operational pattern necessitated by the shortage of vessels suitable for escort. Early in the war the operations of German surface raiders obliged the Admiralty to provide each convoy with a heavy escort—a battleship, a cruiser, or an armed liner.

By mid-October one raider, the pocket battleship *Deutschland*, had sunk two merchant ships and committed a first-class diplomatic blunder by seizing the American freighter *City of Flint*. When the freighter was en route to Germany via Norwegian territorial waters, the Norwegians interned the German prize crew and returned the ship to her master. The incident caused much anti-German sentiment in the United States. It was also the first incident to attract Hitler's attention, militarily, to Norway.

[1]This and the following chapters use 24-hour time, which in World War II came into almost universal use for military purposes. Unless otherwise indicated, all times and dates in the remainder of this book are local.

Most destructive of the early raiders was the pocket battleship *Admiral Graf Spee*, which between 30 September and 7 December 1939 sank nine merchant ships, totaling 50,000 tons. Nine hunting groups, including a French battleship and French and British cruisers and aircraft carriers, were dispatched to hunt her down. Along the east coast of South America ranged Commodore Sir Henry Harwood's group, consisting of the heavy cruisers *Cumberland* and *Exeter* and the light cruisers *Ajax* and *Achilles*.

On 13 December, Harwood's group, less the *Cumberland*, which was refitting in the Falklands, succeeded in intercepting the *Graf Spee* in the approaches to the River Plate. Concentrated fire from the pocket battleship's 11-inch guns, Harwood realized, could blow his cruisers out of the water. To induce the raider to divide her fire, he ordered the *Exeter* to turn northwest and engage while he led the *Ajax* and the *Achilles* on a northeasterly course. The German commanding officer, Captain Hans Langsdorff, thinking he had only a cruiser and two destroyers to deal with, closed the range rapidly so that he could break through to the open sea, thereby sacrificing the advantage of his long-range fire. This move gave Harwood's ships their opportunity. They opened fire, and their 6- and 8-inch shells made several hits on the German ship, inducing Langsdorff to turn away, back toward the South American coast.

The *Graf Spee*'s guns by this time had put the *Exeter* out of action. Harwood ordered her to the Falklands for repairs, while with his two light cruisers he kept dogging the retreating battleship. Langsdorff, overestimating the damage to his vessel, made no effort to resume the action but continued west through the day, with British cruisers on either quarter encouraging him along with occasional salvos from their main batteries. A little after midnight, the *Graf Spee* entered Montevideo harbor. The *Ajax* and the *Achilles* then formed a patrol line just outside Uruguay's territorial waters.

Frenzied diplomatic activities on the part of the German consular representatives were unsuccessful in obtaining permission for the *Graf Spee* to remain in port longer than 72 hours. British propaganda was more successful, giving the impression that a large British fleet had arrived. Actually only the *Cumberland* had joined the *Ajax* and the *Achilles*. From Berlin Langsdorff received the option of fighting his way out or scuttling his ship. He decided to take the latter course. Having landed wounded prisoners and most of his crew, he got under way in the afternoon of 17 December. The British cruisers went to action stations, but before

they could engage her, the *Graf Spee* came to a stop, just outside the three-mile limit, and her skeleton crew transferred to a German freighter alongside. Minutes later the battleship blew up. Langsdorff shot himself shortly afterward. For several months thereafter the Germans abandoned the use of surface raiders.

British elation at the defeat of the *Graf Spee* was somewhat dampened by failure to locate her supply ship, the *Altmark*, which was believed to have British seamen on board, captured by the pocket battleship before her destruction. At length, just three months after the Battle of the River Plate, a flotilla of destroyers under Captain Philip Vian in HMS *Cossack* discovered her in a Norwegian fjord. Dissatisfied with Norwegian assurances that the vessel had been inspected, Churchill ordered Vian to board her and free the prisoners. Eluding a clumsy attempt to ram, Vian laid the *Cossack* alongside the *Altmark* and sent over a boarding party. After a sharp hand-to-hand fight, the German crew surrendered, and the boarders released 298 British seaman who had been battened down in storerooms. The effect of Norway's protests over the violation of her neutrality was much weakened by her obvious failure to make a proper search of the vessel while it was in her territorial waters, and the episode was permitted to die down after the proper exchange of diplomatic protests.

The Invasion of Norway

Both Raeder and Churchill had their eyes on Norway. From Norwegian ports German U-boats or surface raiders would be able to bypass the British blockade and reach the open Atlantic. Between the Norwegian coast and a line of offshore islands, moreover, is a thousand-mile-long sheltered passage known as the Leads. German ships, ignoring Norway's neutrality, could dash across the Skagerrak under their own air cover and follow the Leads until they chose to make a break to the Atlantic. In summer vital Scandinavian iron ore was transported from the Swedish port of Lulea to Germany, safe from the Royal Navy, which could not penetrate the Skagerrak. But the Baltic freezes in winter. Then the iron ore had to be transported overland to the Norwegian port of Narvik, whence ships carried it via the Leads to Germany.

Raeder early brought the Norwegian situation to Hitler's attention, and the Germans made repeated efforts to secure the willing cooperation of the Norwegian government. When these attempts failed, Raeder ordered the naval general staff to prepare plans for the invasion of Norway, and also

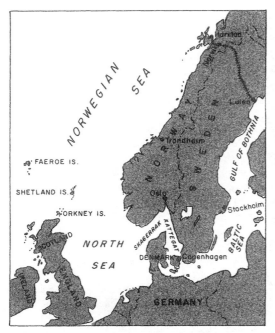

Norwegian Campaign, April–June 1940

of Denmark, to secure undisputed use of adjacent waters. The *Altmark* affair caused the Germans to suspect that the Norwegians had a secret understanding with the British. Then intelligence reached Berlin that the British were planning to mine the Leads. Believing that the Norwegians would acquiesce, Hitler issued the order for the invasion of Norway and Denmark. Landings were to be carried out in the early morning of 9 April 1940, at points from Narvik to Oslo and Copenhagen. In view of British naval superiority, surprise was essential.

Churchill had been insisting for a long while that the Leads must be mined. The Anglo–French Supreme War Council initially opposed any such action but at last, after months of argument, consented to an Admiralty plan to lay minefields off Narvik. This operation was scheduled for the night of 6 April. Had it been carried out then, it could have balked the German scheme. Anticipating that the Germans might react to the mining by invading Norway, the British had a small expeditionary force embarked in ships to proceed with the minelaying forces. Because of last-minute difficulties, the undertaking was postponed for 48 hours, and as intelligence of German activity reached London, the cabinet decided to disembark the troops until the situation was "clarified." Thus, when the German expedition sailed, the troops needed for prompt counteraction in Norway were in England.

The opening clash between the minelaying British and the invading Germans occurred in the gray dawn of 8 April, when H.M. destroyer *Glowworm* encountered a German invasion group headed for Trondheim. Despite hopeless odds, the destroyer attacked the escort, which happened to be the heavy cruiser *Hipper*. At length the *Glowworm*, in a sinking condition, rammed full speed into her adversary, gouging a 130-foot gash in the cruiser's hull. As the destroyer fell away, she blew up and sank. The Germans rescued 38 survivors from the churning sea.

In a rainstorm, before dawn the following morning, the British battle cruiser *Renown* encountered the Narvik-bound invasion force and fought a brief, inconclusive battle with the escorting battleships *Gneisenau* and *Scharnhorst*. In the South, during the 9th, aircraft from the carrier *Furious* sank the light cruiser *Königsberg*, a British submarine sank the light cruiser *Karlsruhe*, and in Oslo Fjord torpedoes from a Norwegian fort sank the heavy cruiser *Blücher*. Nevertheless, by the end of the day, the Germans had achieved all their objectives. Denmark had offered little resistance, and the invaders had a firm grip on all the major ports of Norway.

Only at Narvik was there any serious threat to the German invasion. On Admiralty orders, Captain Warburton-Lee, in the destroyer *Hardy*, accompanied by the destroyers *Hunter*, *Havock*, *Hotspur*, and *Hostile*, entered Ofot Fjord in a snowstorm before dawn on 10 April. Inside, the British found five German destroyers and opened fire with guns and torpedoes, sinking two of the destroyers and also two freighters. Presently five more German destroyers arrived, and the combined force sank the *Hunter* and the *Hardy*, killing Warburton-Lee. The three surviving British destroyers, two of them damaged, escaped to the open sea, sinking an ammunition ship on the way. On the 13th a powerful British naval force, including the battleship *Warspite* and the carrier *Furious*, arrived and finished off the work at Narvik, sinking all eight German destroyers that had survived the earlier attack.

The following day, British troops under Major General Mackesy, supported by naval units commanded by Admiral Lord Cork and Orrery, landed at nearby Harstad on the offshore island of Hinnoy. The object was to set up a base for an early advance on Narvik, but even when the expeditionary force had been reinforced to more than 20,000 men, Mackesy hesitated to move. The cabinet, at length exasperated by the general's repeated delays, appointed Lord Cork to the overall command. Supported by planes from the carrier *Ark Royal*, the expeditionary force on 28 May fought its way into Narvik.

By this time, however, Germany had invaded the Low Countries and France. On the Western Front, total Allied defeat appeared imminent. Accordingly, the troops at Narvik were instructed to destroy installations and prepare for evacuation, which was completed by 8 June. Raeder sent the *Scharnhorst* and the *Gneisenau* to attack the departing forces and their escort. The two battleships surprised and disabled the carrier *Glorious* before she could get her planes into the air. They then sank her and her two escorting destroyers, which made gallant efforts to save their charge. The Germans also sank two freighters and an antisubmarine trawler. The remainder of the expeditionary force reached England safely.

The Fall of France

With the German onslaught through the Netherlands and Belgium, World War II began in earnest, and the Conservative Government of Prime Minister Chamberlain was unequal to the challenge. On 10 May, the day Hitler struck at the Low Countries, Chamberlain yielded his office to Winston Churchill, who told a hushed House of Commons, "I have nothing to offer but blood, toil, tears and sweat."

The German attack began with Army Group B smashing through Holland toward Belgium, its right flank protected by the North Sea. The French and British, pivoting on the end of the Maginot Line at the Franco–Belgian border, swung to the northeast to meet the attack on the line Antwerp–Sedan. This move was just what the Germans anticipated. Seven Panzer divisions of Army Group A penetrated the Ardennes Forest, crossed the Meuse River, broke through the weak hinge of the pivoting Allied line, and, followed by additional German forces, raced to the Channel, trapping the French and British forces that had advanced into Belgium. In a week the Allied situation was critical; in two, it was desperate. Only evacuation by sea could save the Allied troops from capture or annihilation.

Grimly the French and British tried to cut southward through Army Group A, aided by additional forces in France driving north, but incredible inefficiency in the French high command and the overwhelming strength of the German ground and air forces combined to defeat the attempt. Two weeks after the beginning of hostilities in the West, the Allies were in full retreat to the Dunkirk area.

The evacuation from Dunkirk was a masterpiece of improvisation. British boat owners spontaneously aided naval efforts, volunteering themselves and their craft for service. But it was the Royal Navy that bore the brunt of the task, which began on 26 May. Churchill and the Admiralty hoped to take off about 45,000 troops, but the rear guard held the German ground forces back longer than anyone could have expected, and the French Air Force and the Royal Air Force combined to hold back the Luftwaffe, while the vessels—destroyers, Channel ferries, sloops, yachts, motorboats—shuttled back and forth between Dunkirk beach and English ports. In the nine days of the evacuation, more than 338,000 British, French, Dutch, and Belgian troops were delivered to England, but they had to leave their heavy weapons behind.

The Germans scarcely paused to regroup before, on 5 June, they began an attack southward, into France. This time there was no Battle of the Marne to stop them. Premier Paul Reynaud pleaded with Churchill to land more troops in France and to commit the entire resources of the Royal Air Force to stop the Germans. Churchill did what he could, but he adamantly refused to commit 25 fighter squadrons of the RAF, the absolute minimum, his air marshals told him, required for the defense of Britain in the event of a French collapse.

It soon became apparent that there was no possibility of saving France from defeat. Reynaud ordered General Maxime Weygand to surrender on the field. Such a surrender would end the war in France but leave the French Government free to fight on from her other territories and at sea. Weygand refused, saying the honor of the army was involved. Churchill offered, as a last desperate resort, unity between the two nations, the two peoples to share common citizenship and a common government. The French Council of Ministers rejected the proposal.

On 16 June, the defeatists in the French Government forced Reynaud to resign. He was succeeded by Marshal Philippe Pétain, who immediately appealed for an armistice. During the ensuing negotiations, the British put pressure on the French to move their warships beyond possible German control, preferably to British ports, but they stayed where they were, except for two nearly completed battleships, the *Richelieu*, which escaped to Dakar, and the *Jean Bart*, which reached Casablanca.

To make matters worse, on 10 June, in order to have a place at the victors' feast, Mussolini declared war on France, an act that caused an indignant President Roosevelt to declare, "The hand that held the dagger has struck it into the back of its neighbor."

On 22 June, in the forest of Compiègne, in the same railway carriage in which the victorious French had dictated armistice terms to Germany in 1918, the triumphant Nazis read their conditions to the defeated French. France was divided into two zones: occupied France, the Atlantic front and all the northern section, including Paris; and unoccupied France, with a government under Pétain in Vichy. In fact, the Vichy government would be dominated by the Nazi sympathizer Pierre Laval.

By the armistice terms that the French agreed to, their warships were to be assembled in ports to be specified, to be demobilized and disarmed under German and Italian control. Privately, the French naval commander in chief, Admiral Jean Darlan, had assured the British that neither the Germans nor the Italians would ever be allowed to use the French ships, but in view of Darlan's known totalitarian sympathies and also in view of Pétain's weakness of will, the British took cold comfort from his assurances.

The fall of France presented the British with an entirely new strategic situation. They now fought alone, with such limited aid as they could get from the Commonwealth nations, mainly Canada, Australia, and New Zealand, all countries of limited populations and industrial output. They were opposed by the Axis partners, whose control on the Atlantic front now extended from North Cape to the Pyrenees, a long coast impossible to blockade. In the Mediterranean, which previously they had controlled with the French, they were challenged by Italy, which had a not inconsiderable navy and air force.

The British, anticipating Italy's entry into the war, had recently strengthened their naval forces in the Mediterranean. With the arrival of four battleships and the obsolescent carrier *Eagle*, Admiral Sir Andrew Cunningham, Commander in Chief Mediterranean Fleet, shifted his flag from the island of Malta to the battleship *Warspite* and his base of operations from Malta to Alexandria to join the British troops and RAF detachment already there under terms of the Anglo–Egyptian Treaty of 1936. A short time later, the Admiralty assembled at Gibraltar a naval force designated Force H, made up of the battleships *Valiant* and *Resolution*, the battle cruiser *Hood*, the carrier *Ark Royal*, 2 cruisers, and 11 destroyers. Force H, commanded by Vice Admiral Sir James Somerville, would operate in either the Atlantic or the Mediterranean as need arose.

The French Fleet

The prospect that the French warships might be added to the German and Italian navies prompted the British to undertake what Churchill later called a "hateful act." Distrusting Hitler's promise that he would never use the ships of the French Navy, they acted to ensure that those outside of French European ports would be neutralized.

On 3 July 1940, British marines boarded all French ships at Plymouth and Portsmouth and put their crews ashore. A few of the French sailors volunteered to join the Free French forces under General Charles de Gaulle, who had set himself up as head of the Free French Government in Exile. Most refused and were interned in Britain.

On the same date, Admiral Somerville appeared with Force H off Oran, where Admiral Marcel Gensoul commanded the largest French naval squadron outside of French ports. Complying with Admiralty orders, Somerville presented Gensoul with a series of choices: he could join forces with the British; he could sail to a British port, to a French port in the West Indies, or to the United States to have his ships disarmed; or he could sink his ships. Gensoul, incensed by the obvious threat of force, rejected all the alternatives and began to clear his ships for action. Somerville's force thereupon opened fire, capsizing one French battleship, setting fire to another, which then ran aground, immobilizing the battle cruiser *Dunkerque* by a hit in the engine room, and damaging a destroyer. In this quick naval execution, 1,300 French sailors died. The battle cruiser *Strasbourg* and some destroyers managed to clear the harbor and escaped to Toulon. Three days later the *Dunkerque* was further damaged by torpedo planes from the *Ark Royal*.

At Alexandria, where the French and British ships were anchored in the same harbor, friendship between Admirals Cunningham and Godfroy averted tragedy. Cunningham had an advantage over Somerville in that he was in no hurry, not having to fear the arrival of French reinforcements from Toulon. By 5 July, the two commanders had worked out a gentlemen's agreement whereby Godfroy would discharge fuel, remove firing mechanisms from his guns, and make no attempt to break out to sea. Cunningham, for his part, agreed to undertake no measures to seize the French ships by force as had been done in England.

At Dakar torpedo planes from the British carrier *Hermes* attacked the new battleship *Richelieu*, doing enough damage to keep her off the seas for a year. In September a bombardment by Force H in support of an unsuccessful Free French landing at Dakar sank a destroyer and two submarines at a cost to the British of a battleship and two cruisers damaged. The battleship *Jean Bart* at Casablanca was not molested because her main battery had not been mounted. Two French cruisers and a carrier at Martinique were neutralized through the diplomatic efforts of President Roosevelt.

The Vichy government, enraged by the attacks on their ships, ordered reprisals against the British. On 5 July 1940, French planes attacked Gibraltar, but their bombs fell harmlessly into the harbor. On 8 July the French severed diplomatic relations with Britain but stopped short of a declaration of war.

The Battle of Britain

When, following the fall of France, the Germans extended peace feelers to Britain, the British replied with an emphatic negative. In response, Hitler, on 16 July 1940, issued a directive for the invasion of England, Operation Sea Lion. Anticipating such a move, the Royal Navy was prepared to shift the Home Fleet from Scapa Flow to Rosyth, whence it could make a quick dash to the south if invasion forces appeared on the Channel. The Navy even arranged to strip convoys of vital escorts and bring the escort vessels home to defend England's shores. The British realized, however, that in this situation England's first line of defense was the Royal Air Force. There could be no invasion unless the invader first won command of the air over the Channel. That meant destroying the RAF's fighters.

Admiral Raeder, also anticipating the Führer's directive, had his staff at work on an invasion plan. From Hitler he received a plan drawn up by the army. It called for a landing along a 200-mile front extending from Ramsgate near the mouth of the Thames all the way around to the Isle of Wight. Raeder explained that the German navy lacked the ships for a landing of that breadth and that the French ports were too damaged to launch such an operation even if naval strength were no problem. He proposed a much more modest landing between Dover and Beachy Head. On hearing this, the chief of the Army General Staff snorted, "I might just as well put the troops that have landed straight through a sausage machine." Raeder replied coldly that he wanted to put the troops ashore and not at the bottom of the sea.

In the end, the plan adopted was a compromise that suited neither service. But the army and the

navy did agree that no plan was practical unless the Luftwaffe could first knock out the RAF, and thus they passed the ball to Reichsmarschall Hermann Göring, Luftwaffe commander in chief. Göring began the Battle of Britain on 12 August by sending his bombers to knock out the airfields and radar installations that would enable the British Spitfire fighters to shoot down his planes. On the 13th, designated Eagle Day, the air campaign began in earnest, but on that day Göring made a serious mistake in ordering his flyers to waste no more time and effort on British radar installations.

Within a few days German bombers and fighters were appearing by the hundreds over England. They took heavy losses but reported exacting much heavier losses in British planes. The truth was that the British were shooting down nearly twice as many planes as they lost. Fighting over or near their home territory was an advantage, but of greater benefit was the early warning they received from their radar and the even earlier warning they obtained by reading Luftwaffe radio communications sent in a cryptographic system the British called Ultra.[2] With advance information of German times and targets, the Spitfires could almost always be in the air at high altitude when the German planes arrived.

In the night of 24 August, a dozen German bombers lost their way and mistakenly bombed London. The RAF retaliated the next night by bombing Berlin, something Göring had sworn would never occur while he commanded the Luftwaffe. The Reichsmarschall reacted by shifting the weight of his bombing from fighter airfields and installations to British cities, thereby canceling whatever chance he had of knocking out the RAF. Hitler, dubious from the beginning about getting his army safely across the Channel, now regarded it as impossible. He ordered Operation Sea Lion

---

[2]The armed forces of Germany and several other major countries enciphered their most secret messages by means of some variation of the Enigma machine, developed in 1923 in Germany and since then widely used around the world for concealing military and commercial secrets. The Enigma looked and operated something like a typewriter, was electrically driven, and enciphered by means of three or more wired, interchangeable, wheel-like rotors that rotated at different rates as the keys were struck. Early in World War II the British obtained a replica of the German Enigma but were long frustrated by the variable wiring and setting of the rotors, which the Germans frequently changed. They succeeded first in reading the Luftwaffe messages, presumably because an air force must depend heavily on radio communication. The British applied the term Ultra to all messages encrypted on the German Enigma.

postponed until the following spring, and a month later he canceled it entirely. In the course of the Battle of Britain, August to October 1940, the Luftwaffe lost 1,733 aircraft; the RAF, 915 fighters.

In mid-December 1940, Hitler issued an alert for Operation Barbarossa, the invasion of the Soviet Union. Before he could launch the new attack, he was obliged to divert forces to North Africa and Greece to rescue defeated Italian troops. As he strategically faced east, an undefeated and defiant Britain behind his back obliged him to retain 49 divisions in western Europe to guard the Atlantic coast. German forces thus became fatally overextended. There simply were not enough Germans or enough supplies available to conquer, occupy, and defend so much territory.

The Mediterranean Campaigns

The Italian Navy was poorly prepared for combat. Political decisions made by Mussolini and his Fascists had adversely affected military capabilities. Hence, naval leaders were appalled when the Duce led their nation into war. When they pointed out that the navy, among other deficiencies, lacked aircraft carriers, Mussolini assured them that the air force would fulfill the navy's scouting needs. The assurance proved false, in part because the air force lacked adequate training in ship recognition and overwater operations, and in part because airmen gave naval support low priority.

The Italian Navy's weaknesses were demonstrated in an action on 9 July 1940 off Calabria. Admiral Cunningham in the *Warspite*, with 2 other battleships, 5 light cruisers, several destroyers, and the carrier *Eagle*, encountered an Italian force of 2 battleships, 6 heavy and 10 light cruisers, and a number of destroyers under the command of the Italian commander in chief, Admiral Angelo Campioni. The *Eagle* launched planes that slightly damaged one enemy cruiser. The *Warspite*, at a range of 26,000 yards, landed a 15-inch shell near a funnel of the Italian flagship, the battleship *Guilio Cesare*. Campioni, realizing that he was outgunned and fearful of the British carrier, turned away under a smoke screen, calling by radio for support from Italian land-based air. The planes arrived and bombed both fleets impartially without hitting anything.

Ten days later, in the Battle of Cape Spada, two lightly armored Italian cruisers pursuing four British destroyers ran into the Australian cruiser *Sydney* and turned away. The *Sydney*, giving chase, sank one of the cruisers and slightly damaged the other.

In North Africa, Mussolini thought he saw an opportunity to fulfill his dream of establishing a new Roman Empire. On 13 September, Marshal Rodolfo Graziani, on the Duce's orders, began to advance on Egypt. Reaching Sidi Barrani, 60 miles inside the Egyptian border, he started to build an elaborate base to thwart the inevitable counterattack. Nothing the Duce said could force Graziani to move.

With his army thus bogged down in Egypt, Mussolini sought another field of action. On 15 October, over the protests of all his military advisers, he ordered an invasion of Greece. When Italian troops crossed the frontier from Albania on 28 October, the British, fulfilling assurances made earlier to the Greek government, sent RAF and Royal Navy planes to attack Italian shipping and established a naval base at Suda Bay in Crete. The Greeks, however, scarcely needed such assistance; on 8 November the Italian offensive stalled, and a few days later a Greek offensive pushed the invaders back into Albania.

Thus in both his North African venture and his Greek invasion, Mussolini failed in his attempts to turn political opportunism into military success. His dreams of a new Roman Empire were getting nowhere.

Partly to prevent the Italian Navy from assisting in the operation against Greece, Cunningham decided to strike at the naval base at Taranto. On 11 November, the carrier *Illustrious*, escorted by cruisers and destroyers, arrived unobserved off the heel of the Italian boot and after dark launched 12 planes to hit the principal units of the Italian fleet in Taranto harbor. They scored hits on the battleships *Cavour* and *Littorio* at the cost of one plane. An hour later, a second wave of nine planes from the *Illustrious* arrived and scored a hit on the battleship *Duilio* and two more on the *Littorio*, with the loss of one aircraft. The attack reduced the Italian battleship force to three vessels, the *Giulio Cesare*, the *Vittorio Veneto*, and the *Doria*. The *Littorio* and the *Duilio* were out of action for several months; the *Cavour* never went to sea again. Immediately after the attack, the major Italian ships that had survived moved to Naples.

The British situation was also improving in North Africa. Major General Sir Richard O'Connor's Western Desert Force, in Egypt, had been raised to 36,000 men and 275 tanks—the nucleus of the future British Eighth Army. On 9 December O'Connor staged a raid on the Italian position at Sidi Barrani. The raid soon became an all-out drive as the Italians fell back out of Egypt into Libya,

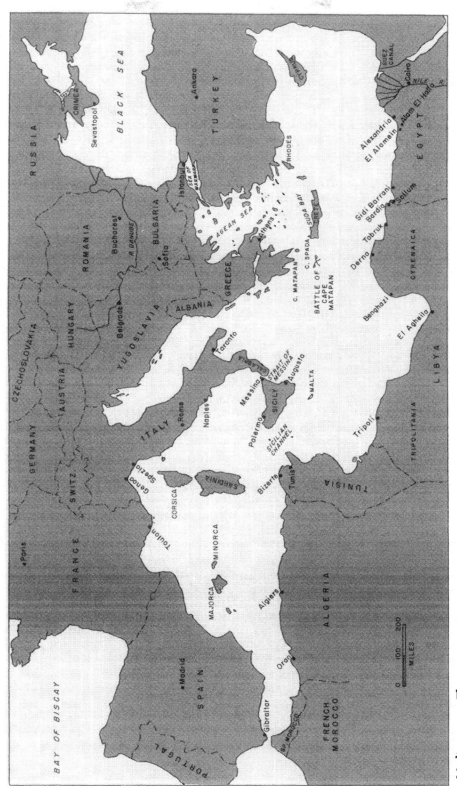

Mediterranean Theater

suffering extraordinarily severe losses. In swift pursuit, the British took Sollum, Bardia, and Tobruk. By 9 February O'Connor's troops stood before El Agheila at the threshold of Tripolitania. The Western Desert Force, which had never numbered more than 40,000 men, had captured 130,000 prisoners, 400 tanks, and 1,290 guns. The British casualties amounted to 476 killed and 1,225 wounded. During the campaign the RAF had provided tactical support, and the Inshore Squadron of Cunningham's Mediterranean Fleet had kept supplies moving from Egypt to O'Connor's advancing troops and armor.

Hitler knew that it was vital for political reasons to restore Axis prestige in the Mediterranean. Moreover, he had to strengthen the Axis Mediterranean defenses in order to forestall any possible threat to the right flank of his forthcoming advance into Russia. To give direct support to Italy in Greece and Albania, Hitler started moving his troops and armor through Yugoslavia, Romania, and Bulgaria. To rescue the Italians in North Africa, he sent a mechanized force under Major General Erwin Rommel to Libya and transferred 500 planes, specially trained to attack ships, from Norway to airfields in Calabria and Sicily.

The tasks assigned the Luftwaffe unit were to protect Axis shipping to North Africa, prevent the passage of British convoys through the central Mediterranean, and neutralize Malta by air attack. German pilots soon demonstrated high competence in carrying out the first two of these assignments. Toward mid-January 1941 their dive-bombers damaged the *Illustrious* and two British cruisers, one so seriously that she had to be scuttled. The *Illustrious*, severely battered, had to go to the United States for repairs that amounted to virtual rebuilding. This action confirmed the British War Cabinet in its view that supplies should continue to be hauled the long way around Africa.

When the Germans began advancing on the Greek peninsula, the British government decided that for political reasons it had to sacrifice O'Connor's triumphs in North Africa in order to reinforce Greece. General Sir Archibald Wavell, Commander in Chief Middle East, sent 58,000 experienced troops there. This transfer of battle-hardened Britons granted the Axis North African forces an unexpected reprieve. Even before Wavell's troops began crossing the Mediterranean, Rommel's Afrika Korps started moving into Libya.

The Germans urged the Italian Navy to intercept the British troop convoys en route to Greece, so Admiral Angelo Iachino, who had replaced Campioni as Italian naval commander in chief, left port on 26 March 1941 with the *Vittorio Veneto*, eight cruisers, and a number of destroyers. Admiral Cunningham, expecting the enemy to try to interfere with the troop movement, was ready when Ultra warned him that the Italian fleet was at sea. At dusk on the twenty-seventh he sortied from Alexandria with the battleships *Warspite*, *Barham*, and *Valiant*, the carrier *Formidable*, and 9 destroyers. The result was the Battle of Cape Matapan, a kind of small-scale Battle of Jutland supplemented by seaborne air power.

On the morning of 28 March 1941 three Italian cruisers sighted a British cruiser-destroyer force and engaged it in a running battle. Admiral Iachino, coming up fast in the *Vittorio Veneto* and unaware that Cunningham had left port, hoped to trap the light British force between his own ships and the Italian cruiser force. Cunningham, apprised by radio of the attack on the cruiser-destroyer force, ordered the *Formidable* to launch a strike against the Italian fleet. The planes made no hits, but the attack enabled the British cruisers to escape and induced Iachino to head for home at 25 knots. Cunningham's heavy ships went after him.

During the next few hours, the *Formidable* launched repeated strikes with bombers and torpedo planes. At 1520 a torpedo hit temporarily stopped the *Vittorio Veneto*; an hour and a half later she was making 19 knots. A strike late in the day by the *Formidable*'s planes stopped the cruiser *Pola* for good. Detaching two cruisers and four destroyers to assist her, Iachino continued his retirement, unaware that the British Mediterranean Fleet was closing in on him. That evening Cunningham's force found the crippled *Pola*, just as the Italian cruiser-destroyer group arrived to assist her. Taking advantage of surprise, the British sank all three cruisers and two of the destroyers. Cunningham's sailors pulled nearly 1,200 Italian survivors out of the water before the arrival of German bombers put an end to the rescue efforts.

On 6 April the Germans, supported by overwhelming air power, invaded Greece. Greek and British troops were forced back, and on the twenty-fourth Greece surrendered. The British were thus confronted with another Dunkirk. Their evacuation had to be carried out under heavy air opposition, mostly over beaches and at night. The withdrawal operation cost the Royal Navy 25 vessels, including 5 hospital ships. Left behind were some 6,000 Britons and all the British tanks and other equipment.

Because of its strategic position, the British were determined to hold Crete, as they had held Malta.

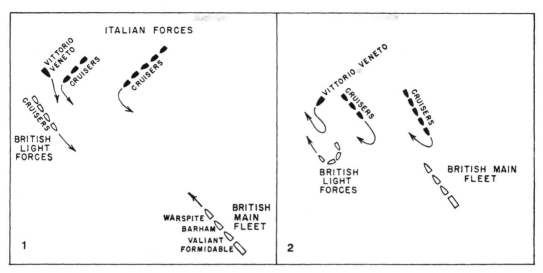

Battle of Cape Matapan, 28 March 1941

They probably would have succeeded had the Germans attempted to capture it by amphibious assault alone. But the Germans were relying heavily on airborne forces to spearhead the invasion. Their primary attack was made by 16,000 troops transported in 530 planes and 100 gliders. Four thousand more troops came in by parachute. Meeting stubborn resistance, the Germans sent in reinforcement convoys on 21 and 22 May. A British cruiser force intercepted both, but two Italian destroyer escorts, the *Lupo* and the *Sagittario*, put up such a fight that the convoys escaped with minimal losses, while the British combatant ships withdrew, believing that heavier Axis naval forces were at hand.

In the Cretan campaign, the Royal Navy lost 3 cruisers and 6 destroyers. Thirteen other ships were damaged, including the *Warspite*, the *Barham*, and the *Formidable*. The Germans lost 220 planes and about 6,500 troops, including a large part of their only airborne division. In view of such heavy casualties among his airborne troops, Hitler forbade their being used in a projected operation against Malta.

Toward the end of 1941, Britain's Mediterranean Fleet suffered several losses from undersea attack. In mid-November, *U–81* sank the carrier *Ark Royal*. A week later, *U–331* torpedoed the battleship *Barham*, which blew up with heavy loss of life. In mid-December, *U–557* sank the cruiser *Galatea*. A few days later, the British lost a cruiser and a destroyer to Italian mines. On the same day, the Italian submarine *Scire* released in the vicinity of Alexandria harbor 3 two-man torpedoes—midget

submarines with detachable warheads. Two of these "human torpedoes" headed for the battleships *Queen Elizabeth* and *Valiant*, while the third damaged a tanker and a destroyer. When captured, one of the Italian torpedomen, in an act of gallantry, warned the *Valiant*'s captain that a warhead fastened to his ship's bottom would shortly explode. This information gave the crew time to evacuate the lower decks. Both battleships, heavily damaged, were out of commission for many months.

The Desert War

While the British vainly attempted to save Greece and Crete, they faced impending disaster on the border of Egypt. On 2 April 1941 General Rommel, heading his Afrika Korps, launched an attack. General Wavell, having sent his most experienced troops to Greece, had relieved them with raw units from home. The Western Desert Force, thus weakened, could not withstand the precision of Rommel's advance. O'Connor was recalled from leave and rushed back to the front, but the Germans captured him and continued their eastward thrust. By the end of May the Afrika Korps had crossed into Egypt.

The arrival of a British convoy, the first successful passage of merchant ships in several months from Gibraltar to Alexandria, encouraged Wavell to mount a counteroffensive. Badly managed, it failed. Churchill thereupon replaced Wavell with General Sir Claude Auchinleck.

During the next year and a half, the desert war in North Africa was a seesaw affair in which, generally, the side that got the most supplies did the advancing. Overall, about 85 percent of the material destined for Rommel reached him, but he suffered through some lean times. A major key to his advance or retreat was Malta and its airfields. Situated near the midpoint, the island afforded air and sea support for British ships in the Mediterranean. It also sat squarely athwart the normal sea routes between Italy and Libya. When Malta was strong, Axis losses rose; when the island was weak, Rommel and his Italian allies received more of everything. It could be kept strong only with supplies of food and fuel and a steady replacement of lost planes. Keeping Malta supplied required a regular escort of convoys to the island, one of the most perilous duties assigned to Force H and the Mediterranean Fleet. Replacing lost planes was the equally risky duty of carriers. These, including the American carrier *Wasp*, approached Malta, sent Spitfires by air, and beat a hasty retreat.

One of the most hard-fought convoy battles of the war took place in August 1942 as the British attempted to make the run from Gibraltar to Malta. Attacked by German and Italian aircraft and submarines and by Italian light units, the convoy suffered the loss of the venerable *Eagle*, 2 cruisers, and a destroyer. Three other warships were damaged. Only 5 of the 14 merchant ships made port.

The Italian Navy, escorting supply ships from Europe to North Africa, also sustained heavy losses. Its misfortune can be attributed in large part to Ultra. The ability to read German and Italian radio traffic enabled the British to intercept much of the Axis seaborne traffic. The British took extraordinary pains to conceal their codebreaking successes. Sometimes they would send out a search plane to "discover" and report an Axis convoy whose existence had already been revealed by Ultra. Thus they could send out an air attack without arousing the enemy's suspicion that Britain had some special source of military intelligence.

In the summer of 1942 the Afrika Korps and its Italian allies, having taken Tobruk and about 40,000 British prisoners, again crossed the frontier into Egypt. Rommel reached El Alamein, 70 miles from Alexandria. He got no farther. Hitler had diverted supplies intended for North Africa to the hard-pressed Russian front. At the same time the British defenders received 300 Sherman tanks and 100 self-propelled guns from the United States. Other factors in the successful British defense were air superiority, skillful use of Ultra information, and the generalship of Sir Claude Auchinleck.

Despite Auchinleck's success, he failed to order his troops, exhausted by their defensive efforts, to advance promptly on the enemy, and an impatient

Churchill replaced him with Sir Harold Alexander. At the same time, General Sir Bernard L. Montgomery succeeded to command of the British ground forces in Egypt, now designated the Eighth Army. Even more than Auchinleck, Montgomery refused to be hurried. A cautious man, he demanded more time and more supplies while incessantly drilling his men.

Meanwhile, new long-range torpedo planes operating out of Malta were making it almost impossible for Axis shipping to evade attack, even by the most circuitous routing. Rommel knew that if he was to win a breakthrough at El Alamein, he would have to attack before further reinforcements and supplies reached the British.

On the night of 30 August 1942 Rommel hurled an attack at the ridge of Alam el Halfa, hoping to outflank the El Alamein defenses. Unfortunately for him, he had signaled his intentions to Berlin and Rome. Thanks to Ultra, Montgomery and Alexander read his messages almost as quickly as the Germans and Italians did. Montgomery accordingly prepared a trap. He heavily fortified the ridge and then let Rommel's armored column through to face massed gunfire that cost it heavily in men and vehicles. By day, while the RAF bombed and strafed Rommel's embattled armor ashore, other RAF planes and the Royal Navy, guided by Ultra information, found and sank 3 tankers bringing oil and gasoline to the German general. On 2 September Rommel called off the attack.

"With the failure of this offensive," he wrote, "our last chance of gaining the Suez Canal had gone. We could now expect that the full production of British industry and, more important, the enormous industrial potential of America . . . would finally turn the tide against us."

The American Drift into War

Promptly following the outbreak of war in Europe, President Roosevelt established a naval neutrality patrol to track and report any belligerent aircraft, ships, or submarines approaching the United States or the West Indies. A month later the United States, in concert with the other American republics, proclaimed a wide safety belt around the Americas south of Canada and warned the belligerents to refrain from military operations inside this area.

Though at this early period most Americans were determined to remain on the sidelines in the conflict, few were neutral in sentiment. Americans in general condemned the totalitarian and aggressive government of Germany and were outraged at its brutal treatment of Jews and other minorities.

Even the American Neutrality Acts were less than strictly neutral, because British and French cargo vessels, in accord with the U. S. "cash-and-carry" policy, could visit the United States and pick up purchased materials, while those of Germany could not penetrate the British blockade. In November 1939 the U. S. government repealed the arms embargo. Britain and France could then purchase munitions from the United States, and Germany could not.

The fall of France awakened the U. S. Congress to the threat from abroad. Considerable doubt existed, in Washington as elsewhere, that Britain could survive the German onslaught. The dreadful prospect that the Royal Navy might be turned over to Germany impressed the U. S. government with the need to build new ships and to prepare for the worst. Congress passed legislation providing for a two-ocean navy and for the first peacetime draft in U. S. history.

Britain entered the war seriously short of vessels suitable for convoy escort. Loss of such vessels during the Norwegian campaign and the Dunkirk evacuation made the shortage critical. To remedy this situation, President Roosevelt in September 1940 made a deal with Prime Minister Churchill whereby the U. S. Navy turned over to Britain 50 of its oldest destroyers in return for 99-year leases on sites for bases at six locations from the Bahamas to British Guiana. Britain added as a gift similar leases on bases in Bermuda and Newfoundland. The United States in turn presented to Britain ten Coast Guard cutters equipped for antisubmarine duty.

Despite strong pacifist sentiment among the American people, the United States began to drift into undeclared war with Germany. In December 1940, Roosevelt proposed the idea of "lend-lease." By this proposal, British ships would still have to pick up the goods; only the "cash" part of the "cash-and-carry" policy would be eliminated. This proposition, unlike the destroyers–bases deal, required congressional approval, which was granted in March 1941 after extended hearings. Lend-lease enabled the country to provide munitions to Britain and, later, to the Soviet Union on a loan basis, thereby averting the old problem of war debts.

In early 1941, American and British officers met secretly in Washington and concluded the ABC-1 Staff Agreement whereby the U. S. Navy would assist the British in escort of convoy across the Atlantic, and the United States, if forced into war with both Japan and the European Axis, would exert her principal efforts against Germany. This policy of "beat Hitler first" was based on Germany's advanced industrial development, the

achievements of her scientists, her proximity to Britain, and her military attainments thus far.

In August 1941 President Roosevelt and Prime Minister Churchill and their senior officers met at Argentia, Newfoundland. Here they worked out details for U. S. escort of convoys, discussed further implementation of the president's "all aid short of war" policy, and drew up an Atlantic Charter setting forth their postwar aims for the betterment of mankind.

The shooting phase of the undeclared war began on 4 September, when a U-boat fired torpedoes at the U. S. destroyer *Greer*, and the *Greer* counterattacked with depth charges. Both missed, but in response to the German attack, President Roosevelt ordered his warships to open fire on any vessel that interfered with U. S. shipping.

To prepare the Neutrality Patrol for its new assignments, it was strengthened and reorganized and given the more appropriate designation U. S. Atlantic Fleet. Its commander, the tough and dedicated Ernest J. King, was promoted to admiral with the title Commander in Chief Atlantic Fleet (CinC-Lant).

In July U. S. marines had begun relieving the British garrison on Iceland, and soon U. S. naval patrol squadrons were flying convoy coverage from both Iceland and Newfoundland. It was between these bases that American warships in September began escorting British merchant ships. The Canadian Navy would escort an eastbound convoy to a point south of Newfoundland and turn it over to U. S. warships, which would shepherd it across to the midocean meeting point (momp) south of Iceland. Here the Americans would hand the convoy over to the Royal Navy for the final run to the ports of Britain. Usually the Americans fueled at Iceland and picked up a westbound convoy for escort back to the Newfoundland area.

First blood in the undeclared war was drawn in the night of 7 October, when a U-boat torpedoed the U. S. destroyer *Kearny*, which was escorting a slow convoy. The destroyer made port, but 11 of her crew had been killed. Two weeks later, the U. S. destroyer *Reuben James*, also on convoy escort, was sunk by a U-boat. More than a hundred of her company, including all her officers, were lost.

In response to these attacks, Congress repealed the 1939 neutrality act forbidding U. S. ships to enter war zones. American merchant ships could now carry lend-lease goods to the ports of Britain. The United States did not officially enter World War II, however, until after the Japanese raided Pearl Harbor, 7 December 1941. The following day the United States declared war on Japan. On 11

December, Germany and Italy, honoring a treaty commitment to Japan, declared war on the United States, whereupon the United States immediately declared war on Germany and Italy.

On the advice of Secretary of the Navy Frank Knox, President Roosevelt appointed Admiral Royal E. Ingersoll CinCLant and ordered Admiral King to Washington as Commander in Chief U. S. Fleet (CominCh). When it was found that King's duties overlapped those of Admiral Harold R. Stark, the Chief of Naval Operations (CNO), Roosevelt sent Stark to London as Commander U. S. Naval Forces, Europe, and appointed King CNO as well as Cominch. No other American naval officer, before or afterward, has ever wielded the authority vested in King. He was quite simply to run the U. S. Navy and report directly to the president.

In addition to running the Navy, King served on the Joint Chiefs of Staff (JCS), which, under the president, directed the operations of the U. S. armed forces. The other members were General George C. Marshall, Army Chief of Staff; General Henry H. Arnold, Commanding General of the Army Air Forces; and, later, Admiral William D. Leahy, Chief of Staff to the President. At intervals the U. S. Joint Chiefs of Staff met with the British Imperial General Staff. Together they comprised the Combined Chiefs of Staff (CCS), the senior executive body controlling Allied military operations.

Chapter 24
The Battle of the Atlantic

Although U-boats had brought Britain to the verge of defeat in World War I, the Admiralty subsequently neglected antisubmarine warfare. The British admirals were lulled into a false sense of security by the Treaty of Versailles, which forbade Germany to build or possess any submarines at all. Hitler's 1935 repudiation of the treaty limitations on German armaments failed to stir them into action. They believed that in the use of convoy they had found the answer to the U-boat menace, and that with the development of the underwater, sound-locating asdic (called sonar in the U. S. Navy) the submarine had ceased altogether to be a threat, since supposedly it could no longer hide under water. The admirals disregarded evidence that except in ideal test conditions asdic was undependable.

As a substitute for the treaty limitations, the British accepted an Anglo–German Naval Agreement whereby Germany was permitted to build surface warships up to 35 percent of British tonnage, and submarines up to 45 percent, or in certain circumstances up to 100 percent, of British tonnage. The British were further lulled in 1936 when the maritime powers, including Britain and Germany, signed a submarine protocol reasserting the prize-law rule that a warship, surface or submarine, before disabling or sinking a merchant ship, must provide for the safety of passengers and crew. Germany was thus apparently repudiating the unrestricted submarine warfare by which she had brought Britain to desperate straits in World War I.

Following the signing of the Anglo–German Naval Agreement, Admiral Raeder appointed Captain Karl Dönitz to head the future German submarine force. Dönitz was well equipped for the job. During World War I, he had commanded U-boats, and thereafter he had served in Germany's small postwar surface fleet. At the time of his appointment to the submarines, he was commanding a cruiser.

Dönitz assumed that in any future war the British would use convoy, and, being a realist, he took for granted that the U-boats would again employ unrestricted warfare. To foil asdic he planned to have his U-boats attack on the surface at night—though, when opportunity presented, individual submarines were to attack by daylight, submerged, at close range. To defeat the convoy Dönitz proposed to have them attack in groups, later called wolf packs. U-boat commanders were to report sightings of enemy ships by radio, and he, from his shore base, would coach the groups by radio to the target. Senior officers objected that such breaking of radio silence could enable the enemy to locate and attack the U-boats. Dönitz replied it was a risk they had to take in order to secure the advantages of group attack.

As Dönitz had anticipated, Hitler in April 1939 scrapped the Anglo–German Naval Agreement. Germany was now free to build as many warships as she wanted of whatever sort she liked. Dönitz asked for 300 U-boats, the minimum according to his calculations needed to starve England, but his request collided with Raeder's Plan Z. Based on Hitler's assurance that there would be no war with England, Plan Z was expected to produce a balanced fleet by 1948. Given priority were six new 56,000-ton battleships. With the outbreak of war, however, construction on these big ships was halted, and the steel was diverted to other purposes. Thus Germany entered the conflict with two 31,000-ton battleships, the *Scharnhorst* and the *Gneisenau*, completed, and two 42,000-ton battleships, the *Tirpitz* and the *Bismarck*, nearing completion; three 20,000-ton pocket battleships, the *Deutschland*, the *Admiral Scheer*, and the *Admiral Graf Spee*; three heavy cruisers; six light cruisers; and a respectable number of destroyers; but only 56 submarines. The four battleships at first remained in port as a fleet in being to inhibit the operations of the British Home Fleet. The pocket battleships and the cruisers were expected to supplement the U-boats by attacking enemy shipping on the oceans.

The Royal Navy, like the Kriegsmarine, was dominated by battleship admirals, who had developed their ideas about naval warfare largely from studying the Battle of Jutland. They too postponed building smaller vessels, destroyers and other ships suitable for convoy escort. Many of the

British escorts early in the war were hurriedly adapted from fishing trawlers and other small craft, ill suited for the rigorous duties they had to perform.

U-boat Operations until the Fall of France

Lieutenant Lemp of *U-30* mistook the passenger liner *Athenia* for a Royal Navy auxiliary cruiser. In sinking her without warning, he supposed he was conforming to prize law and the 1936 submarine protocol. The British drew the conclusion that the Germans had already adopted unrestricted submarine warfare. The Admiralty, which had assumed control of all merchant shipping, ordered ships with speeds under 15 knots to move in convoy. Faster ships sailed independently. By the end of 1939, the Royal Navy had escorted nearly 5,800 vessels with the loss of only 12, and only 4 of these had been sunk by U-boats. During the same period, 102 independently routed merchant vessels were sunk. Dönitz meanwhile had lost nine U-boats, nearly a sixth of his original strength.

The success of convoy contrasts sharply with so-called offensive operations against the U-boats, a throwback to the ineffective antisubmarine patrols of World War I. On 14 September 1939, less than two weeks after Britain's declaration of war, the carrier *Ark Royal* on such a patrol narrowly avoided being torpedoed by *U-39*. Three days later *U-29* sank the 22,500-ton carrier *Courageous*. The Admiralty thereupon canceled the use of carriers for such operations.

In response to the sinking of the *Athenia*, First Lord of the Admiralty Churchill announced that he was arming British merchant vessels. In retaliation Hitler removed some restrictions on U-boats. General removal of restrictions came later, step by step, in reaction to moves by the British.

The most spectacular feat carried out by any U-boat in the fall of 1939 was the penetration of Scapa Flow on the night of 14 October by *U-47* under the command of Lieutenant Günther Prien. Prien successfully navigated the tortuous channel and sank the old battleship *Royal Oak*, with the loss of 786 of her ship's company. Prien's exploit was followed by Luftwaffe raids on Scapa Flow and the Firth of Forth. An embarrassed Admiralty ordered the Home Fleet to retreat to anchorages on the west coast of Scotland, while German propaganda exulted that Britannia had been driven from the North Sea.

The Germans engaged in large-scale minelaying, employing the Luftwaffe, surface vessels, and U-boats to sow offensive minefields in harbor entrances, estuaries, and shallows of the North Sea. When the Home Fleet moved around to the west coast, U-boats laid mines off its new anchorages. The British retaliated by laying undeclared minefields to sink the German surface minelayers, whereupon Hitler removed further restrictions from his U-boats.

Most of the German mines were of the magnetic-impulse type, detonated by the magnetic fields of ships passing overhead or nearby. Impossible to sweep by the usual means, the mines could be rendered less effective through reducing the ships' magnetic fields by use of electrically charged coils or cables applied to their hulls.

The relatively poor score achieved by the U-boats in the early months of the war was a result partly of their small numbers and of their difficulty in reaching and remaining in their chief hunting grounds, the Western Approaches to the United Kingdom. They were barred from the English Channel by a mine barrage the British had laid across the Strait of Dover. To reach the Atlantic they had to go around Scotland. They could not remain long because of the fuel needed to reach and return from the operational area. During the winter of 1939–40 there were never more than ten boats in the Western Approaches, and at times there were no more than two.

In early March 1940 Raeder ordered all available U-boats to be readied for participation in the invasion of Norway. As it turned out, the U-boats played no part at all in the Norwegian campaign, being frustrated by widespread torpedo failures. Off Narvik, Günther Prien launched repeated attacks on anchored transports and cruisers, only to have all his torpedoes run deep. It was, he said bitterly, like having to fight with a dummy rifle.

An investigation revealed that the torpedoes ran deep because air had been forced into their leaky balance chambers. This occurred when air pressure in the U-boats built up during their long daily submergence off Norway awaiting the few hours of darkness. When the much-touted new magnetic detonator failed to operate, its proponents suggested that the failure was an effect of Norway's northern latitudes, but when the magnetic detonator failed elsewhere also, Dönitz ordered it abandoned in favor of the old, reliable contact detonator.

These were disappointing times for the U-boats, but better times were on the way. In the spring of 1940 the foundations were laid for Dönitz's subsequent months of triumph in the Atlantic. The acquisition of Norway's entire coastline and the conquest of the Low Countries and France provided Hitler with the means of turning Britain's maritime flanks.

While secondary U-boat havens were being established in Norway, Dönitz personally supervised the construction of heavily fortified bases on the French Atlantic coast at Brest, Lorient, St. Nazaire, La Pallice, and Bordeaux. Possession of these French bases meant a reduction of more than 50 percent in the transit time of U-boats to their Atlantic hunting grounds.

Because Prime Minister Churchill insisted that the British bomber command concentrate its limited resources on the bombing of Germany, the bombers failed to disrupt the erection of massive concrete pens in these Biscay ports. As a result, the pens were strengthened to the point of invulnerability.

The North Atlantic U-boat Offensive Based on French Ports

In July 1940 U-boats began operating from the French bases. The reduction in cruising time to patrol stations had the effect of increasing the number of submarines available in the operating areas. Dönitz concentrated his strength in the waters off Rockall Bank, 260 miles west of Scotland, and for the first time made effective use of wolf-pack tactics. On sighting a convoy, a U-boat would not attack at once but would trail, decks awash, well to the rear of the target, while it reported the convoy's course, speed, and composition to U-boat Command's new headquarters at Lorient, France. Dönitz would then assume tactical command, ordering the other boats of the pack to make contact with the shadower. With their 17-knot surface speed, the U-boats usually had no difficulty overtaking or intercepting a 7- or 8-knot convoy, timing themselves to arrive well after sunset. In darkness the small silhouette of the U-boats made them all but invisible. With coaching from Dönitz, the pack would attempt a simultaneous surface attack that would scatter the escort and annihilate the convoy. The escorting vessels, attempting to locate their shadowy assailants, usually fired star shell but without much success.

For security reasons, the Germans transmitted in cipher and kept their transmission brief by using code words to replace longer expressions, thus forming a code within a cipher.[1] Later they de-

veloped "spurt transmission," recording the message on tape so that it could be transmitted at high speed, to be recorded and slowed down at the receiving end.

Fast or slow, the U-boat transmissions baffled the British cryptanalysts. Though all three German services used the Enigma ciphering machine, the Kriegsmarine had added such security measures that the British found German naval messages impossible to read long after they had learned to decrypt army and Luftwaffe dispatches.

On the other hand, the Germans had from the beginning been able to decrypt some British naval codes. Younger officers in the Royal Navy urged their communicators to follow the example of the RAF and the U. S. and German navies in adopting fast and relatively secure machine ciphers. But the conservative Admiralty clung to slow and cumbersome hand coding from code books, though such systems were known to be insecure.

Although the British could not read the U-boat chatter, they turned their radio direction finders toward it to locate the U-boats and then rerouted their ships to avoid them. Such measures were not always effective, because the Germans were listening and often merely directed their U-boats to new interception points. The fixes established by the early land-based direction finders were inaccurate for transmissions several hundred miles from shore. Experiments were under way, however, to develop a compact, high-frequency direction finder that could accurately locate distant transmissions and that could be carried to sea on board escort vessels.

The Italians dispatched 27 submarines to the Atlantic and established at Bordeaux a base from which their boats operated under German strategic command. The Germans tried to integrate them into pack warfare, but because the Mediterranean boats were slow and unhandy, the results were unsatisfactory. At length the Italians were allocated the waters south of 45° N as their operating area. Because most British traffic operated north of this parallel, the Italians found few targets.

To meet the submarine threat the Admiralty had ordered additional destroyers and authorized two new ship types—corvettes and frigates. These ships, assisted by trawlers, luggers, and other small vessels, bore the brunt of escort work in the North Atlantic. Casualties to destroyers and other escorts during the Norwegian campaign and the Dunkirk evacuation were heavy. To meet the threat of German invasion, escorts had to be stripped from ocean convoys. Some of the latter sailed protected by a single escort. Sinkings mounted through the

---

[1] A *code* employs a number group or letter group to stand for a word or phrase. A telephone book is thus a kind of code book. In a *cipher* the basic unit is the letter. A very simple cipher would be: A = 1, B = 2, C = 3, etc.

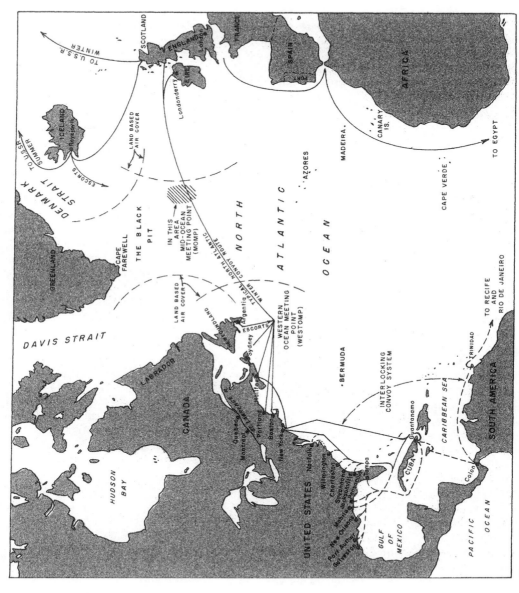

Convoy Routes, 1941–42

late summer and fall of 1940. In July, U-boats sank 196,000 tons of British shipping; in August, 268,000 tons; in September, 295,000 tons; in October, 352,000 tons. Foreseeing the desperate times ahead, Churchill in May 1940 had requested the loan or gift of 50 U. S. destroyers for convoy work.

To cut down the slaughter, the Admiralty in October extended the westward limits of ocean convoy escort to 19° W. The benefit of this move, however, was largely lost by the reduction in the upper speed limit of convoys in order to permit more ships to sail independently. U-boats preferred the easy kills of independent ships rather than employing wolf-pack tactics to tangle with convoys, however inadequately they were escorted. During a five-week period in late 1940, not a single ocean convoy was molested, yet independent losses soared.

In the mid-Atlantic, not only were ships unescorted, but the U-boats had immunity from air attack. Despite long-range air patrols from Britain and from Canada, there remained a broad stretch of the central North Atlantic that land-based aircraft simply could not reach. In this so-called Black Pit (also called the Greenland Air Gap), the U-boats reaped a rich harvest among ships sailing independently.

As convoy escort was extended westward, the U-boats perforce had to make wolf-pack attacks on escorted convoys. Most heavily hit was SC-7, a slow, 34-ship, eastbound convoy intercepted on 18 October some 250 miles northwest of Ireland. Attacking at dusk, Lieutenant Commander Otto Kretschmer in *U-99* with six other experienced boats penetrated the four-ship screen and sank 18 merchantmen carrying nearly a hundred thousand tons of supplies.

Scarcely had this attack ended when eastbound HX-79, a fast, 49-ship convoy carrying American military supplies, ran afoul of Günther Prien's *U-47* and five other U-boats. These boats again swamped the defense and claimed an additional 13 victims. Several of the U-boats had exhausted their torpedoes and begun homeward passage when eastbound HX-79A entered these same waters, at the cost of seven more merchantmen.

These one-sided encounters climaxed Dönitz's first determined foray into the Northwestern Approaches, the "Happy Time," in which U-boats sank 217 merchant vessels, totaling more than 1,100,000 tons, at the cost of six boats. Such success firmly convinced Commander U-boats of the bright prospects for wolf-pack operations, yet because of the limited number of U-boats available and their need for replenishment, they could not maintain

this attrition rate. Fewer than a half dozen U-boats patrolled off Rockall during the last two months of 1940, and heavy weather frustrated efforts to locate the increasingly evasive British convoys. Allied losses from U-boat attack declined during November and December to an average of 180,000 tons. By Christmas 1940 only one U-boat lurked in the Northwestern Approaches, and when Dönitz reckoned accounts at the end of the year, he discovered that construction had barely made good the loss of 31 boats since the war's outbreak. He never ceased to believe, however, that if he had been given the 300 U-boats he requested, England long before this time would have been starved into surrender.

The British were acutely aware that without a continuous flow from the New World of the materials the U-boats were sending to the bottom in such quantity they could not long survive. Something had to be done. Work was speeded up toward developing radar that would enable the escorts to locate the night-attacking U-boats. Efforts were intensified to break the Kriegsmarine's cipher. The Admiralty set up a separate Western Approaches Command with its own commander in chief. Crews of escort vessels were put through a stiff course in defense of convoy and antisubmarine tactics.

Such measures were not long in producing results. Dönitz in late February dispatched several of his most experienced commanders to conduct an all-out blitz in the Northwestern Approaches. The outcome was far from what he had come to expect.

On the evening of 6 March, four of the boats located westbound OB-293, which they attacked intermittently for 24 hours. At dusk on the 7th, Günther Prien in *U-47*, seeking to increase his score to date of 160,000 tons, attempted to penetrate the screen under the cover of a rain squall. The destroyer *Wolverine* spotted Prien's submarine through the gloom and with a barrage of depth charges dispatched the killer of the *Royal Oak*.

Eight days later the remainder of the group located HX-112. Although Ace Joachim Schepke in *U-100* promptly sank a 10,000-ton tanker, the U-boats achieved no further sinkings until the night of the 16th when *U-99*'s commander, Ace Otto Kretschmer, slipped through the screen and, racing up and down the columns, torpedoed four tankers and two freighters before disappearing astern of the main body. At midnight the escort commander, Commander Donald Macintyre in the destroyer *Walker*, detected *U-100* approaching on the surface. Crash-diving, Schepke escaped, but a determined attack by two destroyers forced him to the surface where he was killed when his boat was fatally rammed by the destroyer *Vanoc.*

Minutes later the *Walker* blasted *U-99* to the surface with an accurate pattern of depth charges. Most of the crew, including Kretschmer, were subsequently rescued by Macintyre. The British had captured the U-boat Command's most brilliant tactician, whose score of 266,629 tons sunk was unequaled during the war.

The loss of the three outstanding U-boat aces within less than a week produced profound depression at Lorient headquarters. With other losses, the Germans were suddenly confronted in the Northwestern Approaches with an attrition rate of nearly 20 percent. As foul weather continued to frustrate Luftwaffe reconnaissance over the North Channel, between Ireland and Scotland, Dönitz reluctantly shifted his wolf-pack operations 200 miles to the west, beyond the range of Coastal Command bombers based on Northern Ireland. This move was the first application of his "tonnage warfare," the concentration of U-boat activity in areas where the most Allied merchant tonnage might be sunk at least cost to the U-boat Command. Thus, when defenses became strong in one area, Dönitz would shift his boats to another in order to capitalize on remaining soft spots, even though vital Allied cargoes might meanwhile be delivered to crucial areas. As a result, during several critical periods in the war, the North Atlantic was almost completely uncontested.

On 1 April 1941, the Admiralty received operational control of Coastal Command aircraft and hence was able to integrate air activities more directly with convoy movements. Beginning in April, long-range British aircraft were based on Iceland, whence they were able to cut drastically the size of the Black Pit. In April also, the last of the base-deal American destroyers and cutters were turned over to the Royal Navy. With these additions and increased fuel capacity in the newer escorts, escort could be provided as far as 35° W. The increasing strength of the Royal Canadian Navy permitted the Canadians to undertake escort in the western Atlantic and to establish a link with the British. On 27 May 1941, there sailed from Halifax convoy HX-129, the first North Atlantic convoy to be escorted all the way across the ocean. Now U-boats would have to attack escorted convoys, accepting greater losses, if they were to maintain their rate of sinkings.

The Royal Navy was acquiring a potent new weapon against the U-boat as the new anti-surface-vessel radar became available to its escorts. The destroyer *Vanoc* was one of the first escorts so equipped. It was by means of radar that she had

located and rammed Schepke's *U-100* on the night of 16 March. Between radar and asdic, U-boats would find it difficult to hide on the surface or submerged, by day or night.

More important, the British had at last cracked the Kriegsmarine's Ultra cipher. On 8 May 1941, *U-110,* commanded by Fritz-Julius Lemp, who had sunk the *Athenia,* attacked convoy OB-318. An escort raced toward the U-boat, whereupon she crash-dived, but depth charges damaged her and forced her to the surface, where her panicky crew abandoned ship. Lemp, trying to clamber back on board to scuttle, was shot dead. *U-110* sank, but not before the British had recovered from her a navy-type Enigma machine with spare rotors and full setting instructions.

The Admiralty could now read many of the communications between Dönitz and his talkative submarines. This source of information coupled with radio direction-finding enabled the British to track most U-boats and to locate vessels with which they communicated. The first fruit of the new source of intelligence was the locating in the Atlantic of two supply ships that were enabling U-boats and German surface raiders to extend and prolong their cruises. In early June British cruisers surprised and sank them both. Dönitz's response to the sinkings was to plan to build a fleet of 1,700-ton supply U-boats, the famous "milch cows."

In late August the British obtained another important source of intelligence when *U-570* surrendered to a Coastal Command bomber that had damaged her with depth charges. A trawler towed the U-boat to a British port where her diving capacity, machinery noises, and maneuvering characteristics were intensively studied.

In August U-boats sank only 80,000 tons of Allied shipping, the lowest figure since the Germans had stopped using the defective magnetic torpedo detonator. During the same month, weekly imports to Britain reached nearly a million tons.

The Lords of Admiralty were elated at the turn of affairs. Many officers of the Royal Navy believed that—with British possession of additional escorts and of new means of detection and sources of intelligence, and with U. S. participation in convoy escort—the worst of the Battle of the Atlantic was over, and the U-boat had ceased to be a menace.

They little knew.

The Surface Raiders

For several months following the destruction of the *Graf Spee,* no German surface raiders ventured out into the Atlantic. In the spring of 1940, however, there slipped through the British blockade the first of seven "ghost cruisers," German merchant ships equipped with concealed guns and torpedo tubes and carrying aircraft to extend their hunting range. Disguised to look like neutral merchantmen, they roamed the oceans capturing independently sailing French and British cargo vessels, which they sank after taking off passengers and crews and removing food and fuel for their own use.

The pocket battleship *Admiral Scheer* made her debut in Atlantic waters in October 1940 and set out to break up the North Atlantic convoys. A prime opportunity came her way in early November when she sighted a 37-ship convoy escorted by a single armed merchantman, the *Jervis Bay*. The *Scheer* apparently had a very good chance of sinking nearly all the ships. But the *Jervis Bay*, though overwhelmingly outgunned, interposed herself and attacked the *Scheer* with such ferocity that the battleship was diverted from the chase during the 22 minutes it took her to sink the attacker. By that time the convoy had begun to scatter. The *Scheer* was able to overtake and sink only five ships before nightfall ended the pursuit.

After operations in the West Indies and the Atlantic and Indian oceans, the *Scheer* returned to Germany in April 1941, having sunk 11 ships totaling nearly 100,000 tons, the most successful pocket-battleship cruise of the war. In the spring of 1941 the *Scharnhorst*, the *Gneisenau*, and the heavy cruiser *Admiral Hipper* made brief sweeps into the Atlantic, sinking more than 140,000 tons in two months of operations. When the *Scharnhorst* and the *Gneisenau* headed back home, the Home Fleet deployed to block their return to Germany and perhaps capture or destroy them both. The Kriegsmarine, apprised of the entrapment plan through code breaking, ordered the two battleships to Brest.

Admiral Raeder, encouraged by the success of his warship raiders, decided to send out the newly completed *Bismarck*, reputed to be the most powerful battleship in the world. She would be accompanied by the new heavy cruiser *Prinz Eugen*. On 20 May 1941, a Swedish cruiser reported sighting the two warships in the Kattegat headed toward Norway. The following day British aircraft photographed them in a fjord near Bergen. Admiral Sir John Tovey, Commander in Chief of the Home Fleet, assumed that the raiders would break out at the first opportunity under cloud cover. He therefore deployed his ships to block all the passages from the Norwegian Sea into the Atlantic.

On board the *Bismarck*, Vice Admiral Günther Lütjens elected to break out via Denmark Strait,

north of Iceland, the passage to the open sea farthest from Scapa Flow. Here he was shadowed by the heavy cruisers *Norfolk* and *Suffolk*, using radar. As he reached the Atlantic, he found his ships blocked by the venerable battle cruiser *Hood* and the new battleship *Prince of Wales*. In a short, sharp battle, the *Bismarck* landed on the *Hood* a plunging shell that rammed through her weak deck armor into her magazine. Before the horrified eyes of watchers on the other British ships the battle cruiser disintegrated in a huge fireball. The *Prince of Wales*, too new to have the mechanical difficulties worked out of her, was able to fire only three guns a salvo. She returned the German fire briefly, causing a slow leak in one of the *Bismarck*'s fuel tanks, and then broke off action.

Now with redoubled determination the officers at the Admiralty plotted the *Bismarck*'s destruction. Already they had ordered Admiral Somerville's Force H from Gibraltar to participate in running her down. Now they summoned the battleships *Rodney* and *Ramillies* to break off from convoys and join the chase. The battleship *Revenge* raised steam and proceeded with all possible speed from Halifax.

Shadowed by the *Prince of Wales*, the *Norfolk*, and the *Suffolk*, the *Prinz Eugen* and the *Bismarck* headed south, the latter trailing a long oil streak. Lütjens decided that he must take the *Bismarck* to Brest to have her fuel leak repaired. The *Prinz Eugen* would have to carry on the raiding by herself. Late in the afternoon Lütjens turned on the British ships and fired a few salvos to cover the *Eugen*'s escape. During the night the *Bismarck* succeeded in eluding her shadowers and shaped course for France. With luck she might reach the protection of the Luftwaffe before her hunters rediscovered her.

There followed several hours of intense anxiety at the Admiralty and throughout the Royal Navy, but at 1030 the next day, 26 May, a Catalina, flying patrol from Coastal Air Command, spotted the German battleship 750 miles west of Brest. Now, in rising seas, the British began to close in. For Tovey in the *King George V*, soon joined by the *Rodney*, it was a long stern chase. Admiral Somerville, with Force H coming up from the south, sent the cruiser *Sheffield* forward to locate and shadow the *Bismarck* and ordered his carrier, the *Ark Royal*, to attack, Her first strike miscarried. The second, around 2100, dropped a torpedo that wrecked the *Bismarck*'s steering engine room and jammed her rudder to port. The great ship turned helpless into the wind.

From nearby convoys the cruiser *Dorsetshire* and five destroyers peeled off, and in darkness and tempestuous seas surrounded the *Bismarck*, firing torpedoes, none of which hit. The *Norfolk* finally caught up, and a little before 0900, 27 May, the *King George V* and the *Rodney* arrived and took the German battleship under fire. Soon the 16-inch shells of the *Rodney* began to tell. Within an hour the *Bismarck* was a helpless wreck, afire and rolling sluggishly in the trough of the sea. Tovey now had to break off because he had barely enough fuel left to get home. The *Dorsetshire* remained behind to fire her last three torpedoes. As the third one hit, the *Bismarck* capsized and went down.

The loss of the *Bismarck* put an end to German use of major combat ships for attacks on transoceanic commerce. The *Prinz Eugen* achieved nothing at sea, but she did manage to arrive safely at Brest, joining the *Scharnhorst* and *Gneisenau*. Raeder's standing with Hitler took a decided drop, and the star of Dönitz began its rise as the U-boat battle intensified.

U-boats in American Waters

The Japanese raid on Pearl Harbor took the Germans by surprise. Not until the end of December 1941 was Dönitz able to commit any of his long-range boats to American waters, and then he sent only five—but they were commanded by some of his most experienced aces. When these boats arrived off the U. S. east coast on the night of 13 January, they were amazed to see ships proceeding fully lighted and silhouetted by waterfront lights and the glow of brightly illuminated coastal cities.

The U-boats remained submerged by day. When they surfaced after dusk, they frequently had a choice of targets and usually picked the biggest, dispatching their victims with gunfire or torpedoes or both. By the end of January they had sunk 13 ships. At that time six more U-boats were on the way, but there were never more than a dozen operating at one time along the U. S. coast.

Most of the U. S. Navy's destroyers and other antisubmarine vessels were attached to the fleets or committed to protecting oceanic convoys. Hence coastal shipping had to move independently, without escort. Admiral Sir Dudley Pound, Britain's First Sea Lord, cabled Admiral King, advising him that convoy was the only way to defeat the U-boat and offering to lend him 22 of the Royal Navy's trawlers to help. King was at first reluctant to accept the loan, believing that ships bunched in convoy without strong escort protection are more vulnerable than when proceeding independently, a conclusion disproved by British wartime experience. But King relented, and around the end of

February the trawlers arrived, complete with officers and crews, all veterans of antisubmarine warfare.

Besides the trawlers, Vice Admiral Adolphus Andrews, Commander Eastern Sea Frontier, now had Coast Guard cutters, converted yachts, other small craft, and a few destroyers drawn from the transatlantic convoys. Believing that he still did not have adequate protection for coastal convoys, he resorted to such measures as hunter groups, "offensive" patrols, and Q ships, operations that the British long before had discarded as of slight value.

Sinkings in the Eastern Sea Frontier mounted: in February, 17 vessels amounting to 103,000 tons; during March, 28 vessels of 159,000 tons. Burning tankers were a familiar sight off coastal resorts, and the beaches were becoming covered with black oil. The effect on naval operations caused by these sinkings, especially of the oil-filled tankers, was more severe than that caused by the raid on Pearl Harbor. In these coastal waters not a single U-boat had been sunk. For U-boat Command, this was the "Second Happy Time."

On 1 April, Admiral Andrews established what he called his bucket-brigade system. Lightly escorted convoys proceeded only by day, stopping for the night in harbors and other protected anchorages along the Atlantic coast. In April also the government at long last ordered a blackout of the coasts and a dimout of the coastal cities. The number of ships sunk in the Eastern Sea Frontier that month dropped to 23.

With new construction and the release of destroyers and other escorts from the North Atlantic convoys and from the Atlantic Fleet, Andrews in May was able to set up the first strong coastal convoys. By this time also, more than 300 antisubmarine planes were operating from 19 fields along the coast. The result was dramatic—only six ships sunk in the Eastern Sea Frontier that month. Dönitz had begun shifting his boats southward on the appearance of the convoys, making no effort to contest them by wolf-pack tactics.

The Germans now found profitable hunting in the Caribbean and the Gulf of Mexico. In these areas, where no convoy system yet existed, the U-boats in May sank 41 vessels of 220,000 tons, nearly half being tankers torpedoed off the Passes of the Mississippi. This onslaught was checked by the establishment of an Interlocking Convoy System that enabled ships to transfer at sea from one convoy to another. The system required meticulous scheduling, but it offered the flexibility required by the complicated pattern of Caribbean and Gulf shipping.

Moving once more in search of unprotected ships, the U-boats began attacking independent traffic off Panama, Trinidad, Salvador, and Rio de Janeiro. Their stay in these areas was lengthened by the arrival of the first of Dönitz's "milch cows," the new 1,700-ton U-tankers. The sinking by the Germans of five Brazilian freighters off Salvador provoked Brazil into declaring war, and also emphasized the need to extend the convoy system farther south. Escorts drawn from the U. S. South Atlantic Fleet permitted extension of the system all the way to Rio. By the end of August 1942, Dönitz realized that the Second Happy Time was at an end. He had already begun shifting his U-boat concentration back to the North Atlantic for a renewed blitz on the transatlantic shipping. In the next three months, 1,400 ships were escorted through the Interlocking System, with only three being sunk.

Operations in Arctic Waters

Following Hitler's invasion of the Soviet Union, the British began sending to north Russia convoys of British and American ships laden with military supplies. The convoys usually assembled at Iceland or Scotland, crossed the Norwegian Sea, passed through the relatively narrow sea between North Cape, the northernmost point of Norway, and the Arctic pack ice, and put into the Russian ports of Murmansk or Archangel. The convoys were beset with cold weather, rough seas, and fog, but until the spring of 1942 they suffered negligible losses from U-boat and air attack.

Early in 1942 Hitler, convinced that the Allies were about to attack Norway, began shifting his naval and air strength northward. In addition to U-boats and planes, the new battleship *Tirpitz*, sister of the *Bismarck*, moved to a Norwegian base, as did the *Scheer*, *Hipper*, and *Lützow* (ex-*Deutschland*). He ordered the *Scharnhorst*, *Gneisenau*, and *Prinz Eugen*, still at Brest, to make a break for home via the English Channel. To the great mortification of the British, all three ships made it—passing through the Straits of Dover in broad daylight under protection of the Luftwaffe.

With the German northward shift, the convoys to and from north Russia suffered increasingly severe losses from surface, subsurface, and air attacks. Between March and July 1942, four Russia-bound convoys lost 23 out of 84 cargo vessels. Yet Roosevelt and Churchill insisted that their going through was necessary for keeping the Soviet Union in the war.

Whenever one of the northern convoys sailed, it was protected not only by its close escorts but by a large part of the Home Fleet, which went to sea as support and covering forces to dash to the rescue should any of the Norway-based German ships sortie. Once, in the spring of 1942, the *Tirpitz* with three destroyers darted out from Trondheim to attack a northbound convoy but failed to locate it in the fog.

While British ships were busy capturing Madagascar to safeguard their round-about-Africa convoys, Admiral King lent the Home Fleet a squadron of destroyers, two heavy cruisers, the new battleships *North Carolina* and *Washington*, and the carrier *Wasp*. Thus the German warships, though restrained by a no-risks policy recently imposed by Hitler, through their mere presence in Norway tied down naval power that could have been used more effectively in the Mediterranean and in the Pacific.

At the end of June 1942, British reconnaissance aircraft reported that the *Tirpitz*, *Scheer*, and *Hipper* had shifted to Altenfjord near North Cape. The Admiralty was alarmed because the German ship movement coincided with the advance of convoy PQ-17, which had departed Iceland on 27 June with 34 cargo vessels. The convoy, however, was well protected, with more warships than there were merchantmen—a close escort of 21 ships and, nearby, support and covering forces including seven cruisers, the battleships HMS *Duke of York* and USS *Washington*, and the carrier HMS *Victorious*.

German aircraft began attacking PQ-17 on 2 July, taking losses but achieving no hits until the 4th, when they sank two freighters and damaged a tanker. That evening, Admiral Pound at the Admiralty, noting that PQ-17 was coming opposite Altenfjord and suspecting that the *Tirpitz* was about to attack it, radioed orders for the support force to withdraw westward and the ships of the convoy to scatter and proceed independently to Russian ports. The *Tirpitz* did sortie the next day but turned back when the Luftwaffe planes were unable to locate and attack the *Victorious*, which the Germans knew to be at sea.

As a result of the scattering order, PQ-17 lost 23 more ships, sunk by planes and U-boats. American disappointment over the futile employment of the *Washington* and her escorts led to Admiral King's rapid transfer of these ships to the Pacific, whither the *North Carolina* and *Wasp* forces had already gone. The British suspended the northern convoy sailings until the end of the perpetual daylight of the summer months. Meanwhile Britain and the

United States continued to supply Russia over the long routes via the Pacific Ocean and the Persian Gulf.

After heavily escorted convoy PQ-18, sailing in September 1942, lost 13 ships, the Admiralty sent convoys to north Russia only during the Arctic darkness of dead winter. The first of the winter convoys, JW-51A, reached Murmansk on 25 December without incident. The second, JW-51B, 14 merchantmen escorted by 6 destroyers and 5 smaller vessels, was attacked off North Cape by the pocket battleship *Lützow*, the heavy cruiser *Hipper*, and 6 destroyers. The Germans sank a destroyer and a minesweeper but fled ignominiously when 2 British light cruisers appeared through the gloom. In the succeeding chase, the light cruisers damaged the *Hipper* and sank one of her accompanying destroyers. Hitler, enraged by this fiasco, threatened to scrap his battleships and cruisers and use their steel to make tanks. Admiral Raeder, on the receiving end of this tirade, resigned as naval commander in chief and was replaced by Admiral Dönitz.

By the winter of 1943, Germany's military situation had so worsened that few U-boats could be spared from the Atlantic and few German planes from the Eastern Front. As a result, a series of Arctic convoys, beginning in November, got through unscathed. To stem this flow of munitions, vital to the Soviet army, Dönitz obtained permission from Hitler to again use the surface ships.

The *Tirpitz* was unavailable, having recently been put out of action by midget British submarines that penetrated Altenfjord, so Dönitz passed the assignment to the *Scharnhorst*. On Christmas evening she left the fjord and headed north to attack a convoy that the Luftwaffe and U-boats had reported. British cryptanalysts read the pertinent radio messages and flashed a warning to the fleet, which hastened to intercept. In the darkness three British cruisers twice interposed themselves between the *Scharnhorst* and the convoy, opening fire that knocked out the battleship's forward radar. The *Scharnhorst* turned south and headed blindly back toward Norway, only to run into a second British force, including the battleship *Duke of York*. After a high-speed, eastward chase, the *Scharnhorst* was sunk by British shells and torpedoes.

The British, fearful that a repaired *Tirpitz* might be used against their convoys, attacked her twice again. In April 1944, carrier planes scored 15 hits on her, doing extensive damage. On 12 November 1944, 25 long-range RAF Lancasters, staging through north-Russia airfields, capsized her by direct hits with six-ton bombs.

The Return to the North Atlantic

British assumptions that the U-boat was all but defeated were rudely demolished in the late spring of 1942, when Dönitz began switching his war on shipping back to the North Atlantic. In May and June the U-boats sank more than a million tons of merchant vessels, nearly half of which were sailing in convoy.

Dönitz now had more than 300 U-boats, the number he had said he needed to starve England. The Allies, to be sure, had asdic (sonar) and radar, but the operators were not all well trained, and tempestuous weather, as in the terrible winter of 1942–43, rendered both nearly useless. Moreover the Germans now had a radar detector, which could pick up the radar search signal at a far greater range than the reflected signal could be detected by the search receiver, and submerged U-boats were discharging a device containing a bubble-making chemical whose bubbles echoed back a sonar beam just as a submarine hull would.

Moreover, on 1 February 1942, the Kriegsmarine had radically changed the cipher used with the Enigma machine for communicating with the U-boats, and for ten months the British were unable to read the new version. Thus during a crucial period the convoys lacked the information needed to evade their talkative hunters, while the hunters could usually keep track of their prey. The Americans declined to share their electric ciphering machine, preferring to communicate with the British via the British convoy code, which the Germans were reading with fair regularity.[2]

Dönitz concentrated his attack in the Black Pit area, stationing picket lines of submarines on both sides so that convoys moving in either direction could be attacked throughout its entire width while the U-boats enjoyed virtual immunity from air attack. Sinkings by the U-boats mounted, reaching in November 1942 a peak of more than 700,000 tons.

A convoy conference held in Washington in early 1943 rejected politically explosive proposals for a unified Allied antisubmarine command, and on 1 March adopted Admiral King's formula whereby the British and Canadians retained control of the North Atlantic convoys, while the United States assumed responsibility for Central Atlantic convoys (to the Mediterranean and southward from

[2]Eventually the Royal Navy adopted its own electric ciphering machine, which, like the German and American (and Japanese) machines, was based on the Enigma system. The British and American machines were enough alike that, with the use of adapters, each could decipher material enciphered by the other.

ports south of Halifax) as well as for the Interlocking Convoy System.

In mid-March 1943, 66 U-boats were disposed in picket lines in the North Atlantic. On the 16th and 17th, in a running battle against two convoys, they sank 22 ships. In the course of the month, they sent down 677,000 tons. In London there were forebodings that Britain was approaching defeat at sea. For U-boat Command, however, this was no new "Happy Time," because U-boat sinkings were also mounting ominously. Since the turn of the year, 40 had been sunk.

Despite the doomsaying in London, the increased destruction of U-boats foreshadowed a turn of the tide that was not to be reversed. There were many reasons.

The British, using a primitive form of computer, had once more broken the Kriegsmarine's submarine cipher. Allied scientists had perfected a high-frequency radio direction finder (HF/DF, pronounced "huffduff"), and the British, Americans, and Canadians were installing these devices ashore and afloat to pinpoint the source of U-boat communications. The Allies had developed a microwave radar, which the enemy could not detect. Allied escort vessels now had a new antisubmarine weapon called a hedgehog, which fired ahead of the vessel a mortar-type bomb that exploded on impact, and the British were perfecting another called the squid, which fired ahead-thrown depth charges.

More than enough warships were now available to escort convoys all the way across the Atlantic. The excess permitted Admiral Sir Max Horton, Commander in Chief Western Approaches, to form support groups of six to eight destroyers, frigates, or corvettes and occasionally an escort carrier. These ships, based on Newfoundland and Iceland, had no escort duties but were available to rush to the aid of convoys undergoing heavy U-boat attack. B-24 long-range bombers were now operating against the U-boats out of Newfoundland, Iceland, and Northern Ireland. From these bases they could reach all parts of the North Atlantic, but such was the demand for the bombers on the other war fronts that there were at no time enough of them on patrol to keep the Black Pit air gap completely closed.

In April 1943 U-boats sank 328,000 tons, a little more than half the preceding month's total, and the biggest drop was in numbers of ships while in convoy. That month 14 U-boats were destroyed in the North Atlantic, half by escorts, half by aircraft. For each three merchant ships sunk, a U-boat had gone down. At the end of April, five support groups, two including escort carriers, were available to beef up convoy escorts.

The showdown began on 28 April when 51 U-boats, coached by Dönitz in Berlin, ganged up on slow, westbound convoy ONS-5, 42 ships escorted by a destroyer, a frigate, and four corvettes. The convoy, zigzagging through storms and fogs, at one point was widely scattered. Some of the escorts had to peel off to refuel, but they were more than replaced by two support groups that dashed to the rescue of the beleaguered ships. In the rare intervals when weather permitted, Allied bombers arrived to attack the U-boats or force them down. When the battle ended on 6 May, the U-boats had sunk 12 ships but at the cost of 7 of their own number. The multi-wolf-pack attack on ONS-5 was the biggest of the war, and it suffered the heaviest losses.

In the following three weeks, 12 convoys crossed the Black Pit, losing a total of only 5 ships, while the air and surface escorts sank 13 U-boats. This was a ratio that U-boat Command manifestly could not tolerate. Conceding defeat in the North Atlantic, Dönitz at the end of "Black May" transferred his boats south in conformity with his tonnage warfare strategy.

For the Kriegsmarine, May was a black month also in the Bay of Biscay, which most U-boats based on western French ports had to cross coming and going. Bombers of the RAF Coastal Command, operating from southwest England, in that month sank 7 boats. Impressed, Admiral King sent 36 B-24s and a dozen Catalinas to help with the good work. Improving scores reached a climax in the week of 28 July, when 9 boats were sunk in six days. Between 1 May and the end of 1943, 32 U-boats were sent to the bottom in the Biscay area.

The Central Atlantic

After the United States assumed responsibility for Central Atlantic convoys, Admiral King brought together all U. S. antisubmarine intelligence and control activities into an organization called the U. S. Tenth Fleet. The new fleet was unique in that it had no ships of its own but could give orders to any ship under U. S. control. King assured the fleet such authority by assuming command himself, but in practice he delegated control of its operations to the fleet chief of staff, Rear Admiral Francis S. Low.

As in the North Atlantic, all but the fastest merchant ships in the Central Atlantic moved in escorted convoys. When Dönitz shifted the bulk of his U-boats from the North to the Central Atlantic, he was scarcely bettering their chances for survival, because in the Central Atlantic the U. S. Navy's new hunter-killer groups were just going into action. These groups, organized by Admiral Ingersoll, served both for escort of convoy and for independent antisubmarine operations. They consisted of an escort carrier screened by a few old destroyers or destroyer escorts, smaller destroyers equipped especially for antisubmarine warfare.

The hunter-killer groups in their independent operations were not, as it might appear, simply resuming the ineffective "offensive" patrol operations of World War I and early World War II, nor did they engage in futile needle-in-the-haystack searches. They generally knew what they were looking for and where to find it. The U-boats themselves gave away their locations by making their required radio reports to Dönitz or by requesting instructions for making a fueling rendezvous with a milch cow. Cryptanalysis of the message or bearings provided by HF/DF gave the general location of the transmitting submarine, and the nearest hunter-killer groups sent in teams of Wildcat fighters and Avenger torpedo-bombers to sink it, perhaps determining the exact position of their prey by running down the bearing with their own huffduff. Dönitz's garrulous U-boats were thus talking themselves to death.

The pioneer of the American antisubmarine groups consisted of the escort carrier *Bogue* and four old, flush-deck destroyers. The *Bogue* planes made their first killing during Black May in the North Atlantic while the group was escorting a Halifax–United Kingdom convoy. The group moved south when the U-boats moved and went to work on Wolf Pack Trutz, forming off the Azores. Guided by the Tenth Fleet in Washington, the *Bogue* group located the wolf pack, and two of its planes on 5 June sank *U-217*. On the 12th, seven of the group's planes were involved in the sinking of the milch cow *U-118*.

Hunter-killer groups centered on the escort carriers *Core*, *Santee*, and *Card* soon joined the *Bogue* off the Azores, and together they broke up Wolf Pack Trutz. The Americans sought out especially the milch cows, on which the rest of the U-boats depended for refueling and reprovisioning. On occasion the carrier planes caught a U-boat attached by fueling line to a milch cow and sank both before they could separate and dive. By mid-August the killer groups had sunk 16 U-boats, half of them milch cows. In the same period the submarines in the Central Atlantic had succeeded in sinking only one merchant vessel and shooting down three planes.

Dönitz was obliged to terminate his Central Atlantic operation because of the heavy loss of milch cows. The surviving cows had to remain at sea to refuel boats returning from missions in the Indian and South Atlantic oceans. On such extended cruises, the submarines usually broke radio silence often enough for the Tenth Fleet to track them with considerable accuracy, and coach in the hunter-killers to attack them as they reached the Central Atlantic.

An example is *U-66*. In April 1944, as she was heading north from a patrol in the Gulf of Guinea, her commanding officer, Lieutenant Gerhard Seehausen, radioed a request, monitored by Tenth Fleet, for a refueling rendezvous. He was given a nighttime appointment with *U-488*, but when he approached the rendezvous point in darkness, he was shocked to see destroyer escorts attacking the milch cow, which presently went down. When Seehausen requested another rendezvous, Tenth Fleet was listening and sent in the *Block Island* hunter-killer group. Seehausen, aware that he was being tracked, despondently radioed Berlin: "Refueling impossible under constant stalking! Mid-Atlantic worse than the Bay of Biscay!" The message was spurt-transmitted in less than 15 seconds, but 26 HF/DF stations of the Atlantic network took bearings on it, and in less than an hour the *Block Island* group was on an interception course, sending the destroyer escort *Buckley* ahead, guided by a night-flying plane. The *Buckley* found *U-66*, took her under fire, rammed her, and sent her down blazing.

U-505 was tracked from the time she left Brest until she headed back northward from a cruise in the South Atlantic. Alerted, Captain Dan Gallery's *Guadalcanal* group took an interception course, located the U-boat, and forced her to the surface with hedgehogs and depth charges. After the frightened Germans had poured out of the conning tower hatch, an American party, specially trained by Gallery to meet such an occasion, poured in, seized codes, other important-looking papers, and the latest model Enigma machine, and disconnected demolition charges and closed seacocks. They then pumped out the waterlogged U-boat and towed her triumphantly to Bermuda.

The Final Campaigns

Dönitz hoped for a scientific breakthrough that would allow him to resume a meaningful U-boat offensive. He thought perhaps he had found it with the development of an acoustical torpedo, code-named *Zaunkönig* (wren), that homed specifically on the pitch of an escort's propellers, which had a pitch unlike that of cargo vessels. The *Zaunkönig* was counted on to blast a hole in the screen to permit attack on the merchant vessels with conventional torpedoes. U-boats equipped with the *Zaunkönig* in September 1943 struck at two convoys in the North Atlantic, sinking three escorts, damaging one, and sending six merchantmen to the bottom. As a countermeasure, American and British warships began trailing a noisemaker, called Foxer, which drew the acoustic torpedoes harmlessly into it.

Although Dönitz recognized the peril to U-boats attacking convoys in the North Atlantic, he persisted in having them do so until February 1944, enduring heavy losses while inflicting only slight damage. The combination of close surface escort, land-based air escort, and support groups with escort carriers for local air support had made the North Atlantic convoys virtually immune to attack.

With the Allied invasion of France, the U-boats ceased using French ports, and the westward drive of the Russians expelled them from the Baltic. Eventually they operated only from Norway.

Toward the end of the war, U-boats with breathing tubes, called snorkels, which permitted them to remain underwater while recharging their batteries, staged a blitz in British waters and some even operated in U. S. coastal waters, but there were too few and they came too late to affect the outcome of the war.

Dönitz put his final hopes in the Walter U-boat, in which oxygen was supplied to the diesels from hydrogen peroxide rather than from the air. Such a submarine not only had no need to surface but could move at high speed a considerable distance below the surface. Construction problems and technical difficulties delayed production of the really practical 1,600-ton XXI and 300-ton XXIII Walter boats until 1944. Only one of the former and five of the latter went into active operation before the end of the war. Had they been available earlier and in greater numbers, they could have posed a serious menace to Allied shipping.

German and Italian submarines destroyed 2,775 merchant ships, of which only 28 percent were sailing in convoy. Of Allied shipping losses from all causes, amounting to 23,351,000 tons, U-boats accounted for 14,573,000 tons, or 62.4 percent. The Germans committed 1,175 U-boats to the war and lost 781, American forces accounting for 191. The Italians lost 85 submarines, 21 in the Atlantic. Against these figures, it can be noted that Allied merchant ships successfully completed more than 300,000 voyages across the Atlantic. When Allied shipbuilding capacity reached its peak, the U-boats had no hope of winning. They lost because they dared not maintain the attack on the North Atlantic convoys, which brought the material of victory to Britain. Convoy escorts, surface and air, proved to be the decisive means for offensive action against marauding U-boats.

Chapter 25
The Defeat of Italy and Germany

Japan's attack on Pearl Harbor impelled Prime Minister Churchill to gather his British chiefs of staff and embark for a hastily arranged trip to Washington to confer with President Roosevelt and America's military leaders. Uppermost in Churchill's thought was the ABC-1 Staff Agreement of March 1941, which embodied the "beat Germany first" strategy. Would an infuriated American public now demand of Roosevelt, General George C. Marshall, and other American war planners that they forsake Germany First in order to aim an avenging blow with America's full strength exclusively at Japan? Churchill was quickly reassured. Germany First would remain Allied strategy. Japan would be contained with minimum strength while Hitler's Third Reich became the primary foe.

The Christmas meeting in Washington saw various ideas concerning where best to strike Hitler put before the conference, especially by the nimble-minded Churchill. But no definite attack plan emerged.

This lapse General Marshall set out to make good early in the new year. With his war plans assistant, Brigadier General Dwight D. Eisenhower, and in consultation with the Navy's planners, Marshall proposed two offensives. The first, code-named Operation Sledgehammer, would be launched only if it appeared that Russian resistance might collapse. In the fall of 1942, an Anglo–American force of several divisions would secure a lodgment in western France, perhaps Brittany, and build up strength for a major offensive later. The second, code-named Operation Roundup, required an invasion of France in 1943. Allied forces would seize a beachhead, break out, overrun France, and thrust into Germany, destroying her war-making capacity by means of a double envelopment of the industrial Ruhr Valley. Operation Roundup would thus be a "war-winner."

While they admired the offensive spirit embodied in the Marshall–Eisenhower plans, the British, especially General Sir Alan Brooke, Chief of the Imperial General Staff, found much to criticize in the concept of a direct thrust into Germany. Sledgehammer they ruled out at once. Hitler's Wehrmacht was simply too strong to handle for any Allied force available in 1942. Brooke had growing doubts about Roundup also. Even by 1943 Allied power would not be sufficient to breach Germany's defenses in western Europe. Neither Brooke nor Churchill would espouse an Allied strategy that threatened casualties on the order of World War I, possible stalemate in France, or perhaps even defeat.

The British countered with proposals for attacks somewhere on the periphery of Hitler's empire, bleeding Nazi strength until a greatly weakened Wehrmacht could more easily be overcome by Allied forces landing in western France.

Marshall found the British counterproposal unacceptable. Seconded by Admiral Ernest J. King, U. S. Chief of Naval Operations, he proposed to shift American strength to the Pacific where decisive action could begin immediately. This strategy Roosevelt promptly rejected, decreeing that American troops must be committed to the European theater in 1942. British reluctance, coupled with the president's decree, led to the adoption by the Combined Chiefs of Staff, on 25 July 1942, of Operation Torch, an invasion of Northwest Africa.

Why Africa? Partly because few other strategic options remained. French North Africa was held by Vichy forces, not German, and though risky, attack here was feasible. If Tunis, Algeria, and Morocco were brought over to the Allies, Rommel's Afrika Korps in Egypt would be trapped between the invaders and the British Eighth Army, Malta relieved, and the Mediterranean opened to shipping, with a consequent saving of crucially short merchant tonnage. Moreover, bases would be secured for future attacks on what Churchill called the "soft underbelly" of the Axis. If Germany could not be quickly forced from the war, Italy might be. Success in North Africa, as the British pointed out, would oblige Hitler to withdraw troops from western to southern Europe, making Operation Roundup more feasible, and probably also from the Eastern Front, thereby taking some pressure off the Russians.

Operation Torch: The Invasion of North Africa

Following the British attack at Oran in 1940, Hitler had allowed Marshal Philippe Pétain to build up a Vichy African force to 120,000 troops, plus modern aircraft and some tanks. French naval units in North Africa included destroyers, submarines, and coast defense guns at principal ports. Save for the French Navy, expected to fight hard because of the animosity roused by the attack at Oran, the will of Vichy units to fight was uncertain. Well disciplined, they could be expected to obey orders from Nazi-dominated Vichy. Moreover, they knew that cooperation with the invaders would bring Nazi retaliation against their compatriots in France.

To encourage nonresistance on the part of the French, it was desirable insofar as possible to give Torch an American semblance. Accordingly Lieutenant General Eisenhower was named Supreme Allied Commander, and American troops were assigned to lead most of the assaults. Steps were taken to reach an understanding with French commanders of key Vichy units while maintaining strict secrecy about the operation. Secrecy was imperative, because even modest numbers of Germans flown in by Luftwaffe planes or rushed in by destroyers to North Africa would be a guarantee of real trouble.

Early seizure and use of developed port facilities was essential. Nothing approaching the quantity of supplies needed to sustain many thousands of Allied troops could be muscled ashore across beaches from landing craft. The British wanted to concentrate all Allied landings in the Mediterranean, extending them eastward to Philippeville and Bône. The Americans insisted on seizing only Algiers and Oran inside the Mediterranean and using the troops thus freed to capture Casablanca on Morocco's Atlantic coast. Thus, if Spain should enter the war and with German aid block the Strait of Gibraltar, the Allies in North Africa would still have a port on the ocean for supply or, if need be, retreat.

The British planners accepted the American choice of Casablanca, Oran, and Algiers. Following the landings, the Allied troops would race the Germans for the prize of Tunisia.

Organized as the Western Naval Task Force, American warships would ferry 35,000 American troops across the Atlantic to beachheads northeast and southwest of Casablanca. Ships of the Royal Navy, organized in two task forces, would ferry mingled British and American forces from the United Kingdom to beaches on each flank of Oran and Algiers. Some 39,000 men, mostly Americans, would seize Oran; 33,000 others, one-third of them Americans, would capture Algiers. From headquarters at Gibraltar, General Eisenhower would control all forces, aided by Admiral Sir Andrew B. Cunningham, RN, as overall naval commander.

Because of the Oran incident, Eisenhower and Cunningham expected their hardest fight at that port. Men trained for the now-aborted Operation Sledgehammer were accordingly assigned to Oran. Because the French command at Algiers was supposedly "fixed"—sympathetic with Allied purposes—men less well-drilled were assigned to that assault. Time was short: D-Day was set at 8 November 1942.

Operating from his Norfolk headquarters, Rear Admiral H. Kent Hewitt, USN, commanding Atlantic Fleet amphibious forces, trained the Western Naval Task Force. His army opposite number was flamboyant Major General George S. Patton, Jr., a colorful tank officer, veteran of World War I. Despite divergent personalities, the two worked smoothly together to train the closely integrated teams that would make the Moroccan assault.

The early date set for Torch made it less likely that the Germans would get wind of the operation, but it left insufficient time for preparation. Most in need of further training were coxswains, who had to get the men from ship to shore. By later standards, their landing craft were primitive: a peacetime swamp vehicle, the wooden, gasoline-powered, 36-foot Higgins boat, lacking a bow ramp; the Landing Craft Personnel Ramped, designated LCP(R), a Higgins boat with a ramp; and the Landing Craft Vehicle and Landing Craft Mechanized (LCV and LCM), which could carry ashore jeeps, trucks, and field artillery. The LCM could also transport a light tank.

The main body of the Western Naval Task Force sortied from Hampton Roads on 24 October and was joined at sea by the battleship *Massachusetts* and two heavy cruisers from Casco Bay, Maine, and by the aircraft carrier *Ranger* and four escort carriers from Bermuda. After steering evasive courses to elude known U-boat concentrations, the task force neared the African coast in a strong northwest wind that raised heavy seas. The men were cheered by the news that the British Eighth Army was pressing back Rommel's forces in Egypt after the great British victory on 5 November at El Alamein.

On 7 November the task force split apart, and the center attack group headed for a night landing at Fedala, a small port 15 miles northeast of Casablanca. Included were 15 transports, escorted by the cruisers *Brooklyn* and *Augusta* and ten de-

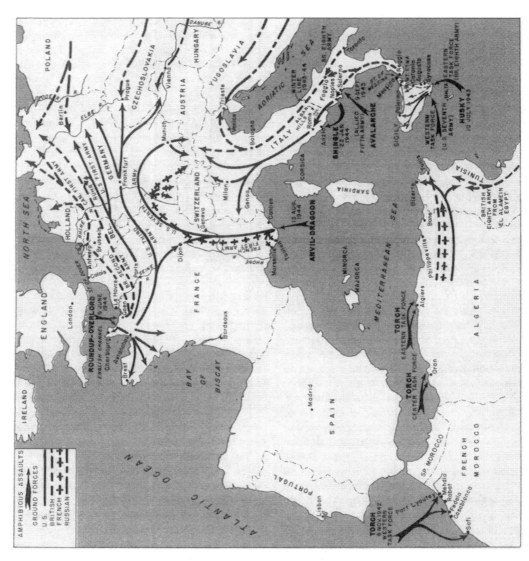

Allied Operations Against the Axis, 1942–45

stroyers. Hovering in the background were the *Massachusetts* group and the *Ranger*, with two escort carriers.

Hewitt had tried to induce the army planners to accept a daylight landing so that ships' guns could first knock out shore defenses and so that coxswains could more easily locate ships and beaches. But the Army had insisted upon night landings—both to achieve surprise and because army officers were not yet convinced that naval gunfire could be effective against shore targets.

Shortly after midnight in the morning of 8 November, anchor chains rattled as the transports of the center attack group reached their assigned positions off Fedala and began to sling out Higgins boats and LCVs. Trouble began at once as the coxswains strove in pitch darkness to collect battalion landing teams from the first line of ships. The landing craft then straggled to the line of departure and circled until blinking light signals from scout boats near the shore directed each to its assigned beach.

At 0500, an hour late, the first waves of landing craft headed in, followed at five- to ten-minute intervals by the second and third waves. French searchlight operators, hearing the noise of the incoming craft, at first flashed lights skyward in quest of planes, then on the sea as they realized the situation. The operators rushed a warning to the coast defense forces, most of whom were in their barracks.

Meanwhile the inexperience of the coxswains had begun taking its toll. Landing craft collided, crashed into rocks and reefs adjoining the designated beaches, or were caught in the surf, spun about, and broached on the shore. They touched down wherever they could, scattering the troops indiscriminately along the beaches. The craft that were able to do so then retracted and returned to the transports for new waves of men. Despite mistakes and difficulties, by dawn 3,500 Americans had landed and seized control of the town. The defending troops quickly surrendered.

The batteries flanking the beach were now manned by French naval gunners who opened fire on landing craft and nearby destroyers. The cruisers and destroyers of the center group quickly returned the fire. As the morning grew brighter, aircraft from the *Ranger* were seen battling French planes over Casablanca, and the *Massachusetts* group approached and exchanged fire with batteries just west of the city and with the 15-inch guns of the unfinished battleship *Jean Bart* in Casablanca harbor.

Beginning at 0815 a cruiser and seven destroyers made a series of sorties from the harbor and fired at the U. S. ships off Fedala. Eight submarines also emerged and fired spreads of torpedoes, which failed to hit anything. The French surface vessels came under concentrated attack by the guns of the center and *Massachusetts* groups and by planes from the *Ranger*; by noon all but one of the French surface ships had been sunk or heavily damaged. Only one submarine made it back into Casablanca harbor. The batteries at Fedala were in American hands. No American vessel had received damage of any consequence. Since half the landing craft had been destroyed, however, not enough troops and supplies could be brought ashore to begin the march on Casablanca that day.

The southern attack group of Hewitt's Western Task Force assaulted Safi, a phosphate-loading port far down the Moroccan coast, which was taken chiefly because it had a quay and large cranes that could offload the medium tanks the LCMs could not handle. Everything went like clockwork. The old battleship *New York* and a cruiser hammered at the shore batteries, while a pair of destroyers, their guns blazing, led the landing craft directly into the harbor. Here the Americans landed and took over key positions. After dawn aircraft from an escort carrier destroyed most of the local French planes on the ground, and that afternoon a converted train ferry brought in the tanks. These were soon heading along the coast road for Casablanca, accompanied offshore by a cruiser and several destroyers.

The northern attack group assaulted Mehdia, on the Moroccan coast 125 miles northeast of Casablanca. Here the object was to capture an all-weather airfield several miles inland at Port Lyautey. The night landings were even more confused than those at Fedala, with a greater proportion of landing craft lost. As a result, by the end of the second day, only half the 9,000 troops assigned to this assault had been put ashore, and they had to fight their way uphill against determined resistance by French colonial forces. Brigadier General Lucian K. Truscott, Jr., commanding the landing force, was reluctant to make use of naval gunfire, considering it dangerous to use against targets near where American troops were operating. He was gratified, however, when cruiser and destroyer fire turned back an armored column coming up the coast road, and when 14-inch shells from the old battleship *Texas* dispersed a column of troop-laden trucks advancing from the interior. The Americans, reinforced by troops brought up the Sebou River by a destroyer, captured the airfield on 10 November.

Inside the Mediterranean, the landing at Oran by well-trained American troops was carried out relatively smoothly against little resistance and was followed by a rapid and orderly advance. By contrast, the landing at Algiers was utterly chaotic, with 90 percent of the landing craft disabled. Fortunately this port put up the lightest resistance of any.

At Fedala, on 9 November, when more than half the 20,000 American troops of the center force had been brought ashore, Admiral Hewitt, according to plan, turned control of the Moroccan attack over to General Patton in order to maintain unity of command. On the morning of the 11th, Patton's troops had nearly surrounded Casablanca and were about to open an all-out attack with sea and air support when the French sent out a flag of truce. They had just received a cease-fire order.

By sheer chance Fleet Admiral Jean Darlan, now commander in chief of Vichy armed forces and number two man in the Vichy government, happened to be in Algiers visiting an ailing son when the Allied invasion took place. General Eisenhower, casting ideological objections aside, had wisely chosen to negotiate with the man who could speak with authority second only to that of Pétain himself. After two days, an agreement was reached. In the afternoon of 10 November Darlan, with Pétain's secret concurrence, ordered all Vichy forces in Africa to cease fire. The word did not reach Casablanca till next morning. United States and British news writers, intensely suspicious of the Nazi-tainted Vichy government, decried Eisenhower's "Darlan deal," but the general had no regrets for an arrangement that saved lives and speeded up the war.

A message Darlan sent to Dakar rallied French authorities there to the Allied cause, but his cable to the French fleet at Toulon had no such effect. In retaliation for the North African cease-fire, Hitler had ordered Vichy France to be occupied, for the moment sparing the dockyard at Toulon. Trusting Hitler's promise that remaining units of the French fleet would not be seized, Admiral Jean de Laborde, the local commandant, rebuffed Darlan's order to sail the ships to North Africa. When the Germans broke their word and attempted to seize the fleet, de Laborde scuttled his ships.

With Morocco and Algeria secure, the Allies had valuable rear bases; but Tunisia, separated from Europe by the 90-mile-wide Sicilian Channel, was the real strategic goal. Beginning 10 November, Darlan sent messages to French commanders at Bizerte and Tunis ordering cooperation with the Allies, but Hitler was quicker. German troops, rushed in by plane and destroyer, overran Bizerte's port and airfield, driving the French Tunisian garrison back to the Algerian border.

Hitler's strategy merely increased the magnitude of Allied victory. An entire Axis field army, which now joined Rommel's retreating Afrika Korps in a wintertime defense of Tunisia, could not fend off an offensive that closed the jaws of an Allied vise from west and south. Rommel's tactical skill inflicted temporary reverses on Eisenhower's troops, notably at Kasserine Pass, but could not stave off inevitable defeat. Rommel personally escaped, being ordered home from Africa by Hitler. In mid-May the last Axis positions in Tunisia were overrun. Some 275,000 Axis prisoners were taken in a victory that approached the recent Russian success at Stalingrad. Reeling back from the Russian post-Stalingrad offensive and driven from Africa, the Nazis had an early foretaste of ultimate disaster.

In anticipation of victory, a new top-level strategy conference had been held at Casablanca in January 1943. This time the conferees, Roosevelt, Churchill, and the Combined Chiefs, were joined by French leaders from North Africa and London, including the redoubtable General Charles de Gaulle. Darlan had been removed from history's stage, victim of an assassin's bullet. Stalin was invited but professed himself too busy to leave Russia.

George Marshall and Sir Alan Brooke promptly renewed their debate of the preceding July, the former pressing hard for his Roundup invasion. Brooke, convinced that executing Roundup in 1943 or even 1944 would merely court stalemate and heavy casualties, argued for more peripheral operations from the newly won French North African base. Deadlock was broken this time by the certainty that if the Combined Chiefs could not agree on strategy, Churchill and Roosevelt would do so, with possibilities that Brooke and Marshall found unpleasant to contemplate. Each yielded a little.

The Americans consented to one more Mediterranean attack, one that must have a maximum effect on the war's outcome. After that, the Americans insisted, detailed planning must commence for Roundup. The British concurred, or seemed to concur. After further discussion, it was mutually agreed that capturing Sicily would have a maximum effect on events. Its seizure might bring about the fall from power of Hitler's junior partner, Mussolini, with the further result that Italian troops, as no longer reliable, would have to be replaced by Germans. Besides aiding the Russians, such an outcome would make victory easier in France. The attack was code-named Operation Husky; the date, July 1943.

All the conferees agreed that top priority must be given to countermeasures against Dönitz's U-boats. Unless losses to submarines could be reduced substantially, all offensives were in jeopardy. As for direct attack against the Axis, General H. H. Arnold and Air Chief Marshal Sir Charles Portal proposed a joint bombing offensive, by which they expected to defeat Hitler through strategic bombing alone. The ground and naval commanders were skeptical about the air forces' chances for success, but were willing to let them try. Admiral King, as his price for delaying the attack on France in favor of another peripheral operation, demanded and received British consent to so increase military resources allotted to the Pacific as to take advantage of the recent Allied reconquest of Guadalcanal, by shifting to at least a limited offensive in that theater.

The day following the Casablanca Conference, President Roosevelt startled the world by announcing that the Allies would accept only "unconditional surrender" of Germany, Italy, and Japan. Terms would be neither offered nor considered. Not even Napoleon at the height of his conquests had so completely closed the door to negotiations. Adopted with Churchill's consent as a catchword to reassure Russian leaders and satisfy Allied publics, as an announced policy it left small incentive for dissident enemy groups to plot an early end to the war. In any case it proved unworkable. Italy and Japan surrendered, but with plenty of conditions. Only Germany's surrender was unconditional.

Operation Husky: The Invasion of Sicily

To command Operation Husky, General Eisenhower received four-star rank and three British assistants to control ground, naval, and air forces: General Sir Harold Alexander, Admiral of the Fleet Cunningham, and Air Chief Marshal Sir Arthur Tedder. A Western Naval Task Force under Vice Admiral Hewitt would land Lieutenant General Patton's U. S. Seventh Army; Vice Admiral Sir Bertram Ramsay's Eastern Naval Task Force would bring in Lieutenant General Sir Bernard Montgomery's "Desert Rats," the British Eighth Army. While an all-British covering force guarded against a still-possible sortie by the Italian fleet, Tedder's Mediterranean air forces were counted on to provide fighter cover, mostly from Malta's airfields.

Finding acceptable landing sites in Sicily sorely vexed Eisenhower's Husky planners. Admiral Cunningham wanted no part of any plan that did not provide maximum fighter cover. Since this meant limiting the attacking range to the combat radius of Spitfire fighters from Malta, the ideal landing sites, beaches near Messina, were out of bounds. Yet only landing in close proximity to the Strait of Messina offered any surety of trapping and capturing the Axis forces in Sicily.

Further complications appeared when planners tried to reconcile logistic requirements for a multi-division assault with General Montgomery's demand that a single, massed landing be thrown at Sicily's southeast tip. Montgomery, who talked recklessly but acted cautiously, wanted to ensure that Patton's Americans would protect his left flank. His demand pleased Cunningham because Spitfires would be based nearby, but it dismayed Eisenhower's supply officers. They could see no way to supply a multi-division attack on the order of Husky, even after an early seizure of Syracuse and Augusta, shallow-water ports on Montgomery's right flank. The ideal landing sites for logistics, beaches on the north coast near Palermo, Sicily's best port, were satisfactory only to General Patton, who typically declared himself ready to land anywhere.

Developments in amphibious technology ended the planning dilemma. New, seagoing beaching craft, which could carry men, tanks, trucks, and artillery from shore to shore, were becoming available in numbers sufficient to keep an attack rolling, even without a major port. These craft—LSTs (Landing Ships, Tank), LCTs (Landing Craft, Tank), and LCIs (Landing Craft, Infantry)—arrived in numbers adequate to land troops and bring in their supplies.[1] Becoming available in quantity also were army DUKWs (called "Ducks"), amphibious trucks that could haul supplies from ships offshore to inland dumps.

Thus Montgomery and Cunningham could have their way: Sicily's southeast tip it could and would be. Unfortunately a landing in this area, so far from Messina, was more likely to push the Axis forces out of Sicily than to trap them in. The selection moreover was based on a misunderstanding growing out of typical poor communications between air forces and ground and sea forces. Marshal Tedder had no intention of providing tactical support to the landings. The business of his air forces was, in his

[1] The first waves of infantry would be carried from ship to shore by the new, very practical landing craft LCVP (Landing Craft, Vehicle and Personnel).

opinion, to fight enemy aircraft on or over their own airfields, never permitting them to reach the beachhead.

There were in Sicily two German and four Italian combat divisions and six Italian coastal divisions, amounting to about 255,000 troops. The Germans, as always, could be expected to put up a good fight. The military potential of the Italian combat troops was less certain, but the real weakness was in the coastal divisions, composed mostly of overage Sicilian reservists. The Sicilians detested the Germans, despised Mussolini, and admired the United States, where many of their friends and relatives lived. They had been assigned to guard the beaches on the theory that they would fight hard to defend their homeland. On the contrary, when the invasion came, they logically concluded that the greater resistance they put up, the more likely their homes were to be bombed or bombarded.

Admiral Hewitt again pleaded with the army to be allowed to deliver a dawn preinvasion bombardment before the infantry hit the beach. But the army commanders again refused, hoping to slip the men ashore before the enemy realized what was happening. The invasion was scheduled for the night of 9–10 July 1943, beginning at 0245, fifteen minutes after moonset.

On 8 July jam-packed North African harbors emptied as the Sicily-bound armada stood out to sea, where it was joined by a convoy bringing a division of Canadian infantry from the United Kingdom. Embarked in 1,375 ships and beaching craft were more than 175,000 men. This was nothing like the 3-to-1 superiority generally considered advisable for an assaulting force, but the Allied commanders hoped to offset the lack of numbers by getting the men ashore as fast as possible. Ultimately 478,000 Allied troops would be committed, about half of them American and half British.

In the evening of 9 July, a sudden, brief storm caused beaching craft to pitch wildly and even the large transports to take water over their bows. Fortunately the tempest abated before midnight, leaving only a heavy swell for the invaders to contend with.

Before moonset airborne British and American troops arrived over Sicily and landed by parachute and glider to delay enemy reinforcement of the beachheads by seizing or blowing up bridges and setting up roadblocks. The seaborne attack forces, in complete darkness, approached their assigned landing beaches remarkably close to schedule. It was to be the most massive amphibious assault in history. The Americans were about to land in three divisions on a 40-mile stretch of Sicily's south coast, while four British divisions, including the Canadian, went ashore on an equally wide stretch of the east coast.

Despite darkness and still-heavy seas, the LCVPs moved smartly from their transports to the line of departure and then, guided by the blinking infrared lights of scout boats, headed for the shore. There was little of the confusion that had prevailed off North Africa.

As, tense and seasick in their pitching landing craft, the infantry assault teams waited for their seagoing ordeal to end, searchlights flashed seaward from ashore. Here and there machine guns opened up and artillery shells raised geysers in the water. Surprise lost, the ships opened fire at the shore defenses. When the LCVPs grounded and dropped bow ramps, the men hesitated momentarily, then rushed ashore, forgetting nausea, and scurried inland to locate their assigned positions and link up with battalions on either flank. By 0485 lead elements of all seven Allied divisions were ashore. Already it was clear that resistance at the beach would be light to nonexistent. The Sicilian reservists were surrendering in wholesale lots.

More dependable German and Italian combat troops and armored columns were moving toward the beach, but most of them had been turned back by evening of the 10th. At Gela, on the south coast, columns of German and Italian tanks were repulsed by shellfire from artillery ferried in by DUKWs and by the 6-inch guns of the cruiser *Boise*. At nightfall Patton's and Montgomery's troops dug in far ahead of their anticipated defense lines.

Tedder's aviators destroyed more than 200 Axis planes and cratered every airfield in Sicily, forcing the Italian and German aircraft to pull back and operate from fields in the Italian mainland. From here they struck frequently at the Allied ships. But the ships, firing the new proximity-fused antiaircraft shells, shot down a good many of them and induced the rest to bomb inaccurately and indiscriminately. Hewitt's losses were limited to a destroyer, an LST, and an ammunition ship. Tragically, a result of the poor communications between Allied naval and air forces, not a few of the aircraft shot down by the naval gunners were American and British planes that happened to be routed over them.

According to plan, Montgomery was expected to lead his Eighth Army in a dash up the coast to Messina, thereby closing the escape hatch out of Sicily, while Patton maneuvered his less-experienced Seventh Army to keep Montgomery's left flank covered. Seldom in the history of warfare has there been a clearer case of military miscasting. Patton was to become famous for the speed of his drives. Montgomery, despite his memorable pursuit of Rommel across the Libyan desert the preceding fall, was more cautious than dashing. He took Syracuse and Augusta, thereby easing his supply problem, but when he met strong German resistance at Catania, he stopped. Instead of calling on the Navy to blast the enemy out of his way or to block the enemy's communications by a landing farther up the coast, he decided to pass around west of Mt. Etna. Redeploying his army for this change of front took the meticulous Montgomery until 1 August. Then when he started moving again, he was slowed by the rugged terrain at the base of the mountain.

Fearing that Montgomery's change of direction would let the enemy escape, Patton with two divisions dashed across Sicily to Palermo, then along the north coast toward Messina. Three times he had his accompanying naval forces carry troops forward in amphibious leaps to catch some of the enemy, but the latter, now in full flight, was always a jump ahead. By 3 August, the Axis forces were crowded into the northeast tip of Sicily and had begun crossing the strait. They completed their evacuation during the night of 16 August. After sunrise on the 17th one of Patton's patrols entered Messina. Two hours later a column of British Eighth Army tanks rumbled into the city.

Though the bulk of the Axis forces escaped, Operation Husky won major advantages for the Allies. It swept away British doubts that the American soldier was a first-rate fighting man. It opened the Mediterranean to Allied shipping. Most important, it took Italy out of the war.

In late July, when the fall of Sicily was impending, the Fascist Grand Council repudiated Mussolini, and the king dismissed him from office and had him imprisoned. Mussolini's successor as head of government, Marshal Pietro Badoglio, announced that the Italians would continue to fight shoulder to shoulder with their German allies. At the same time he put out secret peace feelers to the Anglo-Americans.

Operation Avalanche: The Invasion of Italy

In May 1943, as the Tunisian campaign was drawing to an end, the Allied leaders held yet another strategy-planning session, this time in Washington. Assuming Anglo–American success in Sicily, the main question before the session was: What next? After the usual sharp debates and differences of opinion, the participants again reached a compromise. The Americans reluctantly agreed to join the British in an early invasion of peninsular Italy, provided that only the Allied forces already in the Mediterranean would be used—less seven divisions to be withdrawn to the United Kingdom as a nucleus for building up the cross-Channel attack force. The British at last committed themselves to a 1944 invasion of western France, and they raised no objections to the opening of a new Central Pacific drive against Japan, provided that only Allied forces already in the theater of operations would be used.

General Brooke had insisted upon the Italian invasion as a means of drawing German forces out of France. It did nothing of the sort. While the Sicilian campaign was still in progress, the Germans, anticipating an early Italian surrender, had rushed reinforcements to join Field Marshal Rommel's army in Northern Italy and Field Marshal Albert Kesselring's in the South. The Allied invasion of the mainland drew no more Germans into the peninsula. On the contrary, it was the Allies who had to send additional forces to the Mediterranean. Ultimately, the Italian campaign tied down twice as many Allied troops as German.

Eisenhower's invasion plan tempered daring with prudence. First, Montgomery's British Eighth Army would cross Messina Strait into the toe of the Italian boot, taking Reggio and Taranto. A week later another Allied force, the new Anglo–American Fifth Army, under Lieutenant General Mark Clark, USA, would land four divisions on beaches at the Gulf of Salerno. After linking with Montgomery's troops coming up from the south, the Fifth Army would cross a low range of hills near Mt. Vesuvius and capture Naples, Italy's best port.

Eisenhower's planners had selected Salerno not only because it was the gateway to Naples but also because it was just within range of air support by fighter planes based on Sicily. Kesselring, to whom these specifics were obvious, fully expected an attack at Salerno and ordered a tough panzer division to dig in there.

At 1830 on 8 September, as the Salerno invasion force was approaching the gulf, General Eisenhower broadcast a radio announcement of the Italian Armistice. The Germans at once began disarming the Italians and taking control of their government. Only the Italian fleet and some air units escaped. Most of the disarmed Italians simply vanished, blending into the civilian population. Mussolini, rescued by the Germans, was put at the head of a puppet government in northern Italy. The Italian fleet reached Malta but, lacking radar and other up-to-date equipment, proved of little use to the Allies.

The Salerno-bound Fifth Army greeted Eisenhower's announcement with jubilation—and the conviction that they could now simply walk ashore. Senior officers had trouble convincing the troops that, although the Italians had quit fighting, there were plenty of tough Germans to give them a brutal reception.

Admiral Hewitt, heading the Salerno task force, had his flag on the USS *Ancon*, one of the new amphibious command ships, fitted with elaborate radio and radar gear. He had again argued in vain for a dawn prelanding bombardment of the shore defenses. As he expected, the Germans at Salerno were ready and waiting. In one sector, as the LCVPs approached the beach, a loudspeaker blared in English, "Come on in and give up! We have you covered!"

When the ramps of the first landing craft slammed down, pandemonium broke loose. The defenders of the beach opened up with rifle, machine gun, mortar, cannon, and tank fire, and at dawn German aircraft came sweeping over the landing area, bombing and strafing. Surviving troops of the first assault waves bypassed enemy strong points to gather in prearranged assembly areas. Then came DUKWs bringing ashore howitzers and ammunition. Thus armed, the invaders dueled German tanks at point-blank range. Before the day was over the invaders had tanks of their own. Sailors, struggling with pontoons while shells made geysers in the water around them, managed to rig causeways to facilitate bringing the vehicles ashore.

Of all the Allied assaults of World War II, that at Salerno came nearest to being thrown back into the sea. It was saved partly by sheer valor; it was saved partly by close air support, from carriers and from land-based fighters, which Eisenhower had demanded; but mostly it was saved by naval gunfire. Warships hugged the beaches, blasting enemy targets, undeterred by enemy bombers that sent down radio-controlled glide bombs, even though these severely damaged two cruisers and a battleship. On 16 September, when naval guns turned back an all-out German attempt at a breakthrough, Kesselring knew that he could no longer contain the Allied beachhead. He authorized disengagement from the coastal front, "in order," as he afterward wrote, "to evade the effective shelling from warships."

On 1 October, the Fifth Army occupied Naples, and naval salvage experts began clearing the har-

bor, in which the retreating Germans had sunk ships and dumped cranes, trucks, locomotives, and assorted junk in a vain endeavor to make the port unusable by the Allies. Over on the Adriatic coast, the Eighth Army took the important Foggia airdrome, which, however, proved disappointing because Allied strategic bombers based there were unable to cross the Alps safely with a full load of fuel or bombs.

In mid-November, Hitler dissolved Rommel's command and added the troops to Kesselring's army, now holding a defensive line in the mountains northwest of Naples. Here the Germans made skillful use of mines, demolitions, and natural obstacles. They were aided by atrocious campaigning weather—almost continuous rain or snow that turned all roads to quagmires. Though the Allies had control of the sea, virtual control of the air, and more troops than Kesselring had even in his reinforced army, it took the Fifth and Eighth armies, advancing abreast up the Italian peninsula, eight months to fight their way the hundred miles from Naples to Rome.

Eisenhower considered sending a couple of divisions by sea past the German line for a landing at Anzio, south of Rome. From here the invaders would dash inland to the Alban Hills, whence their guns could intercept supplies flowing by road and railroad to Kesselring's army. Eisenhower, concluding that he lacked sufficient force both to hold a new beachhead and to breach the German line, canceled the Anzio project. Soon afterward he left for England to command the cross-Channel attack.

On Churchill's insistence the Anzio project was revived. In the dark early hours of 22 January 1944, the spearhead of a two-division assault landed at Anzio. It was not enough. It never reached the Alban Hills. Kesselring's troops quickly surrounded the invaders and pinned them to the beach. The situation deteriorated into a wretched stalemate.

As the rains ceased and the roads hardened with the advance of spring, the Fifth and Eighth armies launched an all-out attack on the main German line. On 19 May a French corps of the Fifth Army broke through, and Allied troops surged up the Italian peninsula. On the 25th, an advance American patrol coming up from the south joined hands with a patrol out of Anzio. On the night of 2–3 June, the Germans broke off contact all along the front and hastily withdrew to the north. On 4 June, the triumphant Allies made an unopposed entry into Rome, where they were joyfully received by the inhabitants. Two days later, Allied forces in England crossed the Channel and invaded Normandy, thereby reducing the Italian front to a mere backwater of the European war.

Operation Overlord:
The Invasion of Normandy

Because the code name Operation Roundup for the Allied invasion of western Europe had possibly been compromised, it was given a new name, Operation Overlord, and the amphibious phase was called Operation Neptune. Roosevelt's choice to command the enterprise was General Marshall, but when it became evident that Marshall could not be spared from the Joint Chiefs of Staff, the president appointed General Eisenhower. As Supreme Commander Allied Expeditionary Force, Eisenhower was ordered to "enter the Continent of Europe, and, in conjunction with the other United Nations, undertake operations aimed at the heart of Germany and the destruction of her armed forces."

The officers appointed to head the ground, naval, and air forces immediately under Eisenhower were all British: General Montgomery, Admiral Ramsay, and Air Chief Marshal Sir Trafford Leigh-Mallory. Under Admiral Ramsay the chiefly American Western Naval Task Force was commanded by Rear Admiral Alan G. Kirk, USN; and the British Eastern Naval Task Force, by Rear Admiral Sir Philip Vian, RN. Under General Montgomery, the U. S. First Army was commanded by Lieutenant General Omar Bradley, USA; and the British Second Army, by Lieutenant General Sir Miles Dempsey.

When General Eisenhower took command, most of the planning for Overlord had already been completed by an Anglo–American staff under Lieutenant General Sir Frederick Morgan, who had been appointed to the task following the Casablanca Conference. General Morgan and his assistants had considered possible invasion sites from Norway to Portugal, giving special attention to beaches fronting the English Channel. The obvious choice was the Pas-de-Calais, which afforded the shortest sea invasion route and the best natural beaches and was closest to Germany, the ultimate target. But defenses there were strongest and daily getting stronger. The final decision was for a stretch of Normandy coast between Cherbourg and Le Havre. Shortage of beaching craft decreed that the invasion would have to be narrow, three divisions abreast, but these divisions would be followed by more than 50 before onset of winter. D-day was tentatively set for 1 May 1944.

One of Eisenhower's first decisions as supreme commander was to postpone the invasion to early June. The postponement would cost him a month's good campaigning weather, but it would provide enough additional beaching craft from new construction to permit a five-division landing.[2] The army, having digested the lessons of Salerno, now proposed a daylight landing following a naval bombardment of enemy defenses. The period 5, 6, and 7 June would provide the desired early-morning low tide following a moonlit night for air drops. Eisenhower selected 5 June for D-day, with H-hours ranging from 0630 to 0755 to meet the varying tidal conditions at the five assault beaches.

In preparation for Operation Overlord, the Allied air forces early in 1944 shifted their objective from bombing Germany into submission to gaining control of the air. Thousands of bombers accompanied by as many fighters attacked enemy planes and bombed aircraft factories and aircraft repair depots and storage parks. In mid-April they switched to attacks on enemy communications, bombing and strafing tracks, trains, and railroad marshaling yards. Beginning in early May they took bridges as their main targets; before the end of the month, not a single bridge spanned the Seine between Paris and the English Channel.

Weeks before D-day the entire southern part of England became an armed camp, sealed off from the rest of the country. Troops that were to make the initial landings in Normandy were confined in huge encampments near major ports—Americans from Portland west, British from Portsmouth east. An exception to this arrangement was an encampment near the Strait of Dover. Here forces said to be General Patton's 1st U. S. Army Group were reported by enemy planes as apparently planning to invade the continent via the Pas-de-Calais on the opposite shore, where the German Fifteenth Army was stationed. In fact, no 1st U. S. Army Group existed. The encampment, complete with fake tanks, fake landing craft, and mostly empty tents, was a British hoax, intended to mislead the enemy.

As early as 30 May, the troops in southern England began to board the transports and beaching craft that would carry them across the Channel. By 3 June all troops were embarked; the fire-support ships, including six old battleships, had put to sea from Scapa Flow, Belfast, and the Clyde; and the convoys were beginning to form off the southern

[2]The shortage arose partly from the fact that the Central Pacific drive had developed into a major campaign. The invasion of the Marianas, also scheduled for June 1944, required 79 LSTs.

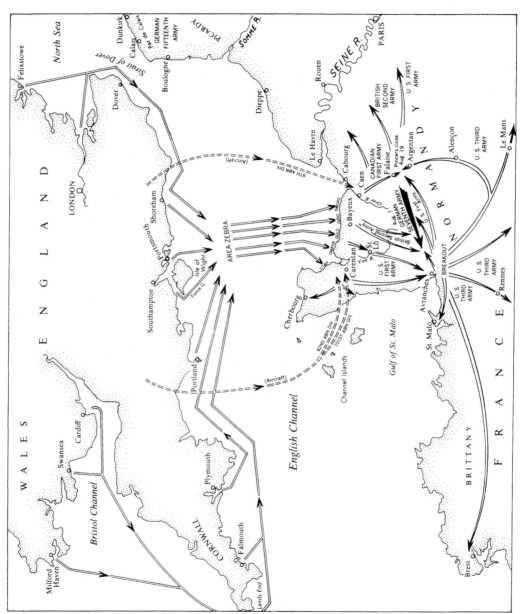

Normandy Invasion and Campaign

ports. Neptune–Overlord, the most complex and most minutely planned military operation in history, was under way. Nothing that could be anticipated was left to chance.

There was nevertheless one element of uncertainty—the weather. Eisenhower, informed by his meteorologists early on 4 June that there would be strong winds, low clouds, and high seas in the target area on the 5th, reluctantly postponed the invasion 24 hours. Ships already at sea were recalled. Toward midnight on the 4th, the meteorologists were able to predict that a break in the weather was on the way. Eisenhower thereupon took the risk of setting the invasion forces again in motion, but deferred his final decision until early the next morning. The meteorologists were then able to predict with confidence that the clearing weather would last at least until the afternoon of the 6th. Thus reassured, the supreme commander, at 0415, 5 June, gave his irrevocable order: "O.K. We'll go."

Ships from all ports of Great Britain headed for Area Zebra, the assembly zone southeast of the Isle of Wight. From here, led by minesweepers, the armada proceeded across the Channel in darkness. As it approached the Normandy coast, three airborne divisions were parachuted behind the beaches to seize and hold bridges and causeways.

Field Marshal Gerd von Rundstedt, Commander in Chief West, on orders from Hitler, had built an "Atlantic Wall" of casemated artillery to sweep every possible landing beach. But he had little confidence in such defenses, believing them vulnerable to naval gunfire. He relied instead on mobile infantry and armored divisions placed well inland, whence they could be rushed to the coast to prevent the Allies from exploiting any beachhead they might succeed in seizing.

His subordinate, Field Marshal Rommel, Commander Army Group B (Seventh and Fifteenth armies), believed that Allied air power would prevent Rundstedt's mobile reserves from reaching the coast in time to achieve decisive results. In his opinion, the invader would be repulsed at the water's edge, or not at all. Denied the armored forces he believed he needed, Rommel concentrated upon static defenses—more casemated artillery, rows of submerged steel, wood, and concrete beach obstacles, all heavily mined. He put his emphasis on the Pas-de-Calais coast, where he thought the invasion would come. The Normandy coast defenses were manned largely by green reserves and foreign volunteers, none of whom were inclined to fight past hope. The tremendous 22-foot tides and shoal beach approaches off Normandy

presented problems for the invader, but they were a disadvantage to the defenders too, because low tide left the beach obstacles high and dry.

The strong winds, low clouds, and high seas of early June lulled the Germans into complacency. Nobody, they believed, would attempt a landing in such conditions. Lacking meteorological stations west of Europe, they had no intimation of clearing weather. Rommel in his command car headed for home, where he planned to spend 6 June, which happened to be his wife's birthday.

At Normandy the first evidence that an invasion was imminent came at 0130 on the 6th, when Allied paratroopers came drifting down out of the night sky between Seventh Army headquarters and the coast. Half an hour later German coastal radar operators began picking up the naval armada. Rommel, notified by telephone, headed back toward Normandy muttering, "How stupid of me! How stupid of me!"

At first light Allied bombers swept over the Normandy beaches. Because of poor visibility, some of them dropped their bombs several miles inland. Off the British beaches, designated Gold, Juno, and Sword, the Royal Navy, waiting for the rising tide to cover offshore reefs, gave the shore defenses two hours of hard pounding. Landing craft then easily penetrated the widely spaced beach obstacles, and British and Canadian troops went ashore against little opposition and began advancing along the highway toward Caen.

At the American Utah Beach, on Cotentin Peninsula at the opposite end of the line, naval gunfire, though less extended, cleared the landing area of its irresolute defenders with equal success. By the end of D-day, 21,300 American troops had landed here against little resistance and established a beachhead six miles wide and six deep. The heaviest losses in this area were caused by mines, which sank a destroyer and five beaching craft.

In contrast to the other Normandy landing areas, the American Omaha Beach proved to be the most heavily fortified stretch of coast that the Allies assaulted during the entire war. Here not reservists but two regiments of first-line veteran troops were manning the defenses, and they had worked to make Omaha Beach a hornets' nest. Because the beach obstacles were too close together for landing craft to penetrate, the initial landings had to be made at low tide when the obstacles were fully exposed. That meant that Omaha Beach defenses got only 35 minutes of preliminary naval bombardment, and here all the aerial bombs were dropped well inland.

Amphibious tanks that led the way to the beach

were nearly all sunk by choppy seas or gunfire. When the LCVPs dropped their ramps, the invading infantrymen had to wade ashore through machine-gun fire, race across a hundred yards of exposed beach, work their way through three rows of mined beach obstacles, and run another hundred yards to a wood-and-concrete seawall, behind which they took temporary refuge.

Beyond the seawall were barbed wire entanglements and, at the far side of a sandy beach, a steep bluff covered with tall grass and bristling with guns. Among the first waves to land were 16 underwater demolition teams of sailors and army engineers who, at the cost of 52 percent casualties, blasted open in the beach obstacles several wide channels through which landing craft could penetrate at high tide.

Waves of infantrymen, coming in at ten-minute intervals, at first merely joined the growing mass of crouching figures behind the seawall. But engineers managed to blow gaps in the barbed wire, machine guns were set up, and under the leadership of surviving officers, small groups of men began rushing across the dry sand and scaling the bluffs. By noon the Americans had begun to penetrate inland.

The American advance was an achievement of sheer courage, but it was made possible by naval guns. The heavy ships sealed off the beachhead with a ring of shellfire, preventing the Germans from reinforcing or shifting their defense forces. But the direct support that cleared the way for the advance was provided by 12 destroyers. Closing the shore to within a thousand yards, actually scraping bottom, these ships delivered call fire as requested by fire-control parties or fired at targets of opportunity. Thus supported, by nightfall some 34,000 troops had gone ashore at Omaha, overrun the bluff, and established a line more than a mile inland. The cost to the invaders had been high: 2,000 killed, wounded, or missing.

Pending the capture of ports, the Allies supplied themselves mostly through a pair of artificial harbors code-named Mulberries A and B. These comprised prefabricated piers protected by breakwaters of steel and concrete caissons and tired old freighters, towed over from England and sunk or anchored off Omaha and Gold beaches. The Omaha harbor, Mulberry A, was soon wrecked by a storm, but it was found that supply could be maintained by beaching LSTs at high tide and unloading them as the tide ebbed and flowed.

Operation Overlord proceeded according to plan if not quite according to schedule. As Montgomery anticipated, the German Seventh Army, defending Normandy, concentrated its efforts in the Caen area, lest the British and Canadians thrust themselves between it and the Fifteenth Army, which was still at the Pas-de-Calais, immobilized by the supposed threat of Patton's phantom army group just across the strait.

The British and Canadians thus served to contain the bulk of the Seventh Army, while the Americans, on the Allied right flank, carried out assigned offensive operations. With a powerful assist from gunfire support ships under Rear Admiral Morton L. Deyo, USN, elements of Bradley's First Army captured Cherbourg on 27 June and soon afterward secured the whole of the Cotentin Peninsula. Other elements headed south with overwhelming air support and broke through to Avranches. A new U. S. Third Army was formed out of excess divisions of the First, and General Patton, abandoning his ghostly duties at Dover, took command. At the end of July, Patton turned Bradley's breakthrough into a breakout. His Third Army, crashing through Avranches, fanned out south, east, and west. It sealed off the Brittany Peninsula and established a broad front for an eastward advance in the direction of the Rhine, toward which Patton with his usual dash now directed the bulk of his army.

The German Seventh Army still had time to escape eastward, but Hitler ordered it to drive west in a futile attempt to penetrate the U. S. First Army and cut Patton's communications. This move enabled the American First and Third armies on 19 August to complete the encirclement of the German Seventh by advancing northward to meet the Canadian First Army driving down from Caen. Though the Germans thus entrapped within this "Avranches-Falaise pocket" were subjected to merciless pounding by aircraft and artillery, they managed on the 20th to break through the Canadians and hold open a corridor long enough for 40,000 troops to escape to the east. But 50,000 Germans who did not get out were captured, and another 10,000 were killed. The Allies in France, now 1,500,000 strong, were already moving on Paris and toward Germany.

The deplorable situation in which the Germans now found themselves inspired a surge of defeatism among Hitler's commanding officers, some of whom contemplated surrendering to the Allies to spare Germany the agony of invasion. Hitler, considering Rundstedt no longer dependable, ordered Field Marshal Günther von Kluge to relieve him, then sacked Kluge when the Seventh Army was trapped. Ordered home and fearing arrest, Kluge took poison. Marshal Rommel, suspected of complicity in an attempt on Hitler's life, was given the choice between poison and a public trial, with the threat that his wife and son would be imprisoned or shot. He chose poison. Rommel was given a state funeral, with full military honors, and Rundstedt was required to read his eulogy.

Operation Dragoon:
The Invasion of Southern France

General Morgan had recommended a diversionary attack on the southern coast of France—to be carried out simultaneously with the Normandy landings. Initially called Operation Anvil, the project raised problems. Even though Operation Neptune was postponed a month, there still were not enough beaching craft, or fire-support vessels either, for simultaneous execution of Neptune and Anvil. The latter would have to be put off till beaching craft and gunnery vessels could be brought around to the Mediterranean. Thus Anvil would forfeit one of its objectives—drawing German defense forces away from Normandy.

Moreover, the Allied generals in Italy opposed Operation Anvil, because many of the troops would have to be withdrawn from the Italian campaign. Strongly backed by Churchill, they proposed to cap their campaign by driving via Trieste through the Ljubljana Gap to Vienna. Churchill argued for the Ljubljana operation on military grounds, but his objective was clearly political—to beat the Russians to the Danube basin.

Eisenhower, deeming the Ljubljana project militarily eccentric, kept insisting on Anvil, and Roosevelt and Marshall supported him. Churchill at last conceded defeat, but, according to legend, he fired a final shot. Because the code-name Anvil had possibly been compromised, it had to be changed. Churchill, it was said, asked that it be renamed Operation Dragoon, inasmuch as he had been dragooned into it. For whatever reason, Dragoon it was, and it was scheduled for 15 August 1944,

Operation Dragoon was Admiral Hewitt's masterpiece, embodying everything he had insisted on from the beginning, plus everything he had learned since: an extended land-based aerial bombing campaign to knock out enemy airfields and strong points, realistic rehearsals of the landing, a night paratroop drop to seal off the beachhead, an intensive two-hour bombing and bombardment of the beach defenses, rocket-firing LCIs preceding the first assault wave to detonate land mines. Beginning at 0800 the assault troops waded ashore at seven selected beaches on a 30-mile front between Toulon and Cannes. All the landings were on time,

and none met any serious resistance. Nine escort carriers stood off the coast, sending in planes to spot for the gunfire-support vessels and to range inland to disrupt enemy communications and break up enemy troop concentrations.

The force that invaded southern France was composed of the U. S. Seventh and the First French armies. While the Frenchmen liberated Toulon and the fine port of Marseille, a far more efficient supply base than Cherbourg, the Americans pursued the retreating Germans up the Rhône Valley and on 11 September, near Dijon, made contact with the U. S. Third Army from Normandy. Thus the thrusts from the English Channel and from the Mediterranean Sea combined, sealing off all German forces in southwestern France. The U. S. Seventh Army and the French First Army, coming abreast, formed the right wing of Eisenhower's ground forces as they advanced on the German frontier.

The German Collapse

By 1 September 1944, when General Eisenhower established headquarters in France and took over the command of the Allied ground forces, the Allies had liberated Paris and crossed the Seine, the Somme, and the Meuse. Under Eisenhower, Montgomery (promoted to field marshal) commanded the 21st Army Group (Canadian First and British Second armies); General Bradley commanded the 12th Army Group (initially U. S. First and Third armies); and Lieutenant General Jacob L. Devers commanded the 6th Army Group (U. S. Seventh and French First armies, up from the invasion of southern France).

Priority in supplies was at first given to Montgomery's army group so that it might quickly capture the coastal launching sites of Germany's new "vengeance weapons," the flying bomb (V-1) and the supersonic rocket (V-2), which were streaking toward London, killing thousands of Londoners and turning great areas of the city into rubble. A scarcely secondary objective of the speeded-up 21st Army Group was capture of the port of Antwerp to ease the critical supply problem.

After the taking of Antwerp, all of Eisenhower's armies, spearheaded by air power, advanced on Germany altogether. They were at length slowed almost to a stop by supply shortage, increasing German resistance, and deteriorating flying weather. In mid-December, Hitler committed Germany's last strategic reserves in a massive drive at the Allied center in the Ardennes. In what is popularly called the Battle of the Bulge, the Germans penetrated 50 miles westward but had little chance of achieving Hitler's objective of splitting the Anglo–American armies apart. Improved flying weather and prompt Allied counterattacks soon obliged the Germans to pull back. In this last, desperate gamble, the Germans had inflicted about 60,000 casualties on the Allies, but the attack had cost them nearly 250,000 men, some 600 tanks and assault guns, and about 1,600 planes.

Early in 1945, the Americans, British, French, and Russians resumed their advance on Germany from east, south, and west. By March Eisenhower's armies were lined up along the steep-banked, swift-flowing Rhine, a formidable barrier. First across were elements of the U. S. First Army, which discovered at Remagen the only Rhine bridge the Germans had failed to destroy. It collapsed in a few days, but nearby, ready for service, were almost a hundred LCVPs and about half as many LCMs, hauled to the front by army trucks and manned by naval personnel. Before the end of March the landing craft had ferried 14,000 troops and 400 vehicles of the First Army across the Rhine and assisted army engineers in constructing pontoon bridges. Farther up the Rhine, General Patton's U. S. Third Army used the craft for a quick buildup on the east bank while bridges were being constructed. Downstream, the craft assisted Montgomery's forces in making their first crossings.

The war in Europe now moved swiftly to a close. The Canadian First and the British Second armies raced for the German North Sea ports. The U. S. First and Ninth armies enveloped the industrial Ruhr, entrapping 325,000 troops, including 30 generals. The U. S. Third Army sped across Germany to Czechoslovakia. The U. S. Seventh Army swept through southern Germany, capturing Munich. The Russians advanced on Berlin and Vienna. The Allied Fifth and Eighth armies shattered the German defenses in northern Italy.

On 28 April, Benito Mussolini, fleeing toward Switzerland, was captured and killed by Italian resistance fighters, who hung up his body by the heels in Milan for public execration. On 1 May, with Russians surrounding Berlin and fighting in the streets, Adolf Hitler, hiding in a bunker under his chancellery, put a pistol to his head and shot himself.

The German armies, reduced to mobs of terrified fugitives, began to surrender to the British and Americans. Early on 7 May, Colonel General Alfred Jodl, acting on behalf of the German high command, placed his signature on the general surrender document at Supreme Commander Eisenhower's headquarters at Reims. At midnight on the 8th World War II officially ended in Europe.

Summary

Early in World War II Great Britain planned to mine the coastal waters (Leads) of Norway to block the winter flow of iron ore from Narvik to Germany and to prevent German ships from using these sheltered waters to bypass the Royal Navy's blockade. To forestall the British, the Germans in April 1940 invaded Norway and Denmark. The Britons fought two naval actions off Narvik and subsequently captured the town but were obliged to withdraw and return to England when Germany invaded the Low Countries and France.

The German armies quickly surrounded the Allied armies, but the Royal Navy, aided by numerous privately owned craft, succeeded in evacuating 338,000 troops through the port of Dunkirk. On 10 June 1940, Italy declared war on France, and on 22 June the defeated French signed an armistice whereby the Germans occupied northern and western France. The rest of France was administered by a government at Vichy headed by Pétain. To prevent French warships from falling into enemy hands, the British seized those in British ports and disarmed those at Alexandria. French naval forces at Oran and Dakar proving uncooperative, British ships and planes attacked them, sinking several ships. After the Italian fleet had twice retreated from equal or inferior British forces, Cunningham in November 1940 staged a night raid with carrier planes on the naval base at Taranto and heavily damaged three Italian battleships.

Meanwhile, Hitler, frustrated by the inability of his Luftwaffe to attain command of the air over the Channel, canceled his plan to invade England and issued orders for an invasion of Russia. Italian troops invaded Egypt from Libya and Greece from Albania; they were repulsed on both fronts. Hitler, despite his decision to attack Russia, felt compelled to come to their rescue. The British sent 58,000 troops from Africa to defend Greece. An Italian fleet attempting to interfere with the British troop convoys was defeated by Cunningham's fleet in the Battle of Cape Matapan (March 1941). When Greece surrendered to the invading Germans, the British withdrew, first from the Greek mainland and then from Crete, taking heavy losses on land and sea.

To North Africa Hitler sent Rommel and the Afrika Korps, which drove back the British and advanced into Egypt. Thereafter for a year and a half the North African war was a back-and-forth affair—the side advancing that was the better supplied. Rommel was increasingly denied supplies by the demands of Germany's Russian campaign and by the buildup on Malta of air power that sank a large part of such supplies as were sent him. In the summer of 1942, he again invaded Egypt and got as far as El Alamein, 60 miles from Alexandria, but for lack of supplies could get no farther. Montgomery, succeeding to command of the British Eighth Army in Egypt, began preparing his forces and building up supplies for an all-out offensive.

At the beginning of the war, the British, in response to the U-boat sinking of the passenger liner *Athenia*, had adopted convoy and armed their merchant vessels, whereupon the Germans moved toward resumption of unrestricted submarine warfare. Dönitz planned to defeat the convoys and offset asdic by organizing his U-boats into wolf packs and coaching them by radio in night surface attacks. Initially, however, he had only 56 boats, not enough for wolf-pack tactics, especially since they had to consume fuel going north around the British Isles to get at ships in the Western Approaches.

After the fall of France and the establishment of German bases in Norway and France, Dönitz was able to use wolf-pack tactics with increasing success. U-boat sinkings of Allied merchantmen rose to a climax in the fall of 1940, then tapered off as Britain acquired more escorts, equipped them with radar, and learned how to break the German U-boat code.

With American entry into the war, the U-boats staged a blitz on U. S. east coast shipping, but were defeated as soon as coastal convoys were established. As the convoys were extended southward, Dönitz, in accordance with his tonnage warfare strategy, moved his boats farther south to less dangerous, more profitable waters. When Germany attacked the Soviet Union, Britain and the United States began supplying Russia with munitions sent around north of Norway to Murmansk and Archangel. These convoys, though heavily protected by warships, lost so many merchantmen to U-boats and planes that after 1942 the Admiralty sent convoys by this route only during the Arctic darkness of dead winter.

Meanwhile, in mid-1942, Dönitz had begun challenging convoys in the North Atlantic by means of overwhelmingly strong wolf packs. This formidable campaign was at length defeated by surface escorts, escort carriers, radar, HF/DF, antisubmarine support groups, and long-range, land-based air escorts. The attack on convoy ONS-5 in the spring of 1943, in which seven U-boats were destroyed, proved the decisive action of the Atlantic battle. Shortly thereafter Dönitz called off his costly attacks in the North Atlantic and dispatched his boats elsewhere, mainly to the Central Atlantic. Here the American hunter-killer groups achieved

great success in sinking U-boats, which they often located by means of HF/DF and cryptanalysis, cleared through the Tenth Fleet, the American antisubmarine organization in Washington.

Destruction of milch cows (U-tankers) by the hunter-killer groups obliged Dönitz to abandon U-boat operations in distant waters. His boats staged one final campaign against North Atlantic convoys, without much success. The belated development of such technological devices as *Zaunkönig* and the snorkel did not reverse the tide. The U-boats could no longer hope for victory, but they doggedly continued the struggle to the end.

Germany also made extensive use of surface raiders, mostly warships, including battleships. Notable was the pocket battleship *Graf Spee*, which early in the war sank nine merchantmen before being defeated by British cruisers in the Battle of the River Plate (December 1939). The battleship *Admiral Scheer* in a six-month cruise sank 11 ships. The appearance on the Atlantic of the giant battleship *Bismarck* in May 1941 caused panic in the Royal Navy. Every major British warship in the Atlantic area set out to hunt her down. She was at last sunk, but not until she had destroyed the battle cruiser *Hood*. In December 1943 the battleship *Scharnhorst*, while hunting a Russia-bound convoy, was sunk off North Cape by a British surface force. Not long afterward, British bombers, staging out of Russia, destroyed the battleship *Tirpitz*.

Though the British and the Americans worked together closely and effectively as Allies to defeat Hitler, they frequently disagreed regarding strategy. The main difference arose over the American desire for an early invasion of western France, followed by a drive into the heart of Germany. The British, having been thrice ejected from the Continent, preferred to continue peripheral strategy, at least until the Allies could be sure of a sufficient preponderance of strength to assure them victory in Europe.

The Anglo–American landings in French North Africa in November 1942 marked tentative American acceptance of peripheral strategy. A major purpose of this and ensuing Allied campaigns in the Mediterranean theater was to divert German strength from western Europe in order to make the eventual cross-Channel attack less costly.

The Allied landings in Northwest Africa coincided with, and were a part of, the turning point of the war. The German armed forces, grossly overextended, had been halted in Russia at Stalingrad and in Egypt at El Alamein. For the Germans, hitherto victorious on land, the rest of World War II consisted of a long retreat to the Fatherland. In North

Africa the Allied drive from the west coincided with a British offensive out of Egypt. The two offensives came together in Tunisia, where in May 1943 they succeeded in trapping 275,000 Axis troops.

In July 1943, the Anglo–Americans invaded Sicily, thereby securing their Mediterranean communications and driving Italy out of the war. The following September they invaded Italy, now German-held, by way of Reggio and Taranto in the South and Salerno farther up the Italian boot. Naval guns secured the precarious Allied toehold at Salerno and at last convinced a doubting army of the value of naval gunfire support.

Brought to a halt by German resistance northwest of Naples, the Allies tried an end run. In January 1944 they landed a force at Anzio near Rome but in insufficient strength to attain its objective—cutting German communications to the principal front, farther south. The main Allied drive at length regained momentum, relieved the Anzio beachhead, and forced the Germans back into northern Italy.

While Allied air forces based on England were winning supremacy of the air over western Europe and isolating the beachhead in Normandy, the Allies were building up strength in the British Isles for the cross-Channel attack. The Americans also wanted to invade southern France to secure the port of Marseille and supplement the cross-Channel forces in their drive into Germany. Opposing the plan to invade southern France, Churchill argued fruitlessly for exploiting the Allied position in Italy with a drive through the Balkans.

The invasion of Normandy took place on 6 June 1944, and the landings in southern France followed on 15 August. The two drives pushed the Germans in France and the Low Countries back into Germany. In the spring of 1945, with the British, Americans, and French driving in from the west, and the Russians advancing from the east, Germany was beaten.

Chapter 26
The Japanese Offensive

The fall of France and of the Netherlands in the spring of 1940 left French Indochina and the Netherlands East Indies orphaned colonies, and so weakened Britain's position that she acceded to Japan's demands to close the Burma Road, China's last connection with the sea. The Imperial Japanese Navy, which had never favored the army's mainland adventure, now saw an opportunity for expansion into the East Indies to obtain oil, tin, rubber, and quinine. Invading Japanese army forces had already worked their way south along the China coast and early in 1939 had occupied Hainan. Shortly after the fall of France, the Vichy-controlled government of Indochina permitted Japanese occupation of the northern part of the country. In September 1940 Japan concluded an alliance with the Axis powers, the Tripartite Pact—an obvious warning to the United States not to interfere in either Europe or Asia.

The Japanese advance into Indochina was, in American eyes, the crucial issue. When in July 1941 the Japanese announced that the Vichy government had agreed to a "joint protectorate" of all Indochina, the United States, Britain, and the Dutch government-in-exile countered by freezing Japanese assets, thus shutting off the supply of oil from the United States, the Persian Gulf, and the East Indies.

This move precipitated the final crisis. Japan had to have oil or see her military machine grind to a halt. In October the Konoye government fell, and a military government headed by General Tojo took over. In November a special Japanese envoy arrived in the United States to assist Ambassador Nomura in negotiations looking toward a resumption of the flow of oil. The failure of these negotiations led directly to Pearl Harbor.

U. S. Preparedness

The greater portion of the U. S. Fleet had long been based on the West Coast, but in the spring of 1940 President Roosevelt, in the hope of deterring Japan from further aggression, directed that it be based at Pearl Harbor. Here it lay somewhat exposed while, after the outbreak of war in Europe,

much of the new naval construction went to the Atlantic. American plane production also was sent chiefly to the Atlantic theater.

On 1 February 1941, the growing Atlantic Patrol Force was renamed the Atlantic Fleet, under Admiral Ernest J. King, while the fleet at Pearl Harbor became the Pacific Fleet, with Admiral Husband E. Kimmel in command. The small American force in the Far East, commanded at that time by Admiral Thomas C. Hart, had for many years been designated the United States Asiatic Fleet. In the Pacific the United States faced the formidable Japanese navy practically alone. Yet at the time of the Pearl Harbor attack the U. S. Fleet was fairly evenly divided between the two oceans.

The British had undertaken to reinforce Singapore, but the crisis in the Far East coincided with a desperate situation in the Mediterranean, where they had suffered severe losses. After considerable hesitation, the Admiralty consented to send the battleship *Prince of Wales* to join the battle cruiser *Repulse* at Singapore in the hope that the presence there of two capital ships would have an additional deterrent effect upon the Japanese.

The Coming of War in the Pacific

In their negotiations, the United States had the advantage over Japan of being able to read the latter's radio communications, because American cryptanalysts had succeeded in constructing machines for deciphering the Japanese diplomatic code, which the Americans called Purple.[1] Hence Washington knew that the Japanese Foreign Office had set the latter part of November 1941 as a deadline for the conclusion of the talks, after which "things are automatically going to happen."

On 26 November the United States handed the Japanese a note demanding that Japan evacuate China. It was not an ultimatum or threat of war, just a simple refusal to export oil, or anything else, to Japan unless she abandoned her conquest of China. President Roosevelt and his advisers did not really

[1]The machines, the system for breaking the code, and the results were given the code name Magic. The machine was a form of the Enigma machine that originated in Germany.

expect the Japanese to do anything of the sort. Japan had expended too many lives and too much treasure and based too many hopes on continued expansion. Denied the oil they believed they needed, they could be expected to take it by force of arms. The nearest plentiful source was the Netherlands East Indies, which were almost defenseless. It was believed in Washington and London that if Japan seized the East Indies, she would also try to capture positions from which her shipping back to Japan could be threatened: Singapore, the Philippines, Hong Kong, and possibly Guam.

On 27 November U. S. patrol planes sighted off Formosa a Japanese expeditionary force capable of carrying several divisions of troops. Admiral Stark, U. S. Chief of Naval Operations, promptly sent a war warning to Admiral Hart at Manila and Admiral Kimmel at Pearl Harbor. Stark explained that "an aggressive move by Japan" was expected within the next few days against the Philippines, Malaya, or Borneo. On 6 December the Japanese expedition was sighted southbound off Indochina. All was proceeding as expected. The Japanese were obviously for the moment bypassing the Philippines.

The Japanese expeditionary force was indeed heading for the Malay Peninsula, for a drive on Singapore. But there was another Japanese force at sea, totally unsuspected by the U. S. government. This force, which included all six of Japan's large carriers, was heading eastward across the Pacific for an attack on Pearl Harbor. It never occurred to the American military planners that Japan would risk her carriers in such an audacious venture.[2]

Yet there was evidence of an impending attack. Responsible U. S. officials knew that the Japanese embassy in Washington had been ordered to destroy all codes except one, the Purple code, which was to be used to decipher a 14-part final message. When the final message began coming in on Saturday, 6 December, American cryptanalysts deciphered it faster than the Japanese could. It was directed to the U. S. secretary of state, breaking off diplomatic relations, the sort of message that in times past the Japanese had followed with a surprise attack on an opposing fleet.

In carrying out such an attack in 1941, the Japanese, to avoid being detected by aircraft, would have to approach their target through the hours of darkness and strike at dawn. The last paragraph of the 14-part message directed the Japanese ambassadors to deliver their message to the State Department at 1300, Sunday, 7 December. One o'clock in the afternoon in Washington would be 0730 at Pearl Harbor.

[2]In addition to the six large carriers, Japan had three light carriers and an escort carrier.

On Oahu the aircraft were lined up in neat rows, making them easy to guard against sabotage—and easy to attack from the air. The eight battleships in the area were all anchored in Battleship Row at Pearl Harbor, to permit weekend liberty. The two carriers then based on Pearl Harbor, the *Lexington* and the *Enterprise*, were out delivering planes respectively to Midway and Wake.

A little after dawn on 7 December, a destroyer stationed off Pearl Harbor reported and sank a midget submarine without alerting the U. S. high command. Radar operators on the opposite coast of Oahu reported planes approaching from the north. These aircraft were interpreted as a flight of B-17s due that morning from the United States.

Officials in Washington were not alone in regarding a carrier attack on Pearl Harbor as too risky. The Japanese Naval General Staff was of exactly the same opinion. The southern drive to obtain oil they accepted as a necessity, but when Admiral Isoroku Yamamoto, commander in chief of the Combined Fleet, proposed a simultaneous attack on Pearl Harbor, they were startled. Yamamoto insisted that the destruction of the U. S. Pacific Fleet was an essential prerequisite to any other Japanese military operations in the Pacific theater. Only by threatening to resign was he able to force acceptance of his plan. In mid-November 1941, on his orders, the Pearl Harbor Striking Force, comprising the carriers *Akagi*, *Kaga*, *Hiryu*, *Soryu*, *Shokaku*, and *Zuikaku*, escorted by the battleships *Hiei* and *Kirishima*, three cruisers, and nine destroyers, moved to a secret base in the Kurils to await further orders. Yamamoto permitted no word of his plan to be transmitted by radio, even in the securest codes, lest some foreign power intercept and decrypt it.

So sure was Yamamoto that war was imminent that on 25 November he ordered the Pearl Harbor Striking Force to sortie, eastbound, from the Kurils. The timing seemed propitious. German armies were threatening Moscow and Alexandria. Much of the U. S. Navy was in the Atlantic, patrolling and escorting British convoys. If the United States declared war on Japan, Germany and Italy were bound by the alliance to declare war on the United States. As Yamamoto expected, an Imperial conference on 1 December ratified Prime Minister Tojo's decision for war. Yamamoto thereupon radioed Vice Admiral Nagumo, commanding the Striking Force: "Climb Mt. Niitaka," meaning "Proceed with the attack."

In the early hours of 7 December, as the Striking Force in darkness was approaching Oahu from the north, Nagumo received the disappointing news that no carriers were at Pearl Harbor. The battleships now became the primary target; together with aircraft, which were to be destroyed mainly to prevent counterattack. At 0600, when the Striking Force was 200 miles north of Pearl Harbor, the six carriers turned into the wind and launched a first wave of 183 planes. After a suspenseful two-hour wait, from the flight leader came the signal: "Tora . . . tora . . . tora," a code word meaning "Surprise achieved." Already a second wave of 170 planes was en route to Pearl Harbor. By 1300 all but 29 of the Japanese aircraft were back on their carriers. The Nagumo force set a retirement course of north–northwest. There was no U. S. counterattack.

The Japanese carrier planes had killed or mortally wounded 2,400 Americans, mostly naval personnel, and injured 1,300 more. They had destroyed 230 planes. They had bombed or torpedoed 18 ships, including all the battleships. The *Arizona* was a total loss. The *Oklahoma* had capsized. The *California* and the *West Virginia* were sunk at their moorings. The *Maryland*, the *Pennsylvania*, the *Tennessee*, and the *Nevada* were all more or less heavily damaged.

In concentrating on ships and aircraft, the Japanese had spared the submarine base, the machine shops, and the 4,500,000 barrels of oil exposed in tank farms near the harbor. The omission proved a serious mistake. From the submarine base would come the first American craft to carry the war to the Japanese. The machine shops were essential for the repair of American vessels damaged then and later. Loss of the oil would have hindered American naval operations far more than the damage done the ships.

The temporary crippling of the U. S. Pacific battle line suddenly elevated America's six attack carriers, the *Saratoga*, *Lexington*, *Enterprise*, *Yorktown*, *Wasp*, and *Hornet*, to the status of capital ships and not, as many high-ranking officers had been insisting, mere reconnaissance vessels or auxiliaries to the battle line. The 34-knot carriers could not in any event have operated with the old 21-knot battleships. In the next few months the carriers, escorted by swift, new cruisers and destroyers, were to prove themselves so convincingly as the queens of battle that when the new, fast battleships began to arrive in the Pacific, they were promptly integrated into the carrier forces as additional antiaircraft escort vessels. The battleships' big, ship-destroying guns had just about lost their usefulness in daytime battles. Only planes could reach a fleet that did its fighting at a range of 200 miles.

While the loss of life was tragic, the damaging of the old battleships further proved a blessing in that it released many trained men to indoctrinate recruits for future expanding carrier and amphibious forces. In due course, all the damaged battleships except the *Arizona* and the *Oklahoma* would be repaired and put back into service, chiefly for shore bombardments.

From the Japanese point of view, the worst consequence of the Pearl Harbor attack was that it defeated their basic objective. The Japanese leaders never had any expectation of actually conquering the Americans. They hoped by sinking a good many American ships to induce a divided United States, as they had induced a divided Russia in 1905, to agree to negotiations that would leave them the fruits of their conquests. But by attacking Pearl Harbor and killing 2,400 Americans, Yamamoto instantly unified the people of the United States in a grim determination, from which they never wavered, to fight on to complete victory.

Command and Strategy

Secretary of the Navy Frank Knox flew to Pearl Harbor for a quick inspection and round of conferences. On his return to Washington, he advised President Roosevelt to relieve Admiral Kimmel of his Pacific Fleet command and replace him with Rear Admiral Chester W. Nimitz, chief of the Bureau of Navigation, an officer with an outstanding record of achievement. The president accepted the secretary's advice.

To Nimitz it appeared that he had inherited a disaster. When his seaplane landed in Pearl Harbor on Christmas morning, the water was covered with black oil from which protruded the tops of battered ships, among them his old flagship *Arizona*, a total wreck. To a crushed Kimmel, Nimitz said, "You have my sympathy. The same thing could happen to anybody."

From the American point of view, the news was nearly all bad. Hours before the raid on Pearl Harbor, the Japanese expeditionary force that had been sighted off Formosa and Indochina had begun landing troops at Singora and Kota Bharu on the Malay Peninsula, and these troops had headed for Singapore against light opposition. On 10 December the *Repulse* and the *Prince of Wales*, advancing to contest the landings, were both sunk by Japanese planes based on Indochina, the first ships to be sunk by aircraft while under way at sea.

By January 1942, Japanese forces had invaded Thailand, the Philippines, and Borneo. They had captured Hong Kong and Guam. Marines on Wake had thrown back the first Japanese invasion attempt, but a second, supported by planes from two of Nagumo's carriers, had succeeded. From the Marshalls, the Japanese had advanced into the

British Gilberts, arousing fears that they intended to proceed through the Ellices to Samoa and block communications between the United States and Australia.

Before assuming his new command, Admiral Nimitz did a good deal of inspecting and consulting. He concluded, to his regret, that it would be impractical for him to command the fleet at sea. In order to keep in touch with the complex U. S. communication network, he would have to remain at his Pearl Harbor headquarters. Among the facilities he visited was the supersecret, underground Combat Intelligence Unit, headed by Lieutenant Commander Joseph J. Rochefort. Served by a great arc of radio listening and direction-finder stations, three such units in the Pacific area and the Communication Security Section in Washington analyzed enemy radio traffic. The local unit's specialty was breaking and reading the Japanese navy's operational code, which the Americans called JN25. Nimitz listened politely to Rochefort's explanation of his unit's functions. The admiral was unimpressed. After all, the unit and its associated stations had provided no warning of the impending raid on Pearl Harbor.

On the last day of 1941, Nimitz assumed his responsibilities as Commander in Chief Pacific Fleet (CinCPac) and put on the four stars that came with the post. To everybody's surprise, Nimitz retained Admiral Kimmel's staff. Perhaps most surprised to be retained was Kimmel's intelligence officer, Lieutenant Commander Edwin T. Layton. It was Layton's duty to gather information from Rochefort's Combat Intelligence Unit and elsewhere, interpret it, and present an intelligence summary at the CinCPac morning conferences. As it turned out, Layton was the only officer besides Nimitz himself who remained attached to CinCPac headquarters throughout the war.

CinCPac's immediate assigned duties were to hold the line in the Pacific, guard U. S. communications with Hawaii, Midway, and Australia, and divert the Japanese from their drive into the East Indies. Nimitz judged that he could best attain these objectives and also restore morale by means of carrier raids against Japan's Pacific island bases. Most of his officers opposed the plan as too risky, and certainly it got off to a bad start when a Japanese submarine torpedoed the *Saratoga*, causing such damage that the carrier had to retire to the Bremerton Navy Yard for repairs. Vice Admiral William F. Halsey, bellicose and self-confident, scouted the defeatism at Pearl Harbor and permanently endeared himself to his new commander by offering to lead the raids himself.

Halsey commanded carrier forces in attacks against the Gilberts, the Marshalls, Wake, and Marcus; and carrier forces under Vice Admiral Wilson Brown raided bases in New Guinea. American newspapers billed these attacks as "great raids" and proclaimed Pearl Harbor fully avenged. The colorful, salty-tongued Halsey emerged a national hero, hailed by the press as "Bull" Halsey, nemesis of the Japanese. But Admiral Nimitz knew that the raids had accomplished little. The Japanese advance in the southwest had not been slowed. To his officers he exhibited his usual demeanor of serene confidence, but to Mrs. Nimitz he wrote: "I will be lucky to last six months. The public may demand action and results faster than I can produce."

On Luzon General MacArthur had abandoned Manila and with his American and Filipino troops retired to the more defensible Bataan Peninsula and nearby Corregidor Island. When it became obvious that no aid could be sent to the defenders and their situation was becoming hopeless, President Roosevelt ordered MacArthur out of the Philippines. A general since 1918, MacArthur had first worn four stars in the early 1930s when he was Army Chief of Staff. The president was unwilling to lose the services of the nation's most experienced army officer.

MacArthur, reluctant to abandon his besieged and starving troops, stalled until 11 March. He then proceeded by night with his family in a PT boat to Mindanao and from there by bomber to Australia. Here he announced to the press: "The President of the United States ordered me to break through the Japanese lines and proceed from Corregidor to Australia for the purpose, as I understand it, of organizing the offensive against Japan, a primary object of which is the relief of the Philippines. I came through and I shall return."

If General MacArthur supposed that he was to be the sole commander of all Allied forces in a prompt relief of the Philippines and a subsequent drive from there to Japan, he was mistaken. For one thing, he had as yet no army. For another, since he had no naval experience, the Joint Chiefs of Staff had seen to it that he would not command the Pacific Fleet. They had restricted his command to the Southwest Pacific Area, which included Australia, the Solomons, New Guinea, and the Philippines.

The North, Central, and South Pacific Areas were to be commanded by Admiral Nimitz as Commander in Chief Pacific Ocean Areas (CinCPOA). Within their respective areas, MacArthur and Nimitz would be supreme commanders over all army and naval forces, American and Allied. But if

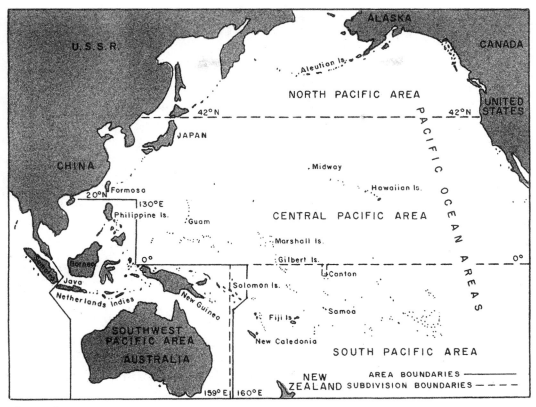

The Pacific Areas

strategy required the Pacific Fleet to enter MacArthur's Southwest Pacific Area, it would remain under Nimitz's command. Since Nimitz was still CinCPac, he was as CinCPOA his own commanding officer.

The Japanese Advance in the South

When Halsey's carriers raided the Gilberts and Marshalls on 1 February 1942, Nagumo's carrier force raced eastward to counterattack. Then, correctly assessing the Halsey raid as a mere hit-and-run affair, Nagumo turned south, supported the Japanese capture of the Australian base of Rabaul in New Britain, raided Darwin, Australia, and entered the Indian Ocean to support the Japanese advance into the East Indies. The Japanese on the Malay Peninsula forced their way south and on 15 February obliged Singapore to surrender.

Meanwhile, Japanese fleets were moving southward down the coasts of Borneo, establishing airfields as they advanced so that land-based planes could support their next moves—aimed at ultimately closing pincers on Java. The chief Allied defense in the East Indies was a small cruiser-destroyer fleet called the ABDA Combined Striking Force and composed of the American Asiatic Fleet, plus a few British, Dutch, and Australian warships. Commanded by Dutch Rear Admiral Karel Doorman, the ABDA Striking Force, everywhere outnumbered and without air cover, made a futile and suicidal effort to gain a little time. Its sole success occurred on the night of 23 February, when four American destroyers dashed up Makassar Strait and attacked a Japanese landing force at Balikpapan, sinking a patrol craft and four transports.

The end came for the ABDA Force in and shortly after the Battle of the Java Sea, which began in the afternoon of 27 February. The force, now reduced to 5 cruisers and 9 destroyers, while speeding to intercept a Japanese convoy bound for Java, encountered and engaged the convoy escort of 4 cruisers and 13 destroyers. There ensued a confused, circling battle that lasted till midnight, with contact lost and regained. When the 4 American destroyers had expended their torpedoes, Admiral Doorman released them, and they made their way eventually to Australia. The rest of the ABDA Force was destroyed—the Dutch cruisers

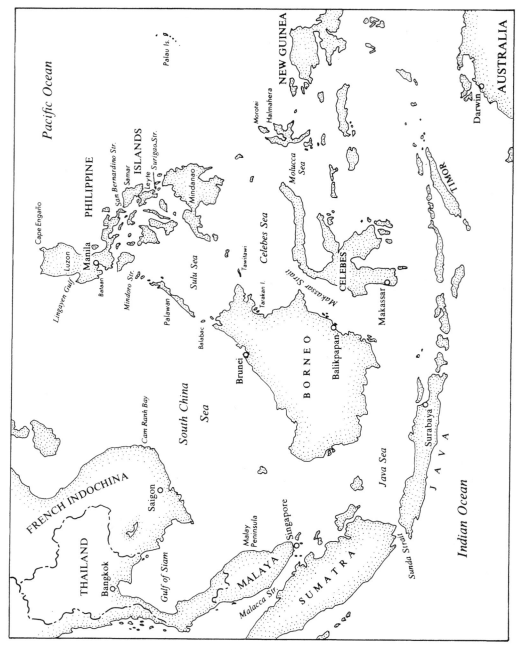

Philippines–East Indies Area

De Ruyter and *Java* and 3 destroyers during the battle; 3 cruisers, the USS *Houston*, HMAS *Perth*, and HMS *Exeter*, and 2 destroyers a little later, while trying to escape from the Java Sea.

Java surrendered to Japanese invasion forces on 9 March, and by the end of the month the Netherlands East Indies were in enemy hands. The Japanese had now attained all their objectives in the South except the complete subjugation of the Philippines, where the Filipino and American troops were to hold out a few weeks longer. The Japanese called their new conquests their Southern Resources Area. The rich oil wells of Borneo, Sumatra, and Java provided them with all the oil they needed, and these and nearby territories provided ample supplies of tin, rubber, quinine, and other strategic materials.

Around the Southern Resources Area, their home islands, and the communication line in between, the Japanese had now established a defense perimeter stretching from Rangoon in Burma, through the East Indies, Rabaul, and the Gilberts and Marshalls to Wake. Between Wake and the Kurils, however, existed a wide gap that gave the Japanese some concern.

For further security, to weaken and discourage nearby British forces, Nagumo's carrier force in early April raided the naval bases at Columbo and Trincomalee on Ceylon. Forewarned of the impending attack, Admiral Sir James Somerville, Commander British Eastern Fleet, had his ships at sea, but Nagumo's aircraft located part of the fleet and sank two destroyers, two cruisers, and the carrier *Hermes*. Somerville withdrew the rest of his fleet to Africa, and the Nagumo force returned triumphantly to Japan.

The Japanese had intended to remain behind their defense perimeter and sink whatever American ships penetrated it, until the Americans were willing to negotiate. But their southern victories were so far ahead of schedule, estimated at six months but completed in 90 days, that the Japanese, feeling invincible, decided to expand their conquests. The region of greatest danger in the southern area appeared to be Australia. Most Australian troops were with the British, defending Egypt, but the Americans might build up sufficient force in Australia to retake the adjacent Southern Resources Area and the Philippines.

There simply were not enough Japanese to conquer and occupy all of Australia, so the Japanese high command planned to isolate it by advancing via the Solomons and the New Hebrides to New Caledonia, Fiji, and Samoa. On these islands they would set up ship, submarine, and air bases to intercept communications between Australia and the United States. As a first step, the Naval General Staff planned to capture the small island of Tulagi in the eastern Solomons and Port Moresby on the south coast of the New Guinea bird tail. From these positions they believed they could secure control over the Coral Sea area.

Admiral Yamamoto agreed to the Tulagi–Port Moresby operations, but he wanted the New Caledonia–Fiji–Samoa phase postponed until he could assault Midway. As Admiral Nimitz had inferred, the American carrier raids had inflicted only moderate damage on the Japanese bases, but the raids had shown increasing boldness. Marcus Island, attacked on 4 March, was less than a thousand miles from Japan. Yamamoto could not rid himself of a nagging worry that those wild Americans might attempt a raid on Tokyo, thereby endangering the life of the sacred emperor, which it was the traditional first duty of the Japanese armed forces to safeguard. Capturing Midway would help to close the gap in Japan's defense perimeter. More important, it would draw out the carrier-centered U. S. Pacific Fleet for destruction.

Again the Naval General Staff opposed a Yamamoto project as too risky. Midway was within bomber range of Pearl Harbor. If captured, it could be kept supplied in the face of American opposition only at extreme hazard. The General Staff was still holding out when what Yamamoto dreaded took place. On 18 April American bombs fell on Tokyo and two other Japanese cities. In compliance with a plan hatched in Washington, the *Hornet*, with 16 long-range B-25s lashed to her flight deck, had approached Japan escorted by Halsey's *Enterprise* group. Unexpectedly encountering picket boats, Halsey ordered the bombers airborne at once, 150 miles short of the intended launching point. The volunteer pilots, led by Lieutenant Colonel James H. Doolittle, USA, all managed to get their heavy planes into the air. Because of the early launching, they did their bombing by day instead of as planned, by night. Not all made it to friendly China. One landed at Vladivostok. Others crash-landed or parachuted into Japanese-occupied territory and were captured. The Japanese executed three of the captives.

Following the bombing of Tokyo, Yamamoto, deeply humiliated, retired to his cabin and spent the day brooding. But the bombing swept away all opposition to his Midway project. The Tulagi–Port Moresby operation was scheduled for early May, the Midway attack for early June. It is a measure of Japanese overconfidence that in support of the May attacks the Imperial Navy allocated only three carriers, the light carrier *Shoho* and Nagumo's new large carriers, the *Shokaku* and the *Zuikaku*.

The Battle of the Coral Sea, 4–8 May 1942

Japanese overconfidence extended even to radio communications. Admiral Yamamoto, who had allowed no word to be broadcast concerning the plan to attack Pearl Harbor, was now, contrary to sound military practice, sending orders by radio concerning future operations. Many of his directives, moreover, were in code JN25, which the Americans were decrypting. Hence, by mid-April, Admiral Nimitz knew that the Japanese were planning an attack on eastern New Guinea and that something was brewing for the Pacific Ocean. Before the end of the month, he knew the Japanese would land on Tulagi in the first week of May, they would follow this landing with an assault on Port Moresby, and a few weeks later they would move against some point in the Pacific.

Nimitz had never been enthusiastic about the Tokyo raid. He saw it as a mere morale builder with no real military significance. Yet, besides the bombers and their pilots, it risked loss of two carriers, their crews, and the Navy's most experienced carrier force commander. Now, with action imminent in the South Pacific, Halsey and his carriers were off to the west on what amounted to a wild-goose chase.

Nimitz assembled what forces he could. He sent Rear Admiral Aubrey W. Fitch with his *Lexington* group to join Rear Admiral Frank Jack Fletcher's *Yorktown* group in the South. To strengthen their screens, he borrowed from MacArthur's Southwest Pacific Area a support force of three cruisers and a handful of destroyers under Rear Admiral Sir John Crace, RN. These moves brought together little enough force to try to stop a Japanese fleet that presumably now had available six large carriers and five light carriers. Halsey, with the *Enterprise* and *Hornet* groups, arrived back at Pearl Harbor on 25 April. He was allowed five days' upkeep for his force and then ordered to proceed to the Coral Sea. Unless the Japanese were seriously behind schedule, he was unlikely to complete the 3,500-mile voyage in time to participate in the inevitable battle.

The *Lexington* and *Yorktown* groups, which had been ordered to join under Fletcher's command, made contact in the southeast Coral Sea on 1 May. Two days later Fletcher received a report of the Japanese landing at Tulagi. Leaving the *Lexington* group to complete fueling, he headed north with the *Yorktown* group, and during the 4th sent his

planes flying over the mountains of Guadalcanal for a series of attacks on the Tulagi area. His relatively inexperienced aviators succeeded in sinking only a few minor Japanese naval craft. Toward the end of the day, Fletcher headed back south, refueled on the 5th, and on the 6th formally merged his groups into a single carrier force, Task Force 17.

By this time Vice Admiral Takeo Takagi's Striking Force, built around the *Shokaku* and the *Zuikaku*, had come swinging around the eastern end of the Solomons and entered the Coral Sea. To westward, the Japanese Port Moresby Invasion Force, supported by the *Shoho*, was coming down from Rabaul, intending to round the tip of New Guinea via Jomard Passage, a break in the Louisiade Archipelago. That evening Fletcher's and Takagi's forces, under cloudy skies, came within 70 miles of each other without making contact. For the Americans, 6 May was in some respects the low point of the war, for word came through that Major General Jonathan Wainwright, whom MacArthur left in command of his beleaguered, half-starved army in Bataan, had been obliged to surrender the Philippines to the enemy.

On the morning of the 7th, Fletcher sent Crace's support force forward to block Jomard Passage in the event his carriers should be put out of action by enemy aircraft. Fletcher's planes, however, found the *Shoho* a little before noon and sent her down with 13 bombs and 7 torpedo hits. Thus deprived of close air support, the Port Moresby Invasion Force reversed course and headed back toward Rabaul. Meanwhile, Takagi's carrier planes, whose business it was to protect the invasion force by eliminating any American carriers in the area, were off to the south attacking the oiler *Neosho* and her accompanying destroyer *Sims*, which had been reported by Japanese scout planes as a carrier and a cruiser. The Japanese sank the *Sims* and left the *Neosho* a drifting derelict.

The climactic action came in the morning of 8 May when the Japanese and American carrier forces located each other at last and attacked almost simultaneously. This was the first battle in history between carrier forces and the first in which the opposing fleets never came within sight of each other. The Japanese and American air strikes were of almost exactly the same strength, but the Japanese had the advantage of greater experience. They also had intermittent cloud cover, while the American force was exposed under cloudless skies.

When the attacking American planes found the Japanese striking force, the *Zuikaku* ducked into a rain squall, but dive bombers pounced upon the *Shokaku* and put her out of action with three

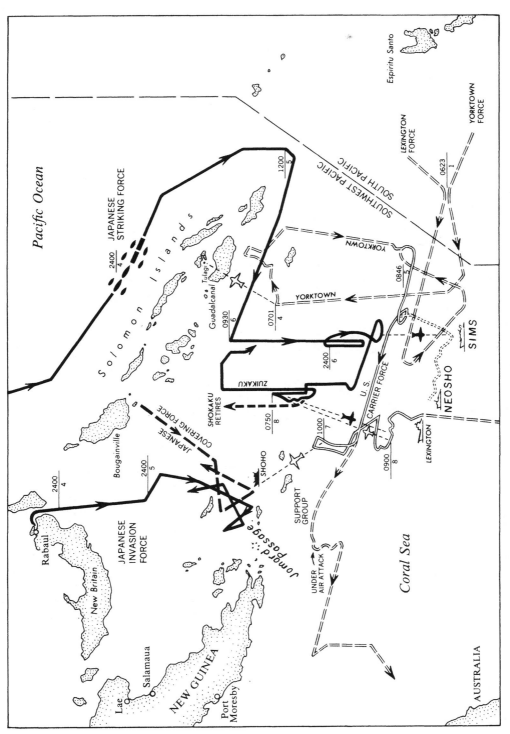

Battle of the Coral Sea, 4–8 May 1942

bombs. Her aircraft were obliged to seek refuge on board her sister carrier. At almost the same time, Japanese bombers achieved a series of near misses on the *Yorktown*, and one struck her with a bomb that penetrated three decks and killed 37 men but failed to impair her flight operations. The *Lexington*, hit by two torpedoes, was able to land her returning planes, but ruptured fuel lines released into her hold dangerous gasoline vapor that at length exploded, setting off such uncontrollable fires that she had to be abandoned. A little before sunset, one of her own destroyers sent her down with four torpedoes.

In terms of enemy tonnage destroyed, Takagi was clearly the tactical victor. But the Americans were the strategic victors in that they had, for the first time, turned back a Japanese advance. Moreover, they had so damaged the *Shokaku* that she would not be available for service for several weeks. And both Japanese carriers had been so nearly stripped of planes by American aircraft and antiaircraft fire that the *Zuikaku* also would be unavailable. Thus, in the forthcoming operation against Midway, the Nagumo force would be deprived of a third of its striking power.

Halsey, with the *Enterprise–Hornet* force, Task Force 16, had raced for the Coral Sea but arrived too late for the battle. Nimitz ordered him and Fletcher to return to Pearl Harbor on the double with their forces, but directed Halsey not to start back until he was sure Japanese search planes from Tulagi had sighted his carriers. If the Japanese believed that all available U. S. carriers were in the South, they might be less wary in their forthcoming Pacific Ocean operation.

The Battle of Midway, 3–6 June 1942

Six months after heading eastward for the Pearl Harbor attack, the Nagumo force was again eastbound across the Pacific. This time it set out from Japan's Inland Sea, departing on 27 May, Japanese Navy Day, the anniversary of Togo's victory at Tsushima—a good omen. The mission was to be another carrier raid, against Midway, with the primary objective of luring out the U. S. carrier fleet for destruction—in order to complete the unfinished business of six months before.

Despite the absence of Nagumo's two newest carriers, there was little of the trepidation that had affected his sailors and aviators in the earlier sortie. Since then they had participated in a long string of victories, and they were not discouraged by the recent Coral Sea battle, because they believed they had sunk both American carriers. Moreover, this

time the Nagumo force was not alone. It was backed by the entire Japanese Combined Fleet. Besides transports, oilers, and other auxiliaries, Japan had at sea 11 battleships, 8 carriers, 23 cruisers, and 65 destroyers. To fend off this vast armada, Admiral Nimitz had available, besides a few land-based planes, only 3 carriers, 8 cruisers, and 14 destroyers.[3]

Such an immense disparity of force should have assured the Japanese a victory that would give them command of the Pacific. And so it doubtless would have, had Admiral Yamamoto kept his ships together. Instead, hoping to achieve a Jutland-type entrapment, he had split up his fleet to the point of absurdity. Ahead of the rest and to northward was the Second Carrier Striking Force, including one new large carrier[4] and one light carrier. These were to raid Dutch Harbor in the Aleutians on 3 June in order to confuse the Americans and perhaps draw some of their forces northward. The Second Carrier Striking Force was followed by two invasion forces with troops to occupy the far-western Aleutian Islands of Attu and Kiska.

At the center of Yamamoto's deployment, the four-carrier Nagumo force, now called the First Carrier Striking Force, would raid Midway on 4 June. Coming up from the southwest, a Midway Occupation Force, supported by a light carrier, 2 battleships, 10 cruisers, and many destroyers, was to put 5,000 troops ashore on Midway, after the atoll had been thoroughly softened up by Nagumo's carrier planes and by its own gunnery vessels.

Several hundred miles behind the Nagumo force was the so-called Main Body, a powerful battleship force, with a single light carrier to provide air cover. These battleships were the centerpiece of Yamamoto's victory plan. Nagumo's air raid on Midway would presumably draw out the U. S. carriers. Stationed west of Pearl Harbor, a cordon of Japanese submarines would both attack the carrier force and report its approach. When the U. S. carriers and their escorting vessels came within range, Nagumo's carriers would attack them, and the battleship force would move in to finish them off.

With the Japanese battleship force was Admiral Yamamoto himself, in the 64,000-ton superbat-

---

[3]He had six old, slow battleships at San Francisco, but in a carrier battle they would have been worse than useless. The *Saratoga*, fully repaired, was at San Diego but could not assemble escorts in time for the battle. The *Wasp* was en route to the Pacific after delivering planes to Malta.

[4]The 24,000-ton *Junyo*, commissioned after the Battle of the Coral Sea.

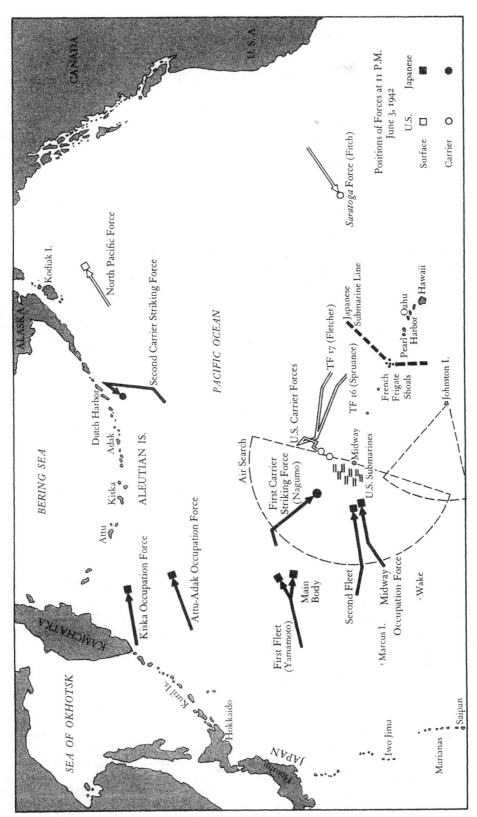

Battle of Midway—the Approach

tleship *Yamato*. He was thus out of touch with his headquarters communication and intelligence center, and, until he made contact with the enemy, he would have to maintain radio silence and thus would be unable to communicate with his scattered forces. Apparently he could not resist participating at sea in what he anticipated would be a decisive battle. It was a mistake Admiral Nimitz never made.

The defect in Yamamoto's battle plan was that its success depended on surprise, and the Americans were not going to be surprised. Under pressure of time, the Japanese commander in chief, as noted above, had communicated his intentions to his widely dispersed fleet by radio, using code JN25. The Pearl Harbor Combat Intelligence Unit and associated stations intercepted and decrypted the messages and passed them on to CinCPac headquarters, so that Nimitz eventually knew more about Yamamoto's plans than some of the Japanese ship captains knew. The information was so nearly complete, in fact, that some of Nimitz's officers suggested that the messages might be fakes, deliberately planted to mislead the Americans.

For want of anything better, Nimitz decided to base his own plans on the assumption that the messages were genuine. On the eve of the Battle of the Coral Sea, he had flown out to Midway with some of his staff and given the two islands of the atoll, Sand and Eastern, a thorough inspection. Thereafter he sent out to Midway everything the commanding officer said he needed to defend the atoll from a major amphibious assault.

To Nimitz it was clear that the Achilles heel of the whole Yamamoto deployment was the Nagumo force, lacking in sufficient antiaircraft defense of its own, and too far away from other elements of the fleet to receive quick assistance. To attack Nagumo's four carriers, Nimitz had only three carriers afloat, but he had also an unsinkable carrier in Midway itself. His best naval planes and best-trained naval aviators had been assigned to the carriers. The army flyers under his command were not trained to fight ships, but he sent to Midway what aircraft he could and hoped for the best.

On the morning of 26 May, Halsey's Task Force 16, the *Enterprise–Hornet* force, arrived at Pearl Harbor. Halsey was ill, suffering from a severe dermatitis brought on by the nervous strain of pioneering carrier warfare for six straight months. To his disgust the doctors ordered him to the hospital. For the second time in 30 days, he had barely missed an opportunity to fulfill his cherished desire to get a crack at the Japanese carriers. Overall tactical command of the carrier forces now fell to

Frank Jack Fletcher. On Halsey's recommendation, Nimitz appointed Halsey's cruiser division commander, Rear Admiral Raymond A. Spruance, to command Task Force 16.

Admiral Fletcher's Task Force 17 arrived at Oahu in the afternoon of the 27th, the *Yorktown* trailing an oil slick ten miles long. In the emergency there was no question of giving her a complete repair job. Pearl Harbor workmen merely braced her bomb-damaged compartments with timbers and patched her hull, perforated by near misses.

Task Force 16, with Spruance in command, departed Pearl Harbor on 28 May and headed for the Midway area. Task Force 17 followed the next day. The Japanese submarines that were to report their approach reached their assigned stations west of Pearl Harbor after both forces had already passed. Task Forces 16 and 17 rendezvoused at sea on 2 June and, under Fletcher's tactical command, took station northeast of Midway to be on the flank of the Nagumo force, which, according to Commander Layton's estimate, would be approaching the atoll from the northwest through an area of perpetual fog where the trade wind met the cold arctic current.

On 3 June, right on schedule, carrier planes bombed Dutch Harbor, and American scout planes reported a large enemy force, 700 miles away, approaching Midway from the southwest. Midway planes attacked the oncoming force that day and the following night without slowing it down or inflicting any serious damage. Fletcher, correctly judging the ships to the southwest to be the Occupation Force, advanced with his own ships to within 200 miles of Midway, ready to attack the Nagumo force, due the next day.

At dawn on 4 June, while under cloud cover northwest of Midway, the Nagumo force launched 108 planes against the atoll, retaining an equal number in reserve. American Catalina scout planes patrolling the edge of the overcast reported both the carrier force and its Midway-bound planes. At Pearl Harbor, Admiral Nimitz remarked to Commander Layton, "Well, you were only five miles, five degrees, and five minutes off."

Fletcher ordered Spruance to advance with Task Force 16 and attack the enemy carriers, while the *Yorktown* recovered her search planes. On Midway all aircraft took off, torpedo planes and bombers to strike the Nagumo force, fighters to fend off the approaching air raid. The American fighting planes proved no match for the agile Japanese Zero fighters, which quickly shot most of them down. The Japanese bombers set fire to han-

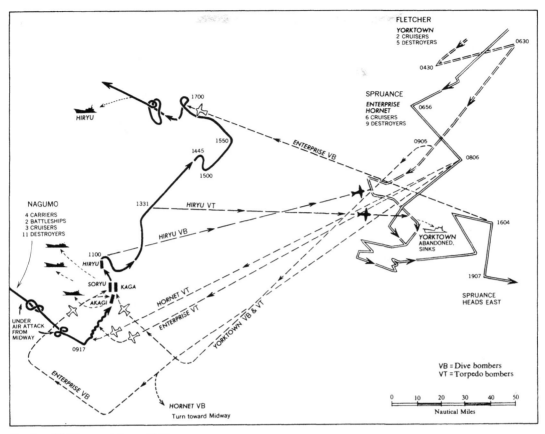

FLETCHER
YORKTOWN
2 CRUISERS
5 DESTROYERS
0630
0430

SPRUANCE
ENTERPRISE
HORNET
6 CRUISERS
9 DESTROYERS
0656
0905
0806

1700
HIRYU
1550
1445
1500

ENTERPRISE VB

NAGUMO
4 CARRIERS
2 BATTLESHIPS
3 CRUISERS
11 DESTROYERS
1331
HIRYU VT
HIRYU VB

1604
YORKTOWN
ABANDONED,
SINKS
1907
SPRUANCE
HEADS EAST

1100
HIRYU
SORYU KAGA
AKAGI
HORNET VT
ENTERPRISE VT
YORKTOWN VB & VT

UNDER
AIR ATTACK
FROM
MIDWAY
0917

VB = Dive bombers
VT = Torpedo bombers

ENTERPRISE VB

HORNET VB
Turn toward Midway

0 10 20 30 40 50
Nautical Miles

Battle of Midway, 4 June 1942

gars and smashed buildings on Midway, but the flight leader, noting as he turned away that the runways were still undamaged, radioed Nagumo that a second attack on Midway was essential.

The Midway-based torpedo planes and bombers, flying northwest, not only were without fighter cover; they had also failed to coordinate. They attacked the wildly maneuvering Japanese carriers in five separate waves. Many were shot down by Zeros and antiaircraft fire, and not a single one of their bombs or torpedoes made a hit.

In the midst of this series of attacks, Admiral Nagumo was shocked to get from one of his search planes a report of ships, "apparently enemy," off to the northeast. On receiving the recommendation for a second attack from his strike leader over Midway, he had ordered his reserve planes to change armament from torpedoes to instant-contact bombs, suitable for shore targets. He now ordered them to change from instant-contact to armor-piercing bombs and torpedoes, for use against ships.

A little before 0830, as the last of the Midway planes were completing scoreless attacks, Nagumo's scout finally identified one of the enemy ships as a carrier. This horrifying news came at the worst possible moment for Nagumo. His first attack wave was arriving from the strike on Midway. His reserve Zeros also were in the air where they had been defending their ships from the Midway-based American planes. Most of the planes in the air were dangerously low in fuel.

Nagumo's aggressive second-in-command urged him to attack the enemy carrier at once with his reserve bombers and torpedo bombers. If he did so, the attacking planes would be without fighter escort and possibly suffer the same fate as the unescorted American aircraft from Midway. Moreover, since it would take some time to complete the launching, many of the planes now in the air would run out of gas and splash, with heavy loss of planes and aviators. On the other hand, to land, refuel, rearm, and launch the planes would give him a powerful, well-protected striking force, but the operation would take about two hours and thus possibly permit the Americans to get the jump on him, a serious disadvantage in carrier warfare.

After consulting with his air operations officer, Nagumo made a fateful decision. He landed his bombers and most of his Zeros. When his aircraft were on board, he changed course from southeast to northeast to close with the Americans. He then reported his intention to Admiral Yamamoto, with the battleships 450 miles to the rear. On the new course, the Nagumo force was attacked successively by torpedo squadrons from each of the American carriers. None of the attackers scored, and most were shot down. Of Torpedo 8, the *Hornet's* squadron, not a single plane survived.

American prospects for victory seemed poor. In eight successive attacks on the enemy force, U. S. aircraft had achieved only a little strafing damage. At 1000 Nagumo's carriers had nearly completed arming and refueling their Midway strike force. The three American carriers had launched, but they were losing their torpedo planes, and their dive-bombers were all flying in wrong directions. The Task Force 16 bomber squadrons, aiming at the estimated position of the Nagumo force, found nothing there because Nagumo had changed course. The *Hornet* bombers turned southeast, toward Midway, and flew completely out of the battle. The *Enterprise* bombers turned northwest but found nothing.

Then American chances changed dramatically for the better. The *Enterprise* flight leader spied a straggling Japanese destroyer and adopted her course. The *Yorktown* bombers, launched later than the others, turned to follow their own torpedo planes. The *Enterprise* and *Yorktown* bomber squadrons, approaching from different directions, arrived over the Nagumo force simultaneously, unobserved by the Japanese and unaware of each other's presence. No amount of planning could have attained such precision.

The Japanese failed to observe the dive-bombers arriving overhead because their attention, and their Zero fighters, had been drawn down to the surface by the attacks of the low-flying U. S. torpedo planes, the last of which had just been snuffed out. Nagumo had finally ordered his counterattack, and his carriers were turning into the wind to launch. Armed and fueled planes were spotted on their flight decks, and other planes were on their hangar decks arming and fueling. Discarded instant-contact bombs were still lying on the hangar decks awaiting return to the magazines. The Nagumo force was thus in the ultimate state of vulnerability.

In five minutes the Japanese strike would be on

its way. Before it could be launched, however, the *Yorktown* and *Enterprise* bombers dived from 15,000 feet and, in seconds, changed the whole course of the war. They released bombs that hit the *Soryu*, the *Kaga*, and Nagumo's flagship, the *Akagi*, setting off lethal fires and explosions in all three.

The *Hiryu*, unscathed, launched bombers and torpedo planes that followed the retiring American bombers and attacked the *Yorktown*, so disabling her that her captain ordered abandon ship. In shifting from the *Yorktown* to a cruiser, Admiral Fletcher turned the tactical command over to Admiral Spruance. Late in the afternoon bombers from the *Enterprise* found the *Hiryu* surrounded by surface escorts. With four hits near the bridge, the bombers left her afire and exploding.

Admiral Yamamoto, too far away to take any direct part in the battle, ordered Vice Admiral Kondo, with the Occupation Force, to send four heavy cruisers forward to bombard Midway. With the rest of his warships he was to speed ahead, add Nagumo's surface ships to his command, and with the resulting force of 4 battleships, 9 cruisers, and 19 destroyers seek out the American forces for a night surface battle. Admiral Spruance, anticipating such a move, withdrew eastward till midnight. As hours passed, with Kondo failing to make contact with the Americans, Yamamoto realized that he was becoming less likely to be the victor of a night battle than the victim of a dawn air attack. At 0015, 5 June, he called off the pursuit.

"How can we apologize to His Majesty for this defeat?" wailed members of the Combined Fleet staff.

"Leave that to me," snapped Yamamoto. "I am the one who must apologize to His Majesty."

At 0255, Yamamoto, bowing to the inevitable, issued the order "The Midway operation is canceled," and directed all Combined Fleet forces to join the Main Body in a westerly retirement.

Kondo's four-cruiser bombardment group, then nearing Midway, reversed course. Heading west, the cruisers spied a surfaced American submarine. In maneuvering to avoid a supposed torpedo, the *Mogami* and the *Mikuma* collided and lost speed. The two undamaged cruisers abandoned them and sped ahead.

The *Hiryu*, after burning all night, sank at 0900. By that time the *Soryu*, the *Kaga*, and the *Akagi* had also gone down. The rest of the Combined Fleet was on a westerly course, heading for a rendezvous northwest of Midway and a general retirement.

Spruance, with Task Forces 16 and 17, less the *Yorktown*, spent 5 June vainly trying to overtake the retreating Japanese ships. In midafternoon he launched 58 dive bombers northwestward, but the strike fell short. The bombers found only a straggling destroyer, which they unsuccessfully attacked. On the 6th, Spruance's search planes discovered to the southwest the two crippled heavy cruisers trailing oil. In a series of attacks, his bombers sank the *Mikuma* and so battered the *Mogami* that she was out of action for a year. At sunset, Spruance, his destroyers low in fuel, turned back eastward—again in the nick of time, for Yamamoto was once more assembling his forces for a night battle.

The Japanese got in the last blows after all. On 6 June, one of their submarines found the *Yorktown* northeast of Midway under tow. The submarine fired a spread of torpedoes that sank a destroyer alongside and so damaged the carrier that she went down on the morning of the 7th. That day the Japanese landed troops on the American islands of Attu and Kiska.

The victory at Midway was by no means cheaply won. It cost the Americans a carrier and a destroyer, 147 planes, 307 lives, extensive damages to Midway installations, and moderate damage to those at Dutch Harbor. The Japanese lost four carriers and a heavy cruiser, 322 aircraft, and 3,500 lives, including many first-line aviators that they could never replace. Although the Japanese losses were not so severe as U. S. wartime estimates indicated, they were enough to reverse the course of the war. The Japanese advance was ended; the Allied advance was about to begin.

Chapter 27
Beginning the Allied Counteroffensive

Imperial Headquarters was profoundly shocked by the news of Midway. On orders from Prime Minister Tojo, the facts were confined to as few people as possible. The wounded were isolated. Officers who knew too much were assigned to distant commands. Documents concerning the battle were classified top secret or destroyed. Newspapers reported one Japanese and two U. S. carriers sunk. They played down the naval battle, however, and played up the occupation of the barren little islands of Attu and Kiska as a major victory.

Imperial Headquarters canceled plans for the capture of Samoa, Fiji, and New Caledonia. But something had to be done about Port Moresby. Bombers from there could attack the Japanese base at Rabaul. Nowhere else were the opposing armed forces thus in contact. Port Moresby would have to be taken. The navy had failed to transport Japanese assault forces there by sea. The army would now attack overland, even though the troops would have to cross the 13,000-foot-high Owen Stanley Range. To fend off any Allied interference with the move, the Japanese began to construct an airfield on Guadalcanal to supplement the nearby seaplane base at Tulagi.

In 1942, the United States lacked the military power to implement its Orange Plan for a drive across the Central Pacific to the rescue of the conquered Philippines. The U. S. armed forces could only react to Japanese moves. When the Japanese seized Rabaul, Admiral King saw it as a jumping-off base for invading Australia or advancing via the Solomons and New Hebrides to cut United States–Australia communications. Port Moresby blocked the way to Australia. To block Japanese eastward moves and eventually serve as a jumping-off place for an Allied westward advance, Admiral King obtained from the Joint Chiefs consent to establish a base at Efate in the New Hebrides. He next set up a separate command in the South Pacific, subordinate to Admiral Nimitz's Pacific Ocean Areas, and appointed Vice Admiral Robert L. Ghormley Commander South Pacific Force and Area (ComSoPac). Ghormley established headquarters at Auckland, New Zealand, and promptly began work on a

second New Hebrides base at Espiritu Santo. (See map, p. 304.)

The American victory at Midway prompted the Allies to shift to at least a limited offensive, and the obvious target was Rabaul. Hardly had the Midway battle ended when General MacArthur made a breathtaking proposal. Give him operational control of the amphibiously trained 1st Marine Division and two carrier forces, and with these and the three army divisions already under his command he would immediately invade New Britain, recapture Rabaul, and force the Japanese back on their base at Truk, 700 miles to the north.

Admiral King was shocked at the suggestion of taking scarce carriers and the Navy's only amphibious troops into the poorly charted, reef-plagued Solomon Sea in the teeth of enemy airfields. Rabaul would have to be approached step-by-step via the Solomons so that airfields could be established to provide fighter air cover for the next step. The successive landings, he asserted, would have to be carried out by marines, trained in amphibious warfare. And since the marines, and nearly all the supporting vessels, would have to come from the Pacific Ocean Areas, the Solomons operation should be under Admiral Nimitz's command, with Admiral Ghormley as his deputy. The Army's contribution would be to provide garrisons for the islands captured by the Navy and the marines.

When MacArthur received word of King's views, he fired back a protest, pointing out that since the Solomons were entirely within his Southwest Pacific Area, the operation should be under his command. General Marshall agreed, but Admiral King argued that if it made sense for the Army to have top command in Europe, where it supplied most of the armed forces, it made equally good sense for the Navy to have top command in the Solomons, where most of the fighting would be done by the Navy and the Navy's marines. Moreover, said King, he was prepared to carry out the campaign with Navy and marines "even if no support of Army forces in the Southwest Pacific is made available." MacArthur radioed back to Marshall that evidently the Navy was trying to reduce

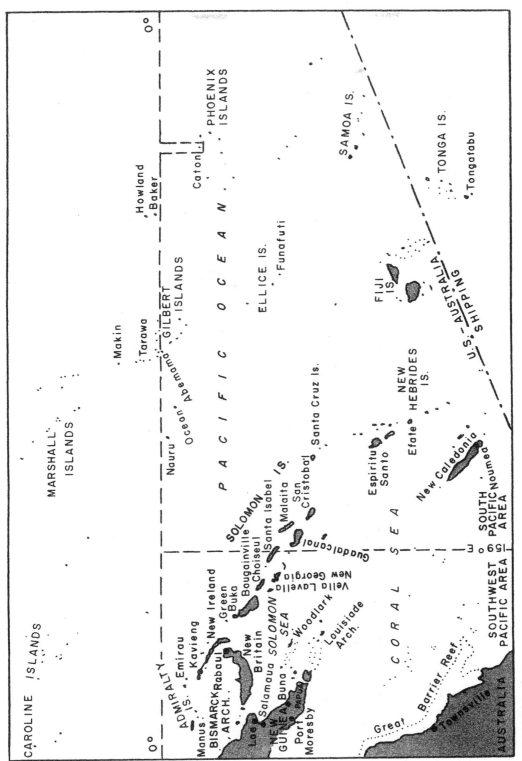

Scene of Early Operations in the South and Southwest Pacific Areas

the Army in the Pacific to a subsidiary role that would consist "largely of placing its forces at the disposal of and under the command of navy or marine officers."

Marshall waited a couple of days to let the disputants, including himself, cool off. Then he suggested to King that they get together and work out a course agreeable to all. The meeting produced a Solomonic compromise, set forth in a joint directive of 2 July 1942. The opening operations, seizure and occupation of the Santa Cruz Islands, Tulagi, and adjacent positions, would be under the strategic control of Admiral Nimitz. To facilitate command problems in the first step, the boundary between the South Pacific and the Southwest Pacific areas was shifted westward to 159° East Longitude, just west of Guadalcanal. As soon as a suitable base had been secured in the Tulagi area, the strategic command would pass to General MacArthur, who would coordinate a move up the Solomons with a second thrust—across the Papuan Peninsula of New Guinea to Salamaua and Lae. The two Allied advances would then converge on Rabaul. Target date for the initial invasions, called Operation Watchtower, was set for 1 August.

Admirals King and Nimitz, with members of their staffs, met 4–5 July at San Francisco to hammer out details. King had brought along Rear Admiral Richmond Kelly Turner, lately director of the Navy Department's War Plans Division. King had picked Turner to command the amphibious forces for the forthcoming operation, in which Frank Jack Fletcher, now a vice admiral, was to be Commander Expeditionary Force.

Before the meeting ended, word came from Pearl Harbor that cryptanalysis had revealed Japanese preparations to land a Pioneer Force on Guadalcanal, evidence that the enemy was about to construct an airfield there.[1] This news gave the Watchtower Operation more urgency. Whoever first operated planes from the airfield would have an enormous, perhaps decisive, advantage. Plans to occupy the Santa Cruz Islands were canceled, and Guadalcanal was substituted.

The time allowed was distressingly brief for assembling forces and preparing for so complex an operation as an amphibious assault. The means were meager. The forthcoming invasion of North Africa had first preference for everything. Japan had seven carriers; the United States had four assigned to the Pacific, and one of these would have

---

[1]To conceal the source of this information, a cover story was later released stating that a scout plane had observed the airfield under construction.

to mount guard in Hawaiian waters. Guadalcanal was believed to be heavily garrisoned with elite Japanese troops. Ghormley had available only the 1st Marine Division. MacArthur's three army divisions could not be touched. Little wonder the perplexed participants in Operation Watchtower began calling it "Operation Shoestring."

Admiral Ghormley and General MacArthur, meeting in Melbourne to coordinate plans, concluded that the proposed operation was little better than foolhardy. MacArthur protested that it would be courting disaster to undertake the invasions until greater Allied strength could be built up in the area.

King sent a sarcastic note to Marshall: "Three weeks ago MacArthur stated that, if he could be furnished amphibious forces and two carriers, he could push right through to Rabaul. . . . He now feels that he not only cannot undertake this extended operation but not even the Tulagi operation." The Joint Chiefs acceded only to Ghormley's request that the target date be deferred to 7 August, though all concerned were aware that every day's delay increased the possibility that the Japanese would have their Guadalcanal airstrip operational, and then the invasion would have to be postponed indefinitely.

The Guadalcanal Campaign

Somehow 82 ships, including three Australian cruisers, were found for Admiral Fletcher's Guadalcanal–Tulagi Expeditionary Force. Steaming from points as widely separated as Wellington, Sydney, Noumea, and Pearl Harbor, they met at sea on 26 July near the Fijis. After a chaotic landing rehearsal, the force steamed westward. In the Coral Sea, it shaped course due north and headed for Guadalcanal through rain squalls that grounded all aircraft, including Japanese search planes.

Under a clearing sky in the dark early hours of 7 August, the *Saratoga*, *Enterprise*, and *Wasp* carrier groups moved into position south of Guadalcanal, while Admiral Kelly Turner's amphibious force slipped up the west coast and entered the body of water later known as Ironbottom Sound— because of the many ships sunk there in the next few months. After a dawn bombardment, Major General Archer Vandegrift's 1st Marine Division began going ashore on Guadalcanal against slight opposition. Contrary to Allied expectations, the Japanese on the island were nearly all Pioneer Force construction workers, most of whom had fled westward during the bombardment. In the afternoon of the 8th, the marines occupied the airstrip,

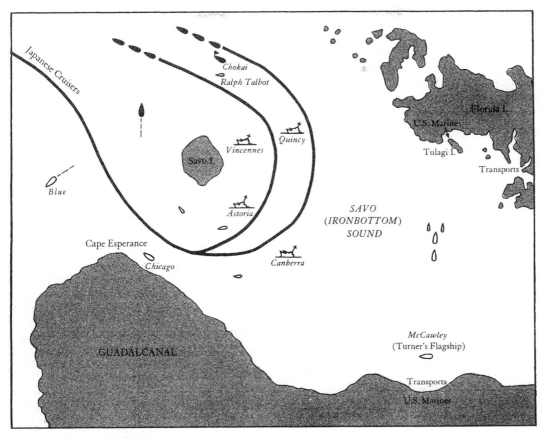

Battle of Savo Island, 9 August 1942

still unfinished. On Tulagi and two adjacent islets on the north side of the sound, the marines met stout resistance but secured these positions also on the 8th.

In quick reaction to the invasions, Japanese aircraft began taking off from the Rabaul area for a series of raids on the shipping in Ironbotton Sound. Thanks to intense antiaircraft fire and a strong combat air patrol from the three American carriers south of Guadalcanal, these raids inflicted only moderate damage, but they did succeed in utterly confusing an already critical logistic problem. In the evening of the 8th some of the cargo vessels were no more than 25 percent unloaded.

The enemy was about to counterattack by sea. Coming down the Slot, the passage between the major Solomons, was a force of five heavy and two light cruisers and a destroyer, commanded by Vice Admiral Gunichi Mikawa. His objective was Ironbottom Sound; his mission, to break up the invasion by a night attack on the transports. His ships had been sighted that morning by an Australian pilot, who identified two of them as seaplane ten-

ders. Kelly Turner, who tended to make up his mind what the enemy was going to do, and act accordingly, concluded that the enemy force was en route to set up a seaplane base in the Central Solomons. He made no special preparations for night action. At sunset three separate Allied cruiser–destroyer forces, in second condition of readiness, began patrolling the entrances to Iron-bottom Sound.

An hour after midnight, the Japanese force slipped unobserved past the stern of the destroyer *Blue*, all of whose lookouts were staring into the darkness ahead. Mikawa, puzzled, detached his own destroyer to keep the *Blue* under observation. As planes from the Japanese cruisers eerily illuminated the area with parachute flares, Mikawa's ships entered the sound and began the action known as the Battle of Savo Island. Firing torpedoes and shells, they dashed past the South Patrol Force. Before the Allied gunners could bring guns to bear or surprised torpedomen could insert firing primers, the Japanese torpedoes had blown a chunk out of the heavy cruiser *Chicago*'s bow and crushed in the side of the Australian heavy cruiser *Canberra*, which lost way and began to blaze under a hail of enemy shells.

The attacking column, still unscathed, split into two divisions and wheeled north, three cruisers passing across the van of the North Patrol Force and four steaming across the rear, searchlights open, guns blazing. In minutes all three cruisers of the North Force, the American heavies *Vincennes*, *Astoria*, and *Quincy*, were afire and listing. The *Quincy* managed to get a couple of shells into the Japanese flagship *Chokai*, smashing the staff chartroom and killing 34 men. Hits made by the other American cruisers did only trifling damage. At 0220, Mikawa ordered, "All ships withdraw," and his attack force headed back up the Slot.

Mikawa, mindful that he had not completed his mission, considered reentering the sound to blast the transports, but he rejected the idea, because he was sure that Fletcher's carriers were already pursuing him and that they would attack him at first light. The farther he could get to the northwest, presumably drawing the American carriers after him, the better the chances would be for a successful counterattack on them by aircraft out of Rabaul. But there was neither attack nor counterattack. Fletcher, citing loss of fighter planes and a need to refuel, had received from Ghormley at Noumea permission to withdraw his carrier groups from the Guadalcanal area. By dawn the carriers were far to the southeast. The Japanese attack force retired up the Slot unmolested.

Inside the sound, the *Quincy* and the *Vincennes* had gone down shortly after the battle. The *Canberra*, helpless, unable to depart, was sunk at 0800 the next morning by American destroyers. The *Astoria* lingered until noon before she plunged. The battle of Savo Island had cost the Allies four desperately needed heavy cruisers and a thousand lives. It was the severest defeat ever suffered by the U. S. Navy in battle. To the Japanese it amply justified their navy's emphasis on training for night combat, an area the Americans had neglected.

Turner, deprived of air cover by Fletcher's departure, felt he had no choice but to withdraw his amphibious force also. Just before dark on the 9th, the last of his ships cleared Ironbottom Sound. The 16,000 marines left behind, subsisting on canned rations eked out by captured rice, completed the building of the airstrip, which they named Henderson Field, to honor Major Lofton Henderson, who had been killed while commanding the marine bombing squadron in the Battle of Midway. On 20 August an American escort carrier approached Guadalcanal from the southeast and flew in 12 dive bombers and 19 fighters. To guard the sea communications to Guadalcanal, Fletcher's carrier force had begun patrolling the waters between Espiritu Santo and the Solomons.

The Japanese were in somewhat of a quandary. On 20 July they had landed 3,000 troops at Buna on the north coast of Papua, with 13,000 more in the follow-up, and the troops had begun their transmontane march on Port Moresby. This operation was the main Japanese concern, but something had to be done about the Americans on Guadalcanal and Tulagi. On the night of 20 August, six destroyers from Truk landed 900 Japanese soldiers west of Henderson Field. These troops attacked prematurely, and the U. S. marines wiped them out almost to a man, with a loss of only 25 of their own.

A larger Japanese reinforcement was on the way. When Admiral Yamamoto learned that American planes were now operating out of the Guadalcanal airfield and that the American carriers were at sea, he sent Vice Admiral Nobutake Kondo down from Truk with a carrier force to support the new Japanese landing and, if possible, destroy Fletcher's carriers. This movement brought about the Battle of the Eastern Solomons, 24 August 1942. Fletcher, having just sent his *Wasp* group south for refueling, was caught under strength. He nevertheless acted promptly and effectively. His planes sank the light carrier *Ryujo* and sent the seaplane carrier *Chitose* flaming out of action. Bombers from the *Shokaku* and the *Zuikaku* counterattacked and severely damaged the *Enterprise*. Kondo, having lost 90 planes, was obliged to retire, and the reinforcement force soon followed. A replacement for the damaged *Enterprise* was already on the way. Nimitz had decided that the *Hornet* was needed more in the Guadalcanal area than off Hawaii and had sent her south.

Following the battle, the Japanese brought in reinforcements only at night. Destroyers and small transports, hovering up the Slot till sunset, darted into Ironbottom Sound so regularly that the disgruntled marines began calling them the Tokyo Express. Allied vessels shunned the sound at night as conscientiously as the enemy shunned it by day.

The Japanese knew that to retake Guadalcanal they first had to recapture the airfield, but they underestimated the task. Supposing that no more than 2,000 Americans were on the island, they sent much the greater portion of their available troops into the Port Moresby operation. Meanwhile, to discourage American reinforcement of Guadalcanal, Japanese submarines patrolled its approaches. These in late August and early September sank the *Wasp* and a destroyer and severely damaged the new battleship *North Carolina* and Fletcher's flagship *Saratoga*.

Because Fletcher was slightly wounded, Admiral Nimitz seized the opportunity to grant him stateside leave for a much-needed rest. Fletcher never returned. Admiral King, reviewing his hard-luck record—three of his carriers sunk, three badly damaged—decided henceforth to keep him ashore. For Fletcher's replacement, he made the obvious choice of Halsey, now fully recovered and anxious for a command at sea.

By mid-September the Tokyo Express had raised the number of Japanese troops on Guadalcanal to 6,000. This force, grossly underestimating the number of Americans present, made a drive for Henderson Field. In an action known as the Battle of Bloody Ridge, the marines threw them back. In doing so they lost 40 men. Japanese losses were 1,200. This crushing defeat shocked Tokyo into realizing that the Americans were on Guadalcanal in considerable force, and that Japan was likely to lose it for good unless stronger measures were taken to recapture it.

On New Guinea, meanwhile, the Japanese troops based on Buna had penetrated a pass in the mountains, descended the southern slope, and, despite savage resistance by MacArthur's Australians, arrived almost within sight of Port Moresby. Imperial Headquarters now ordered their troops to withdraw back across the mountains to Buna and assume a strong defensive posture until Guadalcanal had been recaptured.

Conforming to the new emphasis, the Tokyo Express stepped up operations until it was transporting as many as 900 troops a night down the Slot. A fresh Japanese division moved into the Shortland Islands for transfer to Guadalcanal. In proportion as the enemy strength on Guadalcanal grew, spirits at SoPac headquarters at Noumea sank. Nimitz, becoming aware of this defeatism, flew down to the South Pacific to investigate. He discovered a curious contrast. On Guadalcanal he found the marines gaunt from malaria, fatigue, and sleeplessness, but Vandegrift and his officers were convinced they could hold. At Noumea, a thousand miles to the south, he found Ghormley haggard and exuding gloom. Why, asked Nimitz, was SoPac not using its naval forces to derail the night-running Tokyo Express? If the SoPac staff had doubts that the 1st Marine Division could hold Guadalcanal, why hadn't they sent troops from the army division on New Caledonia to reinforce them? The Japanese, with their hands full on New Guinea and Guadalcanal, were not likely to strike elsewhere.

Thus prodded, Ghormley embarked 3,000 soldiers of his New Caledonia garrison for Guadalcanal, and Rear Admiral Norman Scott with a cruiser–destroyer force sped ahead to run interference. Warned by aviators that an Express was coming down the Slot, Scott proceeded to an intercepting position near Savo Island. In the dark night of 11–12 October, the two forces engaged northwest of Guadalcanal in a confused action called the Battle of Cape Esperance. Scott's force sank a cruiser and a destroyer and lost a destroyer but mistakenly reported sinking "about 15" enemy vessels, thereby providing a terrific, if temporary, lift to the flagging spirits at Noumea.

The force that Scott turned back was in fact en route to give Henderson Field the first of a series of bombardments to pave the way for a large convoy bringing Japanese reinforcements down from the Shortland Islands. The American convoy from Noumea got to Guadalcanal first, discharged its 3,000 troops, and got safely away. That night two Japanese battleships entered Ironbottom Sound and systematically pounded Henderson Field for an hour and a half with hundreds of high-capacity shells, churning up the landing strip and destroying half the aircraft on the island. Two air raids the next day and a bombardment by heavy cruisers the following night added to the destruction. Only a few planes were left to oppose a convoy of six transports, which in the early hours of 15 October brought in some 4,500 Japanese soldiers. The new arrivals raised the enemy force on Guadalcanal to 22,000, the majority fresh troops, to oppose 23,000 Americans, mostly battle-weary, malaria-ridden marines. As the Imperial Army Forces confidently prepared for what they regarded as the inevitable recapture of the airdrome, Admiral Kondo brought down from Truk the most powerful battleship-carrier fleet assembled since the Battle of Midway.[2]

On returning to Pearl Harbor, Nimitz, with King's consent, began to strip the Central Pacific of

[2]The following table gives approximate troop strengths on Guadalcanal on important dates:

	American	Japanese
7 Aug.	10,000	2,200
20 Aug.	10,000	3,600
12 Sept.	11,000	6,000
23 Oct.	23,000	22,000
12 Nov.	29,000	30,000
9 Dec.	40,000	25,000
1 Feb.	50,000	12,000

On 7 August there were also 780 Japanese on Tulagi and nearby islets. Some 6,000 U. S. marines landed on these islands, and a garrison of around 5,000 Americans was maintained in this area throughout the campaign.

troops and planes for the defense of Guadalcanal. Halsey, who was at Pearl Harbor, took off by flying boat for the South Pacific to assume his carrier command.

As the situation in the SoPac area reached a crisis, Nimitz, after consulting with his staff and obtaining King's concurrence, sent radio messages to Ghormley and Halsey. The former he thanked for his "loyal and devoted efforts toward the accomplishment of a most difficult task" and informed him that he was relieved of his command. Halsey's Coronado had hardly landed in Noumea harbor at 1400, 18 October, when he was handed the second message, which he read with astonishment and chagrin: "Immediately upon your arrival at Noumea, you will relieve Vice Admiral Robert L. Ghormley of the duties of Commander South Pacific Area and South Pacific Force." Word that the aggressive and confident Halsey had taken command spread rapidly throughout the South Pacific Area and was received with cheers and jubilation.

On 20 October, the heavily reinforced Japanese on Guadalcanal began their all-out drive on Henderson Field. To the north, Kondo's fleet—4 carriers, 5 battleships, 14 cruisers, and 44 destroyers—cruised back and forth, prepared to fly planes into the airfield as soon as their soldiers had captured it.

Halsey's assuming of the area command left the American carrier forces under the immediate control of Rear Admiral Thomas C. Kinkaid, who had commanded a cruiser division in the battles of the Coral Sea and Midway. Halsey, informed by his scout planes of the presence of the enemy fleet, daringly, not to say rashly, sent Kinkaid north with the *Hornet* and *Enterprise* forces to engage it. He thereby set the stage for the Battle of the Santa Cruz Islands. Just before dawn on the 26th, learning that the opposing fleets were within striking range of each other, he flashed to Kinkaid the electrifying order: "Attack—Repeat—Attack!" But the Japanese launched first and got the jump on the Americans before the American fighters could gain altitude. In a series of attacks, Kondo's planes sank the *Hornet* and heavily damaged the recently repaired *Enterprise*—leaving not a single operational U. S. carrier in the Pacific. The Americans retaliated by bombing two enemy carriers and a cruiser and shooting down nearly a hundred enemy planes, but in the face of overwhelming odds were obliged to retire. It was the American soldiers and marines who saved Guadalcanal. They repelled attack after attack, retaining their grip on Henderson Field while inflicting ten casualties for each loss of their own.

The Japanese, convinced that they had barely missed recapturing the island, further accelerated the operations of their night-running Tokyo Express. Soon their men on Guadalcanal outnumbered the Americans. But the High Command, still dissatisfied with the rate of reinforcement, decided to send down the rest of the division in the Shortlands in a single convoy. At sunset on 12 November, 11 transports and a dozen destroyers under Rear Admiral Raizo Tanaka, started down the Slot with 11,000 troops on board. To clear his way, down from Truk came a force including the battleships *Hiei* and *Kirishima* to bombard Henderson Field.

That same day, Admiral Turner had delivered the second echelon of 6,000 army and marine reinforcements to Guadalcanal. Warned by scout planes of the approaching bombardment force, Turner at dusk withdrew his convoy to the southeast, detaching a force of five cruisers and eight destroyers under Rear Admiral Daniel J. Callaghan to break up the impending bombardment.

Under a moonless but starry sky, the Japanese and American forces entered Ironbottom Sound from opposite directions. Callaghan, belatedly warned by radar that he was on a collision course with the enemy, turned too late, and Japanese and American ships intermingled. There followed a half-hour melee, which for confusion and fury is scarcely paralleled in naval history. Both formations broke, and the engagement became a series of individual ship duels with each side from time to time firing on its own vessels. The American ships were saved from annihilation only by the fact that the Japanese 14-inch guns were provided with bombardment rather than armor-piercing shells. Admirals Callaghan and Scott were both killed. Two Japanese and four American destroyers were sunk, and the flame-gutted cruiser *Atlanta* had to be scuttled. The cruiser *Juneau* while retiring from the battle was sunk by a submarine. The disabled *Hiei* was sent down by planes from Henderson Field. Tanaka's convoy returned temporarily to base.

The following night, with Tanaka again in the Slot, Mikawa's cruisers bombarded the airfield. Coming up from the south now was the *Enterprise*, with workmen still on board repairing her October damages. With the coming of daybreak, 14 November, bombers from the carrier and from Guadalcanal first attacked Mikawa's force, sinking one cruiser and damaging three others. Then, joined by

B-17s from Espiritu Santo, they struck repeatedly at Tanaka's lightly protected transports. By evening six of them had been sunk, and one was limping back to base. Tanaka with his four remaining transports pushed doggedly on toward Guadalcanal. To run interference for him, Kondo himself with the battleship *Kirishima*, four cruisers, and nine destroyers was heading down from the north.

At the same time, up from the south came the new battleships *Washington* and *South Dakota* and four destroyers, detached from the *Enterprise* force. These vessels, commanded by Rear Admiral Willis A. Lee in the *Washington*, reached Guadalcanal first, and late in the evening made a clockwise circuit of Savo Island. Though Lee had detected nothing, Kondo had seen Lee. He hid behind Savo, and as Lee, now to the south, approached on a westerly course, he darted out and with shells and torpedoes sank two American destroyers and disabled the *South Dakota* and the other two destroyers. Lee, left alone with the *Washington*, took advantage of radar control to more than even the score. With his 5- and 16-inch guns he concentrated on the *Kirishima*, which was soon helpless and turning in circles. Kondo ordered his battleship and a disabled destroyer scuttled and with the rest of his forces headed for Truk. His departure ended the three days and nights of fighting known as the Naval Battle of Guadalcanal.

Meanwhile, Tenacious Tanaka, who had steamed unflinchingly through the embattled waters, continued on to Guadalcanal. Here he beached his four transports and disembarked his surviving troops. After dawn the Americans discovered the transports and demolished them with bombs and shellfire.

Though there were fewer Americans than Japanese on Guadalcanal, the latter, lacking adequate artillery and air support, made no renewed effort to capture Henderson Field. Evidently the crisis on Guadalcanal had passed. Admiral Nimitz, the Joint Chiefs, and President Roosevelt reviewed the situation with great relief. General Vandegrift, previously critical of what he called the Navy's excessive caution, now had nothing but praise for the admirals and their forces. "To them," he radioed, "the men of Guadalcanal lift their battered helmets in deepest admiration."

Yamamoto risked no more capital ships in the Solomons campaign. Imperial Headquarters sent no more reinforcements to Guadalcanal. To keep the Japanese garrison on the island precariously alive, Tanaka contrived a streamlined Tokyo Express of fast destroyers that dropped floating drums of food and medical supplies offshore and then darted back up the Slot before daylight. To the Americans it appeared that the struggle for Guadalcanal was about over. Then on the last night of November there occurred the disastrous Battle of Tassafaronga, as if to remind the U. S. Navy that it still had a good deal to learn about night tactics.

A little before midnight on the 30th, Rear Admiral Carleton Wright, a newcomer to the area, led a cruiser–destroyer force into Ironbottom Sound intent on derailing Tanaka's Express, which had been reported approaching from the north by a roundabout route. Making contact by radar, Wright ordered his van destroyers to launch torpedoes, all of which missed. His cruisers concentrated fire on one of Tanaka's eight destroyers. The gunfire set the destroyer aflame, but it also brought disaster to the Americans. Since they had no flashless powder, their gun flashes provided the Japanese torpedo directors with a point of reference. Tanaka's well-drilled team fired a score of their deadly Long Lance torpedoes at the extended American track. Because the Long Lances were well aimed and ran true, and Wright's cruisers maintained course and speed, the torpedoes inevitably found their targets. One or more struck all but one of Wright's five cruisers. The *Northampton* sank, and the *Minneapolis*, *Pensacola*, and *New Orleans* were severely damaged. Tanaka's seven surviving destroyers sped away up the Slot.

The Japanese were maintaining their garrison on Guadalcanal merely to occupy the Americans while they constructed a pair of airfields in the Central Solomons. Keeping the garrison alive, however, became increasingly difficult as Tanaka's destroyers came under intensifying attack by planes at dawn and dusk and by PT boats at night. After PT boats on 11 December wounded Tanaka and sank his flagship, Tokyo at last concluded that Guadalcanal would have to be abandoned. Getting the Japanese soldiers safely off the island posed a serious problem. Solving it took weeks of planning and preparation, and movements of the Combined Fleet to divert American attention. When the Americans on Guadalcanal, reinforced to 50,000 soldiers and marines, closed the pincers on the Japanese positions in early February 1943, they found that their prey had slipped through their fingers. A score of destroyers in three high-speed night runs down the Slot had carried away the 12,000 half-starved survivors of the enemy garrison. Thus on a note of mingled frustration and triumph for both sides, the Guadalcanal campaign came to an end.

Of about 60,000 American soldiers and marines who fought on Guadalcanal, 1,600 were killed and 4,200 wounded. Of more than 36,000 Japanese on the island, about 14,000 were killed or missing, 9,000 died of disease, and 1,000 were captured. These figures do not include the heavy Allied and Japanese losses at sea or in the air while supporting the Guadalcanal operation.

During the months that the Americans were tightening their grip on Guadalcanal, Allied forces a thousand miles to the west were with equal difficulty and equal success wresting from Japan the peninsula of Papua. While Australian troops pursued the retreating enemy via the direct route over the Owen Stanley Mountains, American and Australian forces crossed the mountains by a roundabout trail or flew to airfields on the north coast in areas not held by the enemy. All the Allied forces then converged on the Buna area and in mid-November 1942 began a coordinated offensive to capture it from the Japanese defenders.

Though MacArthur at length committed nearly 33,000 troops to dislodge some 16,000 enemy from Papua, the Japanese held their bit of coastline till late January 1943. Then at last their defenses collapsed, as much from starvation and disease as from outside pressure. In recapturing Papua, 3,300 Allied troops lost their lives and 5,500 were wounded.

South Pacific and Southwest Pacific forces had each captured a base that the Japanese had intended to use as a springboard for further offensive operations. For the Allies two roads to Rabaul were now open. At the Casablanca Conference, Admiral King, strongly backed by General Marshall, won the consent of the Combined Chiefs to take advantage of this situation by allocating more military resources to the Pacific theater.

The Reconquest of Attu and Kiska

More useless islands than bleak, fog-shrouded Attu and Kiska would be hard to find. Yet the Japanese, having publicized their capture as a military triumph, felt compelled to hold on to them. The Americans, for their part, felt uneasy with U. S. territory, however worthless, in enemy hands, and the Combined Chiefs of Staff wanted the Aleutians cleared for use as a route for staging aircraft into Siberia—if and when the Soviet Union joined the war against Japan.

In January 1943, Rear Admiral Kinkaid, transferred from the South Pacific, took over the Aleutian command with the understanding that he was to plan for reconquest of the lost islands as soon as

ships and men for the task became available. Meanwhile, U. S. naval forces and U. S. and Canadian aircraft, by intermittent bombing and bombardment, made the harsh life of the occupying troops harsher. Fighter-escorted bombers from newly established airfields on Adak and Amchitka succeeded in cutting off Kiska from all surface contact with Japan.

In order to isolate the more westerly Attu, Rear Admiral Charles H. McMorris in mid-February began patrolling Attu's supply line with a cruiser–destroyer group. After McMorris's force had sunk an ammunition ship en route to the island from Paramushiro, Japanese Vice Admiral Boshiro Hosogaya began escorting Attu-bound convoys with his entire North Area Force. Contact between McMorris's and Hosogaya's forces resulted in the Battle of the Komandorski Islands, last of the classic daytime surface actions.

An hour before sunrise on 26 March, McMorris in the light cruiser *Richmond*, with the heavy cruiser *Salt Lake City* and four destroyers, made radar contact with the Japanese convoy and promptly gave chase, little guessing that he was in pursuit of a force considerably stronger than his own. As Hosogaya made out the approaching American vessels in the first light of dawn, he ordered his freighters to retire to the northwest, and hastened to put his four cruisers and four destroyers between the Americans and their Aleutian bases. The pursuer now became the pursued—in a three hour westerly chase. At length the *Salt Lake City* took a hit that flooded an engine room. Her engineers, attempting to correct a resulting list, inadvertently let seawater into a fuel line, thereby extinguishing her burners and bringing her temporarily to a standstill. In this desperate situation, McMorris retained one destroyer to make smoke around the stalled cruiser and sent the others charging toward the enemy for a death-defying torpedo attack. The attacking destroyers, steaming boldly into the blazing guns of the Japanese cruisers, were amazed to observe that the enemy was breaking off action. Hosogaya, unable to see the motionless *Salt Lake City* through the smoke, felt that he had stretched his luck far enough. His fuel was running low, and American bombers could be expected any minute from Adak and Amchitka. So he took his entire convoy back to Paramushiro, where his displeased seniors relieved him of his command. Thereafter only submarines attempted to get supplies through to Attu and Kiska.

Admiral Kinkaid kept pressing for an early assault on Kiska. Informed that he could not for several months have all the ships and men he

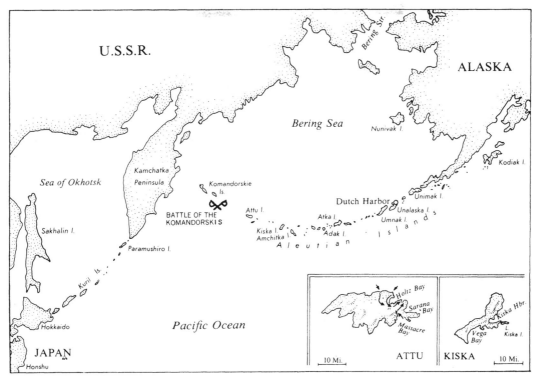

Aleutian Theater of Operations

needed, he requested and received permission to bypass Kiska and seize the smaller, more lightly held Attu.

On 11 May 1943, an assault force including three old battleships, six cruisers, and an escort carrier landed 3,000 troops of the 7th U. S. Infantry Division on the north and south coasts of Attu. The segments of the divided landing force were to meet in the interior and then drive the Japanese garrison of 2,600 into the eastern tip of the island, where fleet guns and carrier planes could pound and strafe them into submission. But the Japanese holed up in the mountains and by use of concealed artillery prevented the juncture of the American forces until 11,000 soldiers had been put ashore. When the Japanese had used up most of their ammunition, a thousand of them came silently down from the hills before dawn on 29 May. At first light they hurled themselves through a gap in the American line, overran two command posts, and broke into a medical station, where they butchered the sick and wounded. At last brought to bay, some 500 of the attackers committed suicide with hand grenades. Surviving Japanese made further attacks that day and the next morning until all the defending garrison except 28 captives had killed themselves or

been killed. American losses by that time amounted to about 600 killed and 1,200 wounded.

In preparation for the assault on Kiska, scheduled for mid-August 1943, army aircraft dropped 1,200 tons of bombs on the island, and battleships and cruisers bombarded the main camp and harbor. On the 15th, transports carrying 29,000 U. S. and 5,300 Canadian troops approached Kiska supported by nearly a hundred men-of-war. After a further spectacular bombardment, the landing force went ashore—only to find the island unoccupied. Three weeks earlier, Japanese cruisers and destroyers had slipped in under a fog and evacuated the entire garrison.

His assignment completed, Kinkaid, promoted to vice admiral, went south to assume command of the U. S. Seventh Fleet under General MacArthur. He was relieved by Vice Admiral Fletcher.

The Central Solomons Campaign

Following the Allied conquests of Guadalcanal and Buna, Halsey's South Pacific and MacArthur's Southwest Pacific forces prepared to launch a coordinated dual drive on Rabaul. Halsey's drive would be spearheaded and supported by Air Command

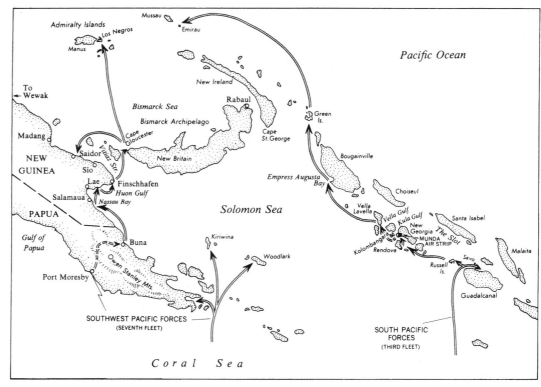

Rabaul Neutralized and Bypassed

Solomons (AirSols) operating from Guadalcanal; MacArthur's, by the Fifth Air Force, operating from three airfields in eastern Papua. Both drives, advancing in a series of steps, would capture or establish airfields as they went and at last bring Rabaul under intensive air attack.

Around 1 April 1943, Admiral Yamamoto came to Rabaul to direct an all-out air offensive, which he counted on to snarl the Allied plans. By stripping his Combined Fleet carriers of 200 planes and adding them to his 100 land-based aircraft, he built up a powerful air armada and sent it in first against the shipping in Ironbottom Sound and then against targets in Papua. In preparation for further aerial offensives, Yamamoto set out with his staff on a tour of the northern Solomons to inspect bases. Rabaul, in an extraordinary lapse of judgment, broadcast the admiral's hour-by-hour itinerary, using code JN25, which the American cryptanalysts were now reading with comparative ease. Counting on Yamamoto's known passion for punctuality, a squadron of long-range P-38s took off from Guadalcanal early on 18 April and shot him down precisely on schedule as his plane was coming in for a landing at Ballale Island, just south of Bougainville. Yamamoto's successor, Admiral Mineichi Koga, con-

tinued the aerial offensive but with steadily diminishing success as he expended his best flyers.

This reckless, and ultimately fateful, expenditure of Japanese planes and aviators did nothing to delay the advance of U. S. Third Fleet[3] into the Central Solomons. At the end of June, the Third Fleet assault ships and craft, comprising Admiral Kelly Turner's Third Amphibious Force, began landing troops on New Georgia, supported by AirSols fighters. The objective on New Georgia was an enemy airfield at Munda Point. Some 34,000 American troops, in six weeks of vicious jungle warfare, finally wrested the field from 8,000 well-entrenched Japanese defenders.

Halsey now inaugurated his bypassing strategy. Instead of invading the next island in the Solomon chain, heavily reinforced Kolombangara, he ordered an assault on lightly held Vella Lavella.

[3]New designation of Halsey's South Pacific naval force. A recent reorganization gave U. S. fleets in the Atlantic and Mediterranean even numbers; those in the Pacific, odd numbers. The fleets were divisible into task forces, task groups, and task units as operations required. Thus TU 31.2.3 was a component of TG 31.2, which was a component of TF 31, which was a component of the Third Fleet.

Here, under cover of fighters operating from the Munda airfield, the Third Amphibious Force, now commanded by Rear Admiral Theodore S. Wilkinson,[4] in mid-August landed 6,000 troops. Profiting from the hard lesson of the Munda campaign, these troops made no attempt to wrest the enemy airfield from its defenders. Instead, they established a defense perimeter, within which Seabees began hacking a new airstrip out of the jungle. In September, New Zealanders relieved the Americans on Vella Lavella and soon pocketed about 600 Japanese in the northwest corner of the island. Because Imperial General Headquarters refused to commit any more troops to the Solomons, Rabaul ordered all Japanese on Vella Lavella and Kolombangara evacuated to Bougainville bases. The evacuations were carried out in late September in the dark of the moon by destroyers, submarines, and barges.

The American invasions of the Central Solomons set again in operation the night-running Tokyo Express, at first to reinforce and supply the Japanese island bases and later to assist in evacuating them. More night battles inevitably followed. The Americans were now better organized and better equipped than in their desperate Guadalcanal nights, and they had had time to study their mistakes. The old scratch teams were replaced by semipermanent task forces. Operating regularly together, commanders and crews developed the skills and confidence that eventually enabled them to expel the Japanese night fighters and their Long Lances from the Solomons. Dependable radar had now become generally available on board Allied vessels, and fleet personnel had learned to use it effectively. The scopes were housed in a special compartment known as Radar Plot, where contacts were plotted and analyzed. Gradually other information, from radio and lookouts, began to be correlated here, and Radar Plot became the Combat Information Center (CIC). Possession of the CIC gave the Allies an enormous advantage over the Japanese. While the Japanese in the Solomons had no radar, they were almost as well served by a radar-detecting device that enabled them to receive and plot the impulses from Allied radar.

During the American drive on Munda airfield, Rear Admiral Walden L. Ainsworth's cruiser–destroyer force twice met an enemy of inferior force in the same waters a little after midnight and fought

the almost identical battles of Kula Gulf (6 July) and Kolombangara (13 July) with similar tactics and similar results. In the first, Ainsworth's force sank a destroyer, and the enemy sank the U. S. cruiser *Helena*. In the second, the Allies sank the cruiser *Jintsu*, while the Japanese sank a destroyer and put the New Zealand cruiser *Leander* out of action. The Allies at this stage showed considerable advance in tactical doctrine over the preceding year but still fell short in battle efficiency and intelligence of enemy capabilities.

On the night of 6–7 August 1943, American naval forces won their first unqualified victory in a nighttime surface action. It was achieved by a task group of six destroyers that were sent to attack an oncoming four-destroyer Tokyo Express. The original commander of the American task group was Commander Arleigh Burke, who had been campaigning to end the practice of keeping destroyers tied uselessly at the ends of cruiser columns during battles. Burke had worked out a plan for just such a mission as had been assigned. "The plan," as he afterward explained it, "was based on hitting the enemy with one sudden surprise after another. This was accomplished by putting two destroyer divisions in parallel columns. One division would slip in close, under cover of darkness, launch torpedoes and duck back out. When the torpedoes hit, and the enemy started shooting at the retiring first division, the second half of the team would suddenly open up from another direction. When the rattled enemy turned toward this new and unexpected attack, the first division would slam back in again."

On the eve of battle, Burke was detached to assume a higher command. Luckily, his successor was Commander Frederick Moosbrugger, who adopted Burke's plan and carried it out with such skill and sense of timing that in the Battle of Vella Gulf he achieved a little classic of naval warfare. Moosbrugger even added a refinement to the Burke plan. When the torpedoes of his first division were speeding toward the unsuspecting enemy column, he contrived to have "the second half of the team" on a T-capping course across its van. Just as the torpedoes struck their targets, both American divisions opened up with gunfire. Under this neatly timed triple blow, three of the enemy destroyers exploded, creating such a pyrotechnical display that PT boatmen 30 miles away in Kula Gulf thought a volcano had erupted on Kolombangara. The fourth enemy destroyer escaped only because the torpedoes that slid under her hull failed to detonate. None of the American vessels was damaged.

[4]Admiral Turner had been ordered to Pearl Harbor to command the Fifth Amphibious Force under Admiral Nimitz.

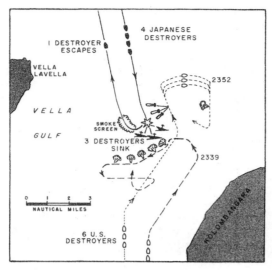

Battle of Vella Gulf, 6–7 August 1943

The progress in night tactics suffered a setback in the destroyer Battle of Vella Lavella, 6–7 October. The Japanese commander muffed a chance to cap the American T and then partially masked his own fire by approaching on a line of bearing. The destroyer most exposed by this maneuver was sunk by American shells and torpedoes. The American commander, ignoring the lesson of Tassafaronga, maintained course and speed after opening fire. Japanese torpedoes blew the bows off two of his destroyers, one of which had to be scuttled.

The Bougainville Campaign

On 1 November 1943, Admiral Wilkinson's Third Amphibious Force bypassed the complex of Japanese bases in and near southern Bougainville and landed 14,000 marines halfway up the Bougainville west coast at Cape Torokina, Empress Augusta Bay. Because fighter-escorted bombers could readily reach Rabaul from this point, headquarters commanders at Rabaul reacted promptly. They hurled two air raids at the new lodgment, but the attacks were broken up by AirSols fighters from Guadalcanal, New Georgia, and Vella Lavella. As in their response to the American invasion of Guadalcanal, the Japanese sent down a cruiser–destroyer force, now under Rear Admiral Sentaro Omori, to attack the American transports.

The resulting Battle of Empress Augusta Bay turned out to be no repetition of the Savo Island battle. Allied patrol planes early spotted and this time correctly reported the oncoming Japanese force. At 0200, 2 November, as Omori's ships, in intense darkness under a rain squall, were

approaching the beachhead, a similar force, under American Rear Admiral Stanton Merrill, was coming up from the south thoroughly alerted and knowing what to expect. Merrill arrived first and stretched his column, four cruisers, with four destroyers in the van and four in the rear, across the entrance to the bay. On detecting the approaching enemy, Merrill, following an oft-rehearsed plan, released his two destroyer divisions for torpedo attacks on the enemy's flanks. With his cruisers he steamed back and forth, firing steadily, and at length, with each reversal of course, pressing nearer the enemy and forcing him away from the bay. Except for Merrill's cruisers, all segments of both sides fell into some degree of confusion, with a number of collisions, but the net result was that Omori was repulsed with the loss of a cruiser and a destroyer. One American destroyer was severely damaged.

Captain Arleigh Burke, commanding Merrill's van destroyers, requested permission to pursue the retreating Japanese, but Merrill, expecting an air attack at dawn, ordered him instead to collect his destroyers and rendezvous with the cruisers for a retirement to the south. The air attack came as expected, about a hundred planes, but by a combination of accurate antiaircraft fire and deft ship handling, the Americans shot down 17 of the attacking planes and avoided all but two minor bomb hits.

While the marines at Torokina were establishing a defensive perimeter, within which Seabees began constructing airstrips, the Tokyo Express resumed operations. After midnight on 25 November, Captain Burke with a squadron of five destroyers, in the Battle of Cape St. George, put an end to such enemy movements. Using his battle plan that had won Moosbrugger a victory the preceding August, Burke's squadron, in two divisions, sank two Japanese destroyers with a combination of torpedoes and shellfire. Burke then chased three transport destroyers to within 60 miles of Rabaul, sinking one.

The New Guinea Campaign

General MacArthur, in his concurrent march on Rabaul via New Guinea, did not have to concern himself with derailing a night-running Tokyo Express. Enemy ships en route from Rabaul to the Japanese lodgments at Lae and Salamaua had to pass over open seas at least partly by daylight. The preceding March a Japanese convoy with 7,000 troops had attempted the passage to Lae. Fifth Air Force bombers, in a series of attacks called the

Battle of the Bismarck Sea, destroyed all eight of the transports and four of the eight escorting destroyers. Thereafter Japanese reinforcements to New Guinea bases went by submarines, or by barges, which proved an easy prey for PT boats.

At the end of June 1943, while South Pacific forces were invading the Central Solomons, MacArthur's Southwest Pacific forces put troops ashore without opposition on Kiriwina and Woodlark islands off the Papuan Peninsula and at Nassau Bay on the New Guinea north coast. The island invasions were carried out by Rear Admiral Daniel E. Barbey's Seventh Amphibious Force, the assault arm of "MacArthur's Navy," the miniscule U. S. Seventh Fleet.

In early September the Seventh Amphibious Force landed a division of Australian troops east of Lae. Another Australian division, airborne, landed west of Lae at an airstrip American paratroopers had recently captured. As the Australians advanced on Lae from east and west, the defenders, pounded by destroyer guns, took to the jungle and began a starving, month-long march across the Huon Peninsula to the coastal town of Sio. From Lae, Barbey's force in late September carried a brigade group of Australians around the tip of the peninsula to Finschhafen, where they surprised and expelled the enemy garrison, which also fell back on Sio.

Before advancing westward through Vitiaz Strait, MacArthur wanted both shores in Allied hands in order to secure his sea communications from air or surface attack. At the end of December, the 1st Marine Division stormed ashore near Cape Gloucester on the far side of the strait, quickly captured the airfield, and chased the Japanese on New Britain almost to Rabaul.

In early January 1944, Barbey landed 7,000 Americans at Saidor. The Japanese at Sio, cut off from supply by land and sea, abandoned the town to the Australians, who had been advancing through the jungle from Lae. The fugitives set out on foot for Madang. Two thousand of them, starving and diseased, died on the way. Hardly had the survivors arrived at their destination when the Australians, attacking from the interior, compelled the whole Madang garrison to fall back to Wewak.

The Neutralization of Rabaul

Following the costly, long-drawn-out Guadalcanal campaign, Admiral King began to question the wisdom of expending time and lives to wrest Fortress Rabaul from its 100,000 well-supplied defenders. At far less cost, once airfields were operational on Bougainville, Rabaul could be bombed

into impotence, while Southwest Pacific forces broke through the barrier of Bismarck-based air and sea power and captured the Admiralty Islands on the far side. In the Admiralties was ample level ground for airfields and base installations, and here also was Seeadler Harbor, a finer anchorage than Rabaul's Simpson Harbor. In August 1943, the Combined Chiefs of Staff, then meeting at Quebec, concurred with King in deciding that Rabaul was to be neutralized and bypassed rather than captured.

The "taking out of Rabaul" began on 12 October with a massive 349-plane raid staged by the Fifth Air Force out of New Guinea. Other powerful raids followed, whenever weather permitted. To help protect the base, Admiral Koga again stripped planes from his Combined Fleet, sending 173 carrier aircraft down from Truk.

Admiral Halsey next ordered carrier strikes against Rabaul, in order to destroy the numerous planes still operating from there and to bomb seven heavy cruisers that Koga had sent down from Truk to redeem Omori's failure in the Battle of Empress Augusta Bay. In an attack on 5 November, Rear Admiral Frederick Sherman's carrier group, built around the veteran carrier *Saratoga* and the new light carrier *Princeton*, shot down numerous enemy aircraft and damaged six of Koga's seven cruisers.

Halsey next borrowed from Nimitz's Fifth (Central Pacific) Fleet Rear Admiral Alfred E. Montgomery's carrier group, built around the new *Essex, Bunker Hill,* and *Independence,* and on 11 November sent it in for another attack on Rabaul. This time the Japanese countered with an air attack against the American force but suffered heavy losses while inflicting only minor damage with strafing and near misses. Koga now withdrew from Rabaul all ships and his remnant of carrier aircraft. The American naval forces had demonstrated that they could stand up against a powerful enemy base, and they had shot down so many carrier planes that the Combined Fleet was paralyzed, unable for many months to contest the drive that Nimitz was about to unleash across the Central Pacific.

By mid-November the Third Amphibious Force, effectively supported by AirSols, had landed about 34,000 soldiers and marines at the Torokina beachhead on Bougainville. The invaders in six weeks of hard fighting expanded the defense perimeter until it enclosed 22 square miles. Within this area Seabees and a New Zealand engineer brigade had by the end of 1943 constructed a fighter and a bomber strip, thus extending Halsey's bomber line to reach all the Bismarcks. In January 1944, AirSols, operating from the new airfields at

Torokina, stepped up raids against Rabaul to one or more a day. A month later AirSols bombers were averaging a thousand sorties a week.

In mid-February the U. S. Fifth Fleet, advancing rapidly across the Central Pacific, made a devastating raid on Truk. Koga thereupon recognized Rabaul as no longer defensible and began pulling aircraft out of the Bismarcks to where they could be used more profitably. Fortress Rabaul had been knocked out, but to keep it so, Halsey and MacArthur completed their ring of steel around the enemy stronghold.

In February the Third Fleet placed nearly 6,000 New Zealand and American troops ashore on the Green Islands 115 miles due east of Rabaul. After the invaders had destroyed the small Japanese garrison, Seabees built an airstrip on the main island, thereby bringing the entire Bismarck Archipelago within the radius of fighter-escorted AirSols bombers.

At the end of February, MacArthur ordered a thousand-man American reconnaissance-in-force on Los Negros, easternmost of the Admiralty Islands, northwest of the Bismarcks. Though there were 4,300 Japanese in the Admiralties, Allied fleet guns and air support enabled the invaders to turn the reconnaissance into a regular invasion. They seized part of the airdrome and drew around it a tight perimeter into which poured fresh echelons of troops and Seabees with bulldozers. The troops quickly expanded the beachhead, and the Seabees made the airstrip operational.

In mid-March the Third Fleet landed marines on Emirau, 70 miles northwest of Kavieng. Soon 18,000 men had gone ashore on this island, which the Japanese had never occupied, and work was under way on a PT base and another airstrip.

The boxing in of Rabaul was completed, but this time there was scarcely a pause in Allied offensive operations. As the marines occupied Emirau, MacArthur's soldiers were invading Manus, main island of the Admiralty group. By the end of March, 3,300 Japanese had been killed or captured in the Admiralties, as against 300 Americans killed, and work on the naval and air base was under way—not merely to keep Rabaul neutralized but to support further operations westward.

Development of the base facilities in the Admiralty Islands (or simply Manus, as they came collectively to be called) was the last major cooperative effort of the South and Southwest Pacific commands. The South Pacific Area, left far behind by the war, was gradually being reduced to garrison status. Its army forces, plus a few warships, were allotted to MacArthur; its marines and most of its naval forces went to Nimitz. MacArthur had hoped to enlist Halsey to command his growing Seventh Fleet, but Admiral King had other plans. Halsey was ordered to Pearl Harbor for a seagoing command under Nimitz.

For MacArthur, the capture of Manus marked the end of one campaign and the beginning of another. Even before the Admiralties were secured, he was planning a tremendous 400-mile leap westward to Hollandia. Beyond Hollandia he would leap forward again and again until at length he reached the Philippines in fulfillment of his promise: "I shall return."

Chapter 28
The Dual Advance

The several Orange Plans for the relief or reconquest of the Philippines, it will be recalled, had all envisaged a drive across the Central Pacific. In anticipation of eventually opening such an offensive, the U. S. Navy, just before and just after the declaration of war, had ordered the construction of 22 new aircraft carriers. But the Japanese threat to Australia and United States–Australia communications had diverted Allied forces to the Solomons and Papua for an offensive directed against the Japanese bastion at Rabaul.

Admiral King had grown increasingly impatient at the slowness of these southern operations—six months to take Guadalcanal and Buna, more months to climb the chain of the Solomons and complete the conquest of Papua, with Rabaul still to be taken. At this rate it would take many years for the Allied forces to reach Japan. King began to talk about bypassing Rabaul and using the forces thus freed to open an advance across the center.

General MacArthur favored a single line of advance, but across the South. He proposed that, once Rabaul had been captured or neutralized, the transpacific advance on Japan should be via coastal New Guinea and the Philippines by forces under his command. This drive, along what he called the New Guinea–Mindanao Axis, would be mainly an army offensive, carried forward by a series of amphibious operations, bypassing enemy concentrations, and continuously supported by land-based air. The Navy, besides transport and convoy, would carry out such supporting functions as shore bombardments and securing the flank of the Army's advance.

Opponents of the New Guinea–Mindanao Axis argued that it was a roundabout approach to Japan, requiring long and vulnerable communication lines; that it was a slow means of approach, with each successive advance limited to the attack radius of fighter aircraft and of fighter-escorted bombers. It would take little advantage of the carrier forces that were arriving in the Pacific.

On the other hand, a drive through the islands of the Central Pacific, spearheaded by the carriers, could take tremendous leaps westward, threatening the enemy's whole island empire and obliging

him to fragmentize his strength to defend each position. The widely spaced island groups could not in general be mutually supporting and, once isolated by America's growing carrier air power, they could not be reinforced. The advance across the center would cut Japan's communications to the Southwest Pacific and protect shorter Allied lines to the same area. It would speedily bring the war into Japanese waters and force the enemy fleet out for a decision that presumably would leave Japan herself open to attack.

The Joint Chiefs of Staff and their subcommittees, after carefully weighing the alternatives, decided to open a Central Pacific drive as the main line of advance, but also to permit MacArthur's Southwest Pacific forces to continue along the New Guinea–Mindanao Axis. The Southwest Pacific forces would serve to protect Australia and at the same time contain the Japanese with whom they were in contact, preventing them from opposing the Central Pacific drive. At the Washington conference of May 1943, the British Chiefs raised no objection to the Joint Chiefs' plan, having been assured that the new advance could be carried out with additional resources already earmarked for the Pacific: carriers, fast battleships, dive-bombers, and torpedo planes—weapons least needed in the European theater. It was tacitly understood that consent was the price the British must pay to induce the Americans to invade Italy, and that henceforth the Americans alone would run the war in the Pacific.

Because a dual drive must be closely coordinated, some officers expressed the opinion that it was now imperative to appoint a supreme commander in the Pacific theater. But it was clear the Army, and probably the American public too, would oppose subordinating MacArthur to Nimitz, or any other available flag officer; and King had no intention of giving MacArthur control of the Pacific Fleet. Thus for the Pacific war there was to be no overall command closer than the Joint Chiefs in Washington. As it turned out, instant worldwide radio communications overcame most of the disadvantages of the divided command—at least until the two offensives came into actual contact.

The original plan for opening the Central Pacific drive called for an invasion of the Marshall Islands, but every discussion of ways and means for conquering this archipelago came around to the fact that it was out of reach of Allied land-based planes, and nobody knew whether there would be enough carriers or experienced carrier aviators to support an invasion without supplementary land-based air support. These was also the question of photoreconnaissance. In 1943 it was generally believed that only land-based planes could carry out the extensive aerial photography needed to reveal defense installations, beach gradients, coral reefs, and water depths.

The Marshalls could, however, be reached by planes based on the Japanese-held Gilbert Islands, and the Gilberts could be reached by planes from actual or potential Allied air bases on Canton Island, Baker Island, and the Ellice Islands. Hence it was decided that the Americans would first take the Gilberts, from which land-based planes could support a subsequent invasion of the Marshalls.

It was understood from the beginning that the main target in the Gilberts was to be the island of Betio in the Tarawa Atoll, where the Japanese were known to have an airfield, but when Admiral Nimitz received his orders from the Joint Chiefs on 20 July, he was startled to find that they also called for an invasion of Nauru, nearly 400 miles from Tarawa. Supporting invasions so far apart would dangerously divide the fleet, and Nauru, once taken, was so located as to be of no use to the Americans. Fortunately, Nimitz, backed by his principal commanders, was able to persuade the Joint Chiefs to drop Nauru from the plan and substitute Makin, just 100 miles from Tarawa. On Butaritari Island in the Makin Atoll there was room to build a bomber strip that would be less than 200 miles from the southern Marshalls. The revised plan also included conquest of lightly held Abemama, another potential air base. D-day for Tarawa and Makin was 20 November 1943.

Power for the New Drive

The Central Pacific drive was unique in the history of warfare. Nothing in the past gave any sure clue as to how armed forces could advance in great leaps across an ocean studded with hostile island air bases. Carrying out the offensive required new methods of training, new techniques of combat, support, supply, and maintenance, and a whole arsenal of new weapons. Yet when the drive began in the autumn of 1943, less than two years after the attack on Pearl Harbor, the means were at hand.

That was perhaps the most remarkable achievement of World War II.

The main combat arm of the Central Pacific forces was the U. S. Fifth Fleet, a complex of men, ships, and aircraft organized for the purpose of projecting power at a distance.[1] By autumn it comprised 6 large carriers, chiefly of the new 27,000-ton, 32-knot *Essex* class; 5 light carriers of the new 11,000-ton *Independence* class; 8 escort carriers; 5 new and 7 old battleships; 9 heavy and 5 light cruisers; 56 destroyers; 29 transports and cargo vessels; and a large number of landing and beaching craft.

Commanding this considerable and growing fleet was Vice Admiral Raymond A. Spruance, a man of outstanding intellect and an austere and exacting officer. His work on the staff of the Naval War College had established his reputation as a strategist. The Battle of Midway had demonstrated his brilliance as a tactician. Since then, as Admiral Nimitz's chief of staff, he had played a major part in planning the operations he was to lead.

Spearheading the Fifth Fleet was Task Force 58, the fast carrier force. It normally operated in four circular task groups, each of which typically contained two large and two light carriers surrounded by an escort of 1 or 2 fast battleships, 3 or 4 cruisers, and 12 or 15 destroyers. Highly flexible, the carrier groups could operate together or independently. Such was the floating air base that was to lead the way across the Pacific to the shores of Japan. But the fast carrier force of 1943, commanded by Rear Admiral Charles A. Pownall, was only a miniature version of the armada that later wiped out Japanese air power and shattered Japan's Combined Fleet.

The amphibious component of the Fifth Fleet was the Fifth Amphibious Force, commanded by Rear Admiral Richmond Kelly Turner. In an invasion this force comprised transports, cargo vessels, landing and beaching craft, and also the destroyers, escort carriers, cruisers, and old battleships assigned for close support.

The troops assigned to the Fifth Amphibious Force, both army and marine, were designated V Amphibious Corps. The Corps commander was Major General Holland M. Smith, USMC, whose typical reaction to an inept or slovenly performance had earned him the nickname "Howlin' Mad Smith." Though "Howlin' Mad" was as stubborn

[1]At first the title U. S. Fifth Fleet applied only to the *ships* of the Central Pacific force, but it was later extended to include also the amphibious troops and the land-based planes. United States naval personnel sometimes referred to the Central Pacific fleet as the Big Blue Fleet.

and outspoken as "Terrible Turner," and though the two had frequent disagreements, they still made an effective team, for both were amphibious experts.

Finally, the Fifth Fleet had its own land-based air force, composed of army, naval, and marine corps planes under the operational control of Rear Admiral John H. Hoover.

To free the Fifth Fleet from rearward bases, affording it the strategic momentum to thrust rapidly across the Pacific, seizing command of the sea as it went, Service Force Pacific provided roving fueling groups and mobile service squadrons. The former consisted of oilers for refueling ships at sea. The latter comprised tenders, repair ships, floating drydocks, ammunition ships, and other auxiliaries that could quickly set up advanced bases by dropping anchor in any lagoon or other protected anchorage.

All the senior officers of the Fifth Fleet had been nominated by Admiral Nimitz, who had selected them solely on the basis of their competence. Not all the officers at Pearl Harbor, or in Washington, were pleased with his selections. Pownall, heading the carrier force, was an aviator, but critics questioned why Spruance, not an aviator, should be commanding a carrier-spearheaded fleet. The Army was disappointed that no army officers were appointed to these senior posts, though at least half the amphibious troops and possibly half the flyers would be army personnel. Critical eyes would be watching the performance of Nimitz's nominees.

As the new men-of-war arrived at Pearl Harbor, they were formed into task groups and sent against live targets for warm-up and training. In early September a three-carrier group struck Marcus Island, doing great damage to installations and destroying several Japanese bombers. On 18–19 September, another three-carrier group joined bombers from Canton and Funafuti in a raid on the Gilberts. The main purpose of this attack was to ease enemy pressure on American air bases in the Ellices, which had been bombed by planes from Tarawa and Makin. This aim was more than fulfilled, for the Japanese immediately evacuated all air units from Tarawa and left at Makin only four amphibious planes for reconnaissance. Equally important, the defenders shot off a great deal of ammunition that they could not replenish, and the attackers succeeded in getting some excellent photographs of both Tarawa and Makin. Eighteen days later, a six-carrier force, the largest yet organized, staged a massive raid on Wake, so denuding that base of aircraft that the Japanese had to send up additional planes from the Marshalls. Lastly, in

early November, as we have seen, carrier groups under Admirals Sherman and Montgomery assisted Halsey's Bougainville campaign by raiding Rabaul.

An important result of the considerable increase of American carrier strength was the decision to abandon the practice of operating each carrier in a separate formation. Maneuvering several carriers within a single ring of escorts was difficult, and it sacrificed some flexibility, but these handicaps were more than offset by the defensive advantages of concentrated combat air patrols and massed VT-fused antiaircraft fire.

The Americans, unaware of the paralysis of the enemy fleet through loss of carrier planes, took elaborate care to achieve surprise, in order to gain a foothold before Koga could strike. So as not to disclose the target, Hoover's B-24s delayed regular raids until mid-November, when the Fifth Fleet was already at sea en route to the assault.

Reconquest of the Gilbert Islands

The invasion of the Gilberts was more complex and on a larger scale than any operation thus far undertaken by the Americans in the Pacific theater. The four task groups of Task Force 58 set out for their assigned supporting and covering positions—two groups from Pearl Harbor, the other two from the South Pacific, where they had just completed their raids on Rabaul.

A Northern Attack Force brought troops of the 27th Infantry Division to assault Makin Atoll. Admiral Turner and General Holland Smith were both with this force, because it was originally destined for Nauru, thought to be the most strongly defended of the target islands. When Makin was substituted for Nauru, the attack force merely headed for the new destination, its command structure unchanged.

The rest of the Fifth Amphibious Force, designated the Southern Attack Force, picked up the 2nd Marine Division at Wellington, New Zealand, where it had been training. The ships and men rehearsed landing operations in the New Hebrides and then headed for Tarawa.

The submarine *Nautilus*, carrying a single company of marines, set out to scout lightly held Abemama, which was to be invaded after Makin and Tarawa had fallen.

Because of Makin's exposed position near the Marshalls, a one-day conquest here was deemed essential so that the supporting fleet could be quickly withdrawn. Accordingly, 6,500 troops were assigned to seize little Butaritari, main island

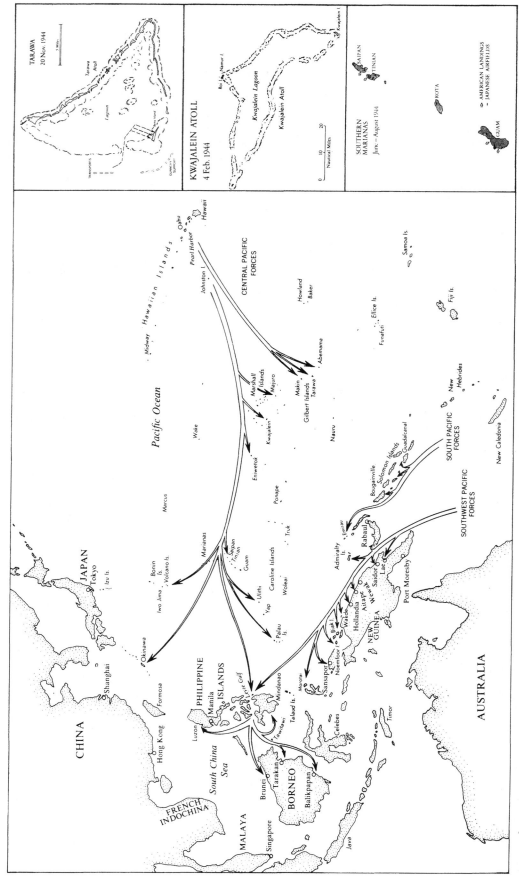

TARAWA
20 Nov. 1944

5 Mile.

Tarawa
Atoll

Lagoon

Betio Island

TRANSPORTS

GUNFIRE
SUPPORT

KWAJALEIN ATOLL
4 Feb. 1944

Roi I. Namur I.

Kwajalein I

Kwajalein Lagoon

Kwajalein Atoll

0   10   20

Nautical Miles

SOUTHERN
MARIANAS
June – August 1944

SAIPAN

TINIAN

ROTA

GUAM

▲ AMERICAN LANDINGS
▬ JAPANESE AIRFIELDS

CHINA

JAPAN

Tokyo

Izu Is.

Shanghai

Hong Kong

Formosa

South China
Sea

FRENCH
INDOCHINA

MALAYA

Singapore

Java

BORNEO

Brunei

Tarakan

Balikpapan

Celebes

Timor

PHILIPPINE
ISLANDS

Luzon

Manila

Mindanao

Leyte Gulf

Tawitawi

Talaud Is.

Morotai

Sansapor

Noemfoor

Biak I.

Wakde

Hollandia

Aitape

Sarmi

Wewak

Saidor

Lae

NEW
GUINEA

Port Moresby

AUSTRALIA

New Caledonia

New
Hebrides

Okinawa

Iwo Jima

Bonin
Is.

Volcano Is.

Marianas

Saipan

Tinian

Guam

Ulithi

Yap

Palau
Is.

Wolesi

Caroline Islands

Truk

Ponape

Marcus

Wake

Eniwetok

Nauru

Kwajalein

Marshall
Islands

Majuro

Makin

Tarawa

Gilbert Islands

Abemama

Howland

Baker

Funafuti

Ellice Is.

Fiji Is.

Samoa Is.

Admiralty
Is.

Emirau

Rabaul

Bougainville

Solomon Islands

Guadalcanal

SOUTH PACIFIC
FORCES

SOUTHWEST PACIFIC
FORCES

Pacific Ocean

Midway

Hawaiian Islands

Oahu

Pearl Harbor

Hawaii

Johnston I.

CENTRAL PACIFIC
FORCES

Across the Pacific

and headquarters of the atoll, which was known to be lightly fortified and defended. In fact, the occupation forces on Butaritari amounted to no more than 800 men, comprising 284 naval infantry commanded by a junior grade lieutenant and an assortment of noncombatants. Nevertheless, to the disgust of Holland Smith, the invading U. S. troops lost momentum and bogged down. Instead of clearing the island in a single day they took almost four. Despite the vast numerical superiority of the Americans over the Japanese, the American casualty rate was excessive: 64 dead and 152 wounded. Moreover, on 24 November, when the fleet should already have withdrawn from the Makin area, a torpedo from a newly arrived Japanese submarine struck the escort carrier *Liscome Bay*, which simply blew apart as the blast set off her stored aircraft bombs. Of her crew of about 900, nearly 650 were killed by the explosion or by the flaming oil that spread from her shattered hull. Nowhere has the Navy's insistence upon speed in amphibious assault been more sharply vindicated. Marine General Holland Smith began to lose confidence in army amphibious troops, particularly those of the 27th Division.

Meanwhile, the *Nautilus* had put her company of marine scouts ashore on Abemama to estimate what forces would be needed for a later assault on this target. When the marines found only 25 defenders, they called on the submarine for gunfire support and went ahead and captured the atoll themselves.

Interest in the Gilberts operation centers chiefly on Tarawa, where at the cost of heavy casualties the Americans learned the techniques that were to carry them across the powerfully defended beaches of the Central Pacific. The storming of Tarawa proved a bitter school for amphibious assault, completing the lessons of the Solomons and New Guinea operations and the prewar exercises of the Navy and the Fleet Marine Force.

The main target for Rear Admiral Harry Hill's Southern Attack Force was narrow, two-mile-long Betio, the sole fortified island in the Tarawa Atoll. The Japanese had only about 3,000 combat effectives to oppose the 16,000 men of Major General Julian C. Smith's reinforced 2nd Marine Division. The defenders, like the invaders, were elite troops, but the chief strength of the island lay in the difficulty of its approaches and the nature of its fixed defenses. It was surrounded by a wide shelf of coral, barely submerged at low tide. On this shelf the Japanese had laced together concrete, coral, and metal obstacles with barbed wire to force approaching craft into lanes covered by shore-

based artillery. Along the beach at the high-water line ran a four-foot-high seawall of tough green coconut logs, almost impervious to anything but heavy-caliber fire. Behind the wall were numerous gun emplacements and partly underground bomb shelters and steel-reinforced concrete command posts, most piled high with sand to absorb shellfire.

The American planners, by consulting former inhabitants and studying aerial and submarine photographs, had learned all they could about Betio. They concluded that the island had no favorable landing beaches and that all were formidably defended. Faced with a choice of evils, they selected a 1,500-yard stretch of beach on the north coast, inside the lagoon. They overlooked, or disbelieved, a vital piece of information that was actually written into Admiral Turner's operation plan: "During high water neap tides, the reef of the north coast of Betio is covered by from one to two feet of water"—not deep enough for standard landing craft. D-day, 20 November, was known to be within a period of neap tides.

To avoid prohibitive losses and achieve sustained momentum, attacking forces would have to destroy most of Betio's defenses before the landing took place. Experienced officers did not count heavily on the effectiveness of a week of bombing by Hoover's B-24s or of air raids by Task Force 58 planes immediately preceding D-day. They pinned their hopes mainly on close-range preinvasion gunfire from Hill's three old battleships and five cruisers. On the morning of 20 November, these ships, in a two-and-a-half-hour bombardment, poured 3,000 tons of projectiles into Betio. The whole island appeared to be aflame, and an enormous pall of smoke and dust billowed into the air. The wooden barracks was consumed, an ammunition dump was blown up, and some guns were knocked out, but most of the Japanese sat snug in their bombproofs.

The landing craft, entering the lagoon against headwinds in a choppy sea, were late arriving at the line of departure. Beginning at 0825 the first three assault waves, the new, track-driven amtracs (amphibious tractors) carrying troops, crossed the line at four-minute intervals and headed for the beach, 6,000 yards away. The fourth, fifth, and sixth waves, standard landing craft, LCMs and LCVPs, carrying troops, tanks, and light artillery, soon followed. At 0845 Admiral Hill, fearful of hitting the landing craft, which were concealed from the fleet by dense smoke, ordered his ships to cease fire. The first wave was then still 15 minutes from the shore. Japanese manning the seaward beaches made use of this respite to join the defenders on the lagoon shore and take the approaching landing craft under fire with their rifles and machine guns.

The amtracs, from the moment they left the line of departure, had come under scattered fire, which became steadily more severe as they approached the shore. The reef, as Turner's staff had predicted, was under only two or three feet of water, but the tracked craft merely lumbered onto and across it. As they did so, they ran into a crescendo of machine-gun, rifle, and antiboat fire that threw the waves into confusion and killed or wounded many of the passengers. Far heavier casualties were suffered by the fourth, fifth, and sixth waves, whose conventional landing craft grounded on the edge of the reef. Some of the marines jumped out into the deep water and drowned, pulled down by their heavy gear. Others were ferried to the shore by returning amtracs of the first waves. Most got out into the shallow water and waded 600 yards to the beach through withering machine-gun and rifle fire. A few Sherman tanks, discharged by LCMs onto the reef, made it to the island, but LCVPs bringing in 37- and 75-mm guns had no choice but to retract and wait for the tide to rise.

The low water had one good effect: it left a strip of sandy beach on which the marines who reached the shore could huddle with some protection afforded by the seawall. Nevertheless, casualties at this time were extremely high. Even standing erect made one the target of deadly fire from several directions. Yet after the first shock, marines began climbing the wall and clearing out gun emplacements and rifle pits with charges of TNT.

While still boated, the assault commander, Colonel David M. Shoup, ordered his regimental reserve committed without delay. He then radioed General Julian Smith, in the battleship *Maryland*, for immediate gunfire and air support. The division commander not only saw that Shoup got the support he requested but also committed half the division reserve. As further reports of the critical situation ashore reached him, Julian Smith radioed General Holland Smith, then off Makin, requesting and receiving permission to commit the corps reserve.

Nearly a third of the 5,000 Americans who reached Betio before dark on 20 November were casualties, but about half of the western shore was in American hands, and at the base of the pier the marines had established a perimeter 300 yards deep. During the hours of darkness, the invaders maintained remarkable fire discipline; scarcely a shot was fired. A good many of the Japanese climbed trees or otherwise took position for sniping after dawn.

At first light on the 21st, the battle resumed and soon again reached full fury. Call strikes from the carriers and call fire from the gunnery vessels developed steadily increasing accuracy. Thus supported, the marines were able to advance the whole length of Betio's western shore, over which elements of the corps reserve soon began to pour. Then and later the principal task of the invaders was clearing out enemy-occupied pillboxes and shelters. Tanks and artillery were useful in this perilous business, but generally the job had to be completed by infantrymen with flamethrowers and hand-delivered charges of TNT.

When in the afternoon of the 23rd Julian Smith announced the end of organized enemy resistance, the defenders had been practically wiped out. More than a hundred Korean laborers were captured, but of the Japanese, only one officer and 19 enlisted men had surrendered. The rest fought to the last or committed suicide. Of the 18,300 Americans who landed on Betio, some 3,000 were casualties. Of these, more than a thousand were killed or died of wounds.

The American public and high command were profoundly shocked. As an essential jumping-off place for a major campaign, Tarawa ranked in importance with Guadalcanal and Papua, both of which had cost far more lives. But losses in taking these positions had been spread over six months. Tarawa's thousand fatalities were suffered in just three days.

Lieutenant General Robert C. Richardson, Commanding General U. S. Army Forces Central Pacific, blamed the dilatory capture of Makin and the costly conquest of Tarawa on command incompetence. To Admiral Nimitz he recommended replacing the V Amphibious Corps with an army corps, a substitution that would have the effect of transferring control of the amphibious soldiers and marines from Holland Smith to himself. Nimitz ignored the recommendation.

Admiral Nimitz was worried about the forthcoming invasion of the Marshalls, but key positions in these small islands had to be taken lest bombers based on them render the nearby Gilberts untenable. He was far more worried about the proposed Fifth Fleet invasion of the Marianas, which would come later. The Marianas targets—Saipan, Tinian, and Guam—were each much larger than any island in the Gilberts or Marshalls. They were within range of Japanese land-based air support but far beyond the reach of any Allied land-based planes.

It had cost a thousand lives to take flat, 2-mile-long Betio. What would it cost to take mountainous, 25-mile-long Guam?

When the Central Pacific drive was first scheduled, General MacArthur had protested that taking strongly defended islands would be too costly and pointed to the Japanese defeat at Midway as evidence. He was not sorry to see the Gilberts and Marshalls conquered, however, because Japanese on these islands could advance via the Ellices to Samoa and cut his communications with the United States. But he was adamantly opposed to further American advances along the Central Pacific Axis. Such a westward advance without land-based air support, he believed, would be too costly in lives, ships, and planes. Besides, the buildup of force at the center might divert supplies from his own force and thereby retard his movement across the south, and a quick drive across the center could render his own roundabout advance via New Guinea and the Philippines superfluous.

The bloodletting at Tarawa gave MacArthur the ammunition he needed to advance his view. He urged the Joint Chiefs to direct Nimitz, after taking the Marshalls, to cancel further operations in the Central Pacific and transfer the Fifth Fleet southward to support his own drive to Mindanao. When they rejected this recommendation, MacArthur, in defiance of regulations, tried to bypass the Joint Chiefs with a letter to Secretary of War Henry L. Stimson, to be shown to the president. "Give me central direction of the war in the Pacific," he urged, "and I will be in the Philippines in ten months. . . . Don't let the Navy's pride of position and ignorance continue this great tragedy to our country."

This plea had no more effect than the former one, but the general was soon presented with a new and unexpected opportunity. Admiral Nimitz invited senior officers in the Pacific theater to convene at Pearl Harbor to discuss strategy. MacArthur sent two generals and an admiral, with instructions to argue for a single line of advance—via the New Guinea–Mindanao Axis. At the meeting, held on 27 and 28 January 1944, MacArthur's representatives had no difficulty convincing the CinCPOA staff, all of whom opposed tackling the Marianas. Nimitz, thus supported by the opinions of officers whose judgment he respected, said that he would forward their recommendations with a favorable endorsement. He sent his planning officer to Washington with a copy of the conference notes and instructions to use his powers of persuasion with the Joint Chiefs. An elated MacArthur sent his chief of staff to Washington with the same mission.

Invasion of the Marshall Islands

Planning for the Marshalls invasion, which was well under way before the assault on the Gilberts, originally called for simultaneous assaults on Maloelap and Wotje atolls, the two Marshallese bases nearest Pearl Harbor, and on Kwajalein, Japanese headquarters at the center of the archipelago. Holland Smith, made cautious by the heavy losses at Tarawa, convinced Spruance and Turner that not enough troops and support were available to capture three bases at the same time. They recommended to Nimitz a two-step operation: Maloelap and Wotje first, Kwajalein later. Nimitz made a counterproposal: bypass the two outer atolls and assault only Kwajalein. The Fifth Fleet flag and general officers all considered this proposal too risky. At a meeting on 14 December 1943, Nimitz polled them. They all recommended taking Maloelap and Wotje first. When the poll was completed, Nimitz said quietly, "Well, gentlemen, our next objective will be Kwajalein." The only modification he would permit was occupation of undefended Majuro Atoll in the eastern Marshalls, to provide a protected fleet anchorage in the area of operations, for use until Kwajalein was secured.

The daring decision to go directly to the heart of the Marshalls proved sound. The Japanese had given the outer atolls priority in defense materials and personnel. The fortification of Kwajalein remained comparatively light, certainly nothing like what the marines had found on Betio. Though the Kwajalein garrison numbered about 8,000, not quite 2,200 were trained combat troops. However, most of the 8,000 were given arms, and they sold their lives as dearly as possible.

The officers who had commanded the main segments of the Fifth Fleet in the Gilberts operation would command them also in the Marshalls assault—with one exception. Admiral Pownall, the only officer whose appointment had not been criticized, had to be relieved of his command. With two groups of Task Force 58, he staged a preinvasion raid on Kwajalein. He planned two successive strikes, but when aviators returned from the first and reported numerous undamaged enemy planes still on the airfield, Pownall canceled the second strike and ordered a retirement. That evening, the aircraft he had spared caught up with the retreating fleet and, attacking by moonlight, put a torpedo into the stern of the new carrier *Lexington*. Nimitz, displeased by this lack of aggressiveness and good judgment, relieved Pownall of his command but characteristically, to spare him disgrace, kicked him upstairs to the recently vacated post of Commander Air Forces Pacific, arranging that his responsibilities should be limited to administrative and logistic duties. To replace Pownall, Nimitz secured the appointment of veteran naval aviator Rear Admiral Marc A. Mitscher, but only as senior carrier division commander. If he failed to measure up in the forthcoming Marshalls operation, he could be quietly shunted aside without a formal relief.

One of the striking facts about the war in the Pacific is that the techniques and weapons for amphibious attack fully matured between Tarawa and the invasion of the Marshalls. The most important lesson learned by the U. S. armed forces was the one Admiral Porter had learned nearly 80 years before, following the first, unsuccessful attack on Fort Fisher—that strong defenses can be destroyed only by extended, deliberate, aimed fire. The same rule was found to apply to aerial bombing.

As soon as the airfields on Makin, Abemama, and Tarawa were operational, Admiral Hoover's bombers began their attack on the Marshalls and soon stepped up to a raid-a-day schedule, in six weeks dropping more than 2,000 tons of bombs and taking hundreds of reconnaissance photographs. On 29 January 1944, an expanded Task Force 58 arrived in the Marshalls with 750 planes to compound the destruction. Hoover's and Mitscher's aircraft, together with Task Force 58's gunnery vessels, battered shore defenses, churned up airfields, and destroyed every Japanese plane in the archipelago.

As the Fifth Amphibious Force, 300 ships bringing 84,000 troops, approached the Marshalls, Admiral Hill's Special Attack Group detached itself and occupied Majuro. Into Majuro's lagoon followed a mobile service squadron prepared to look after the needs of the naval forces. Thus was set up one of a series of temporary forward bases that freed the fleet from immediate dependence upon Pearl Harbor and extended its reach step by step across the Pacific.

On 30 January the Northern Attack Force, under Rear Admiral Richard L. Conolly, and the Southern Attack Force, under Admiral Turner's direct command, reached Kwajalein Atoll and added their guns and escort carrier planes to step up the final intensive preparation. The primary invasion targets, Roi and Namur, a pair of connected islands at the north end of the lagoon, and

Kwajalein Island, 44 miles to the south, were pounded with four times the weight of bombs and shells that had been hurled against Betio. Aircraft picked their targets and bombed precisely. Gunnery ships varied range and trajectory, and shifted from demolition to armor-piercing shells as the situation required.

On 31 January, U. S. troops seized islets near Roi–Namur and near Kwajalein Island and sited artillery on them to cover the main landing beaches. That day and the following night, newly organized underwater demolition teams reconnoitered the approaches to the beachheads. The next morning, 1 February, after a final blasting of the target islands, the landing forces headed for their assigned beaches. The amtracs were now armed and armored and accompanied to the shore by LCI gunboats and amphibian tanks. Coordinating the operations were Conolly and Turner in the new amphibious command ships.

Not everything went smoothly. The assault on Roi–Namur was marred by disorder and poor timing. The landing force was Major General Harry Schmidt's newly organized 4th Marine Division, untried in battle and lifted directly from the United States with inadequate opportunity to practice landings. Once ashore, however, the marines quickly overran both islands, which were declared secure in the early afternoon of 2 February. They had suffered casualties of 196 killed and about 550 wounded.

The landings on Kwajalein Island by Major General Charles H. Corlett's 7th Infantry Division were almost flawless. Thereafter these well-trained veterans of Attu advanced very slowly. They had to defeat a fairly large defense force, and, having chosen a landing beach at the narrow western end, they had to advance on a narrow front the whole length of the island. But the main reason for their plodding advance appears to have been infantry tactics inherited from the static conditions of World War I. When they completed their conquest of the island in the afternoon of 4 February, their casualties, 177 killed and about a thousand wounded, were scarcely less severe than those of the fast-stepping marines.

Because he had not had to commit the 10,000 troops of the corps reserve, Admiral Spruance could push on without delay to the conquest of Eniwetok Atoll. But Eniwetok was in an exposed position, only 1,000 miles from the Marianas, less than 600 from Ponape, and less than 700 from Truk, whose reputation for impregnability had earned it the title "Gibraltar of the Pacific." To prevent interference with the Eniwetok operation, land-based planes from Tarawa neutralized Ponape, and Mitscher took three groups from Task Force 58 southwest to attack Truk. Admiral Koga had prudently withdrawn the bulk of the Combined Fleet to the Palau Islands in the western Carolines, but he had left behind a small force to protect cargo vessels at Truk. Mitscher's ships and planes destroyed about 200 enemy aircraft and sank 15 naval vessels, including 2 cruisers, as well as 19 cargo vessels and 5 tankers—at a cost of 25 planes and severe damage to one carrier. Mitscher next headed for the Marianas with two of his task groups. They were detected while still distant, but their radar-aimed VT-fused antiaircraft shells kept the attacking planes from hitting any U. S. ship. The subsequent strikes at Saipan, Tinian, and Guam wiped out at least 150 bombers. Aerial photoreconnaissance got invaluable pictures of beaches and airfields suitable for assault.

Meanwhile, Harry Hill's force had captured the three main islands of Eniwetok Atoll. None of the troops, army and marine units originally assigned to corps reserve, had had any battle experience; hence there was some confusion during the landings. Once ashore, however, the well-trained marines overran two of the islands, each in a single day. But the soldiers, drawn from the 27th Infantry Division that had proved laggardly at Makin, got off to such a slow start on their assigned island that one of the marine landing teams had to be rushed in to take over the brunt of the fighting.

For their achievement in conquering the Marshalls, and in recognition of their increased responsibilities in an expanding fleet, Mitscher, Holland Smith, Turner, and Spruance were each awarded an additional star, and Mitscher was appointed Commander Fast Carrier Force Pacific.

The success of the Marshalls and associated operations swept away Admiral Nimitz's doubts and his dread of heavy personnel losses. He was now confident that the Fifth Fleet could not only conquer the Marianas but support MacArthur as well. Hence, a scolding letter dated 8 February 1944, which he received from Admiral King, was superfluous. King first congratulated Nimitz on the Marshalls victory. He then got down to the source of his displeasure: Nimitz's 28 January endorsement of the proposal to bypass the Marianas. "I have read your conference notes with much interest," King wrote, "and I must add with indignant dismay." The Japanese-held Marianas blocked all potential communications across the Pacific. Capture of the Marianas would "dry up" the Carolines, since men and material flowed from Japan southward by sea and air chiefly under protection of aircraft based on

the Marianas. King continued: "I assume that even the Southwest Pacific advocates will admit that sometime or other this thorn in the side of our communications to the western Pacific must be removed."

General Arnold sturdily backed King's insistence on capture of the Marianas. On these islands Arnold planned to establish airfields whence the new B-29 long-range bombers could reach Japan.

The New Guinea–Mindanao Axis

Admiral Nimitz soon had an opportunity to support General MacArthur's leap-frogging drive along the coast of New Guinea. Toward the end of March 1944, he sent Task Force 58 to lure out the Combined Fleet for a showdown battle or to blast it off the flank of MacArthur's line of advance by raiding its new anchorage in the Palaus. Japanese patrol planes spotted the approaching American carrier force, whereupon Admiral Koga, still unready for battle for lack of replacement aviators, promptly withdrew the bulk of his fleet. When Task Force 58 planes struck the Palaus on the 30th and 31st, they sank a destroyer, and sank or heavily damaged 35 other vessels—mostly auxiliaries and freighters. Koga himself, heading by plane from the Palaus to new headquarters in the Philippines, ran into a storm and crashed. The Combined Fleet was once more without a commander in chief.

In mid-April Task Force 58 was again at sea, this time in direct support of MacArthur's forthcoming advance. This advance was a daring 400-mile leap by sea from the Admiralties, past the Japanese Eighteenth Army base at Wewak, to a landing at Hollandia. A subsidiary force landed at Aitape to block the coast road. By far the largest amphibious operation up to then in the Southwest Pacific Area, it involved 113 ships and 84,000 troops. So thoroughly had the Fifth Air Force and the Seventh Fleet (including escort carriers lent by Nimitz) softened up the enemy defenses that support by Task Force 58 proved unnecessary.

General MacArthur was now launched upon his westward drive to capture Japanese airstrips and convert them to his own use, ever advancing his fighter-escorted bomber line until it could cover his invasion of Mindanao, southernmost of the Philippine Islands. In mid-May his amphibious forces landed at Wakde Island just off the New Guinea coast 130 miles northwest of Hollandia. Admiral Soemu Toyoda, Koga's offensive-minded successor, concluding that the Allies were committed to a single line of advance, via New Guinea, drew up a plan, Operation A-Go, for fleet action in the western Carolines area. To Tawitawi, between the Philippines and Borneo, he sent the new Mobile Fleet, actually the bulk of the Combined Fleet, now organized around the carriers in imitation of Task Force 58. Commanding the Mobile Fleet was Vice Admiral Jisaburo Ozawa, Japan's senior naval air officer. At a favorable opportunity, Ozawa was to sortie and engage Task Force 58, his inferiority being offset by land-based air, chiefly from three airfields the Japanese had constructed on Biak Island in the mouth of Geelvink Bay. When MacArthur's fast-moving forces landed on Biak on 27 May, the Japanese reacted sharply, lest the island airfields provide support for Mitscher rather than for Ozawa. First, they transferred much of their Central Pacific air power to the New Guinea area. Next, Ozawa endeavored to rush surface units to Biak with reinforcements. After two such attempts had been turned back, one by aircraft, the other by a Seventh Fleet cruiser–destroyer force, Ozawa sent Vice Admiral Matome Ugaki with a really formidable escort, including the superbattleships *Yamato* and *Musashi* and six cruisers. These were to fight their way through to Biak at all costs, land their troops, and bombard the invaders.

On 11 June, while this force was en route to Biak, the strategic picture changed abruptly. The U. S. Fifth Fleet raided the Marianas preparatory to invading Saipan. Apparently the showdown battle would be fought not off New Guinea but in the Philippine Sea off the Marianas. On Toyoda's radioed orders, Ozawa sortied from Tawitawi; and Ugaki, dropping off his transports, headed north to join Ozawa and the rest of the Mobile Fleet east of the Philippines.

Ozawa's defeat in the Battle of the Philippine Sea took the pressure off MacArthur, who could now proceed unmolested with his campaign. Before Biak was secured, he had invaded Noemfoor Island, 50 miles farther west. At the end of July, his forces went ashore at Cape Sansapor, near the western end of New Guinea. In a little more than three months, they had advanced nearly a thousand miles, seizing five enemy bases en route. Only the northern Molucca and the Talaud islands now stood between MacArthur and Mindanao, 500 miles to the northwest.

The Battle of the Philippine Sea—
the Approach of the Fleets

Toyoda had based the Mobile Fleet at Tawitawi partly to be near the source of Borneo oil, little of which was reaching Japan because of the slaughter of Japanese tankers by American submarines. The

Americans soon learned the fleet's location, and their submarines converged upon the area in such numbers that Ozawa dared not leave port for maneuvers. His aviators, who had been sent to the carriers with minimum basic training, ceased training altogether and merely loafed, losing their fighting edge.

When the order came from Admiral Toyoda to rendezvous in the Philippine Sea, there was not enough processed oil available for distant operations. The oilers that accompanied the Mobile Fleet carried crude Borneo oil, pure enough to be piped directly into fuel bunkers but dangerously volatile. Ozawa threaded through the straits of the Philippines and in the afternoon of 17 June joined forces with Ugaki in the Philippine Sea. They refueled with the dangerous crude and the following day resumed their advance toward the Marianas.

Ozawa, estimating correctly that Task Force 58 was twice as strong as the Mobile Fleet and had far better-trained flyers, pinned his hopes on certain advantages—or supposed advantages.[2] The easterly trade wind would give him the lee gage, permitting him to launch and recover aircraft while advancing on the enemy. Having appraised Spruance as a cautious man, on the basis of his tactics at Midway, he estimated that Task Force 58 would maintain a close covering position off the beachhead. His own planes, unencumbered with heavy body armor and self-sealing fuel tanks, had an optimum striking radius of more than 300 miles, compared to 200 miles or less for American carrier planes. Ozawa expected Japanese aircraft based on Rota and Guam to attack the Americans first, greatly reducing Task Force 58's superiority before the Mobile Fleet went into action. Then he intended to stand off beyond the reach of the American planes and, making use of the Guam airfields as refueling and rearming stations for his bombers, shuttle-bomb the American carriers into final defeat.

In the afternoon of 18 June, planes from the Japanese carriers located Task Force 58 some 200 miles west of Saipan. Ozawa thereupon began taking disposition for an attack the next morning. He held back his Main Body, including all his large carriers, well beyond the radius of the American planes, and sent forward a Van Force of three light carriers and all his heavy ships a hundred miles closer to Task Force 58, to serve as an antiaircraft screen. Thus no American planes could reach his

[2]Mobile Fleet: 9 carriers, 5 battleships, 13 cruisers, 28 destroyers, 430 carrier aircraft. Task Force 58: 15 carriers, 7 battleships, 21 cruisers, 69 destroyers, 891 carrier aircraft.

Main Body, and if they attempted to do so, they would be shot down by the Van Force.

On 6 June, Task Force 58, with Admiral Spruance in the *Indianapolis* and Vice Admiral Mitscher in the *Lexington*, had departed Majuro and headed for the Marianas, followed at a distance by the Fifth Amphibious Force, which now included 535 ships, carrying more than 127,000 troops, two-thirds of whom were marines. At the same time, on the opposite side of the globe, American forces were invading Normandy. Together these operations constituted the most gigantic military effort unleashed by a single nation at one time in all history.

Though there would be no land-based air support for the Marianas operation, no one seriously doubted after the Marshalls invasion that the Fifth Fleet was capable of conducting any foreseeable amphibious assault without assistance. On 11 June, from a point 200 miles east of Guam, Mitscher hurled his carrier air groups against the Southern Marianas. Enemy plane losses were heavy and retaliation was light, because, as we have seen, much of Japanese Central Pacific air power had been drained south in defense of Biak. Many of the aviators thus suddenly transferred had succumbed to malaria and jungle fever.

On 14 June Mitscher detached two carrier groups northward to attack landing fields on Iwo Jima and Chichi Jima and thus cut air communications from Japan, thereby completing the isolation of the Marianas. The other two carrier groups steamed around to a covering position west of Saipan, where the Fifth Amphibious Force put the 2nd and 4th Marine Divisions ashore on 15 June.

Such splitting of the fleet calls to mind the divided condition of the Japanese naval forces in their approach to Midway two years earlier. But the Japanese had no chance of taking the Americans by surprise, because Filipino coastwatchers and U. S. submarines were keeping Spruance informed of the Mobile Fleet's approach. Knowing that battle was imminent, he postponed the invasion of Guam, transferred 8 cruisers and 21 destroyers from the Fifth Amphibious Force to Task Force 58, and ordered the two detached carrier groups to complete their strikes on the 16th and rejoin the other two groups. He left tactical command of Task Force 58 in Mitscher's hands but let it be known that he expected Mitscher to inform him in advance of his intentions.

When the two detached groups rejoined Task Force 58 on the 18th, Mitscher formed a fifth group, of surface vessels including his seven fast battleships, and stationed it in the direction of the enemy to serve as an antiaircraft screen, and to engage in surface combat if an opportunity presented. Until nightfall Task Force 58 steered west, but its search planes found nothing. At dusk it reversed course and headed back toward the Saipan beachhead. Two hours later Pearl Harbor sent Mitscher radio-direction-finder bearings that placed the Mobile Fleet 355 miles west–southwest of his own position. To Mitscher it seemed imperative that he now turn and race toward the Mobile Fleet so that by daybreak his planes would have it within their reach. He also preferred to get some distance from the Guam airfields and possible shuttle-bombing. To Spruance he proposed by voice radio that Task Force 58 "come to a westerly course at 0130 in order to commence treatment of the enemy at 0500."

Spruance's orders mentioned only one objective: "capture, occupy and defend Saipan, Tinian and Guam." He therefore considered that the overriding mission of Task Force 58 was to shield the U. S. beachhead and amphibious shipping. Aware that in past major battles the Japanese had divided their naval forces, Spruance sought a position around which no enemy segment could make an end run—get behind his back and strike at the invasion forces. He rejected Mitscher's proposal. Task Force 58 continued on an easterly course.

The Battle of the Philippine Sea, 19–20 June 1944

Dawn 19 June found Task Force 58 under clear skies, with Mitscher's flagship *Lexington* 110 miles southwest of Saipan. At 0619 the force at last reversed direction but was unable to close the Mobile Fleet, because it had to turn repeatedly into the easterly trade wind in order to launch and receive planes. Between 0720 and 0900 comparatively feeble attempts by land-based aircraft to attack the U. S. carriers were frustrated by Hellcat fighters, which shot down at least 35 of the would-be attackers.

A little before 1000 Task Force 58 radars detected aircraft at 150 miles approaching from the west, obviously from the Mobile Fleet. American fighter directors, operating with superb efficiency, vectored out some 450 Hellcats and stacked them at high altitude, whence they swooped down on their ill-trained, outnumbered opponents. A few Japanese aircraft penetrated as far as the American battleship group, where they were blasted with deadly VT-fused ammunition. While bombers from the U. S. carriers kept the Guam airfields unusable for shuttle-bombing, three more massive

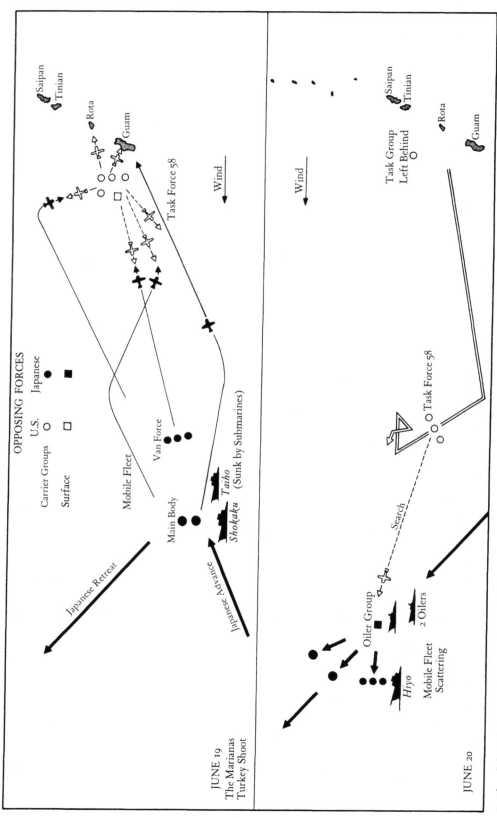

OPPOSING FORCES

	U.S.	Japanese
Carrier Groups	○	●
Surface	□	■

Saipan
Tinian
Rota
Guam

Task Force 58

Wind

Mobile Fleet

Van Force

Main Body

Taiho
Shokaku (Sunk by Submarines)

Japanese Retreat

Japanese Advance

JUNE 19
The Marianas
Turkey Shoot

Saipan
Tinian
Rota
Guam

Task Group
Left Behind

Wind

Task Force 58

Search

Oiler Group

2 Oilers

Hiyo

Mobile Fleet
Scattering

JUNE 20

Battle of the Philippine Sea, 19–20 June 1944

raids arrived from the Mobile Fleet and suffered the same scourging as the first. For the American aviators, observing enemy planes falling like autumn leaves or streaking aflame into the sea, this was the "Great Marianas Turkey Shoot." When the sun set, the Japanese fleet had lost 346 planes and thus again was in a state of virtual paralysis.

During the eight-hour annihilation of Japanese naval air power, other disasters were overtaking the Mobile Fleet. Two American submarines slipped through the weak screen of the Main Body and fired torpedoes into two carriers, the new *Taiho*, Ozawa's flagship, and the Pearl Harbor veteran *Shokaku*. From ruptured fuel lines, explosive vapors of the Borneo crude permeated both vessels. In midafternoon the two carriers exploded like giant firecrackers, with tremendous loss of life. Among the survivors was Admiral Ozawa, who had transferred to the carrier *Zuikaku*. At sunset the Mobile Fleet was in retreat, course northwest.

Now that the enemy's wings were clipped, Spruance was ready to advance and attack. Leaving one carrier group behind to protect the Saipan beachhead from land-based aircraft, the other groups proceeded on course west–southwest, assuming that the Mobile Fleet was retiring the way it had come. United States search planes finding nothing in that direction, Mitscher at noon, 20 June, altered course to northwest. Finally, a little before 1600, an *Enterprise* search plane reported the enemy 275 miles away. It was a long haul for U. S. carrier aircraft, but Mitscher decided to launch a deckload, 216 planes, even though they would have to return in darkness.

A little before sunset the aviators from Task Force 58 found the enemy carrier groups scattering fanwise to the northwest. Promptly attacking, the Americans sank two oilers and the carrier *Hiyo* and damaged two other carriers. Ozawa managed to launch 75 planes which, together with antiaircraft fire, shot down 20 U. S. planes. Japanese losses were much heavier. When the sun set at the end of this brief action, the Mobile Fleet had only 35 aircraft left.

Under darkening skies that soon became pitch black, the Americans headed back toward their carrier decks. Flyers with damaged planes began to ditch. Those who neglected fuel-conserving measures soon followed.

In an effort to shorten the return flight of its surviving planes, Task Force 58 was racing toward them. Then, as the carriers turned back into the wind to take them on board, Mitscher risked attracting submarines by ordering all his ships to turn on lights. Nevertheless, there was wild confu-

sion as newly arrived aircraft swarmed into the landing circles on their last drops of fuel. To prevent collisions, landing signal officers were obliged to wave off far more than they landed. When planes exhausted their fuel and splashed, destroyers moved busily through the fleet seeking survivors.

After completing recovery of planes, Task Force 58 shaped course toward the scene of the twilight air battle, proceeding at 16 knots through the night and the next day along the path of the returning flyers. By this means destroyers and float planes rescued all but 49 of the aviators who had participated in the battle of 20 June. Overall American losses, from all causes, in the two-day battle were 130 aircraft and 76 flyers.

Admiral Mitscher's official report of the Battle of the Philippine Sea ended on a bitter note: "The enemy had escaped. He had been badly hurt by one aggressive carrier air strike, at the one time when he was within range. His fleet was not sunk." Aviators at Pearl Harbor were convinced that Spruance had ignored the greatest opportunity of the war. "This," they said, "is what comes of placing non-aviators in command over aviators." They scoffed at the possibility of a segment of the Japanese fleet getting undetected between Task Force 58 and the beachhead. Even if it got there, it would have found seven old battleships, three cruisers, and five destroyers on guard. These vessels would have defeated the segment, said the aviators, or at least damaged it enough for Task Force 58 to overtake and destroy it.

On the other hand, had Mitscher closed with the enemy, he would have had to divide his planes—some for attack and some for defense—thus making his own carriers more vulnerable, and his attacking planes might have suffered catastrophic losses over the Japanese Van Force. The limitations imposed by Spruance may have prevented Mitscher's aviators from sinking more Japanese carriers, but they enabled them to kill more Japanese flyers, and lack of trained flyers, more than anything else, hurt the Japanese in the ensuing campaigns. Both King and Nimitz always insisted that Spruance acted correctly.

Conquest of the Southern Marianas

Mountainous, 14-mile-long Saipan could not be bombarded into impotence as the flat islets of Kwajalein Atoll had been. Despite two days of prelanding naval bombardment, the 20,000 marines put ashore on 15 June had by nightfall penetrated only halfway to the D-day objective line, and more than 10 percent had been killed or wounded. The following day Admiral Turner ordered ashore his reserve, the 27th Infantry Division. By 17 June, the American offensive had overcome fierce Japanese resistance and had begun to roll.

It was unfortunate but possibly unavoidable that the 27th Division, which had demonstrated its laggardness and poor training at Makin and again at Eniwetok, should have been assigned to operate with marines. Worse, on the 19th, when the two marine divisions pivoted for a drive to the north, Holland Smith ordered the 27th Division to the center of the new front—the rugged spine of the island, where the terrain was most difficult. Predictably, the soldiers began falling behind, exposing the inner flanks of the marine divisions on each side. Holland Smith, thereupon, with the concurrence of Spruance and Turner, summarily relieved the 27th Division commander, Major General Ralph C. Smith.

General Richardson, who from the beginning had taken an exceedingly dim view of marines commanding soldiers, went storming out to Saipan, where he reviewed the 27th Division and awarded decorations. He then proceeded to upbraid Holland Smith and Turner. "Howlin' Mad" incredibly managed to hold his tongue, but "Terrible Turner" blasted back. When Richardson complained hotly to Spruance, the latter tried to make light of the situation. "That's just Kelly Turner's way," he assured Richardson, "and no one takes him seriously." Admiral Nimitz tried to sit on the story, but too many people knew about it. The media got the facts, took sides, and—to the acute distress of Nimitz and other senior officers—fought out the Smith v. Smith controversy in public.

The capture of Saipan cost 16,500 American casualties, including 3,400 killed. The subsequent conquests of Tinian and Guam were much less costly, partly because these islands were lightly garrisoned compared to Saipan, but chiefly because they received more sustained and more systematic bombardment. Guam, the biggest island, received 13 days of naval gunfire. The landing force here was the new III Amphibious Corps, commanded by Major General Roy S. Geiger, USMC. Included were the 3rd Marine Division and the 77th Infantry Division. In their recapture of Guam, they demonstrated that soldiers and marines could fight effectively shoulder to shoulder under marine command.

The conquest of the Southern Marianas cost more than 5,000 American and nearly 50,000 Japanese lives, not counting several thousand Japanese civilian residents on Saipan who committed suicide rather than fall into the hands of the "barbarous Americans." Japan had lost her direct staging line to the Carolines. The United States had acquired logistic bases for further conquests westward and northward, submarine bases for stepping up attacks on Japanese communications with the Southern Resources Area, and air bases from which B-29s could blast the industrial concentration in and about Tokyo.

The loss of the Southern Marianas was the beginning of the end for Japan, and informed Japanese officials knew it. The Tojo government fell and was succeeded by a cabinet to whom the emperor made known his desire for early peace negotiations. Yet so binding was the Japanese military code, so rigid were the demands of Oriental "face," that for a whole year no official in Japan could bring himself to initiate steps for ending hostilities.

The Change of Command

While the Spruance–Turner–Smith–Mitscher team was busy conquering the Marianas, Nimitz ordered Halsey up from the South Pacific to make plans for supporting MacArthur in his forthcoming invasion of the Philippines, scheduled for 15 November 1944. In the new operations Halsey and his subordinates would relieve the Spruance team, whereupon the Fifth Fleet would be redesignated Third Fleet, and the Fast Carrier Force would change its title from Task Force 58 to Task Force 38. Admiral Mitscher would remain in command of the Fast Carrier Force, at least through the initial Philippines invasion, for the simple reason that there was nobody else Admiral Nimitz was yet ready to trust to carry out so crucial a mission, particularly since it might result in another battle at sea. The Spruance team, after taking stateside leave, would set to work planning invasions of Iwo Jima and Okinawa, which they would conduct after the recapture of the Philippines. This double-echelon system, unique in the history of warfare, was counted on to speed up the war. It was feasible only because the Pacific theater enjoyed a surplus of skillful commanders.

Chapter 29
Submarines in the Pacific War

The Pacific Ocean phase of World War II opened with an antisubmarine operation. About an hour before Admiral Nagumo's planes appeared over Oahu, the U. S. destroyer *Ward* detected a Japanese midget submarine near the entrance to Pearl Harbor. The *Ward* attacked the midget, sank it, and reported the encounter—but the message did not reach Admiral Kimmel. The midget was one of five that had been piggybacked into the area by larger Japanese submarines to supplement the attack of their carrier planes. None of the five returned to its mother boat.

After the Pearl Harbor raid, only U. S. submarines were immediately available to carry the war to Japan. As soon as Washington learned of the attack, the Chief of Naval Operations, in a sharp break with U. S. traditions, ordered unrestricted submarine warfare against the Island Empire. The little-publicized, unremitting campaign of attrition by the "dolphin navy" was for many months dogged by bad luck and faulty equipment, but at length, by cutting Japan's logistic lines and thus virtually starving her into submission, the submarines made a major contribution to U. S. victory in the Pacific.

United States submarines in the Pacific theater at the outbreak of war were divided between the Pacific Fleet Submarine Force, at Pearl Harbor, and the Asiatic Fleet Submarine Force, based at Cavite in Manila Bay. Included were small, numbered S-class boats, with a relatively short cruising radius, and the much more battleworthy fleet boats, named after fish and other marine creatures. The *Gato*, prototype of the more modern fleet boats, was 312 feet long, with a cruising radius of 12,000 miles. She carried 24 torpedoes and had ten tubes—six forward and four aft. A 3-inch gun and light automatic weapons completed her armament. This was the type of submarine that took the war to Japan. As more of these fleet boats became available, the S-class were withdrawn from combat service. At the outbreak of war, the Pacific Fleet had 21 fleet boats, but more than half were in the United States undergoing repair, modernization, or shakedown. The Asiatic Fleet had 23 fleet-type submarines and 6 S-boats. There were also 13 Netherlands submarines in the Far East.

The Japanese initially had 60 submarines: 46 I-class and 14 RO-class. The I-class were big submarines; the RO-class, medium; the HA-class, developed later in the war, small. In addition, as noted, Japan used some midget submarines. The Japanese torpedo was at first more dependable than the American, with greater speed, longer range, and a more powerful warhead. Oxygen-driven, it was an adaptation of the surface-carried Long Lance, cut down from 24 to 21 inches in diameter to fit Japanese submarine tubes. The Japanese had inefficient sound gear, however, and their submarines lacked radar until late in the war.

The Japanese boats were in general not used in the submarine's most effective role—as commerce raiders. Their captains' conception of the warrior role led them to favor military targets. While American submarines were wearing down Japan's fighting potential by unremitting attacks on her cargo ships, the Japanese disregarded the vulnerable tankers and freighters on which the Allied fleets depended and went after the usually well-screened warships.

Early U. S. Submarine Operations

The first Pacific Fleet submarine to go on war patrol was the *Gudgeon*, which departed Pearl Harbor on 11 December 1941, followed in the next few days by the *Pollack* and the *Plunger*. Arriving off Japan in early January, the *Pollack* sank two enemy freighters; the *Plunger*, one. The *Gudgeon* achieved no sinkings on patrol station but had better luck while en route back home, because the Japanese submarines, like the German, had the risky habit of breaking radio silence.

The Japanese talkativeness enabled Rochefort's Combat Intelligence Unit at Pearl Harbor to track enemy submarines by radio direction-finding and warn U. S. and Allied cargo vessels out of their path. In late January the unit was tracking *I-173*, which helped the trackers to spot its position by shelling Midway while passing. The Combat Unit noted that *I-173* and the homeward-bound *Gudgeon* were almost on a collision course and passed the word to the American submarine. The

Gudgeon submerged and waited. Presently, on schedule, along came *I-173*, on the surface, hatches open, men smoking and sunbathing on deck. The *Gudgeon* fired three torpedoes into her and she went down fast—the first combatant vessel ever sunk by an American submarine.

When Japanese bombers on 10 December 1941 attacked the Cavite naval base on Manila Bay, most of the Asiatic Fleet submarines saved themselves by submerging, but the *Sealion*, moored at a pier, took two direct hits and was out of the war. Most of the surface ships in the Philippines retreated to Java, but the submarines and the old tender *Canopus* remained behind under the command of Captain John Wilkes.

In a futile effort to thwart the impending Japanese invasion of the Philippines, Wilkes stationed his 28 remaining boats in a defensive cordon around Luzon. These craft made 31 determined attacks, firing 66 torpedoes at warships, transports, and cargo vessels bringing the enemy landing force, but succeeded in sinking only three freighters.

When MacArthur abandoned Manila on Christmas Day 1941, the submarines were left without a base and were fast running out of fuel. By the end of December, all had retired to Surabaya, major port of Java. With them went Wilkes, Admiral Thomas C. Hart, commander in chief of the Asiatic Fleet, and their staffs.

Thereafter, while continuing their patrol missions, the submarines began a series of runs to Bataan and Corregidor, delivering food, medical stores, and ammunition to the defenders and bringing out submarine parts, torpedoes, valuables, and key personnel. The *Trout*, requesting 25 tons of ballast to replace cargo brought in, received 2 tons of gold bars, 18 tons of sacked silver coins, and 5 tons of U. S. mail and negotiable securities. On her way back to base, the *Trout*, not allowing her cargo to interfere with essentials, torpedoed a freighter and a submarine chaser. Among the persons evacuated were Philippine President Manuel Quezon and Vice President Sergio Osmeña, army and naval aviators, and, not least important, the codebreakers. These cryptanalysts, if left behind and captured, might have been forced to reveal their important secrets. Last of the submarines to call at Corregidor was the *Spearfish*, which on the night of 3 May brought away 12 officers, 12 army nurses, an army wife, and 17 footlockers full of financial and other records. Some 48 hours later Major General Jonathan Wainwright, MacArthur's replacement in the Philippines, was obliged to surrender his forces.

The second military objective assigned to the Asiatic Fleet submarines was defense of the Malay Barrier, the line of islands running from Sumatra through Java to Timor. In carrying out this task they were no more successful than in their defense of Luzon. Between January and the end of March 1942, they sank eight ships, including a destroyer, but failed to slow the Japanese advance. In the same period three of the U. S. submarines were lost.

With the defeat of the ABDA naval force in the Battle of the Java Sea, Surabaya became untenable. Captain Wilkes moved his headquarters and base to Fremantle, Australia. Awarded the Distinguished Service Medal, in May he was duly rotated back to the States. His replacement was Rear Admiral Charles A. Lockwood, who reorganized the Asiatic Fleet submarines into the Southwest Pacific Submarine Force, with a subsidiary base at Brisbane.

In early June, Admiral Nimitz, anticipating the Battle of Midway, assigned 19 submarines to backstop the defending carrier forces by covering the approaches to the atoll. They accomplished little. The *Nautilus* hit the carrier *Kaga* with a dud torpedo and thought she had sunk the *Soryu*. That night the heavy cruisers *Mogami* and *Mikuma* collided while maneuvering to avoid the U. S. submarine *Tambor*. Crippled and slowed, the *Mikuma* later became the victim of American carrier planes.

Thus the early performance of the American submarines fell far short of what had been expected. They had entered the war hampered not only by an undependable torpedo but also by a faulty doctrine. The U. S. peacetime doctrine, anticipating attacks on warships only and overestimating the submarine's vulnerability, imposed excessive caution. The effect was aggravated by overcautiousness of some of the initial submarine skippers, men who had to be replaced by hotspurs ready and willing to take the risks that are a necessary part of submarine warfare. Out went the unproductive early practice of making underwater sonar-guided attacks, as well as use of brief and infrequent periscope observations in daylight submerged attacks. Bolder tactics developed, made practical by the reliable torpedo data computer, which the U. S. submarines already possessed, and by radar, which they were rapidly acquiring.

In mid-August 1942, two companies of U. S. marines raided Makin Atoll in the Gilberts, hoping thereby to divert Japanese forces away from supporting their fellow countrymen in the struggle for Guadalcanal. The marines were transported to the target and brought away on board the *Nautilus* and the *Argonaut*, two of America's largest and slowest submarines. The operation boosted American morale, but from the strategic point of view it was a failure. The Japanese were not diverted from Guadalcanal, and they began to build up formidable defenses in the Gilberts, especially on Tarawa, which were to cost many American lives little more than a year later.

Over his distant subsidiary base at Brisbane, Admiral Lockwood had only administrative control. Operational control of the 11 antique S-boats based on Brisbane was exercised by Captain Ralph W. Christie. At the time of the American invasion of Guadalcanal, Christie sent his boats to cover the approaches to the Japanese bases in the Bismarcks and the upper Solomons. His strategy paid prompt dividends. On the morning of 10 August 1942, several of the cruisers that had wreaked havoc on the Allied invasion forces two nights before in the Battle of Savo Island were returning in triumph to Kavieng. Submarine S-44, patrolling the area, fired four torpedoes into one of the victors, the heavy cruiser *Kako*. Her boilers exploded and she went down in five minutes. A lowly, 17-year-old S-boat had thus bagged the first major combatant ship to be sunk by an American submarine.

The U. S. submarines kept well clear of the operating area and thus minimized the risk that American boats might be attacked by their own surface forces.[1] One exception to this practice occurred when, during the desperate days of October 1942 on Guadalcanal, the *Amberjack* delivered a load of aviation gasoline to Tulagi, the only instance during the war when an American submarine was used as a tanker.

The most famous story of this period concerns the *Growler*, patrolling near the Bismarcks one dark night in February 1943. Her target, a 900-ton Japanese provision ship, rushed at her. The command "Left full rudder!" came too late for the *Growler* to avoid collision; she plowed into the ship at 17 knots. The Japanese vessel sprayed the *Growler*'s bridge with machine-gun bullets, killing several men and severely wounding the captain, Commander Howard W. Gilmore. Gilmore nevertheless made his voice heard: "Clear the bridge!" The four living men scrambled through the hatch.

---

[1]This was an important consideration, because air and surface forces were inclined to shoot first and ask questions afterward. As a result of failure or misunderstanding of recognition signals, at least 28 U. S. submarines were bombed or strafed by American aircraft. Five others were shelled by U. S. surface craft. The *Dorado* and the *Seawolf* were sunk with all hands by "friendly" forces. Nine other submarines were damaged.

Unable to follow, Commander Gilmore gave his last command: "Take her down!" For this "distinguished gallantry and valor" he was posthumously awarded the Medal of Honor.

In January 1943 Rear Admiral Robert English, Commander Submarines Pacific, under Nimitz, was killed in a plane crash. Admiral Lockwood was transferred to Pearl Harbor to take over English's command, and Ralph Christie, promoted to rear admiral, assumed the Fremantle post. Captain James Fife relieved Christie at Brisbane.

Lockwood immediately set about establishing a submarine base nearer than Pearl Harbor to the submarine patrol areas. He chose Midway Island, which he equipped with tenders and a minimum shore installation. This change aroused an outcry from the submariners, who complained that there was nothing at Midway "but sand and gooney birds." Lockwood agreed that the submariners had a point. He arranged schedules so that the boats returned regularly to Pearl Harbor for rest and relaxation, and he took over the Royal Hawaiian Hotel in Honolulu for their exclusive use as a de luxe rest camp.

Japanese Submarines versus American Warships

A Japanese submarine, patrolling north of Singapore on 9 December 1941, reported the presence of the British *Prince of Wales* and *Repulse*, thus setting them up for destruction by naval planes based on Saigon. A month later *I-6* fired a torpedo into the U. S. carrier *Saratoga*, putting her out of the war for five months, just long enough for her to miss the Battle of Midway.

In the Battle of Midway Japanese use of submarines in support of fleet operations is well exemplified. Boats were sent out individually or positioned in cordons to scout and intercept American fleet movements. The two cordons between Pearl Harbor and Midway arrived on station too late to observe or intercept the American carriers. The only Japanese submarine that achieved any positive results in this battle was *I-168*, which sank the damaged *Yorktown* and a destroyer.

During the Guadalcanal campaign, Japanese submarines were a major menace to U. S. naval forces. At the end of August 1942, the *Saratoga*, while patrolling the southeast approaches to Guadalcanal, was again torpedoed, this time by *I-26*, and was once more out of the war, for three crucial months. In mid-September, in the same general area, *I-15* and *I-19* intercepted an American convoy of six well-escorted transports coming up from Espiritu Santo with reinforcements. Typically, the Japanese submarines disregarded the transports and went after the escorts. *I-19* fired three torpedoes into the *Wasp*, which blazed up fatally and had to be abandoned and sunk. *I-15* fired at the *Hornet* and missed, but put a torpedo into the *North Carolina* and another into the destroyer *O'Brien*. The battleship, though severely damaged, survived, but the *O'Brien* sank before she could reach drydock. In the remainder of the whole Solomons campaign, the Japanese force sank only two more American warships, the destroyer *Porter* during the Battle of the Santa Cruz Islands in late October 1942, and the light cruiser *Juneau* following the night cruiser action the next month. On the other hand, during 1942 the Japanese lost 23 submarines, 2 being sunk by U. S. submarines.

In 1943 the Japanese submarines sank three important U. S. naval vessels: the destroyer *Henley*, the submarine *Corvina*, and the escort carrier *Liscome Bay*. The *Liscome Bay*, sunk 16 November in the Gilberts, was the last warship to be destroyed by the Japanese submarines until July 1945, when *I-58* sank the heavy cruiser *Indianapolis* just two weeks before the end of the war.

In late 1943 the U. S. submarines, having at last obtained a dependable torpedo, were just beginning their war against enemy warships.

Correcting the Deficiencies of the U. S. Submarine Torpedo

Because navies between the world wars had anticipated that in future conflicts they would send submarines against warships only, and since major warships carried heavy side armor, it was assumed that a torpedo exploding beneath the hull would be far more effective than one striking the side of a ship. Hence the British, the Germans, and the Americans developed magnetic exploders that were supposed to detonate warheads under enemy vessels. In practice, they often failed. For that matter, the American impact detonators also often failed.

The defects in the American detonators would have been discovered long before the war, had sufficient funds been available for testing. But in the 1930s, when each torpedo cost about $10,000, the Newport Torpedo Station was operating on a tight budget. Hence tests were made with practice warheads that were not expected to detonate. The trials thus tested nothing but the gyro steering mechanism and the steam propulsion units.

The U. S. Mark 6 exploder was activated by a sharp change in the earth's magnetic field in the vicinity of a steel hull. The exploder was supposed to operate when the torpedo was ten feet or less beneath the ship, but many torpedoes failed to explode when set properly for depth and when passing directly under the target. Reports such as that of the *Sargo*, which suffered 13 misses out of 13 easy shots, caused Admiral Lockwood, while still ComSubSoWesPac, to conduct a series of tests. Shots fired through a submerged fishnet ran an average of 11 feet deeper than set. The Bureau of Ordnance finally conceded that torpedoes with armed warheads, replacing the lighter practice heads, did indeed run deeper than set.

When the error was corrected, and the torpedoes ran nearer the surface, the magnetic exploders tended to activate as soon as they entered the target's horizontal magnetic field. The result was a string of premature explosions. The submarine captains, observing these explosions through their periscopes, were often deceived into believing they were making hits. But evidence was piling up that the Mark 6 was a failure at any depth. Admiral Christie, who had helped to develop it, refused to accept the evidence; his Southwest Pacific submarines continued for some time using the Mark 6 intact. But Admiral Lockwood, now ComSubPac, in late June 1943 at last ordered the magnetic component inactivated. Henceforth his submariners would rely on the simpler contact exploder.

It was high time. The United States had been in the war a year and a half. The British and the Germans had pinpointed the flaws in their magnetic exploders in the early days of the war and had promptly ceased using them.

American submariners, with the magnetic exploder deactivated, now fired torpedoes directly at their targets, expecting explosion on contact. The numbers of prematures declined, but duds sharply increased. The Bureau of Ordnance put the blame on the submarine commanders, who manned the periscopes and called out data for aiming the torpedoes. Crews lost faith in their captains, and some of the latter, embarrassed and discouraged, applied for transfer to other duty.

Not Lieutenant Commander Lawrence Daspit, captain of the *Tinosa*. He stopped a huge whale factory with two torpedoes fired into her stern at long range from an unfavorable track angle. He then brought the *Tinosa* around to an ideal firing position on the ship's beam. He next, deliberately and in single shots, fired nine carefully checked and aimed torpedoes at her. Nine hit and nine failed to explode. Wrathfully Daspit took his one remaining torpedo back to Pearl Harbor and demanded that it be examined.

Lockwood again ordered tests. When the testers managed to recover a dud that they had fired underwater against a Hawaiian cliff, they found the trouble in the firing-pin assembly. "The war head," wrote Lockwood, "was crushed in at the forward end and, when we got the exploder mechanism out of it, we found the firing pin had actually traveled up its badly bent guides and hit the fulminate caps, but not hard enough to set them off." On a glancing blow, however, the pin usually functioned. These findings explained the *Tinosa's* experience. Installing stronger firing-pin assemblies of the toughest steel and lightening the firing pin solved the problem. With U. S. participation in the war nearly half over, American submarines at last had a reliable weapon.

Soon after the steam torpedo was brought to satisfactory performance, the Mark 18 electric torpedo began to appear. It brought problems of its own. Late in 1944, for instance, the *Tang* was sunk by her own circling Mark 18. But the submariners were now alert for such problems, and most of them were dealt with effectively. The low speed of the Mark 18 (28 knots v. 45 for the Mark 14 steam torpedo) delayed acceptance of the electric torpedo, but in the minds of submarine officers its wakeless feature came to offset its slowness. Eventually most U. S. submarines used electric torpedoes.

Across the Pacific

At the time of the U. S. invasion of the Gilbert Islands in November 1943, the Americans assumed that any Japanese surface opposition would emanate from Truk and refuel in the Marshalls. Lockwood stationed his submarines accordingly. As we have seen, the Combined Fleet was in no condition to counterattack. It remained at Truk. The lurking U. S. submarines sank only a supply ship and a tanker.

Two of the American submarines were lost to enemy action. One was the *Corvina*, already mentioned; the other was the *Sculpin*. On 19 November, the *Sculpin*, between Truk and the Marshalls, was detected while closing on an enemy convoy. A depth-charge attack from the convoy escorts inflicted so much damage that she had to surface. Her crew fought her deck guns as long as they could and then scuttled her. Thirteen officers and men rode the *Sculpin* down, among them Captain John P. Cromwell, whom Admiral Lockwood had sent to take command of a wolf pack, should one be formed. Because Cromwell possessed important information about war plans, he had elected to go

down lest the Japanese extract his information through torture or truth serums. For his decision he was posthumously awarded the Medal of Honor.

The survivors of the *Sculpin's* crew were taken to Truk and there transferred to the escort carriers *Unyo* and *Chuyo* for transportation to Japan. On 3 December, in typhoon weather, the U. S. submarine *Sailfish* made a skillful approach and sank the *Chuyo*. Twenty *Sculpin* survivors went down with her.

So long as the Combined Fleet refrained from contesting the American advance, U. S. submarines in fleet-related operations made only limited contributions. Thus, during the first part of 1944, most of the important sinkings of enemy ships were achieved by independently operating boats. In June, however, when the Japanese elected to counterattack, the American submarines played really major roles in the Marianas campaign and the Battle of the Philippine Sea. Before the invasion of Saipan, Admiral Lockwood and Admiral Christie positioned their submarines in accordance with the request of Admiral Spruance. Three boats scouted the Tawitawi area as the Japanese fleet assembled there. Others operated off the principal Philippine Straits through which it was likely to pass to reach Saipan. Four patrolled the Philippine Sea off the Marianas, each boat's activities being centered on one corner of an imaginary 60-mile square. Others were in motion, relieving patrollers or returning to base after being relieved; two of these transients played major roles in the development of the battle. There was also on routine patrol a wolf pack called Blair's Blasters after group commander Captain L. N. Blair. The boats off Tawitawi and the straits were Christie's Fremantle craft; the others were Lockwood's from Pearl Harbor.

On 31 May 1944, the submarine *Silversides* informed Blair's Blasters, patrolling nearby, that a convoy was coming their way, apparently heading from Japan to Saipan. By the time the *Silversides* and the wolf pack had joined forces, two more convoys had appeared in the area. Early on 1 June the *Pintado*, of the Blasters, had picked off a freighter from the first convoy. The *Shark*, also of the wolf pack, sank a cargo ship late on 2 June and another on the morning of 4 June. On the evening of the 5th she got two more, one a 7,000-ton transport. That same night the *Pintado* sank two ships. As a result of these sinkings, half a division of Japanese reinforcement troops were drowned, many other soldiers reached the Marianas without guns or battle gear, and the commander on Saipan had to ration munitions. Blair's Blasters had thus greatly lessened the opposition the American assault troops would have to overcome in the forth-coming invasion.

In three days in early June the submarine *Harder*, under Commander Samuel D. Dealey, set a remarkable record, sinking three destroyers and damaging at least two more in the vicinity of Tawi-tawi. On the morning of 10 June, as she was patrol-ling in the Sulu Sea off Tawitawi, she witnessed the sortie of Admiral Ugaki's battleship force for the relief of Biak and radioed a timely warning to Allied commands.

When the Japanese naval commander in chief, Admiral Toyoda, suspended the Biak operation and ordered the two segments of the Mobile Fleet to rendezvous in the Philippine Sea, Christie's and Lockwood's careful positioning of their submarines began to pay off. On 13 June the submarine *Redfin* saw the carrier force, under Admiral Ozawa, sortie from Tawitawi and flashed a warning. In the early evening of the 15th, the submarines *Flying Fish* and *Seahorse* sighted the two segments of the Mobile Fleet 300 miles apart in the Philippine Sea. Early on the 17th, the *Cavalla* made contact with a tanker convoy, and Admiral Lockwood ordered her to follow, on the chance that the tankers would lead her to the Japanese combat vessels. The *Cavalla* lost the tankers, but that evening she sighted the Mobile Fleet, now united and heading for the Marianas. Unfortunately visibility was so poor that the *Cavalla* could not assure Admiral Spruance that she had seen the entire Mobile Fleet.

As a result of these sightings, Spruance post-poned the invasion of Guam and prepared for the Battle of the Philippine Sea, and Lockwood shifted his four "square" submarines 250 miles southwest-ward. Now that the approximate location of the Japanese fleet was known, Lockwood gave his sub-marines permission to shoot first and transmit con-tact reports afterward. Thus it was that the *Alba-core*, assigned to the southwest corner of the new square (which Lockwood called his "invisible trap"), found herself at the right place at the right time to sink the carrier *Taiho*. Three hours later the ubiquitous *Cavalla* put three torpedoes into the carrier *Shokaku* and sent her down.

In contrast to the precision with which Christie and Lockwood stationed their submarines for the Marianas campaign, the Japanese had theirs all in the wrong place. MacArthur's landing on Biak had led them to expect that the next Fifth Fleet opera-tions would be against the Palaus instead of the Marianas, for it was the Palaus that Spruance had hit in support of MacArthur's invasion of Hollandia. Hence the Japanese sent submarines to operate north of the Admiralties, their version of the "in-visible trap." In setting up their screen they not

only selected the wrong area but also failed to allow for improvements in American submarine warfare. By mid-1944 the war in the Atlantic against the U-boat had been won, and escorting vessels were bringing the weapons and experience of the Battle of the Atlantic to the Pacific. Of some 25 I-boats and RO-boats operating in connection with the Marianas campaign, 17 were sent to the bottom by American destroyers, destroyer escorts, and air-craft. The U. S. destroyer escort *England* alone, in the last two weeks of May, achieved six kills.

The Japanese submarine command, recogniz-ing its growing ineffectiveness, followed the exam-ple of the Japanese airmen in initiating suicide operations. The undersea counterpart of the kami-kaze was the kaiten, a one-man midget submarine, or "human torpedo," piggybacked to the attack area by a conventional submarine. The operator then entered the midget and steered it to the target, where he detonated the warhead, blowing up the midget, himself, and, he hoped, the target vessel. The kaiten certainly had enough power. The final model, 54 feet long, carried a warhead containing 3,000 pounds of high explosive, six times the weight of the explosive in the U. S. Mark 14 torpedo. As in the kamikaze program, there was no lack of young would-be suicides eager to serve in the kaitens. Nearly 900 sacrificed their lives in the program, but the only confirmed victim was an oiler loaded with 400,000 gallons of aviation gaso-line, sunk at her berth in Ulithi lagoon in Novem-ber 1944.

The American drive across the Pacific bypassed scores of Japanese-occupied islands in the Solo-mons, the Bismarcks, the Gilberts, the Marshalls, and the Carolines. To supply these isolated garri-sons, the Japanese navy began at the insistence of the army to use its submarines as cargo carriers. Some of the new HA-class, designed specifically to carry cargo, were built without torpedo tubes. The army, dissatisfied with the navy's efforts, be-gan building and manning its own cargo-carrying submarines. As the Allied forces operated at ever-increasing distances from their continental bases, the effectiveness of the Japanese submarines, pressed into unsuitable service, steadily declined. Seldom in the history of warfare has a primary weapon been used with less grasp of its true poten-tial.

American Submarines versus Japanese Warships

We have seen how the submarines *Cavalla* and *Albacore* contributed mightily to the American vic-tory in the Battle of the Philippine Sea by sinking the big carriers *Shokaku* and *Taiho*. In the great Battle for Leyte Gulf (24–25 October 1944), described in the next chapter, submarines gave the first warning of the approach of the Japanese fleet and struck both opening and closing blows, sinking two heavy cruisers and one light cruiser and putting two heavy cruisers out of action.

In 1944 alone, U. S. submarines sank a battleship, 7 aircraft carriers, 2 heavy cruisers, 8 light cruisers, 31 destroyers, and 7 submarines. They also severely damaged a carrier and 4 heavy cruisers. Many of the successes, particularly against large warships, were achieved by submarines operating independently of the surface fleet. Most noteworthy were the sinkings of the battleship *Kongo* and the carrier *Shinano*.

The 31,000-ton *Kongo*, which went down in November 1944, was the only battleship sunk by an American submarine. On the 21st, Commander Eli T. Reich's *Sealion II* encountered her victim 40 miles north of Formosa. It was just past midnight, with the sky overcast but the visibility fair. Identifying the contact as comprising at least two battleships, two cruisers, and several destroyers heading for Japan, Reich elected to make a surface approach, using radar. By the time he gained the desired attack position and made visual contact with the enemy, the sea was rising, whipped by a night wind. At 0256 Reich fired six bow torpedoes at the leading battleship, at a range of 3,000 yards. Throwing the rudder hard right, he brought his stern tubes to bear on the second battleship and at 0259 got away three more torpedoes. Then he took the *Sealion* away at flank speed. To his great disappointment, the enemy force continued on course at 18 knots, apparently unimpaired. The *Sealion* gave chase, taking water over the bridge and a good deal down the conning tower hatch. At 0450 the battleship at which the bow tubes had been fired slowed to 12 knots and dropped astern of the task force with two destroyers standing by. Shortly afterward this ship, the veteran *Kongo*, went dead in the water. As the *Sealion* maneuvered into attack position, a blinding flash lit up the night, followed by an ear-splitting thunderclap. Evidently the *Kongo*'s magazines had exploded. She went down fast.

The *Sealion*, again in almost total darkness, set out in pursuit of the other battleship but was unable to overtake her in the now heavy seas. Only after the war did the submarine's crew learn that one of her stern-tube torpedoes fired at 0259, missing its intended battleship target, had sunk a destroyer.

The *Sealion*'s achievement was overshadowed a week later when the *Archerfish*, under Commander Joseph F. Enright, sank the *Shinano*, of 62,000 tons displacement, one of the largest warships in the world. Begun as a sister ship to the superbattleships *Yamato* and *Musashi*, she was converted into an aircraft carrier, commissioned 18 November 1944, and sunk ten days later. When the *Archerfish* found her 150 miles south of Tokyo, she was on her way from Tokyo Bay to the Inland Sea for fitting out in comparative safety from the B-29 raids then beginning against Japanese cities.

The submarine made radar contact with the carrier and her four escorts at 2048. There ensued a stern chase, which the *Archerfish* would inevitably have lost had the target not zigzagged. At 0300 a radical change in the *Shinano*'s base course put the submarine ahead of her, and a zig at 0316 made the *Archerfish*'s position perfect except for a rather large gyro angle. At 0317, with range at 1,400 yards, Enright fired four bow and two stern torpedoes, all of which probably hit.

The *Shinano* might not have sunk had the crew not been inexperienced and the ship unready for sea. Doors that should have been watertight had no gaskets; water leaked freely around them and out of unsealed conduits. Steam pumps had not yet been installed, and piping was incomplete—and there were too few hand pumps. When the morale of the crew failed and discipline broke down, loss of the ship was inevitable. At 1018 her captain ordered abandon ship, and half an hour later the *Shinano* went down, taking the captain and 500 of his ship's company.

The Lifeguard League

While the U. S. fleet boats were decimating the Japanese navy, they were simultaneously performing a lifesaving mission. When planning was in progress for the Gilbert Islands invasion, Admiral Lockwood adopted a suggestion that submarines might well be employed to rescue downed flyers. Thus was born the Lifeguard League, which before the end of the war rescued 504 airmen.

Submarines were stationed in appropriate locations, and airmen were briefed accordingly. The pilot of a crippled plane would set it down as near a submarine as possible, and he and his crew would take refuge on board. Lifeguarders performed notable service also for army flyers, especially crews of B-29s shot down while engaged in operations against Japan from bases in the Marianas.

The rescues were by no means always easy or free of danger. The *Harder*, for example, rescued a downed fighter pilot from a tiny island in the Carolines under trying circumstances. After her commanding officer, Commander Dealey, had taken his boat into the shoals as far as he dared, three of his crew went ashore on a rubber raft in the face of enemy sniper fire and brought the flyer out. Probably the most dramatic story is that of the *Stingray*, under Lieutenant Commander Samuel Loomis, which in June 1944 received a report of a downed aviator close to the beach at Guam. When the *Stingray* reached the designated position, she found the pilot on his rubber raft acting as an involuntary target for a Japanese shore battery. Not daring to surface, Loomis raised both periscopes, one for observation, the other for the pilot to tie his raft to, for towing. The pilot failed to grasp what was expected of him, and the *Stingray* made three fruitless approaches in the midst of numerous shell splashes. At last on the fourth try, Loomis ran the periscope into the pilot, and he hung on. When the *Stingray* had towed him well out of range of the guns, she surfaced and took him on board. "We are on speaking terms now," Loomis noted, "but after the third approach I was ready to make him captain of the head."

The Assault on Japanese Merchant Shipping

While Japan's submarines were achieving less and less, American submarines, as we have seen, were sinking increasing numbers of Japanese warships. Even more significant in the outcome of the war was the achievement of American submarines against the cargo ships of Japan, which carried the life blood of her existence. They sank 1,113 merchant vessels of over 500 tons, with an additional 65 "probables," for a total of 5,320,094 gross register tons.

When the American order for unrestricted submarine warfare against enemy shipping was issued a few hours after the Japanese attack on Pearl Harbor, it was a break with tradition for U. S. submarines. After all, the United States had entered World War I in protest against the German use of unrestricted submarine warfare.

Yet the order from Washington was realistic. In modern total war there is no effective distinction between contraband and noncontraband. All the shipping of a country is enrolled in the war effort. The tankers and cargo ships of Japan, bringing in vital oil, rice, tin, rubber, iron, and coal, were as much a part of Japan's war machine as her battleships and aircraft carriers. Japan's shipping problem was complex because, having no industry in her resources areas and no resources in her industrial area, she had to bring all raw materials to

Japan for processing and then distribute the processed materials to the forces in the field. Thus Japan was extraordinarily dependent upon shipping and hence extraordinarily vulnerable to unrestricted submarine warfare.

Until the spring of 1942 Japanese shipping sailed independently and unescorted. Increasing losses then induced Japan to establish limited convoys, consisting of only four or five ships escorted by a single old destroyer or smaller vessel. When in late 1943 the Japanese adopted somewhat larger convoys, the Americans countered with wolf-pack operations. Compared to the North Atlantic convoys, which averaged 70 well-escorted ships, the Japanese convoys were still minuscule; hence American wolf packs seldom comprised more than three submarines, a practice that promoted close-knit cooperation. After some initial attempts at rigid station-keeping, the American skippers made themselves virtuosos of undersea warfare, making kills at all hours, from all depths and angles. The curve of sinkings soared.

The American cryptanalysts broke what they called the "maru code," employed by the marus, the Japanese merchant vessels. The Japanese shipping officials used it to control convoys, assigning them in advance routes, destinations, and daily noon positions. Information from this invaluable source was sent via ComSubPac to U. S. submarines, greatly improving their chances for finding and sinking enemy merchantmen and their escorts.

In November 1944 Lockwood again moved forward, this time to Guam, establishing new headquarters in the tender *Holland*. Submarines fueled at Guam made extended patrols in the Luzon Straits and the East China Sea, sinking so many tankers that nearby beaches became as covered with black oil as those of the U. S. east coast had been in early 1942. They thus at last cut off Japan completely from her Southern Resources Area.

In June 1945 American submarines were able to strike against Japan's other major lifeline, that from the continent, by invading the Sea of Japan itself. Until that time heavy minefields at all entrances to the sea had kept most submarines out. The solution to this problem was a new electronic device, the short-range FM sonar, which could detect mines at a quarter of a mile. In Operation Barney, nine boats penetrated into the Sea, where they sank the submarine *I-122* and 28 merchant ships for a total of 55,000 tons. Eight of the nine boats came home safely.

Chapter 30
The Defeat of Japan

Both Admiral Nimitz's Central Pacific drive and General MacArthur's Southwest Pacific drive were directed toward the China–Luzon–Formosa triangle, with three objectives: (1) to tap the immense reserves of Chinese manpower for use directly against Japan; (2) to blockade Japan by cutting off the flow of vital materials, mainly oil, from the Southern Resources Area to Japan; and (3) to obtain a base suitable for supporting an advance against Japan. Though the Joint Chiefs never entirely abandoned the first of these objectives, it became increasingly clear that the Chinese were not going to break through the Japanese-held coastal areas to join hands with the Allies.

Admiral King questioned the desirability of seizing Luzon, if it had to be reached via a costly drive from south to north through the Philippine Islands. Let MacArthur carry out his scheduled invasion of Mindanao, he suggested, and establish air bases there to reduce enemy air power on Luzon. Then let him join forces with Nimitz's Central Pacific command in an invasion of Formosa, which would provide a base as good as Luzon for blocking Japanese communications with the East Indies, and also be 375 miles nearer Japan.

At the mere suggestion of bypassing Luzon, General MacArthur raised such strong objections that in late July 1944 President Roosevelt joined him and Admiral Nimitz in a conference at Honolulu to consider the question. MacArthur pointed out that thousands of Filipino guerrillas were already harassing the Japanese occupation forces, that nearly the entire Filipino population could be counted on to join the American campaign of liberation, that to bypass and seal off these friendly people and the American prisoners of war on Luzon would expose them to frightful privations and mistreatment at the hands of their Japanese captors, and that for the United States to fail to honor her promise to liberate the Filipinos at the earliest possible moment would be construed in the Orient as a second American abandonment of the Philippines. The president found these arguments convincing, but a final decision had not been reached when the Combined Chiefs of Staff met with

Roosevelt and Churchill at the Second Quebec Conference on 11 September 1944.

Admiral Halsey provided the solution. Just as the Quebec conference met, his flagship, the *New Jersey*, joined the fast carrier force, now called Task Force 38. The next day he ordered an air raid on the central Philippines. The results were startling. At the cost of eight planes, Task Force 38 aviators destroyed about 200 enemy aircraft and sank a dozen freighters. Convinced that the central Philippines were "a hollow shell with weak defenses," Halsey radioed a recommendation that a planned seizure of Yap and the Palaus be abandoned forthwith and that the ground and amphibious forces for these operations be turned over to MacArthur for the invasion of Leyte at the earliest possible date. MacArthur and Nimitz concurring, the Joint Chiefs ordered the Leyte invasion to be carried out on 20 October—two months ahead of schedule. Nimitz directed the Yap invasion force, then at sea, to alter course and report to General MacArthur's headquarters in the Admiralty Islands. He radioed no such order to the Palau-bound forces, believing this archipelago was needed as a staging point for Leyte.

In addition to Yap Island and Peleliu and Angaur islands in the Palaus, the Joint Chiefs had ordered the capture of a number of small positions flanking the approaches to the Philippines. With the change of plan, several of these invasions were canceled. The rest were unopposed or lightly opposed—with the sole exception of Peleliu. Here the Japanese, having learned that naval gunfire rendered defense of the beachhead futile, made no serious attempt to oppose the landing. Instead, the 7,000 elite troops defending Peleliu holed up in the interior, in natural and man-made caves. It took the veteran 1st Marine Division until February of the following year to dig them out, a slow and painful process that cost the Americans 10,000 casualties, including nearly 2,000 killed—a high price indeed for an island that proved of little value. On the other hand, Ulithi Atoll, which the Americans occupied on 23 September without opposition, provided an invaluable anchorage and logistic base for U. S. operations during the last few months of the war.

On Nimitz's orders, the Third Amphibious Force, comprising all the Third Fleet amphibious vessels, reported for temporary duty with the Southwest Pacific forces. They were integrated into Vice Admiral Kinkaid's Seventh Fleet, which thereby became the largest fleet in the world, with more than 700 ships. Between 10 and 15 October, the leading elements of this armada sortied from Manus and from Hollandia and other New Guinea ports and shaped course for Leyte.

Already planes from every Allied airfield within range, including the 20th Bomber Command based in western China, were isolating Leyte by knocking out possible sources of support from west and south. Halsey's floating airfields were blocking support from the north by bombing ships and wharves and attacking airdromes in Okinawa, Formosa, and Luzon.

Torpedo bombers from Japan pounced upon Halsey's fleet and took heavy losses, but they succeeded in putting two U. S. cruisers out of action. The Japanese aviators, elated by this moderate success and confused about what they had achieved, sent home exaggerated reports that set off victory celebrations in Tokyo. Admiral Toyoda, taking the reports at face value, sent out his better-trained squadrons of carrier planes and a force of cruisers and destroyers under Vice Admiral Kiyohide Shima "to mop up remaining enemy elements." Radio Tokyo announced to the world that the American carrier fleet had been just about wiped out and that Japanese ships and aircraft were en route to annihilate the remnant, which was in disorderly flight.

To counter this propaganda, Nimitz released Halsey's report to Pearl Harbor: "The Third Fleet's sunken and damaged ships have been salvaged and are retiring at high speed toward the enemy." Japanese search planes meanwhile had dampened the Japanese celebrations by reporting that the Third Fleet was not noticeably impaired. On receipt of this news, Shima prudently retired to the Ryukyu Islands, southwest of Japan.

The Third Fleet, having wiped out the greater portion of Japanese land-based air power and the only effective part of Japanese carrier air power, proceeded to take station off the Philippines in order to participate in the forthcoming invasion. With support from both the Third and Seventh fleets, the assault, it appeared, was completely safe from outside enemy interference. Yet seeds of trouble were present, because no provision was made for an overall commander at the scene of

action. Halsey was responsible to Nimitz; Kinkaid, to MacArthur. There was no unifying command closer than Washington.

It was clear that the Seventh Fleet, which was escorting the invasion forces to Leyte, was to furnish close support for the assault. But which fleet was to provide cover, that is, fend off hostile naval forces from the beachhead? Nimitz's operation plan directed Halsey to "cover and support forces of the Southwest Pacific," but it also contained a loophole: "In case opportunity for destruction of major portion of the enemy fleet offer or can be created, such destruction becomes the primary task." This clause, inserted so that Halsey would not feel tied to Leyte, as Spruance had felt tied to Saipan, proved, as Samuel Eliot Morison noted, "the tail that wagged the dog."

Within the Third Fleet, too, there was an undesirable command situation. In lending the Third Amphibious Force to the Seventh Fleet, Nimitz had stripped the Third Fleet down to the four task groups of Task Force 38, of which Admiral Mitscher was to remain in command until after the invasion of Leyte. Thus Mitscher and Halsey were commanding the same force, just as Mitscher and Spruance had commanded the same force in the Battle of the Philippine Sea. In the Leyte operation, Mitscher never knew what his authority and responsibilities were because Halsey from time to time bypassed him and assumed direct tactical command of the force.

Since the Japanese fleet had not come out in strength to fight a pitched battle while Task Force 38 was destroying Japanese planes over Formosa, Halsey assumed that it would not come out at all. He began refueling and planned to send his groups one at a time to Ulithi to reprovision, rearm, and rest their crews. In the evening of 22 October, he detached Vice Admiral John S. McCain's Task Group 38.1—an unfortunate choice because McCain's group had more carriers, hence more planes and more punch, than any of the other three groups.

On 17 October U. S. Rangers began landing on islands flanking the entrance to Leyte Gulf. On the 18th Seventh Fleet gunfire-support ships entered the gulf and began a two-day pounding of enemy coast defenses on Leyte. On the morning of the 20th, the Third and Seventh amphibious forces filed into the gulf and began sending troops ashore supported by close-in fire-support groups. The day was clear, the water calm, and there was only a little mortar fire from the shore. The assault on Leyte proved one of the easiest of the war.

In the early afternoon, General MacArthur,

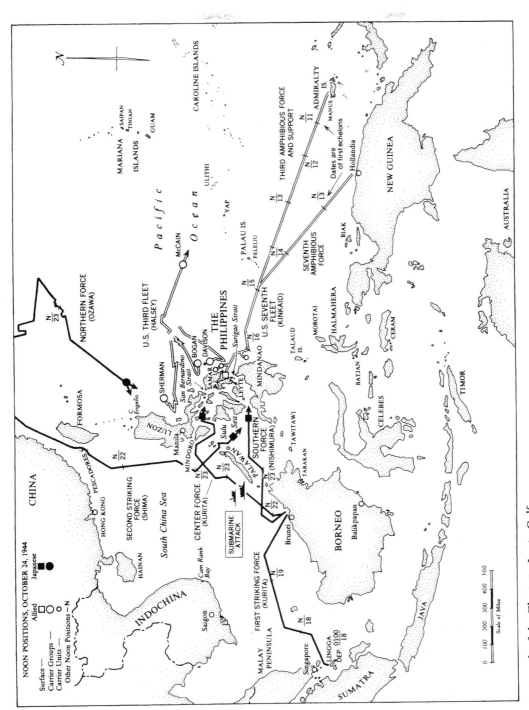

Approach of the Fleets to Leyte Gulf

who had been watching from the light cruiser *Nashville*, climbed down into a landing craft with Sergio Osmeña, who had succeeded to the presidency of the Philippines, and other officials, and headed for the beach. When the craft hit bottom 50 yards from shore, the coxswain dropped the ramp. MacArthur stepped off into knee-deep water and led the way in, taking long strides. He had returned.

The Battle for Leyte Gulf, 24–25 October 1944

When Admiral Toyoda, in Tokyo, received a report on 17 October that troops had landed at the mouth of Leyte Gulf, he promptly ordered execution of SHO-1, the naval defense plan for the Philippines. He had no choice, because his surface fleet was at Lingga Roads near Singapore, close to the source of oil, and his carrier fleet was at home in the Inland Sea, where it could train aviators without much fear of submarine attack. Should the Americans capture the Philippines, the Combined Fleet would be permanently divided.

In ordering SHO-1, Toyoda put into motion forces that triggered the Battle for Leyte Gulf, actually four separate engagements that involved more tonnage and covered a greater area than any other naval battle in history. No battle was ever more closely observed by distant commands. The forces involved did much radio reporting and communicating among themselves. The weather was generally clear with little static. Directly or by relay most of the radio communications were heard in Leyte Gulf, Pearl Harbor, Washington, and Tokyo.

In compliance with Toyoda's order, the surface fleet, under Vice Admiral Takeo Kurita, departed Lingga early on 18 October, entered Brunei Bay two days later to take on fuel, and on 22 October sortied in two segments. Kurita himself, with 5 battleships (including the superbattleships *Yamato* and *Musashi*), 12 cruisers, and 15 destroyers, headed for Leyte Gulf via the South China Sea, the Sibuyan Sea, and San Bernardino Strait. His second-in-command, Vice Admiral Shoji Nishimura, set out across the Sulu Sea with 2 battleships, a cruiser, and 4 destroyers, intending to pass through the Mindanao Sea and Surigao Strait. He and Kurita planned to penetrate Leyte Gulf simultaneously from north and south on the morning of 25 October and clamp pincers on the amphibious shipping off the beachhead. To bring the two arms of the pincer into closer balance, Toyoda ordered Vice Admiral Shima, still in the Ryukyus,

to head south with his 3 cruisers and 4 destroyers and join Nishimura.

To attract Halsey away from the path of this double envelopment, Admiral Ozawa was coming down from the Inland Sea with a carrier force. The Japanese had correctly estimated that Spruance could not be drawn away prematurely from the Saipan beachhead. They now judged that Halsey, whom they appraised as bold, not to say rash, could be lured away from Leyte if tempted with an attractive bait, such as aircraft carriers. Ozawa selected for bait the four most expendable of his ten carriers: the veteran *Zuikaku* and the light carriers *Chitose*, *Chiyoda*, and *Zuiho*. With these vessels and a screen of 2 battleships, 3 cruisers, and 8 destroyers, he headed for the Philippines, convinced that he was on a suicide mission, for the Battle of the Philippine Sea and the recent battle over Formosa had left him no trained pilots for his planes.

The Americans, as they became aware of the enemy units, called Ozawa's decoy fleet the Northern Force; Kurita's ships, the Center Force; and the Nishimura and Shima groups, the Southern Forces.

They learned first of the approach of Kurita's Center Force. In the early hours of 23 October, the American submarines *Darter* and *Dace* sighted it west of Palawan, and the *Darter* radioed a warning. Both submarines then attacked with torpedoes and sank two heavy cruisers, including the flagship, and so disabled another that she had to return to Brunei. Kurita, grimly suspecting that he was about to enter a hornets' nest, shifted his flag to the *Yamato*.

Halsey, on receiving the *Darter's* warning, ordered his three available task groups, commanded by Rear Admirals Gerald F. Bogan, Ralph E. Davison, and Frederick C. Sherman, to move in close to the Philippines. A little past 0800 on the 24th, Task Force 38 scout planes reported the Center Force entering the Sibuyan Sea. Halsey at once directed McCain, then nearing Ulithi, to reverse course and prepare for action. He gave his other three groups their combat orders in one word, "Strike!" These groups launched five successive air attacks against Kurita as his Center Force doggedly plowed across the Sibuyan Sea toward San Bernardino Strait. Four of Kurita's battleships were damaged, and a heavy cruiser was put out of action. The monster *Musashi*, struck repeatedly by torpedoes and bombs, by early afternoon was trailing far astern. The final attack of the day concentrated on the *Musashi*, which at length capsized, carrying down more than a thousand men. Kurita, complaining bitterly about lack of air support, temporarily reversed course and retired out of range of Halsey's planes.

Kurita lacked air support because Japanese air command on Luzon had launched every plane it could muster against Sherman's task group. Most of the Japanese aviators, poorly trained, were shot down, but one hurled into the light carrier *Princeton* a single bomb that started such uncontrollable fires that she had to be abandoned. Ozawa's Northern Force, having reached a position off Cape En-

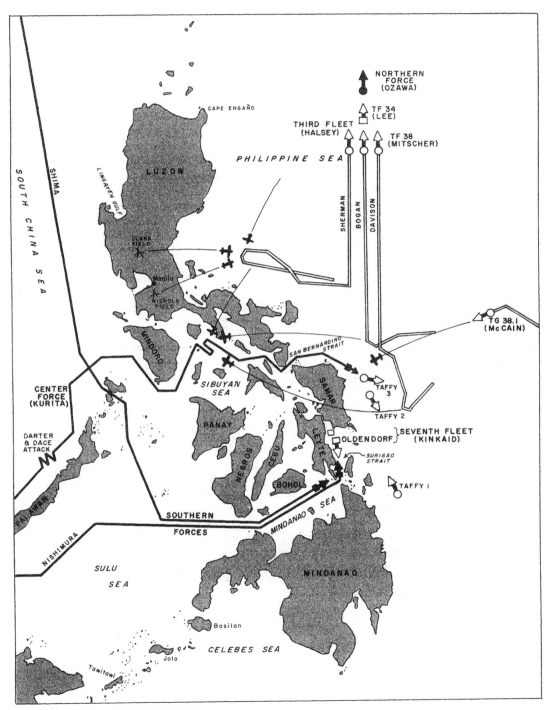

Battle for Leyte Gulf, 23–25 October 1944

gaño, launched 76 planes against Sherman. These aircraft took heavy losses without making a single hit. The survivors, untrained in deck landings, fled to Luzon airfields.

In midafternoon Halsey radioed a battle plan whereby 4 battleships, 6 cruisers, and 14 destroyers from Bogan's and Davison's task groups would be formed as Task Force 34 under Vice Admiral Willis Lee "to engage decisively at long ranges." Admirals Nimitz and Kinkaid read this message with satisfaction. Here was a detached group adequate to deal with the Japanese Center Force. Though they heard no subsequent "execute," they assumed that the execute signal had been sent by short-range voice radio, since Davison's and Bogan's groups were close together, and Halsey's flagship *New Jersey* was in the latter group.

To the north, Ozawa was doing his best to attract Halsey's attention—making smoke, breaking radio silence. But Sherman, in the closest American group, was for a long time too busy launching and warding off air attacks and trying to save the *Princeton* to send scout planes northward. At last in the late afternoon he did so, and the scouts found the Japanese carrier force only 190 miles away. Mitscher, who was in the *Lexington* in Sherman's group, passed the information to Halsey, in Bogan's group. Sherman, anticipating action, sent a cruiser to sink the derelict *Princeton* with torpedoes.

Mitscher's information electrified Halsey. He was sure that in so extensive an operation the Japanese would use their carriers. Now he knew where they were. He strode into flag plot, put his finger on the charted position of the Japanese Northern Force 300 miles away, and said to his chief of staff, "Here's where we're going. . . . Start them north."

Halsey's intention was to approach the enemy under cover of darkness so as to have him well within range of his planes before first light. To Nimitz and Kinkaid he radioed: "Am proceeding north with three groups to attack enemy carrier force at dawn." Both recipients interpreted this dispatch to mean that Halsey was sending three *carrier* groups north, and that he had formed Task Force 34 (which included the *New Jersey*) to remain behind, standing guard over San Bernardino Strait.

So convinced was Halsey that he was doing the right thing that he disregarded reports from night-flying aircraft that the Center Force was again heading east for San Bernardino Strait, and that navigation lights in the strait, long blacked out, were lighted. When some of Mitscher's staff, ap-

palled at leaving the strait unguarded, urged him to protest to Halsey, Mitscher replied, "If he wants my advice, he'll ask for it."

Halsey had not formed Task Force 34, because he accepted the overoptimistic reports of his aviators that the Center Force had been battered into impotence. He believed that Kinkaid's Seventh Fleet could now repel the Center Force as well as the smaller Southern Forces, which American search planes had sighted that morning. In any event, he considered it imperative that he destroy the carriers, the warships with the longest reach and the hardest punch. He had missed his chance at fighting enemy carriers at Coral Sea and again at Midway, and he was convinced that Spruance, who had had them within his reach, had muffed his good luck. Now here was an opportunity Halsey felt bound to seize.

Bogan's and Davison's task groups, northbound, were joined by Sherman's at 2345, 24 October. An hour later the Japanese Center Force, with battered hulls but with guns and fire-control apparatus unimpaired, emerged from San Bernardino Strait behind Halsey's back.

When search planes early on 24 October sighted the Southern Forces eastbound in the Sulu Sea, Admiral Kinkaid assumed that they were headed to attack his amphibious shipping in Leyte Gulf. Taking for granted that Halsey would block San Bernardino Strait, he ordered Rear Admiral Jesse B. Oldendorf, commanding his fire-support ships, to plug Surigao Strait with everything he had. Oldendorf did just that. Aware of his superiority in firepower, he determined not merely to repulse but to annihilate the approaching enemy forces. To that end he prepared a perfect trap. He sent PT boats down to the southern end of the strait to open the attack and also give warning of the enemy's approach. At the northern end, where it led into the Leyte Gulf, he stationed his 21 destroyers for high-speed torpedo runs down the sides of the strait and his 6 old battleships and 8 cruisers steaming back and forth in position to cap the T on any oncoming enemy column.

In the late afternoon, Admiral Kurita radioed Admiral Nishimura, then in the Mindanao Sea, that he had been delayed by air attacks and could not arrive in Leyte Gulf on schedule. Nishimura thereupon sped ahead in order, apparently, to enter the gulf under cover of darkness. Admiral Shima's force was therefore unable to catch up and join Nishimura's, a circumstance that proved the former's salvation.

An hour before midnight, Nishimura's force, four destroyers, two battleships, and a heavy cruiser in column, entered Surigao Strait and ran the gauntlet of PT boats without suffering damage. At 0230 it blundered into Oldendorf's trap—destroyers firing torpedoes from right and left, battleships and cruisers firing shells from dead ahead. Under this double onslaught, Nishimura's two battleships and two of his destroyers went down. His cruiser, ablaze, and two damaged destroyers managed to wobble away. Shima, observing that Nishimura had met with disaster, prudently turned away and with his three cruisers and four destroyers retired at top speed back down the strait.

By this time the sun was rising, and out in the Pacific, off the east coast of Samar, the four battleships, eight cruisers, and two destroyer squadrons of Kurita's Center Force were beginning to deploy from night search disposition to circular antiaircraft formation. A lookout in the crow's nest of the flagship *Yamato* reported masts looming over a misty but brightening horizon to the southeast. Presently the masts and then the hulls of carriers and escorting vessels became visible from the *Yamato*'s bridge.

Kurita believed he had come upon a task group of Halsey's Task Force 38, but Halsey by then was 300 miles away to the north engaging Ozawa. What Kurita saw in the morning haze was a Seventh Fleet task unit, code-named Taffy 3, comprising six little 18-knot escort carriers, three destroyers, and four destroyer escorts, commanded by Rear Admiral Clifton A. F. Sprague. Taffy 2 and Taffy 1, of similar composition, were, respectively, just over the horizon to the southeast and 130 miles away to the south. On antisubmarine, antiaircraft patrol, these units alone barred the way to Leyte Gulf.

Rattled, Kurita made the fateful mistake of ordering "General Attack" while his fleet was still undergoing deployment, thus throwing his ships into confusion, with the faster ones forging out ahead. At 0658 the Japanese opened fire.

Clifton Sprague was no less surprised than Kurita. At first incredulous and then appalled, he made smoke, fled east into the wind to launch planes, and ducked into a convenient rain squall, at the same time calling for help by radio in plain English. Kinkaid, in Leyte Gulf, received the call and relayed word of the attack to Halsey, immediately following it with another message in plain English—evidently intended as much to frighten the Japanese as to prod Halsey into action: "Request Lee proceed top speed cover Leyte. Request immediate strike by fast carriers."

Kurita at first sped east to seize the weather gage and thus prevent Sprague from launching planes. Nearby Taffy 2, however, did launch planes

to attack the Japanese, and subsequently its carrier decks acted as indispensable refueling and rearming stations for aircraft arriving from Leyte and from Taffy 1.

Sprague turned south and then southwest, toward Leyte Gulf, hoping that Oldendorf's heavies were approaching from that direction to rescue him and destroy the Center Force. The latter pursued Sprague and began making hits on his carriers.

Sprague's destroyers and destroyer escorts now turned on the pursuing Japanese and began making suicidal attacks with shells and torpedoes. Three of the little ships were sunk by enemy gunfire and two others heavily damaged, but not before they had put torpedoes into three Japanese cruisers. In the annals of naval warfare, few men-of-war have performed their duty more gallantly or against heavier odds than Sprague's escorts. As it turned out, the most decisive result of their attack was that the flagship *Yamato*, accompanied by another battleship, turned north to evade torpedoes and fell far behind in the chase. Kurita thus lost sight of the fleeing carriers and was not able again to get a clear picture of the tactical situation.

Sprague's carriers began to take hits. That they were not all sunk can be attributed to poor Japanese gunnery, expert American damage control, and the fact that the attackers were using armor-piercing shells, which passed through the unarmored carriers generally without exploding. Nevertheless, the carrier *Gambier Bay*, at length having taken more hits than her damage-control parties could handle, lost power, began to list, and at 0907 capsized and sank.

The really decisive operation against the Center Force was carried out by aircraft, which kept up an almost continuous attack. They sank three heavy cruisers, two of which had previously been torpedoed by Sprague's escorts. Under this unremitting onslaught, the rest of the Japanese fleet fell into increasing confusion. Kurita, having lost touch with Sprague's carriers and with most of his own force, concluded that the prey had escaped and that the time had come to bring order out of chaos. At 0911 he headed north, summoning his ships by radio to converge on the *Yamato*.

Taffy 3, bewildered by the sudden retreat of the enemy vessels, which a few minutes before seemed to have every advantage on their side, shaped course for Leyte Gulf, now 25 miles away. Its ordeal, however, was not ended. A few minutes before 1100, five Japanese planes swooped down upon Sprague's battered carriers. These were units of the newly organized Kamikaze ("Divine wind") Special Attack Corps, so named from the typhoons that in 1274 and 1281 saved Japan by scattering Kublai Khan's invasion fleets. Its members were suicidally inclined aircraft pilots who, unable to hit ships with torpedoes or bombs, made up in guts what they lacked in skill by hurling their planes and themselves into their targets.

One of the suicide pilots, diving at the *Kitkun Bay*, succeeded in striking her only a glancing blow, but his bomb exploded and did considerable damage. Two more kamikazes crashed into the *Kalinin Bay*, already scarred by 14 shell hits, and started fires. One rammed through the flight deck of the *St. Lo*, caught fire, and detonated bombs and torpedoes on the hangar deck. The resulting series of explosions nearly blew the *St. Lo* apart. She sank a little before noon.

Kurita, meanwhile, having reassembled the remnant of his Center Force, was trying to decide what to do next. He had learned from Shima that Nishimura had met with disaster. He had no word at all from Ozawa. From Manila came a false report of American carriers northeast of Samar, and Kurita decided to attack them. Spurred on by bombers arriving from McCain's distant carrier group, he reached the supposed location of the carriers and found an empty sea.

By this time the Japanese destroyers were low in fuel, and Kurita and his staff were utterly exhausted after three days under attack from surface, subsurface, and air. Kurita saw retirement from the field of battle as his only alternative. Toward dusk the Center Force headed for San Bernardino Strait, which it entered at 2130.

The preceding evening, as Task Force 38, on Halsey's order, started north, the force's night-flying search planes were recalled from watching the Center Force in the Sibuyan Sea and sent scouting northward in search of the Northern Force. When Sherman's group joined Bogan's and Davison's around midnight, Halsey turned the tactical command over to Mitscher. At about 0200, the search planes made radar contact with the Northern Force, whereupon Mitscher, with Halsey's approval, ordered Admiral Lee to form Task Force 34, now enlarged to include all six battleships—among them the *New Jersey*, with Halsey on board. Task Force 34 took station ten miles ahead of Task Force 38 in anticipation of a possible night battle, or to pick off enemy cripples and stragglers after dawn.

In the course of 25 October, Task Force 38 attacked Ozawa's Northern Force six times. It was no contest. Ozawa on his four old carriers had left only 29 planes, all with inexperienced, virtually untrained aviators, to oppose Mitscher, who on his

ten carriers had 787 aircraft with superbly trained flyers. In two morning attacks, the Americans sank the light carrier *Chitose* and a destroyer and left the light carrier *Chiyoda* dead in the water, afire, and listing. They bombed the light carrier *Zuiho* and a cruiser and torpedoed the veteran carrier *Zuikaku*, Ozawa's flagship. The torpedo explosion in the *Zuikaku* knocked out her steering engines and her radio transmitter. The damage to her steering apparatus caused her to fall behind, out of control, and obliged Ozawa to shift to a cruiser. Because of the breakdown in her transmitter, long undetected, Kurita failed to get the word that the decoy scheme was working.

Halsey, forging ahead with Task Force 34, scanning the horizon for the masts of Japanese stragglers, was having his attention diverted from the impending surface action by news from the south. At 0800 he received a much-delayed radio message that the Southern Forces had been repulsed in Surigao Strait. He assumed that the Seventh Fleet was now free to give Leyte Gulf whatever cover it might need, and was exasperated shortly afterward by a whole series of calls for help from Kinkaid. It was not his business, he believed, to protect the Seventh Fleet. In his opinion he was doing exactly what he should be doing: going after the enemy carrier force. When Kinkaid pointed out that his old battleships were short of ammunition Halsey ordered McCain's task group to go "at best possible speed" to the aid of Sprague and notified Kinkaid that he had done so.

At Pearl Harbor, where most of the messages had been intercepted, Admiral Nimitz's staff was urging him to intervene, to order Halsey to send help to Sprague. Nimitz said no; he was opposed, except under extraordinary circumstances, to interfering with the tactical commander at the scene of action.

Kinkaid's calls for help became increasingly strident. At last Captain Bernard Austin, assistant chief of staff, suggested that Nimitz at least ask Halsey the simple question: Where is Task Force 34? Nimitz thought for a minute, then told Austin that was a good idea and to go ahead and send the question.

Nimitz realized by now that Task Force 34 could not possibly be off San Bernardino Strait and, knowing Halsey, he guessed correctly where it was—up north chasing the Japanese carrier force. He considered that the situation now justified his interfering with the man on the scene. He intended the question as a nudge: "Where *ought* Task Force 34 to be—and hadn't it better get there as soon as possible?"

When the message reached Halsey a little after 1000, it looked less like a nudge than a bludgeon. As placed in his hands, it read: FROM CINCPAC ACTION COM THIRD FLEET INFO COMINCH CTF SEVENTY-SEVEN X WHERE IS RPT WHERE IS TASK FORCE THIRTY-FOUR RR THE WORLD WONDERS.[1]

Austin had added Admiral King and Admiral Kinkaid (CTF 77) as information addressees, his yeoman had stuck in the RPT (repeat) phrase for emphasis, and the communicator, to baffle enemy cryptanalysts, had routinely tacked on padding, random phrases (TURKEY TROTS TO WATER GG . . . RR THE WORLD WONDERS) fore and aft, where they covered the vulnerable opening and closing of the message. The communicator on board the New Jersey removed the opening padding, but the end read so much like a part of the message that he left it on despite the double-consonant divider, trusting that someone in flag country would point out to Halsey that the closing phrase was marked as padding.

Nobody did. To Halsey it looked like heavy-handed sarcasm, with King and Kinkaid called in to witness his humiliation. Wrathfully he snatched off his cap, hurled it to the deck, and sounded off loudly and profanely. He held on course a little longer, but the pressure was too great. Shortly before 1100 he ordered Task Force 34 to reverse course. As he passed Task Force 38, still north-bound, he detached Bogan's carrier group to provide air cover for Task Force 34.

While Halsey headed south, Davison's and Sherman's groups continued north and finished off the *Zuiho*, the *Chiyoda*, and the *Zuikaku*, last survivor of the carrier attack on Pearl Harbor. Ozawa, minus his bait carriers but with 10 of his 13 surface vessels, returned to Japan. His decoy mission had succeeded, but fruitlessly because he did not get the word to Kurita.

When Halsey arrived off San Bernardino Strait a little after midnight, he found that Kurita's Center Force had already passed back through and was again in the Sibuyan Sea. The fast battleships of the Third Fleet had steamed 300 miles north and then 300 miles back south between the two major enemy forces, without quite making contact with either force.

[1]Meaning: "From CinCPac (Admiral Nimitz). For action by Commander Third Fleet (Admiral Halsey). For information to CominCh (Admiral King) and Commander Task Force 77 (Admiral Kinkaid). Where is, repeat, *where is* Task Force 34?"

Liberation of the Philippines

The Battle for Leyte Gulf, by shattering the Japanese fleets, brought the purely naval war to an end; there could be no more stand-up fights at sea. The Army Air Force was unable, however, to relieve the Navy in support of Lieutenant General Walter Krueger's Sixth Army on Leyte because monsoon rains had turned the island into a quagmire, defeating attempts by engineers to extend or complement the airstrip at Tacloban. So Task Force 38, with Admiral McCain replacing Admiral Mitscher but with Admiral Halsey still in overall command, was obliged to remain off the Philippines, pounding the all-weather airfields on Luzon and attacking a new "Tokyo Express" that was bringing supplies and reinforcements to Leyte.

It was grim service. In November alone, kamikazes crashed into seven carriers, killing nearly 300 Americans and injuring hundreds more. In the Seventh Fleet during the same period, suicide planes damaged two battleships, two cruisers, two transports, and seven destroyers, of which one sank. Despite continuing suicide attacks, Task Force 38 by mid-December was keeping fighters over Luzon around the clock, permitting few enemy planes to take off and destroying hundreds on the ground. On the 18th the carrier force suffered a different sort of attack when a typhoon struck, sinking three destroyers, damaging three other ships, shattering 186 planes, and killing 800 men.

On 15 December, as the Leyte campaign was drawing to an end in favor of the U. S. Sixth Army, Americans landed on the island of Mindoro on the dry side of the Philippines in order to set up usable air fields to cover the forthcoming landings on Luzon.

The Southwest Pacific Forces, on 9 January 1945, invaded Luzon at Lingayen Gulf, where the Japanese had landed three years before. The expeditionary force was about the same as for the invasion at Leyte: the Sixth Army and the Seventh Fleet supplemented by the Third Amphibious Force. There was little opposition to the landing, because the Japanese army was withdrawing to the north to take a stand in the mountains. There was none at all from the Japanese fleet, but the suicide planes were more numerous and more deadly than ever. They damaged 43 Allied ships, 18 seriously, and sank 5. One cruiser was hit by five planes. The kamikazes killed 738 men of the Allied forces and wounded nearly 1,400.

Halsey, with Task Force 38, made a foray into the South China Sea west of the Philippines to scare away any Japanese ships that might contemplate interfering with Mindoro–Lingayen communications. He then reported to Ulithi and turned over the fast carriers, battered and behind schedule, to Spruance. Kinkaid returned most of the ships that Nimitz had lent the Seventh Fleet. These vessels, together with the fast carrier force (now again Task Force 58, with Mitscher in command), and ships newly arrived from the European theater formed an enlarged U. S. Fifth Fleet.

The period of collaboration between the Southwestern Pacific and the Central Pacific forces was now over. The Fifth Fleet was to advance northward in the direction of Japan. MacArthur was planning a drive southward for recovery of the rest of the Philippines and the East Indies.

On 28 February, just as Manila was falling to the XIV U. S. Army Corps, other Southwest Pacific forces were landing on Palawan. They next invaded Mindanao, where they completed the work of a Filipino guerrilla army that already controlled most of the island. By mid-April Admiral Barbey's Seventh Amphibious Force had staged no fewer than 38 invasions in the central and southern Philippines. In accordance with the new doctrine, the Japanese never seriously opposed the landings. They held the cities as long as they could, blew them up when forced out, and then withdrew to the hills, where most of them died of starvation and disease. Usually only a small fraction of the original garrisons survived till the general surrender at the end of the war.

The Return to Borneo

With the conclusion of naval operations in the European theater, American warships began transferring to the Pacific; British warships, to the Indian Ocean. The Joint Chiefs of Staff suggested that the Royal Navy support General MacArthur and the Australians in the reconquest of Borneo, which would provide a handy source of oil for future operations. The British at first agreed, but when the Americans announced their intention of invading Japan in 1945, Prime Minister Churchill insisted that the Royal Navy, which heretofore had experienced nothing in the Far East but defeat and humiliation, should be in on the kill—if only for reasons of prestige. President Roosevelt agreed, and the Royal Navy's carrier force proceeded to the Pacific to join the forces under Nimitz, leaving MacArthur's operations to be supported only by the stripped-down Seventh Fleet, which, however, proved entirely adequate.

During May and June 1945, Barbey's Seventh Amphibious Force landed troops, mostly Australian, at Tarakan, Brunei, and Balikpapan. As in the central Philippines, there was no resistance at the beach but hard fighting inland. The invasion of the oil-rich port of Balikpapan, however, was unique in several respects: it was carried out against the most formidable beach defenses that the Southwest Pacific forces encountered during the entire war; it was preceded by 16 days of naval bombardment, the longest for any amphibious assault of the war; and it was the final invasion of the war. After the Seventh Fleet had fired 38,000 rounds of shell and 7,300 rockets against the coast defenses, the assault troops walked ashore without a single casualty.

With the completion of the Borneo campaign, General MacArthur planned to advance on Java. The Joint Chiefs, however, called a halt to his southward drive. All available Allied strength was to be concentrated for an invasion of Japan, for which MacArthur was to command the ground forces, and Nimitz the sea forces.

The Capture of Iwo Jima

To command the northward advance of the Central Pacific forces, Nimitz, promoted to fleet admiral, shifted from Pearl Harbor to forward headquarters on Guam. Vice Admiral Turner and Lieutenant General Holland Smith had each been elevated an echelon: the former to Commander Amphibious Forces Pacific Fleet; the latter to General Fleet Marine Force Pacific, a post that would not require him to exercise tactical command of troops.

The Fifth Fleet's initial objective was Iwo Jima, in the Volcano Islands, halfway between the B-29 bases in the Southern Marianas and Tokyo. From Iwo Jima fighter planes could accompany the long-range B-29s over Japan. Iwo could also serve as a way station for B-29s in need of refueling, a refuge for damaged bombers, and a base for air–sea rescue.

Iwo is a triangular heap of lava and ashes with a dormant volcano, Mt. Suribachi, at one corner, a rough plateau opposite, and a ridge in between. A little larger than Peleliu, it had three times as many defenders and a far more elaborate system of caves, pillboxes, and concealed gun positions. As soon as the Americans captured Saipan, the Japanese identified Iwo as a future American target, because of its location and its relatively flat surfaces—suitable for airfields. Able Lieutenant General Tadamichi Kuribayashi, commanding the island's defenses, had made Iwo the most formidably defended eight square miles in the Pacific.

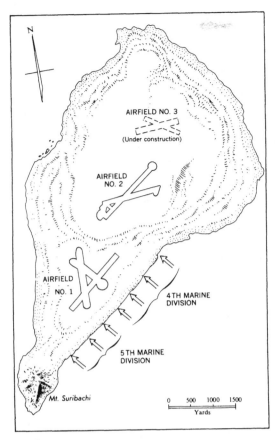

Iwo Jima

the gunnery vessels, now including additional battleships and cruisers from Task Force 58, opened the heaviest prelanding bombardment of the war. After 85 minutes of deliberate, aimed shelling, the ships checked fire while more than a hundred Task Force 58 planes roared over the island, firing rockets and machine guns and dropping general-purpose and napalm bombs. The fleet then resumed with a fast neutralizing fire to drive the defenders underground. Just before H-hour, 0900, the ships again checked fire to permit planes to strafe the beaches.

At 0830 the first wave of nearly 500 landing craft, carrying eight battalions of the 4th and 5th Marine Divisions, had headed for the shore. The amtracs and armored amphibians were expected to carry the troops well beyond the beach, but most of them were stopped by the steep-rising shore of soft volcanic ash, into which their treads sank without taking hold. Marines who succeeded in scrambling ashore began crawling up a series of terraces, in the face of intense rifle and machine-gun fire from pillboxes on the central ridge.

This was the beginning of the costly process, reminiscent of Peleliu, of digging out the deeply entrenched defenders with rifles, grenades, flamethrowers, and explosive charges. Instead of the estimated four days, the conquest of Iwo Jima required nearly a month of vicious fighting and mutual slaughter. In the supporting fleet, kamikazes crashed into several ships, disabling the carrier *Saratoga* and sinking the escort carrier *Bismarck Sea*. Casualties among the assault forces exceeded those among the defenders: on the island and in the fleet, 19,000 Americans were wounded, and nearly 7,000 were killed or died of their wounds. Yet the conquest of Iwo Jima proved its worth not only in stepping up the efficiency of the bombing of Japan but also as a haven for planes damaged or short of fuel. By the end of the war, some 2,400 B-29s, with crews numbering about 27,000, made emergency landings on the island.

The Okinawa Campaign

Capturing the 60-mile-long island of Okinawa in the Ryukyus had been recommended by Admiral Spruance and agreed upon by Admiral Nimitz and the Joint Chiefs. From Okinawa the blockade of Japan could be tightened, and the bombing of Japanese cities intensified. It could also serve as a staging base for a proposed invasion of Kyushu. The operation was carried out by forces under Admiral Spruance, commanding the Fifth Fleet; Admiral Mitscher, commanding Task Force 58; Admiral

At dawn on 16 February 1945, Rear Admiral William H. P. Blandy's gunnery ships and escort carriers arrived off Iwo and began blasting Kuribayashi's island fortress. Simultaneously Task Force 58, with Spruance and Mitscher on board, arrived off Tokyo, 600 miles to the north, for the first fleet attack on Japan since the Halsey–Doolittle raid of early 1942. In two days of strikes Task Force 58 destroyed several hundred aircraft that might have been used against the American forces at Iwo. Task Force 58 then turned back to join the bombardment of the island target. At the same time Rear Admiral Harry Hill's invasion force approached, bringing the assault troops under Major General Harry Schmidt, USMC, the new commanding general of the V Amphibious Corps. Also in the invasion force were Secretary of the Navy James Forrestal, who came as an observer, and General Holland Smith, in overall command of the expeditionary troops—a mainly advisory role.

On D-day, 19 February, Admiral Turner took personal command of the support force. At sunrise

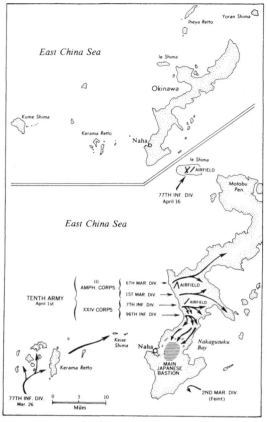

East China Sea

Okinawa

Turner, who commanded the landing force until the beachhead was secured; and Lieutenant General Simon Bolivar Buckner, USA, commanding the U. S. Tenth Army. The Tenth Army, comprising the 1st, 2nd, and 4th Marine Divisions and four army infantry divisions, provided 183,000 combat troops to oppose the 77,000 defenders under Lieutenant General Mitsuru Ushijima.

On the morning of 1 April 1945, after a prolonged neutralizing fire directed at selected beaches on the Okinawa west coast, the Tenth Army began going ashore. Because the Japanese were adhering to their new defense plan of mere delaying tactics at the beach, the invaders met only sporadic small-arms and mortar fire. In mid-April, however, elements of the Tenth Army heading south against growing opposition came at last in contact with the main defense citadel. This was a warren of hills, caves, and pillboxes somewhat like an enlarged Iwo Jima but dug not into soft lava but into solid earth and stone. For six weeks the Americans, suffering and inflicting heavy casualties, moved forward scarcely at all.

Off to the north, between Okinawa and Kyushu, steamed Task Force 58, providing air cover to the American troops and especially to their incoming supplies. Performing a similar function to the southwest, between Okinawa and Formosa, was a British fleet of 4 carriers, 2 battleships, 5 cruisers, and 15 destroyers. Commanded by Vice Admiral Sir Bernard Rawlings, RN, and serving in the U.S. Fifth Fleet, it was designated Task Force 57.

From the beginning, Japanese bombers and suicide planes had struck at the American ships off Okinawa, at first individually and then in a series of mass raids. A kamikaze so damaged the *Indianapolis* that Spruance sent her to the Mare Island Navy Yard, California, for major repairs, and shifted his flag to a battleship. Mitscher lost a large part of his staff and had to change flagships twice in four days as the carriers *Bunker Hill* and *Enterprise* were successively put out of action by crashing kamikazes. All four British carriers were hit, but, thanks to their armored flight decks, all were able to continue operations. Most often hit, because they were the first ships sighted by oncoming suicide planes, were the destroyer types stationed at sea to give early warning.

To participate in the suicide operations, the superbattleship *Yamato*, a cruiser, and eight destroyers sortied from the Inland Sea for a one-way passage to Okinawa, planning to sink as many ships as possible before being destroyed. But submarines reported the sortie, and Task Force 58 planes pounced on them southwest of Kyushu. The planes quickly sent the *Yamato*, the cruiser, and a destroyer down and so wrecked three other destroyers that the surviving vessels sank them before returning to base.

Supporting the Okinawa campaign proved to be the most costly naval operation in history. Thirty-four U. S. ships and craft were sunk and 368 damaged, many beyond repair. More than 4,900 sailors were killed. Many of the 4,824 listed as wounded were in fact hideously burned by the gasoline fires that usually accompanied kamikaze strikes.

The strain on the senior commanders, who never left the scene of action, became almost unbearable. At last Admiral Nimitz, toward the end of May, sent in Halsey, McCain, and Hill to replace Spruance, Mitscher, and Turner, whereupon the Fifth Fleet again became the Third Fleet.

On 21 June the U. S. forces declared Okinawa secured. The next day General Ushijima acknowledged defeat by committing suicide. The Tenth Army had suffered 7,613 killed and 31,800 wounded.

The Japanese Surrender

On 22 June 1945 Emperor Hirohito of Japan at a meeting of his Supreme War Council gave utterance to what others in authority had been unwilling or afraid to state officially: Japan must find a way to end the war. It was high time. Clouds of American bombers were turning Japan's cities into ashes. The strangling blockade was bringing the nation's production of war materials to a standstill. The surrender of Germany had dispelled the vain hope that some decisive weapon might yet be obtained from that quarter, and at the same time released the combined forces of the Allied world for operations against Japan. Okinawa, the last offshore Japanese outpost, had fallen to the Americans.

Ending the war was not simple. Powerful factions in Japan and in the armed forces abroad favored a war to the bitter end, and neither the rulers nor the people would accept a peace that did not preserve the imperial system. Negotiations therefore had to be carried out in secret, and terms short of "unconditional surrender" had to be obtained. Since of the major powers only Russia was even ostensibly neutral with respect to the Pacific war, it was appropriate that peace feelers be extended through Moscow. But when the Japanese ambassador in Moscow approached the Soviet foreign office on the subject of peace terms, he found the Russians disposed to stall. At the July conference of the victors over Germany held at Potsdam, Premier Stalin said nothing to President Truman or to Prime Minister Churchill about Japan's request for mediation. The Russians had no intention of helping the Japanese to get out of the war until they themselves could get into it and thereby share the fruits of victory.

But President Truman knew about the peace feelers, for American intelligence was reading the coded radio messages passing between the Japanese foreign minister in Tokyo and the Japanese ambassador in Moscow. On 26 July the governments of the United States, Britain, and China gave Japan her answer in the Potsdam Proclamation, which specified that for Japan "unconditional surrender" was to apply only to the armed forces. The proclamation further stated that Japan was to be stripped of all her territorial gains and possessions except the four home islands, and that points in Japan would be occupied until a "peacefully inclined and responsible government" had been established in line with the people's desires expressed in a free election.

The Potsdam Proclamation came a little too suddenly for the Japanese Cabinet, for they had not taken steps to prepare the Japanese people for surrender, and they had not settled disagreements among themselves. The chief stumbling block, however, was the failure of the proclamation to spell out what the Allies intended to do about the Japanese emperor.

On 16 July 1945, the world's first man-made atomic explosion was set off at Alamagordo, New Mexico, and within a few hours Admiral Spruance's former flagship, the *Indianapolis,* newly repaired from the battering she received off Okinawa, was en route from San Francisco to the Marianas with uranium for the first military atomic bomb. Bombers from Okinawa and the Marianas were now appearing over Japan in waves of 500 or more, burning out vast areas in Japan's major cities. On 10 July, Task Force 38 had raided airfields near Tokyo. From this date on, with a single break, the Third Fleet carrier forces paraded up and down the Japanese coast with virtual impunity while Japan hoarded her aircraft to throw back the expected invasion. On 17 July, Halsey's 105 men-of-war were joined by 28 British warships, designated Task Force 37. This combined fleet, the most powerful striking force in history, then raided the naval bases at Yokosuka on Tokyo Bay and at Kure on the Inland Sea, sinking or heavily damaging the remnants of the Imperial Japanese Fleet.

On 30 July, the Third Fleet ended the first phase of its intensive operations against Japan with a raid on the airfields and factories in central Honshu. On this date also, the *Indianapolis,* having delivered her uranium to Tinian, touched at Guam, and then headed for Leyte. She was sunk in the Philippine Sea by a Japanese submarine with the loss of nearly 900 lives.

On 28 July, Japanese Prime Minister Suzuki announced to the press that his government would disregard the Potsdam Proclamation. President Truman, interpreting this statement as a rejection, ordered the first atomic bomb dropped. The order was carried out on 6 August by a B-29 flying from Tinian. Most of Hiroshima, the target city, was seared and flattened. The Russians now realized that if they were to get into the war at all, it must be soon. On 8 August the Soviet foreign minister at Moscow handed the Japanese ambassador his long-awaited answer. It was a declaration of war. Within a few hours the Red Army marched into Manchuria. On the 9th another atomic bomb devastated the city of Nagasaki. Also on the 9th the Third Fleet, having ridden out a typhoon, returned to Japanese waters and raided airfields in Hokkaido and northern Honshu. On the 10th Russian forces entered Korea.

These startling events both ended the procrastination of the Japanese government and solved one of its most difficult problems. The imperial councilors had been at a loss as to how to present the facts to a nation long deluded with propaganda. There was a strong chance that any attempt to surrender would precipitate mutiny in the armed services and civil war among the people. But the power and mystery of the new bomb, the swift advance of the Red Army, and the resumption of Third Fleet raids persuaded all but the most hotheaded that further resistance was useless. After midnight on the morning of 10 August, Emperor Hirohito rose with deep emotion before his Supreme Council and advised immediate acceptance of the Potsdam Proclamation. The Cabinet unanimously agreed but only on the condition that the imperial system remain unimpaired. This decision they forwarded via Switzerland and Sweden to Washington, London, Moscow, and Chungking. On receipt of the Japanese decision, American Secretary of State James Byrnes, acting on behalf of the Allied governments, drafted a reply accepting the condition but imposing two stipulations: that during the occupation the emperor must submit to the authority of the Supreme Allied Commander in Japan, and that the Japanese people should decide the emperor's ultimate status through free election.

While the Allies were considering the Japanese condition and the Japanese were considering the Allied stipulations, the Third Fleet raided northern Honshu again and struck at the Kurils. It then turned south and on 13 August once more attacked Tokyo. On the 14th the Japanese Cabinet, again on the emperor's advice, accepted the Allied stipulations. On 15 August, when one carrier strike was already over Tokyo and another had just been launched, Admiral Halsey received Admiral Nimitz's order to "cease fire."

President Truman appointed General MacArthur Supreme Commander of the Allied Powers and directed him to conduct the surrender ceremony and command the subsequent occupation of Japan. The general was in no hurry. He allowed hotheads in Japan and Japanese-occupied territory time to face the fact of defeat and realize the futility of further resistance. He ordered the Japanese government to send representatives to him in Manila to receive instructions. On 28 August, the first American occupation troops arrived by plane at Atsugi airfield near Tokyo. The next day ships of the U. S. Third Fleet, including the *Missouri*, the

South Dakota, and the British flagship *Duke of York,* entered Tokyo Bay. That afternoon Admiral Nimitz arrived by seaplane and broke his flag on the *South Dakota*. General MacArthur flew in to Atsugi the following day and set up temporary headquarters in the customhouse building at Yokohama.

On 2 September on board the *Missouri*, in the presence of flag and general officers who had led the war against Japan, Japanese Foreign Minister Shigemitsu signed the instrument of surrender on behalf of the emperor and the Japanese government, and General Umezu, Chief of the Army General Staff, signed on behalf of the Japanese General Headquarters. General MacArthur then signed the acceptance as Supreme Commander. Admiral Nimitz next affixed his signature as representative for the United States. He was followed by representatives for China, the United Kingdom, the Soviet Union, Australia, Canada, France, the Netherlands, and New Zealand.

When the signing was completed, General MacArthur said: "Let us pray that peace be now restored to the world and that God will preserve it always. These proceedings now are closed."

As he finished speaking, the sun broke through the morning haze and hundreds of U. S. planes roared over Tokyo Bay.

Summary

In late 1941 the United States in effect told Japan to withdraw her army from China or do without U. S. oil. Japan chose a third alternative. She invaded the oil-rich East Indies. To minimize the risks in this operation, she also staged a carrier attack on the U. S. Pacific Fleet at Pearl Harbor and proceeded to seize Guam, the Philippines, Hong Kong, and Singapore.

The attack on Pearl Harbor failed to achieve its purpose. The Japanese carrier planes sank only a few old battleships, of no immediate use to the United States. During Japan's drive into the East Indies, which together with adjacent positions she called her Southern Resources Area, the U. S. carrier forces raided Japanese bases in the Central and South Pacific and staged an air attack on Tokyo and other cities of Japan.

In the spring of 1942, as Japan's conquest of her Southern Resources Area drew to a close far ahead of schedule, the Japanese devised two plans of further conquest: (1) seizure of Port Moresby, New Guinea, to facilitate a further drive southeastward to cut United States–Australia communications; and (2) seizure of Midway and points in the Aleutians to provide forward observation posts and, more important, to draw out the U. S. carrier fleet for destruction by Japan's Combined Fleet. Both operations were foiled, partly through U. S. breaking and reading Japanese coded radio messages.

In the Battle of the Coral Sea (5–8 May 1942), a U. S. two-carrier force turned back the Japanese Port Moresby invasion force and repulsed an enemy two-carrier force but lost the carrier *Lexington*. The Americans had put both enemy carriers temporarily out of commission so that they were unable to participate in the forthcoming attack on Midway.

In the Battle of Midway (3–7 June 1942), a U. S. three-carrier force turned back the Japanese Midway invasion force and sank four Japanese carriers and a heavy cruiser but lost the carrier *Yorktown*. This weakening of Japanese naval power proved the turning point of the war, enabling the Allies to shift to the offensive.

All the Orange Plans had proposed recapturing the Philippines, if lost, by a drive across the Central Pacific, but the threat to United States–Australia communications diverted Allied efforts to the South. In a campaign to recapture the Japanese southern base at Rabaul, South Pacific forces under Admiral Ghormley and, later, Admiral Halsey (both subordinate to Admiral Nimitz) captured Guadalcanal and advanced up the Solomons, while Southwest Pacific forces under General MacArthur seized Papua, points controlling Vitiaz Strait, and the Admiralty Islands. In defending Rabaul and the Solomons, the Japanese expended their carrier air power to the point where the Japanese fleet was temporarily paralyzed.

To speed up the war, the Joint Chiefs bypassed Rabaul and reverted to the Orange Plan. Beginning in late 1943 the Central Pacific forces (called U. S. Fifth Fleet when commanded by Admiral Spruance and U. S. Third Fleet when under Admiral Halsey) captured the Gilberts, including Tarawa; the Marshalls, including Kwajalein; and Saipan, Tinian, and Guam in the Marianas. The U. S. attack on the Marianas at last drew out the Japanese fleet and produced the Battle of the Philippine Sea (19–20 June 1944), in which the Japanese lost three carriers and most of their carrier planes.

The U. S. Third Fleet support of the invasion of the Philippines by MacArthur's Southwest Pacific forces brought about the Battle for Leyte Gulf (24–25 October 1944), which left the Japanese fleet a mere remnant, incapable of fighting any more battles.

While MacArthur's Southwest Pacific forces were completing their conquest of the Philippines and recapturing Borneo, Nimitz's Central Pacific forces were capturing Iwo Jima and Okinawa. B-29 bombers from the Marianas and Okinawa and fighters from Iwo Jima staged devastating fire raids on Japanese cities. American submarines from Guam, Allied submarines from Subic Bay, and American aircraft from Luzon and Okinawa prevented oil and other vital supplies from reaching Japan from her Southern Resources Area, while submarines in the Sea of Japan denied the Japanese the coal and iron of the continent. These catastrophes plus Third Fleet raids on Japan proper, Russia's entry into the war, and the dropping of two atomic bombs finally induced Japan to surrender. The instrument of surrender was signed on board the *Missouri* in Tokyo Bay on 2 September 1945.

Chapter 31
The Beginning of the Cold War

Even before the end of the war in Europe, the grand alliance began breaking up. At Yalta, where Roosevelt, Churchill, and Stalin met for the last time, accords were reached that meant one thing to the Soviets and another to the Western democracies. Roosevelt and Churchill spent many hours winning agreements that Stalin in a few days or a few weeks ignored.

With the death of President Roosevelt at Warm Springs, Georgia, in April 1945, the process of disintegration speeded up. The new president, Harry S. Truman, knew nothing of the strategy of the war or of the agreements, or of the personalities of Churchill and Stalin. The hopes of men rested with the United Nations, whose organizational meetings were convening in San Francisco as President Roosevelt's body was laid to rest at his family estate at Hyde Park.

Because Stalin was not yet ready to make a break with the United States, the Soviet Union abandoned some of her more recalcitrant positions, and the United Nations Charter was signed. The United Nations had as its principal machinery two deliberative bodies, the General Assembly and the Security Council. In the former, each member, regardless of size or population, had one vote—except that in accordance with an agreement reached at Yalta, the Soviet Union got three votes, including one each for Byelorussia and the Ukraine. Roosevelt had not sought multiple votes for the United States in the Assembly, because the real power was in the Security Council, where the five major powers—the United States, the Soviet Union, Britain, France, and China—had the veto power. Six other nations, without veto power, were members of the Security Council, on a rotating basis. The General Assembly was conceived to be a guiding and advisory body, while the Security Council might employ a wide range of measures for the settlement of international disputes, ranging from mediation and conciliation to "such action by air, sea, or land forces as may be necessary to maintain or restore international peace."

America's hopes for the United Nations sped her process of demobilization and slashed her military budgets. Taking a shortsighted view of the

world situation, politicians concluded that the U. S. monopoly of the atomic bomb meant that conventional weapons could be neglected, a view that was discredited in 1950 by the outbreak of the Korean War. The USSR, meanwhile, showed herself ready to take advantage of the postwar situation to expand her borders or to make sure that her neighbors were "friendly" nations, whose governments were Communist and sympathetic to the Soviet Union. Thus Albania, Bulgaria, East Germany, Hungary, Poland, and Romania became Russian satellites. As Churchill was to put it, an Iron Curtain had descended across Europe.

Reorganizing U. S. Defenses

With demobilization came a reappraisal of the U. S. defense establishment. Military leaders advocated both unification and also further division of the services. At the same time the shrinking of budgets to peacetime levels caused a scramble of each service to get more than its share.

Air Force leaders believed they had earned the right to a separate existence—apart from the Army. In World War II they had had their own representative, General Arnold, in the Joint Chiefs of Staff. Their strategic bombing of Germany and Japan (including dropping the atomic bombs) had been virtually independent missions.

The impetus toward unification of the services was based on the need to avoid waste and duplication and possible operations at cross purposes. The practicality of unified command had been convincingly demonstrated during the recent war in the Pacific Ocean Areas, where the services were in effect merged under the overall command of Admiral Nimitz.

The services were agreed that the most likely—indeed, the only possible—enemy was the Soviet Union or a Soviet-inspired satellite. But the strategies proposed for countering the threat differed. In the resultant highly vocal discussions, the so-called unification battle of 1945–47, Air Force enthusiasts were most outspoken and created the most headlines, but the Navy's point of view, as espoused by Secretary James V. Forrestal, generally prevailed.

The airmen were convinced of the deterrent effect of the atomic bomb and of the effectiveness of strategic bombing. They counted on assuming the Navy's traditional role of first line of national defense, even though almost all of their planning was offensive or at least retaliatory in nature. They relied on the B-36 bomber, which they stated was capable of delivering an atomic bomb anywhere in the world. In their opinion the major portion of U. S. defense funds should be devoted to the air arm, with the other services substantially reduced.

Some Air Force enthusiasts sought control over all aviation, no matter how used, espousing the simplistic notion that each service should have control of all weapons in its particular field: the Air Force, all air; the Army, all ground forces; the Navy, all ships—and since the Soviets at that time had no fleet to speak of, they proposed sharply reducing the Navy.

The idea of relying on the Air Force to win the next war by strategic bombing was as appealing to the public as it was appalling to naval leaders. The notion, held by some civilians, that the atomic bomb, and the big bomber to deliver it, had rendered all other weapons obsolete, overlooked the fact that diplomatic protest is not sufficient to settle some international disputes and atomic devastation is too extreme for most.

Forrestal pointed out that strategic bombing, with or without the atomic bomb, could not win a major war, particularly against a continental power. Sooner or later troops would have to be employed, if only as occupation forces. They would have to be transported to the scene of the action and kept supplied, both tasks requiring the use of sea power. Also, the massive-retaliation theory, as it came to be called, lacked flexibility. Forrestal feared that if the Air Force view prevailed, the United States would lack the capacity to respond to piecemeal takeover of countries along the littorals of Eurasia.

Naval leaders pointed out that the rigid division of weapons and functions advocated by some groups would make it impossible for the Navy to carry out its mission. It needed to duplicate, or at least adapt, two types of military force that would come under the control of other services if the extreme Air Force view prevailed. The Navy needed an air arm that would be under naval control and that could be used to support the naval mission. The other requirement was for a highly mobile body of troops, trained in sea-to-land operations, which could be used to seize, protect, and

garrison bases needed for naval operations, and to protect American lives and interests in troubled areas of the world. To this end, the Marine Corps had been established, and its achievements had become a part of the national heritage of the United States.

Forrestal opposed the idea promoted by the Army of a single chief of staff, as one who might be oversold on one pet theory of war to the detriment of the United States in her ability to respond to challenges. He pointed to the outstanding success of the Joint Chiefs of Staff in directing operations in World War II and urged that the institution be retained.

Since service personnel might be suspected of bias in favor of their own service, Forrestal disarmed criticism by appointing a civilian committee, headed by Ferdinand Eberstadt, to study the problem of national defense. The findings of the committee were convincing. The Eberstadt Report became the basis for the National Military Establishment, created by the National Security Act of 1947. A secretary of defense, a member of the president's cabinet, headed the Military Establishment. The components of the Establishment were the departments of the Army, Navy, and Air Force, each with its secretary, not of cabinet rank.

The Joint Chiefs of Staff were retained to direct operations. The Navy kept not only its carrier aviation but also its land-based reconnaissance wing and a Marine Corps of limited size with its own air wing. The Army was left with its traditional functions virtually unchanged. Secretary of the Navy Forrestal became the first secretary of defense and set about administering the law that he had helped to keep within reasonable bounds despite the efforts of extremists. By the Defense Reorganization Act of 1949, the National Military Establishment was replaced by a regular executive department, the Department of Defense.

The Revolt of the Admirals

The B-36 bombers proved in fact to lack sufficient range to reach all parts of the Soviet Union from the United States. The Navy proposed to supplement them by transporting bombers closer to the target by sea, and requested funds to build a carrier large enough to handle planes that could carry the heavy atomic bomb. The Air Force, jealous of its supposed monopoly of strategic bombing and delivery of the atomic bomb, lodged a sharp objection. Secretary of Defense Forrestal overruled the Air Force and obtained an appropriation to build what was to be the first of the supercarriers, the 65,000-ton *United States*.

Before the big carrier's keel was laid at Newport News on 18 April 1949, Forrestal had been succeeded by Louis Johnson, a World War I army officer, former assistant secretary of war, and a recent director of the aircraft corporation that built the B-36. Johnson came to office determined to build up the Air Force and trim the Navy. One of his first acts as secretary of defense was to halt construction on the *United States*, whereupon Secretary of the Navy John L. Sullivan resigned in protest.

The president's defense budget for the forthcoming fiscal year was a skimpy $16 billion, and Johnson refused to spend even that much. He proceeded to cut away at the nation's military muscle, principally at the expense of naval and marine corps air, in the happy delusion that he was cutting away fat. Dreaming of still more drastic savings, he shocked Admiral Richard L. Conolly by remarking, "Admiral, the Navy is on its way out. . . . There's no reason for having a Navy and a Marine Corps. . . . We'll never have any more amphibious operations. That does away with the Marine Corps. And the Air Force can do anything the Navy can do nowadays, so that does away with the Navy."

The Navy's aviators, first to feel the effect of Johnson's meat-ax economies, began sounding the alarm. Captain John G. Crommelin led off, defying regulations, to charge publicly that the Air Force, with a determined assist from Johnson, was trying to take over all air power. His statement was endorsed by Vice Admiral Gerald F. Bogan, commanding a task force in the Pacific Fleet; by Admiral Arthur W. Radford, then CinCPac and the Navy's senior aviator; and by the Chief of Naval Operations, Admiral Louis E. Denfeld, not an aviator.

Representative Carl Vinson blocked an attempt by Johnson to abolish marine corps aviation, and he provided the admirals a forum by calling them to testify before his Armed Services Committee, which had been investigating the B-36. Admiral Radford led off with a blast against the B-36, which he called a billion-dollar blunder and a popular "symbol of a theory of warfare, the atomic blitz, which promises . . . a cheap and easy victory." As officers of all three services expressed their views before the committee in emphatic language, tempers flared in and out of the committee room.

As far as the public was concerned, the "revolt of the admirals" ended when President Truman dismissed Admiral Denfeld from office, replacing him as CNO by Admiral Forrest P. Sherman, but the dispute was effectively terminated only by the Korean War, which brought more liberal defense budgets and discredited Johnson and his opinions.

The Policy of Containment

In March 1947, in response to continued Soviet aggression, President Truman proclaimed a new policy, one of helping free peoples everywhere "against aggressive movements that seek to impose upon them totalitarian regimes" and of supporting peoples "who are resisting attempted subjugation by armed minorities or by outside pressures."

Although the Soviet Union was not mentioned by name, no one doubted that this policy, which came to be known as the Truman Doctrine, was directed against Russia, which directly or indirectly was threatening both Greece and Turkey. In Greece, where civil war was in progress, the Communist rebels were receiving substantial aid from Yugoslavia, which at that time was considered a Russian satellite, acting with the approval of and in support of the Russian Politburo. Russia also was demanding of Turkey rights that amounted to complete control of the Dardanelles. The Truman Doctrine served notice on the Soviet Union that the United States would support Greece and Turkey against any expansion by Communist forces into their territory. The U. S. government sent supplies, including munitions, and military advisers to aid the Greek government against the rebels. Visits of U. S. naval forces to the Mediterranean, begun in 1946, were stepped up to serve as a diplomatic show of force.

In June 1947 Secretary of State George C. Marshall proposed a corollary to the Truman Doctrine of providing military and diplomatic aid to threatened nations. Marshall offered a program of economic aid to help the war-impoverished European states to help themselves, to enable them to eliminate the poverty and misery that are a breeding ground for Communist movements. Speaking at Harvard University, he put forward a plan for reconstruction of European countries through their own efforts, supported by American economic aid. The program came to be called the Marshall Plan, and was translated into the European Recovery Program.

The Soviet Union perceived clearly enough that the Recovery Program was a sovereign antidote to the spread of Communism and denounced it as American economic imperialism. She not only refused to participate but intimidated Finland and Czechoslovakia, as well as her satellites, into declining American assistance.

At first Congress balked at the cost of underwriting the revival of western Europe, but the Communists themselves inadvertently assured that the program would be funded and that it would succeed. In Czechoslovakia the Communist party, through a series of manipulations and power plays, succeeded in taking over the government. President Edvard Benes resigned in protest, and Foreign Minister Jan Masaryk threw himself or was thrown from a window and was killed. The brutal seizure outraged the people of America and Europe. Congress appropriated funds to implement the Recovery Program, and the countries of free Europe united efforts to make it work.

Because of Czechoslovakia's inland position, far from the pressures of sea power, there was little the United States could do to help, but Congress, faced with this example of naked Communist aggression, passed the long-debated Selective Service Act, as a step toward drafting young men in order to build the U. S. armed forces up to authorized strength.

Even before Truman and Marshall had put forth their plans, George Kennan, counselor of the American embassy in Moscow, had written an anonymous article, eventually published in the July 1947 issue of *Foreign Affairs*, recommending such assistance programs, and he had given them an enduring name—containment. "The Soviet pressure against the free institutions of the Western world," Kennan wrote, "is something that can be contained by the adroit and vigilant application of counterforce at a series of constantly shifting geographical and political points, corresponding to the shifts and maneuvers of Soviet policy."

The policy of containment was to dominate U. S. relations with the Communist world for the next 30 years.

The Berlin Blockade

The most dangerous situation to confront the United States since the end of World War II occurred in June 1948, when the Soviet Union clamped a blockade on Berlin, preventing all material from entering or leaving by road, rail, or canal. This blockade resulted partly from the division of Germany into four zones of occupation after World War II. The Russian Zone surrounded all of Berlin, but the capital itself was under quadripartite rule in a manner similar to that of the occupied German nation. Hence, the three western powers, France, Great Britain, and the United States, held their Berlin garrisons as on an island surrounded by Soviet-held territory and by Soviet troops. The Soviet Union obviously had as her aim the complete ousting of the western powers from Berlin. The ostensible reason given for the blockade was the imminence of a currency reform in the western zones, which the Russians said was sure to disorganize the East Zone currency. The blockade became so tight that no land or canal traffic was allowed to flow between the western zones and Berlin.

This situation presented U. S. leaders with a grave problem. Russia, obviously making a major bid for supremacy in Germany, was forcing a show of strength. It was obvious that if the free nations backed down now, Russia would assume they were acting from fear and would proceed to further and even more serious aggression. The challenge was clear.

The response of the western powers was an airlift. Soon large quantities of foodstuffs, coal, and other supplies were being delivered to the former German capital on a round-the-clock schedule by British and American planes. The Russians did not oppose the airlift in any serious way although Russian fighters occasionally made dry runs on airlift planes. The American and British pilots were careful to stick to the routes prescribed in the original agreement on Berlin in 1945. United States naval as well as air force planes were used in the airlift to supply foodstuffs, medical supplies, and coal. The blockade came to an end early in May 1949, when the western powers and Russia agreed to hold another session of the Council of Foreign Ministers to reconsider the German problem. In the 11 months of the blockade the Anglo–American airlift transported 2,343,315 tons of supplies.

The North Atlantic Treaty Organization

As the cold war progressed, the United States and several of the western European nations began to realize that their national security was at stake and that military cooperation between free countries was essential to combat the Soviet threat. Hence in 1949 the United States and 11 other nations agreed upon a treaty, the North Atlantic Pact, by which it was provided that the member nations would consider an attack on any one of them as an attack against them all. The signatory nations were Belgium, Canada, Denmark, France, Iceland, Italy, Luxembourg, the Netherlands, Norway, Portugal, the United Kingdom, and the United States. The year after its inception the North Atlantic Treaty Organization (NATO) invited Greece and Turkey to become members. Later West Germany also joined.

The teeth of the pact are in Article 5, which states:

The parties agree than an armed attack against one or more of them in Europe or North America shall be considered an attack against them all. And consequently they agree that, if such an armed attack occurs, each of them, in exercise of the right of individual or collective self-defense recognized by Article 51 of the Charter of the United Nations, will assist the party so attacked by taking forthwith, individually and in concert with the other parties, such action as it deems necessary, including the use of armed force, to restore and maintain the security of the North Atlantic area.

Provisions of the treaty called also for a command organization of military forces to be made available for military operations as necessary. The employment of this force was to be directed by a council known as the North Atlantic Council, which would sit permanently in Paris. This council represented the political planning level and was to be responsible for grand strategic direction.

The Far East

At the end of World War II, the victorious Allies seemed to have nothing to fear. Japan was badly beaten; the other Eastern powers were allied to the common effort. Yet within five years, all of China was shut off from the Free World behind a "Bamboo Curtain" like the Iron Curtain in Europe, and outright war was in progress in the Far East. China was wracked by civil war. Step by step the Communists won territory until at length the Nationalists fled to Formosa and established a "temporary" government seat there. Similar civil war broke out in Indochina in 1946. In Korea, the artificial division of the country at the 38th parallel led to open warfare in June of 1950.

China

The government of Chiang Kai-shek, which had fought the war against Japan, came under severe criticism both inside and outside China. Local unrest bred by uneven distribution of food and other consumer goods was seized upon by Chinese Communists. As time went on, the Communists under Mao Tse-tung became well organized and were armed with surrendered Japanese weapons, with captured Chinese Nationalist weapons, and with American weapons originally supplied to Chiang. In the course of events, sporadic guerrilla fighting spread into organized civil war between the Nationalists and the Communists.

Attempting to halt the deterioration of the situation in China, the United States supplied more money and arms to the Nationalists and sent a special representative to strive to resolve the conflict. General of the Army George C. Marshall was chosen for this mission; his instructions were to attempt to bring about a coalition government of the Nationalists and the People's Party—as the Communists called themselves. The efforts of Marshall met with very little success, and the Communists gained strength as time went on. By October 1948, they had occupied all of Manchuria, and during 1949 and 1950 they took over the rest of the country. In December 1949, the Nationalist Government moved to Formosa.

Mao immediately established a *rapprochement* with Soviet Russia, and a 30-year pact of "friendship, alliance, and mutual assistance" was signed by the two Communist powers in February 1950. Thus, within five years, nearly 500 million persons came under the domination of the Communist world. An American "White Paper" issued late in 1949 pointed out American efforts to stem the tide, noting that equipment for 39 divisions and over two billion dollars in aid had been given to the Chinese Nationalists and that most of the arms and money had gone ultimately into the hands of Mao and his followers. The loss of arms and money was serious enough, but loss of China behind the Bamboo Curtain was to have consequences of the utmost gravity.

Korea

At the Potsdam Conference it had been decided that on a temporary basis Russia would occupy North Korea and the United States South Korea. The actual line of demarcation, the 38th parallel, was decided on the spot as a convenient division line for the acceptance of the Japanese surrender. No one on the non-Communist side thought of it as an actual boundary. In the last four days of World War II, Russian forces moved into North Korea and seized Japanese forces there. Immediately the Soviets began organizing Socialists and Communists in their zone and set up the Korean People's Interim Committee as the basis of a government in opposition to the Democratic Party of Kim Koo and Syngman Rhee. Much political maneuvering ensued, with the Russians refusing to recognize Rhee and his party or even to allow the U. S. and, later, UN officials to visit north of the 38th parallel. In September 1947, the Soviet Union, having organized the North Korean government and army to its liking, proposed that all occupation forces be withdrawn by January 1948. This proposal was rejected. The United Nations named a commission to hold free elections in all of Korea in 1948, but the members of that commission were summarily refused permission to enter North Korea. Making the best of a bad situation, South Koreans established in South Korea the Republic of Korea with Syngman Rhee as president and the capital at Seoul. This government was elected in July 1948, and, on 15 August, the United States turned the government over to the Republic. American troops were withdrawn by the end of June 1949. About 500 U. S. advisers remained behind to train a hastily organized South Korean army.

In May 1948, the Communists of North Korea proclaimed the People's Democratic Republic of Korea with its capital at Pyongyang. When the Russians withdrew shortly afterward, they left behind a well organized and trained North Korean army and a substantial body of advisers to complete the training.

Indochina

When the Japanese occupied Indochina in 1941, she had been a French colony for nearly half a century, and France had exercised control over parts of Indochina long before that. For three years the occupying Japanese left day-to-day administration in the hands of the local French government, but after the Americans invaded the nearby Philippines, they seized complete control, interning the French administrators and disarming or killing whatever French troops failed to escape across the border into China. The Japanese then combined the three eastern states of Indochina into what they called the autonomous realm of Vietnam and appointed as their puppet head of state the playboy emperor Bao Dai.

In southern China, closely watching these moves, was 55-year-old Ho Chi Minh, a Moscow-trained Marxist revolutionary, founder of the Indochinese Communist party and long an exile from his native Vietnam. Around himself he had organized a militant, Communist-dominated Vietnam League for Independence, or Vietminh, composed of various Vietnamese nationalist groups.

When Japan accepted the Allied surrender terms, the Vietminh invaded Vietnam, disarmed the Japanese, and called on the Vietnamese people to support their crusade for independence. On 19 August 1945, the Vietminh entered Hanoi and forced Bao Dai to abdicate. On 2 September, while the Japanese were signing the instrument of surrender in Tokyo Bay, Ho Chi Minh mounted the outdoor balcony of the Hanoi opera house and to a cheering crowd announced the founding of the Democratic Republic of Vietnam, with himself as president.

In late 1945 French troops began arriving in Indochina with the aim of reestablishing the old colonial control. When this proved beyond their means, the French government offered to recognize, subject to referendum, Ho's Democratic Republic of Vietnam as a free state within the Indochina Federation and the French Union. Mutual distrust, however, led to increasingly hostile acts that culminated in French shelling of the Vietnamese port of Haiphong. The Vietminh retaliated by attacking French garrisons, thus initiating the seven-year (1947–54) French–Vietminh War.

The French army largely succeeded in expelling the Vietminh from the cities, but Ho's forces remained strong in the countryside. The French navy became involved, providing limited carrier air support for shore operations and improvising riverine forces to penetrate the interior.

A special difficulty for the French was that they could win little cooperation from the Vietnamese people, to most of whom the French represented hated colonial imperialism. Understanding nothing of Marxist philosophy, the Vietnamese gave their support to Ho Chi Minh as the deliverer of their country from imperial domination.

There were, however, enough anti-Communists in Vietnam to organize in the southern city of Saigon a party in opposition to the Vietminh. They invited Bao Dai to return from exile in Hong Kong and head their government. The French, embarrassed to be fighting a nakedly colonial war, acquiesced. In 1949 they signed an agreement with Bao whereby he became chief of state of a French-sponsored Vietnam. The United States and the United Kingdom extended recognition to the Bao Dai government.

Almost from the beginning of the French–Vietminh War, both the French and Ho Chi Minh had been appealing for aid from the United States. Ho, favorably impressed by the recent U. S. freeing of the Philippines, hoped that the Americans would respond to the cause of freedom. But recent experience with the Soviet Union had bred among Americans distrust of all Communists, including Ho and his followers.

President Truman was faced with the unhappy choice of disregarding his containment policy or supporting French imperialism. For three years he remained aloof from the struggle in Vietnam. Then in April 1950 the Chinese Communist government, having recently gained control of all mainland China, signed an agreement with Ho Chi Minh's Democratic Republic of Vietnam to provide the latter with arms and other supplies. A few days later Truman approved an allocation of funds to support the French in Indochina, and soon a steady stream of war materials—planes, naval craft, munitions, and other supplies—began flowing from the United States to the embattled French.

President Eisenhower followed his predecessor's example, explaining the supposed necessity of his action by what he called "the falling domino principle." As he put it, "If Indochina fell, not only Thailand but Burma and Malaya would be threatened, with added risks to East Pakistan and South Asia as well as to all Indonesia." Eventually the United States was footing nearly 80 percent of the financial costs of the French war against the Vietminh.

Japan

Unlike Germany, Japan was not divided between occupying powers at the end of the war. The Allied Command named the United States as the occupying power and General of the Army Douglas MacArthur as Supreme Commander. By the terms of the surrender, Japan agreed to a democratic government and to free elections. Under the direction of General MacArthur, a cabinet headed by Baron Kijuro Shidehara granted the franchise to women, lowered the voting age from 25 to 20, and dissolved the vast family and corporate trusts that had constituted much of Japan's economic and military strength. A new constitution was ratified and became effective 3 May 1947. Under it Japan renounced her right to wage war and the idea of the divinity of the emperor, and also abolished the House of Peers. A new Diet became the "highest organ of state power and sole law-making authority."

In American strategic planning for the Far East, Japan was established as one of a series of key positions running through Okinawa and Formosa to the Philippines. Areas of friction with the Russians developed over the Kuril Islands and fishing rights in the waters between Japan and Siberia. Further friction developed from Russia's efforts to organize a Communist party in Japan. Although small, the party was well organized and so active that, on 6 June 1950, General MacArthur ordered the government to ban Communist members of the Council from public activities "for perversion of truth and incitation to mass violence."

Naval Developments

To solve postwar naval problems required much imagination and boldness in a time when national feeling was concentrated on peace. Officers and men of the U. S. Navy were being released from active duty so fast that it was sometimes difficult to get ships to ports where they could be decommissioned. The first step taken in the United States to prepare for possible future trouble was to organize a strong reserve of both ships and trained personnel. Some ships that had outlived their usefulness or whose cost of maintenance would exceed their replacement value were disposed of by sale or transfer. Others were sold outright to private citizens. Some were scrapped. A few were used as target ships in atomic tests at Bikini Atoll in the Marshall Islands. Most ships that were worth retaining in the fleet but that had to be decommissioned for want of funds and personnel were put in "mothballs."[1]

The establishment of an adequate, well-trained Naval Reserve was of utmost importance. Drilling units were set up in the various naval districts, some with drill pay for 48 drills a year. The Organized Reserve consisted of units with authorized complements of 200 enlisted men and 15 officers. In addition there were many volunteer specialized units in electronics, intelligence, base construction (Seabees), aviation, and many others. Fourteen days' paid training duty afloat or ashore annually was authorized for reservists in the programs. Some of these cruises were in fleet ships, others in district ships, usually destroyer escorts assigned to the various naval districts and kept in partial commission with a skeleton crew on board. The reservists would fill out the crew and help take the ship to sea.

The active fleet operations were extended to include the Navy's traditional role of implementing diplomacy. Beginning in 1947 the U. S. Sixth Fleet remained on continuous duty in the Mediterranean, showing the flag and helping to support Western interests. One carrier was always on duty there; a second carrier, several cruisers, and destroyers completed the carrier task force. In addition there was maintained an amphibious force of transports carrying the Fleet Marine Force. Logistic supply was handled primarily from the United

---

[1]"Mothballing" was intended to preserve ships from the deterioration usually considered inevitable in long periods of idleness. Gun mounts were covered in a moisture-proof "cocoon" of vinylite plastic. Machinery spaces were sealed and electrically dehumidified. Ships' records were transferred intact to storage, and propulsion machinery was greased and otherwise protected from moisture. The success of the program became apparent with the outbreak of war in Korea when the mothballed ships were returned to full service in a matter of a few weeks.

States on a simulated wartime basis. This force existed not only as an arm of diplomacy but as a force to strike offensively in time of war, to protect American lives and interests, to act as goodwill ambassadors, and to keep control of all that vital waterway, essential for Western communication lines. With the establishment of NATO, joint naval operations came into increasing prominence. NATO signals and tactics were developed for joint operations of ships of NATO navies, and joint maneuvers were successfully held on several occasions.

The U. S. Navy spent much time and effort in combating the submarine menace for future operations. Hunter-killer groups, sonobuoys, high frequency radio direction finders, sonar, and other devices were refined and improved.

Developments were also extensive in naval aircraft design and operation. The jet fighter completely replaced the old propeller-driven types. Jet bombers became common, and the speed of aircraft, both fighter and bomber, far outstripped anything available in the war years. *Essex*-type carriers received strengthened flight decks to accommodate jet planes and heavier bombers. One of the most radical changes in design was the angled carrier deck, which was developed by the British and was installed in the USS *Antietam* and other U. S. carriers. The landing section of the deck was angled about eight degrees to port so that a plane coming in for a landing would not crash through the barriers into planes parked on the forward part of the flight deck. This kind of angling also permitted simultaneous landing and launching operations from one carrier, planes being sent off forward at the same time others were landing aft.

Changes in munitions were also of prime importance. Automatic 6- and 8-inch guns were developed and installed in cruisers. Automatic 3-inch guns began to replace 40-mm mounts as antiaircraft weapons. In the field of rocket weapons both the Army and the Navy conducted extensive developmental programs.

The helicopter was another important development in the Navy's aircraft program. Its flexibility of operation and the small space needed for landing and take-off meant that it could operate successfully from cruisers and battleships as well as carriers. It made a good scout and was able to relieve destroyers of some of the more onerous mail-delivering duties as well as the duty of plane guard in carrier operations. In Korea these craft were to play many other important roles from air strike control planes to rescue missions. Supply or evacuation of isolated positions was but one of the vital services they performed. The lives of many wounded were saved by these "whirly-birds" operating from hospital LSTs and hospital ships, for they were able to pick a wounded man up from an advance dressing station and fly him directly to the hospital vessel.

Nuclear Weapons

The U. S. armed services required more precise knowledge of their atomic bomb. They wanted to know how to use it effectively in offense, and they needed to know its capabilities and limitations so that countermeasures might be taken to minimize its effects in event an enemy used it. Hence the War and Navy departments scheduled a test of the weapon, to be conducted by a joint task force under the command of Vice Admiral W. H. P. Blandy in the summer of 1946 at Bikini Atoll in the Marshall Islands. More than 200 ships, 150 planes, and 42,000 men participated. Placed in the target area to provide study for blast damage and radiation contamination were 75 vessels, most American, some German and Japanese. Included were elderly battleships, carriers, cruisers, destroyers, attack transports, submarines, and smaller types.

Each of the vessels carried scientific instruments, an assortment of equipment, and live animals to measure or reflect the effects of the blast and subsequent radiation. Drone airplanes were prepared to fly through the resulting cloud and send back scientific data. Drone boats were to take samples of the water after the explosion.

Two bombs were exploded, the first, dropped from a B-29; the second, several weeks later, suspended below the surface. Eleven ships were sunk, and others were battered and burned. The water of the lagoon was made so dangerous by radioactivity that four days after the second blast it was unsafe for personnel to spend any "useful length of time" on board the target vessels.

The United States did not long enjoy monopoly of the atomic bomb. Partly as the result of the work of traitors, and partly as a result of Soviet scientific knowledge, the Russians in 1949 exploded an atomic bomb of their own—several years earlier than Western scientists had thought possible. In subsequent years Great Britain, France, Communist China, and India developed and tested atomic bombs.

Far more destructive than the atomic bomb is the hydrogen (or thermonuclear) bomb, a prototype of which the United States tested at Eniwetok Atoll in 1951. The Soviet Union soon followed with its own hydrogen bomb test. Subsequently Britain and Communist China staged tests of this terrible weapon.

Summary

After World War II, the U. S. administration, seeking "a bigger bang for a buck." supported a move to merge the armed services and thus avoid expensive duplication and possible cross purposes. Secretary of the Navy James Forrestal led a successful fight for retention of the Joint Chiefs of Staff and the Navy's air components and Marine Corps. The National Security Act of 1947 provided for a National Military Establishment (later, Department of Defense), headed by a secretary of defense of cabinet rank. Its components were the departments of the Army, Navy, and Air Force, each with its secretary, not of cabinet rank.

Forrestal, as first secretary of defense, sponsored construction of a supercarrier, the *United States*, which could handle planes able to carry the atomic bomb. Forrestal's successor, Louis Johnson, stopped work on the *United States* and slashed budgetary provisions for naval and marine corps air. In the ensuing "revolt of the admirals," naval officers denounced Johnson's alleged notion that B-36 bombers armed with atomic bombs were all that was needed to safeguard the United States.

In 1947 the United States inaugurated her policy of "containment," which thereafter dominated U. S. relations with the Communist world. It began with the so-called Truman Doctrine of helping free peoples (initially Greece and Turkey) to resist aggression, the Marshall Plan of providing economic aid for the rebuilding of war-ravaged Europe, and the policy of keeping the carrier-centered U. S. Sixth Fleet in the Mediterranean.

When the United States, Britain, and France announced issuance of a common currency for their zones in Germany and their sectors in Berlin, the Soviets retaliated by blocking overland access to Berlin. Britain and the United States responded with an airlift that kept West Berlin supplied for 11 months, until the blockade was lifted.

In 1949, the United States, Canada, and nine nations of western Europe, plus Greece and Turkey (and, later, West Germany), formed the North Atlantic Treaty Organization (NATO), pooling land, sea, and air forces and declaring that an attack on any one of them would be considered an attack upon them all.

Communism threatened to engulf much of the Far East. General MacArthur ensured that it made no serious headway in Japan, but Chiang Kai-shek and his Nationalist Government in China were less effective. Despite massive logistic aid from the United States, the Nationalists were unable to stem the advance of Mao Tse-tung's Communists. In 1949, as the Communists completed their conquest of mainland China, the Nationalist Government retreated to Formosa, which thereafter became more generally known as Taiwan.

To facilitate acceptance of the Japanese surrender, Korea at the end of World War II was divided at the 38th parallel, with the Russians occupying the North and the Americans the South. Because the North Koreans, under Russian tutelage, barred a UN commission from holding free elections in their territory, Korea became divided into two nations. When the occupying forces withdrew in 1948–49, North Korea had a much more powerful army than that of South Korea.

Upon the withdrawal of the occupying Japanese from Indochina at the end of World War II, Ho Chi Minh's Vietnam nationalists moved in and established a Communist-dominated Democratic Republic of Vietnam, with its capital at Hanoi. Returning French forces, unable to oust the Vietminh, accepted the founding in southern Vietnam of an anticommunist counter-state, with its capital at Saigon. The United States long remained aloof from the ensuing French–Vietminh War. But beginning in 1950, when the Communist Chinese started providing the Vietminh with weapons, the United States more and more assumed the burden of supporting the French armed forces in Vietnam.

The United States did not long enjoy the monopoly of either the atomic bomb or the far more destructive hydrogen bomb. More quickly than Western scientists had believed possible, the Soviet Union and Communist China acquired both.

Chapter 32

Implementing the U. S. Policy of Containment

Hasty demobilization and meager defense spending following World War II so weakened U. S. military power as to make it difficult if not impossible for the government to back up its policy of containing the spread of Communism. By the end of 1949, the administration had apparently abandoned any thought of extending direct protection to Formosa or any part of continental Asia. On 12 January 1950, Secretary of State Dean Acheson, speaking extemporaneously before the National Press Club, stated that the U. S. line of defense "runs along the Aleutians to Japan and then goes to the Ryukyus. . . . The defense perimeter runs from the Ryukyus to the Philippines." In thus pointedly excluding Korea and Taiwan (Formosa) from the perimeter, Acheson was merely stating the policy of the president, the secretary of defense, and the Joint Chiefs of Staff. The following May, Tom Connally, chairman of the Senate Foreign Relations Committee, stated that should the Soviets seize South Korea, the United States was unlikely to intervene.

All such statements were highly interesting to the Soviets. Since World War II they had been maneuvering to get a free hand in Korea, either directly or through their client state of North Korea. The 1905 United States–mediated Treaty of Portsmouth, ending the Russo–Japanese War, had recognized Japan's paramount position in Korea, thus opening the way for Japan's eventual annexation of that country. Now the United States was drafting a peace treaty for Japan, preparatory to withdrawing American occupation forces. The Soviets expected the new treaty to recognize Russia's paramount position in Korea. "When they saw it wasn't going to work out that way," said George Kennan, "they concluded: 'If this is all we are going to get out of a Japanese settlement, we had better get our hands on Korea before the Americans let the Japanese back in there.' "

By June 1950 the North Koreans, with Russian help, had built up a formidable military force: 130,000 men under arms, plus 100,000 trained reserves. Their army was provided with Soviet weapons, including 150 tanks, and was supported by an air force of 180 World War II Soviet combat planes.

South Korea's armed forces were far less formidable. By mid-1950 her army numbered about 94,000 men, but they were mostly recent recruits, hastily assembled in response to North Korea's warlike preparations. They were not combat ready, and they had no tanks, no medium artillery, and no aircraft. They were but feebly backed by U. S. forces afloat and ashore, because most of America's military power that had not been amputated by the Truman–Johnson economies had now been committed to NATO. In Japan were General MacArthur's occupation forces, consisting of Lieutenant General Walton H. Walker's U. S. Eighth Army, comprising four undermanned, undertrained divisions; and Vice Admiral C. Turner Joy's U. S. Naval Forces Far East, which comprised only a light cruiser and a division of four destroyers. Available but not under MacArthur's command was the U. S. Seventh Fleet. Based in the Philippines, commanded by Vice Admiral Arthur D. Struble, it included only the carrier *Valley Forge*, a heavy cruiser, a squadron of destroyers, and a division of submarines. Fortunately for these lightweight naval forces, North Korea's navy consisted only of 45 small craft.

The Korean War, 1950–53

On the morning of 25 June 1950, North Korean troops poured across the 38th parallel in a full-scale invasion of South Korea. The North Koreans and their Chinese and Russian sponsors evidently believed there would be no sharper external reaction than diplomatic protest. In New York, however, the United Nations Security Council promptly convened in emergency session and without a veto, by virtue of a Russian boycott, condemned the North Korean invasion as a breach of world peace and forthwith ordered military sanctions.

In a startling shift of policy, President Truman, infringing on Congress's constitutional authority to declare war, decided to commit the U. S armed forces to the defense of South Korea. He delegated

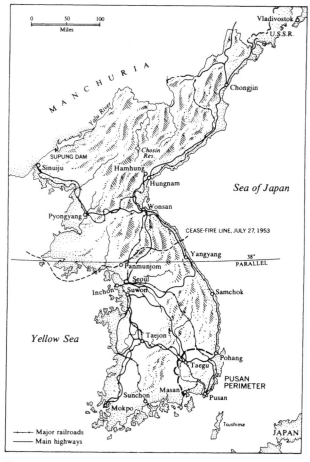

Korea

responsibility for the "police action," as he later called it, to the Joint Chiefs of Staff, who appointed General MacArthur Commander in Chief Far East and placed the Seventh Fleet under his command. The United Nations called on its member states to assist the United States, and eventually 16 of them provided combat elements, and 5 others sent medical units.

The North Korean invaders, spearheaded by an armored brigade, drove south toward Seoul. The surprised defenders, lacking antitank weapons, fell back in a hopeless rout. When the Reds entered the capital on 28 June, the South Korean army was shattered, half its troops missing, captured, or dead.

The retreating South Koreans had managed to blow the bridges over the Han River just south of Seoul. The invaders were thus obliged to pause while they ferried their tanks and guns across. During the interval, the first American troops, two battalions of the 24th' Infantry Division, arrived from Japan via the Korean port of Pusan and ad-

vanced to meet the Communists. Then, digging in, falling back from one roadblock to another, blowing bridges, they succeeded in slowing the Red drive, which was further hampered by difficulties of supply. At last the invaders, overestimating American strength, deployed across country instead of smashing through to Pusan, as they well might have done.

As the Americans slowly retreated, inflicting far more casualties than they took, they were strongly supported on their right by the Republic of Korea army, which was beginning to recover from its early reverses. In the time gained by the fighting retreat, the rest of the 24th and two more American divisions had arrived in Korea, reconstituting the Eighth Army, and General Walker, in command, was able to draw around the port of Pusan a defense perimeter. Within this so-called Pusan Perimeter, by taking advantage of his interior position, he was able to hold back superior forces. The retreat was halted, but the American people were shocked to see their military forces, recent major victors over three world powers, now so whittled down by penny-pinching as to be thrust into a corner by the forces of one minor power.

The operations of the U. S. Seventh Fleet, with British warships attached, had been and remained indispensable in maintaining the United Nations defense in Korea. Planes from the *Valley Forge* and the British light carrier *Triumph* joined land-based aircraft in wrecking bridges, marshaling yards, hangars, oil refineries, and fuel storage depots, and utterly eliminating the small North Korean air force. Throughout the war, Seventh Fleet surface vessels kept the east coast road and railroad unusable for supplying North Korean forces. Thus, all the supplies reaching the North Koreans at the Pusan Perimeter had to come through Seoul, on the far side of the mountainous interior. At the Perimeter itself, carrier planes gave close support to the Eighth Army, an employment for which Air Force pilots had not been trained.

Though bitter fighting continued all along the Pusan front, by mid-September the situation there was stabilized. The UN troops lacked the power to break out of the Perimeter, but the North Koreans needed all their forces and a continuous flow of ammunition and other supplies to hold them in.

General MacArthur had foreseen the stalemate and had been preparing to take advantage of it. Engaged in the Perimeter operation were about 90 percent of North Korea's troops—absolutely dependent upon supplies flowing steadily from the north. Now was the time to place an armed force in their lightly defended rear to cut their supply line. Such a thrust could of course be carried out only by amphibious assault. Before the end of July the Joint Chiefs of Staff had authorized such an attack and had agreed to send marines to spearhead the operation.

When, in mid-August, MacArthur informed the Joint Chiefs that he intended to invade at the port of Inchon, the chiefs had second thoughts. At first glance Inchon seemed the perfect choice. It is the port of Seoul, through which all southbound supplies had to pass. Recapture of the South Korean capital would at the same time depress the morale of the North Korean forces and render their situation untenable.

But Inchon sits behind many square miles of islands, shoals, and mud flats, and is approachable from seaward only through narrow, winding Flying Fish Channel or East Channel, both of which could be readily mined. A ship disabled by mine or bomb in one of these channels would trap those ahead and block those behind it. There were no beaches at Inchon. Ships heading for the main invasion point would have to pass the fortified island of Wolmi Do,

and the marines would be obliged to clamber over a seawall onto an industrial area with a clutter of railroad tracks and probably fight their way from building to building. The tidal range of Inchon— one of the greatest in the world—averages 30 feet, but only twice a day, three days out of each lunar month, would the tide be high enough for the troop-bearing LSTs, which required a minimum of 29 feet to maneuver. MacArthur had selected 15 September, when the tide would be high enough at sunrise and again at sunset.

When MacArthur's plan to invade Inchon, via Flying Fish Channel, became known among the senior officers involved, it caused intense concern at Pusan, Tokyo, and Washington. General J. Lawton Collins, Army Chief of Staff, and Admiral Forrest C. Sherman, Chief of Naval Operations, hastened from Washington to Tokyo—intent on learning how the general intended to overcome the handicaps of Inchon and, if necessary, talk him out of so quixotic an enterprise. At a meeting in the evening of 20 August at MacArthur's headquarters in the Dai Ichi building in Tokyo, MacArthur listened quietly as officer after officer pointed out that a landing at Inchon was impossible.

General MacArthur then arose and in an eloquent 30-minute monologue won the reluctant consent of all concerned. He had no plan to overcome the drawbacks of an Inchon landing. He left all that to the Navy, which had never let him down. One of his reasons for selecting Inchon, he said, was precisely because of its handicaps. The North Koreans would never suspect anyone of being so audacious as to attempt a landing there. Hence the assault force would have the priceless advantage of surprise. He drew a parallel with the capture of Quebec in 1759, when General Wolfe chose for his landing the "impossible" Anse du Foulon. From this little inlet his troops, by ascending the cliff and appearing at dawn on the Plains of Abraham, so rattled the Marquis de Montcalm that the latter abandoned the safety of the city walls and dashed out with his forces onto the plain, where they were quickly defeated.

MacArthur's principal victory at this point was winning over Admiral Sherman, who returned to Washington and secured the consent of the rest of the Joint Chiefs. For his assault force, MacArthur was allocated a reconstituted 1st Marine Division, which included four battalions of South Korean marines. His follow-up force would be the U. S. Seventh Infantry Division, brought up to strength by the attachment of some 5,000 South Korean troops. Together, these two divisions constituted the X Corps, the command of which MacArthur entrusted to his chief of staff, Major General Ed-

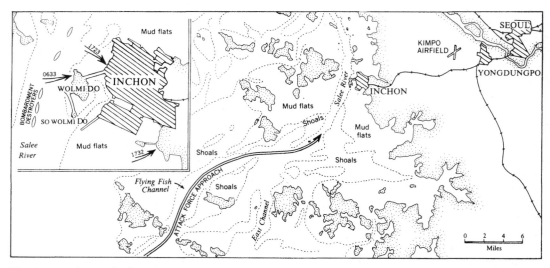

The Approaches to Inchon

ward M. Almond, USA. The X Corps, comprising altogether 71,000 officers and men, would be transported and supported by a hurriedly assembled international fleet of 230 ships. The tight schedule permitted no opportunity for rehearsal.

The Navy sacrificed complete surprise in favor of softening up the intended beachhead. Beginning 5 September, the *Triumph* and a pair of U. S. escort carriers ranged along Korea's west coast, launching strikes against Inchon and also, to mislead the North Koreans, against other possible landing points. On the 13th the U. S. fast carriers *Valley Forge* and *Philippine Sea* began sending in planes to pound the island fortresses of Wolmi Do and adjacent So Wolmi Do, guarding Inchon's inner harbor.

Meanwhile, six U. S. destroyers, backed by two American and two British cruisers, negotiated Flying Fish Channel and took the two sentinel islands under direct fire for an hour. The treatment was repeated on the 14th. That evening the ships of the attack force, under Rear Admiral James H. Doyle, in total darkness entered Flying Fish Channel and felt their way by radar toward the city. Included were the bombardment vessels of the past two days and the amphibious command ship *Mount McKinley* with General MacArthur and Admiral Doyle on board.

Before dawn the amphibious vessels and gunnery ships anchored off Wolmi Do. At first light, marine Corsairs from the distant escort carriers *Badoeng Strait* and *Sicily* began making strafing runs over the island. Next, the destroyers, cruisers, and rocket ships opened fire. The control vessel hoisted, then lowered, the red flag, and LCVPs, carrying a battalion of marines, headed for the

beach, accompanied by a vessel firing rockets and 40-mm shell. The marines began going ashore a little after 0630, and as they fought their way up a steep hill, landing craft brought in tanks. General MacArthur, watching intently from the deck of the *Mount McKinley*, saw the American colors raised on the hilltop. When the report came in, "Wolmi Do secured," he turned with a broad smile to the other officers. "That's it," he said. "Let's get a cup of coffee." Later in the morning, while naval guns and planes forced defending gunners to take cover, marines raced along a causeway from Wolmi Do and captured little So Wolmi Do.

Ships and aircraft now had several hours to work over the city defenses while the tide ebbed and flowed. In the late afternoon, an hour before high tide, a regiment of marines, carried over the mud flats in amtracs, landed south of the city and raced for the railroad connecting Inchon to Seoul. Another regiment, in LCVPs, approached the industrial area north of the inner harbor. Here the fleet and planes had concentrated their fire. Beyond the seawall the approaching marines could see little but smoke and flame. As their landing craft crashed into the wall, they raised crude scaling ladders and clambered over. At peak of tide, an hour after the infantry landings, eight LSTs abreast approached the wall, now partly obliterated, and landed bulldozers, which broke down enough of the remaining wall to enable tanks and other heavy equipment to be landed.

The North Koreans at Inchon put up a sturdy resistance, but there were too few of them. They were nearly wiped out, while the assault phases on all beaches cost the marines only 21 killed and 186 wounded. The marines had not, after all, suffered from the lack of rehearsal. The key UN officers afloat and ashore had participated in amphibious operations in World War II and had learned their lessons well.

On 17 September the marines took Kimpo airfield, the largest in Korea, and advanced to attack Seoul. On the 18th the 7th Infantry Division landed at Inchon and drove south toward Suwon, which it captured on the 22nd. Seoul fell to the marines on the 26th. As MacArthur had predicted, the UN capture of Seoul put the North Koreans at the Pusan Perimeter in an impossible situation, without any hope of supply or reinforcement. General Walker's Eighth Army, timing its attack to coincide with the Inchon landing, found the North Korean army melting away. Many North Koreans were killed, a good number escaped northward through the mountains, and more than 125,000 were taken as prisoners of war. On the day that Seoul fell to the marines, an armored spearhead of the Eighth Army made contact with the 7th Infantry Division south of Suwon.

General MacArthur's audacious gamble had paid off in one of the most triumphant military operations in history. In 15 days impending defeat had been turned into overwhelming victory. On the day of the Inchon assault, MacArthur had signaled: "The Navy and Marines have never shone more brightly than this morning." Now at the end of the campaign the never-defeated MacArthur stood at the apex of his career.

On 27 September, the Joint Chiefs authorized MacArthur to "conduct military operations north of the 38th parallel," if necessary to achieve "the destruction of the North Korean armed forces." The Eighth Army, after mopping up the liberated countryside, advanced northward from Seoul, while Republic of Korea troops marched into North Korea along the east coast road. MacArthur, intent on achieving another amphibious end run, had Almond's X Corps embarked at Inchon and brought around to North Korean ports on the east coast. The 1st Marine Division was to make a landing at Wonsan, but the North Koreans had thickly mined Wonsan harbor, as they should have mined Inchon. By the time the mines were swept, the South Korean army had taken Wonsan from the rear, and the Eighth Army had captured Pyongyang, the North Korean capital.

The Communist Chinese government had for some time been warning that if UN troops approached the Chinese border on the Yalu River, China would intervene. MacArthur and his intelligence staff did not take the threat seriously, believing that if the Chinese intended to enter the war, they would have done so while the UN forces had

their backs to the sea at Pusan. In a conference with President Truman at Wake Island on 15 October, General MacArthur expressed the opinion that the Chinese threat was a bluff. There was no simple way to verify rumors of a Chinese buildup of force along the border because the Joint Chiefs strictly forbade MacArthur to send planes, or any other armed force, across the Yalu to violate Chinese territory or airspace.

On the strength of his intelligence estimates, and secondarily to test Chinese intentions, MacArthur sent General Walker's Eighth Army northward from Pyongyang and General Almond's X Corps north from Hungnam. As the two forces drove toward the Yalu, they were separated from each other by 80 miles of mountainous terrain, so that liaison between them had to be handled through Tokyo. Given the uncertainty of China's designs, MacArthur's strategy was dubious, to say the least, but after the brilliant success of Inchon, nobody felt qualified to question his judgment.

Into the gap between the Army and the Corps, the Chinese in the night of 25 November hurled a 180,000-man offensive. In bitter cold both UN drives were in full retreat after efforts at mutual support had failed. The Eighth Army fell back, trading space for time, past Pyongyang, past the 38th parallel, and past Seoul.

The retreat of the X Corps was less precipitate. Elements of the 1st Marine Division had reached the Chosin Reservoir. There Chinese, numbering 120,000, surrounded them, threatening them with total extinction. The marines, using a perimeter defense, held their position until they could organize for retirement southward. The ensuing withdrawal, over difficult terrain, through snow and cold, under constant attack and harassment, was one of the great retreats of history. The marines, skillfully supported by carrier aircraft from the Seventh Fleet, fought their way through eight Chinese divisions, bringing out most of their equipment and the survivors of three army battalions that had also been cut off in the reservoir area. In mid-December the last of Almond's X Corps reached Hungnam, where they were safe under the protection of Seventh Fleet guns and planes. From Hungnam 100,000 troops, together with their equipment, and almost as many civilian refugees were evacuated by sea.

The X Corps, disembarked at Pusan, was merged into the Eighth Army, which in late January established itself on a firm defense line a few miles south of Seoul. Commanding the Eighth Army was Lieutenant General Matthew B. Ridgway, replacing General Walker, killed in an automobile accident. The Chinese and North Korean troops, who considerably outnumbered their UN opponents, now had the support of Russian-built MIG-15 jets based in Manchuria. Their Chinese and North Korean pilots, however, could never wrest command of the air from the well-trained American flyers. On the other hand, denial of permission for UN planes to fly over Manchuria, even for a moment, provided the MIGs a sanctuary toward which they could streak when attacked by UN jets.

The Communists' advantage in numbers was more than offset by their difficulties in keeping themselves supplied. Seventh Fleet bombardments of coastal roads forced them to rely on inland communications. Strikes by carrier- and land-based UN planes so successfully interdicted use of the inland trails, roads, and railroads by day that the Reds had to depend largely on supplies transported by night, and often backpacked. Seventh Fleet carrier planes, in their campaign against Communist supply routes, performed the extraordinary feat of bombing three of the Yalu bridges with such precision that only the Korean halves were destroyed, thus avoiding violation of Manchurian airspace. The Reds, denied adequate ammunition and other supplies, could not maintain an offensive. Hence the well-supplied UN forces were able to turn the tide and drive their opponents back across the 38th parallel, inflicting heavy casualties.

MacArthur, eager to push the Chinese and the North Koreans back to the Yalu, proposed blockading the China coast, bombing points in China, and making use of the trained Nationalist Chinese troops on Taiwan—either in Korea or against mainland China to relieve the pressure on the UN forces in Korea. When the Joint Chiefs turned down these proposals as likely to expand the war, MacArthur busied himself holding press conferences and releasing news bulletins in support of his recommendations. President Truman, annoyed, issued an order requiring military commanders to clear all policy statements with the Pentagon.

The president, the State Department, and the Joint Chiefs had in fact about decided to seek a cease-fire as soon as South Korea had been well cleared of the enemy. By mid-March 1951 the time seemed at hand. The president circulated among the participating UN governments, for approval, a proposal to the Communists for an armistice—one that provided for a return to the status quo. The proposal was meticulously worded to avoid any hint of threat or accusation.

A copy of the armistice message went to General MacArthur, for information only. MacArthur promptly torpedoed the president's initiative by issuing on his own what amounted to an ultimatum, threatening Red China with new reprisals that would doom her "to the risk of imminent military collapse." He stood ready at any time, he said, to meet the enemy commander in chief in the field to accept his capitulation. The Chinese government scornfully rejected the general's taunting overture, and the president was obliged to shelve his cease-fire proposal.

Congressman Joseph Martin had recently delivered an inflammatory speech accusing the president of holding back the Nationalist Chinese troops from opening an Asian second front. "If we are not in Korea to win," the congressman had concluded, "then the Truman administration should be indicted for the murder of thousands of American boys." Martin sent a copy of his speech to General MacArthur, and the general, in a letter that the congressman promptly made public, endorsed the charges.

For President Truman this was too much. To the vast relief of his UN allies, he dismissed MacArthur from all his Far East commands, replacing him with General Ridgway. Lieutenant General James Van Fleet relieved Ridgway in command of the Eighth Army.

In the third week of April 1951, the Communists launched their spring offensive. The Eighth Army gave way slowly, hitting hard, and inflicting such heavy losses that it was able at last to turn its withdrawal into an advance. Its primary object now was inflicting as many casualties as possible. By mid-June the Red losses had become so severe that Jacob Malik, Soviet delegate at the United Nations, proposed cease-fire negotiations, and both sides agreed.

The truce talks began the following month, carried out mostly in the village of Panmunjom. They lasted two years, the Communists finagling to attain with words the victory they had been unable to achieve by force of arms. A limited war continued, involving minor attacks and clashes between outposts.

Finally, on 27 July 1953, the armistice was signed, dividing Korea not along the 38th parallel, but along the more defensible line on which the armies faced each other. South Korea thus lost 850 square miles in the west but gained 2,350 in the east. For this small exchange of territory the cost was grim. The South Koreans had lost 70,000 killed in action; the Americans, 34,000; and the other UN participants, 5,000. The Chinese are estimated to have suffered 960,000 battle casualties; the North Koreans, 640,000. The Korean civilians were the chief victims of the struggle. Approximately 3,000,000 North Koreans and 500,000 South Koreans were killed or died from war-related causes.

New Naval Weapons

The Korean War discredited a good many post–World War II notions about national power—particularly Louis Johnson's delusion that amphibious forces, aircraft carriers, the Marine Corps, and indeed the Navy itself were obsolete, and that all that was needed to safeguard American interests around the world was a few squadrons of B-36s armed with atomic bombs. Before the war was six weeks old, President Truman had fired Johnson, replacing him as secretary of defense by General of the Army George Marshall—a change hailed with thanksgiving throughout the Army and Navy.

In August 1951 the U. S. Navy ordered the construction of a supercarrier to take the place of the *United States*, whose building Johnson had canceled. Ironically, the new carrier was christened ·the *Forrestal*, after the defense secretary who had authorized the *United States*. Displacing 78,000 tons, she was followed in the 1950s and 1960s by seven somewhat similar carriers. In 1961 the 89,600-ton *Enterprise*, the world's first nuclear-propelled carrier, was commissioned. The next nuclear-powered carrier was the *Nimitz*, 91,400 tons, commissioned in 1975, the first of her class. A critical feature of the nuclear carriers was their ability to cruise 13 years or more without refueling.

The new carriers were designed to carry out the attack-and-support functions performed by carriers in World War II and the Korean War. But they also had an additional function—that of deterrence against nuclear attack on the United States. To perform this function they had to be big enough to handle the big planes that could carry nuclear weapons—the Skyhawk (A-4), the Intruder (A-6), the Corsair (A-7), and the high-flying Phantom fighter (F-4). These weapons posed a constant threat of nuclear counterattack should the Soviet Union contemplate a preemptive strike against U. S. airfields and missile sites. The need for such means of deterrence became more acute after the Russians acquired the superdestructive thermonuclear (hydrogen) bomb in 1953. The need became critical in 1957 when, for a time, the Soviet Union had an intercontinental ballistic missile (ICBM) and the United States had none.

Meanwhile, submarines were undergoing a structural evolution that at length enabled them in large measure to take over the deterrence mission. The evolution was begun during World War II by

the Germans, seeking increased underwater speed and endurance. Improved hull design boosted speed, and use of the snorkel increased endurance. At war's end the Germans were experimenting with liquid hydrogen peroxide, instead of the atmosphere, as a source of oxygen for their diesel engines.

In the United·States the experiments that led to the construction of the atomic bombs suggested that the heat generated by nuclear fission might be a source of power for propelling submarines. A devoted naval research and development team, headed by the hard-driving, irascible genius Hyman Rickover, produced the submarine *Nautilus*, the first nuclear-powered vessel of any type. In Long Island Sound, on 17 January 1955, she marked an epoch in naval operations as she got under way propelled by atomic energy.

The *Nautilus*'s submerged cruising capacity was dramatically demonstrated in the summer of 1958 by Commander William R. Anderson, who commanded her on a voyage from Pearl Harbor to England, passing under the arctic ice pack. The following year the nuclear-powered submarine *Skate*, under Commander James Calvert, not only duplicated the *Nautilus*'s voyage but broke through 12 feet of arctic ice to surface at the North Pole—thereby incidentally demonstrating the stoutness of the new submarines, a structural toughness that enabled them to dive to a depth of 1,500 feet or more. In 1960 Captain Edward L. Beach took the nuclear-powered *Triton* around the world submerged, following generally the route of Magellan.

The early nuclear-propelled submarines were all rendered obsolete by experiments with the diesel-driven research submarine *Albacore*. Whale-shaped, fully streamlined, with a blunt, rounded bow, she made the unprecedented speed of 33 knots submerged. Her hull design was adopted for the *Skipjack*-class of nuclear-propelled attack submarines, the first of which was laid down in May 1956, and, with some modification, for all nuclear-powered strategic missile submarines.

Submarines continued to be equipped with torpedo tubes. The torpedoes were guided by acoustical homing systems. They were fired by water pressure, replacing the former air-pressure firing, which could reveal the submarine's presence and location by releasing bubbles. Also fired from the torpedo tubes was a submarine rocket (Subroc), which left the water and could speed through the air 25 to 30 miles before dropping a homing torpedo or nuclear depth charge.

Admiral Arleigh Burke, not long after he became Chief of Naval Operations in the summer of

1955, set up a Special Projects Office in the Bureau of Ordnance and selected Rear Admiral William F. Raborn to head it. Its function was to devise means of firing ballistic missiles from the sea. Ship-based rockets would provide an alternate deterrent, swifter and hence more effective than carrier-based aircraft.

Raborn's committee experimented gingerly with the Jupiter, an intermediate-range ballistic missile (IRBM) developed by the Army. As a ship-board operational weapon, however, the Jupiter presented appalling problems. Weighing 55 tons, it stood as high as a six-story building. Its liquid-oxygen fuel component was a frightful fire hazard. Fortunately, some experiments in 1956 demonstrated the feasibility of a solid propellant. Soon thereafter the Atomic Energy Commission devised means of greatly reducing the size and weight of a thermonuclear warhead. The Navy immediately wedded the new warhead and a solid-fuel body to create the Polaris, an IRBM 32 feet long, weighing 15 tons.

Here was a missile that could be fitted into the big, new nuclear-propelled submarines. The Navy stopped work on two of the *Skipjack* class and ordered inserted between the bow and stern sections an additional 130-foot section to accommodate two rows of eight missile tubes, together with missile fire control and inertial navigation systems. The submarines thus converted were named *George Washington* and *Patrick Henry*. On 20 July 1960, the *George Washington* fired the first Polaris missile from underwater. By that date the U. S. Air Force had developed the Atlas, the first American ICBM, and the Soviet navy had a nuclear-propelled ballistic missile submarine of its own. Eventually the French and British navies each acquired a few nuclear-powered ballistic missile submarines.

The first U. S. submarine built expressly to carry the Polaris missile was the *Ethan Allen*, commissioned in August 1961. She and others of her class had subsequently to be modified to carry Polaris missiles of increasing size and range. Enlarged versions had to be built to accommodate the Poseidon and Trident missiles, with ranges respectively of 3,200 and 4,000 miles. During the late 1960s and the 1970s, the United States had 41 nuclear-propelled missile submarines, named for famous Americans. Each submarine had two crews, called the Blue and the Gold, which would alternate in 60-day cruises, generally submerged. At all times, an average of 25 of these submarines were on patrol. Difficult to locate, able to reach any

point in the world with their pretargeted, multiple-warheaded (MIRV) missiles, they became the nation's most dependable deterrent.

The first cruiser constructed for the U. S. Navy after World War II was the *Long Beach*, laid down in December 1957. She was unique also in being the first nuclear-propelled surface warship and the first ship built with guided missiles as her main battery. She was one in a series of guided-missile cruisers, some converted World War II light and heavy cruisers, more built from the keel up. A few of the latter were nuclear-propelled. Their primary function was to defend aircraft carriers from air, missile, and submarine attacks.

The destroyer continued to be the most versatile of warships. Some post–World War II destroyers were armed mainly with guns; others, mainly with nonnuclear missiles. Their functions varied from protecting carriers to attacking submarines, for which they had a potent weapon in the Asroc, an antisubmarine rocket. A slower, less fully armed destroyer type was the frigate, designed mostly for ocean escort of merchant convoys and amphibious forces.

The example of Inchon silenced those who asserted that large-scale amphibious operations were a thing of the past. The U. S. Marine Corps was left intact with its air arm, and the Navy began laying down assault vessels of various sorts. A new type was the amphibious assault ship, combining the capabilities of several earlier types. During the 1960s seven of the *Iwo Jima* class were launched. These were 17,000-ton ships with flight decks. They were capable of carrying more than a battalion of marines and launching them in helicopters. During the 1970s five of the larger *Tarawa* class were launched. Displacing as much tonnage as World War II *Essex*-class carriers, which they somewhat resembled, they were intended to handle VSTOL (Vertical Short Take-Off and Landing) aircraft as well as helicopters. They could accommodate a reinforced marine battalion, together with their vehicles, and had a docking well for landing craft and amtracs.

The Nuclear Deadlock

The competition between the United States and the Soviet Union to surpass or at least rival each other in destructive power resulted in a nuclear deadlock that the *New York Times* called a "balance of terror." The deadlock imposed ill-defined but definite limits on international intervention. An example was the reaction to Russia's brutal suppression in November 1956 of Hungary's revolt against her Soviet-dominated government. Though the General Assembly of the United Nations condemned the Russian action, the Western governments realized they could do nothing short of risking a general war that could escalate into a nuclear holocaust.

On the other hand, the United States in 1958 was able without undue risk to support friendly governments in Lebanon and Taiwan against Communist intrusion. In each situation President Eisenhower had forehandedly obtained authority from Congress to employ armed force.

When Communist elements from Syria fomented revolution in Lebanon, Lebanese President Chamoun on 14 July appealed to the United States for military aid to ensure that his country's forthcoming scheduled election should be lawful and orderly. In the next two days, under cover of planes from the carrier *Essex*, 5,000 U. S. marines landed on the beaches near Beirut and joined the Lebanese army in restoring order. Thanks largely to this prompt and decisive show of strength, the Lebanese election was held in accordance with the law. Soon afterward the marines departed.

A potentially more dangerous situation was developing on the other side of the world. On 23 August the Communist Chinese, as if in preparation for an invasion, began heavily bombarding the island of Quemoy—just off the mainland but claimed by Taiwan and garrisoned by about 100,000 Nationalist Chinese troops. On orders from Chief of Naval Operations Admiral Burke, the U. S. Seventh Fleet moved to the vicinity of Taiwan, where it was reinforced until by late September it comprised 150 warships, including six carriers. United States Air Force and Marine Corps fighters from the Philippines and Japan operated from Taiwan airfields, joining the U. S. carrier planes in guarding Taiwan, thereby freeing the Nationalist air force to deal with Communist air power in the vicinity of Quemoy. The Sidewinder air-to-air, heat-seeking missile supplied by the U. S. Navy to the Nationalist fighters proved itself in combat against Communist MIGs. The U. S. Navy also provided expert schooling to Chiang Kai-shek's little navy in the vital task of resupplying the beleaguered garrison across beaches under fire, and furnished a screen of fighting ships off Quemoy when this task was carried out. The threat of war at length subsided, with the Nationalists more firmly entrenched than ever on Quemoy and their other offshore islands.

The U. S. government soon had cause to worry about a situation nearer home. In Cuba the rebel leader Fidel Castro in 1959 seized control of the state. At first, Washington welcomed him as a desirable alternative to the harsh regime he had overthrown, but it soon became known that with help and advice from Moscow he was setting up a Communist dictatorship at America's doorstep. While broadcasting tirades against the United States, Castro coolly confiscated a billion dollars worth of U. S. investments in Cuba and ordered the U. S. embassy staff at Havana drastically reduced. The United States broke diplomatic relations with Cuba, and President Eisenhower directed the Central Intelligence Agency (CIA) to train anti-Castro Cuban exiles for an invasion of their homeland. Accordingly, the CIA established a secret camp for 1,400 trainees in Guatemala. Eisenhower left to his successor, President Kennedy, the decision whether to use them.

Kennedy was advised that the invasion would trigger a revolt in Cuba and that the people would join the invaders in a attack on their hated government. Thus assured, Kennedy consented to the operation but forbade use of U. S. military forces to support it. The president had been badly advised. The invasion on 17 April 1961 set off no revolt. The invaders, landing in the ill-chosen Bay of Pigs, walked into a trap and were all killed or captured.

The Bay of Pigs fiasco humiliated the United States, established Castro more firmly in power, drew Cuba further into the Soviet orbit, and convinced Premier Khrushchev that Kennedy's failure to use U. S. armed forces showed lack of nerve. Khrushchev therefore undertook the gamble of setting up in Cuba launching pads for intermediate-range missiles with nuclear warheads. The CIA, learning that something unusual, involving Russians, was afoot, sent high-flying U-2 observation planes over Cuba. On 14 October 1962, one returned with photographs of a missile site in an advanced state of construction.

President Kennedy, after considering the alternatives, called on the Navy to set up a modified blockade, which he called a quarantine, to intercept weapons-bearing ships en route to Cuba. After briefing congressional leaders and informing the heads of other NATO powers of his decision, the president on the evening of 22 October went on television and explained to the American people, and indirectly to the Russians, what the Soviets were doing and what he intended to do about it. On the morning of the 24th, having given the Russians two days to react, Kennedy directed the Navy to proceed with the quarantine. "Send the order in

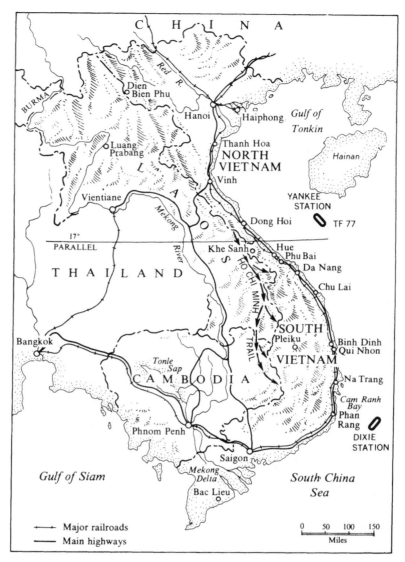

Vietnam

the clear," he said, as a means of notifying the Russians as well as U. S. ships and stations.

Nearly 200 vessels, destroyer types supported by cruisers and carriers, promptly took station on the "quarantine line," a great arc centered on and 500 miles away from the eastern end of Cuba. The whole world seemed to hold its collective breath as it waited for the showdown, with the possibility of nuclear war. That afternoon, U. S. aircraft patrolling the Atlantic reported Russian freighters stopped, or turning back, short of the line of American warships. At the White House Secretary of State Dean Rusk said, "We're eyeball to eyeball and I think the other fellow just blinked."

Khrushchev, perceiving that he had no choice between capitulation and nuclear warfare, agreed to remove the missiles. To take some of the sting out of the Russian defeat, Kennedy promised not to invade Cuba. Nevertheless Russia was humiliated, and Khrushchev was discredited. Soviet leaders, considering the part played by U. S. sea power in the Cuban crisis, in the Lebanon and Quemoy incidents, and in the Korean War, became convinced that they could not attain national objectives while relying solely on submarines for naval power. To them recent events provided persuasive arguments for building a surface navy.

The Vietnamese War, 1960–75

The end of the Korean War enabled Communist China to step up sharply her flow of weapons to Ho Chi Minh's Vietnamese forces. Armed with Chinese artillery, some 50,000 Vietnamese in early 1954 surrounded a 13,000-man French garrison at Dien Bien Phu and in a 55-day siege pounded it into submission.

Exhausted, the French and Vietnamese were glad to accept an armistice. A 14-nation conference, assembled at Geneva, divided Vietnam into two parts, separated by a demilitarized zone at the 17th parallel. All French troops were to withdraw from positions north of the zone; all Vietnamese troops, from positions south of the zone. The effect was to create two nations: Ho Chi Minh's Democratic Republic of Vietnam, or North Vietnam, with her capital at Hanoi; and Bao Dai's State of Vietnam, or South Vietnam, with her capital at Saigon. Accords reached at Geneva specified that Vietnam was to be reunited in two years by national plebiscite.

President Eisenhower, in line with the U. S. policy of containing Communism, began providing South Vietnam with arms and other needs and sent advisers to help establish and train a South Vietnamese army and navy. As the U. S. advisers moved into South Vietnam, the French armed forces moved out of Indochina, thereby relinquishing all claim to Vietnam—and Cambodia and Laos as well.

Ngo Dinh Diem, the tough, autocratic premier of South Vietnam, soon deposed Emperor Bao Dai. Confirming himself by referendum as head of state, he declared South Vietnam a republic and himself her first president. He refused to permit his country to participate in the national plebiscite stipulated by the Geneva accords, pointing out that the votes in the North, which would be government-dictated, could overwhelm the less populous South.

Such was Ho Chi Minh's reputation as a freedom fighter that he was revered throughout Indochina. His politics were less popular. He and his deputies were obliged to use brutal methods, involving considerable bloodshed, to consolidate Communist control of North Vietnam. By 1960, however, the Hanoi government had sufficiently solved its internal problems to turn its attention toward unifying the whole country through conquest of South Vietnam. They began by encouraging dissident movements in the South and by infiltrating part of their own armed forces through the demilitarized zone. They thus initiated in South Vietnam an insurrection whose partisans called themselves the National Liberation Front, but who were generally known as the Vietcong. The Vietcong set about gaining control of the peasantry by alternating propaganda and persuasion with terror and massacre.

Ngo Dinh Diem, as client of the United States, had to be reasonably circumspect in extending his jurisdiction over South Vietnam. Moreover, as a devout Catholic he was opposed to using murder as a political expedient. But as Vietcong guerrilla operations spread, sometimes with the connivance of religious sects and local authorities, Diem grew increasingly despotic. He established concentration camps, abolished village governments, and declared nationwide martial law.

Aside from the Vietcong, Diem's greatest internal opposition came from militant Buddhist leaders. To force them into line, security police headed by Diem's brother, Ngo Dinh Nhu, closed pagodas and arrested Buddhist clergy and their student supporters. In retaliation, Buddhist monks and nuns dramatically advertised their grievances to the world by burning themselves to death in public places.

The U. S. government became increasingly displeased by Diem's tyranny, and the American advisers were exasperated by Diem's passive use of the South Vietnamese army they had armed and trained. On 1 November 1963, on a hint from Washington, South Vietnamese generals deposed Diem. They then shocked the Americans by also killing Diem and his brother. Thereafter for several years South Vietnam was headed by a series of unstable military governments.

President Kennedy's response to the spreading Vietcong insurrection was to send South Vietnam increasing quantities of war materials and more and more advisers. After the Bay of Pigs fiasco he felt he had to show some success against the Communists, and his military counselors repeatedly assured him that a little more effort would restore peace in Vietnam. At the time of his assassination in November 1963, there were nearly 17,000 U. S. advisers in South Vietnam, and some were in effect exercising military command. Helicopters with American pilots were supporting Vietnamese troops and returning enemy fire, U. S. naval vessels with sophisticated electronic equipment were visiting the Gulf of Tonkin to listen in on North Vietnam internal radio communications, and a beefed-up U. S. Seventh Fleet was operating out of the Philippines as a warning to Communist China to keep hands off Taiwan and Vietnam.

On 2 August 1964, North Vietnamese torpedo

boats came out and made hostile runs on the U. S. destroyer *Maddox*, then snooping in the Gulf of Tonkin. In the night of the 4th, the *Maddox* and the U. S. destroyer *Turner Joy*, while operating in the gulf in a rain squall, believed they were objects of another torpedo attack. Both ships did a good deal of shooting but only at radar targets, which apparently were phantoms. At any rate, Hanoi always insisted that no North Vietnamese vessels were out that night.

On orders from President Johnson, who took the alleged second attack seriously, bombers from Seventh Fleet carriers *Ticonderoga* and *Constellation* carried out the first U. S. raid on North Vietnamese territory by bombing torpedo-boat bases and an oil storage depot. The United States thus initiated the longest war in U. S. history and, next to World War II, the costliest in lives and money.

To give further military operations legal sanction, Johnson pushed through Congress the Tonkin Gulf Resolution granting him a free hand "to repel any armed attack against the armed forces of the United States and to prevent further aggression." Congress again had surrendered its war-making power to the president.

In February 1965 Johnson, in retaliation for a Vietcong mortar attack on a U. S. military advisers' barracks at Pleiku, ordered carrier plane attacks on barracks and port facilities in North Vietnam. Three days later the Vietcong shelled another U. S. barracks, and the carriers staged a more massive raid on North Vietnam.

Johnson now ordered in the U. S. marines to defend the bases. On 8 and 9 March, at the coastal air base of Da Nang, the first echelon of two marine battalions came ashore—not as advisers but as acknowledged combat troops. Soon U. S. Army combat troops also were arriving in South Vietnam in ever-increasing numbers.[1] Both they and the marines made frequent offensive forays into the interior. At the end of 1965, 180,000 Americans were in Vietnam, fighting in all–U. S. combat units.

Another 50,000 Americans served with the U. S. carriers and supporting vessels in the South China Sea. Two to four carriers with their escorts regularly steamed back and forth at "Yankee Station" at the mouth of the Gulf of Tonkin, ready to send strikes against military targets north of the

demilitarized zone or to support operations below. A single carrier operated at "Dixie Station" off South Vietnam until mid-1966, when enough land-based aircraft were available to take over support of maneuvers in that area. Newly arrived carrier pilots usually gained their first experience against live targets by operating from "Dixie Station" before going north to face the formidable Soviet-supplied antiaircraft defenses of North Vietnam.

Seventh Fleet cruisers and destroyers, joined briefly by the recommissioned battleship *New Jersey*, bombarded enemy positions near the coast. United States naval and coast guard vessels cooperated with the growing South Vietnamese navy in interdicting Communist coastal and river traffic. An Army–Navy riverine force raided Vietcong positions on the rivers, sometimes using novel craft reminiscent of the U. S. Civil War gunboats on the Mississippi.

Against a unified North Vietnam liberally supplied with weapons and ammunition by China and the Soviet Union, the Americans could make little progress. The United States was allied to a divided nation headed by an unstable government. United States mechanized forces were often at a disadvantage against elusive enemy guerrillas, who could take sanctuary in neutral Laos or Cambodia. For fear of bringing China or Russia into the war, the Americans refrained from crossing the demilitarized zone and generally avoided bombing North Vietnam's cities or blockading her harbors.

The nature of the war began to change as regular army troops from North Vietnam came pouring through the supposedly inviolable demilitarized zone. To stem the flow, U. S. marines established a line of strong points across the Vietnam narrows a little south of the demilitarized zone, anchoring the line at Khe Sanh just short of the Vietnam–Laos border. The enemy merely sidestepped the marine strong points, passing troops and transporting supplies via Laos, along the so-called Ho Chi Minh Trail.

At the end of January 1968, the North Vietnamese and Vietcong launched their Tet offensive—no shadowy guerrilla operation but an all-out drive to capture the main cities of South Vietnam.[2] At the same time 60,000 well-armed Communist troops surrounded the 5,000 marines at Khe Sanh, vowing to make it an American Dien Bien Phu. Khe Sanh, gravely threatened, was saved by the prowess of the marines, plus massive air support,

---

[1]In response to a U. S. appeal to make the containment of North Vietnam an international crusade, South Korea sent two divisions of troops, the Philippines sent 2,000 soldiers, and Australia, New Zealand, and Thailand sent token forces.

[2]*Tet*: the Vietnamese New Year, a three-day holiday commencing with the first new moon following 20 January.

which now included devastating strikes by B-52s operating out of Guam and Thailand air bases.

By April the Tet offensive had failed, with terrible casualties on both sides. The South Vietnamese and the Americans had relieved the besieged cities, and South Vietnam had achieved a new unity. The United States, on the contrary, had become divided. Many Americans were demanding a withdrawal of U. S. forces from the costly, apparently endless war. American cities and campuses were the scenes of large-scale antiwar demonstrations. President Johnson, feeling himself repudiated, announced that he would not run for reelection. To persuade Hanoi to negotiate, he stopped all bombing of North Vietnam. Negotiations did in fact begin in Paris, but the Communists refused to make any concessions whatever until all foreign troops had been withdrawn from Vietnam.

When President Nixon took office in January 1969, there were more then half a million U. S. fighting men in Vietnam, including 85,000 marines and 38,000 sailors. By that date the war had cost the lives of more than 40,000 Americans. Nixon had come to office with the promise to "Vietnamize" the conflict, gradually turn it over to the Vietnamese and bring the Americans home. This now seemed possible, because South Vietnam at last had a reasonably stable government, most of the population had been brought under government control, and the South Vietnamese army and navy were growing and developing military skills. By the end of August 25,000 American troops had left Vietnam, with many more scheduled soon to follow.

To simplify South Vietnam's future defense problems, South Vietnamese and U. S. troops in April 1970 invaded Cambodia to break up the North Vietnamese sanctuary there and seize munitions and other stores. Some 40,000 South Vietnamese troops remained in Cambodia to neutralize Communist operations in that country against South Vietnam—and also against the central Cambodian government. In February 1971, the South Vietnamese army, with U. S. air support, invaded Laos to disrupt the infiltration routes of the Ho Chi Minh Trail.

In early 1972, the Americans remaining in Vietnam retired entirely from ground combat, and the U. S. and South Vietnam governments offered the Communists a plan for ending hostilities. This plan Hanoi and the Vietcong scornfully rejected, remaining so intransigent that the Paris peace talks were soon suspended as futile.

The Communists turned down the proffered peace terms because, now supplied more generously than ever with modern weapons from China and Russia, they were about to launch a new drive by which they fully expected to bring the war to a conclusion on their own terms. In March they staged a massive, three-pronged invasion of South Vietnam—into the South, into the central highlands, across the demilitarized zone. Unlike the guerrilla warfare of the past or even the Tet offensive, the new invasion featured heavy artillery and columns of tanks. The South Vietnamese fell back on all fronts.

The United States now resumed full-scale bombing of all North Vietnam, flying bombers in from South Vietnam, Guam, Thailand, and the Seventh Fleet. On orders from President Nixon, American planes mined the harbors of North Vietnam and completed the blockade of the country by concentrating on roads and railroads connecting with China.

The South Vietnamese, thus supported, halted their retreat, held fast, and began to counterattack. By July they were advancing everywhere and had regained control of their northern provinces. In September the situation had become sufficiently stabilized that Nixon restricted the bombing of North Vietnam to the panhandle below the 20th parallel. All parties recognized that the war had reached military stalemate.

When the publicized Paris peace talks were suspended, U. S. presidential adviser Henry Kissinger continued to conduct secret negotiations with North Vietnamese politburo member Le Duc Tho. When these negotiations reached an impasse in mid-December 1972, Nixon ordered 12 days of utterly unrestricted bombing of North Vietnam. Huge areas of Hanoi and Haiphong were reduced to rubble.

In a new series of talks in January 1973, Kissinger and Le Duc Tho at last ironed out their differences. A new agreement, accepted by the interested powers, was initialed by the negotiators and subsequently signed by the Vietnamese foreign ministers and the U. S. secretary of state. It called for a cease-fire, withdrawal of all U. S. troops from Indochina, prompt release of military prisoners, creation of an international commission to supervise the peace, and the right of the people of South Vietnam to determine their own political future.

The United States rapidly dismantled her bases in Vietnam and withdrew the last of her troops. Thereafter North and South Vietnamese forces engaged in desultory combat that the small international commission was unable to mediate or suppress. At the end of 1974, North Vietnam began a drive that, as it gathered force, took as its objective the final conquest of South Vietnam. In early 1975 the Communists in Cambodia launched an offensive to overthrow the established Cambodian government.

Without U. S. air support, the armed forces of South Vietnam and Cambodia proved utterly incapable of stemming the Communist onslaught. By March 1975 the North Vietnamese had overrun half of South Vietnam, and in Cambodia the Communists had nearly surrounded Phnom Penh, the Cambodian capital. On 17 April the Cambodian government surrendered to the Communists. On the 30th, Russian-built tanks led the North Vietnamese army into Saigon, and what was left of the South Vietnamese government capitulated. The government of Laos, bowing to North Vietnamese pressure, quietly submitted to a takeover by the Laotian Communists. Ho Chi Minh was now dead, but his dream of an independent, Communist Indochina had been realized.

The U. S. crusade in Vietnam had been futile as well as foredoomed. It had cost 56,000 American and possibly two million Vietnamese lives and 135 billion American dollars. It had discredited the U. S. policy of containment. When none of the rest of Southeast Asia followed Indochina into the Communist camp, the domino theory seemed likewise discredited.

Summary

When Communist North Korean troops in June 1950 crossed the 38th parallel to invade South Korea, the United Nations called on its members to apply military sanctions. The U. S. government, assuming the principal burden, ordered General MacArthur to repulse the invaders. After the North Koreans had forced the defending Eighth Army into the southeast corner of Korea, MacArthur had the Seventh Fleet land the marine-spearheaded X Corps at the port of Inchon on the Korean west coast. From here the marines advanced and captured Seoul, thereby blocking supplies to the North Korean army, which quickly disintegrated under Eighth Army counterattack.

Both the Eighth Army and the X Corps now invaded North Korea. When the two forces, widely separated, advanced toward the Yalu River, hordes of Chinese troops attacked them and forced them to retreat. In January 1951, the Eighth Army, having absorbed the X Corps, established itself on a firm defense line south of Seoul and began to thrust the Chinese and North Korean troops back across the 38th parallel. In the midst of this campaign, President Truman dismissed MacArthur for insubordination, replacing him with General Ridgway. Heavy losses at length induced the Communists to negotiate. In July 1953, after two years of haggling, the opponents signed an armistice, dividing Korea along the current battle line, which straddled the 38th parallel.

The most striking post–World War II additions to the U. S. Navy were big carriers, some nuclear-propelled, able to handle planes that could carry nuclear weapons; and fast, nuclear-propelled submarines bearing ballistic missiles of ever-increasing size and range—Polaris, Poseidon, Trident—that could be fired from underwater.

In 1958, carrier-supported U. S. marines landed in Lebanon at the request of the Lebanese president to help quell Communist-inspired disorder and ensure an orderly election, and the Seventh Fleet stood off Taiwan to warn Communist China to keep hands off Taiwan and the Taiwanese island of Quemoy. In 1961 an attempt by U. S.-trained Cuban exiles to invade Cuba at the Bay of Pigs was defeated. The following year, the U. S. Navy, by stationing a line of warships on the approaches to Cuba, induced the Russians to abandon their project of placing missiles with nuclear warheads on the island.

In 1954, after the French army was defeated at Dien Bien Phu by Ho Chi Minh's Communist-dominated Vietnamese forces, an international conference arranged a cease-fire and divided Vietnam by a demilitarized zone at the 17th parallel. Because the division apparently confined the Communists to North Vietnam, the United States sent arms and advisers to help South Vietnam build up armed force to keep them there. In 1964, President Johnson, charging that two American destroyers in international waters had been attacked by North Vietnamese torpedo boats, ordered U. S. carrier planes to bomb targets in North Vietnam and obtained from Congress a resolution authorizing him to use U. S. armed forces to "prevent further aggression."

By the end of 1968, Johnson had more than half a million Americans in Vietnam—fighting armed South Vietnamese political dissidents called Vietcong and North Vietnamese who infiltrated through the demilitarized zone or via neutral Laos. The U. S. Navy provided carrier air support, shore bombardment, and vessels to patrol South Vietnamese coasts and rivers.

In 1969 President Nixon, bowing to pressure from the American public, began withdrawing Americans from Vietnam as the growing South Vietnamese army and navy proved able to take over the burden of the war. In 1972, after the Americans had retired entirely from ground combat, the South Vietnamese army, with U. S. air support, threw back a massive Communist offensive. At the end of the year, Nixon, by unrestricted bombing of North Vietnam's cities, induced the North Vietnamese to accept an agreement by which, in return for withdrawal of U. S. troops from Vietnam, they promised to release all prisoners of war and let the people of South Vietnam determine their own political future. After the Americans had dismantled their bases and departed, the North Vietnamese overran South Vietnam and united the country under Communist rule. The governments of adjacent Cambodia and Laos also submitted to Communist domination.

Chapter 33
New Weapons, New Challenges

The humiliating end of the U. S. involvement in Vietnam had unhappy consequences for American self-confidence and for American policy-making in the field of foreign affairs. It also caused widespread misgivings about American dependability. Other circumstances fostered doubts that the United States possessed the leadership and the power to defend the free world, or even herself, from Soviet aggression. Confidence in U. S. leadership was undermined by the forced resignation of President Nixon, the caretaking administration of President Ford, and the vacillations of President Carter. Reliance on U. S. power was eroded by the decline of American military strength concurrent with a steady increase in Soviet arms—at a time when the Soviet Union was avowedly moving to preempt the strategic materials of Africa and the oil of the Persian Gulf, on which the free world had come to depend.

The U. S. Navy

In the 1950s and early 1960s, as the U. S. Air Force B-52 bombers built up to planned strength, as the ICBM silos were emplaced, and as the missile-armed nuclear submarines were developed, the United States came to rely on the concept of the "triad" for defense against nuclear attack. The redundancy of three weapons systems capable of destroying any enemy was deemed worth the cost, because it forced upon the enemy a much-enlarged problem to devise countermeasures, and it provided insurance that if one leg of the triad were to be rendered vulnerable through some breakthrough in weapons technology, the United States would still retain a convincing measure of strategic deterrence.

Soon, however, not one but two legs of the triad began to appear less dependable. Improved surveillance techniques, mainly through use of satellites, and ever-more-accurate guidance systems made the fixed-site missile silo vulnerable. The B-1 supersonic intercontinental bomber, designed to replace the aging, subsonic B-52, was rejected as too costly. At the end of the 1970s, there remained to the United States only one unassailable deter-

rent: her nuclear submarine force with its barrage of long-range missiles.

President Johnson, underestimating the rate at which the Soviets were arming themselves, cut back on all weapons not useful in the costly Vietnam War. The Soviets were thus enabled to approach equality with the United States in deployment of ballistic missiles. In 1972, in the first Strategic Arms Limitation Talks (SALT I), the United States, facing the facts, in effect agreed to relinquish strategic superiority in exchange for assured parity.

In a period in which the Soviet Union was outbuilding the United States also in conventional weapons, President Nixon set about relaxing international tensions. He restored relations with a formerly hostile mainland China, which had split with the Soviet Union. He visited Peking as a guest of the nation and subsequently exchanged visits with the Soviet Union's Leonid Brezhnev, secretary general of the Russian Communist party. By thus playing off one potential enemy against the other, he did much to bring about the period of détente and easing of tensions that was climaxed in 1979 by the signing of the SALT II treaty by Presidents Carter and Brezhnev.[1]

Thus lulled, the U. S. public was less concerned with keeping up its armed might than with lowering taxes and at the same time enhancing the social welfare programs, which by 1980 consumed 21 percent of the gross national product. By the same date, the U. S. Navy had shrunk to its weakest state in 40 years, outnumbered by the Soviet Navy in every class of ship except aircraft carriers and major amphibious warfare vessels.

While the Soviet Union and every country of western Europe except Britain and Ireland continued to rely on conscription, the United States in 1973 replaced her draft with an all-volunteer force. A feature of the volunteer plan was comparability; service personnel received salaries comparable to those of their civilian counterparts. But military

---

[1]Brezhnev was elected president in June 1977 and thus became the first Soviet official to hold simultaneously the posts of party leader and chief of state.

pay failed to keep up with inflation. By 1980 it lagged 40 percent behind salaries in the civilian sector. The effect on retention was disastrous. Reenlistment rates, which until 1977 had risen steadily under the all-volunteer system, declined precipitously in the career-petty-officer brackets— a particularly serious situation at a time of increasingly sophisticated weaponry.

Despite its weakened condition, the U. S. Navy was counted on for three specific offensive capabilities: an intercontinental ballistic missile barrage from its nuclear-powered submarines, a formidable strike capacity aboard its far-ranging carrier task forces (after 1978 referred to as "battle groups"), and conduct of amphibious warfare. All major U. S. fleet unit projects were evaluated for their utility in these offensive roles.

In 1980 the older among America's original 41 nuclear-propelled strategic-missile submarines were approaching the end of their service lifetimes. None had been commissioned since 1967, a period during which the Soviet Navy had built more than 60 such craft. Replacements for the aging American missile submarines were to be a new *Ohio* class. The *Ohio* herself, launched in 1978, was at that time the largest undersea craft ever built—560 feet long, displacing 18,700 tons submerged. Her main battery was 24 Trident missiles, with an effective range of up to 4,000 miles. Trident-2, under development, was expected to have a 6,000-mile range. The Tridents were designed to carry multiple independently targeted (MIRV) warheads.

Though many Soviet attack submarines had been armed with cruise missiles since the 1960s, the U. S. Navy did not deploy a cruise missile that met its exacting standards until the late 1970s. The first to be adopted was the Harpoon, designed for use against ships and carried by submarines, surface vessels, and aircraft. Fired from a submarine's torpedo tube, the Harpoon would surface and skim the waves at close to the speed of sound, to deliver its 510-pound warhead as far as 60 miles away. Under development was the Tomahawk cruise missile, able to deliver a 1,000-pound warhead, conventional or nuclear, against a ship or land target at ranges out to 375 miles.

The aircraft carrier continued as the capital ship of the U. S. Navy's all-purpose surface force. The newer ones were the biggest war vessels ever built. A second *Nimitz*-class carrier, the *Dwight D. Eisenhower*, was commissioned in 1977. A third, the *Carl Vinson*, was launched in 1979. The Department of Defense projected a force level of 12 carriers into the indefinite future. Of this number, 4 would normally be forward deployed—2 in the

Sixth Fleet in the Mediterranean and 2 in the Western Pacific with the Seventh Fleet. The Iran crisis of 1978, however, broke the pattern, requiring one or more carrier battle groups in the Indian Ocean. In 1979–80, the *Nimitz*, during her deployment to the Indian Ocean, rang up some sort of record with 144 consecutive days under way.

As the F-14 Tomcats gradually replaced the F-4 Phantoms in the carrier squadrons, the United States could claim the best air defense plane in the world. With a ceiling of 60,000 feet and a speed of Mach 2.4, this aircraft carried a multi-target radar and the Phoenix long-range air-to-air missile. Its radar missile system tracked 24 targets simultaneously, and it could attack 6 of these at one time. When inflation drove the cost of the Tomcat up to $25 million, the Navy was obliged to complete replacement of some of the F-4 fighter squadrons with the less expensive F-18 Hornet, a very good aircraft but of lower capability than the F-14 in the interceptor role. However, the Hornet was designed for attack missions also, and would replace the A-7 Corsair in naval light attack squadrons. The E-2 Hawkeye, a carrier-based early warning aircraft, proved to be the world's best electronic and control plane. It had a powerful radar and effective passive detection systems, as well as secure UHF and HF links. With its on-board computer, the Hawkeye was a complete information center.

Despite the impressiveness of the big carriers and their attack and defense systems, not all naval leaders were satisfied with the concentration of so much of the Navy's offensive power in a single vessel. One such officer was Admiral Elmo R. Zumwalt, Chief of Naval Operations 1970–74, who wrote: "Because of the high accuracy of anti-ship missiles, the large carrier represents too many dollars per ship to be optimal as a combatant in a sea control war."

Zumwalt proposed the construction of "sea-control ships," small helicopter carriers designed to commercial rather than combatant ship specifications to minimize costs. They would carry helicopters for antisubmarine warfare and VSTOL aircraft for air defense. Lack of a VSTOL fighter with adequate range, weapons, and all-weather radar, plus opposition from Congress, killed the sea-control ship concept.

President Ford included an additional *Nimitz*-class carrier in his 1977 budget, but it became a political casualty of his loss of the 1976 election. His successor, President Carter, proposed, as a less costly alternative to the *Nimitz*es, the building of 50,000-ton carriers with conventional propulsion. But the smallest ship the Navy could design that could safely handle such high-performance aircraft as the F-14 was about 60,000 tons. Because of the marginal performance (two screws, 27-knot speed, and limited damage protection) of the ship Carter proposed, and the fact that it violated the Defense Appropriations Act of 1975, which required all major combatant vessels for the Navy's strike forces to have nuclear propulsion, Congress overruled the administration and authorized the building of a fourth *Nimitz*. President Carter thereupon, in an unprecedented action, vetoed the entire Defense Appropriations Act. Congress persisted, however, and despite the threat of a presidential veto, added the fourth *Nimitz* to the 1980 budget, which the president ultimately accepted.

Admiral James L. Holloway III, Admiral Zumwalt's successor as CNO, proposed another alternative: eventual adoption by the Navy of VSTOL aircraft operating from a variety of vessels. If such aircraft could be developed with mission performance capabilities equal to those of their conventional counterparts, they could be effectively operated from virtually any sea-based platform, large or small—thus greatly expanding the alternatives available in carrier design, and increasing the flexibility of sea-based tactical aviation.[2]

Achievement of high-performance VSTOL aircraft could not be expected before 1995. In the meantime the Navy would have to continue using conventional aircraft and find some way to extend the service life of its big angle-decked carriers. Holloway's solution to the latter problem was the Service Life Extension Program (SLEP). This program called for the *Forrestal*-class carriers to be withdrawn from the active fleet, one at a time, and put out of commission for 2 years while they were refurbished as necessary to extend their useful life another 15 years—for a total of 45 years of active service in the fleet. In 1980 the first of the carriers entered SLEP. This was the *Saratoga*, which had been commissioned in 1956.

Paradoxically, the greatest threat to the orderly implementation of the VSTOL program came from enthusiasts in Congress and among civilians in the Department of the Navy who wanted to scrap ongoing aircraft developments and immediately begin construction of small carriers to handle the only VSTOL aircraft then available, the Harrier, whose capabilities fell far short of what was anticipated in the future. Naval officers wanted no part of

such downgrading of expectations, and Congress, by authorizing the fourth *Nimitz*, rejected precipitous abandonment of current capabilities. Holloway's successor as CNO, Admiral Thomas B. Hayward, pursued a program of VSTOL research and development that promised to lead to an orderly transition.

The Soviet Navy

World War II vindicated the trust Russia's leaders placed in ground forces for their national security. But in the ensuing cold war they found themselves confronting the maritime powers, which had demonstrated their capacity to execute and support amphibious assaults over great distances. Faced with the possibility of assaults on their own territory, the Soviets set about expanding their coast-defense forces: short-range aircraft and submarines, together with their surface support. In the post-Stalin period the Soviet planners, observing the reckless extent to which the United States was slashing her naval power, began to discount the likelihood of seaborne invasion and shifted emphasis to long-range aircraft and missiles.

The Soviet Union's race for military supremacy was precipitated by three American actions. In mid-1960 the nuclear submarine *George Washington* fired a Polaris missile from beneath the surface. Early the following year President Kennedy announced an acceleration of the Polaris program and a doubling of the production rate of ICBMs. In October 1962, the United States, possessing overwhelming nuclear superiority, forced Khrushchev's humiliating backdown in the Cuban missile crisis. The Soviet First Deputy Minister of Foreign Affairs grimly told an American official, "You Americans will never be able to do this to us again."

To the Soviets the expansion of the American Polaris and missile programs looked like a possible preparation for nuclear war, a war in which they would be in a no-win situation. Even if the first nuclear exchange wiped out U. S. continental defenses, the Americans would still have at sea submarine-based missiles for a second strike. The Soviet Navy had a few diesel-electric submarines that could fire a missile with a nuclear warhead, but only from the surface. To offset the American second-strike competence, the Soviets began forthwith to build long-range, nuclear-powered, missile-equipped submarines that would match or surpass the Polaris craft in numbers and striking power. They also put on the pressure to rival or outdo the U. S. land-based missile buildup. The U. S. Central Intelligence Agency (CIA) became

---

[2]The VTOL (vertical takeoff and landing) aircraft used by the Soviets on their *Kiev*-class carriers was the approximate equivalent in combat capability of the American F-86 of the Korean War era.

aware of the Soviet submarine project, but for 11 successive years it underestimated by 50 percent or more the number of land-based missiles the Russians were able to deploy—with the result that the Department of Defense unilaterally curtailed U. S. nuclear programs.

The Americans considered their fleet of 41 ballistic missile submarines adequate for the sea-based leg of their triad, but the Soviets pressed on considerably past that number, probably because of the limited size and effectiveness of their intercontinental bomber force. Each navy managed to keep itself fairly well informed concerning the other's submarine-building operations, with the result that each tried to outdo the other, in capabilities if not in numbers. The 18,700-ton *Ohios* were a counterpart to the Soviet 11,300-ton "Delta" class. In response to the *Ohios*, the Soviets began building a new "Typhoon" class of about 25,000-tons displacement, each Typhoon having 20 tubes for SLBMs (submarine-launched ballistic missiles).

The newest attack submarines in both navies were designed to fire both torpedoes and cruise missiles. The high-speed *Los Angeles* class, 6,900 tons submerged, making better than 30 knots under water, was developed to counter the Soviet "Victor" class. In reaction to the *Los Angeles* and her sister ships, the Soviets began building their "Oscar" and "Alfa" classes. The former displaced about 13,000 tons and carried 24 launching tubes. The latter displaced about the same tonnage as the *Los Angeles* but had a titanium hull that withstood the pressures at phenomenal depths. Submerged, the Alfas could outspeed the *Los Angeles,* but they were extraordinarily noisy and hence easy to track.

The expansion of the Soviet submarine fleet was the responsibility of Admiral Sergei Gorshkov, a brilliant strategist and innovator whom Khrushchev had brought to Moscow at the age of 45 to command the Soviet Navy. Gorshkov believed that the U-boats had been defeated in the two world wars because the Germans had been unable to afford them adequate air and surface support. He was determined that his own submarines should be amply supported, and he assumed that the United States and other NATO powers would similarly support theirs. He resolved therefore to have weapons in the air and afloat to destroy surface ships as well as submarines—preferably far from the Soviet Union.

To attack ships distant from Russia, Gorshkov planned to use the Backfire, a true supersonic bomber somewhat similar to the B-1 that the United States had decided against as being too expensive for its strategic value. The Backfire could

carry conventional or nuclear weapons, in the form of nine tons of bombs and two air-to-surface missiles. For surface or subsurface attack, Gorshkov would use submarines equipped with torpedoes and cruise missiles. For antisubmarine and surface warfare, he developed a formidable fleet of missile-bearing destroyers and cruisers. Some of the latter carried ASW helicopters, which they could launch from a flight deck aft.

The largest Soviet combatant ships in service in 1981 were the 36,000-ton *Kiev* and *Minsk,* carriers for powered-lift aircraft.[3] These vessels had about the same displacement, manpower, and aircraft capacity as the U. S. *Tarawa* class, but lacked the latter's accommodations for, and means of launching, large landing craft. The Soviets affected to disdain the Western-type carrier (conventional takeoff and landing) as vulnerable and useful mainly for supporting "imperialist aggression," but in 1981 persistent rumor had it that they were building their own 60,000-ton nuclear-propelled model.

A major function of the new Soviet fleet was to serve as an instrument of state policy, which had as its ultimate aim the achievement of a universal Communist state through world revolution. Gorshkov had studied naval history (through Marxist spectacles) and well understood that the old game of "showing the flag" was in fact a matter of displaying one's weapons as a means of winning friends and discouraging potential enemies. The Soviet fleet had to be strong enough to demonstrate its ability to "support wars of national liberation" and "thwart imperialist aggression." The Soviets, obsessively secretive about most military matters, were happy to display their naval might in extended cruises and in a pair of worldwide exercises in the seventies—called by the West *Okean*-70 and *Okean*-75.

Initially the Soviet Navy gave low priority to the interdiction of enemy sea communications, but in the 1976 edition of the *Soviet Military Encyclopedia,* published shortly after *Okean*-75, Admiral Gorshkov gave such interdiction the Soviet Navy's number three priority, after strategic and counterforce missions.

The following table compares force levels of major combatant ships as of 1980. Other types (mine, patrol, etc.) are not easily comparable because of wide variations in size, strength, and mission. It should be noted, moreover, that though the *Iwo Jimas* (7), the *Tarawas* (5), and the *Kievs* (2)

[3]Powered-lift aircraft: a general term including helicopters, VSTOL, VTOL, and all other aircraft whose engines provide lift directly via propellers or jet thrust.

were capable of similar air operations, the American vessels were designed primarily for amphibious operations; the Russian, for fleet tactical operations. The Soviet *Moskvas*, with the aft placement of the flight deck, were unsuitable for VSTOL operations and were strictly helicopter carriers.

U. S.		USSR
13	Carriers	0
0	Carriers (VSTOL)	2
7	Carriers (helicopters)	2
5	Amphibious assault ships	0
	Submarines:	
5	Diesel (general purpose)	179
74	Nuclear (general purpose)	87
0	Diesel (ballistic missile)	19
41	Nuclear (ballistic missile)	71
28	Cruisers	39
153	Destroyers and frigates	213

Africa and the Persian Gulf

For two centuries the Indian Ocean had been virtually a British lake, and for a time much of the surrounding territory—east Africa, south Asia, and Australia—was part of the British Empire or under British protectorate. Following World War II, Britain, weakened by her losses and exertions in the struggle, began liquidating what remained of her empire in Asia and Africa. In 1968 the British government announced its intention of removing all its forces from east of Suez. The United States and the Soviet Union thereupon prepared to establish naval patrols in the Indian Ocean.

A major aim of the United States in establishing such a patrol was maintaining stability in the littoral countries, but the U. S. Navy's principal task would be to prevent interference with tankers bearing oil from the Persian Gulf or with ships conveying such strategic materials as copper, cobalt, chromium, manganese, and industrial diamonds—all lacking or in insufficient supply in the United States, western Europe, and Japan, but abundant in Africa south of the Sahara.

The oil wells of the Persian Gulf states—mainly Saudi Arabia, Kuwait, Iraq, and Iran—were relative late comers to world petroleum production. As wells in other parts of the world ran dry, these producers became increasingly important. By 1980, the Persian Gulf countries had become the world's leading oil exporters—20 million barrels a day. A loaded tanker left the gulf on an average every 16 minutes. These tankers brought 73 percent of Japan's oil, 63 percent of western Europe's,

and 15 percent of America's. It was estimated that within four or five years the Soviet Union also would need to import oil from the same source.

The Persian Gulf states and other members of the Organization of Petroleum Exporting Countries (OPEC), taking advantage of their growing monopoly, began raising their price. The general charge for crude in 1970 was $1.80 a barrel (42 gallons); by 1981 it had risen to $40. The steep and rapid rise upset the world's economic balance and forced up nearly everywhere an already soaring inflation. The only restraining factor in OPEC price hikes was possible bankruptcy of the countries on which OPEC depended for protection.

The Royal Navy during its long sway in the Indian Ocean operated from naval bases at Aden, Trincomalee, and Singapore. By the late 1960s neither Britain, the United States, nor the Soviet Union controlled a foot of Indian Ocean coastline—though the Soviets did have a treaty with Iraq that gave them naval access to the port of Basra at the head of the Persian Gulf, and the U. S. Navy since shortly after World War II had maintained a Middle East Force of destroyer types based on independent Bahrain, an archipelago inside the gulf. With the prospect of British withdrawal, the United States looked about for a strategically less vulnerable position on which to base an enlarged force. She selected Diego Garcia.

Diego Garcia is an atoll in the British Chagos Archipelago, in the middle of the Indian Ocean, about 2,500 miles southeast of the Persian Gulf. By arrangement with the London government, U. S. Seabees in 1971 arrived at the atoll and began work. They built warehouses, barracks, a radio station, and a mile-long jetty. They constructed fuel tanks, laid out a 12,000-foot airstrip and 17 miles of asphalt road, and dredged the lagoon to provide an anchorage for a large battle group.

The United States chose not to establish a military presence in the Persian Gulf area, but depended on Saudi Arabia and Iran to stand guard while America provided them with military equipment and trained their officers and technicians. Of the two countries, Saudi Arabia was considered less dependable. With her sparse native population, small army, and thousands of foreigners operating her oil wells and refineries, she appeared particularly vulnerable to attack from without or coup from within.

Iran, on the contrary, appeared in the early 1970s a model of stability, governed by the comparatively progressive Shah Mohammed Reza Pahlavi, who was rapidly Westernizing his country. The United States therefore counted on the shah

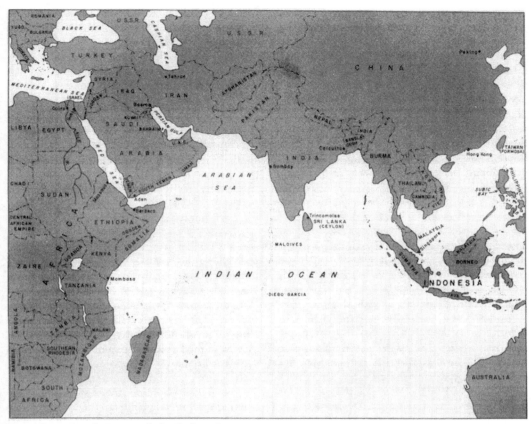

East Africa, South Asia, and the Indian Ocean

and his men to stand guard over the world's chief fountain of petroleum, and made her most sophisticated weapons available to them. Thousands of young Iranian officers and civilians went to the United States for training and education, and thousands of American experts and skilled workmen established themselves in Iran to advise and assist in the country's defenses and burgeoning commerce and industry. Other Americans went to Iran to man electronic monitoring stations to keep watch on missile activities in the nearby Soviet Union.

The Soviet Union's response to Britain's withdrawal from east of Suez was to detach a task force from her Pacific fleet based on Vladivostok and send it on a four-month, flag-showing cruise—to India, Pakistan, Ceylon, Iraq, Iran, South Yemen, and Somalia. The Soviets thereafter maintained a continuous presence in the Indian Ocean.

Moscow followed up the initial display of naval might with diplomatic initiatives, playing on each country's suspicion of her neighbors. As a result,

the Soviet Union was enabled to negotiate treaties of friendship and cooperation with India, South Yemen, and Somalia. At the same time, the Soviets were funneling aid to Marxist guerrillas in Portugal's rebellious African colonies of Mozambique and Angola.

The treaties made Indian Ocean ports available to the Soviet fleet: several in India, Aden in South Yemen, and Berbera in Somalia, which flanks the Gulf of Aden, gateway to the Red Sea. The British had left behind a naval base at Aden. At Berbera, on the opposite shore, the Soviets began building another base, including an airstrip, fuel storage facilities, and antiship missile sites.

One goal of the Soviet treaty system was to exploit Western retrenchments. Another was to isolate Russia's rival China by creating an Asian security system from which China would be excluded. To Somalian President Siad Barre, Soviet President Brezhnev confided a third objective. "Our aim," said Brezhnev, "is to gain control of the two great treasure houses on which the West depends—the energy treasure house of the Persian Gulf and the mineral treasure house of central and southern Africa."

In 1974 the dictatorship at Lisbon was overthrown, and the republican government that replaced it promptly granted independence to Portugal's African colonies. In Mozambique, the Marxist Liberation Front, with ample Soviet aid, had already dominated the other rebellious factions. It at once assumed control as the People's Republic of Mozambique. In Angola, independence found three factions fighting among themselves for the right to form a new government. The United States, determined not to get involved in another Vietnam-like conflict, withheld assistance from the pro-Western factions. The Soviets, however, airlifted in 15,000 Cuban troops to fight along with the Marxist Popular Front, which won, and formed the Angolan People's Republic. The presidents of the two new Marxist states promptly signed treaties of friendship with Moscow.

In 1977, the Soviet client state of Somalia, laying claim to the Ethiopian province of Ogaden, sent troops across the border and routed the defenders. The Soviets, calculating where their best interests lay, suddenly shifted sides. To Ethiopia they airlifted $4 billion worth of arms and 3,000 military technicians and sent 20,000 Cuban troops, who temporarily repulsed the Somalis. The Soviets thus lost 3 million Somali allies and their naval base at Berbera but gained 30 million Ethiopian allies and use of the Ethiopian Red Sea port of Massawa, where they began building a new naval base.

As the decade of the 1970s drew to a close, tragic Cambodia had again been overrun and conquered, this time by the Soviet client state of Vietnam, which defeated the previous conqueror, Pol Pot's genocidal Khmer Rouge regime. At the same time, fugitives from the oppressive Vietnamese rule were fleeing to sea from Vietnam itself, or being set adrift, often in leaky, unseaworthy boats. United States naval vessels based on Subic Bay were much involved in rescuing these wretched "boat people."

At the opposite end of the Asian littoral, South Yemen had become an avowed Marxist state, little more than a Soviet satellite, heavily armed with Russian planes, tanks, and artillery. A line drawn from Angola through Ethiopia showed South Yemen to be a spearhead pointed at the Persian Gulf—with only Saudi Arabia barring the way.

In Afghanistan, to the northeast, Soviet-backed insurgents deposed and murdered the president and set up a Marxist, anti-Western government under a Soviet puppet. Here was another spearhead, or second pincer jaw, aimed at the Persian Gulf. In this direction only Iran barred the way.

But the Iranian government was becoming increasingly unstable. The shah's drive to Westernize Iran had alienated many of his people, particularly among the clergy. The police, to suppress incipient revolt, used increasingly harsh measures. At last, in February 1979, the Iranians rebelled, ousted the shah, and forced him into exile. His government was replaced by a virulently anti-American Muslim theocracy headed by a vengeful old clergyman, the Ayatollah Ruhollah Khomeini. In the confusion of the turnover, thousands of potential victims, including many Americans, fled the country. Six U.S. naval ships carried away 440 people, including 200 American citizens, from southern Iranian ports.

One of the first acts of the new regime was to cancel $7 billion worth of aircraft, ships, missiles, and other arms on order from the United States. Included were four destroyers, which the U. S. Navy was happy to add to its own fighting fleet. With the summary execution of its ranking officers, the Iranian army disintegrated. Though the Soviet Union, through inflammatory radio broadcasts and support of the Iranian Communist Party and other dissident factions, was partly responsible for the shah's ouster, she did not immediately profit from the revolution, because the new regime was opposed to all outside influences and was almost as anti-Soviet as it was anti-American. Khomeini's precept was "Neither Western nor Eastern."

In the fall of 1979, President Carter admitted the exiled shah into the United States for emergency surgery. Muslim students thereupon seized the U. S. embassy in Tehran and took hostage the Americans in the compound, including 15 marines. The captors demanded as the price for their release the surrender to Iran of the shah's "stolen" fortune and the forced return of the shah himself to stand trial for his "crimes."

The U. S. government retaliated by freezing Iran's assets in the United States, amounting to several billion dollars, by suspending all trade with Iran except for food and medicines, and by expelling all Iranian military personnel from the country. Iranian students in American schools were allowed to remain. President Carter ordered the *Nimitz* battle group to the Indian Ocean to join the U. S. Seventh Fleet forces already there. The Iranians warned that a U. S. attack on Iran would be followed by the immediate execution of the American hostages, then numbering 53.

In April 1980 an aborted attempt to rescue the hostages raised questions about the capabilities and state of materiel of the U. S. armed forces. Of eight helicopters sent on the mission from the *Nimitz*, three while over Iran experienced mechanical malfunctions, obliging the leader to cancel the operation. During the withdrawal in darkness from the staging site in the Iranian desert, a helicopter crashed into a transport plane, which caught fire, killing eight Americans. Later, when the Iranians callously displayed the charred remains of the Americans on their national television, Carter angrily ordered all the personnel at the Iranian embassy in Washington to be out of the United States within 72 hours.

Meanwhile, in Afghanistan the Muslim tribesmen had risen against their Marxist ruler, who was ousted and executed in a palace revolt. On Christmas Eve 1979, the Soviets, in a carefully planned massive operation, invaded Afghanistan by land and air and installed another puppet as head of government. For the first time since World War II, the Soviets had used Russian troops to penetrate a state outside the Warsaw pact nations of central Europe. No serious barrier now stood between them and their objectives—a warm-water port on the Indian Ocean and control of the oil from the Persian Gulf states.

President Carter called on the Soviets to withdraw their army from Afghanistan without delay. He terminated Senate consideration of the SALT II treaty that he had signed with President Brezhnev, canceled the year's annual shipment of wheat to Russia, barred U. S.–Soviet exchange of high-technology materials and information, asked Congress to reinstate registration for the draft, and induced the athletes of the United States and several other countries to boycott the forthcoming Olympic games, scheduled to be held in Moscow. To the world he announced: "An attempt by any outside force to gain control of the Persian Gulf region will be regarded as an assault on the vital interests of the United States. It will be repelled by any means necessary, including the use of force."

Rearming the United States

Events in the Middle East early convinced President Carter that the United States required a means of applying military pressure quickly at a distance. He turned the problem over to the Department of Defense, which recommended the establishment of a Rapid Deployment Force (RDF). The RDF was to consist of three heavily mechanized brigades of U. S. marines, plus transport and support, ready at all times to go by sea or air wherever needed. It could serve as a spearhead, to be followed by additional forces as circumstances required. Planning, training, and achieving coordination with the other services were to be the responsibility of a Rapid Deployment Joint Task Force, with headquarters at MacDill Air Force Base in Tampa, Florida.

The overthrow of the shah's government made activation of the RDF urgent and also created a need for bases nearer the Persian Gulf than Diego Garcia. A Defense–State Department team toured the gulf area seeking facilities for use by U. S. forces. Saudi Arabia turned them down, but Oman, Kenya, and Somalia offered airfields and ports. The United States promptly accepted the cooperation of Oman and Kenya, but Somalia presented a problem. She offered the Soviet-built base at Berbera, but requested in return $90–100 million in military equipment—to be used by her without any restriction whatever. Fearful of being drawn into Somalia's border war with Ethiopia, the United States at first declined the offer. But the need was too great. The Americans at length began sending Somalia military supplies, but stated that use of them by the Somalis for anything but self-defense would result in an immediate cutoff. The base problem thus settled, additional movements of U. S. forces were soon under way. By February 1981, advance elements of the RDF were in the Indian Ocean area supported by 34 warships.

Meanwhile, Iran's diatribes against the United States had grown less strident. The Iranians had long since found retention of the American hostages less an advantage than an encumbrance. Most of the world condemned it. Trade sanctions, imposed by a number of major nations, had left Iran feeling isolated. She was experiencing shortages, particularly in spare parts for the arsenal of weapons the shah had purchased from the United States. The shah had died, thereby removing the main focus of Iranian anger. In September 1980, when Iraq invaded Iran intent on annexing the latter's chief oil-producing province at the head of the Persian Gulf, the Iranians found no nation willing to assist in Iran's defense. Ronald Reagan, elected president of the United States, managed to make them apprehensive concerning his intentions toward their country. Within an hour of his inauguration, 20 January 1981, Reagan announced to the world that the hostages were freed and on their way home. Besides liberating the Americans, the Iranians had also considerably abated their demands, which at one time had included 24 billion dollars in ransom money. What the Iranians finally accepted, with Algeria acting as go-between, was a pledge by the United States to release Iran's frozen assets, to freeze the shah's assets, if any, in the United States, and to refrain from interfering in Iran's internal affairs.

The incoming Reagan administration set to work at once implementing two announced programs: cutting the budgets of most U. S. government departments to the bone and at the same time rearming the country. Reagan proposed the largest, most expensive peacetime military buildup in the nation's history, to cost $1.5 trillion in five years. The Air Force would get its manned, supersonic bomber, and the Navy would be built up from 456 to 600 ships, including 15 carrier-centered battle groups. To attract volunteers to man this expanding defense force, Reagan proposed raising military pay to make it truly comparable to civilian wages.

Summary

In the early 1960s the United States came to rely for defense against nuclear attack on the deterrent effect of a triad: bombers, ICBMs, and missile-armed nuclear submarines. But U. S. rejection of the B-1 bomber as too costly and improved Soviet missile guidance systems (which made American fixed-site missile silos vulnerable) left the United States only her missile-armed submarines as unassailable deterrents. Lulled by SALT I and détente (and lack of adequate information), the Americans permitted the Soviets to outbuild them in conventional weapons. By 1980 the U. S. Navy was outnumbered by the Soviet Navy in every class of ship except aircraft carriers and major amphibious warfare vessels.

The U. S. and Soviet navies competed in building bigger nuclear submarines with missiles of increasing range. The 11,330-ton Russian "Deltas" were followed by the 18,700-ton U. S. *Ohios*, which in turn were succeeded by the 25,000-ton Soviet "Typhoons." The U. S. Navy continued to build *Nimitz*-class carriers and developed its SLEP refurbishing program for keeping its *Forrestal*-class carriers operational. Some senior American officers, however, declared concentration of U. S. naval power in big carriers undesirable in the face of the increasing accuracy of antiship missiles. Admiral Holloway, when CNO, proposed development of high-capability VSTOL aircraft that could be operated from virtually any type of ship.

At a time when the United States, western Europe, and Japan were coming to depend ever more heavily on central and southern Africa for strategic materials and on the Persian Gulf for oil, Britain withdrew all her forces from the Indian Ocean, where for centuries she had been dominant. To fill the vacuum, U. S. and Soviet naval forces moved in, the former to protect shipping and maintain stability in the littoral countries, the latter to exploit Western retrenchments, isolate China by forming agreements with other Asian states, and gain control of the Persian Gulf and central and southern Africa.

In pursuit of her goals, the Soviet Union brought in Cuban troops to establish Marxist governments in Angola, Mozambique, and Ethiopia, armed South Yemen as a client state, and occupied Afghanistan with her own forces. The United States developed a naval base at the British atoll of Diego Garcia, while depending on the government of the shah of Iran to stand guard over the Persian Gulf. When the shah was overthrown by an anti-American regime, the United States obtained use of ports and airfields in Kenya, Somalia, and Oman, and began moving her Rapid Deployment Force into the Indian Ocean. Ronald Reagan, on taking office in 1981 as president of the United States, began the biggest, most costly military buildup in U. S. history.

Bibliography

The Age of Galley Warfare
(Chapter 1)

Burn, Andrew R., *Persia and the Greeks: The Defense of the West, c. 546–478 B.C.*; New York: St. Martin Press, 1962. Casson, Lionel, *The Ancient Mariners*; New York: Minerva Press, 1959. Gravière, Edmond Jurien de la, *La Guerre de Chypre et la Bataille de Lepante*, 2 v.; Paris: E. Plon, Nourrit, et Cie., 1888. Grundy, George B., *The Great Persian War*; New York: Charles Scribner's Sons, 1901. Lewis, Archibald R., *Naval Power and Trade in the Mediterranean, A.D. 500–1100*; Princeton: Princeton University Press, 1951. Morrison, J. S., and R. T. Williams, *Greek Oared Ships, 900–322 B.C.*; Cambridge: Cambridge University Press, 1968. Rodgers, Vice Admiral William L., USN (Ret.), *Greek and Roman Naval Warfare*; Annapolis: U. S. Naval Institute, 1937, and *Naval Warfare under Oars*; Annapolis: U. S. Naval Institute, 1939. Rose, J. Holland, *The Mediterranean in the Ancient World*; Cambridge: Cambridge University Press, 1933. Shepherd, Arthur M., *Sea Power in Ancient History*; Boston: Little, Brown, 1924. Southworth, John Van, *The Ancient Fleets*; New York: Twayne Publishers, 1968. Starr, Chester G., *The Roman Imperial Navy, 31 B.C.–A.D. 324*; Ithaca: Cornell University Press, 1941. Tarn, William W., *Hellenistic Military and Naval Developments*; Cambridge: Cambridge University Press, 1930. Thiel, J. H., *A History of Roman Sea Power Before the Second Punic War*; Amsterdam: North-Holland, 1954, and *Studies on the History of Roman Sea Power in Republican Times*; Amsterdam: North-Holland, 1946. Torr, Cecil, *Ancient Ships*; Cambridge: Cambridge University Press, 1894. Also the works of the classical historians and commentators available in various editions and translations; for GREECE: Arrian, Diodorus Siculus, Herodotus, Polybius, Quintus Curtius, Thucydides, and Xenophon; for ROME, including the Eastern Empire: Appian, Dio Cassius, Julius Caesar, Livy, Polybius, Suetonius, and Tacitus.

The Oceanic Age
(Chapter 2)

Baker, J. N. L., *History of Geographical Discovery and Exploration*; London: George G. Harrap, 1931. Beazley, C. Raymond, *Prince Henry the Navigator*; New York: G. P. Putnam's Sons, 1895. Branch, W. J. V., and E. Brook-Williams, *A Short History of Navigation*; Annapolis: Weems School of Navigation, 1942. Brendon, J. A., *Great Navigators and Discoverers*; London: George G. Harrap, 1929. Graham, Gerald S., *Empire of the North Atlantic: The Maritime Struggle for North America*; Toronto: University of Toronto Press, 1950. Hewson, J. B., *A History of the Practice of Navigation*; Glasgow: Brown, Son, & Ferguson, 1951. Montross, Lynn, *War Through the Ages*; New York: Harper & Brothers, 1946. Mordal, Jacques, *Twenty-Five Centuries of Sea Warfare*; New York: Clarkson N. Potter, 1959. Morison, Samuel Eliot, *Admiral of the Ocean Sea: A Life of Christopher Columbus*; Boston: Little, Brown, 1942. Oman, Sir Charles W. C., *The Art of War in the Middle Ages*; Ithaca: Cornell University Press, 1953. Waters, D. W., *The Art of Navigation in Elizabethan and Early Stuart Times*; New Haven: Yale University Press, 1958.

The Rise of English Sea Power
(Chapters 2–8)

General

Navy Records Society, London (the nearly 100 volumes are invaluable collections of source and authoritative materials on the British navy). Albion, Robert G., *Forests and Sea Power: The Timber Problem of the Royal Navy, 1652–1862*; Cambridge, Mass.: Harvard University Press, 1926. Clowes, Sir W. L., and others, *The Royal Navy: A History from the Earliest Times to the Present*, 7 v.; London: Sampson Low, Marston, 1897–1903. Corbett, Sir Julian S., *England in the Mediterranean: A Study of the Rise and Influence of British Sea Power within the Straits, 1603–1713*, 2 v.; London: Longmans, Green, 1904; ed., *Fighting Instructions, 1776–1794*; London: Navy Records Society, 1905, and *Signals and Instructions, 1530–1816*; London: Navy Records Society, 1908. Fortescue, Sir John, *A History of the British Army*, 13 v.; London: Macmillan, 1899–1920. Hakluyt, Richard, *The Principal Voyages, Traffiques, & Discoveries of the English Nation*, 12 v.; New York: Macmillan, 1903. Lewis, Michael, *The Navy of Britain: A Historical Portrait*; London: George Allen & Unwin, 1948. Mahan, Alfred T., *The In-*

fluence of Sea Power upon History, 1660–1783;
Boston: Little, Brown, 1890, 1918, 1935. Marshall,
John, Royal Naval Biography, 12 v.; London:
Longman, Rees, Orme, Brown & Green, 1823–25.
Richmond, Sir Herbert W., The Navy as an Instru-
ment of Policy, 1558–1727, Cambridge: Cambridge
University Press, 1953, and Statesmen and Sea
Power; Oxford: Clarendon Press, 1946. Rivera y
Casares, P. D. de, Historia de las Organizaciones
Navales de España y Francia: Madrid: Editorial
Alhambra, 1932 (?).

Early Period (Chapter 2)
Beadon, Roger, Robert Blake; London: Edward
Arnold, 1935. Clark, G. N., The Dutch Alliance
and the War against French Trade, 1688–1697;
London: Oxford University Press, 1934. Corbett,
Sir Julian S., Drake and the Tudor Navy, with a
History of the Rise of England as a Maritime
Power, , 2 v.; New York: Longmans, Green, 1898;
and The Navy during the Spanish War, 1585–1587;
London: Navy Records Society, 1894. Duro,
Cesario Fernandez, La Armada Española, 9 v.;
Madrid: Rivadeneyra, 1895–1903. Laughton, Sir
John Knox, ed., State Papers Relating to the Defeat
of the Spanish Armada, 2 v.; London: Navy Re-
cords Society, 1894. Lewis, Michael, The Spanish
Armada; New York: Macmillan, 1960. Mattingly,
Garrett, The Armada; Boston: Houghton Mifflin
1959. Owen, John H., War at Sea under Queen
Anne, 1702–1708; Cambridge: Cambridge Uni-
versity Press, 1938. Penn, C. D., The Navy under
the Early Stuarts, and Its Influence on English
History; London: J. Hogg, 1920. Richmond, Sir
Herbert W., The Navy in the War of 1739–1748, 3
v.; Cambridge: Cambridge University Press, 1916.
Williamson, James A., The Age of Drake; London:
A. & C. Black, 1938, Maritime Enterprise, 1485–
1558; London: Oxford University Press, 1913, and
Sir John Hawkins: The Time and the Man; Oxford:
Clarendon Press, 1927.

The Seven Years' War (Chapter 3)
Corbett, Sir Julian S., England in the Seven Years'
War: A Study in Combined Strategy, 2 v.; London:
Longmans, Green, 1918. Furneaux, Rupert, The
Seven Years' War; London: Hart-Davis MacGib-
bon, 1973. Graham, Gerald S., Empire of the
North Atlantic: The Maritime Struggle for North
America; Toronto: University of Toronto Press,
1950. Mackay, Ruddock F., Admiral Hawke; Ox-
ford: Clarendon Press, 1965. Pitt, William, First
Earl of Chatham, Correspondence, Kimball, G. S.,
ed., 2 v.; New York: Macmillan, 1906. Richmond,
Sir Herbert W., The Navy in India, 1763–1783;
London: Ernest Benn, 1931. Sherrard, O. A., Pitt
and the Seven Years' War; London: Bodley Head,
1955. Stacey, C. P., Quebec, 1759–The Siege and
the Battle; New York: Macmillan, 1960. Tunstall,
Brian, Admiral Byng and the Loss of Minorca;

London: Philip Allen, 1928. Willson, Beckles, Life
and Letters of James Wolfe: Heineman, 1909.

The War of the American Revolution (Chapters 4–5)

American Navy

Allen, Gardner W., A Naval History of the American Revolution, 2 v.; Boston & New York: Houghton Mifflin, 1913. Clark, Thomas, Naval History of
the United States from the Commencement of the
Revolutionary War to the Present Time; Phil-
adelphia: M. Carey, 1814. Clark, William Bell,
George Washington's Navy, being an Account of
His Excellency's Fleet in New England Waters:
Baton Rouge: Louisiana State University Press,
1960. Jackson, John W., The Pennsylvania Navy,
1775–81: The Defense of the Delaware; New
Brunswick: Rutgers University Press, 1974. Knox,
Commodore Dudley W., USN (Ret.), The Naval
Genius of George Washington; Boston: Houghton
Mifflin, 1932. Maclay, Edgar S., History of Amer-
ican Privateers; New York: D. Appleton, 1899.
Middlebrook, Louis F., History of Maritime Con-
necticut during the American Revolution 1775–
1783, 2 v.; Salem: Essex Institute, 1925. Miller,
Nathan, Sea of Glory: The Continental Navy Fights
for Independence; New York: David McKay, 1974.
Morgan, William James, Captains to the North-
ward, the New England Captains in the Continen-
tal Navy; Barre, Mass.: Barre Gazette, 1959.
Paine, Ralph D., Ships and Sailors of Old Salem;
New York: Outing Publishing., 1909. Paullin,
Charles O., The Navy of the American Revolution,
its Administration, its Policy, and its Achieve-
ments: Cleveland: Burrows Brothers, 1906, and
History of Naval Administration, 1775–1911;
Annapolis: U. S. Naval Institute, 1968. Rogers,
Ernest D., ed., Connecticut's Naval Office at New
London, 2 v.; New London: New London County
Historical Association, 1933. Stewart, Robert A.,
The History of Virginia's Navy of the Revolution;
Richmond, Va.: Mitchell & Hotchkiss, 1934.

British Navy

Broomfield, J. H., "The Keppel-Palliser Affair,
1778–1779," Mariner's Mirror, v. 47, no. 3 (1961),
pp. 195–207. Dupuy, Trevor H., and Grace P.
Hayes, The Military History of Revolutionary War
Naval Battles; New York: Watts, 1970. James, Cap-
tain William M., The British Navy in Adversity;
London: Longmans, Green, 1926. Johnson, Frank,
The Royal George; London: C. Knight, 1971.
Mackesy, Piers, The War for America, 1775–1783;
Cambridge, Mass.: Harvard University Press,
1964. Mahan, Alfred T., The Major Operations of
the Navies in the War of American Independence;
London: Sampson Low, Marston, 1913. Stout, Neil
R., The Royal Navy in America, 1760–1775. A
Study of Enforcement of British Colonial Policy in

the Era of the American Revolution; Annapolis: Naval Institute Press, 1973. White, Thomas, Naval Researches, or a Candid Inquiry into the Conduct of Admirals Byron, Graves, Hood, and Rodney in the Actions off Grenada, Chesapeak, St. Christopher's, and of the Ninth and Twelfth of April 1782, Being a Refutation of the Plans and Statements of Mr. Clerk, Rear Admiral Ekins, and Others: Founded on Authentic Documents or Actual Observation; London: Whittaker, Treacher & Arnett, 1830.

French Navy

Bonsal, Stephen, When the French Were Here: A Narrative of the French Forces in America and Their Contribution to the Yorktown Campaign, Drawn from Unpublished Reports and Letters of Participants in the National Archives of France and the MS Division of the Library of Congress; Garden City: Doubleday, Doran, 1945. Chevalier, E., Histoire de la Marine Française Pendant la Guerre de l'Independance Américaine; Paris: Librairie Hachette et Cie., 1877. Doniol, Henri, Histoire de la Participation de la France à l'Établissement des États-Unis d'Amérique, Correspondance Diplomatique et Documents, 5 v. and supplement; Paris: Imprimerie Nationale, 1886–1892. Dull, Jonathan R., The French Navy and American Independence: A Study of Arms and Diplomacy, 1774–1787; Princeton: Princeton University Press, 1975. Fleming, Thomas J., Beat the Last Drum: The Siege of Yorktown, 1781; New York: St. Martin's Press, 1963. Jouan, René, Histoire de la Marine Française des Origines jusqu'à la Révolution; Paris: Payot, 1932. Lacour-Gayet, G., La Marine Militaire de la France sous le Règne de Louis XVI; Paris, Librairie Spéciale pour l'Histoire de la France, 1905. Landers, H. L., The Virginia Campaign and the Blockade and Siege of Yorktown 1781, Including a Brief Narrative of the French Participation in the Revolution Prior to the Southern Campaign; Washington, D.C.: USGPO, 1931. Larrabee, Harold A., Decision at the Chesapeake; New York: Clarkson N. Potter, 1964. Loir, Maurice, La Marine Française; Paris, 1893. Perkins, James B., France in the American Revolution; Boston and New York: Houghton Mifflin, 1911. Patterson, Alfred T., The Other Armada: The Franco–Spanish Attempt to Invade Britain in 1779; Manchester: Manchester University Press, 1960. Scott, James B., De Grasse à Yorktown; Paris: Editoriale Internationale, 1931. Troude, O., Batailles Navales de la France, 4 v.; Paris: P. Levot, 1867–1868

Biographies, Memoirs, Diaries

Anderson, Troyer S., The Command of the Howe Brothers During the American Revolution; New York and London: Oxford University Press, 1936. Barnes, John S., ed., Fanning's Narrative, Being the Memoirs of Nathaniel Fanning, an Officer of the Revolutionary Navy, 1778–1783; New York: Naval History Society, 1912. Barrow, Sir John, The Life of Richard Earl Howe, K.G., Admiral of the Fleet and General of the Marines; London: John Murray, 1838. Beatson, Robert, Naval and Military Memoirs of Great Britain from 1727 to 1783; 6 v., London: Longman, Hurst, Rees, and Orme, 1804. Brown, Gerald S., The American Secretary: The Colonial Policy of Lord George Germain, 1775–1778; Ann Arbor: University of Michigan Press, 1963. Burgoyne, Lieutenant General John, A State of the Expedition from Canada as laid before the House of Commons by Lieutenant-General Burgoyne and verified by evidence with a collection of authentic documents; London, 1780. Calmon-Maison, L'Amiral d'Estaing; Paris, Calmann-Lévy, 1910. Clark, William Bell, Captain Dauntless: The Story of Nicholas Biddle of the Continental Navy; Baton Rouge: Louisiana State University Press, 1949, Gallant John Barry, 1745–1803: The Story of a Naval Hero of Two Wars; New York: Macmillan, 1938, and Lambert Wickes: Sea Raider and Diplomat; New Haven: Yale University Press, 1932. Cornwallis-West, G., The Life and Letters of Admiral Cornwallis; London: Robert Holden, 1927. Cunat, Charles, Histoire du Bailli de Suffren; Rennes: A. Marteville et Lefas, 1852. De Koven, Mrs. Reginald, The Life and Letters of John Paul Jones, 2 v.; New York: Charles Scribner's Sons, 1913. Field, Edward, Esek Hopkins, Commander-in-Chief of the Continental Navy During the American Revolution; Providence: Preston & Roinds, 1898. Fitzpatrick, John C., ed., The Diaries of George Washington 1748–1799, 4 v.; Boston and New York: Houghton Mifflin Co. for the Mount Vernon Ladies' Ass'n. of the Union, 1925. Freeman, Douglas Southall, George Washington, A Biography, 7 v.; New York: Charles Scribner's Sons, 1948-57. Hannay, David, Rodney; London and New York: MacMillan and Co., 1891. Hennequin, T. F. G., Essai Historique sur la Vie et les Compagnes du Bailli de Suffren; Paris: Librairie de Paytieux, 1824. Hudleston, Francis J., Gentleman Johnny Burgoyne: Misadventures of an English General in the Revolution; Indianapolis: Bobbs-Merrill, 1927. Hunt, Robert M., The Life of Sir Hugh Palliser, Bart., Admiral of the White and Governor of Greenwich Hospital; London: Chapman and Hall, 1844. Keppel, Rev. Thomas, The Life of Augustus, Viscount Keppel, Admiral of the White, and First Lord of the Admiralty in 1782–3, 2 v.; London: Henry Colburn, 1842. Lewis, Charles L., Admiral de Grasse and American Independence; Annapolis: U. S. Naval Institute, 1945. Lorenz, Lincoln, John Paul Jones, Fighter for Freedom and Glory; Annapolis: U. S. Naval Institute, 1943. Macintyre, Donald G. F. W., Admiral Rodney; New York: Norton, 1963. Martelli, George, Jemmy Twitcher: A Life of the Fourth

Earl of Sandwich, 1718–1792; London: Cape, 1962. Miller, Charles H., Admiral Number One: Some Incidents in the Life of Esek Hopkins, 1718–1802, First Admiral of the Continental Navy; New York: William-Frederick Press, 1962. Morison, Samuel E., John Paul Jones, a Sailor's Biography; Boston: Little, Brown, 1959. Mundy, Godfrey B., The Life and Correspondence of the Late Admiral Lord Rodney, 2 v.; London: John Murray, 1830. Partridge, Bellamy, Sir Billy Howe; London: Longmans, Green, 1932. Ralfe, J., The Naval Biography of Great Britain, Consisting of Historical Memoirs of those Officers of the British Navy who Distinguished Themselves during the Reign of His Majesty George III, 4 v.; London: Whitmore and Fenn, 1828. Spinney, David, Rodney; London: Allen & Unwin, 1969. Stone, William L., trans. and ed., Memoirs and Letters and Journals of Major-General Riedesel during his Residence in America, 2 v.; Albany: J. Munsell, 1868. Thiéry, Maurice (Agnew, Anne, trans.), Bougainville, Soldier and Sailor, London: Grayson and Grayson, 1932. Valentine, Alan C., Lord George Germain; Oxford: Clarendon Press, 1962. Weelen, Jean-Edmond (Lee, Lawrence, trans.), Rochambeau, Father and Son, A Life of the Maréchal de Rochambeau by Jean-Edmond Weelen, and the Journal of the Vicomte de Rochambeau; New York: Henry Holt, 1936.

Primary Sources

Barck, Dorothy C., ed., Letter-Books and Order-Book of George, Lord Rodney, Admiral of the White Squadron 1780–1782, 2 v.; New York: Naval History Society, 1932. Barnes, G. R., and J. H. Owen, eds., The Private Papers of John, Earl of Sandwich, First Lord of the Admiralty 1771–82, 4 v.; London: Navy Records Society, 1932–38. Barnes, John S., ed., Logs of Serapis—Alliance—Ariel under the Command of John Paul Jones 1779–80; New York: Naval History Society, 1911. Beck, Alverda S., ed., The Letter Book of Esek Hopkins, Commander-in-Chief of the United States Navy; Providence: Rhode Island Historical Society, 1932, and The Correspondence of Esek Hopkins, Commander-in-Chief of the United States Navy; Providence: Rhode Island Historical Society, 1933. The Bedford Club, Operations of the French Fleet under the Count de Grasse in 1781–2, as Described in Two Contemporaneous Journals; New York: Bedford Club, 1864. Bonner-Smith, David, ed., The Barrington Papers; London: Navy Records Society, 1937. Chadwick, French E., ed., The Graves Papers and Other Documents Relating to the Naval Operations of the Yorktown Campaign, July to October 1781; New York: Naval History Society, 1916. Clark, William Bell, and William James Morgan, eds., Naval Documents of the American Revolution; Washington, D.C.:

USGPO, 1964–. Fitzpatrick, John C., ed., Writings of George Washington, 39 v.: Washington, D.C.: USGPO, 1931–44. Hannay, David ed., Letters Written by Sir Samuel Hood (Viscount Hood) in 1781–2–3; London: Navy Records Society, 1895. Institut Français de Washington, ed., Correspondence of General Washington and Comte de Grasse, 1781 August 17–November 4; Washington, D.C.: USGPO, 1931 (Senate Document No. 211; 71st Congress, 2nd Session, 1931). Johnson, Amandus, trans. and ed., The Naval Campaigns of Count de Grasse during the American Revolution 1781–1783, by Karl Gustaf Tornquist; Philadelphia: Swedish Colonial Society, 1942. Keim, De B. Randolph, ed., Rochambeau; Army of de Rochambeau on Land and Naval Exploits of de Ternay, des Touches, de Barras, and de Grasse in American Waters 1780–81; Washington, D.C.: USGPO, 1907 (Senate Document No. 537, 59th Congress, 1st Session, 1907). Laughton, Sir John Knox, ed., Letters and Papers of Charles, Lord Barham, Admiral of the Red Squadron, 1758–1813, 3 v.; Navy Records Society, 1907–1911. Log of the Bon Homme Richard; Mystic: Marine Historical Association of Mystic, Conn., 1936. The Naval Miscellany, v. I, Navy Records Society, 1902. Neeser, Robert W., ed., Letters and Papers Relating to the Cruises of Gustavus Conyngham, a Captain of the Continental Navy 1777–1779; New York: Naval History Society, 1915. The Despatches of Molyneux Schuldham, Vice-Admiral of the Blue, Commander-in-Chief of British Ships in North America January–July 1776; New York: Naval History Society, 1913. O'Beirne, Thomas L., Narrative of the Fleet under Lord Howe; New York: New York Times and Arno Press, 1969. Paullin, Charles O., ed., Out-Letters of the Continental Marine Committee and Board of Admiralty, August 1776–September 1780, 2 v.; New York: Naval History Society, 1914. Sparks, Jared, ed., Correspondence of the American Revolution, Being Letters of Eminent Men to George Washington, from the Time of His Taking Command of the Army to the End of his Presidency, 4 v.; Boston: Little, Brown, 1853. Stevens, Benjamin, F., The Campaign in Virginia 1781, The Clinton-Cornwallis Controversy, 2 v.; London: 4 Trafalgar Square, 1888. Facsimiles of Manuscripts in European Archives Relating to America 1773–1783, 25 v.; London: 4 Trafalgar Square, 1889–1898.

The War of the French Revolution (Chapter 6)

Bradford, Ernle, Nelson, The Essential Hero; New York: Harcourt, Brace, Jovanovich, 1977. Bryant, Arthur, The Years of Endurance; London: Collins, 1942, and The Years of Peril; London: Collins, 1944. Burne, Alfred H., The Noble Duke of York; London: Staples Press, 1949. Closmadeuc, G. Thomas de, Quiberon, 1795; Paris: Plon, 1899.

Desbrière, Edouard, *1793–1805 Projets et Tentatives de Débarquement aux Îles Britanniques*, 4 v.; Paris: Chapelot, 1900–1902. Howarth, David, *Trafalgar: The Nelson Touch*; New York: Atheneum, 1974. Jackson, T. S., *Logs of the Great Sea Fights*, 2 v.; London: Navy Records Society, 1899–1900. James, Admiral Sir William, *Old Oak: The Life of John Jervis*; London: Longmans, Green, 1950. James, William, *The Naval History of Great Britain from the Declaration of War by France in 1793 to the Accession of George IV*, 6 v.; London: Richard Bentley, 1837. Lloyd, Christopher C., *St. Vincent and Camperdown*; New York: Macmillan, 1963. Mahan, Alfred T., *Types of Naval Officers*; Boston: Little, Brown, 1901. Marcus, G. J., *The Age of Nelson: The Royal Navy, 1793–1815*: New York: Viking, 1971. Pellew, George, ed., *Life and Correspondence of Henry Addington, Viscount Sidmouth*, 3 v.; London: John Murray, 1847. Rose, J. Holland, *Lord Hood and the Defence of Toulon*; Cambridge: Cambridge University Press, 1922. Sherwig, John M., *Guineas and Gunpowder: British Foreign Aid in the War with France, 1793–1815*; Cambridge, Mass.: Harvard University Press, 1969. Smith, D. B., *The St. Vincent Papers*, 2 v.; London: Navy Records Society, 1921, 1926. Tonnèle, Jean, *L'Angleterre en Méditerranée*; Paris: Charles-Lavauzelle, 1952. Warner, Oliver, *The Glorious First of June*; New York: Macmillan, 1961.

Nelson and Bonaparte (Chapter 7)

Anderson, R. C., *Naval Wars in the Baltic during the Sailing Ship Epoch*; London: Gilbert Wood, 1910, and *Naval Wars in the Levant, 1559–1853*; Princeton: Princeton University Press, 1952. Barrow, John, *Life and Correspondence of Admiral Sir William Sydney Smith*, 2 v.; London: Richard Bentley, 1848. Bruun, Geoffrey, *Europe and the French Imperium, 1799–1814*; New York: Harper & Brothers, 1938. Bunbury, Sir Henry (Fortescue, Sir John, ed.), *Narratives of Some Passages in the Great War with France*; London: Peter Davies, 1927. *The Cambridge Modern History*, Chapters 2–13 seriatim. Carlan, J. M., *Navios en Secuestro: La Escuadra Española del Oceano en Brest (1799–1802)*; Madrid: Instituto Historico de Marina, 1951. Corbett, J. S., and H. W. Richmond, eds., *The Spencer Papers*, 4 v.; London: Navy Records Society, 1913–1914 and 1923–1924. Garcot, Maurice, *Kléber*; Paris: Berger Levrault, 1936. *Histoire de l'Expédition Française en Égypte*, 10 v.; Paris: Denain, 1830–1836. Hoskins, H. L., *British Routes to India*; New York: Longmans, Green, 1928. James, Admiral Sir William M., *The Durable Monument: Horatio Nelson*; London: Longmans, Green, 1948. Maurice, Sir J. F., ed., *The Diary of Sir John Moore*, 2 v.; London: Longmans, Green, 1904. Napoleon I, *Correspondence*, 28 v.; Paris:

Plon avec Dumain, 1857–1859. Nicholas, Sir Harris, ed., *Dispatches and Letters of Lord Viscount Nelson*, 7 v.; London: Henry Colburn, 1846. Puryear, V. J., *Napoleon and the Dardanelles*; Berkeley: University of California Press, 1951. Warner, Oliver, *Victory: The Life of Lord Nelson*; Boston: Little, Brown, 1958.

The War of the French Empire (Chapter 8)

British Admiralty Bluebook, *The Tactics of Trafalgar*; London: H. M. Stationer's Office, 1913. Corbett, J. S., *The Campaign of Trafalgar*; London: Longmans, Green, 1910. Creswell, John, *Generals and Admirals*; London: Longmans, Green, 1952. Désbrière, Edouard, *Trafalgar*; Paris: Chapelot, 1907. Hamilton, Sir R. V. ed., *The Byam Martin Papers*, 3 v.; London: Navy Records Society, 1898–1902. Leyland, John, *The Blockade of Brest, 1803–1805*, 2 v.; London: Navy Records Society, 1898–1901. Mahan, Alfred T., *The Life of Nelson*, 2 v.; Boston: Little, Brown, 1907. Marliani, M. de, *Combate de Trafalgar*; Madrid: Impreso de Orden Superior, 1850. Napier, W. F. P., *History of the War in the Peninsula, 1807–1814*; Philadelphia: Carey & Hart, 1842. Newbolt, Henry, *The Year of Trafalgar*; London: John Murray, 1905. Parkinson, C. Northcote, *War in the Eastern Seas, 1793–1815*; London: George Allen & Unwin, 1954. Ross, John, *Admiral Lord de Saumarez*, 2 v.; London: Richard Bentley, 1838. Thomazi, A., *Trafalgar*; Paris: Payot, 1932.

The Beginnings of the U. S. Navy (Chapter 9)

Allen, Gardner, *Our Navy and the Barbary Corsairs*; Boston: Houghton Mifflin, 1905, and *Our Naval War with France*; Boston: Houghton Mifflin, 1909. Barnes, James, *Commodore Bainbridge*; New York: Appleton, 1897. Cooper, James Fenimore, *History of the Navy of the United States of America*; Philadelphia: Lea and Blanchard, 1847. Dearborn, Henry A., *The Life of William Bainbridge*; Princeton: Princeton University Press, 1931. Ferguson, Eugene S., *Truxtun of the Constellation*, Baltimore: Johns Hopkins Press, 1916. Knox, Commodore Dudley Wright, USN (Ret.), *A History of the United States Navy*; New York: G. P. Putnam's Sons, 1948, and ed., *Naval Documents Related to the Quasi-War between the United States and France*, 7 v.; Washington, D.C.: USGPO, 1935–38, and *Naval Documents Related to the United States Wars with the Barbary Powers*, 7 v.; Washington, D.C.: USGPO, 1939–45. Lewis, Charles Lee, *The Romantic Decatur*; Philadelphia: University of Pennsylvania Press, 1937. Long, David G., *Nothing Too Daring: A Biography of Commodore David Porter*; Annapolis: U. S. Naval Institute, 1970. McKee, Christopher, *Edward Preble*; Annapolis: Naval Institute Press,

1972. *The Autobiography of Charles Morris;* Annapolis: U. S. Naval Institute, 1880. Paullin, Charles Oscar, *Commodore John Rodgers: Captain, Commodore, and Senior Officer of the American Navy, 1773–1838;* Annapolis: U. S. Naval Institute, 1967. Smelser, Marshall, *The Congress Founds the Navy, 1787–1798;* South Bend: University of Notre Dame Press, 1959. Symonds, Craig L., *Navalists and Antinavalists: The Naval Policy Debate in the United States, 1785–1827;* Newark, University of Delaware Press, 1980.

The War of 1812 (Chapter 10)

Adams, Henry, *The War of 1812;* Washington: Infantry Journal, 1944. Brackenridge, H. M., *History of the Late War, between the United States and Great Britain;* Baltimore: Cushing and Jewett, 1818. Grant, Bruce, *Isaac Hull: Captain of Old Ironsides;* Chicago: Pelligrini, 1947. Guttridge, Leonard F., and Jay D. Smith, *The Commodores:* New York: Harper and Row, 1969. Horsman, Reginald, *The War of 1812;* New York: Alfred A. Knopf, 1968. James, William, *Naval Occurrences of the Late War between Great Britain and the United States of America;* London: Thomas Egerton, 1817. Lloyd, Alan, *The Scorching of Washington: The War of 1812;* Washington: Robert B. Luce, 1974. Lord, Walter, *The Dawn's Early Light;* New York: Norton, 1972. Lossing, Benson J., *A Pictorial Field Book of the War of 1812;* New York: Harper & Brothers, 1868. Mackensie, Alexander S., *Life of Stephen Decatur;* Boston: Little, Brown, 1846; and *Life of Commodore Oliver Hazard Perry;* New York: Harper, 1840. Mahan, Captain A. T., *Sea Power in Its Relation to the War of 1812,* 2 v.; Boston: Little, Brown, 1905. Mahon, John K., *The War of 1812;* Gainesville: University of Florida Press, 1972. Roosevelt, Theodore, *The Naval War of 1812;* New York: G. P. Putnam's Sons, 1903. Smith, W. H., *Life and Services of Captain Philip Beaver;* London: John Murray, 1829. Tucker, Glenn, *Poltroons and Patriots: A Popular Account of the War of 1812,* 2 v.; Indianapolis: Bobbs-Merrill, 1942.

Navies in Transition (Chapter 11)

Technology

Bathe, Greville, *Ship of Destiny;* St. Augustine, Fla. : n.p., 1951. Baxter, James Phinney, *Introduction of the Ironclad Warship;* Cambridge, Mass.: Harvard University Press, 1933. Bennett, Frank M., *The Steam Navy of the United States;* Pittsburgh: Warren, 1896. Brodie, Bernard, *Sea Power in the Machine Age:* Princeton: Princeton University Press, 1941. Chapelle, Howard I., *History of American Sailing Ships,* and *The History of the American Sailing Navy:* New York: W. W. Norton

& Company, Inc., 1935, 1949. Cowie, J. S., *Mines, Minelayers and Minelaying;* London: Oxford University Press, 1949. Dahlgren, J. A. *Shells and Shell Guns;* Philadelphia: King and Baird, 1856. Preble, George Henry, L. R. Hammersley, *A Chronological History of the Origin and Development of Steam Navigation:* Philadelphia: L. R. Hammersley, 1883. Robertson, Frederick Leslie, *The Evolution of Naval Armament:* London: Constable, 1921. Tennent, Sir J. Emerson, *The Story of the Guns;* London: Longmans, Green, 1864.

Miscellaneous Naval Operations

Allen, Gardner, *Our Navy and the West Indies Pirates;* Salem, Mass.: Essex Institute, 1929. Bourchier, Lady, *Memoir of the Life of Admiral Codrington;* London: Longmans, Green, 1873. Buker, George E., *Swamp Sailors: Riverine Warfare in the Everglades, 1835–1842;* Gainesville: University Presses of Florida, 1975. Hayford, Harrison, ed., *The Somers Mutiny Affair;* Englewood Cliffs: Prentice-Hall, 1959. Johnson, Robert Erwin, *Thence Round Cape Horn: The Story of United States Naval Forces on the Pacific Station, 1812–1882;* Annapolis: U. S. Naval Institute, 1967. Lewis, Charles Lee, *Matthew Fontaine Maury: Pathfinder of the Seas;* Annapolis: U. S. Naval Institute, 1927. Long, David F., *Nothing too Daring: A Biography of Commodore David Porter, 1780–1843;* Annapolis: Naval Institute Press, 1970. Parkinson, C. Northcote, *Edward Pellew, Baron Exmouth, Vice Admiral of the Red;* London: Methuen, 1934. (See also Clowes, *Royal Navy,* above, under "Rise of English Sea Power, Chapters 2–8.")

The Mexican War

Bancroft, Hubert Howe, *History of the Pacific States,* XXII; San Francisco: History Company, 1886. Bauer, K. Jack, *The Mexican War, 1846–1848;* New York: Macmillan, 1974, and *Surfboats and Horse Marines: U. S. Naval Operations in the Mexican War, 1846–1848;* Annapolis: U. S. Naval Institute, 1969. Bayard, S. J., *A Sketch of the Life of Commodore Robert F. Stockton;* New York: Derby and Jackson, 1856. Conner, P. S. P., *The Home Squadron under Commodore Conner in the War with Mexico;* Philadelphia: n.p., 1896. DeVoto, Bernard, *The Year of Decision: 1846;* Boston: Little, Brown, 1943. Morison, Samuel Eliot, *"Old Bruin": Commodore Matthew Calbraith Perry, 1794–1858;* Boston: Little, Brown, 1967. Price, Glenn W., *Origins of the War with Mexico: The Polk–Stockton Intrigues;* Austin: University of Texas Press, 1967. *Report of the Secretary of the Navy, 1846:* Washington, D.C.: USGPO, 1847 *Senate Executive Document 33, 30th Congress, 1s Session,* Washington, D.C.: USGPO. Smith, Justin A., *The War with Mexico,* 2 v.; New York Macmillan, 1919.

The Crimean War

Barker, A. J., *The Vainglorious War;* London Weidenfeld and Nicholson, 1970. Bazancourt, Baron C. de, *The Crimean Expedition to the Capture of Sebastopol,* 2 v.; London: Sampson Low, Son, 1856. Daly, Robert W., "Nakhimov: Black Sea Admiral," *Marine Corps Gazette,* April 1953, 54–61. Furse, Col. George Armand, *Military Expeditions beyond the Seas,* 2 v.; London: William Clowes & Sons, 1897. Heath, Sir Leopold George, *Letters from the Black Sea during the Crimean War, 1854–1855;* London: Richard Bentley and Son, 1897. Hibbert, Christopher, *The Destruction of Lord Raglan: A Tragedy of the Crimean War, 1854–1855;* Boston: Little, Brown, 1962. Kinglake, William, *The Invasion of the Crimea,* 8 v.; Edinburgh: William Blackwood & Sons, 1863–1887. Russell, William Howard, *General Todleben's History of the Defence of Sebastopol: a Review;* New York: D. Van Nostrand, 1865, and *The War,* 2 v.; London: George Routledge & Sons, 1856.

The American Civil War (Chapters 12–14)

General

Anderson, Bern, *By Sea and By River: The Naval History of the Civil War;* New York: Holt, Rinehart, and Winston, 1960–62. Boynton, Charles B., *History of the Navy During the Rebellion;* New York: D. Appleton, 1867. Butler, B. F., *Autobiography and Personal Reminiscences;* Boston: A. M. Thayer, 1892. Du Pont, H. A., *Rear Admiral Samuel Francis Du Pont;* New York: National Americana Society, 1926. Farragut, Loyall, *The Life of David Glasgow Farragut;* New York: D. Appleton, 1879. Johnson, R. U., and C. C. Buel, eds., *Battles and Leaders of the Civil War,* 4 v.; New York: Century, 1887–1889. Jones, Virgil Carrington, *The Civil War at Sea,* 3 v.; New York: Holt, Rinehart, & Winston, 1960–62. Lewis, Charles L., *David Glasgow Farragut: Our First Admiral;* Annapolis: U. S. Naval Institute, 1943. Mahan, A. T., *Admiral Farragut;* New York: D. Appleton, 1892. Moore, F., ed., *The Rebellion Record,* 11 v.; New York: George Putnam's Sons, 1861–1864, and Van Nostrand, 1864–1868. Morgan, James Morris, *Recollections of a Rebel Reefer;* Boston: Houghton Mifflin, 1917. Niven, John, *Gideon Welles: Lincoln's Secretary of the Navy;* New York: Oxford University Press, 1973. *Official Records of the Union and Confederate Armies in the War of the Rebellion,* 128 v.; Washington, D.C.: USGPO, 1880–1902. *Official Records of the Union and Confederate Navies in the War of the Rebellion,* 30 v.; Washington, D.C.: USGPO, 1894–1922. Porter, D. D., *Naval History of the Civil War;* New York: Sherman Publishing Co., 1886. *Report of Joint Committee on the Conduct of the War,* 9 v.; Washington, D.C.: USGPO, 1863–1866.

Scharf, J. T., *History of the Confederate States Navy;* New York: Rogers and Sherwood, 1887. Thompson, R. M., and R. Wainwright, *Confidential Correspondence of G. V. Fox,* 3 v.; New York: Naval History Society, 1918–1919. Welles. G., *The Diary of Gideon Welles,* 3 v.; Boston: Houghton Mifflin, 1911. West, R. S., Jr., *Gideon Welles: Lincoln's Navy Department;* Indianapolis: Bobbs-Merrill, 1943, *Mr. Lincoln's Navy;* New York: Longmans, Green, 1957, and *The Second Admiral: A Life of David Dixon Porter;* New York: Coward-McCann, 1937.

The Blockade and the Cruisers (Chapters 12 and 14)

Albion, Robert G., and Jennie Barnes Pope, *Sea Lanes in Wartime;* New York: Norton, 1925. Bennett, F. M., *The Monitor and the Navy under Steam;* Boston: Houghton Mifflin, 1900. Bradlee, F., *Blockade Running during the Civil War and the Effect of Land and Water Transportation on the Confederacy;* Salem: Essex Institute, 1925, and *The Kearsarge–Alabama Battle;* Salem, Mass.: Essex Institute, 1921. Bulloch, J. D., *The Secret Service of the Confederate States in Europe,* 2 v.; New York: George Putnam's Sons, 1883. Church, W. C., *The Life of John Ericsson,* 2 v.; New York: Charles Scribner's Sons, 1891. Daly, Robert W., *How the Merrimac Won;* New York: Crowell, 1957. Ellicott, J. M., *The Life of John Ancrum Winslow,* New York: George Putnam's Sons, 1902. Evans, Robley D., *A Sailor's Log;* New York: Appleton, 1901. Gilchrist, Robert C., *The Confederate Defense of Morris Island;* Charleston: News-Courier Book Press, 1947. Hayes, John D., ed., *Samuel Francis Du Pont: Civil War Letters,* 3 v.; Ithaca; Cornell University Press, 1969. Johnson, John, *The Defense of Charleston Harbor;* Charleston: Walker Evans & Cogswell, 1890. Jones, Samuel, *The Siege of Charleston;* New York: Neale, 1911. King, J. E., "The First Fort Fisher Campaign, 1864–65," *U. S. Naval Institute Proceedings,* v. 77 (August 1951), 843–855. Lewis, Charles L., *Admiral Franklin Buchanan;* Baltimore: Norman, Remington, 1929. Owsley, F. L., *King Cotton Diplomacy;* Chicago: University of Chicago Press, 1931. Parker, Foxhall A., *The Battle of Mobile Bay;* Boston: A. Williams, 1878. Robinson, W. M., *The Confederate Privateers;* New Haven: Yale University Press, 1928. Schwab, J. D. *The Confederate States of America, 1861–1865: A Financial and Industrial History;* New York: Charles Scribner's Sons, 1901. Semmes, R., *Memoirs of Service Afloat;* New York: P. J. Kennedy & Sons, 1869. Soley, J. R., *The Blockade and the Cruisers;* New York: Charles Scribner's Sons, 1883. Vandiver, Frank, ed., *Confederate Blockade Running Through Bermuda;* Austin: University of Texas Press, 1947. Watson, William, *The Adventures of a Blockade Runner;* London: T. Fisher Unwin, 1892.

Worden, J. L., and others, *The Monitor and the Merrimac*; New York: Harper & Brothers, 1912. (See also Baxter, *Introduction of the Ironclad Warship*, above, Chapter 11.)

The War in the West (Chapter 13)

Fiske, John, *The Mississippi Valley in the Civil War*; Boston: Houghton Mifflin, 1900. Gosnell, H. A., *Guns of the Western Waters*; Baton Rouge, Louisiana State University Press, 1949. Mahan, A. T., *The Gulf and Inland Waters*; New York: Charles Scribner's Sons, 1883. Milligan, John D., *Gunboats Down the Mississippi*; Annapolis: U. S. Naval Institute, 1965. Walke, H., *Naval Scenes and Reminiscences of the Civil War*; New York: F. R. Reed, 1887.

Naval Developments of the Late Nineteenth Century (Chapter 15)

Alden, John D., *The American Steel Navy*; Annapolis: Naval Institute Press, 1972. Buhl, Lance C., "Mariners and Machines: Resistance to Technological Change in the American Navy, 1865–1869," *Journal of American History*, v. LXI (1974), 703–727. Dorwart, Jeffery M., *The Office of Naval Intelligence*; Annapolis: Naval Institute Press, 1979. Hagan, Kenneth J., *American Gunboat Diplomacy and the Old Navy, 1887–1889*; Westport, Conn.: Greenwood Press, 1973. Herrick, Walter R., Jr., *The American Naval Revolution*; Baton Rouge: Louisiana State University Press, 1966. Karsten, Peter, *The Naval Aristocracy: The Golden Age of Annapolis and the Emergence of Modern American Navalism*: New York: Free Press, 1972. Livezey, William E., *Mahan on Sea Power*; Norman: University of Oklahoma Press, 1947. Long, John D., *The New American Navy*, 2 v.; New York: Outlook, 1903. Mahan, Alfred T., *From Sail to Steam*; New York: Harper & Brothers, 1907. Mitchell, Donald W., *History of the Modern American Navy: From 1883 through Pearl Harbor*; New York: Knopf, 1946. Parkes, Oscar, *British Battleships, 1860–1950*; London: Seeley Service, 1957. Seager, Robert II, *Alfred Thayer Mahan*; Annapolis: Naval Institute Press, 1977. Sloan, Edward W., III, *Benjamin Franklin Isherwood, Naval Engineer: The Years as Engineer-in-Chief, 1861–1869*; Annapolis: Naval Institute Press, 1965. Spector, Ronald, *Professors of War: The Naval War College and the Development of the Profession*; Newport: Naval War College Press, 1977. Sprout, Harold, and Margaret Sprout, *The Rise of American Naval Power*; Princeton University Press, 1944. Swann, L. A., Jr., *John Roach, Maritime Entrepreneur: The Years as Naval Contractor, 1862–1886*: Annapolis: Naval Institute Press, 1965. Wilson, H. W., *Ironclads in Action*, 2 v.; Boston: Little, Brown, 1896. (See also Bennett, *The Steam Navy of the United States*, and Brodie, *Sea Power in the Machine Age*, above, Chapter 11.)

The Rise of Japanese Naval Power (Chapter 16)

General

Ballard, R. N., *The Influence of the Sea on the Political History of Japan*; New York: E. P. Dutton, 1921. Falk, E. A., *Togo and the Rise of Japanese Sea Power*; New York: Longmans, Green, 1936.

Rise of, To 1870

Brown, D., "The Impact of Firearms on Japanese Warfare, 1543-1598," *Far Eastern Quarterly* (May 1948), pp. 236–253. Cole, A. B., ed., *With Perry in Japan*; Princeton: Princeton University Press, 1942. Dulles, F. R., *China and America*; Princeton: Princeton University Press, 1946. Eldridge, F. B., *The Background of Eastern Sea Power*; Melbourne: Georgian House, 1945. Fay, Peter Ward, *The Opium War, 1840–42*; Chapel Hill: University of North Carolina Press, 1975. Marder, A. J., "From Jimmu Tenno to Perry: Sea Power in Early Japanese History," *American Historical Review*, v. LI (October 1945), 1. *Narrative of the Expedition of an American Squadron to the China Seas and Japan*; Washington, D.C.: USGPO, 1856. Sadler, A., "The Naval Campaign in the Korean War of Hideyoshi, 1592–1598," *Asiatic Society of Japan Transactions* (June 1937). Underwood, H. H., *Korean Boats and Ships*; Seoul: Chosen Christian College, 1934. Walworth, A., *Black Ships Off Japan: The Story of Commodore Perry's Expedition*; New York: Knopf, 1946.

Sino–Japanese War

Marble, F., "The Battle of the Yalu," *U. S. Naval Institute Proceedings*, v. XXI no. 3 (1895), 479. McGiffin, P. N., "The Battle of the Yalu," *Century Magazine*, v. L (August 1895), 585. Porter, R. P., *Japan: The Rise of a Modern Power*, London: Oxford University Press, 1914. Rawlinson, John L., *China's Struggle for Naval Development, 1839–1895*; Cambridge, Mass.: Harvard University Press, 1967. Wallach, R., "The War in the East," *U. S. Naval Institute Proceedings*, v., XXI (1895) no. 21, 691. Wilson, H. W., *Battleships in Action*, 2 v.; New York: Little, Brown, 1928. "Vladimir" (pseud. Volpicelli, C.), *The China-Japan War*; London: Sampson Low, Marston, 1896. (See also Morison, *Matthew Calbraith Perry*, above, Chapter 11.)

Russo–Japanese War

"Battle of the Sea of Japan," *Journal of the U. S Artillery*, v. XXIV (July–August 1905), 72. Bodley R. V. C., *Admiral Togo*; London: Jerrolds, 1935. Cotten, L. A., "The Naval Strategy of the Russo-Japanese War," *U. S. Naval Institute Proceedings* v. XXXVI (March 1910), 41. Great Britain, Committee of Imperial Defence, Historical Section, *Official History of the Russo-Japanese War*, 3 v. appendix, 3 map cases; London: H. M. Stationer

Office, 1910–1920. Hargreaves, Reginald, *Red Sun Rising: The Siege of Port Arthur*; Philadelphia: Lippincott, 1961. Hoadley, W. T. (trans.), "The Battle of the Yellow Sea: Official Version of the Japanese General Staff," *U. S. Naval Institute Proceedings*, v. XL (September–October 1914), 153. Hough, Richard, *The Fleet that Had to Die*; New York: Viking, 1958. Jane, F. T., *The Imperial Russian Navy*; London: Thacker, 1899, and *The Imperial Japanese Navy*; London: Thacker, 1899. Klado, N., *The Battle of the Sea of Japan*; London: Hodder & Stoughton, 1906, and *The Russian Navy in the Russo-Japanese War*; London: Hurst and Blackett, 1905. Lloyd, A., *Admiral Togo*; Tokyo: Kinkodo, 1905. Mahan, A. T., "Retrospect upon the War between Japan and Russia," *Naval Administration and Warfare*; Boston: Little, Brown, 1918. McCully, Newton A., *The McCully Report: The Russo-Japanese War*; Annapolis: U.S. Naval Institute, 1977. Mizuno, H., *This One Battle*; Tokyo: Daitoa Shuppan Kabushiki Kaisha, 1944. "Naval Attacks upon Port Arthur," *Journal of the U. S. Artillery*, v. XXVII (January–February 1907), 54. Nebogatoff, "Battle of Tsushima," *Journal of the Royal United Service Institution*, v. L (October 1906), 1262. Nojine, E. K., *The Truth about Port Arthur*; London: John Murray, 1908. Novikov-Priboy, *Tsushima*; London: George Allen and Unwin, 1936. Ogasawara, N., *Life of Admiral Togo*; Tokyo: Saito Shoin, 1934. Okomoto, Shumpei, *The Japanese Oligarchy and the Russo-Japanese War*; New York: Columbia University Press, 1970. Semenoff, V., *Rasplata*; London: John Murray, 1909, and *The Battle of Tsushima*; London: John Murray, 1906. Theiss, F. *The Voyage of Forgotten Men*; Indianapolis: Bobbs-Merrill, 1937. Walder, David, *The Short Victorious War: The Russo-Japanese Conflict, 1904–1905*; London: Hutchinson, 1973. Warner, Denis, and Peggy Warner, *The Tide at Sunrise: A History of the Russo-Japanese War, 1904–1905*; New York: Charterhouse, 1974. Westwood, J. N., *Illustrated History of the Russo-Japanese War*; Chicago: Regnery, 1974, and *Witnesses of Tsushima*; Tokyo: Sophia University, in cooperation with The Diplomatic Press, Tallahassee, 1970. White, R. D., "With the Baltic Fleet at Tsushima," *U. S. Naval Institute Proceedings*, v. XXXII (June 1906), 597.

USGPO, 1898–1900. Chadwick, French E., *The Relations of the United States and Spain: The Spanish-American War*; New York: Charles Scribner's Sons, 1911. Corbett, Julian S., and Henry Newbolt, *History of the Great War*, 5 v.; London: Longman's, 1920–23. Mahan, A. T., *Lessons of the War with Spain and Other Articles*; Boston: Little, Brown, 1899. Mayo, Lawrence S., ed., *America of Yesterday, As Reflected in the Journal of John Davis Long*; Boston: Little, Brown, 1923. West, Richard S., Jr., *Admirals of American Empire*; Indianapolis: Bobbs-Merrill, 1948. Wilson, Herbert W., *The Downfall of Spain*: London: Sampson Low, Marston, 1900. (See also Long, *The New American Navy*, Mitchell, *History of the Modern American Navy*, and Seager, *Alfred Thayer Mahan*, all Chapter 15, above.)

Philippines Campaign

Dewey, George, *Autobiography of George Dewey*; New York: Charles Scribner's Sons, 1913. Fiske, Bradley A., *From Midshipman to Rear-Admiral*; New York: Century, 1919; and *Wartime in Manila*; Boston: Gorham, 1913. Sargent, Nathan, *Admiral Dewey and the Manila Campaign*; Washington, D.C.: Naval Historical Foundation, 1947. Spector, Ronald, *Admiral of the New Empire: The Life and Career of George Dewey*; Baton Rouge: Louisiana State University Press, 1974.

Caribbean Campaign

Alger, Russell A., *The Spanish-American War*; New York: Harper & Brothers, 1901. Clark, Charles E., *My Fifty Years in the Navy*; Boston: Little, Brown, 1917. Evans, Robley D., *A Sailor's Log, Recollections of Forty Years of Naval Life*; New York: D. Appleton–Century, 1901. Goode, William A. M., *With Sampson through the War*; New York: Doubleday and McClure, 1899. *Record of Proceedings of a Court of Inquiry in the Case of Rear-Admiral Winfield S. Schley, U. S. Navy*; Washington, D.C.: USGPO, 1902. Rickover, H. G., *How the Battleship* Maine *was Destroyed*; Washington, D.C.: Department of the Navy, Naval History Division, 1976. Schley, Winfield S., *Forty-Five Years under the Flag*; New York: D. Appleton, 1904. Sigsbee, Charles, *The "Maine," An Account of Her Destruction in Havana Harbor*; New York: D. Appleton–Century, 1899.

The Spanish–American War (Chapter 17)

General

Annual Report of the Secretary of the Navy, 1898; Washington, D.C.: USGPO, 1898. *Annual Report of the Secretary of War, 1898;* Washington, D.C.: USGPO, 1898. *Appendix to the Report of the Chief of the Bureau of Navigation, 1898;* Washington, D.C.: USGPO, 1898. U. S. Naval Intelligence Office, *Information from Abroad: Notes on the Spanish-American War;* Washington, D.C.:

The Rise of American Naval Power (Chapter 18)

Beale, Howard K., *Theodore Roosevelt and the Rise of America to World Power*; Baltimore: Johns Hopkins Press, 1957. Braistead, William R., *The United States Navy in the Pacific, 1897–1909* and *1909–1922*; Austin: University of Texas Press, 1958 and 1971. Challener, Richard, *Admirals, Generals, and American Foreign Policy, 1898–1914*; Princeton: Princeton University Press, 1973. Craven,

Thomas T., *History of Aviation in the United States Navy: From the Beginning Until the Spring of 1920*; Washington, D.C.: Naval History Division, 1977. Davis, G. T., *A Navy Second to None*; New York: Harcourt, Brace, 1919. Evans, Robley D., *An Admiral's Log*; New York: Appleton, 1910. Fiske, Bradley A., *From Midshipman to Rear Admiral*; New York: Century, 1919. Hart, Robert A., *The Great White Fleet*; Boston: Little, Brown, 1965. Harrod, Frederick S., *Manning the New Navy: The Development of a Modern Naval Enlisted Force, 1899–1940*; Westport: Greenwood, 1977. Marder, Arthur J., *The Anatomy of British Sea Power, 1880–1905*; Knopf, 1940, and *The Road to War, 1904–1914* (v. I of *From Dreadnought to Scapa Flow: The Royal Navy in the Fisher Era, 1904–1919*; New York: Oxford University Press, 1961–70). Morris, Richard Knowles, *John P. Holland, 1841–1914: Inventor of the Modern Submarine*; Annapolis: U. S. Naval Institute, 1966. Stafford, E. P., *The Far and the Deep: A Half Century of Submarine History*; New York: Putnam, 1967. Williamson, Samuel, *The Politics of Grand Strategy: Britain and France Prepare for War, 1904–1914*: Cambridge, Mass.: Harvard University Press, 1969. (See also Brodie, *Sea Power in the Machine Age*, above, Chapter 11; Bennett, *The Steam Navy of the United States*, Chapter 11; Long, *The New American Navy*, Chapter 15; Mitchell, *History of the Modern American Navy*, Chapter 15; and Sprout and Sprout, *The Rise of American Naval Power*, Chapter 15.)

World War I (Chapters 19–21)

General

History of the Great War, Based on Official Documents: Corbett, Julian S., and Henry Newbolt, *Naval Operations*, 5 v.; London: Longmans, Green, 1920–1931. Fayle, C. Ernest, *Seaborne Trade*, 3 v.; New York: Longmans, Green, 1920, 1923. Hurd, Archibald, *The Merchant Navy*, 3 v.; New York: John Murray, 1921–1929. Churchill, W. S., *The World Crisis*, 4 v.; New York: Charles Scribner's Sons, 1923–27 (available also in condensed one-volume edition). Keyes, Roger, *The Naval Memoirs of Admiral of the Fleet Sir Roger Keyes*; New York: E. P. Dutton, 1934. Marder, Arthur J., *From the Dreadnought to Scapa Flow: The Royal Navy in the Fisher Era, 1904–1919*, 5 v.; New York: Oxford University Press, 1961–70. May, Ernest R., *The World War and American Isolation, 1914–1917*; Cambridge, Mass.: Harvard University Press, 1959. Raeder, Grand Admiral Erich, *My Life*; Annapolis: U. S. Naval Institute, 1960. Scheer, Reinhard, *Germany's High Seas Fleet in the World War*; London: Cassell, 1920. (See also Wilson, H. W., *Battleships in Action*, v. II, above, Chapter 16.)

Surface Actions (Chapter 19)

Bacon, R. H., *The Life of John Rushworth, Earl Jellicoe*; London: Cassell, 1936. Bellairs, C. W., *The Battle of Jutland*; London: Hodder & Stoughton, 1920. Bennett, G., *The Battle of Jutland*; Newton Abbot: Davis and Charles, 1964, and *Coronel and the Falklands*; New York: Macmillan, 1962. Bingham, Barry, *Falklands, Jutland, and the Bight*; London: John Murray, 1919. Bywater, H. C., "Gunnery at Jutland," *U. S. Naval Institute Proceedings*, v. LI (September 1925), 1780. Chalmers, W. S., *The Life and Letters of David, Earl Beatty*; London: Hodder & Stoughton, 1951. Chatfield, A. E. M., *The Navy and Defence*; London: William Heinemann, 1942. Cruttwell, C. R. M. F., *A History of the Great War, 1914–1918*; London: Oxford University Press, 1936. Fawcett, H. W., and G. W. W. Hooper, eds., *The Fighting at Jutland*; London: Hutchinson, 1920. Fisher, John A., *Memories and Records*, 2 v.; New York: George H. Doran, 1920. Frost, H. H., *The Battle of Jutland*; Annapolis: U. S. Naval Institute, 1936 (reissued 1970). Frothingham, T. G., *The Naval History of the World War*, v. II; Cambridge, Mass.: Harvard University Press, 1924. Gibson, L., and J. E. T. Harper, *The Riddle of Jutland*; New York: Coward McCann, 1943. Gill, C. C., *What Happened at Jutland: The Tactics of the Battle*; New York: George H. Doran, 1921. Groos, O., *Der Krieg in der Nordsee*, v. V. Berlin: E. S. Mittler & Sohn, 1925. Hirst, Lloyd. *Coronel and After*; London: Peter Davies, 1934. Jameson, Sir William, *The Fleet that Jack Built*; New York: Harcourt, Brace, 1962. Jellicoe, J. R., *The Grand Fleet, 1914–1916: Its Creation, Development, and Work*; New York: George H. Doran, 1919. Liddell Hart, B., *A History of the World War, 1914–1918*; New York: Little, Brown, 1935. Macintyre, Donald, *Jutland*; New York: W. W. Norton, 1958. Marder, Arthur J., *The War Years: To the Eve of Jutland* and *Jutland and After*: v. II and III of *From the Dreadnought to Scapa Flow*, 5 v.; New York: Oxford University Press, 1961–70. Milne, A. Berkeley, *The Flight of the Goeben and the Breslau*; London: E. Nash, 1921. Pastfield, J. L. R., *New Light on Jutland*; London: William Heinemann, 1933. Patterson, A. Temple, *Jellicoe: A Biography*; London: Macmillan, 1969. Raeder, Erich, *Cruiser Warfare in Foreign Waters*, 2 v.; Newport: U. S. Naval War College, 1923–35. Rawson, G., *Earl Beatty, Admiral of the Fleet*; London: Jarrolds, 1930. Roskill, Stephen, *Admiral of the Fleet Earl Beatty: The Last Naval Hero*; New York: Atheneum, 1981. Scott, Percy, *Fifty Years in the Royal Navy*; London: George H. Doran, 1919. Steinberg, Jonathan, *Yesterday's Deterrent: The Story of Tirpitz and the Birth of the German Battle Fleet*; London: Macdonald, 1968. Tirpitz, Alfred, *My Memoirs*, 2 v.; Dodd, Mead, 1919. Verner, Rudolf, *The Battle Cruisers at the Action of the*

Falkland Islands; London: J. Bale & Danielsson, 1920. Von Hase, G. O. I., *Kiel and Jutland*; London: Skeffington & Son, 1921. Von Schoultz, G., *With the British Battle Fleet: War Recollections of a Russian Naval Officer*; London: Hutchinson, 1925. Waldeyer-Hartz, H., *Admiral von Hipper*: London: Rich & Cowan, 1933. Young, Filson, *With the Battle Cruisers*; London: Cassell, 1921.

The Campaign for Constantinople (Chapter 20)

Aspinall-Oglander, Cecil F., *Roger Keyes*; London: Hogarth Press, 1951, and with A. F. Becke, *Military Operations: Gallipoli*, 2 v.; London: William Heinemann, 1929. Bacon, Sir Reginald H., *The Life of Lord Fisher of Kilverstone*, 2 v.; Garden City: Doubleday, Doran, 1929. Brodie, Charles G., *Forlorn Hope*; London: Frederick Books, 1956. Bush, Eric W., *Gallipoli*; London: George Allen & Unwin, 1975. Dardanelles Commission, *First Report*; London: H. M. Stationery Office, 1917. *Gallipoli Studies at Marine Corps Schools, Quantico*, 1932, microfilm, U. S. Naval Academy Library. Gilbert, Martin, *Winston S. Churchill*, v. 3, 1914–16, *The Challenge of War*; Boston: Houghton Mifflin, 1971. Hamilton, Sir Ian, *Gallipoli Diary*, 2 v.; New York: George H. Doran, 1920; condensed version, London: Edward Arnold, 1930. Higgins, Trumbull, *Winston Churchill and the Dardanelles*; New York: Macmillan, 1963. James, Robert Rhodes, *Gallipoli*; New York: Macmillan, 1965. Jenkins, Roy, *Asquith: Portrait of a Man and an Era*; New York: Chilmark Press, 1964. Keyes, Roger, *The Fight for Gallipoli*; London: Eyre & Spottiswoode, 1941. Liman von Sanders, Otto, *Five Years in Turkey*; Annapolis: U. S. Naval Institute, 1927. Marder, Arthur J., *Fear God and Dread Nought: The Correspondence of Admiral of the Fleet Lord Fisher of Kilverstone*, 2 v.; Cambridge, Mass.: Harvard University Press, 1952, and *Portrait of an Admiral: The Life and Letters of Sir Herbert Richmond*; London: Jonathan Cape, 1952. Mason, A. T., "An Introduction to the Gallipoli Campaign," *Marine Corps Gazette* (February and May, 1936). Moorehead, Alan, *Gallipoli*; New York: Harper & Brothers, 1956. Murray, Joseph, *Gallipoli as I Saw It*; London: W. Kimber, 1965. Oxford and Asquith, Herbert Henry Asquith, Earl of, *Memoirs and Reflections*, 2 v.; Boston, Little, Brown, 1928. Roskill, Stephen, *Hankey, Man of Secrets*, 3 v.; New York: St. Martin, 1971. Stewart, A. T., and J. E. Peshall, *The Immortal Gamble*; London: Black, 1917. Wester-Wemyss, Rosslyn, *The Navy in the Dardanelles*; London: Hodder & Stoughton, 1924. (See also Churchill, *The World Crisis*, and Marder, *From the Dreadnought to Scapa Flow*, v. II, listed in "World War I, General," above.)

The War Against Shipping (Chapter 21)

Annual Report of the Secretary of the Navy, 1914–1919; Washington, D.C.: USGPO, 1914–16. Bacon, Reginald, *The Dover Patrol, 1915–1917*, 2 v., New York: George H. Doran, 1919. Bauer, Hermann, *Reichsleitung und U-Bootseinsatz, 1914 bis 1919*; Lippoldsberg: Klosterhaus, 1956. Carnegie Endowment for International Peace, *Official German Documents Relating to the World War*, 2 v.; New York: Oxford University Press, 1923. Cowie, J. S., *Mines, Minelayers, and Minelaying*; London, Oxford, 1949. Gayer, A., "Summary of German Submarine Operations in the Various Theaters of War from 1914 to 1918," W. P. Beehler, trans., *U. S. Naval Institute Proceedings* (April 1926), pp. 621–659. Gibson, R. H., and Maurice Prendergast, *The German Submarine War, 1914–1918*; New York: Richard R. Smith, 1931. Gleaves, Albert, *A History of the Transport Service*; New York: George H. Doran Co., 1921. Grant, Robert M., *U-Boat Intelligence, 1914–1918*; London: Putnam, 1969, and *U-Boats Destroyed*; London: Putnam, 1964. Guichard, Louis, *The Naval Blockade, 1914–1918*; New York: D. Appleton, 1930. Hezlet, Sir Arthur, *The Submarine and Sea Power*; New York: Stein and Day, 1967. Hubatsch, Walther, *Kaiserliche Marine*; Munich: J. F. Lehmans, 1975. Jellicoe, John R., *The Crisis of the Naval War*; London: Cassell, 1920, and *The Submarine Peril*; London: Cassell, 1934. Kittredge, Tracy B., *Naval Lessons of the Great War*; New York: Doubleday, Page, 1921. Low, A. M., *Mine and Countermine*; London: Oxford, 1940. Lundeberg, Philip K., "The German Naval Critique of the U-Boat Campaign, 1915–1918," *Military Affairs*, v. XXVII (1963), 105–118, and "Undersea Warfare and Allied Strategy in World War I," *Smithsonian Journal of History*, v. I:3 (1966), 1–30; v. I:4 (1966), 49–72. Michelson, Andreas, *Der U-Bootskrieg, 1914–1918*; Leipzig: K. F. Koehler, 1925. Morison, Elting E., *Admiral Sims and the Modern American Navy*; Boston: Houghton Mifflin, 1942. Sims, William S., and Burton J. Hendrick, *The Victory at Sea*; New York: Doubleday, Page, 1921. Spindler, Arno, *Der Handelskrieg mit U-Booten*, 5 v.; Berlin and Frankfurt: E. S. Mittler, 1932–66. Tupper, Reginald G. O., "The Blockade of Germany by the Tenth Cruiser Squadron," *Journal of the Royal United Service Institution*, v. LXVII (February 1923), 1. (See also Mitchell, *History of the Modern American Navy*, above, Chapter 15.)

Disarmament and Rearmament (Chapter 22)

Atwater, E., *American Regulation of Arms Exports*; New York: Columbia University Press, 1941. Buckley, Thomas N., *The United States and the Washington Conference, 1921–1922*; Knoxville: University of Tennessee Press, 1970. Buell,

R. L., *The Washington Conference;* New York: D. Appleton, 1922. Bywater, H. C., *Navies and Nations;* Boston: Houghton Mifflin, 1927. Davis, F., *The Atlantic System: the Story of Anglo-American Control of the Seas;* New York: Reynal & Hitchcock, 1941. Davis, H. I., ed., *Pioneers in World Order: An American Appraisal of the League of Nations;* New York: Columbia University Press, 1944. Engely, G., *The Politics of Naval Disarmament;* London: Williams and Norgate, 1932. Grew, J. C., *Report from Tokyo: a Message to the American People;* New York: Simon and Schuster, 1944. Hurley, Alfred F., *Billy Mitchell: Crusader for Air Power;* Bloomington: Indiana University Press, 1975. Johnstone, W. C., *The United States and Japan's New Order;* London: Oxford University Press, 1941. Levine, I. D., *Mitchell, Pioneer of Air Power;* New York: Duell, Sloan & Pearce, 1943. Miller, H. B., *Navy Wings;* New York: Dodd, Mead & Company, 1937. Perkins, D., *America and Two Wars;* Boston: Little, Brown, 1944. Rippy, J. F., *The Caribbean Danger Zone;* New York: G. P. Putnam's Sons, 1940. Roskill, Stephen, *Naval Policy Between the Wars;* v. 1, New York: Walker, 1968; v. 2, Annapolis: Naval Institute Press, 1976. Sprout, H., and M. Sprout, *Toward a New Order of Sea Power;* Princeton: Princeton University Press, 1940. Strakhovsky, L. I., *Intervention at Archangel;* Princeton: Princeton University Press, 1944.

World War II (Chapters 23–30)
General

Abbazia, Patrick, *Mr. Roosevelt's Navy: The Private War of the U. S. Atlantic Fleet, 1939–1942;* Annapolis: Naval Institute Press, 1975. Adams, Henry H., *Years of Deadly Peril: The Coming of the War, 1939–1941, 1942: The Year that Doomed the Axis, Years of Expectation: Guadalcanal to Normandy,* and *Years to Victory;* New York: David McKay, 1967–73. Buell, Thomas B., *Master of Sea Power: A Biography of Fleet Admiral Ernest J. King;* Boston: Little, Brown, 1980. Clark, Ronald, *The Man Who Broke Purple: The Life of Colonel William F. Friedman, Who Deciphered the Japanese* [Diplomatic] *Code in World War II;* Boston: Little, Brown, 1977. Connery, Robert H., *The Navy and the Industrial Mobilization in World War II;* Princeton: Princeton University Press, 1951. Craven, Wesley Frank, and James Lee Cate, eds., *The Army Air Forces in World War II, 7 v.;* Chicago: University of Chicago Press, 1948–58. Greenfield, Kent R., ed., *Command Decisions;* New York: Harcourt, Brace, 1959. Kahn, David, *The Codebreakers: The Story of Secret Writing;* London: Weidenfeld & Nicholson, 1967. (Abridged version; New York: New American Library, 1973.) Karig, Walter, and others, *Battle Report,* 6 v.; New York: Rinehart, 1944–52. King,

Fleet Admiral Ernest J., and Walter Whitehill, *Fleet Admiral King: A Naval Record;* New York: Norton, 1952. Leahy, Fleet Admiral William D., *I Was There;* New York: McGraw-Hill, 1950. Liddell Hart, B. M., *History of the Second World War;* London: Cassell, 1970. Masterman, John C., *The Double-Cross System in the War of 1939 to 1945;* New Haven: Yale University Press, 1972. Matloff, Maurice, and Edwin M. Snell, *Strategic Planning for Coalition Warfare, 1941–1942;* Washington, D.C.: Department of the Army, 1953, and (without Snell) *Strategic Planning for Coalition Warfare, 1943–1944;* Washington, D.C.: Department of the Army, 1959. Millis, Walter, ed., *The Forrestal Diaries;* New York: Viking, 1951. Morison, Samuel Eliot, *History of United States Naval Operations in World War II,* 15 v.; Boston: Little, Brown, 1947–62, *Strategy and Compromise,* Boston: Little, Brown, 1958, and *The Two-Ocean War;* Boston: Little, Brown, 1963. Pogue, Forrest M., *George C. Marshall: Ordeal and Hope, 1939–1942;* New York: Viking, 1966, and *George C. Marshall: Organizer of Victory, 1943–1945;* New York: Viking, 1973. Roscoe, Theodore, *United States Destroyer Operations in World War II;* Annapolis: U. S. Naval Institute, 1953. United States Naval War College, *Strategical and Tactical Analyses;* Washington, D.C.: Bureau of Naval Personnel, 1947. *United States Strategic Bombing Survey;* Washington, D.C.: USGPO, 1945–47. Winterbotham, F. W., *The Ultra Secret;* New York: Harper & Row, 1974. Winton, John, *Air Power at Sea, 1939–1945;* New York: Crowell, 1976. (See also Fiske, *Midshipman to Rear Admiral,* above, Chapter 17.)

World War II, Atlantic Theater (Chapters 23–25)
General

Ansel, Walter, *Hitler Confronts England;* Durham: Duke University Press, 1960. Auphan, Paul, and Jacques Mordal, *The French Navy in World War II;* Annapolis: U. S. Naval Institute, 1957. Bekker, Cajus, *Hitler's Naval War;* Garden City: Doubleday, 1974. Bennett, Geoffrey M., *Naval Battles of World War II;* London: Batsford, 1975. Bryant, Arthur, *The Turn of the Tide,* Garden City: Doubleday, 1957. Churchill, Winston S., *The Second World War,* 6 v.; Boston: Houghton Mifflin, 1948–53. Cresswell, John, *Sea Warfare, 1939–1945;* New York: Longmans, Green, 1950. Cunningham, Andrew B., *A Sailor's Odyssey;* New York: E. P. Dutton, 1951. De Belot, Raymond, *The Struggle for the Mediterranean, 1939–1945;* Princeton: Princeton University Press, 1951. Dönitz, Karl, *Ten Years and Twenty Days;* New York: World Publishing, 1959. Eisenhower, Dwight D., *Crusade in Europe;* Garden City: Doubleday, 1948. James, Sir William R., *The Brit-*

ish Navies in the Second World War; New York: Longmans, Green, 1947. Kammerer, Albert, *La passion de la flotte française*; Paris: Librarie Arthème Fayard, 1951. Kemp, P. H., *Key to Victory: The Triumph of British Sea Power in World War II*; Boston: Little, Brown, 1957. (British edition of Kemp, called *Victory at Sea*; London: Frederick Muller, 1957.) Kesselring, Albert, *A Soldier's Record*; New York: William Morrow, 1954. Liddell Hart, B. H., ed., *The Rommel Papers*; New York: Harcourt, Brace, 1953. Lohmann, W., and H. H. Hildebrand, *Die Deutsche Kriesgsmarine, 1939–1945*, 3 v.; Bad Nauheim: H. H. Podzun, 1956–64. Macintyre, Donald, *The Naval War Against Hitler*; New York: Scribner's, 1971. Martenssen, Anthony T., *Hitler and His Admirals*; New York: E. P. Dutton, 1949. Masterman, John C., *The Double-Cross System in the War of 1939 to 1945*; New Haven: Yale University Press, 1972. Montgomery, Bernard, *El Alamein to the River Sangro*; London: Hutchinson, 1948, and *The Memoirs of Field Marshal Montgomery*; Cleveland: World Publishing, 1958. Pack, S. W. C., *Cunningham the Commander*; London: Batsford, 1974, and *Sea Power in the Mediterranean*; London: Barker, 1971. Parmet, Herbert S., *Eisenhower and the American Crusades*; New York: Macmillan, 1972. Playfair, Ian S. O., *The Mediterranean and the Middle East*; London: H. M. Stationery Office, 1954. Richards, Dennis, and Hilary St. George Saunders, *Royal Air Force, 1939–1945*, 3 v.; London H. M. Stationery Office, 1953–54. Roskill, Stephen W., *The War at Sea*, 3 v.; London: H. M. Stationery Office, 1954–61. Ruge, Friedrich, *Der Seekrieg: The German Navy's Story, 1939–1945*; Annapolis: U. S. Naval Institute, 1957. Schofield, Brian B., *British Sea Power: Naval Policy in the Twentieth Century*; London: Balsford, 1967. Verrier, Anthony, *The Bomber Offensive*; New York: Macmillan, 1969. Von der Porten, Edward P., *The German Navy in World War II*; New York: Ballantine Books, 1969. Warner, Oliver, *Admiral of the Fleet Cunningham of Hindhope*; Columbus: University of Ohio Press, 1967.

The German–Italian Offensive (Chapter 23)

Bragadin, Marc Antonio, *The Italian Navy in World War II*; Annapolis: U. S. Naval Institute, 1957. Chatterton, Edward Kemble, *The Epic of Dunkirk*; London: Hurst & Blackett, 1940. Derry, T. K., *The Campaign in Norway*; London: H. M. Stationery Office, 1952. Divine, David, *The Nine Days of Dunkirk*; New York: Ballantine Books, 1959. Macintyre, Donald, *Narvik*; London: Evans Bros., 1959. Pack, S. W. C., *The Battle of Matapan*; New York: Macmillan, 1961, and *The Battle for Crete*; Annapolis: Naval Institute Press, 1973. Pope, Dudley, *The Battle of the River Plate*; London: William Kimber, 1956, and *73 North*;

London: Weidenfeld & Nicholson, 1958. Schofield, Brian B., *The Attack on Taranto*; Annapolis: Naval Institute Press, 1973. U. S. Office of Naval Intelligence, *Fuehrer Conferences on Matters Dealing with the German Navy*, 3 v.; Washington, D.C.: USGPO, 1946. Wheatley, Roland, *Operation Sea Lion*; Oxford: Clarendon Press, 1958.

The Battle of the Atlantic (Chapter 24)

Admiralty, *The Battle of the Atlantic*; London: H. M. Stationery Office, 1946. Baxter, James Phinney, III, *Scientists Against Time*; Boston: Little, Brown, 1948. Beesley, Patrick, *Most Secret Intelligence*; London: Hamish Hamilton, 1977. Berthold, Will, *The Sinking of the Bismarck*; London: Longmans, Green, 1958. Brennecke, Jochem, *The Hunters and the Hunted*; New York: Norton, 1957. Brown, David, *Tirpitz: Floating Fortress*; Annapolis: Naval Institute Press, 1977. Campbell, Ian, and Donald Macintyre, *The Kola Run*; London: Frederick Miller, 1958. Chalmers, William S., *Max Horton and the Western Approaches*; London: Hodder & Stoughton, 1954. Creighton, Kenelm, *Convoy Commodore*; London: William Kimber, 1956. Farago, Ladislas, *The Tenth Fleet*; New York: Ivan Bolensky, 1962. Frank, Wolfgang, *The Sea Wolves*; New York: Rinehart, 1955. Gallery, Daniel, *Clear the Decks!*; New York: Morrow, 1951, and *Twenty Million Tons under the Sea*; Chicago: Henry Regnery, 1956. Grenfell, Russell, *The Bismarck Episode*; New York: Macmillan, 1949. Herzog, Bodo, *Die Deutschen U-boote, 1906–1945*; Munich: Lehmann, 1959. Hughes, Terry, and John Costello, *The Battle of the Atlantic*; New York: Dial Press, 1977. Lane, Frederic C., and others, *Ships for Victory: A History of Shipbuilding under the U. S. Maritime Commission in World War II*; Baltimore: Johns Hopkins Press, 1951. Lewis, David D., *The Fight for the Sea*; New York: World Publishing, 1961. Macintyre, Donald, *U-Boat Killer*; New York: Norton, 1956. Müllenheim-Rechberg, Baron Burkard, *Battleship Bismarck: A Survivor's Story*; Annapolis: Naval Institute Press, 1980. Raeder, Erich, *My Life*; Annapolis: U. S. Naval Institute, 1960. Riesenberg, Felix, *Sea War: The Story of the U. S. Merchant Marine in World War II*; New York: Rinehart, 1956. Rohwer, Jürgen, *The Critical Convoy Battles of March 1943*; Annapolis: Naval Institute Press, 1977. Slessor, John, *The Central Blue*; New York: Praeger, 1957. Watts, Anthony J., *Loss of the Scharnhorst*; London: Allan, 1970. Woodward, David, *The Tirpitz and the Battle for the North Atlantic*; New York: Norton, 1954. (See also, above, in "World War II, Atlantic Theater, General," Dönitz, *Ten Years and Twenty Days*, and in "World War II, General," Morison, *U. S. Naval Operations*, v. I.: *The Battle of the Atlantic*, and v. X: *The Atlantic Battle Won*.)

The Defeat of Italy and Germany (Chapter 25)

Ansel, Walter, *Hitler and the Middle Sea*; Durham: Duke University Press, 1972. Blumenson, Martin, *Salerno to Cassino*; Washington, D.C.: Center for Military History, 1969. Eisenhower Foundation, ed., *D-Day: The Normandy Invasion in Retrospect*; Lawrence: University of Kansas Press, 1971. Garland, Albert N., and Howard McGraw Smyth, *Sicily and the Surrender of Italy*; Washington, D.C.: Department of the Army, 1965. Higgins, Trumbull, *Soft Underbelly: The Anglo-American Controversy over the Italian Campaign: 1939–1945*; New York: Macmillan, 1968. Howe, George F., *Northwest Africa: Seizing the Initiative in the West*; Washington, D.C.: Department of the Army, 1957. Mason, Donald, *Salerno*; New York: Ballantine Books, 1977. Mitchie, Allan A., *The Invasion of Europe: The Story Behind D-Day*; New York: Dodd, Mead, 1964. Murphy, Robert D., *Diplomat among Warriors*; Garden City: Doubleday, 1964. Schofield, Brian B., *Operation Neptune*; Annapolis: Naval Institute Press, 1974. Sheehan, Neil, *Anzio: Epic of Bravery*; Norman: University of Oklahoma Press, 1964. Stoler, Mark A., *The Politics of the Second Front: American Planning and Diplomacy in Coalition Warfare, 1941–1943*; Westport, Conn.: Greenwood Press, 1976. Tute, Warren, Terry Hughes, and John Costello, *D-Day*; New York: Macmillan, 1974. (See also, above, in "World War II, General," Morison, *U. S. Naval Operations*, v. II, IX, and XI.)

World War II, Pacific Theater (Chapters 26–30)
General

Agawa, Hiroyuki, *The Reluctant Admiral: Yamamoto and the Imperial Navy*; Tokyo: Kodansha International, 1979. Barbey, Daniel E., *MacArthur's Amphibious Navy: Seventh Amphibious Force Operations, 1943–1945*; Annapolis: U. S. Naval Institute, 1969. Ballantine, Duncan S., *U. S. Naval Logistics in the Second World War*; Princeton: Princeton University Press, 1949. Belote, James H., and William M. Belote, *Titans of the Seas: The Development and Operations of Japanese and American Carrier Task Forces During World War II*; New York: Harper and Row, 1975. Brown, David, *Carrier Operations in World War II: The Pacific Navies*; London: Ian Allan, 1974. Bulkley, Robert J., *At Close Quarters: PT Boats in the United States Navy*; Washington, D.C.: Department of the Navy, 1962. Buell, Thomas B., *The Quiet Warrior: A Biography of Admiral Raymond A. Spruance*; Boston: Little, Brown, 1974. Clark, J. J., with Clark G. Reynolds, *Carrier Admiral*; New York: McKay, 1967. D'Albas, Emmanuel E., *Death of a Navy: Japanese Naval Action in World War II*; New York: Devin-Adair, 1957. Dull, Paul S., *A Battle History of the Imperial Japanese Navy, 1941–1945*; Annapolis: Naval Institute Press, 1977.

Dyer, George C., *The Amphibians Came to Conquer: The Story of Admiral Richmond Kelly Turner*; Washington, D.C.: Naval History Division, Department of the Navy, 1972. Forrestel, E. P., *Admiral Raymond A. Spruance, USN: A Study in Command*; Washington, D.C.: Naval History Division, Department of the Navy, 1966. Frank, Benis M., *Halsey*; New York: Ballantine Books, 1974. Halsey, William F., and J. Bryan, III, *Admiral Halsey's Story*; New York: McGraw-Hill, 1947. Holmes, W. J., *Double-Edged Secrets: U. S. Naval Intelligence Operations in the Pacific during World War II*; Annapolis: Naval Institute Press, 1979. Horikoshi, Jiro, and Masutake Okumiya, *Zero! The Story of the Japanese Air Force*; New York: E. P. Dutton, 1956. Hoyt, Edwin P., *How They Won the War in the Pacific: Nimitz and His Admirals*; New York: Weybright and Talley, 1970. Isely, Jeter A., and Philip A. Crowl, *The U. S. Marines and Amphibious War*; Princeton: Princeton University Press, 1951. James, D. Clayton, *The Years of MacArthur*, v. II (1941–45); Boston: Houghton, Mifflin, 1975. Jones, Ken, and Hubert Kelly, *Admiral Arleigh (31-Knot) Burke: The Story of a Fighting Sailor*; Philadelphia: Chilton, 1962. Kenney, George C., *General Kenney Reports*; New York: Duell, Sloan, & Pearce, 1949. Manchester, William, *American Caesar: Douglas MacArthur, 1880–1964*; Boston: Little, Brown, 1978. Merrill, James M., *A Sailor's Admiral: A Biography of William F. Halsey*; New York: Crowell, 1976. Morton, Louis, *Strategy and Command: The First Two Years*; Washington, D.C.: Department of the Army, 1962. Potter, E. B., *Nimitz*; Naval Institute Press, 1976, and, with Fleet Admiral Chester W. Nimitz, USN, *Triumph in the Pacific: The Navy's Struggle Against Japan*; Englewood Cliffs, N.J.: Prentice-Hall, 1963. Reynolds, Clark G., *The Fast Carriers: The Forging of an Air Navy*: New York: McGraw-Hill, 1968. Russell, William H., "The Genesis of FMF Doctrine: 1879–1899," *Marine Corps Gazette* (March–July 1951). Shaw, Henry I., and others, *History of U. S. Marine Corps Operations in World War II*, 5 v.; Washington D.C.: Historical Branch, U. S. Marine Corps, 1958–68. Sherman, Frederick C., *Combat Command: The American Aircraft Carriers in the Pacific War*; New York: E. P. Dutton, 1950. Sherrod, Robert, *History of Marine Corps Aviation in World War II*; Washington, D.C.: Combat Forces Press, 1952. Smith, Holland M., "Amphibious Tactics," *Marine Corps Gazette* (June 1946–March 1947), and, with Percy Finch, *Coral and Brass*, New York: Scribner's, 1949. Taylor, Theodore, *The Magnificent Mitscher*; New York: Norton, 1954. Toland, John, *The Rising Sun: The Decline and Fall of the Japanese Empire 1936–1945*: New York: Random House, 1970 Turnball, Archibald D., and Clifford L. Lord, *History of United States Naval Aviation*; New Haven

Yale University Press, 1949. Wilson, Eugene E., *Slipstream*; New York: McGraw-Hill, 1950, and *Kitty Hawk to Sputnik to Polaris*; Barre, Mass.: Barre Publishing Co., 1960.

The Japanese Offensive (Chapter 26)

Barde, Robert Elmer, *The Battle of Midway: A Study in Command*; University of Maryland dissertation, 1971. Bartlett, Bruce, *Cover-Up: The Politics of Pearl Harbor, 1941–1946*; New Rochelle: Arlington House, 1978. Belote, James H., and William M. Belote, *Corregidor: The Saga of a Fortress*; New York: Harper & Row, 1967. Bennett, Geoffrey M., *The Loss of the Prince of Wales and Repulse*; Annapolis: U. S. Naval Institute, 1973. Brownlow, Donald Grey, *The Accused: The Ordeal of Rear Admiral Husband Edward Kimmel, U. S. N.*; New York: Vantage, 1968. Butow, Robert J. C., *Togo and the Coming of the War*; Princeton: Princeton University Press, 1961. Department of Defense, *The "Magic" Background of Pearl Harbor*, 8 v.; Washington, D.C.: USGPO, 1978. Frank, Patrick, and Joseph D. Harrington, *Rendezvous at Midway: U.S.S. Yorktown and the Japanese Carrier Fleet*; New York: John Day, 1967. Fuchida, Mitsuo, and Masatake Okumiya, *Midway: The Battle that Doomed Japan*; Annapolis: U. S. Naval Institute, 1955. Glines, Carroll, *Doolittle's Tokyo Raiders*; Princeton: D. Van Nostrand, 1964. Hough, Richard A., *The Battle of Midway: Victory in the Pacific*; New York: Macmillan, 1970. Johnston, Stanley, *Queen of the Flattops*; New York: Dutton, 1942. Kimmel, Husband E., *Admiral Kimmel's Story*; Chicago: Henry Regnery, 1955. Lord, Walter, *Incredible Victory*; New York: Harper & Row, 1967. Lundstrom, John B., *The First South Pacific Campaign: Pacific Fleet Strategy, December 1941–June 1942*; Annapolis: Naval Institute Press, 1976. Millis, Walter, *This Is Pearl: The United States and Japan, 1941*; New York: Morrow, 1947. Millot, Bernard, *The Battle of the Coral Sea*; Annapolis: Naval Institute Press, 1974. Morton, Louis, *The Fall of the Philippines*; Washington, D.C.: Department of the Army, 1953. *Narrative Statement of Evidence at Navy Pearl Harbor Investigation*, 3 v.; Washington, D.C.: Department of the Navy, 1945. *Pearl Harbor Attack: Hearings Before the Joint Committee*, 79th Congress, 40 v.; Washington, D.C.: USGPO, 1946. Richardson, James O., and George C. Dyer, *On the Treadmill to Pearl Harbor: The Memoirs of Admiral James O., Richardson*, Washington, D.C.: Naval History Division, Department of the Navy, 1973. Smith, William Ward, *Midway: Turning Point of the Pacific*; New York: Crowell, 1966. Toland, John, *But Not in Shame: The Six Months After Pearl Harbor*; New York: Random House, 1961. Trefousse, Hans Louis, ed., *What Happened at Pearl Harbor?*; New York: Twayne, 1958. Tuleja, Thaddeus V., *Climax at Midway*; New York:

Norton, 1960. U. S. Office of Naval Intelligence, *The Japanese Story of the Battle of Midway*; Washington, D.C.: USGPO, 1947. Wohlstetter, Roberta, *Pearl Harbor: Warning and Decision*; Stanford: Stanford University Press. (See also, above, in "World War II, General," Morison, *U. S. Naval Operations*, v. III and IV.)

Beginning the Allied Counteroffensive (Chapter 27)

Griffith, Samuel B., *The Battle for Guadalcanal*: Philadelphia: Lippincott, 1963. Leckie, Robert, *Challenge for the Pacific: Guadalcanal, the Turning Point of the War*; Garden City: Doubleday, 1965. Merillat, Herbert L., *The Island: A History of the First Marine Division on Guadalcanal*; Boston: Houghton Mifflin, 1944. Miller, John, *Cartwheel: The Reduction of Rabaul*: Washington, D. C.: Department of the Army, 1959. Miller, Thomas G., Jr., *The Cactus Air Force*; Harper & Row, 1969. Newcomb, Richard F., *Savo: The Incredible Naval Debacle off Guadalcanal*; New York: Holt, Rinehart & Winston, 1961. (See also, above, in "World War II, General," Morison, *U. S. Naval Operations*, v. V, VI, and VII.)

The Dual Advance (Chapter 28)

Bryan, J., and Philip Reed, *Mission Beyond Darkness*; New York: Duell, Sloan, & Pearce, 1945. Crowl, Philip A., *Campaign in the Marianas*; Washington, D.C.: Department of the Army, 1960, and, with Edmund G. Love, *Seizure of the Gilberts and Marshalls*: Washington, D.C.: Department of the Army, 1969. Heinl, Robert D., and John A. Crown, *The Marshalls: Increasing the Tempo*; Washington, D.C.: Headquarters, U. S. Marine Corps, 1954. Lockwood, Charles A., and Hans Christian Adamson, *Battles of the Philippine Sea*: New York; Crowell, 1967. Sherrod, Robert, *Tarawa: The Story of a Battle*; New York: Duell, Sloan, & Pearce, 1944. (See also, above, in "World War II, General," Morison, *U. S. Naval Operations*, v. VII and VIII.)

Submarines in the Pacific War (Chapter 29)

Beach, Edward L., *Submarine*; New York: Henry Holt, 1952. Blair, Clay, Jr., *Silent Victory: The U. S. Submarine War Against Japan*; Philadelphia: Lippincott, 1975. Hashimoto, Mochitsura, *Sunk: The Story of the Japanese Submarine Fleet, 1942–1945*; London: Cassell, 1954. Holmes, W. J., *Undersea Victory: The Influence of Submarine Operations on the War in the Pacific*; Garden City: Doubleday, 1966. Lockwood, Charles A., *Sink 'Em All: Submarine Warfare in the Pacific*; New York: Dutton, 1951, and, with Hans Christian Adamson, *Hellcats of the Sea*; New York: Greenberg, 1955. Mars, Alistair, *British Submarines at War, 1939–1945*; London: William Kimber, 1971. O'Kane, Richard H., *Clear the Bridge! The War Patrols of* the U.S.S. Tang; Chicago: Rand McNally, 1977. Orita, Zenji, with Joseph D. Harrington, I-Boat Captain; Canoga Park, Cal.: Major Books, 1976. Roscoe, Theodore, United States Submarine Operations in World War II; Annapolis: U. S. Naval Institute, 1949.

The Defeat of Japan (Chapter 30)

Appleman, Roy E., and others, Okinawa: The Last Battle; Washington, D.C.: Department of the Army, 1948. Belote, James H., and William M. Belote, Typhoon of Steel: The Battle for Okinawa; New York: Harper and Row, 1970. Butow, Robert J. C., Japan's Decision to Surrender; Stanford: Stanford University Press, 1954. Cannon, M. Hamlin, Leyte: The Return to the Philippines; Washington, D.C.: Department of the Army, 1954. Craig, William, The Fall of Japan, New York: Dial Press, 1967. Falk, Stanley L., Decision at Leyte; New York, Norton, 1966. Field, James A., The Japanese at Leyte Gulf; Princeton, Princeton University Press, 1947. Frank, Benis M., Okinawa: Touchstone to Victory; New York: Ballantine Books, 1969. Hoyt, Edwin P., The Battle of Leyte Gulf: The Death Knell of the Japanese Fleet; New York: Weybright & Talley, 1972. Inoguchi, Rikihei, Tadashi Nakajima, and Roger Pineau, The Divine Wind: Japan's Kamikaze Force in World War II; Annapolis: U. S. Naval Institute, 1958. Johnson, Ellis A., and David A. Katcher, Mines Against Japan; Silver Spring, Md.: Naval Ordnance Laboratory, 1973. Newcomb, Richard F., Abandon Ship: Death of the U.S.S. Indianapolis; New York: Henry Holt, 1958. and Iwo Jima; New York: Holt, Rinehart, & Winston, 1961. Winton, John, The Forgotten Fleet: The British Navy in the Pacific, 1944–1945; New York: Crown-MacCann, 1970. Woodward, C. Vann, The Battle for Leyte Gulf; New York: Macmillan, 1947. (See also, above, in Chapter 28, Lockwood and Adamson, Battles of the Philippine Sea, and in "World War II, General," Morison, U. S. Naval Operations, v. XII, XIII, and XIV.)

The Beginning of the Cold War (Chapter 31)

Acheson, Dean, Present at the Creation: My Years in the State Department; New York: Norton, 1969. Adams, Henry H., Harry Hopkins: A Biography; New York: Putnam, 1977. Albion, Robert Greenhalgh, and Robert Howe Connery, Forrestal and the Navy; New York: Columbia University Press, 1962. Caraley, Demetrios, The Politics of Military Unification; New York: Columbia University Press, 1966. Donovan, Robert J., Conflict and Crisis: The Presidency of Harry S. Truman; New York: Norton, 1977. Harriman, W. Averell, and Elie Abel, Special Envoy to Churchill and Stalin, 1941–1946; New York: Random House, 1975. Millis,

Walter, ed., The Forrestal Diaries; New York: Viking, 1951. Rogow, Arnold A., James Forrestal; New York: Macmillan, 1963.

Implementing the U. S. Policy of Containment (Chapter 32)

Bonds, Ray, The Vietnam War; New York: Crown Publishers, 1979. Cagle, Malcolm W., and Frank A. Manson, The Sea War in Korea; Annapolis: U. S. Naval Institute, 1957. Field, James A., Jr., History of United States Naval Operations, Korea; Washington, D.C.: USGPO, 1962. Fitzgerald, Frances, Fire in the Lake: The Vietnamese and the Americans in Vietnam; Boston: Little, Brown, 1972. Geer, Andrew C., The New Breed: The Story of the U. S. Marines in Korea; New York: Harper, 1952. Heinl, Robert D., Victory at High Tide; Philadelphia: Lippincott, 1968. Hewlett, Richard G., and Francis Duncan, Nuclear Navy, 1946–1962; Chicago: University of Chicago Press, 1974. Hooper, Edwin Bickford, and others, The United States Navy and the Vietnam Conflict; Washington, D.C.: Naval History Division, Department of the Navy, 1976–. Jackson, J. H., The World in the Postwar Decade, 1945–55; New York: Houghton Mifflin, 1957. Karig, Walter, and others, Battle Report, v. VI; New York: Rinehart, 1952. Kissinger, Henry A., Nuclear Warfare and Foreign Policy; New York: Harper, 1957. Marshall, S. L. A., The River and the Gauntlet; New York: Morrow, 1953. Millet, Allan R., ed., A Short History of the Vietnam War; Bloomington: Indiana University Press, 1978. Polmar, Norman, Atomic Submarines; Princeton: D. Van Nostrand, 1963. Ridgway, Matthew B., The Korean War; Garden City: Doubleday, 1967. Schlesinger, Arthur M., Jr., The Bitter Heritage: Vietnam and American Democracy, 1941–1946; New York: Fawcett, 1967. Taylor, Maxwell D., The Uncertain Trumpet; New York: Harper, 1960. Thomas, R. C. W., The War in Korea, 1950–1953; Aldershot, England: Gale & Polden, 1954. Tran Van Don, Lt. Gen., Our Endless War Inside Vietnam; San Rafael, Cal.: Presidio Press, 1978. Truman, Harry S., Memoirs, 2 v.; Garden City: Doubleday, 1955. U.S. Naval History Division, Riverine Warfare: The U.S. Navy's Operations in Inland Waters; Washington, D.C.: USGPO, 1969. Westmoreland, William C., A Soldier Reports; Garden City: Doubleday, 1976. Whitmore, William F., "The Origin of Polaris," U. S. Naval Institute Proceedings (March 1980), pp. 55–59.

New Weapons, New Challenges (Chapter 33)

Alden, John D., "Tomorrow's Fleet," U. S. Naval Institute Proceedings (January 1980). pp. 117–126 Couhat, Jean L., Combat Fleets of the World 1980/81; Annapolis: Naval Institute Press, 1980

Edwards, Mickey, "Soviet Expansion and Control of the Sea Lanes," *U. S. Naval Institute Proceedings* (September 1980), pp. 46–51. Gorshkov, Sergei G., *Red Star Rising at Sea*; Annapolis: U. S. Naval Institute, 1974, and *The Sea Power of the State*; Annapolis: Naval Institute Press, 1979. Harrison, Kirby, "Diego Garcia: the Seabees at Work," *U. S. Naval Institute Proceedings* (August 1979), pp. 54–61. Hayward, Thomas B., "The Future of U. S. Sea Power," *U. S. Naval Institute Proceedings* (Naval Review Issue, May 1979), pp. 66–77. Herrick R. W., *Soviet Naval Strategy;* Annapolis: U. S. Naval Institute, 1974. Hickman, William F., "Soviet Naval Policy in the Indian Ocean," *U. S. Naval Institute Proceedings* (August 1979), pp. 43–52. Holloway, James L., III, "The Transition to V/STOL," *U. S. Naval Institute Proceedings* (September 1977), pp. 18–24. Johnson, Maxwell O., "U. S. Strategic Options in the Persian Gulf," *U. S. Naval Institute Proceedings* (February 1981), pp. 53–59. Lacouture, John E., "Seapower in the Indian Ocean: a Requirement for Western Security," *U. S. Naval Institute Proceedings* (August 1979), pp. 30–41. Manthorpe, William H. J., "The Soviet Navy in 1976," *U. S. Naval Institute Proceedings* (Naval Review Issue, May 1977), pp. 203–214. MccGwire, Michael, "The Rationale for the Development of Soviet Seapower," *U. S. Naval Institute Proceedings* (Naval Review Issue, May 1980), pp. 155–183. *Newsweek*, "Reagan's Defense Buildup," 16 March 1981, pp. 22–23. Nitze, Paul H., and others, *Securing the Seas: the Soviet Naval Challenge and Western Alliance Options*; Boulder, Colorado: Westview Press, 1979. Nixon, Richard, *The Real War*; New York: Warner Books, 1980. Polmar, Norman, *The Ships and Aircraft of the U. S. Fleet*, 11th edition; Annapolis: Naval Institute Press, 1978. Rozinski, Herbert, *The Development of Naval Thought*, Newport, R. I.: Naval War College Press, 1977. *Time*, "The Navy under Attack," 8 May 1978, pp. 14–24, and "A Bonanza for Defense: the Administration Proposes a Record Military Buildup," 16 March 1981, pp. 26–31. Uhlig, Frank, Jr., "The Shape of the United States Navy in 1990," *Navy International*; London, 1978, pp. 14–18. Wegener, Edward, *Soviet Naval Offensive*; Annapolis: U. S. Naval Institute, 1975. West, F. J., "A Fleet for the Year 2000: Future Force Structure," *U. S. Naval Institute Proceedings* (Naval Review Issue, May 1980), pp. 66–81. Woolsey, R. James, "The Central Issues of Sea-based Aviation," *U. S. Naval Institute Proceedings* (Naval Review Issue, May 1979), pp. 143–149. Zumwalt, Elmo R., Jr., "Total Force," *U. S. Naval Institute Proceedings* (Naval Review Issue, May 1979), pp. 88–107.

Index

Ships names are printed in italics, followed in parentheses by nationality. Within the same parentheses are generally, for sailing ships, the number of guns rated or carried. Later ships are identified by type. Officers are listed with nationality and highest rank associated with their names in this book, but grades within ranks (e.g., *lieutenant* commander, *vice* admiral) are not supplied. Lieutenants, captains, colonels, and generals are army unless otherwise indicated. The following designations and abbreviations are used.

Ships

AC	armored cruiser
BB	battleship
CB	battle cruiser
CA	heavy cruiser
CGN	guided missile cruiser (nuclear)
CL	light cruiser
Cr	cruiser
CV	aircraft carrier
CVE	aircraft carrier, escort
CVL	aircraft carrier, light
CVN	aircraft carrier, nuclear
DD	destroyer
DE	destroyer, escort
LHA	amphibious assault ship
LPH	amphibious assault ship, general purpose
Pr Cr	protected cruiser
mer	merchant ship
SS	submarine
SSN	submarine, nuclear
SSBN	fleet ballistic missile submarine, nuclear

Nationalities

Austr	Australian
Br	British
Can	Canadian
Conf	Confederate
Fr	French
Ger	German
It	Italian
Jap	Japanese
Mex	Mexican
Sp	Spanish
U.S.	United States

Ranks

pres	president
adm	admiral
col	colonel
commo	commodore
capt	captain
comdr	commander
lieut	lieutenant